Families, Professionals, and Exceptionality

A Special Partnership

Third Edition

Ann P. Turnbull
H. Rutherford Turnbull, III

Beach Center on Families and Disability,
The University of Kansas

Merrill,
an imprint of Prentice Hall

Upper Saddle River, New Jersey   *Columbus, Ohio*

Library of Congress Cataloging-in-Publication Data
Turnbull, Ann P., 1947–
   Families, professionals, and exceptionality : a special partnership / Ann P. Turnbull,
H. Rutherford Turnbull, III.—3rd ed.
    p.   cm.
   Includes bibliographical references and index.
   ISBN 0-13-568551-6
1. Parents of exceptional children—United States. 2. Exceptional children—United
States—Family relationships. 3. Counselor and client. I. Turnbull, H. Rutherford.
II. Title.
HQ759.913.T87 1996
649'.15—dc20

96-24585
CIP

Cover Art: Cindy Higgins, © 1995, Beach Center on Families and Disability, The
   University of Kansas. Used by permission.
Editor: Ann Castel Davis
Developmental Editor: Linda Ashe Montgomery
Production Editor: Stephen C. Robb
Design Coordinator: Julia Zonneveld Van Hook
Cover Designer: Brian Deep
Production Manager: Patricia A. Tonneman
Production Supervision: Proof Positive/Farrowlyne Associates, Inc.
Illustrations: Proof Positive/Farrowlyne Associates, Inc.

This book was set in Garamond and Swiss by Proof Positive/Farrowlyne Associates, Inc.
and was printed and bound by R. R. Donnelley & Sons Company. The cover was printed
by Phoenix Color Corp.

© 1997 by Prentice-Hall, Inc.
Simon & Schuster/A Viacom Company
Upper Saddle River, New Jersey 07458

Earlier editions © 1990 by Macmillan Publishing Company and © 1986 by Merrill
Publishing Company.

Printed in the United States of America
10 9 8 7 6 5 4 3 2

ISBN: 0-13-568551-6

Prentice-Hall International (UK) Limited, *London*
Prentice-Hall of Australia Pty. Limited, *Sydney*
Prentice-Hall Canada, Inc., *Toronto*
Prentice-Hall Hispanoamericana, S. A., *Mexico*
Prentice-Hall of India Private Limited, *New Delhi*
Prentice-Hall of Japan, Inc., *Tokyo*
Simon & Schuster Asia Pte. Ltd., *Singapore*
Editora Prentice-Hall do Brasil, Ltda., *Rio de Janeiro*

To our children, J. T., Amy, and Kate, who have taught us about and exemplified empowerment, and to our very own "A-dad," who set the standards of excellence to which we aspired.

—The Turnbulls

Preface

Welcome to *Families, Professionals, and Exceptionality: A Special Partnership*. This, the third edition of our book, does not simply update the content of previous editions. It preserves the family systems perspective of the previous editions, and adds a new concept, the concept of empowerment through collaboration. In addition, this edition infuses a multicultural approach into both of these basic concepts.

Text Organization

This text is organized into three parts. "Part 1, Understanding Empowerment," describes the concept of empowerment historically and currently. "Part 2, Understanding Families," describes families as interactive systems, enabling you to understand them from a systems perspective. "Part 3, Collaborating for Empowerment," explains how you can empower families, professionals, and yourself using seven opportunities for partnerships and committing to eight obligations to develop a reliable alliance. In addition to presenting concepts and implementing techniques, we synthesize the literature on empowerment, relying on the concepts and research data reported in several disciplines. Through our synthesis, we create a framework that transforms this complex concept and its implementing techniques into an approach that is easy to understand and apply. Throughout the text we emphasize mutual empowerment, believing that whatever empowers one person should and can empower another. As one person in a collaborative partnership becomes more empowerful, so will all of them. Empowerment, after all, is a value that families, professionals, and you as an individual can pursue and obtain through collective action.

Text Features

We bring together theory, research, and the best practices related to family-professional partnerships from both general and special education. The effort to merge these two bodies of knowledge is, we believe, a "first." We hope the merger will also shape family-professional partnerships in general and special education into an inclusive whole for the benefit of all students, all families, and all professionals. With this merger comes the opportunity for families of all students to participate in tomorrow's schools in a more empowered and effective way.

In each chapter, we feature "family voices," portraying a family in the opening and closing vignette and relying on families' voices throughout the chapter. The vignette and subsequent quotations, contained in the "My Voice" features or in shorter quotations, are not ornamental. Rather, they are instrumental, linking the concepts and content of the chapter to real families, real professionals, and real schools. Through these voices, you will acquire a richer, real-life understanding of the family systems approach for your work with and for families.

These families and professionals speak with many dialects and accents; represent a broad spectrum of American life; and show how people of every economic and social stratum, of every color, race, and ethnic origin, in every part of this country empower themselves, their family members, and their colleagues in schools and communities. To repeat: Empowerment is for everyone, and these voices show exactly how everyone can become more empowerful through collaboration.

The chapters are strong theoretically and empirically in terms of their research base. Just as important (because we want this book to make a difference for you and others, personally and professionally), each chapter is highly applied, setting out techniques for you and others to use in collaborating for empowerment. The "Together We Can" and "Tips" features exemplify the applied nature of each chapter.

Acknowledgments

We have been privileged to have an "empowerment team" who assisted us with the preparation and production of this book. First and foremost, Opal Folks, Lois Weldon, and Ben Furnish, all at the Beach Center, have been valuable colleagues. It has delighted us to witness Opal and Lois "fighting" over who gets to prepare the next draft of each chapter. Their enthusiasm for the work and their spirited, friendly, and synergistic "can do" attitude show that they are not only mother and daughter but also incredibly productive and morale-boosting partners.

While completing his course work and comprehensive examinations for his doctorate in theater and film, Ben Furnish persevered as our "Sherlock Holmes," tracking down references, securing permissions, ensuring that all the photographs were in hand, and putting a final and necessary editing touch on each chapter. His diligence and commitment to quality are unsurpassed.

We are especially thankful to Cindy Higgins, the Beach Center's associate director, for her creation of the cover image for this text and for understanding how to translate the concepts of empowerment and collaboration into a powerful visual image.

All the Beach Center staff members have supported our efforts and have assisted in sharing information and resources at various stages of writing. It has been a pleasure for us to incorporate the research of many Beach Center staff members into this volume, and we gratefully acknowledge the information that they have produced and their collaborative, supportive partnerships.

Special thanks go to the Beach Center's own Richard Viloria for assisting us in preparing many of the figures and boxes throughout the text and to Ana Moshkina for helping us secure library resources.

Without the team, we could not have done this book nearly so efficiently and effectively. We are grateful to them all for their diverse and manifold contributions.

This being the third edition, we also acknowledge the help of the following Beach Center and Kansas University colleagues in the first two editions: Jean Ann Summers, Mary Jane Brotherson, Holly Benson, Betsy Santelli, Marilyn Shank, Chris Walther-Thomas, Julie Sergeant, Gloria Graves, Chuck Rhodes, Mary Beth Johnston, Laurie Ford, and Lori Unruh.

We also want to acknowledge the team at Merrill/Prentice Hall. Ann Davis (senior editor), Linda Montgomery (developmental editor), Pat Grogg (editorial assistant), Steve Robb (production editor), and Dawn Potter (copy editor), have been effective collaborators and reliable allies whose expertise and conscientiousness have significantly enhanced the quality of our work. We gratefully acknowledge their individual and collective contributions.

In terms of substance, we particularly acknowledge and affirm the seminal work of Joyce Epstein from The Johns Hopkins University. Dr. Epstein is a prolific researcher and contributor to the general education literature about family-school-community partnerships. Although there has been a separation of family related literature concerning general and special education, Dr. Epstein's work has tremendous implications for the field of special education. We are grateful to have the opportunity to merge it with special education literature throughout this text.

One of our favorite features in *Families, Professionals, and Exceptionality* is the opening and closing vignette of each chapter. So we send out a special thanks to these "voices" and their families: Patricia McGill Smith, Glenn Gabbard, Hortense Walker and Theresa Cooper, Susan Rocco, Marta Cofresi, Nila Benito, Richard and Betty Battles, Tricia Baccus, Sue Manos, Lorrie Baxter, Nancy Lunsford, Nancy Ward, Pam Gorian, Lisa Lieberman and Craig Ackerson, Scefinia Hill, Jane and John Hoyt, and Delfy Roach. In addition, we especially acknowledge their children, whose lives and experiences form the core of this book. Finally, we appreciate the efforts of Pat Boyd, Kathleen Judd, Nancy Krafcik, John McIntyre, Mark Mlawyer, Julie Sergeant, and Mary Ellen Sullivan in connecting us to some of these families.

In closing, we would like to thank the following reviewers for their valuable suggestions: Beth Harry, University of Miami, who made especially helpful conceptual comments; Martha Cook, University of Alabama; Melanie B. Jephson, Stephen F. Austin State University; Alec F. Peck, Boston College; and Ellen Williams, Bowling Green State University.

—The Turnbulls

Dear Reader,

The most effective professional—indeed, the person who makes the biggest difference in one's own life and in others' lives, too—is empowerful and collaborative.

Empowerful: To be an empowered person is to know what you want, to have the motivation to "go for it," and to have the knowledge and skills to turn your motivation into effective action, into the realization of a goal.

Collaborative: To be collaborative is to share resources among individuals, work jointly with others, and create a context that enhances collective action.

Empowerment and collaboration are the keys to our personal lives. As parents of J. T., our 28-year-old son who has mental retardation and autism, we have benefited from his own empowerment, as he has from ours. We have also benefited from collaboration with many families and professionals.

There was a time, not many years ago, when J. T. had "failed" special education, the sheltered workshop, and group-home living. The direction of his life was straight down—into an increasingly deep, dark hole of disappointment, segregation, and disability.

Today, some seven years later, J. T. works in competitive employment, with support, at the University of Kansas. He earns enough at his job to pay the principal, interest, taxes, and insurance on the house he lives in. He lives there with two roommates, neither of whom has a disability. He participates in recreation throughout our community and has become a well-known and welcome customer at bakeries and restaurants, music hangouts, and fitness centers.

How did all this come about? Because, through his own challenging behavior, J. T. conveyed that he wanted out of a segregated, low-expectations system. Because we witnessed what one teacher, Mary Morningstar at Walt Whitman High School in Bethesda, Maryland, could help J. T. accomplish. Because we believed that J. T. deserved an enviable life and because he and we dreamed of a different future. Because, through working with Mary and countless other professionals and friends, we have discovered that the "power of one"—the energy and talents of one person—expand exponentially when matched to the energy and talents of others.

There has developed in our lives and in J. T.'s a synergy—a combination of action and actors—that has a ripple effect. As J. T. and we are motivated to act, develop necessary knowledge and skills, and then take action—that is, as we act empowerfully—we do so with others as collaborators. And they in turn expand their own visions for themselves, families, students, and professionals. And then they and we collaborate to help that enlarged vision become a reality.

J. T.'s life is an evolving testament to the power of motivation, the potency of knowledge, and the utility of skills—a dynamic example of empowerment through collaboration.

With J. T., Mary Morningstar, and our lives with them as the living foundation, we wrote this book to enable you to have great expectations, to motivate you to pursue them, to provide you with knowledge and skills to do so, and to encourage you to do likewise with others.

What expectation? An expectation of life for people with disabilities and their families such as J. T. and we have, one replete with friendships born of common endeavor.

We hope you will absorb, share, and apply this book and its teachings for the benefit of families, students, other professionals, and yourself. Becoming a more empowerful and collaborative person, a person who can make a sustainable difference in your own life and through your life for others: That is our hope for you.

—The Turnbulls

Table of Contents

Families, Professionals, and Exceptionality

A Special Partnership

Part One

Understanding Empowerment

Part 1 introduces you to our central theme—empowerment. In chapter 1, we trace the history of parent-professional relationships, showing how parents' roles and professionals' views of parents' roles have evolved. As philosopher George Santayana has cautioned us, we will surely repeat our histories unless we understand them. Repeating some of the parent-professional history is not desirable, but moving from that history into different kinds of futures is.

Just as parent-professional relationships have changed, so, too, have the schools—the places where the relationships are played out. In chapter 2, we describe the recent changes in special and general education, paying particular attention to efforts to reform both types of education and to make schools more inclusive for children with disabilities and gifts/talents. Because schools are the contexts where history is reflected and the future shaped as well as the contexts in which professionals, families, and students are joined inseparably, they are particularly important to understand.

Having laid a foundation, we address our main theme in chapter 3—empowerment of families, professionals, and students. Here, we state for the first time our simple, straightforward message: You can be a better professional if you seek to empower families and students, your professional colleagues, and yourself. Having said as much, we introduce the conceptual framework for empowerment and link it to the context of the schools.

In chapter 4, we describe eight obligations that you have for establishing reliable alliances with families. These obligations focus on the affective or attitudinal qualities and skills that you bring to your work and that are at the heart of empowering partnerships.

At the end of part 1, you should be able to trace the history of parent-professional relationships, describe the schools as the contemporary context for empowerment, define empowerment and its components, and explain the eight obligations of reliable alliances.

Chapter One

Historical and Current Roles of Families and Parents

It's a long way from Omaha, Nebraska, a long way from being the single mother of a newborn with a disability to Washington, D.C., and being the executive director of a national network of parent-directed organizations that advocate for children with disabilities. But Patricia McGill Smith is quite a traveler, and in more ways than one. Patty and her daughter Jane, who has mental retardation and pervasive developmental disorders, are more than just zip-code travelers. They are travelers across the historical and current roles of families, having assumed many roles in the nearly 25 years that Jane has been alive.

When Jane was born, Patty searched and searched for reasons to explain why her daughter had a disability. Was it because Patty had had a stressful pregnancy, during which her mother was extremely ill and her father died? That seemed not to be the case, and "blaming it on God didn't seem to work, either," says Patty.

Lacking an explanation, however, did not mean that Patty lacked an ability to help herself and then others. Soon after Jane was born, Patty became a paid staffer at the local Association for Retarded Children. She helped to connect parents of newborns to parents of older children with disabilities for information and emotional support and thus created new services for parents and children.

Nonetheless, Patty still faced convoluted issues about how to support Jane without overlooking the needs of her six other children. It was a few years after Jane was born before Patty could talk with her other children about Jane's disability. Until then, those brothers and sisters were "left to swim in the morass that I was in,

only I didn't know it. I was just so completely caught up with my own emotions and my own fears and my own sadness that it didn't dawn on me to think in terms of the brothers and sisters and the support they needed. It was six or seven years before I ever really, really sat down and talked to them, to really ask, 'How do you deal with this fact? What are your feelings? How did it impact your life?'"

What triggered those heart-to-heart conversations was Patty's realization that she was spending "so much of my time and energy, every waking hour, just on Jane." Sadly, she recalls, it got so bad that she could not remember watching her daughter Mariann growing up. That lack of memory, more than anything else, was the source of Patty's courage when she told one of Jane's teachers that, despite the teacher's insistence, she would not attend one of Jane's extracurricular presentations but was going to watch her son Matt pitch his first Little League game. Fortunately for Patty, another professional told her, several years later, that she was right to split her time among all her children: None of them was Jane's mother and none should have to assume so much responsibility. Indeed, Patty's best advice to her children was simply the truth: "You need to know that Jane takes more time, more energy, more resources, more of everything we've got, and I don't regret giving it to her, but you need to know that our family is imbalanced. This is the way it is, and we must all work together."

Patty's growth into a national advocate began when she was hired as the parent consultant at Meyer Children's Rehabilitation Institute at the University of Nebraska Hospital in Omaha. "I moved from the kitchen table to a paid staff position, as a parent. I probably was the first parent in the country to be paid for giving a parent perspective on the health care of children with disabilities. For me, that was a dramatic turn of events in parent-professional relationships." Later, Patty became the deputy assistant secretary of special education, U.S. Department of Education, working with assistant secretary Madeleine Will (herself the mother of a young man with mental retardation); and still later she became executive director of the National Parent Network on Disability.

Not every parent will become an advocate, and Patty's advice to parents is simple: "You can learn so much and you can do so much, but you don't have to because, whatever age or stage you are in your life, do what's the right thing for you. Take care of yourself so you can take care of your family."

Collaboration, Patty is quick to point out, comes from creating the "trust bond" between parents and professionals. The trust bond comes when parents and professionals open up to each other—when professionals tell parents why and how they became professionals, who has had the greatest influence on them, and what they like about their jobs. These three simple conversation topics, Patty says, let professionals enter into a personal dialogue with families, potentially creating the trust bond that lets families and professionals collaborate. This collaboration benefits professionals in a special way: "They get the personal satisfaction, they experience the growth and the development that the parent's experiencing because you're both walking through this same developmental stage."

3

Why is it important for you to know about the history of family and parent roles in the care and education of children and youth with exceptionalities? First, history helps us understand contemporary issues and approaches, many of which are legacies from the past. Second, many of the challenges that families and professionals now face can be overcome if we heed history's lessons. Third, history teaches us that today's approaches may seem as improbable to the next generation of families and professionals as earlier approaches seem to us now.

Families and parents have had nine major roles over time: (1) the source of their child's disability, (2) organization members, (3) service developers, (4) recipients of professionals' decisions, (5) teachers, (6) political advocates, (7) educational decision makers, (8) family members, and (9) collaborators. These roles do not represent discrete eras, each with a clear beginning and end. Rather, the roles overlap. There is, however, a general and approximate chronological order to them.

Parents As the Source of Their Child's Disability

The eugenics movement (1880–1930) pointed to parents as the source or cause of their child's disability (Barr, 1913). To eliminate or reduce the number of "unfit" parents, the eugenicists argued, would improve the human race through selective breeding. The eugenics movement was based on (1) genealogical investigations such as Goddard's (1912) study of the Kallikak family, (2) Mendel's laws of heredity, and (3) studies by MacMurphy (1916) and Terman (1916) indicating that delinquent behaviors were strongly associated with "feeble-mindedness" (Scheerenberger, 1983).

The eugenics movement resulted in laws that restricted marriage by persons with intellectual disabilities and required them to be sterilized and institutionalized (Ferguson, 1994). Upholding a compulsory sterilization law, U.S. Supreme Court Justice Oliver Wendell Holmes, Jr., wrote: "Three generations of imbeciles are enough" (*Buck v. Bell*, 1927). By the same token, only 9,334 persons with mental retardation were institutionalized in 1900, but 68,035 were in institutions in 1930 (Scheerenberger, 1983).

The parents-as-cause perspective extended beyond mental retardation to autism (Bettelheim, 1950, 1967); asthma (Gallagher & Gallagher, 1985); learning disabilities (Oliver, Cole, & Hollingsworth 1991; Orton, 1930; Thomas, 1905); and emotional disorders (Caplan & Hall-McCorquodale, 1985). Nowhere is professional blaming behavior more evident than with respect to autism. It was typical in the 1940s and 1950s for professionals to describe parents of children and youth who had autism as rigid, perfectionist, emotionally impoverished, and depressed (Kanner, 1949; Marcus, 1977). Indeed, a leading professional, Bruno Bettelheim (1950, 1967), contended that a child who had autism—characterized by severe withdrawal—was simply responding to the stress created by the parents' "extreme and explosive" hatred of the child. Bettelheim even advocated a "parentectomy"— namely, institutionalizing the child and thereby replacing natural parents with institutional staff and professionals allegedly more competent and caring.

By contrast, the current definition of autism states that "no known factors in the psychological environment of a child have been shown to cause autism" (National Society for Autistic Children, 1977). This definition is the one accepted by professionals, families, and Congress (in the federal special education law). In box 1–1, Frank Warren (1985), the father of a young man with autism and a national advocate, totally rejects the Bettelheim position. He comments on Bettelheim's position in light of the new definition.

Congenital malformations occur in approximately 3 percent of all births. Only 25 percent of those malformations are known to have genetic causes. Another 10 percent are known to have environmental causes, and 65 percent have causes that are currently unknown (Beckman & Brant, 1986; Buyse, 1990). Of course, some disabilities in children may be traced to the parents. For example, some conditions (such as cystic fibrosis) are clearly genetic in nature. Excessive use of alcohol or drugs by pregnant women may cause children to have disabling conditions such as fetal alcohol syndrome or cocaine addiction (Conlon, 1992; Poulsen, 1994). Likewise, pregnant women who use intravenous drugs put their children at risk for human immunodeficiency virus (HIV), the cause of acquired immunodeficiency syndrome (AIDS). In fact, 80 percent of children with pediatric AIDS have acquired HIV from their mothers (Conlon, 1992). Malnutrition during pregnancy or in the child's early life may lead to mild mental retardation or motor impairment (Baumeister, Kupstas, & Woodley-Zanthos, 1993; Coulter, 1987). Nonetheless, some children who are exposed to extremely detrimental environments early in life develop relatively unscathed by their experiences, whereas other children who are subjected to less stressful environments may fail to thrive and experience developmental delays (Werner & Smith, 1992).

Shame on You!

That means we didn't do it. . . . We, the parents of autistic children, are just ordinary people. Not any crazier than others. Not "refrigerator parents" any more than others. Not cold intellectuals any more than others. Not neurotic or psychopathic or sociopathic or any of those words that have been made up. It means, Dr. Bettelheim, that you, and all those others like you who have been laying this incredible guilt trip on us for over 20 years, you are wrong and ought to be ashamed of yourselves.

Source: Warren, F. (1985). "A society that is going to kill your children." In H. R. Turnbull & A. P. Turnbull (Eds.), *Parents speak out: Then and now* (2nd ed.) (p. 217). Englewood Cliffs, NJ: Merrill/Prentice Hall.

Our best advice to you is this: Avoid blaming parents! If you need to know the cause of a disability, investigate it. If you learn that the parent may have been a cause, use that information to design supports and services that can be particularly helpful to the family and find ways to identify and affirm their positive contributions to their child. As you do so, you may be able to contribute to preventing disabilities in their other children and avoid exacerbating their child's existing disability. But do not blame. The only thing that blaming can do is create a barrier to collaboration between you and the family; and without collaboration you will be less effective in assisting the family, and the family will derive less benefit from you. In short: Blame is a barrier, but empathy is conducive to collaboration.

Parents As Organization Members

Parents and other family members began to organize on a local level in the 1930s and on the national level in the late 1940s and 1950s. Many parents and families believed that public and professional responses to their children's educational and other needs were inadequate; additionally, many sought emotional support from others who were facing similar challenges. They were the predecessors of people such as Patty Smith (the Omaha mother). In 1933, five mothers of children with mental retardation in Cuyahoga County, Ohio, organized a group to protest the public schools' exclusion of their children. Their efforts led to a special class that they themselves sponsored. Much later, in 1950, 42 parents and other concerned individuals from 13 states met in Minneapolis to establish the National Association of Parents and Friends of Mentally Retarded Children (later called the National Association for Retarded Children, then the National Association for Retarded Citizens, and now The Arc).

The group known as the United Cerebral Palsy Associations (UCP) has a similar history. It was founded in 1949 largely through the efforts of Leonard H. Goldenson, the father of a child with cerebral palsy. Here is what he says about UCP's beginnings:

> One day, realizing the cost of driving our child into New York City from Westchester, my wife said to me, "Leonard, I know we can afford to do this but what about the poor people? How can they afford to do it?" And she added, "Why don't we look into the possibility of trying to help others in this field?"
>
> It was on that basis that I started to investigate the whole field of cerebral palsy.
>
> Upon investigation, I found there were probably only twenty-some-odd doctors in the entire United States who knew anything about cerebral palsy. I found there were only a few local parents groups in the country that were trying to do something about it. But the parents were so involved with their own children and had to take so much time with them, they could not get out to raise money and inform the public about the subject. (Goldenson, 1965, pp. 1–2)

Other parent groups include the National Society for Autistic Children, founded in 1961 and now called Autism Society of America; the National Association for Down Syndrome, founded in 1961; the Association for Children with Learning Disabilities, founded in 1964; and the Federation of Families for Children's Mental Health, founded in December 1988. The federation's mission statement appears in figure 1–1.

Despite their impact on service delivery and political advocacy, parent organizations cannot be all things to all parents. Elizabeth Boggs, one of the founding members of The Arc, writes:

> I am proud to be the only person who has been continuously active in some volunteer capacity with the National Association for Retarded Citizens [now called The Arc] since I participated in its founding in 1950. . . . The cause has taken me to 44 states, plus Puerto Rico and 10 foreign countries. It is hard to put a job title on the role I've played. One could say that I've been a social synergist with a predisposition toward communication and collaboration rather than confrontation. (Boggs, 1985, pp. 39–40)

By contrast, Janet Bennett, also a parent, sees organizational membership in a much different light.

> My first phone call to my local unit produced a pleasant enough response from the office secretary and a promise of some information to be mailed. This material consisted of a short summary of the unit's programs and services and a long questionnaire on which I could indicate areas in which I would be delighted to volunteer. . . . The message was clear: a parent in my circumstances, trying to cope with a trauma of uncertain dimensions, should marshal her forces, muster her energies, and get out and work for the cause. . . .

> If I had had an unretarded baby, I'd never in a million years have thought of volunteering for anything during that period. Now that I had Kathryn, why in the world would I be expected to do anything of the kind. Yet in the face of minimal help from the organization, it was telling me I should help it. And numb from shock and diminished self-confidence, I did my best to comply. (Bennett, 1985, pp. 163, 164)

Moreover, parent organizations tend to consist primarily of white, middle-class parents. Minority parents and parents who are very rich or very poor typically have not joined them. A 1987 survey of The Arc membership revealed that 95 percent of the respondents were white and only one-fourth of all members had incomes under $20,000 (Haller & Millman, 1987).

Here's the simple point to remember: Some parents, but not others, are helped by and participate in parent organizations. Share information with parents about appropriate local, state, and national organizations but encourage them to determine the level and type of their own participation. One caution: Despite the increased emphasis on noncategorical services in schools and special education, most parent organizations are based on disability categories. If you teach in

FIGURE 1–1

Federation of Families for Children's Mental Health Mission Statement

- To ensure the rights to full citizenship, support and access to community-based services for all children and youth with emotional, behavioral, or mental disorders and their families.

- To address the unique needs of children and youth with emotional, behavioral, or mental disorders from birth through the transition to adulthood.

- To provide information and engage in advocacy regarding research, prevention, early intervention, family support, education, transition services, and other services needed by these children, youth, and their families.

- To provide leadership in the field of children's mental health and develop necessary human and financial resources to meet its goal.

Source: Steering Committee for the Federation of Families for Children's Mental Health. (1989, March). *Mission statement.* Alexandria, VA: Author. Reprinted by permission.

schools that do not categorize children by type of disability, parents may need information about the type of disability so they can get support from the appropriate parent organizations.

Parents As Service Developers

Parents have played a major role in developing services for their minor and adult children. During the 1950s and 1960s, they and the organizations they created focused on establishing education programs for children who had moderate and severe disabilities but were excluded from public schools. These parents organized classes in community buildings and church basements, solicited financial support from charitable organizations, and did the job the schools should have been doing. During those two decades and especially since then, parents and their organizations have spearheaded recreation, out-of-home residential living, and employment services. In all these endeavors, parents have had four jobs: They have created public awareness, raised money, operated services, and advocated for others to take over service operations.

Samuel Kirk (1984), a distinguished special educator, describes the profound impact of parent organizations in developing special education services:

> I found a satisfaction in associating with many intelligent and knowledgeable parents in these organizations. I found that through association with other parents they learned what the best programs were for their children. If I were to give credit to one group in this country for the advancements that have been made in the education of exceptional children, I would place the parent organizations and parent movement in the forefront as the leading force. (p. 41)

Although some family members prefer to be service developers and providers, professionals should not expect them to start and maintain services that are the professionals' responsibility. For example, professionals should not expect parents to start a supported employment program for students with disabilities; after all, parents of children without disabilities are not expected to start and maintain a college preparatory curriculum in their local high school. Of course, families should have full opportunities to collaborate with professionals in creating educational, vocational, and recreational programs; but they should not have to assume the full responsibility for starting and operating any program. There is one very good reason: Many parents simply do not have the time to develop and operate services. They often already devote extraordinary time just to meeting their own needs and satisfying the demands of their for-pay jobs (Knoll, 1992). In other words, parents should be supported to be parents, first and foremost. Service development should be an option, not an expectation, for them.

Parents As Recipients of Professionals' Decisions

Even as recently as the 1970s, and certainly long before then, professionals expected parents to comply passively and gratefully with their decisions about the programs in which their children should participate and how those programs should operate. As Kolstoe (1970), an author of a leading textbook on the methods of educating students with disabilities, wrote in 1970:

> Should it be judged that special class placement will probably be of most benefit to the child, then placement should be made without delay. Both the child and his parents should be told that the

child is being transferred into the special class because the class is special. . . . The entire program should be explained so the parents will understand what lies ahead for the child and so they can support the efforts of the teachers with the child. (Kolstoe, 1970, p. 42)

This was not a novel perspective for students who were regarded as gifted, as a 1960s text shows:

> Some "guts" to speak straight from the shoulder would be helpful to the educators in this situation. Then the lay groups probably would realize they must delegate some of their authority to the educators to make necessary decisions for improving the education of students. For example, an overwhelming majority of parents do not have the sophistication in educational matters to decide whether or not their youngster would be better off educationally if placed in a differential program for the gifted. . . . Parents could better spend their time: a) supporting parent organizations for raising funds and influencing state and federal legislation, and b) learning techniques to aid their own youngsters toward high achievement. (Lucito, 1963, pp. 227–228)

Some professionals still believe that they and the school systems know what is best for a student, so they still expect families to assume a totally deferential role, especially regarding the student's evaluation, program, and placement. Professionals with this expectation create a psychological barrier to effective family-professional collaboration—for example, parents may feel intimidated and angered by the professionals' authoritarian approach (Turbiville, Turnbull, Garland, & Lee, 1996). This psychological barrier can be particularly strong and problematic for culturally diverse families (Harry, Allen, & McLaughlin, 1995). Try to be an equal partner with families when making decisions and do not expect them to be the passive recipients of your decisions. Cultivate the approach that Patty Smith advocates, creating a trust bond and joint decisions. Throughout this book, we will be providing you with information about how you can collaborate in various decision-making situations.

Parents As Teachers

The role of parents as teachers emerged during the late 1960s, peaked during the 1970s, and was moderated during the mid to late 1980s. At the root of the parent-as-teacher role was evidence that family environment influences children's intelligence (Hunt, 1972). The data showed that families from economically deprived backgrounds had problems associated with their home lives, and these problems created child-rearing environments that lacked the opportunities typically available in middle- and upper-class homes (Zigler & Muenchow, 1992). Thus, President Kennedy's New Frontier and President Johnson's Great Society programs (for example, Head Start) included training parents to teach their children; in turn, the children would make more progress, a theory largely credited to researcher Urie Bronfenbrenner.

> Bronfenbrenner's notion of parent involvement and the ecological model of child development emerged from two sources—his own childhood and his cross-cultural research. Born in Moscow, he emigrated to the United States in 1923. His father, a physician, took a job as director of an institution for the "feeble-minded" in Letchworth Village, New York.
>
> From time to time, Bronfenbrenner's father would anguish over the commitment to the institution of a person who was not retarded. Sadly, after a few weeks there, these people of normal intelligence would begin to mimic the mannerisms of the rest of the residents. When one of these patients came to work in the Bronfenbrenners' household, however, she gradually resumed a "normal" life. To young Urie, it was an important lesson in how family and community expectations influence human behavior.
>
> After such an upbringing, Bronfenbrenner decided to become a psychologist. During the course of cross-cultural studies in western and eastern Europe, he was struck by the observation that Russian parents, both fathers and mothers, seemed to spend more time with their children than did American parents. When he was asked to present his findings at a National Institute for Child Health and Human Development meeting in 1964, a woman named Florence Mahoney commented, "Why, the president ought to hear about this."
>
> A few weeks later the White House called, and Bronfenbrenner and his wife were soon presenting their observations on Russian childrearing complete with slides to Lady Bird and her daughters. The Johnsons were impressed, especially by the pictures of Russian preschools. One of the Johnson daughters asked, "Why couldn't we do something like this?" (Zigler & Muenchow, 1992, pp. 16–17)

Bronfenbrenner's approach—called *ecological* because it linked family environment to human development—was the basis on which professionals prepared parents for increasing their children's progress and achievement. The 1970s brought an emphasis on parents' learning behavioral principles and child development so they could teach their children how to develop. Enthusiasm for this approach was sparked by encouraging research results that parents can be effective teachers of their children (Bricker & Bricker, 1976; Shearer & Shearer, 1977). Professionals, more emphatically than parents, endorsed the parent-as-learner-and-teacher role. Because parents *could* be effective teachers, many professionals believed that parents *should* be teachers. They also believed that "good" parents were those who frequently served as teachers, not "just" parents, for their children (Benson & Turnbull, 1986).

The use of the term *parent* is actually a misnomer in this context. It is more correct to substitute "mothers" for "parents" because literature of this period contains almost no reference to the role that fathers might play in their children's development (Turbiville, Turnbull, & Turnbull, 1995).

Given the optimism that research data justified (Baker, 1989), it was only natural for early childhood education programs to insist that parents should be effective teachers of their own children (Shearer & Shearer, 1977). And just what should parents be taught? Karnes and Teska (1980) have identified the competencies that parents need to acquire to fulfill their "teacher" role:

> The parental competencies required for direct teaching of the handicapped child at home involve interacting with the child in ways that promote positive behavior; reinforcing desired behavior; establishing an environment that is conducive to learning; setting up and maintaining a routine for direct teaching; using procedures appropriate for teaching concepts and skills; adapting lesson plans to the child's interests and needs; determining whether the child has mastered knowledge and skills; keeping meaningful records, including notes on child progress; participating in a staffing of the child; communicating effectively with others; and assessing the child's stage of development. (p. 99)

Surprisingly, these are fewer than half the skills the authors regarded as essential to the parent-as-teacher role. Now, compare these skills to the ones you have to master through your own professional training program and ask yourself whether it is realistic to expect parents to develop so many didactic skills.

Some parents find teaching to be very satisfying. Others say it produces unintended consequences, such as guilt and stress if they are not constantly working with their son or daughter (Robbins, Dunlap, & Plienis, 1991). Indeed, many of today's parents of children and youth with disabilities, unlike parents during the 1970s and early 1980s, seem to place less importance on their roles as teachers. There are reports of low attendance rates at parent training sessions (Chilman, 1973; Rosenberg, Reppucci, & Linney, 1983; Shank & Turnbull, 1993). Instead, many families want more information (not necessarily formal training sessions) on various topics (Cooper & Allred, 1992). That is why many families today welcome information on topics such as advocacy, homework, and future planning. Consider information exchanges (a more collaborative term than parent training) and invite fathers, brothers and sisters, and extended family members rather than only mothers.

If you believe that you or your professional colleagues have information to share with parents so they can be more effective in raising their children or supporting their families, we urge you to ask the parents what they want to know and how they want to learn it and then to offer them whatever they want. Of course, you should explain what you can offer and why you think they should say yes to your offer. But in the parent-as-teacher role, collaboration (joint planning of parent education programs) will do everyone more good than a professional-knows-best approach. Many educational programs are best provided by a parent-professional instructional team with families and professionals as co-learners (Winton & DiVenere, 1995).

Parents As Political Advocates

Parents have been tremendously successful as advocates in the political process, but they have had to work for many years at the federal, state, and local levels and in legislatures, courts, and executive agencies. It was because educational services for most students with disabilities were woefully inadequate throughout 1950–1970 that parents took on a new role—as political advocates. In the early 1970s, parents of students with mental retardation and the Pennsylvania Association for Retarded Children won a lawsuit against the state to obtain a free appropriate education for children with mental retardation (*Pennsylvania Association for Retarded Citizens (PARC) v. Commonwealth of Pennsylvania*, 1971, 1972). Thereafter, parents and the organizations to which they belonged brought right-to-education suits in almost every state, usually successfully. Buoyed by their success in court, parents sought federal legislation to implement the courts' decisions (Turnbull, 1994). Parent organizations representing all areas of exceptionality, particularly The Arc, joined forces with professionals, particularly the Council for Exceptional Children, and successfully advocated for comprehensive federal legislation requiring the states to provide all students with disabilities a free appropriate public education.

The parent groups were immensely successful as political advocates, convincing Congress to pass the Education for All Handicapped Children Act (P.L. 94-142) in 1975 and four major amendments since then (1978, 1983, 1986, and 1990). (We discuss this legislation, now referred to as the Individuals with Disabilities Education Act, in detail in chapter 9.) It is a tribute to parent advocacy—always greatly aided by and sometimes led by professional organizations—that Congress passed these laws, that the parent organizations were able to form coalitions with each other and professional groups, and that all of this has been accomplished over such an extended period of time in a continuous and consistent manner. Box 1–2 describes the results of the policy collaboration between parents as advocates and professionals—the collaboration that convinced Congress to enact the 1975 federal special education law.

Lowell Weicker (1985), a former United States senator from Connecticut and the father of a son with Down syndrome, played an important role in the advocacy movement. In the mid 1980s, he described the impact of political advocacy on attempts by President Reagan's administration to deemphasize the federal role in special education, attempts that he and the parent advocacy movement thwarted:

> The administration did not get its way. Why? Because the disabled people in this country and their advocates repudiated a long-held cliché that they were not a political constituency, or at least not a coherent one. It was assumed that in the rough and tumble world of politics they would not hold their own as a voting block or as advocates for their cause. But that assumption was blown to smithereens in the budget and policy deliberations of 1981, 1982, and again in 1983. In fact, I would be hard-pressed to name another group within the human service spectrum that has not only survived the policies of this administration but has also defeated them as consistently and as convincingly as the disabled community has. Indeed, it has set an example for others, who were believed to be better organized. (p. 284)

As the federal role in disability services changes and as state and local governments and even the private-sector providers play more significant roles in implementing disability policy and funding disability services, parents once again will be obliged to be advocates.

Collaborating for New Policies and Laws

Congress enacted P.L. 94-142, Education for All Handicapped Children Act, in 1975 because of a ground swell of public opinion led by desperate families, assisted greatly by professionals, and buoyed up by governors and state legislators.

What kind of ground swell arose from the families? One that produced literally thousands of letters, hundreds upon hundreds of pages of written testimony, scores of personal visits from families to their senators and representatives, and hundreds of witnesses before congressional committees that took testimony in Washington, D.C., and in the states.

The ground swell was carefully orchestrated by a coalition of family-advocacy organizations representing a wide spectrum of disabilities, including mental retardation, cerebral palsy, deafness, blindness, physical disabilities, learning disabilities, and emotional disorders. It was lead by The Arc; its governmental-affairs committee chairman, Elizabeth M. Boggs (the mother of child with severe disabilities); that committee's staff director, Paul Marchand (a special educator); and the Council for Exceptional Children under the direction of its governmental-affairs staffers Fred Weintraub and A1 Abeson.

It revealed in excruciating detail the effects on children and their families when schools will not admit the children as students, misclassify them, fail to offer an appropriate education, disregard parents' participation in individualized evaluations and programs, and refer students to warehouse-like institutions.

The ground swell revealed the desperation, anger, and frustration that parents felt; the urgent needs their children had; and the recalcitrance of public school officials to admit, much less educate effectively, the great majority of children with disabilities.

Beginning in 1972 and not stopping until Congress enacted (over President Ford's veto) P.L. 94-142 in 1975, parents practiced the old lawyer's adage: "When you have the law, argue the law"—but they didn't have the law on their side. "When you have the facts, argue the facts"—and they did have the facts on their side. "And whatever you do, scream like hell"—and they certainly did that and very successfully, too.

Parents As Educational Decision Makers

The role of parents as educational decision makers grows directly out of the 1975 law, P.L. 94-142, Education of All Handicapped Children Act, now called Individuals with Disabilities Education Act (IDEA). This revolutionary law grants active decision-making rights to parents of children and youth with disabilities. But the law is also very traditional because it recognizes the critical role that families play in their children's development and the necessity of subjecting schools to parental oversight. Although children who are gifted are not included in the federal laws for children with disabilities, 33 states have mandates, accompanied by some level of funding, for gifted education (Coleman, Gallagher, & Foster, 1994).

In granting these decision-making and accountability rights to parents, Congress adopted the basic premise that families of children and youth with disabilities could make no assumptions that the public schools would allow parents to enroll their children, much less that schools would educate the children appropriately (Turnbull, Turnbull, & Wheat, 1982). Thus, Congress viewed parents as persons who should or could ensure that professionals provide an appropriate education; this view reflected a major reversal in expectations about parents' roles. No longer were parents to be passive recipients of professionals' decisions concerning services to their children. Now they were to be educational decision makers and monitors, doing what Patty Smith has been doing for all of Jane's life.

Parents' relationships with professionals may have indeed become more equal than a couple of decades ago; however, the majority of parents participate in educational decision making in a passive rather than an active style (Goldstein, Strickland, Turnbull, & Curry, 1980; Lynch & Stein, 1982; Malekoff, Johnson, & Klappersack, 1991). Why is this so? We address the reasons for passive participation more fully in chapter 2 and throughout this entire book.

Sometimes parents do not have the motivation (such as energy or hope) to be educational decision makers; at other times they have the motivation but do not have the knowledge and skills (such as information or problem-solving skills); and in a vast number of cases parents have motivation, knowledge, and skill, but the educational context disempowers rather than empowers them to be partners. This is particularly so for culturally diverse parents who have felt disenfranchised by the educational system (Harry et al., 1995; Harry & Kalyanpur, 1994). But the roles of parents as educational decision makers—particularly moving from a passive role to one of educational decision maker—are changing. The current emphasis is on collaboration.

Families As Collaborators

In their current role, families are regarded as collaborators. An important word in that sentence is *families*. Until the early 1990s, all roles typically focused on parents. This is the first time that we have used *family* to describe a role. The reason for the change is that there has been increasing recognition that partnerships do not need to be limited—and should not be limited—to parents only (especially to mothers only). Partnerships can and should involve relationships between professionals and other family members, such as grandparents, brothers and sisters, and even close family friends, who are vital resources in supporting and enhancing educational outcomes for students with exceptionalities. Just consider Patty and Jane Smith; the entire Smith family should have the opportunity to be collaborators with Jane's professional providers.

Although families from different cultures define themselves in many and varied ways, we have chosen to define *family* as "two or more people who regard themselves as a family and who perform some of the functions that families typically perform. These people may or may not be related by blood or marriage and may or may not usually live together" (Turnbull, Turnbull, Shank, & Leal, 1995, pp. 24–25). Thus, four generations of women who are living together might call themselves a family unit; another family might describe a broad network of parents, grandparents, aunts and uncles, cousins, and a host of others who are part of close-knit family relationships.

Beginning in the mid 1980s, both professionals and parents began to emphasize that successful family life requires that the needs of all family members should be identified, addressed, and balanced (Friesen & Koroloff, 1990; Morgan, 1988; Patterson, 1991; Turnbull & Summers, 1987). This premise is consistent with family systems theory, which views the family as a social system with unique characteristics and needs. Family systems theory asserts that the individual members of a family are so interrelated that any experience affecting one member will affect all (Carter & McGoldrick, 1980; Goldenberg & Goldenberg, 1980; Minuchin, 1974). Certainly Patty Smith, when discussing Jane's siblings, makes that fact clear. It has helped us, and we hope it will help you, to combine family systems theory with research on the impact of children and youth on families (Benson & Turnbull, 1986; Turnbull, Summers, & Brotherson, 1984; Turnbull, Brotherson, & Summers, 1985). In chapters 5 through 8, we will introduce you to family systems theory and its implication for families.

Why is family systems theory important to you? Briefly, it will help you know families; and when you know families in an individual and personalized way, you can be attuned to their strengths, great expectations, priorities, and needs. In turn, the family systems approach can help you work more effectively and collaboratively with the family members who are most able to promote students' positive educational outcomes.

Now that you have learned the definition and composition of *family* and have been introduced to a family systems perspective, we need to clarify what we mean by collaboration. (We will refer to this definition throughout this book, particularly in chapter 3 when we talk about collaboration for empowerment.) *Collaboration* refers to the dynamic process of connecting families' resources (that is, motivation and knowledge/skills) to an empowering context to make decisions collectively.

The role of parents as collaborators differs from the role of parents as decision makers and certainly from that of parents as recipients of professionals' judgments. The role of parents as collaborators presumes that families will be equal and full partners with educators and school systems and that this collaboration will affect the student and school system operations as well. Sometimes family views will prevail; at other times they will not. Always families, in alliance with educators, will grapple with the difficult task of providing a free appropriate education to each student.

State-of-the-art collaboration involves a wide range of stakeholders in promoting the most successful educational experiences for students. Those stakeholders are families, students with exceptionalities, classmates, teachers, administrators, paraprofessionals, and related service providers. This kind of collaboration benefits not only family members but also educators, who derive support and assistance from professional colleagues and families. For example, a general classroom teacher who has primary responsibility for educating a student with autism is not left to generate solutions to all challenges but instead has a dynamic team of supporters, helpers, and friends who provide assistance to find the most successful solutions to those challenges.

Students with exceptionalities are key collaborators; their participation is referred to as self-determination. *Self-determination* means choosing how to live one's life consistently with one's personal values and preferences (Turnbull, Blue-Banning, Anderson, Turnbull, Seaton, & Dinas, 1996; Turnbull & Turnbull, 1985). For too many years, it has been assumed that either professionals or parents or both know what is in a student's best interest and that they should represent a student's interest when it comes to educational decision making.

Collaboration for self-determination encourages students, even from their earliest years, to develop the attitudes, knowledge, and skills to express their preferences and to make decisions based on their strengths, needs, and future aspirations. To this end, families and professionals create an empowering context to enable students to act on those attitudes, knowledge, and skills. Indeed, many secondary school programs have developed curricula and model opportunities for students to be involved in their own educational planning and decision making (Powers, Singer, & Sowers, 1996; Sands & Wehmeyer, 1996). As we will point out later, however, self-determination is culturally rooted in a value system that particularly emphasizes individual achievement and autonomy, so some families may reject self-determination as a culturally inappropriate goal.

What are the benefits of collaboration when we take into account a broader definition of family, self-determination, and the prospects of a much larger number of collaborators? Collaboration has two important benefits. First, it benefits the student by bringing to bear on the student's behalf the multiple perspectives and resources of the collaborators to improve educational outcomes. Second, it benefits the collaborators by making available to each the resources (that is, motivation and knowledge/skills) of the others and thereby increasing their own resources through the process of being supported by others and learning from others. A fundamental premise of this book is that collaboration is mutually beneficial: It is the most effective way of being a professional.

Because collaboration occurs in a school context, we turn next (in chapter 2) to that context, which is general and special education in today's schools and the family-professional partnership approaches associated with each. In chapter 3, we develop our theme of collaboration as a means to empowerment.

Summary

Parents and families have carried out many roles, some of them unwelcome or unjustified, some born out of necessity, and some of them eagerly embraced. These roles were the sources of their child's problems, organization members, service organizers, recipients of professionals' decisions, learners and teachers, political advocates, educational decision makers, and collaborators.

No one role can characterize all parents, and some parents have played all or most roles. Families vary in the roles they assume, and professionals vary in the roles they consider appropriate and in turn recommend to and expect from families. This much is clear, however: The pendulum of role playing has swung back and forth along several dimensions:

- From viewing parents as part of the child's problem to viewing them as collaborators in addressing the challenges of exceptionality
- From insisting on passive roles for parents to expecting active and collaborating roles for families
- From viewing families as a mother-child dyad to recognizing the preferences and needs of all members of a family
- From responding to family needs in a general way to individualizing for the family as a whole and for each member of the family

Families and professionals alike may feel caught up in time-zone changes, much like world travelers.

Dorothy "Tot" Avis (1985), a parent who is also a professional in the disability field, describes the concept of "deinstitutionalization jet lag," referring to parents who were told years ago that the state institution was best for their child and who now are told that the community is preferable. Families and professionals alike experience "family-role jet lag." Expectations and philosophies have drastically changed since the eugenics movement and the formation of parent organizations. Understanding the distance that families have traveled paves the way for the journey into mutually beneficial family-professional collaboration. This journey starts by considering a major theme that runs throughout this book—collaboration.

What does it mean to have time-traveled and role-traveled, as Patty and many other parents and professionals have? It means understanding the roles that families have assumed and continue to assume and seeing that they—and the professionals who work with them—will, together, have different roles in the future.

Very little about family-professional relationships is static; very much is dynamic. Among the most dynamic aspects of the relationships are those that rely on collaboration, not professional dominance or parent dominance within the relationships.

As Patty has said, "My experience has been that having professionals work with, around, above, behind, anywhere with me, has been the most absolutely wonderful thing that has happened to me. I have never thought that I, as a parent and a parent leader, ever could do it on my own, and I never did. My greatest successes have been in collaboration with other parents and with professionals, too. That collaboration has made all the difference."

Chapter Two

Schools As Systems: The Context for Family-Professional Collaboration

*I*t's a long way—geographically and metaphorically—from the playground at a Lexington, Massachusetts, elementary school to the White House and the United States Senate and House of Representatives in Washington, D.C.

But for Megan Gabbard, who has cerebral palsy and speech and motor impairments, and her parents, Glenn and Ruth Ann Gabbard, the distance is remarkably short. That is because the Gabbards and other parents are acting like the Minutemen who fired the shot heard 'round the world. They are taking matters into their own hands. Case in point: the playground, Megan's education, and Congress's enactment of school reform legislation in 1994.

Consider the playground. Designed by the parents of all the other students in Megan's elementary school and financed by their joint fund-raising efforts, the playground is accessible to all students, whatever their disabilities. It is a symbol of a school in which Megan and all other students with disabilities are included in general education programs.

Symbolically, the playground is a community for all children. Factually, it is the product of school reform dialogue between parents and educators concerned primarily with general education issues and those concerned primarily with special education issues.

Both the playground and school reform, Glenn explains, created long-needed opportunities for collaborative partnerships between these two different groups. Just as the playground's design, financing, and use brought special and general education constituencies into face-to-face conversation, so, too, school reform

gives parents of children in special education a chance to "be part of discussions that they were not previously party to"—discussions about outcome-based assessments of students and their schools, about how well or poorly the schools were preparing students for life after school.

Finally, school reform extends the notion of inclusion so that it is no longer a placement/curriculum issue but a governance issue. As Glenn says, "inclusion has been niched within special education, but it now means that kids with disabilities can participate in the restructuring opportunities that are provided in regular schools. . . . The specialized categories and programs such as special education can, under a restructuring framework, be included in a community, rather than being niched into separate systems."

Thus, inclusion techniques that benefit Megan and other special and general education students, such as cooperative learning, heterogeneous grouping, blended grades, shared technologies, and even playground design and funding, have two roles: The techniques lay the groundwork for school restructuring processes that involve parents of all children, and they are likely to benefit the dialogue around school reform.

Glenn cautions that one barrier to inclusion and school reform is the "when and where" of special and general education staff: When and where they were trained affects whether the staff want or can practice inclusion. Some special education staff simply don't believe Megan should be included. To Glenn's chagrin, their exclusionary view reinforces the general educators who believe the same. That attitude, however, runs contrary to the welcome that parents of children in general education have given to Megan. So attitudes are a problem. If a school does not have the expectation of innovation, then school reform will face hard times.

Another barrier may be structural. Will school teams really affect dialogue and result in improvements? Glenn has his doubts: Strategic planning for Megan and for schools themselves has to include special and general educators and parents of all children. A barrier is that these individuals have not had much practice at teaming, acknowledging conflict, and resolving conflict. "Open discussion and working-through are hard for any group"; but when they succeed, they create compatibility between these individuals and can lead to the kind of playground—and the kind of school—that provides access to and quality for all.

Glenn says, "My fear is that often the restructuring efforts simply add new layers on existing power structures and don't really make significant change." In addi-

tion, the "school system in general has not provided sufficient training to people at all of those levels about what it means to really reposition your authority in a school. . . . It's kind of counter-intuitive to some people to change the authority structure in a school. We have to learn how to team and be intentional about learning it. Otherwise it becomes a fad and people will dismiss it."

Dismissing the opportunities for teaming may be all too easy. "At the national level, one barrier to local teaming is that parents of children with disabilities are portrayed as a special interest group and not as consumers." That has a lot to do with how special education is funded. The challenge, Glenn concludes, is to create a dialogue among all consumers of education about the community of all learners.

"There is an intractable quality to some of these discussions about special education funding. Unless there is a more open discussion about how we could create newer systems, then the resentment of the special education 'interest group' will continue, weighted down by the *perception that parents of children with disabilities are rabid advocates and nothing more. We have to find new ways to talk about issues, and new issues to talk about.*

We have to discuss these issues without stigma, saying that we are committed to inclusion and community for all."

That's the playground metaphor: inclusion, a community for all, and new ways of talking and new issues to talk about. Will school restructuring ensure a new playground for all consumers of education? Not necessarily, but it can.

In chapter 1, you learned about the eight roles that parents have played in the education of children and youth with exceptionalities and that the most contemporary role is viewing families as collaborators. To help you collaborate, we will describe in this chapter the context of general and special education—how it has changed over the last two decades and how today it requires general and special education professionals to collaborate with each other and with families, students, and community representatives. We will focus on the general education reform movement, the special education reform movement, and current school restructuring efforts.

General Education Reform Movement

Contemporary school reform has been on the agenda since the early 1980s and has occurred in three phases (Turnbull, Turnbull, Shank, & Leal, 1995):

- *Enhancing the curriculum:* improving education by increasing academic excellence across basic subjects
- *Restructuring school governance:* creating local flexibility and innovation
- *Reshaping service delivery:* integrating educational, social services, mental health, public health, and other services into one delivery system

These three phases are illustrated in figure 2–1.

Enhancing the Curriculum

The major purpose of enhancing the curriculum was to ensure excellence. This impetus was supported by a national commission report, *A Nation at Risk*

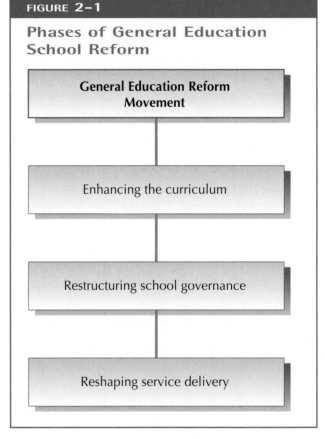

FIGURE 2–1

Phases of General Education School Reform

General Education Reform Movement

Enhancing the curriculum

Restructuring school governance

Reshaping service delivery

(National Commission on Excellence in Education, 1983), that emphasized the United States' loss of economic competitiveness with countries such as Japan and Germany because U.S. students were scoring lower than their peers from these and other countries. *A Nation at Risk*, as well as other national reports, recommended curriculum reform (for example, requiring more math and science) and called upon school staff to increase their effectiveness in educating students. Enhancing the curriculum was a top-down strategy in which federal leaders recommended curriculum guidelines for state and local educators.

The excellence-in-education movement undoubtedly made more educators, families, and community leaders aware that schools' and students' educational performance was not up to par. Although the schools were the first source of reform, many people expected parents to assume more responsibility for extending learning to the home.

Restructuring School Governance

A different and subsequent change strategy was a bottom-up approach that sought to reform school policies, improve school organizations, and allocate governance authority to local schools and away from district, state, and federal education agencies. As Glenn Gabbard pointed out, restructuring meant that the people of Lexington, Massachusetts, not bureaucrats in Washington, D.C., would design the playgrounds—actually and metaphorically.

Restructuring gave significantly more opportunities to parents to advocate for systems change as members of site-based management teams. But simply having opportunities for decision making that are closer to the local level does not guarantee an authentic family voice. School power structures typically give the greatest decision-making authority to administrators and teachers. As we will discuss in detail later in this chapter, and as Glenn has also noted, school organization typically has reflected hierarchical authority, formalized procedures, regulated paperwork reporting, and centralized power (Lortie, 1975; Meyer & Rowan, 1978; Skrtic, 1991; Ware, 1994). Even schools that set out to develop decision-making structures characterized by parity among educators and families often encounter unanticipated challenges (Gruber & Trivette, 1987).

A promising model for restructuring has come from Yale University professor James Comer. In his model, school planning and management teams are comprised of parents, teachers, administrators, related service providers, and nonprofessional support staff (for example, custodians and clerks). The teams are responsible for (1) developing and implementing a comprehensive plan to improve school morale and the academic program, (2) organizing and delivering staff development consistent with the school's goals, and (3) identifying and remedying problems as they arise (Comer, 1986; Comer & Haynes, 1991).

A key to the Comer bottom-up strategy is using "a 'no-fault' problem-solving approach; consensus decision-making based on child development principles; and collaborative management that does not paralyze the school principal" (Comer & Haynes, 1991, p. 273). This phase of general education school

reform led to "islands of excellence" within restructured school governance, with parents having a strong role in advocating for systems change. Box 2–1 describes how one collaborative educator has used the Comer model to restructure his school and invite parents to volunteer in his school.

Reshaping Service Delivery

Throughout the 1990s, school reform has focused on using the schools as the "one-stop shopping" site where children and youth and their families who face multiple challenges and risks can have all their service needs met (Kagan, 1993). To educate multiply challenged students, reformers advocate providing school-linked comprehensive services—an integrated and comprehensive linkage of social, mental health, and public health services offered within the schools. The reformers assert that a single point of service delivery and coordination will be more cost- and time-efficient and more effective for children and families. Reform focuses on meeting families' basic needs.

In the school-linked comprehensive services model, community service councils represent all human service agencies within the community, services and supports are available and coordinated through a single point of entry, and paperwork hassles for families are minimized (Kagan, 1993; Sailor, 1994). In chapter 13, we will discuss how you can collaborate with families through school-linked comprehensive services.

Family-Professional Collaboration Model within General Education

While the three phases of general education school reform were developing, another and equally important change was underway. It focused on home-school relationships and has become particularly relevant because it addresses an issue that cuts across all three phases of school reform. This issue is collaboration—partnerships—between the student's family and the student's teachers. As you are about to learn, the home-school partnership approach is especially relevant to family-professional collaboration for empowerment and the education of children with educational exceptionalities.

Joyce Epstein's research and demonstration models are the widely recognized and useful bases for new approaches to developing school, family, and community partnerships (Epstein, 1992, 1994, 1995; Epstein & Connors, 1994a, 1994b). She uses the term *partnership* to emphasize the equal role that all stake-

Drawing a Circle of Collaborators

Practicing "Comer schooling" came easily for Dwight Fleming. He was born, grew up, and now works as a school principal in the northeast quadrant of Hartford, Connecticut, a deprived urban area where the greatest majority of the families are African-American. It's a place characterized by single parenthood, poverty, homelessness, housing developments, incarceration, and hard work for low wages (when work is available).

Dwight's work focuses on, among other things, how to connect parents, their children, and the school.

"Each parent is a potential service provider or connector. My job is to help them become part of the education team, a team that consists of the school, the student, and the parents. I want them to see school as a positive experience for their children and the children to see it as a safe place to learn and grow."

To help a parent become part of the team, Dwight allows the family to define itself and to share itself:

"I don't care who's taking care of the kid at home...a mother, aunt, grandparent, father, sister, whoever. I find a way to get them to spend time at King School, and then to feel good about being there and then share their talents. You know, everyone has talents."

How does Dwight "find a way" to get the parents to come to school?

"I smile at parents, pay attention to what they say, invite them to come here, tell them we'd like to have them involved here, walk them around, show them what other parents have done, give them some ideas about what we need to have done, and let their imaginations go to work. I make them feel like somebody. Everybody is somebody special. I work one-to-one."

Thinking of his work as a collaborator, Dwight says:

"I begin to draw a circle, starting with the student and then extending to family and friends and neighbors. In each of these contacts, I offer hope, not pity."

And he tells them, "My job, the King School's job, is to give the student the best education we can and to protect that child's development and future."

In a word, parent participation is a one-to-one business based on inclusion, hope, and assurances. Does it work? Comer's data say so, and Dwight Fleming's experiences say so, too.

"It does kids good to see neighborhood people in school and then after school. They know they're being supported and watched. And with neighbors looking in during school and after school, I can find out a lot about students that I couldn't learn just by the student being here and by talking with the family."

Sources: Comer, J. P. (1986). Parent participation in the schools. *Phi Delta Kappan*, 67(6), 442–446; Turnbull, A. P., Turnbull, H. R., Shank, M., & Leal, D. (1995). *Exceptional lives: Special education in today's schools*. Englewood Cliffs, NJ: Merrill/Prentice Hall.

holders have in working together for students' benefit. Figure 2–2 illustrates the partnership through "overlapping spheres of influence" (Epstein, 1987, 1992).

Epstein describes this model as follows:

> The spheres can, by design, be pushed together to overlap to create an area for partnership activities or pushed apart to separate the family and school based on forces that operate in each environment.

> The external model of the spheres of influence shows that the extent of overlap is effected by forces of (a) time, to account for changes in age and grade levels of students and the influence of historic changes, and (b) efforts in behavior to account for the backgrounds, philosophies and practices that occur in each environment. The *external model* recognizes pictorially that there are some practices that schools and families (and other spheres) conduct separately and some practices that they conduct jointly in order to influence children's learning and development. (Epstein, 1994, p. 40)

Epstein's model targets students as the beneficiary of the overlapping spheres of influence.

> School and family partnerships do not "produce" successful students. Rather, the partner-

FIGURE 2-2

Overlapping Spheres of Influence of Family, School, and Community on Children's Learning

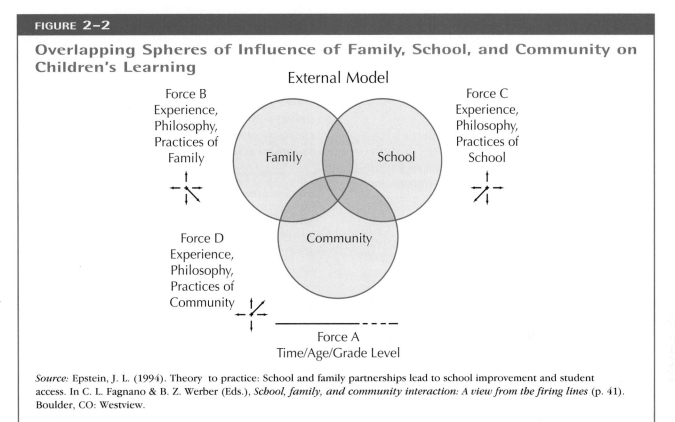

Source: Epstein, J. L. (1994). Theory to practice: School and family partnerships lead to school improvement and student access. In C. L. Fagnano & B. Z. Werber (Eds.), *School, family, and community interaction: A view from the firing lines* (p. 41). Boulder, CO: Westview.

ship activities that include teachers, parents, and studentsengage, guide, energize, and motivate students so that *they* produce their own success. The model assumes that student learning, development, and success, broadly defined—not just achievement test scores—are the main reasons for school and family partnerships. Further, productive connections of schools, families, and communities, and pertinent individual interactions of teachers, parents, and students are conducted in order to help students increase their academic skills, self-esteem, positive attitudes toward learning, independence, other achievements, talents, accomplishments, and other desired behaviors that are characteristic of successful students. (Epstein, 1994, p. 42)

Epstein describes six types of partnerships that can promote outcomes associated with successful students (see figure 2-3). She and others have conducted extensive research and implemented comprehensive systemic models at all school levels—elementary, middle, and secondary—mostly in urban schools, but not entirely so, based on her framework (Dolan & Haxby, 1995; Epstein, 1992; Epstein, 1995; Epstein & Connors, 1994a, 1994b). As comprehen-

sive as their work is in so many aspects, issues related to partnership opportunities that have been most prevalent in special education (such as involvement in IEP conferences) are noticeably absent from research and literature describing the model.

How does Epstein's framework of school, family, and community partnerships interact with the three phases of general education reform? Throughout all the partnership types, but particularly in parenting (type 1), communicating (type 2), and extending learning in home (type 4), there is a strong emphasis on supporting students to master the curriculum and attain higher standards of academic achievement; this emphasis is consistent with enhancing the curriculum. Likewise, decision making (type 5) strongly encourages collaboration among families, educators, students, and community representatives to formulate and implement policy at the school-building level; this emphasis is consistent with restructuring school governance and is reflected in Glenn Gabbard's description at the beginning of this chapter. Finally, parenting (type 1), where the major emphasis is on supporting families to meet their basic obligations, is consistent with reshaping service delivery.

FIGURE 2–3

Epstein Model for Partnership

Type 1: Parenting—Assisting families with basic obligations of parenting skills and setting home conditions for learning at each age and grade level,

Type 2: Communicating—Increasing the effectiveness of the school's basic obligations to communicate clearly about school programs and children's progress through school-to-home and home-to-school communications,

Type 3: Volunteering—Improving the organization, work, and schedules of volunteers and audiences to involve families at the school or in other locations to support the school and students,

Type 4: Extending Learning in Home—Involving families with their children in learning activities at home, including homework and other curricular-linked activities and decisions,

Type 5: Decision Making—Including families in decision making, governance, and advocacy, and

Type 6: Collaborating with Community—Coordinating the work and resources of community businesses, agencies, colleges or universities, and other groups to strengthen school programs,

Source: Epstein, J., & Connors, L. J. (1994). *Trust fund: School, family, and community partnerships in high school* (Report No. 24) (p. 5). Boston: Boston University, Center on Families, Communities, Schools, and Children's Learning.

Special Education Reform Movement

Significantly and sadly, there is a distinct separation between general education and special education reform. As we will discuss later in this chapter, general and special education reform activities in the late 1990s are just beginning to converge, and we believe that such convergence is beneficial for all students. The history of special education, however, has played itself out on a separate reform track. The major special education reform phases include (1) reshaping the provision of a free appropriate public education and (2) restructuring student placement. Figure 2–4 highlights the phases of the special education reform movement.

Reshaping the Provision of Free Appropriate Public Education

As you learned in chapter 1, 1975 was a landmark year in special education. That was the year that Congress enacted the Education of All Handicapped Children Act, P.L. 94-142, now called Individuals with Disabilities Education Act (IDEA). IDEA's cornerstone is the provision of a free appropriate public education, and upon that cornerstone many school reforms have been built.

Before IDEA was passed, special and general education were even more separate than they have been during the last decade. Many students with disabilities were educated in separate classes and separate schools; indeed, it was relatively common for students, particularly those with more severe disabilities, to be excluded from public schools completely. Many schools simply had no policy to educate students with the most severe disabilities. It was within this context (as you learned in chapter 1) that parents and professionals joined forces to make their voices heard as advocates for IDEA.

IDEA provides a federal mandate and federal money to state and local education agencies to assist them in educating students from birth to age 21. Like almost all laws, IDEA has many purposes, so it is divided into many discrete parts. Part B provides for the education of students ages 3 through 21, and Part H provides for the education of infants and toddlers, birth to age 3. Part B and Part H are alike in many ways, but we will indicate their relevant differences as we explain their basic provisions.

In order to qualify for the federal funding, states must adhere to six principles of educating students with disabilities. We will briefly highlight the requirements of the six IDEA principles (each of which creates rights for Megan Gabbard and her parents) and emphasize their implications for family-professional collaboration.

Zero Reject   Zero reject is a principle against the exclusion from school of any student ages 3 through 21 who has a disability. In other words, it is a principle for the inclusion in school of every student ages

FIGURE 2-4

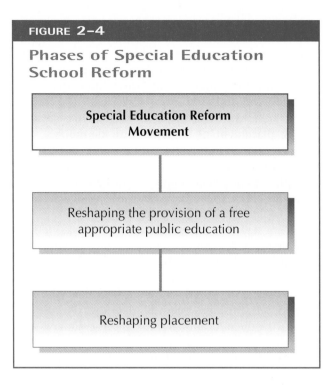

Phases of Special Education School Reform

Special Education Reform Movement

Reshaping the provision of a free appropriate public education

Reshaping placement

3 through 21 without regard to the type or extent of the student's disability. Part B has an explicit zero-reject rule, but Part H (birth to age 3) allows, or gives discretion to, states to educate some or all infants and toddlers; Part H, unlike Part B, does not have a zero-reject provision. For collaboration purposes, the zero-reject principle means that professionals and families can collaborate to secure education services.

Nondiscriminatory Evaluation
Nondiscriminatory evaluation is a principle in favor of a fair, unbiased evaluation of the student's educational needs and strengths (see chapter 11). It assures that a multidisciplinary team will assess the student's needs and strengths across all relevant domains and subjects. The team must use more than one assessment instrument in ways that account for the student's functioning in and outside of school. With respect to at least the first evaluation, parents must consent to have the evaluation administered. For collaboration purposes, it creates opportunities for professionals and families to do the following:

- Secure a full understanding of the student's needs and strengths
- Take into account the observations of parents and others (including educators) as they develop that understanding
- Ensure that the evaluation is useful to and used by the student's teachers and other involved pro-

fessionals and by the family as they work together to provide a free appropriate public education

Appropriate Education
Appropriate education is a principle in favor of a beneficial education (see chapter 12). The principle requires professionals to comply with important processes in providing an appropriate education. These processes include relying on the evaluation and, through it, developing an individualized family service plan (IFSP) for infants and toddlers (birth to age 3) or an individualized education program (IEP) for all other students and providing related services (such as physical, speech, and occupational therapy) as needed to make the other special education services effective. For collaboration purposes, the appropriate education principle creates opportunities for professionals and parents to develop the individualized approaches (that is, set annual goals and short-term objectives, specify evaluation measures, determine what related services will be provided, and set forth the student's placement). Certainly, the IFSP/IEP process is viewed as the key to the student's education, and the process for developing that plan is expected to afford professionals and parents a significant collaboration opportunity.

Least Restrictive Placement
Least restrictive placement (also called least restrictive environment) is a principle that presumes that a student with a disability will be included (placed) in general education (environment) to the greatest extent appropriate for the student. It is not a hard-and-fast rule in favor of inclusion in all general education academic, social, and physical programs and environments; but it assures the student those kinds of placements if they are more beneficial to the student than segregated or separate placements. This principle creates an opportunity for professionals and families to collaborate to determine what programs and environments are appropriate and beneficial and what can be done to make them more accommodating to and beneficial for the student.

Due Process
Two other principles—procedural due process and parent participation—assure that the schools and parents are accountable to each other; they are checks and balances. The due process principle gives professionals and parents the opportunity to challenge each other's decisions about special education evaluation, individualized plans, and placement. Although it creates an adversarial process (a quasi-judicial hearing before an independent hearing officer, followed by appeals to the state or federal

courts), it also sometimes affords mediation of disagreements. In all cases, it creates opportunities for professionals and families to hold each other accountable and, as each sees what the other is doing to educate the student, to challenge the other.

Parent Participation
The parent participation principle grants the student's parents the right to have access to school records concerning the student and to control access to those records by others, to be eligible to participate on special education advisory committees, and to use the other principles for the student's benefit. In the broadest of ways, it legalizes and legitimizes the role of parents as education decision makers (see chapter 1) and thus permits parents and professionals to become collaborators with each other.

These six principles were bound to have significant effects on students, their families, school systems, professionals, and indeed every community in America. There is no doubt that the effects have been positive; likewise there is no doubt that IDEA's promises have been only partially fulfilled. One promise was of a life (during and after schooling has concluded) characterized by independence, productivity, and inclusion; that promise has been only partially kept (Koyanagi & Gaines, 1993; Peraino, 1992; Wagner, Newman, D'Amico, Jay, Butler-Nalin, Marder, & Cox, 1991; Wagner, D'Amico, Marder, Newman, & Blackorby, 1993).

A second promise was of a partnership between families and educators, one in which (as you learned in chapter 1) parents would be education decision makers, partners in shared decision making; that, too, is an only partially kept promise, as we will discuss throughout this chapter and as Glenn Gabbard has pointed out.

One reason for the partially kept promise relates to timing and school practices. Significantly, the regulations implementing IDEA were issued on August 23, 1977, and were effective on November 1, 1977, just a brief while later. Given this short time frame, schools attempted to implement meaningful procedures related to IEP and other requirements. But their initial efforts targeted paper compliance: meeting the letter of the law and doing the requisite paperwork rather than building a foundation for empowering and authentic relationships leading to meaningful family collaboration (Goldstein, Strickland, Turnbull, & Curry, 1980). Once routinized family participation became the norm, collaboration of the type we hope you will practice became the exception to the norm. You can take action to change the norm, as we suggest later in the chapter and as we demonstrate throughout this book.

Restructuring Placement

The second phase of special education reform was less concerned with providing free appropriate public education to students with disabilities than with assuring the students more integrated placements. There have been two major efforts aimed at restructuring placement of students with disabilities: the Regular Education Initiative and the current emphasis on inclusion. Both efforts rest on IDEA's least restrictive placement principle and are motivated by educators and parents who have been dissatisfied with the slow implementation of that principle.

The Regular Education Initiative was led by Madeleine Will, then assistant secretary of education and director of the U.S. Office of Special Education and Rehabilitative Services. Her son has a cognitive disability. She and the educators and families who supported her position believed that the linchpin for improving the educational outcomes for students with disabilities was to merge special and general education into a unified system and dismantle their separateness.

Although this effort was referred to as the Regular Education Initiative, it really was a special education initiative. Many educators joined Will in advancing a merger of regular and general education (Jenkins, Pious, & Peterson, 1988; Pugach & Lilly, 1984; Wang, Reynolds, & Walberg, 1986). But many others, particularly those primarily associated with learning disabilities, emotional disabilities, and hearing impairment, raised serious concerns (Hallahan, Keller, McKinney, Lloyd, & Bryan, 1988; Kauffman, Gerber, & Semmel, 1988; Schumaker & Deshler, 1987).

Throughout the REI debate, the major emphasis was on creating instructional flexibility and adaptation within general education classrooms for students with mild disabilities. This reform effort was professionally dominated. There was limited concerted effort to form family-professional partnerships to advance the Regular Education Initiative, and family-professional collaboration took a back seat to the REI debate over placement. Indeed, while attention was directed to the Regular Education Initiative, routinized implementation of IDEA's principles for family decision making persisted, and paperwork compliance was the norm.

Undergirding the Regular Education Initiative was a concern about outcomes for special education students. This concern escalated when, in 1991, the National Longitudinal Study reported the following (Wagner et al., 1991):

- Approximately one-third of all special education students (from a sample of 6,000 students with disabilities ranging in age from 13 to 21) were failing one or more classes.

- Of the students who were failing, approximately one-fifth were failing in six or more classes.
- Less than one-half of the special education graduates were fully employed after leaving high school.
- Approximately one-fifth of youth with serious emotional disorders were arrested.

Additional bleak news about student outcomes focused particularly on students with emotional and behavioral disorders. Compared to the statistic that approximately one-third of all students with disabilities were receiving failing grades, 44 percent of students with serious emotional disorders were receiving failing grades. Additionally, compared to a 71 percent graduation rate for students without disabilities and a 54 percent graduation rate for students with disabilities, students with emotional and behavioral disorders have a 36 percent graduation rate (Koyanagi & Gaines, 1993).

This report gave credence to the post-REI reformers—inclusion advocates—who had become impatient with REI, especially as it related to students with severe disabilities. Many professionals working within the area of severe disability long have had a strong philosophical orientation toward placement in least restrictive settings. They focused on changing classroom instruction for the benefit of all students and on comprehensive school restructuring of all policies and procedures. As Glenn Gabbard said, they also emphasized creating a dialogue with general education. The inclusion movement, started in the early 1990s, incorporated the following principles (Sailor, 1991; Turnbull, Turnbull, Shank, & Leal, 1995, p. 116):

- All students receive education in the school they would attend if they had no disability.
- A natural proportion (that is, representative of the school district at large) of students with disabilities occurs at each school site.
- A zero-reject philosophy exists so that typically no student will be excluded on the basis of type or extent of disability.
- School and general education placements are age- and grade-appropriate so that no self-contained special education classes will exist.
- Cooperative learning and peer instruction are the preferred instructional methods.
- Special education supports exist within the general education class and in other integrated environments.

Although many parents typically have strong opinions about inclusion (both pro and con), the inclusion reform effort has focused more on two-way special and general education collaboration than on creating three-way general education/special education/family collaboration (Stainback & Stainback, 1990). Because of the overwhelming task of merging separate educational systems and making accommodations to create supportive placements in inclusive settings, family-professional collaboration again has not been a high priority in special education reform. That is not to say, however, that it has been ignored or that three-way collaboration cannot occur between general education, special education, and families— as we will show you throughout this book and as the actual and metaphorical playground in Lexington, Massachusetts, demonstrates.

Nature of Family-Professional Collaboration

Within the special education field, family-professional collaboration has had different models at the early intervention/early childhood stage and at the elementary and secondary school stage.

Early Intervention and Early Childhood Stage There is extensive literature favoring family-centered practices during the early years. This family-centered emphasis represents a philosophical paradigm shift:

> The term parent involvement sums up the current perspective. It means we want parents involved with us. It means the service delivery system we helped create is at the center of the universe, and families are revolving around it. It brings to mind an analogy about the old Ptolemaic view of the universe with the earth at the center. . . . Copernicus came along and made a startling reversal—he put the sun in the center of the universe rather than the Earth. His declaration caused profound shock. The earth was not the epitome of creation; it was a planet like all other planets. The successful challenge to the entire system of ancient authority required a complete change in philosophical conception of the universe. This is rightly termed the "Copernican Revolution." Let's pause to consider what would happen if we had a Copernican Revolution in the field of disability. Visualize the concept: The family is the center of the universe and the service delivery system is one of the many planets revolving around it. Now visualize the service delivery system at the center and the family in orbit around it. Do you see the difference? Do you recognize the revolutionary

change in perspective? We would move from an emphasis on parent involvement (i.e., parents participating in the program) to family support (i.e., programs providing a range of support services to families). This is not a semantic exercise—such a revolution leads us to a new set of assumptions and a new vista of options for service. (Turnbull & Summers, 1987, pp. 295–296)

According to the extensive literature on family-centered practices, four major characteristics tend to define practices as family-centered (Bailey, Buysse, Edmondson, & Smith, 1992; Beckman, Robinson, Rosenberg, & Filer, in press; Dunst, Johanson, Trivette, & Hamby, 1991; Shelton, Jeppson, & Johnson, 1989). These practices generally

> (a) include families in decision making, planning, assessment, and service delivery at family, agency, and system levels; (b) develop services for the whole family and not just the child; (c) are guided by families' priorities for goals and services; and (d) offer and respect families' choices regarding the level of their participation. (Murphy, Lee, Turnbull, & Turbiville, 1995, p. 25)

A family-centered approach was incorporated into 1986 amendments to IDEA. IDEA requires professionals who serve children with disabilities from birth to age 3 to collaborate with the child's family to develop an individualized family service plan (IFSP) that assures services for the family and the child alike. One of the requirements for the IFSP is to document family concerns, resources, and priorities and to provide the family with services, consistent with members' preferences, so the family can increase its capacity to meet the child's special needs.

When a student becomes 3 years old, the early intervention services end and two new types of services begin. During the ages of 3, 4, and 5, the student receives early childhood special education; and during the ages of 6 through 21, the student receives special education.

Similarly, the name and nature of the student's individualized plan change when the student achieves certain ages. During the ages of birth through 2 ("zero to three"), the student and family have an IFSP—an individualized family services plan. During the ages of 3 through 21, the student, but not the family, has an IEP— an individualized education plan.

Under the IFSP and in model early intervention programs, both the student and the family receive services. By contrast, under the IEP and in typical special education (ages 3 through 21), the student is the primary focus of services; the family may receive only some related services, such as school social work services, school psychology services, or school health services.

So the name of the individualized plan differs (IFSP or IEP), and the services under each (family and student jointly or student primarily and family secondarily) change with the student's age and transition from early intervention to early childhood special education.

With these two changes, there also is a challenge for families. So many families become accustomed to having family-focused services during state-of-the-art early intervention programs that they experience a real "culture shock" when their children enter early childhood special education or elementary school.

This is because the services in those programs focus on the student, not the family; the family's centrality is replaced by the student's. More than that, the professionals in first-class early intervention/IFSP programs typically have received more training in family-centered service delivery, are more able to work with the family, and are indeed acculturated to doing just that. By contrast, the professionals in early childhood education (ages 3 to 5) and beyond (ages 6 through 21) lack the training, the skills, and the culture to work with families as effectively or willingly as early intervention specialists.

Yet the families who were reared in the truly family-centered early intervention programs are beginning to demand from other providers the same quality of family-centered services to which they had become accustomed under early intervention. For the families and new providers, the challenge is to retain at least the kind of collaboration that early intervention provided.

Despite the rhetoric and promising practices about family-centered services, research continues to underscore professional dominance in decision making and child rather than family orientation. Staff often use a standard format for communicating with families in IFSP and IEP meetings and assume that they know parents' needs and preferences and do not need to communicate with them directly (Minke, 1991). Although many professionals report that they understand the importance of a family-centered approach and the legal requirements for serving families, they describe their services as primarily child-oriented (Katz & Scarpati, 1995; McBride, Brotherson, Joanning, Whiddon, & Demmit, 1993).

Using the Epstein types of parent participation as a model, family-professional collaboration within early intervention/early childhood special education closely parallels the following types: (type 1) parenting, (type 2) communicating, (type 4) extending learning in home, (type 5) decision making, and (type 6) collaborating with community.

Elementary, Middle, and Secondary School Stage
What family-partnership types are most prevalent in elementary, middle, and secondary schools? How does family-professional collaboration in special education at the elementary, middle, and secondary school levels compare and contrast with the Epstein partnership model?

Families helped to answer these questions by testifying before the National Council on Disability, an independent federal advisory agency, as it conducted hearings in 10 regions throughout the United States during the fall of 1994. The overwhelming testimony from families was that IDEA should be fine-tuned and its implementation improved (National Council on Disability, 1995). Based on our synthesis of the professional literature and our work with families locally and nationally, we believe that a useful way to think about family perspectives (albeit overly simplistic) is to regard families as falling on a continuum, as illustrated in figure 2–5.

At one end of this continuum are families who have a high participation rate. Like Megan Gabbard's family, these families are assertive, knowledgeable, and empowered, and they invest tremendous time and energy in attempting to get an appropriate education for their son or daughter. Typically, they are frustrated with the school system and believe that the provision of a free appropriate public education requires them to be eternally vigilant.

In the middle range are families who generally participate by taking advantage of the legal formalities mandated by IDEA (evaluation and IFSP/IEP development) but who do not have a lot of knowledge about the nature of their child's program and the outcomes that their child is achieving. Typically, these families are satisfied with their child's program.

At the other end of the continuum are families whose participation is at a low level. Typically, these families feel disenfranchised by the system and rarely participate in any meaningful way. Often they feel intimidated, angry, and devalued and perceive that their child is receiving an inferior education. (Just as family participation falls on a continuum, so does the participation of professionals. Additionally, remember that the same family and professional can move back and forth on the continuum at different times and under different circumstances depending upon the issues that are being addressed and the willingness of individuals in the context to encourage collaboration.)

The following testimonies at the National Council on Disability hearings were most likely provided by families on the high-participation end of the continuum:

> I have come to call myself Bonnie, the bitch, because of what I've had to become to fight the system for the handicapped child, and yet I have contacted multiple state offices. I have followed through with every lead that anybody has ever given me. I have talked with the Governor's office here in the state. I've gone so far as to call the White House. . . . I guess my feeling at this point is, "Is there anybody out there who really cares?" I don't know what more to do. I, as a parent, have pursued every option. (testimony by Bonnie Weninger, in National Council on Disability, 1995, p. 123)

> Special education is sometimes perceived as being a kind of white middle class issue. I just want to point out and underscore what a number of parents here said tonight. The kind of resources it takes for a family to get appropriate programs and services is so totally overwhelming in terms of time, energy, money, and skills, that it's really not surprising that the people who tend to be the most visible are the parents with the most resources. (testimony by Diane Lipton, in National Council on Disability, 1995, pp. 34–35)

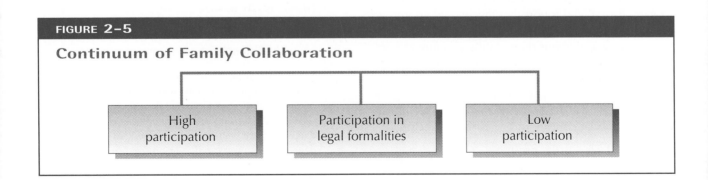

FIGURE 2–5

Continuum of Family Collaboration

High participation | Participation in legal formalities | Low participation

We really need to put the responsibility again on the educators and not make all the parents professionals, because parents also have jobs, and the amount of time, energy, emotions that every parent . . . has put into the education of our children's special needs [is] just tremendous. It shouldn't be that way. We really need to distribute that kind of energy more evenly. It's very frustrating. (testimony by Birgit Schweingruber, in National Council on Disability, 1995, p. 108)

There are, of course, parents and other family members who are in the middle of the continuum. A study of 21 parents of elementary students reported a rather high level of satisfaction with special education (Green & Shinn, 1994). Each of the students in this study had been identified as having a learning disability and received services in a resource room for less than half the school day.

- Parents rated their satisfaction with special education, giving a mean rating of 4.8 on a scale of 5.0.
- The majority of parents emphasized that getting extra help and attention was the primary benefit of special education.
- A majority also endorsed the positive characteristics of special education teachers, such as "warm, caring person" and "immense patience" (Green & Shinn, 1994, p. 274).
- Ninety percent of the parents reported that they had seen positive changes in their child since receiving resource room services, with 75 percent of the comments emphasizing changes related to self-esteem or an improved school attitude; for example, "she looks forward to school now and thinks more of herself" and "he feels good about himself" (Green & Shinn, 1994, p. 275).
- Only two parents made reference to their child's improved academic skills.

The researchers concluded that the parents' perceptions of progress and satisfaction were not necessarily related to the students' academic performance or gain. Parents did report that they would appreciate having more objective information about their child's performance and about their child's standing as compared to other students in the general education program. Almost three-quarters of the parents indicated that school personnel had not discussed ultimate goals or exit criteria with them when the child was initially placed in special education. The authors concluded:

This outcome is the proverbial "good news-bad news" situation. . . . "good news" for local schools and the special education community is that parents report liking what special educators do and what they think they do. . . . The "bad news" is that parental satisfaction with the services provided to their children may not be related to their children's academic performance. Simply stated, improved achieved outcomes were not the basis for parent satisfaction in this sample. (Green & Shinn, 1994, p. 278)

A third group of parents, representing the right side of the continuum, apparently feels disenfranchised by the school system; consequently, their participation is low. The seminal work of Beth Harry and her colleagues speaks poignantly and with disturbing candor of the conflicts that exist for many parents who perceive their disenfranchisement from the special education system, particularly those from culturally diverse backgrounds (Harry & Kalyanpur, 1994; Harry, Allen, & McLaughlin, 1995; Harry, 1992a, 1992b). A Puerto Rican mother said:

It is only their opinions that matter. If I do not want the child in a special class or if I want her in a different school, they will still do what they want. Because that is what I tried to do, and Vera [the social worker] talked with them too and tried to help me, but—no! Our opinions are not valued. Many parents do not want their child in a special class or in a school so far away, but they keep quiet. It is very hard to struggle with these Americans. In America, the schools are for Americans. (Harry, 1992b, p. 486)

The paperwork associated with special education can be overwhelming for many of these same parents:

So many papers! I have a lot of work to do—in the mornings I do my work and then in the afternoon I take care of my mother and do her groceries and wash her clothes. I have a lot of boxes with a lot of papers and I told my husband I would throw them away and he said, "No, no!" So I took them to the LAA [Latin American Association] and gave them to them. I can't stand having so many papers! (Harry, 1992b, p. 482)

Harry describes the factors contributing to the disenfranchisement of these minority parents:

The combination of the "direct," informal manner of American professionals, with their assumptions of the validity of detached, scientific information (Wright et al., 1983), can be alienating rather than reassuring for people accustomed to a slower pace, more personal yet more generalized approach. . . .

The bureaucratic structure of schools, and, certainly of the special education system, with its formal procedures and systems, presents people from such cultures with a formidable challenge. When these systems are implemented without regard for the need for personalized information, and, as has been emphasized earlier, without opportunity for dialogue, the result is often confusion and alienation on the part of parents and increasing impatience on the part of professionals. When they are implemented in a vein of compliance rather than communication the results can be disastrous (Harry, 1992b). (Harry & Kalyanpur, 1994, p. 160)

If we relate the testimony and research data to the Epstein model, we learn that the special education emphasis has been on type 2 (communicating) and type 5 (decision making). One difference with respect to decision making, as Epstein describes it for general education, is that special education decision making has primarily concentrated on advocacy for the student, not on advocacy at the systems level (participation in school-based councils, PTAs, and other school restructuring efforts such as those going on in Lexington, Massachusetts). A trend we detect is that parents of students without exceptionalities seem to have not been as involved in student-focused advocacy as in systems advocacy. Advocacy and decision-making activities are again separated into those that are generally appropriate for families in general education and those that are generally appropriate for families in special education.

The two additional types of partnerships that have primarily dominated the time and energy of parents whose children are in special education are evaluating for special education (chapter 11) and individualizing for appropriate education and placement (chapter 12).

Contemporary School Restructuring

Nature of School Restructuring

Having reviewed the general and special education reform phases and observed that they have operated independently of each other and, at least so far as special education is concerned, not wholly satisfactorily, let's now consider the reform that is most affecting today's schools. It seeks school restructuring and deliberately brings general and special education together. The paradigm of this kind of restructuring, and the challenges it poses, are those that Glenn Gabbard speaks about in the beginning of this chapter.

The evolutionary and separate movements of general education reform and special education reform converged when in 1994 Congress enacted Goals 2000: Educate America Act. The Goals 2000 legislation seeks simultaneously to incorporate top-down and bottom-up education reform to improve outcomes for all students. Goals 2000 sets forth eight national education goals, which are described in figure 2–6.

The act calls for states to establish standards for all students. Unlike previous general education reform efforts, which excluded from consideration students with exceptionalities, Goals 2000 specifically includes all students. The Senate committee that recommended Goals 2000 noted, "In far too many districts around the country, two separate educational systems have developed with little or no coordination—one system for regular or general education and one separate and distinct system for special education." Accordingly, Goals 2000 should "serve as a vehicle for making the promise of . . . IDEA a reality for students with disabilities," and those students

---

FIGURE 2–6

The National Education Goals

By the year 2000:

- All children ready to learn
- 90 percent graduation rate
- All children competent in core subjects
- First in the world in math and science

- Every adult literate and able to compete in the workforce
- Safe, disciplined, drug-free schools
- Professional development for educators
- Increased parental involvement in learning

---

therefore must be "an integral part of all aspects of education reform" and entitled to the "same high expectations, treatment, and leadership offered to their non-disabled peers" (Sen. Report 103-85, 103rd Congress, 1st Session).

The two most notable aspects of this school restructuring effort are its emphasis on (1) student outcomes and the assessment of those outcomes and (2) site-based management (including increased family partnerships) as a strategy of restructuring school governance.

In lieu of complying with IDEA solely by concentrating on its processes, school reform now addresses students' academic gains, the kinds of jobs they are prepared for as adults, and the quality of their self-esteem and social relationships. Goals 2000 school restructuring has the bottom line of improving student outcomes and standards—what all students are learning, the progress all are making toward reaching the expectations they hold for themselves, and the expectations that all families share with them.

A second major characteristic of the current school restructuring movement is site-based management. As exemplified by the Lexington school that Megan Gabbard attends, this management approach gives increasing autonomy and flexibility to schools so they may use local problem solving and innovation and thus involve all stakeholders—families, students, educators, and community citizens. The primary goal of site-based management is to meet the educational needs of all students—those previously served in general and special education—by creating a unified system:

> The teaching-learning process is critical in restructuring schools. Curricula are organized to support the learning of challenging content and to promote personal success skills such as critical thinking, problem solving, group membership, use of technology, and life-long learning skills. However, the curricula do not control the instruction; rather, teachers work together to determine how to accommodate students with learning differences. Some of the accommodations may include lower performance expectations for some students, but content is always meaningful in length to the expectations of the regular classroom. There is no "your student/my student" mentality in the school; there is a common mission of school improvement. (McLaughlin, 1996, pp. 642–643)

Because the mentality of "your student in general education/my student in special education" is inappropriate, it is necessary to reconceptualize collaboration (McLaughlin, 1996). Instead of "your family in general education/my family in special education," there emerges a unified conceptualization—"our students/our families, typical and exceptional." Remember Megan Gabbard and her peers and their playground? If so, you understand the meaning of "our"! In figure 2–7, we show how the phases of the general education reform movement (the lefthand column) have paralleled the phases of the special education reform movement (the righthand column) and today have merged into the contemporary school restructuring phase (bottom). This phase, as we will show first in chapter 3 and then throughout this book, seeks to empower all educators, families, and students through collaboration. This collaboration—"our students/our families, typical and exceptional"—is desirable to secure improved educational outcomes for all students and necessary to effect school restructuring.

Convergence of General and Special Education Model of Family-Professional Collaboration

For all these changes to happen, educators need to combine the empirical knowledge base and experiential lessons of general education with the special education family-professional collaboration models. Our suggestion of the most appropriate convergence is set out in figure 2–8.

The figure includes seven opportunities for family-professional partnerships and eight obligations for reliable alliances. In identifying these seven opportunities for family-professional partnership (depicted in the lefthand column), we relied on five of the partnership types specified by Epstein (see figure 2–3) and merged her final type—collaborating with community—into all other opportunities; it is not a separate opportunity. Thus, instead of the six types from the Epstein model, there are eight, which are then combined with two additional partnership opportunities in special education—evaluating for special education and individualizing for appropriate education.

If any of these opportunities is missing in the programs you develop for family collaboration, you should consider adding them and bringing all these opportunities together into a comprehensive program in which the whole is likely to be greater than the sum of the parts. If you do this, you probably will see increased benefit for all stakeholders because you will be offering a broad array of family-professional collaborative opportunities.

Depicted in the righthand column of figure 2–8 are the components of a reliable alliance. Research and experience over the last 20 years in special education show that professionals and families need to create reliable alliances rather than hierarchical relationships as they carry out all seven opportunities to be partners with families. That certainly is the import of the testimony given to National Council on Disability (1995). In addition, "there seems to be a natural imbalance between the helper and the helped, the powerful and the powerless, the expert and the novice that is difficult to overcome" (Sonnenschein, 1984, p. 130). Yet transforming the hierarchical imbalance is essential—it becomes an obligation—if students, families, and professionals are to collaborate and consequently experience greater empowerment.

An alternative to professional hierarchies is becoming a reliable ally of families. What is a reliable alliance? What does it mean to be a reliable ally? Consider the people in your life on whom you depend for nonjudgmental, unconditional, and

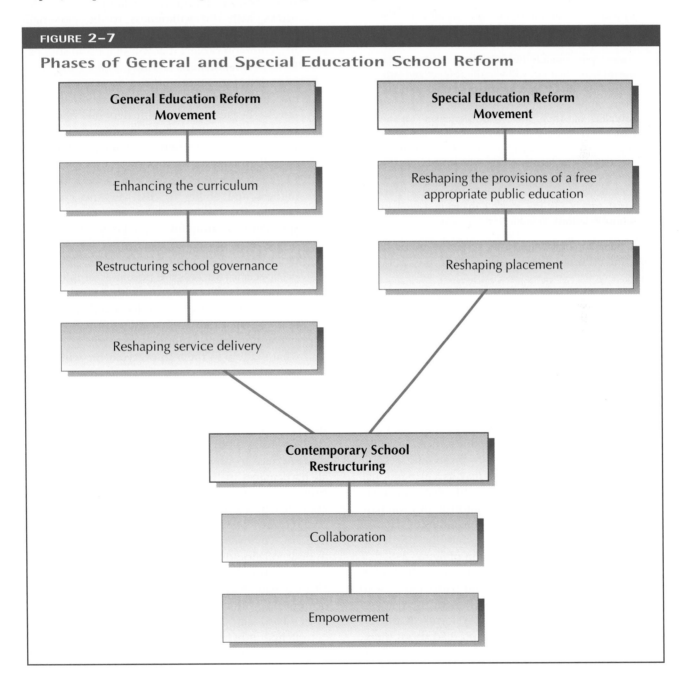

FIGURE 2–7

Phases of General and Special Education School Reform

General Education Reform Movement

Special Education Reform Movement

Enhancing the curriculum

Reshaping the provisions of a free appropriate public education

Restructuring school governance

Reshaping placement

Reshaping service delivery

Contemporary School Restructuring

Collaboration

Empowerment

ever-available support. You know that you can turn to them in good times and bad to get the help that you need. They probably make you feel better about yourself, provide support and information to you within the context of a personal relationship, and therefore strengthen your belief in yourself. This is the essence of a reliable ally for all people.

A survey of families and professionals, not limited to those in special education, underscored what professionals think that parents want from them and what parents actually want:

> In a classic example of misunderstood cues, the reported preferences of parents are not what school personnel think they are. School personnel passionately believe that a professional, businesslike manner will win the respect and support of parents. The response of parents to questions about their contacts with the school revealed that they view "professionalism" on the part of teachers, school psychologists, guidance counselors, or principals as *undesirable.* Parents mention their dissatisfaction with school people who are "too businesslike," "patronizing," or who "talk down to us." . . . Parents reported a "personal touch" as the most enhancing factor in school relations. (Lindle, 1989, p. 13)

A parent whose child was receiving home-based early intervention services described the personal touch:

> At first, I was tense with a professional coming to my home. But it was a nice little conversation. The professional's mannerism and the way she asked questions was like we were sitting down for a cup of coffee. She got a lot of information without asking. (Summers, Dell'Oliver, Turnbull, Benson, Santelli, Campbell, & Siegel-Causey, 1990, p. 87)

The bottom-up school restructuring approach, incorporating site management, now more than ever before creates an obligation for educators and families to establish a personal touch by becoming reliable allies for each other. We believe that, as a professional, you have certain obligations to build reliable alliances with families across all seven opportunities for partnerships. We will discuss those obligations in detail in chapter 4, but for now just note that they are incorporated into the righthand column of figure 2–8.

For you to make this shift from hierarchial interactions to reliable alliances in your partnerships with families, you should be insightful about the use and misuse of power. There are many forms of power, and you should ask yourself, as you read about them, which of these might enhance or impede your teaching of students and your collaborating with families. Zipperlen and O'Brien (1993, pp. 23–24) list the types of power:

- *Power-over* other people arises from the ability and willingness to make decisions for others and to enforce their compliance by authoritative control of rewards and punishments.
- *Power-with* other people arises from people's ability and willingness to listen to and be influenced by another's perceptions and suggestions and to offer their perceptions and suggestions in turn. Power-with requires the kind of respect that grows with the willingness to be personally involved with one another and to share by choice in a common project that will shape and shift patterns of relationships among people. Differences provide information and the occasion to clarify and strengthen relationships by negotiating creatively. Because power-with depends upon and reinforces cooperation, its exercise depends on people's mutual restraint and willingness to learn from their experience together.
- *Power-from-within* arises from a person's willingness and ability to discover and creatively express the abilities and concerns that they find spiritually meaningful. . . . Power-from-within one gives a person courage to act when important values are threatened, even if the short-term prospects for success are poor. . . . People acting on the basis of power-from-within need to exercise personal discipline to sharpen their discernment of what ultimately matters to them and to strengthen their abilities to creatively express what matters to them in everyday life with other people.

One of the major goals in restructuring is to abandon power-over roles and to develop collaborative relationships among all stakeholders, including families and professionals. These relationships will be characterized by power-with so that the end result for all participants in the relationships will be a power-from-within. Because moving from a power-over approach to a power-with and a power-from-within one requires a systemic shift in how many schools operate, we now will focus on a major systems barrier to new collaborations.

For you to be successful in developing a reliable alliance with families—establishing power-with and power-from-within relationships—you have to confront a hard fact: Traditional school organization has entrenched power-over structures and procedures. These power-over approaches are characterized by standard routines, often highly superficial, for

FIGURE 2-8

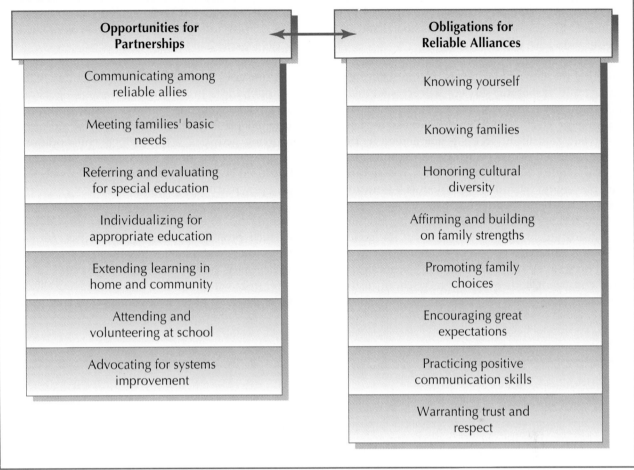

Opportunities and Obligations

Opportunities for Partnerships	Obligations for Reliable Alliances
Communicating among reliable allies	Knowing yourself
Meeting families' basic needs	Knowing families
Referring and evaluating for special education	Honoring cultural diversity
Individualizing for appropriate education	Affirming and building on family strengths
Extending learning in home and community	Promoting family choices
Attending and volunteering at school	Encouraging great expectations
Advocating for systems improvement	Practicing positive communication skills
	Warranting trust and respect

meeting the IDEA mandates. (We have already given some examples, and we will continue to do so throughout the book.) Your ability to provide families with a range of opportunities for partnerships and your obligations to form reliable alliances (see figure 2–8) will be influenced by the willingness of the school district to participate in school restructuring and, in doing so, to move away from the traditional bureaucratic compartmentalization of each professional's role and adopt a dynamic and flexible organization for bringing teams together to address mutual problems and devise creative solutions (Skrtic, 1991). Glenn Gabbard has told you what can happen if restructuring takes on a partnership approach, but he has also described the barriers.

As you interview for jobs and select the school system where you will work, or as your present school system employer considers restructuring, explore the extent to which the system provides the seven oppor-

tunities for family-professional partnerships and undertakes the eight obligations of reliable alliances. The more you have the opportunity to work in an empowering organization characterized by flexibility, fluidity, and decentralized management, the more you will have your own reliable allies to support you in your quests to establish reliable alliances with families. When you find yourself working in bureaucratic (power-over) organizations, you can and should commit yourself to working collaboratively, to the extent possible, with administrators, teachers, families, and others. After all, finding and creating those reliable alliances, while difficult in power-over structures, is a necessary step in transforming those structures. It is the first step in creating the actual and the metaphorical playgrounds that benefit students such as Megan Gabbard. More than a necessary step in contemporary school restructuring, it is a necessary step in empowerment, which we define and demonstrate in chapter 3.

Summary

Parents play a new role in today's schools—as collaborators with professionals. That role has emerged from and indeed furthers the reforms that general and special education have experienced.

In general education, the reforms consist of enhancing the curriculum, restructuring school governance, and reshaping service delivery systems. In special education, the reforms consist of assuring that each student with a disability has access to a free appropriate education (access is guaranteed by their legal rights based on six principles of the Individuals with Disabilities Education Act) and restructuring their placement through the Regular Education Initiative and the inclusion initiative.

Collaboration between families and professionals is a powerful technique for carrying out the general and special education reforms. Collaboration can and should occur at all stages of a student's school career and is consistent with contemporary school restructuring activities.

Those restructuring activities are based on eight national educational goals agreed on by the governors in 1989 and enacted by Congress as the heart of its 1994 Goals 2000 law.

As restructuring has occurred, general and special educators have a chance to collaborate with parents of children in all school programs—general and special alike. Indeed, there are seven opportunities for family-professional partnerships—seven normally occurring activities within which collaboration can and should be the norm. Additionally, there are eight obligations for reliable alliances that can be infused into every partnership opportunity.

The bottom line for educators in today's schools is simply this: to move from relationships with families in which professionals have power over families to relationships with families in which professionals and families have power with each other and in which power from within the relationships is naturally occurring and beneficial to professionals and families alike.

On a newly constructed school playground in Lexington, Massachusetts, there are not only new structures—equipment and programs that are accessible to all children—but also new human dynamics that planned, financed, built, and benefit from those structures.

The new dynamics represent the interests of parents of children who have disabilities and parents of children who are seemingly typical and the interests of general and special educators.

More than that, the new dynamics find shape and form in the activity of joint planning, joint financing, joint construction, and joint benefit—a collaboration that creates a win-win result for all those players.

Not surprisingly—after all, Lexington is the site of the "shot heard 'round the world"—these players have found new ways to talk about new issues. As they developed new forms of dialogue and new topics, they created a new human dynamic—the synergistic dynamic of collaboration.

Megan Gabbard now can enter the playground; more than that, she can be herself there, in the company of all kinds of other children. To say she is included is correct; to say that she is the symbol of a new human dynamic is also correct. In Lexington, the shot heard 'round the world sounds like collaboration.

Chapter Three

Empowerment

In south-central Los Angeles, two women live the "African-American experience," but with a difference. Theresa Cooper and Hortense Walker are mothers of young children with disabilities, and they have embarked on a many-dimensioned ministry to families.

Theresa's son Eric is 8 years old and has an auditory processing problem; he hears but struggles with interpreting what he hears. Hortense's son, also named Eric, is 4 years old and has cerebral palsy. Together, Theresa and Hortense respectively direct and serve as volunteer staff of Loving Your Disabled Child (LYDC).

LYDC is housed on the second floor of a modest church. It is a community center where parents can get support, training, and information; and it is funded with federal and state money. Its location tells a great deal about LYDC and about Theresa and Hortense, and its funding reveals a lot, too. LYDC straddles several worlds—one that is grounded in a religious ministry, another that is based in the secular world, and a third that is family and disability related.

How do these worlds merge, and what differences do the mergers make? Theresa, the professional, says that being Eric's parent gives her "such a compassion and such a will to help the other families beat the system and make it." Hortense, the volunteer, says that she knows how to "connect" with other families.

That connecting skill was hard to come by. When Hortense's son was born, the message she got from professionals consisted of "bad news, bad news, bad news. No one was positive. That was very stressful: There is no one to tell you, 'Do you understand that you can have a

functional and happy life with this child? That as parents you can love this child and raise this child. There are things you won't have, but then there are things that you will have.' No one had that compassion for me. No one centers on the family. No one was meeting our needs."

No one, that is, until Hortense went to LYDC. There she found parents whose children had disabilities more severe than Eric's, yet these parents were "laughing and talking with each other, smiling, having confidence that life was just fine." And they gave her hope—indeed, all of LYDC gave her hope and became the support group she needed.

To give parents hope, Theresa explained, she likes making connections with people, finding out "what's in them that I can help enhance or bring out, identifying their strength and playing on that, building that up so that they can do what they need to do."

Theresa sends a loud and clear message: "You can still have those hopes and dreams but just modify them."

Theresa and Hortense see LYDC and their work as a ministry of hope, curing, and caring: "We have to minister to a person's hurt." They do that, as LYDC's first director did, by being an example. "The director at that time [when Theresa and Hortense came to LYDC] had two children with disabilities, but she was just so normal, so peaceful . . . it was just something: You can't have that peace naturally." If not naturally, then how?

For them, the answer is being a Christian: "We are to be Christlike." So it does not surprise Theresa and

Hortense that they are peaceful and bring peace to others: "They see the Godliness in us. It's all about denying ourselves to help someone else. It's all about someone else, it's not about yourself."

And what if that other person is perplexed about what to do? What if parents want to institutionalize their child? "We lay out the options, tell them our views, and say, 'It's up to you,' because it really is up to the person who has the problem. We take the position of the person who has the problem." And when, and only when, the person asks for advice, they say what they would do. A big part of helping is letting other parents make their own choices.

Has it made a difference that they are African Americans? Yes. "We are living the African-American experience." They know the families' needs and how to respond, whether it is to bring food to the family when a child has died or to provide bus fare so the family can come to LYDC and also not go hungry.

Part of the African-American experience is experiencing prejudice. White teachers or consultants will come to LYDC, but only during the day; their African-American counterparts, on the other hand, will come at night, when the families can come to LYDC.

Coming to LYDC . . . what does that mean? It means coming to Theresa and Hortense, but it signifies more than that: It entails encountering a ministry that is characterized by empowerment of self and others and that is based on collaboration.

The recurring theme in this book, exemplified by Theresa and Hortense, is empowerment through collaboration. This theme will permeate your partnerships with families. The more you understand empowerment—its implications for yourself, your professional colleagues, and families—and how to collaborate for empowerment of families, yourself, and other professionals, the more effective you are likely to be.

Professional literature, popular media, and everyday conversations are replete with the word *empowerment*. What does the word really mean? For starters, we encourage you to define empowerment. One way to do this is to think of the people whom you consider to be most empowered and the people whom you regard as most disempowered. Try to limit your thinking to families and professionals. What are their respective characteristics? Would you describe yourself as being more or less empowerful than your professional peers, your own family members, families whom you respect, and others whom you know? What are the characteristics of Theresa and Hortense?

Now what do you know about the meaning of empowerment?

Definition and Rationale

Empowered people strive to have control over their lives; they try to take action to get what they want and need (Cochran, 1992; Cochran & Dean, 1991; Dunst, Trivette, & LaPoint, 1992; Rappaport, 1981). Often they succeed magnificently; sometimes they succeed only partially; sometimes they fail. Why do they have these different experiences with empowerment?

The answers are that empowerment—the ability to get what one wants—depends on the context in which one finds oneself and that empowerment changes over time. In other words, empowerment takes different forms in different contexts; what one does or experiences in one context (such as a neighborhood) may not be the same as what one does or experiences in another context (such as school-board meetings). Empowerment also differs among individuals in the same context; some individuals may be more empowerful than others in the same context. And empowerment may change over time for the same individual; an individual may become more and more empowerful over time because becoming empowerful is a developmental process (Kieffer, 1984; Zimmerman, in press).

Think about the most empowered and most disempowered people you know. The highly empowered people probably take frequent action to satisfy their preferences and needs and to build on their strengths. They have the means, knowledge, or opportunity to act; they know what they want and take action to get it. As a professional, you can and should be a person who provides families with some of the means they need to become more empowerful. Is there any doubt in your mind that Theresa is a person who empowers others? What a role model she should be for you!

By contrast, the most disempowered people probably often feel stuck, knowing that they face problems but feeling very unclear about what to do and sometimes being unable to take any action at all. In a sense, Hortense was stuck—mired in hopelessness—until she met Theresa and the other parents at LYDC.

How does empowerment apply to special education or, for that matter, to any provider-of-services system? If a father of a daughter who is gifted wants information on summer enrichment programs, being empowered means taking the necessary steps to make sure that, consistent with his daughter's preferences and family resources, he has access to that information, reviews it, and selects a summer program. For the foster parent of a child with a severe disability, empowerment may mean finding help to obtain and pay for necessary medical care for the child, obtaining the help, determining if her needs have been met, and taking further action if necessary. The professional collaborating with these and other families can and should provide the information or refer families to an appropriate source and then provide support according to their preferences. This support should ensure that their needs are satisfactorily addressed, just as Theresa and Hortense meet the needs of the families involved in LYDC, whether those needs are for the basics of life, such as food and clothing, or for disability-related services.

Empowerment is important not just for families who have a member with an exceptionality but also for you, for other professionals, and for students in special education. *Mutual empowerment*—empowerment of yourself and others—should be your goal in all your roles and responsibilities. In this book, we focus on the role that professionals such as yourself play in supporting families to be empowered. Yet we also want you to know that all the techniques you will learn in this book apply not just to your work with families but also to your work on your own behalf, your work with other professionals, and your work with students.

For example, special or general education teachers are empowered when they know how to secure the related services their students need and to collaborate with related service providers; all of that enables the teachers to be successful with their students. Similarly, school administrators, school faculty, community employers, and related service providers who work in agencies other than the school (such as local rehabilitation agencies) are empowered to secure programs for students in transition from special education to jobs and inclusive adult education programs when they collaborate to create school-to-work programs. Here, too, they secure the result they all want—namely, satisfying careers for students.

Likewise, students with exceptionalities are empowered when, during conferences to develop or evaluate their individualized education program, they clearly and succinctly share their preferences, strengths, and needs and suggest ways to address them. Student participation in IEP conferences can benefit teachers, administrators, families, and students, as we show in chapter 12. Mutual empowerment can and should be the result, over time, of one person's acting empowerfully in collaboration with others.

Most of the special education literature about family-professional partnerships emphasizes how important it is for professionals to empower families (Dunst, Trivette, & Deal, 1988; Garlow, Turnbull, & Schnase, 1991; Knoll, Covert, Osuch, O'Connor, Agosta, Blaney, & Bradley, 1990; Turnbull, Garlow, & Barber, 1991; Weiss, 1989). We repeat, however, that professional empowerment—your own and your colleagues' empowerment—is just as important. So as we describe how professionals can collaborate with families or other professionals to empower families, bear in mind that the concepts we present and the techniques we suggest are just as useful to you as an individual and a professional as they are to families. Because the concepts and techniques can help families and you, they also can help other professionals.

We encourage you to set a goal during this course—indeed, throughout the rest of your life—to become more empowerful and to support others to be empowerful. You will be most successful in enabling families, students, and others to achieve greater empowerment if you yourself are empowered. As you will read throughout this book, this type of win-win situation, where there is mutual empowerment, enables everyone to benefit from and contribute to each other. One of the truly remarkable aspects of LYDC is that its one professional staffer

(Theresa), its parent volunteer (Hortense), and the other parents involved all contribute to each other. Not surprisingly, this reciprocity enables them to get something they want—whether it is emotional support and the motivation to press on or information and new skills.

Having said this, let us now return to our single narrow purpose: teaching you how to foster families' empowerment.

Empowerment Framework

Overview

In a nutshell, empowerment—increasing control over one's life, taking action to get what one wants—occurs where there is a transaction between an individual and the context in which he or she is taking action. For our purposes, the individual is the family, and the context is special and general education or other service-delivery systems. The transaction in this case is collaboration. When families and schools or other provider systems are connected through collaboration, then empowerment—action to get what one wants—is probable. Hortense exemplifies the individual or family members, and LYDC exemplifies the context. The collaboration between the family and the professionals in a service-delivery context empowers everyone involved: Hortense is more likely to get what she wants, and LYDC and its staff (Theresa) are more likely to sense what Hortense wants and to respond to her.

It may help to think about the family and the education context as the two uprights on a soccer goal (see figure 3–1). Each is a vertical pole planted in a foundation but not connected. Standing alone, each is nothing more than a pole. Each may serve a role, but it is not to be an essential part of some action that we call the game of soccer. When connected by a horizontal crossbar, however, each of the vertical uprights acquires a new and different role. No longer is each simply a stand-alone pole; now each is an essential component of a goal. When there is a goal, there can be action: People can play soccer.

Think of collaboration as the crossbar in special education. It connects the two poles (that is, the families and the education contexts) to each other and thus creates the possibility that families and professionals can collaborate to take action. In the following sections, we discuss the family factors, the

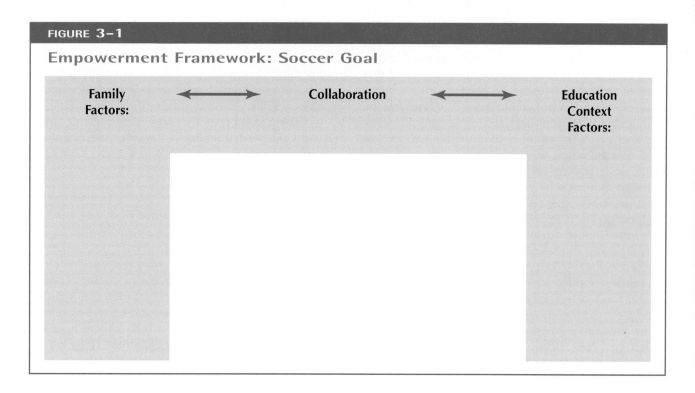

FIGURE 3-1

Empowerment Framework: Soccer Goal

Family Factors: ← Collaboration → Education Context Factors:

education context factors, and collaboration. We begin by showing in figure 3–2 the full model of empowerment. As we discuss each part of it, we break the model apart, concentrating on only that part. After we discuss each part, we reassemble the model. So bit by bit you will learn and build on your learning.

Family Factors

The first part of the empowerment model is family factors. As illustrated in figure 3–3, the family factors of empowerment are *motivation* and *knowledge/ skills*. (Study figure 3–3, paying particular attention to the family factors. We will describe the education context factors later in this chapter.) When families are motivated to take action and when they have the knowledge/skills to act, then they can affirm: "It's within us to be empowerful."

Motivation   Motivation includes five elements: (1) self-efficacy, (2) perceived control, (3) hope, (4) energy, and (5) persistence in pursuing goals. We briefly introduce each element here and discuss them throughout the rest of this book.

Self-efficacy refers to the belief in one's own capabilities (Bandura, 1977, 1982; Jones, Ross, & Marquis, 1995; Ozer & Bandura, 1990; Zimmerman, 1990, 1992;

Zimmerman & Rappaport, 1988). Feelings of self-efficacy clearly influence behavior; people tend to avoid activities and situations when they believe they cannot succeed, but they undertake activities when they think they can be effective. How does self-efficacy relate to families and professionals? Families' self-efficacy refers to their beliefs about their own ability to care for their children and to contribute to their children's positive outcomes. Teachers' self-efficacy refers to their beliefs concerning the degree to which they can make a difference in enhancing student learning (Ashton & Webb, 1986; DiBella-McCarthy, McDaniel, & Miller, 1995).

Research on parent and teacher self-efficacy shows that there is a positive relationship among families, teachers, student development, and home-school interaction (Hoover-Dempsey, Bassler, & Brissie, 1992):

1. Higher levels of parents' self-efficacy are related to increased parent involvement in volunteering at school, participating in educational activities, and communicating with teachers on the telephone.
2. Teachers with higher self-efficacy reported higher levels of parent participation, suggesting that higher-efficacy teachers may encourage more active parent collaboration.
3. Teachers with higher self-efficacy characterized parents as also having higher efficacy.

FIGURE 3–2

Empowerment Framework: Collaborating for Empowerment

Family Factors:
It's Within Us to Be Empowerful

Collaborating for Empowerment:
Through Collaboration, We Act Empowerfully

Education Context Factors:
It's Within Us to Make Our Contexts Empowering

Motivation	Knowledge/Skills		Opportunities for Partnerships	Obligations for Reliable Alliances
			Opportunities arise when . . .	*Reliable alliances consist of . . .*
Self-efficacy: believing in our capabilities	*Information:* being in the know		Communicating among reliable allies	Knowing yourself
Perceived control: believing we can apply our capabilities to affect what happens to us	*Problem solving:* knowing how to bust the barriers		Meeting families' basic needs	Knowing families
				Honoring cultural diversity
Hope: believing we will get what we want and need	*Coping skills:* knowing how to handle what happens to us		Referring and evaluating for special education	Affirming family strengths
Energy: lighting the fire and keeping it burning	*Communication skills:* being on the sending and receiving ends of expressed needs and wants		Individualizing for appropriate education	Promoting family choices
			Extending learning in home and community	Envisioning great expectations
Persistence: putting forth a sustained effort			Attending and volunteering at school	Communicating positively
			Advocating for systems improvement	Warranting trust and respect

FIGURE 3-3

Empowerment Framework: Collaborating for Empowerment

Family Factors:
It's Within Us to Be
Empowerful

**Collaborating for
Empowerment:
Through Collaboration,
We Act Empowerfully**

Education Context Factors:
It's Within Us to Make Our
Contexts Empowering

Motivation

Self-efficacy: believing in
our capabilities

Perceived control:
believing we can
apply our capabilities
to affect what
happens to us

Hope: believing we will
get what we want
and need

Energy: lighting the fire
and keeping it
burning

Persistence: putting forth a
sustained effort

Knowledge/Skills

Information: being in the
know

Problem solving: knowing
how to bust the
barriers

Coping skills: knowing
how to handle what
happens to us

Communication skills:
being on the sending
and receiving ends of
expressed needs and
wants

40   *Chapter 3*

The relationship between the individual family member and the teacher seems to be a mutual one in that a teacher with higher self-efficacy encourages parents to believe more in their capabilities (that is, augment their self-efficacy). The augmented self-efficacy that parents have, in turn, reciprocally encourages teachers to be even more efficacious. Simply put, if you believe in your own effectiveness, you probably will act; and any action you take will probably encourage others to be more effective. It is this interaction between families and teachers—between families on the one hand and yourself and your colleagues on the other—that makes empowerment (or, at least, beliefs in self-efficacy) a reciprocal matter.

Perceived control, believing you can apply your capabilities to affect what happens to you, is a second element of motivation. Research underscores the importance of families' having choices about issues concerning their child (Allen & Petr, 1996; Donahue-Kilburg, 1992; Dunst, Trivette, Gordon, & Starnes, 1993). A parent of a child with cerebral palsy describes the role of choice this way:

> Choice is really important. Parents need to know there are choices and be able to make decisions. Choice is having the freedom to decide what you need for your family and to be able to ask for it. Making choices on everyday things are building blocks for empowerment. (Jones, Garlow, Turnbull, & Barber, 1996, p. 101)

As you learned in chapter 1, professionals traditionally have expected families to acquiesce to professional direction and advice. This approach, however, can be disempowering. A more empowering approach is for all stakeholders in educational decision making to share their expertise and resources for the mutual benefit of all (Allen & Petr, 1996; Jones et al., 1996; Turbiville, Turnbull, Garland, & Lee, 1996). This is the essence of a power-with and power-from-within approach rather than a power-over approach. It is the sort of approach that Theresa practices when she learns what strengths people have and how she can enhance them.

Hope is the third element of motivation. Although there are many definitions of hope (Snyder, 1994), we define it as your belief that you will get what you want and need. Hope involves having a vision, a sense of expectation. How does hope differ from perceived control? Perceived control involves your belief that you can affect what will happen to you. Hope is the extension of perceived control. Hope is expecting that, by using your capabilities, you will indeed get what you want and need.

When some people encounter events they think they cannot affect, they may experience learned helplessness, a psychological state in which people expect events in their life to be externally controlled and anticipate that they will likely fail rather than succeed in what they try to do (Seligman, 1990). The opposite of learned helplessness is learned hopefulness, a psychological state in which people perceive that, through affecting what happens to them, they will achieve positive outcomes (Zimmerman, 1990). Families frequently report how important hope becomes as they face the challenges of exceptionality.

Hope! That's what Hortense needed and what Theresa and LYDC supplied in full measure. And what a difference that supply has made. By contrast, another mother has described how she wished a neurosurgeon had been more hopeful in communicating to her about the impact of her child's head injury:

> We knew it was serious. We didn't need a doctor to say that. What we needed to hear is there's always hope but it's very serious. . . . And I don't think they have to be able to do any more than that. Perhaps shake your hand or hold it, look you straight in the eye and say, "This is very serious. But there's always hope." But you see, that wasn't given to us at all. (Singer & Nixon, 1996, p. 29)

Families emphasize the importance of having hope as a catalyst for not giving up but persevering, even when times are tough and progress is not very noticeable.

Energy is the fourth element of motivation—lighting the fire and keeping it burning. Energy has two components: (1) what it takes initially to "light the fire" and (2) what it takes to "keep it burning." In terms of lighting the fire, taking the first steps of action to get what one needs or wants, research has pointed to the importance of a "mobilizing episode" (Kieffer, 1984, p. 19). A mobilizing episode for families might be the initial diagnosis of a disability, having their child excluded from the neighborhood school, or being told that their child is not "college material." These episodes create strong reactions of injustice or outrage that jog people from a "business as usual" approach to one of taking significant action. Mobilizing episodes can also be positive; for example, a child may get a new power wheelchair, parents may attend a conference and be especially inspired and informed by a speaker about what is possible in supported employment, or teachers may have an opportunity to serve as a consulting teacher for others. Whatever the mobilizing episode, the key is that action takes energy, and energy is necessary for people to get initially mobilized.

The initial burst of energy is necessary but not sufficient. There must be energy to carry out actions one after another, each building toward the ultimate goal. Because empowerment is time- and labor-intensive, initial and subsequent bursts of energy are necessary. One way to encourage empowerment is to encourage a wellness approach to everyday living. Covey (1990) includes the habit called "sharpening the saw" as one of his seven habits of highly effective people. Physical renewal—exercise, nutrition, and stress management—is an essential element of sharpening the saw.

The final element of motivation is *persistence*—putting forth sustained effort over time. Persistence is closely related to energy for keeping the fires burning, but persistence requires tenacity—a never-say-die, bulldog attitude. It entails refusing to give up when one's initial efforts do not immediately result in one getting what one wants or needs. Sometimes in specific actions, such as finding the best medication regimen for a child with diabetes or working through challenging behavior for a youngster with an emotional disorder, a family will go through periods of trial and error before obtaining a successful solution. Persistence is required to work through discrete, time-limited, or relatively short-term challenges.

Persistence is also needed in working toward long-term goals. One of those goals is an appropriate education for students. This goal begins when students are in early intervention programs and continues through their transition from high school into adulthood. Many parents will be advocates throughout their child's adult years and need to be persistent to run the marathon of long-term disability challenges (Turnbull, 1988). The capacity for sustained effort is a critical element of an individual's motivation.

In summary, the five elements of motivation are self-efficacy, perceived control, hope, energy, and persistence. Reflect on the people you think are especially strong in each of these five elements. What do you think jump-starts and then continues to propel their motivation? What are the catalysts for their motivational strength? Could it be that they are connected to others who enhance these five factors? Could it be—shouldn't it be—that families and professionals connect and collaborate for empowerment?

Knowledge and Skills   Motivation is only one of the family factors of empowerment. The second factor is knowledge/skills (Jones et al., 1996). Many families who are highly motivated also have knowledge/skill strengths as well. It is possible, however, to have strong motivation but to be slightly or significantly lacking in knowledge/skills. Empowered families have sufficient knowledge/skills to get what they want and need. Figure 3–2 identifies the four elements of knowledge and skills: (1) information, (2) problem solving, (3) coping skills, and (4) communication skills.

Information is a high-priority need for families (Bailey, Blasco, & Simeonsson, 1992; Hadadian & Merbler, 1995). Families say that their greatest needs for information relate to (1) future services, (2) present services, (3) how to teach their child, (4) the nature of their child's disability, (5) experiences of other parents who have a child with similar needs, (6) handling the emotional and time demands of parenthood, (7) community resources, and (8) legal rights (Cooper & Allred, 1992; Gowen, Christy, & Sparling, 1993). Families and professionals alike need state-of-the-art information that is accessible, relevant, and time-efficient. They need to be "in the know." One of Theresa's and Hortense's goals is to put families in the know by offering training or other information sessions and by making other consultants or experts available to families. Ironically, one of the greatest barriers to empowerment is the large gap between research and the accessibility and affordability of this information for families and professionals (Turnbull & Friesen, 1995; Turnbull & Turnbull, 1993). We encourage you to acquire, use, and exchange state-of-the-art information with families and professionals. Everyone wants and needs to be in the know.

Problem solving consists of the ability to establish and implement a plan to get what you want in spite of problems standing in the way (Cochran, 1992; Cornell Empowerment Group, 1989; Heller, 1990; Jones et al., 1996; Knackendoffel, Robinson, Deshler, & Schumaker, 1992; Turnbull, Patterson, Behr, Murphy, Marquis, & Blue-Banning, 1993; Zimmerman, 1992). Problem solving is a way of busting the barriers that stand between what "is" and what is "ideal." As parents might say, "Our son with spina bifida wants to be a disc jockey. The fact that he's in a wheelchair shouldn't stop him. Let's see what it will take for him to volunteer at the local radio station."

As we point out in chapter 4, problem solving consists of (1) developing a vision; (2) agreeing on a specific goal; (3) brainstorming options for addressing the goal; (4) evaluating benefits and drawbacks of each option; (5) selecting the most appropriate option; (6) specifying an implementation plan, including next steps, person responsible, resources needed, and time lines; (7) implementing the plan; (8) evaluating how closely the results of action match the goals; and (9) modifying the plan and continuing to make progress. This is a lot of work, so much that families and professionals can and should collaborate to refine their problem-solving skills (Johnson & Pugach, 1991; Shank & Turnbull, 1993).

The third element of the knowledge/skills factor is *coping skills*—knowing how to handle what happens to you. Olson and associates (1983) have categorized coping skills into five types. We briefly define them here, including citations to literature related to families who have a member with an exceptionality.

1. *Passive appraisal:* setting aside worries about a problem

   When things really get bad I go and soak in the bath for an hour. My husband was told I was on the verge of a nervous breakdown but I haven't had it yet! (Lonsdale, 1978, p. 108)

2. *Reframing:* changing the way one thinks about a situation in order to emphasize positive rather than negative aspects (Behr, 1989; Blue-Banning, Santelli, Guy, & Wallace, 1994; Summers, Behr, & Turnbull, 1988)

   My only daughter is profoundly retarded. She's loved and in return she's lovely. She's not able to walk or talk, but she can smile and laugh. She is loved. (Turnbull, Blue-Banning, Behr, & Kearns, 1986, p. 130)

3. *Spiritual support:* deriving comfort and guidance from one's spiritual beliefs (Fewell, 1986; Weisner, Belzer, & Stolze, 1991)

   We are Catholic, and I know we can draw on that. There are always divine interventions when I was ready to self-destruct. (Turnbull & Ruef, in press, a)

4. *Social support:* receiving practical and emotional assistance from friends and family (Beckman, 1991; Dunst, Trivette, Gordon, & Pletcher, 1989)

   At a critical time, one of my good friends said, "Don't give up, don't lose faith." It was real energizing to know that others believed in my daughter, too. (Turnbull & Ruef, in press, a)

5. *Professional support:* receiving assistance from professionals and agencies (Friesen, Koren, & Koroloff, 1992)

   It was the first day of summer vacation and my son was off the wall, because he really needed structure. I was freaking out, and I couldn't deal with it. I called the teacher and told her I didn't know what to do. She came across town and took him to her house and said, "Do something fun for two hours." (Turnbull & Ruef, in press, b)

We encourage you to reflect on the coping strategies that Theresa and Hortense use, especially their reliance on their spiritual support and social support, and to think about your own coping skills and challenging situations that you have faced. Families and all members of collaboration teams vary in their capabilities to cope, in the number of different coping strategies that they use, and in the quality or effectiveness of each strategy. Moreover, the strategies that families use will change from time to time depending on the issues families face and the contexts in which they face them. Throughout this book, we discuss these coping strategies.

We want to add a caveat, however, about the term *coping*. Although it is a frequently used term and concept in the professional literature, families often do not embrace it nearly as strongly. For example, a parent described her view of coping like this:

For the first 33 years of my life I wasn't once accused of "coping," not even "well." I just got on with, actually enjoyed it, and did many things with varying degrees of success. Then my daughter with Down syndrome was born and ever since I've been "coping well." Mind you, that's not how it felt. After the initial vacuum of shock I thought I just went on getting on with life with the usual success-failure rate. But I must have been "coping well" because everybody kept telling me I was. . . . Why do I feel so offended by the praising people who tell me I'm "coping well"? I guess because I see it as an attempt to reduce me to a unidimensional figure—"the mother of a child with Down syndrome who copes." . . . "Cope" comes from an Old French word meaning "to strike (a blow)" and I still feel like "coping" the next well-meaning person who says it to me. (Boyce, 1992, p. 37)

Professional terminology can create barriers in professional-family relationships. So we encourage you to communicate with families by using terms that are meaningful to them. *Coping* may not be a meaningful and positive term to some families.

The last knowledge/skills element is *communication skills*. Communication skills—being on the sending and receiving ends of the needs and wants that you, families, and other professionals express—are at the heart of empowerment and substantially contribute to the collaborative process. In chapter 4, we describe in detail nonverbal communication skills, verbal communication skills, influencing skills, and group communication skills. We also point out how and why families' cultural values and traditions strongly influence their preferred communication skills and require both speakers and listeners to make accommodations.

In summary, knowledge/skills consists of four elements—information, problem solving, coping skills, and communication skills. For families to be empowered, it is necessary for them to have sufficient knowledge/skills. When motivation and knowledge/skills are present simultaneously, families will be far more likely to affirm, "It's within us to be empowerful."

Education Context Factors

We have been discussing only one of the two factors involved in empowerment—family factors. But as we said in our overview of empowerment and displayed in figure 3–1, empowerment is like a soccer goal: It needs another upright. For our purposes, this upright is the education context—the schools and professionals involved in a child's education. We now turn our attention to the education context, beginning with the soccer-goal analogy.

Just as a soccer game requires a playing field (a context for the action of the game of soccer) so do the context factors of empowerment require an arena in which they can be carried out. This is because empowerment is contextual and involves family-professional partnerships (Cornell Empowerment Group, 1989) and collaboration (Fine, 1990; Turnbull & Turnbull, 1985). It also requires the family to participate within the context in which they seek to become more empowerful (Florin & Wandersman, 1984; Kieffer, 1984; Zimmerman & Rappaport, 1988). Indeed, some service-delivery contexts deliberately seek to enable families to become more empowerful (Jones et al., 1996).

Figure 3–4 displays the education context factors. These factors enable educators and other professionals to affirm, "It's within us to make our contexts empowering." Families may indeed possess a great deal of motivation and knowledge/skills; but if the education context and educators/professionals they encounter refuse to respond positively, their empowerment will be constrained and even negated. By contrast, if the education context is empowering, then the families, and even their children, become agents of each others' empowerment. That is the way it is at LYDC: Theresa models or exemplifies her own power and thereby teaches other family members, such as Hortense, to act powerfully. Hortense in turn becomes an agent for the empowerment of other families who enter the LYDC context. A circle or chain of empowerment begins with just one person.

In chapter 2, we introduced and discussed the context factors of seven opportunities for partnerships and eight obligations for reliable alliances (illustrated in figure 3–4). We define these seven opportunities for partnerships in figure 3–5. At the end of each definition, we refer to the chapter that focuses exclusively on that type of partnership and describe how you can create an empowering context for each partnership.

In chapter 2, we also introduced the eight obligations for a reliable alliance, briefly defined in figure 3–6. To create an empowering context, you need to infuse these eight obligations into all seven opportunities for partnerships—that is, into *all* your interactions with families. The more you incorporate the eight obligations of a reliable alliance into your interactions with families, the more empowering you will make the context and the more you will empower families.

In summary, professionals like you and your colleagues, operating in school contexts, must transform policies, procedures, and programs from power-over approaches to power-with and power-within approaches. You and your contexts can be part of the empowerment process for families if you focus on the seven opportunities for partnerships and eight obligations for reliable alliances with families that we introduced in chapter 2 (illustrated in figures 3–5 and 3–6) and that we further describe throughout the remaining chapters.

Collaboration

How do the two poles of the soccer goal—the family and education context factors—connect? They do so by the horizontal bar: collaboration. When families and educators are connected, they together can affirm, "Through collaboration we act empowerfully." Collaboration is the crossbar that creates a goal; it is the connector. We remind you of the definition of collaboration that we included in chapter 1 so you will see how it ties to the empowerment framework illustrated in figures 3–2 and 3–7. As we said in chapter 1, collaboration refers to the dynamic process of connecting families' resources (motivation and knowledge/skills) with an empowering context to make decisions collectively. When collaboration incorporates families' resources (motivation and knowledge/skills) with an education context that consists of partnerships and reliable alliances, empowerment results: Families and professionals can take action to get what they want and need. As the crossbar in figure 3–7 shows, "Through collaboration, we can act empowerfully."

In figure 3–7 you will see that the crossbar represents professionals who help create connections by supporting and augmenting families' motivation and

FIGURE 3-4

Empowerment Framework: Collaborating for Empowerment

Family Factors:
It's Within Us to Be
Empowerful

**Collaborating for
Empowerment:
Through Collaboration,
We Act Empowerfully**

Education Context Factors:
It's Within Us to Make Our
Contexts Empowering

Opportunities for Partnerships	Obligations for Reliable Alliances
Opportunities arise when . . .	*Reliable alliances consist of . . .*
Communicating among reliable allies	Knowing yourself
Meeting families' basic needs	Knowing families
Referring and evaluating for special education	Honoring cultural diversity
Individualizing for appropriate education	Affirming family strengths
Extending learning in home and community	Promoting family choices
Attending and volunteering at school	Envisioning great expectations
Advocating for systems improvement	Communicating positively
	Warranting trust and respect

FIGURE 3-5

Seven Opportunities for Partnerships

1. *Communicating among reliable allies:* involves two-way and three-or-more-way communication among all stakeholders to create reliable alliances (chapter 9)
2. *Attending to families' basic needs:* involves supporting families and their children in meeting their basic emotional, informational, financial, safety and health, and daily care needs (chapter 10)
3. *Referring and evaluating for special education*: involves implementing local, state, and federal policy and best practice in referring students for special education services and evaluating students to determine the nature of their exceptionality and their specific strengths, needs, and preferences, all as the basis for individualized instruction (chapter 11)
4. *Individualizing for appropriate education:* involves developing and implementing meaningful, relevant, and comprehensive individualized education programs (chapter 12)
5. *Extending learning in the home and community:* involves building links among the many activities in environments in which students and families live in order to best support learning and development (chapter 13)
6. *Attending and volunteering at school:* involves families in observing school events, participating in the life of the school, and contributing to accomplish the school's important tasks (chapter 14)
7. *Advocating for systems improvement:* involves building coalitions to address priority school needs in designing and implementing policy, model programs, and best practices in enhancing student learning and family participation (chapter 15)

FIGURE 3-6

Obligations for a Reliable Alliance

1. *Knowing yourself:* involves having accurate self-knowledge—knowing and appreciating your own perspectives, opinions, strengths, and needs
2. *Knowing families:* involves being able to identify the unique aspects of each family's characteristics, interactions, functions, and life cycle and to respond in ways that are personalized and individually tailored to respect families' uniqueness
3. *Honoring cultural diversity:* means relating to others in personalized, respectful, and responsive ways in light of values associated with factors such as ethnicity, race, religion, income status, gender, sexual orientation, disability status, occupation, and geographical location
4. *Affirming and building on family strengths:* means identifying, appreciating, and capitalizing upon families' strengths
5. *Promoting family choices:* involves selecting the family members to be involved in collaborative decision making, deciding which educational issues should take priority over others, choosing the extent to which family members are involved in decision making for each educational issue, and selecting appropriate goals and services for the student
6. *Envisioning great expectations:* means recognizing that one can have an exceptionality and also have an enviable life
7. *Practicing positive communication skills:* means using nonverbal skills (such as physical attending and listening), verbal communication skills (such as furthering responses, paraphrasing, and summarizing), and influencing skills (such as providing information, providing support, and offering assistance) in ways that most sensitively and respectfully connect with families
8. *Warranting trust and respect:* means having confidence that everyone is pulling in the same direction in a supportive, nonjudgmental, and caring way

FIGURE 3–7

Empowerment Framework: Collaborating for Empowerment

Collaborating for Empowerment:
Through Collaboration, We Act Empowerfully

Family Factors: It's Within Us to Be Empowerful		**Education Context Factors:** It's Within Us to Make Our Contexts Empowering	
Motivation	**Knowledge/Skills**	**Opportunities for Partnerships** *Opportunities arise when . . .*	**Obligations for Reliable Alliances** *Reliable alliances consist of . . .*
Self-efficacy: believing in our capabilities	*Information:* being in the know	Communicating among reliable allies	Knowing yourself
Perceived control: believing we can apply our capabilities to affect what happens to us	*Problem solving:* knowing how to bust the barriers	Meeting families' basic needs	Knowing families
	Coping skills: knowing how to handle what happens to us	Referring and evaluating for special education	Honoring cultural diversity
Hope: believing we will get what we want and need	*Communication skills:* being on the sending and receiving ends of expressed needs and wants	Individualizing for appropriate education	Affirming family strengths
Energy: lighting the fire and keeping it burning		Extending learning in home and community	Promoting family choices
Persistence: putting forth a sustained effort		Attending and volunteering at school	Envisioning great expectations
		Advocating for systems improvement	Communicating positively
			Warranting trust and respect

knowledge/skills. These professionals create those connections by engaging with families in a collaborative partnership characterized by a genuine and authentic relationship—what we call a reliable alliance. This is just the kind of relationship Hortense Walker has had with one of the professionals in Eric's life . . . but not with another, as box 3–1 describes.

Throughout this book, we discuss collaboration in its many different forms. When you collaborate with a single family and have the outcome of empowerment

---

TOGETHER WE CAN
BOX 3–1

Collaborating for Empowerment

To ask Hortense Walker about the family and context factors and collaboration as a connector, it is best to ask about the characteristics of the most and least effective professionals she and her family have worked with.

Their best experiences came with Eric's teacher in an early intervention program. Before Eric entered the program at age 18 months, Marlene (the teacher) visited the Walker home and quickly became encouraging so that she and Hortense easily bonded.

How was she encouraging? By not being a "hammer" and insisting that Eric should be in the program but by explaining how the program would help Eric and the whole family and then letting the family decide whether to enter it. She gave them a reason to enroll Eric (motivation) and information on which to make a decision. She acknowledged to them that they have the power within themselves to be empowerful to make decisions.

How was she able to create a bond? She was considerate of the family, keeping her appointments and gently prompting Hortense and her husband Michael to ask questions they were afraid to ask, questions about Eric and his impact on the family.

"We came to see Marlene as a person whose first objective was to meet the needs of our family as a whole. She emphasized the positives of the program for us and for Eric. We just ate up her time and her knowledge. She felt appreciated by us, and she was. That made the difference."

In a very real sense, Marlene became the context: She offered herself as a resource, and in doing so she created opportunities for partnerships. Clearly, by her offer and especially the manner in which she made the offer, she displayed her sense of obligation to be a reliable ally.

By contrast, the least effective professional, a social worker at the regional service center, never asked Hortense and Michael what they needed. "Eric was very young, throwing up everything he ate, very skinny, and never asleep. I'd work all day and then sleep just an hour a night," recalled Hortense. But the social worker visited only once and never asked if Hortense needed respite. "She was rationing the respite to families whose children were more severely involved than Eric."

Yet in Hortense's mind, Eric was indeed a child with a severe disability, and Hortense herself was fast approaching the end of her rope.

The result of that interaction with the social worker? "I grew up in a home that respected professionals. I was raised by my grandmother and oldest sister; my mother died at childbirth, and I was the last of nine children. My oldest sister is 20 years older than I. They taught me to respect doctors and teachers and to do as they say."

The social worker taught Hortense just the opposite. Now, Hortense questions everyone closely and doesn't let anyone take her or her family lightly.

Well, almost everyone. With Marlene, it's not necessary to question closely. After all, Marlene acknowledges Hortense's and her family's power. In doing so, she creates a different kind of life for them, one in which they are invited by her to be collaborators and in which they gladly accept her invitation.

---

for the family and for yourself, you will begin to enhance your own motivation and knowledge/skills. You will realize that you are competent to make a significant difference in the lives of students and families; and when you realize that, you will acquire a genuine feeling of satisfaction about being an effective individual and teacher.

As one collaboration occurs, and then another, and then still another, you may experience the height of collaboration, which is collective empowerment. You and the families will experience success in your relationships with each other because you are getting what all of you want and need. You will become mutually empowerful; and as you attain this stage, you may experience a qualitative change in yourself and your relationship with families. This change—this difference in quality—is what some people call synergy.

Synergy is "the capacity of an individual or group to increase the satisfaction of all participants by intentionally generating increased energy and creativity, all of which is used to co-create a more rewarding present and future" (Craig & Craig, 1974, p. 62). When all members of a collaborating team—families and professionals—are able to become personally and individually more empowerful and more able to reach a common goal, the outcome is that the whole becomes greater than the sum of the parts. That is the essence of synergy. Synergy basically means the collective empowerment of all, the enabling of each collaborator to reach the goals that each wants and that all want. When everyone is working collaboratively and expanding his or her own empowerment, they create a "synergistic community" (Katz, 1984, p. 222), an alliance in which each person's efforts significantly and exponentially advance individual and group goals.

This synergistic community—this alliance of reliable people—is the ideal context. A synergistic context is what we found when we visited LYDC and, over a series of long conversations, came to know and appreciate Theresa and Hortense. Theresa, Hortense, and other LYDC families have created that circle or chain of empowerment; more than that, they have created a context that expects and nurtures empowerment.

So, you might ask, what keeps the ideal from being the reality? At least part of the answer is that sometimes people fear that if others around them are more empowered, then they, by necessity, will have less power. In such a game, what one group gains, another group loses; there is no "win-win" possibility.

In this scenario, a context cannot respond to and empower all its members.

For example, some people may erroneously assume that, in a team meeting comprised of a parent, a student with an exceptionality, a teacher, and a school psychologist, the professionals and student will lose power if the parent gains power to exercise choices and exert some control. This assumption rests on the notion that there is only a fixed amount of power; if one person has a bigger piece of the "power pie," others will have to be satisfied with smaller pieces. This is a prevailing perspective in Western cultures. A cultural strength of some non-Western thinking, however, is that resources are regarded as abundant rather than limited (Katz, 1984).

One of the characteristics of synergistic communities, then, is that empowerment can be an expanding and renewable resource distributed equitably among those who are working toward a common goal (Katz, 1984; Swift & Levin, 1987). Let's return to box 3–1 and recall the two professionals whom Hortense described. As Marlene provided choices to Hortense in decision making, Hortense became more empowered and so did Marlene: Both got what they wanted and needed. On the other hand, the social worker who attempted to hold on to her power cut herself off completely from a reliable alliance with Hortense. In effect, she was unable to take action to help get what either she or Hortense wanted or needed. The lesson of box 3–1 is very straightforward: A synergistic community is one in which the respective empowerment of families and professionals converges to create mutual empowerment for everyone.

Do individual empowerment and especially mutual empowerment occur rapidly? No, particularly because (as we pointed out in chapter 1) professionals and families have had longstanding relationships that too often denigrate, or disempower, families but elevate professionals. History is a powerful teacher; it teaches that new collaborations, different relationships, and radically changed thinking are desirable but difficult to achieve.

Indeed, empowerment is a developmental process. Empowerment—empowering individually and mutually—takes time; it does not happen automatically just because one wishes for it to occur. In fact, an in-depth study of highly empowered community leaders concluded that their journeys toward empowerment took three to four years (Kieffer, 1984).

How can you, a single professional, orchestrate your own empowerment, enable families do the same for themselves, and thereby spark a mutual empowerment or synergistic community that expands a context's responsiveness? The answer is the one we have already given and restate now: When the family ("within us") factors combine with the education context ("within our contexts") factors, as they do through collaboration (see figure 3–7), then mutual empowerment can exist: the "win-win" ability of each of you to get what you want and need.

You have a key role in creating an empowering context in which families, you, and other professionals can be mutually empowerful. To get to that result, we suggest that you put into place the seven opportunities for family-professional partnerships (chapters 9 through 15) and try to infuse each of those partnerships with the eight obligations of a reliable alliance (chapter 4 and all others).

Summary

Professionals who work effectively with families not only understand the roles that families have played over the years (chapter 1) and the contexts in which they work with families (chapter 2) but also accept new responsibilities. These responsibilities are (1) to enable families to enhance their motivation and knowledge/skills and to do the same for themselves and other professionals and (2) to create an empowering context, one in which opportunities for partnerships and obligations for reliable alliances coexist. To achieve this result, professionals need to collaborate with families, other professionals, and other interested individuals. Professionals, through their role as collaborators, have opportunities and obligations to create mutual empowerment.

Empowerment consists of identifying one's most important needs and preferences and then taking steps to satisfy them. Empowerment occurs within a two-part framework. One part consists of family factors—a family that is motivated, that has knowledge/skills, that can truthfully say, "It's within us to be empowerful." The other part of empowerment consists of education context factors—schools and professionals that take advantage of opportunities for partnerships and undertake obligations for reliable alliances, who can truthfully say, "It's within us to make our contexts empowering." Of course, the connector between the individual and the context factors is collaboration. Empowerment can occur when professionals and families collaborate by enhancing motivation, expanding knowledge and skills, taking advantage of opportunities for partnerships, undertaking obligations to create reliable alliances, and taking action to get what they want.

There are two kinds of knowledge: that which derives from research, which we call "head" or "book" knowledge, and that which derives from simply living, which we call "heart" or "street" knowledge. At Loving Your Disabled Child, both kinds of knowledge combine. They do so in a way that empowers everyone, and that is collaborative.

Theresa Cooper and Hortense Walker practice heart knowledge, but they reflect the book knowledge that we have described in this chapter. They practice mutual empowerment, demonstrating and thus inculcating into others the attitudes and skills that facilitate empowerment, enabling action by others, and creating a context within LYDC that responds to what its families want and need.

They collaborate with LYDC's families, sometimes in unexpected ways. There is an implicit promise of collaboration in this relatively atypical message that Theresa gives the parents: "Parents need to know that they can love their child who has a disability and that their love can grow. . . . Your marriage can stay together, your children can love their brother or sister, there can be just an overabundance of love, and the family can be stable and together."

The promise is that Theresa and Hortense and other LYDC families will help each other be loving and strong.

Doesn't collaboration begin when two or more people have expectations of the kind that Theresa speaks about? Isn't it established when they find ways to solve their problems and then celebrate their successes?

Theresa and Hortense think so, and that's why they do not find it unusual that LYDC parents talk and laugh when they come together. They may not have solved all their problems, not by any means; but their empowering attitudes, their abilities to reinforce each other's strengths, their skills in sharing information and referring each other to services, and their celebrations—all these are hallmarks of empowerment and collaboration.

Chapter Four

Building Reliable Alliances

*W*hen it comes to creating empowering relationships and building reliable alliances, Susan Rocco has more than a few lessons to teach other parents and professionals. Some of those lessons were hard to come by, but not all.

For example, when she wanted her son Jason to be removed from his self-contained school and included in a general education program in Honolulu, Susan had to know a great deal about herself and about the culture of her adopted state.

After all, at age 10, Jason was a bit of a challenge: As handsome as he was, he nevertheless had a serious pervasive developmental delay, severe mental retardation, mild cerebral palsy, and epilepsy. Although he usually expressed his strong preferences in what Susan calls "prosocial" ways, he sometimes was fairly stubborn and challenging, especially as he began to feel the effects of hormone changes and adolescence.

What Susan knew about herself was that "you get more flies with honey than vinegar." She abandoned the cultural mores that she had learned on the U.S. mainland and adopted the nonassertive, nonconfrontational mores of Hawaii. She also had to trust professionals in order to secure their trust in her.

About the cultural mores, Susan says that "being able to just play the game by those social rules and genuinely trying to connect with people and get them to know Jason" was a key to Jason's admission to an inclusive setting in a new school.

As for getting people to know her and Jason and to trust her: She knew she had created a powerful alliance with his teachers in his "sending" school. All those teachers knew Jason and encouraged Susan to go for it because they would back her up. They did just that, meeting with his teachers in his inclusive school and persuading them to give Jason and another student, his friend Sheryl, a reception before spring semester ended and before he showed up for school in the fall.

That was a smart strategy because it was necessary to create partnerships with the "receiving" school and its staff—a partnership similar to the one Susan had created with one of Jason's sending teachers, Cindy.

To create partners at Jason's school, Susan found that she had to validate the teachers' efforts, writing compliments to them and sending copies to their administrators.

"I had come to an understanding that the teachers had a really hard job and that the more I could have them thinking positively about Jason and me, the better we would be."

Having Cindy and Sheryl's parents as inclusion pioneers also was important. "Had I not had those relationships and that level of trust in my partners, including Cindy, it might have been just scary to attempt to include Jason. I could do it with my friends holding my hand, but it might have been very difficult had I been the only parent trying this radically different thing."

This "radically different thing"—being an inclusion pioneer—didn't come naturally to Susan. Inspired by experiences of other parents in Hawaii and elsewhere and by the research and demonstration efforts of a few special education professors, Susan finally just bit the bullet. "I just really had my doubts about Jason being able to handle a pod-type of classroom with Jason's new teacher, Mrs. Ching, and yet I thought, why not go for it? Let's try it."

That sense of great expectations paid off as Jason's peers "took ownership" of him and his education and began to regard him as a capable young man. Their attitude was infectious, and Mrs. Ching herself began to develop a friendly, almost fun relationship with Jason. Her relationship with Jason made it increasingly possible for Susan and Mrs. Ching to deal directly with each other rather than through Cindy as the go-between. Indeed, as the school year concluded, Mrs. Ching, a teacher with 20 years of experience, told Susan that Jason was the teacher and Mrs. Ching the learner—so much so that Mrs. Ching is now considering going into special education.

As Susan looks to the future, she admonishes herself to be far less "left-brained," far less logical, planned, and depersonalized, and far more "right-brained" and affective.

"I used to think that I should be more businesslike and more professional about certain things. . . . But I now really truly think that's all baloney, that your best shot is to make friends with somebody. That's my goal. It doesn't always get friendship, but in order for you to have a level of trust with one another, you just have to spend time as people together without the anxiety of meeting Jason's needs hanging over your head."

As you learned in chapter 3, empowerment occurs when collaboration connects families and their characteristics to education contexts and their characteristics. We described the education context factors as opportunities for partnerships and obligations for reliable alliances. This chapter focuses on the context factors—"It's within us to make our contexts empowering." More often than not, these alliances are characterized by open, genuine, and reciprocal relationships.

These relationships and their ensuing alliances depend on

- Knowing yourself
- Knowing families
- Honoring cultural diversity
- Affirming and building on family strengths
- Promoting family choices
- Encouraging great expectations
- Practicing positive communication skills
- Warranting mutual respect and trust

Knowing Yourself

The first obligation for a reliable alliance is self-knowledge—knowing yourself. The more you know yourself, the better you can understand and appreciate the personalities and behaviors of others (Seligman & Darling, 1989). What you need at the outset is a willingness to understand your own perceptions and to reflect on how they may be affecting your relationships with families.

What does it mean to understand your own perceptions? The way in which people view the world varies widely and depends on a complex interaction of internal and external forces (Webster, 1977). The complexity of this interaction prevents any two people from perceiving the world in exactly the same way. Why and how is this so?

First, we perceive the world through our sensory receptors. Although this fact accounts for much consistency in perception among people, it is possible that differences exist even at this basic level. Such differences are obvious when we interact with persons who experience deafness or blindness.

Through our sensory receptors, we filter and edit information to understand what we hear, feel, see, and smell. This part of perception, called *interpretation,* characteristically takes the form of impressions, conclusions, assumptions, expectations, or prejudices.

Interpretations differ from observations: Two people may observe the same event but interpret it differently. For example, some of the characteristic behaviors of autism are rocking, hand flapping, jumping up and down, and repeating words (Turnbull, Turnbull, Shank, & Leal, 1995). These behaviors are generally considered to be inappropriate. An alternative interpretation of these behaviors was described by an African-American family who consistently focused on their son's similarities with others rather than his differences:

> On one occasion, as the family sat watching a high-speed chase scene on television, Chas jumped up and began to make a loud humming noise. He flapped his hands rapidly and paced back and forth. His mother looked at him calmly after it was over and said, "You really got excited at that Chas, didn't you?" He was not told to stop flapping his arms; rather his mother responded naturally, seeing what might be interpreted as "autistic behavior" as a characteristic related to his likes and dislikes. (O'Connor, 1995, pp. 74–75)

When we acknowledge our tendency to interpret sensory data, we realize that our interpretations may not always be accurate and may not be the same as families' interpretations.

As Susan Rocco learned after moving to Hawaii from the mainland, cultural differences can be a major factor contributing to alternative perceptions. For example, African-American mothers described differences in parenting styles that can lead to quite different perceptions about appropriate discipline:

> A black person does not raise their kids like a white person. Mostly the white kids, they tell their parents what they want to do and if their parents don't do it, they get cussed out. If my kids were to talk back to me, I wouldn't stand for anything like that in the first place. The environments are just entirely different. (Kalyanpur & Rao, 1991, p. 527)

This difference in discipline philosophy gets complicated when it leads to issues such as alternative ways to define abuse. (In chapter 9, we discuss maltreatment and how, by meeting families' basic needs, you can help prevent it. To do that, however, you need to know yourself, families, and their cultures.)

One parent said: "Spanking is when you just hit them a few times and don't leave no bruises on that number. But when you just hit them and hit them hard and you leave scars and they swell up bad, that's not spanking. I call it abusing a child. That's a load of difference" (Kalyanpur & Rao, 1991, p. 527). This mother commented that she would never be able to confide in the social worker who made home visits that she spanks her child because the social worker would interpret it as "beating up the child" (Kalyanpur & Rao, 1991, p. 528).

To develop reliable alliances with others, you need to be willing to admit that your perceptions may be inaccurate, or at least incomplete, as well as different from theirs. By understanding your own perceptions and recognizing that differences in perceptions are natural results of different human experiences, you may be able to alter your approach when these differences exist. When in Hawaii (or Rome), do as the Hawaiians (or Romans) do; or at least know how you and they differ. Instead of viewing differences as problems or as "parents being wrong," regard differences as opportunities for families and you to broaden your respective understandings of one another and for you to try to walk in the family's shoes, sand and all. Consider the family with empathy, remembering that empathy means an intuitive and sensitive understanding of the feelings and perspectives of another person. To comprehend another's feelings, thoughts, and motives, you first need to understand yourself; then, empathetically understanding another may come more easily.

Knowing Families

Just as it is important to know and understand yourself in order to create an empowering context and reliable alliances, so, too, you need to understand families. By their nature, families are complex. There are literally hundreds of ways that families can vary, so your challenge is to avoid simplistic general understandings of families and instead appreciate each family in terms of the dimensions of its own life.

You have already been briefly introduced to the family systems approach; we first brought it to your attention in chapter 1. A family systems approach enables you to be attuned to a family's characteristics (such as cultural background, size and form, special challenges), interactions (relationships within and between marital, parental, sibling, and extended family), functions (tasks or responsibilities that the family carries out such as affection, socialization, economics, and daily care), and life cycle issues (developmental and nondevelopmental changes that the family experiences). The family systems approach in turn will enable you to develop a comprehensive and relevant appreciation of families' individuality and thereby to work more effectively and collaboratively with everyone in the family. You will have an opportunity to learn about family characteristics, interactions, functions, and life cycle in chapters 5 through 8.

Honoring Cultural Diversity

To honor cultural diversity, your first step is to try to stand in the shoes (sand and all) of the families you work with, to the greatest extent possible. In the following situation, imagine you are an Inuk mother of a toddler with profound deafness. A communication specialist is giving you guidance about child development.

> This Inuk boy lived in an isolated northern village [in Alaska] and had not developed any spoken language. The mother had just reluctantly attempted to follow the therapist's model of working on sound-object association using an airplane, a car, and a boat. The therapist offered the following suggestion:
>
> Therapist: "See—look! He's really interested in letting the cars zoom down the ramp. What you could do would be to talk about just what he's interested in doing—whatever he's looking at or playing with. Like, 'Whee! Up, up, up, up. Wait! One, two, three-GO! Whee! That's fun! Let's do it again!'"
>
> [The therapist demonstrated the kind of interactive play that she used with the families with whom she worked, talking and pausing for the child's responses.]
>
> Inuk mother: "I just can't talk to my son in that way. It doesn't feel right." (Crago & Eriks-Brophy, 1993, pp. 123–124)

What are the fundamental elements that do not "feel right" to the mother? What does it really mean to "feel right" within relationships? Feeling right is one of the major outcomes of reliable alliances that honor cultural diversity. And as we show throughout this chapter and the entire book, reliable alliances are the essential ingredients of empowering contexts.

The matter of feeling right is by no means a trivial one when minority families are involved. Here is what a Native American professional says about trying to persuade members of her own tribe to enroll their children with disabilities in an early intervention program:

I felt that the families were a little bit reluctant. [Even though] I'm a member of their own tribe, that they still considered me an intruder of some type, because a lot of other times when programs came in, they felt that there were too many people hounding them or hovering over them and wanting them to do this and do that, but as I explained to them, I'm also the parent of a child with disabilities, and that made it a little bit easier. I share their culture and beliefs, and I encourage them to use traditional medicines, never doubting that, and that always comes first, but at the same time, getting them to believe that in reality, too, there is something different. And that's how I've gained a lot of the parents' trust. (testimony by Norberta Sarracino, in National Council on Disability, 1995, p. 38)

*D*efinition and Rationale

Culture refers to many different factors that shape one's sense of group identity, including race, ethnicity, religion, geographical location, income status, gender, sexual orientation, disability status, and occupation (Turnbull & Turnbull, 1996). It is the framework within which individuals, families, or groups interpret their experiences and develop their visions of how they want to live their lives (Anderson & Fenichel, 1989). Often the term *culture* is used synonymously with the words *race* and *ethnicity*. The U.S. Department of Education classifies people into five groups based on race and ethnicity, identified in figure 4–1.

Aside from race and ethnicity, there are many other factors that shape one's sense of culture or group identity. A white religious fundamentalist from the Midwestern Bible Belt who has never been unemployed but is the father of a child with a learning disability may very well have world views and ways of collaborating (or not) with professionals that are different from, say, those of an African-American Muslim from the inner city of a large Eastern metropolis whose child has cerebral palsy. Further, the African-American Muslim may have world views different from those of a newly immigrated intact Vietnamese family who were highly paid professionals and leaders in their Roman Catholic church and whose child has extraordinary mathematical or scientific talents.

In each of these three families, there are different cultural (not just racial or ethnic) attributes. These attributes may vary within families. One family may change its religion or choose atheism, another's eco-

---

FIGURE 4–1

Five Federal Classifications Based on Race and Ethnicity

- *American Indian or Alaskan Native*: A person having origins in any of the original peoples of North America and who maintains cultural identification through tribal affiliation or community recognition.
- *Asian or Pacific Islander:* A person having origins in any of the original peoples of the Far East, Southeast Asia, the Pacific Islands, or the Indian subcontinent. This area includes, for example, China, India, Japan, Korea, the Philippine Islands, and Samoa.
- *Hispanic:* A person of Mexican, Puerto Rican, Cuban, Central or South American, or other Spanish culture or origin—regardless of race.
- *Black* (not of Hispanic origin): A person having origins in any of the Black racial groups of Africa.
- *White* (not of Hispanic origin): A person having descended from any of the original peoples of Europe, North Africa, or the Middle East.

Source: U.S. Department of Education, Office for Civil Rights. (1987). *1986 elementary and secondary school civil rights survey: National summaries.* Washington, D.C.: DBS.

---

nomic status may improve or decline precipitously, and still another's may be influenced by racial or religious intermarriage. Disability status can strongly influence one's cultural affiliations, such as the strong group identity known as deaf culture (Commission on Education of the Deaf, 1988).

Honoring cultural diversity is a means for establishing reliable alliances with people from different cultural backgrounds, ensuring that those alliances are characterized by respectful and comfortable exchanges of communication, supports, and services (Chan, 1992; Hall, 1976), and creating empowering contexts. These alliances take into consideration the values, decision-making styles, family roles, language, background knowledge, and influences of significant others. How can you honor cultural diversity so that families with whom you interact will "feel right"—feel that your approach has responded to and affirmed their values and priorities?

*F*ramework to Enhance Cultural Competence

To begin with, you will want to enhance your own cultural competence. As Susan Rocco might have said, "You need to get to know Mrs. Ching, and she needs to get to know you." Figure 4–2 describes a five-step process for doing just that.

Enhancing Self-Awareness   To be more culturally self-aware, look at figure 4–3. As you think of the three or four attributes that best define yourself, you may focus on your race. Others, however, may focus on their respective geographic region, gender, sexual orientation, religion, socioeconomic characteristics, or disability characteristics. The important thing, of course, is for you to be keenly aware of who you are and what factors shape your own cultural views and to understand that your cultural beliefs and traditions may work very well for you but not necessarily for others. The most dangerous trap for culturally unaware people is assuming that their way is the only right way.

Enhancing Culture-Specific Awareness
One way to enhance your awareness about others' cultures is to learn more about the five racial groups identified in figure 4–1 who live in your own community. What are each group's fundamental values, child-rearing practices, family patterns? How might they answer the questions in figure 4–3?

As you become more aware of traditions, customs, and values of various racial and ethnic groups, we caution you against stereotyping. Is it possible to characterize "the Hispanic family" or "the Asian family" accurately and fully? Absolutely not. For one thing, the group called Hispanics represents 26 separate nationalities, each with differing degrees of acculturation, educational status, income, geographic location, and occupation (Bruder, Anderson, Schultz, & Caldera, 1991). Similarly, Asian Americans originate from three major geographic areas and at least 15 different countries (Chan, 1992, p. 182):

- East Asia: China, Japan, Korea
- Southeast Asia: Cambodia, Laos, Vietnam, Burma Highland, Malaysia, Singapore, Indonesia, the Philippines
- South Asia: India, Pakistan, Sri Lanka

These three regions and 15 countries represent three major religious orientations—Confucianism, Taoism, and Buddhism—and countless other diversities. That is why it is unwise to assume that there is any such thing as a stereotypical Asian family. The best you can do, in a broad way, is to become familiar with general traditions, customs, and values of the families from culturally diverse backgrounds in your community. It is important to recognize, however, that there is tremendous family variation within racial and ethnic groups. Do not let your general culture awareness lead you into overgeneralizations.

Enhancing Culture-Generic Awareness
Once you understand your own and others' culture, your next step is to recognize crosscutting or generic traits of a number of racial and ethnic groups. For example, in chapter 5 you will learn about perspectives pertaining to individualism versus collectivism, system-centered versus relationship-centered orientation, and a taking-charge perspective toward change versus an

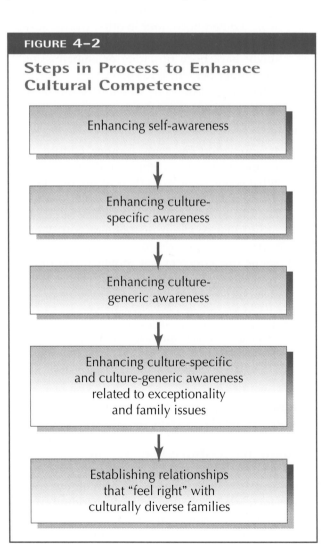

FIGURE 4–2

Steps in Process to Enhance Cultural Competence

Enhancing self-awareness

Enhancing culture-specific awareness

Enhancing culture-generic awareness

Enhancing culture-specific and culture-generic awareness related to exceptionality and family issues

Establishing relationships that "feel right" with culturally diverse families

FIGURE 4–3

Cultural Self-Awareness

Origins

1. When you think about your roots, what country(ies) other than the United States do you identify as a place of origin for you or your family?
2. Have you ever heard any stories about how your family or your ancestors came to the United States? Briefly, what was the story?
3. Are there any foods that you or someone else prepares that are traditional for your country(ies) of origin? What are they?
4. Are there any celebrations, ceremonies, rituals, holidays that your family continues to celebrate that reflect your country(ies) of origin? What are they? How are they celebrated?
5. Do you or anyone in your family speak a language other than English because of your origins? If so, what language?
6. Can you think of one piece of advice that has been handed through your family that reflects the values held by your ancestors in the country(ies) of origin? What was it?

Beliefs, Biases, and Behaviors

1. Have you ever heard anyone make a negative comment about your country(ies) of origin? If so, what was it?
2. As you were growing up, do you remember discovering that your family did anything differently from other families that you were exposed to because of your culture, religion, or ethnicity? Name something that you remember that was different.
3. Have you ever been with someone in a work situation who did something because of his or her culture, religion, or ethnicity that seemed unusual to you? What was it? Why did it seem unusual?
4. Have you ever felt shocked, upset, or appalled by something that you saw when you were traveling in another part of the world? If so, what was it?
   How did it make you feel? Pick some descriptive words to explain your feelings.
   In retrospect, how do you wish you would have reacted?
5. Have you ever done anything that you think was culturally inappropriate when you have been in another country or with someone from a different culture? In other words, have you ever done something that you think might have been upsetting or embarrassing to another person? What was it?
   What did you do to try to improve the situation?

Imagine

1. If you could be from another culture or ethnic group, what culture would it be? Why?
2. What is one value from that culture or ethnic group that attracts you to it?
3. Is there anything about that culture or ethnic group that concerns or frightens you? What is it?
4. Name one concrete way in which you think your life would be different if you were from that culture or ethnic group.

Source: Lynch, E. W. (1992). Developing cross-cultural competence. In E. W. Lynch & M. J. Hanson (Eds.), *Developing cross-cultural competence: A guide for working with young children and their families* (pp. 355–369). Baltimore: Brookes. Paul H. Brookes Publishing Co., P.O. Box 10624, Baltimore, MD 21285-0624. Reprinted by permission.

acceptance perspective toward tradition. These perspectives are parts of the world views of individuals who sometimes share racial and ethnic affiliation; again, there are variations within and across groups.

Once you have characteristics such as these in mind, you can begin to understand the dimensions along which people representing different cultural characteristics can vary. These generic issues do not relate to exceptionality specifically or to family issues associated with exceptionality. Rather, they serve as guides to alliances that feel right to others and that can become reliable because they do indeed feel right.

Enhancing Culture-Specific and Culture-Generic Awareness Related to Exceptionality and Family Issues As your own cultural competence increases, so will your understanding of how you can foster reliable alliances with families from cultures other than your own. For example, in chapter 11 you will learn that families from culturally diverse backgrounds interpret the definition and meaning of exceptionality in alternative ways. You will need this information as you collaborate with families when conducting evaluations, sharing evaluation results, and planning individualized programs. For example, you will understand how to collaborate with this grandmother, whose daughter and granddaughter spent many years in special education programs. The grandmother commented:

> [Special educators] say that word 'handicap' means a lot of things, it doesn't just mean that a person is crazy. But for us, Puerto Ricans, we still understand this word as 'crazy.' For me, a person who is handicapped is a person who is not of sound mind or has problems in speech or some problems of the hands or legs. But my children have nothing like that, thanks to God and the Virgin! (Harry, 1992c, p. 31)

As this example shows, culture influences the definition and meaning of exceptionality. As you will learn later, it also influences respective professional and family roles, communication patterns, expectations for independence and achievement, and anticipated outcomes of education. As you gain more culture-specific and culture-generic awareness related to exceptionality and family issues, consider the cultural characteristics that can affect a family's responses to collaboration and to the educational services you provide. Box 4–1 includes suggestions for enhancing your own cultural competence with families.

Establishing Feel-Right Alliances with Culturally Diverse Families   The more you honor cultural diversity, the more you will be able to establish feel-right alliances. How could the speech

---

TIPS   BOX 4–1

Enhancing Your Own Cultural Competence with Families

Being More Culturally Competent

- Learn about the families in the community that you serve. What cultural groups are represented? Where are they from? When did they arrive? How closely knit is the community? What language(s) is spoken? What are the cultural practices associated with child rearing? What cultural beliefs surround health and healing, disability and causation?

- Work with cultural mediators or guides from the families' cultures to learn more about the extent of cultural identification within the community at large and the situational aspects of this identification and regional variations.

- Learn and use words and forms of greeting in the families' languages if families are limited- or non-English proficient.

- Allow additional time to work with interpreters to determine families' concerns, priorities, and resources and to determine the next steps in the process. Remember that building rapport may take considerable time but is critical to effective intervention.

- Recognize that some families may be surprised by the extent of parent/professional collaboration that intervention programs expect in the United States. Do not expect every family to be comfortable with such a high degree of

involvement. However, never assume that they do not want involvement and are not involved from their own perspective. Likewise, do not assume that they will become involved or will feel comfortable doing so.

- For limited- or non-English proficient families, use as few written forms as possible. If forms are used, be sure that they are available in the family's language. Rely on the interpreter, your observations, and your own instincts and knowledge to know when to proceed and when to wait for the family to signal their readiness to move to the next step.

Source: Lynch, E. W., & Hanson, M. J. (1992). Steps in the right direction: Implications for interventionists. In E. W. Lynch & M. J. Hanson (Eds.), *Developing cross-cultural competence: A guide for working with young children and their families* (pp. 355–370). Baltimore: Brookes. Paul H. Brookes Publishing Co., P.O. Box 10624, Baltimore, MD 21285-0624. Reprinted by permission.

therapist have done a better job of creating a feel-right alliance with the Inuk mother? Unfortunately, much of the professional literature in the field assumes that what feels right to middle- and upper-middle-class white mothers feels right to all family members representing the broad range of cultural diversity.

The research on families of children with exceptionalities has concentrated on middle- and upper-middle-class white mothers. For example, a review of all articles published in four journals (*Journal of Early Intervention, Topics in Early Childhood Special Education, Infant-Toddler Intervention*, and *Infants and Young Children*) that had the word *parent* or *family* in the title and were published during a 12-month period (1992–1993) showed that the sample populations in the research studies included 1,602 mothers and 135 fathers—a 12 to 1 ratio in favor of mothers. The percentage of Euro-American representation in the research samples was typically 75 to 80 percent or more. During this time, no studies had the word *father* in the title. There has been a clear tendency to conduct research on Euro-American mothers and to apply the results to all family members of all races (Turnbull, Turbiville, Turnbull, & Gabbard, 1993). Generalizing the results of this research is unwarranted.

Furthermore, the research on culturally diverse families has often ignored families' strengths and confused the effects of race with the effects of socioeconomic factors. Often the research has not been done by minority researchers, who may well have the keener cultural understanding that seems necessary for interpreting data in a nondiscriminatory way (Marion, 1979; Ruiz & Padilla, 1977; Harry, 1992a).

Moreover, the vast number of special education textbook writers, federal and state policy leaders, school-board members, state and local educational agency administrators, and teachers and related service providers have been and still are from the Euro-American, middle-class culture. Quite naturally, these people, often lacking cultural competence, frequently have assumed that "good parents" are ones who fit the Euro-American mold and behave in Euro-American ways (Harry, 1992b, 1992c).

We strongly encourage you to do the following:

- Reject stereotypical, culture-biased thinking
- Enhance your ability to honor cultural diversity so you will form feel-right alliances with culturally diverse families
- Become a more effective collaborator for empowerment

Affirming and Building on Family Strengths

As you read in chapter 1, many professionals have tended to focus on families' deficiencies rather than their strengths. Yet highlighting and appreciating families' strengths is one of the key aspects of supporting families to enhance their own self-efficacy. Remember that self-efficacy is an element of motivation in chapter 3's empowerment framework. Building reliable alliances depends on your respecting families' inherent strengths and building upon them through the collaborative process (Dunst, Trivette, & Deal, 1994).

All families have strengths. For gifted children, family strengths include spending time in out-of-school activities with adult interaction, having stimulating adult conversation around the dinner table, and modeling engagement in intellectual activities (Csikszentmihalyi, 1992; Friedman, 1994; Snow, Barnes, Chandler, Goodman, & Hemphill, 1991). Even families who face major challenges, such as substance addiction or child or spousal maltreatment, can have strengths in other areas of their lives. Figure 4–4 includes a list of strengths that you might consider as you interact with families. If you regard the family as having only challenges or needs—not strengths—you may have difficulty becoming a reliable ally. If, on the other hand, you recognize and affirm their strengths, you will likely become a more reliable ally. Reflect on those relationships with people whom you regard as reliable allies. Do they believe in your strengths or focus on your weaknesses? Your own preferences are probably like almost everyone else's: We all tend to be more comfortable with and effective around people who value our strengths and do not "put us down." That was the way Jason Rocco's teachers responded to him and Susan; and, remember, Susan made a point of emphasizing their strengths.

Promoting Family Choices

Because perceived choice is a critical factor contributing to the motivation of individuals and families to take action in their lives (chapter 3), it is necessary in building reliable alliances and creating empowering contexts to increase families' opportunities to express their choices and have those choices heard and heeded by professionals such as yourself (Summers, Dell'Oliver, Turnbull, Benson, Santelli,

FIGURE 4–4

Samples of Families' Strengths

- Lots of caring, extended families
- Being very optimistic
- Being very knowledgeable
- Making the child feel loved and accepted
- Maintaining an orderly, well-organized, and safe home
- Having a yard or park for playing
- Encouraging the child to notice, hear, and smell different interesting things around the house
- Encouraging wellness and health in all family members through exercise, balanced diet, and healthy habits
- Seeking out support from friends or counseling as needed
- Finding unique ways to use informal teachable moments as part of a typical home life
- Communicating thoughts and feelings to family members in a supportive and authentic way
- Having a sense of humor
- Being persistent in seeking help and support from others
- Having a strong religious faith
- Having interesting hobbies to share with children

Source: Adapted from Turbiville, V., Lee, I., Turnbull, A., & Murphy, D. (1993). *Handbook for the development of a family friendly individualized service plan (IFSP).* Lawrence, KS: University of Kansas, Beach Center on Families and Disability.

Campbell, & Siegel-Causey, 1990). There are many different areas in which family choice can be exercised, including the following (Allen & Petr, 1996):

1. Selecting the family members to be involved in collaborative decision making
2. Choosing the degree of control that family members will exercise pertaining to decision making for each educational issue
3. Deciding which educational issues should have priority over others
4. Selecting appropriate goals, objectives, educational approaches, and methods of evaluation for the student

Promoting family choices requires planning and delivering educational services in a way that maximizes flexibility for the family. When nearly 100 families were asked what they need to make their days easier, what would contribute to the well-being of their families and children, and how the public sector could best support them (Knoll, 1992), they did not respond by listing a series of "whats," such as specific services or resources that they would like to have. Instead, they described the "hows" and the process through which professionals and agencies furnish resources. The process they mentioned most frequently was flexibility in all aspects of services. Flexibility connotes that professionals and agencies recognize that each family is different—each has its own characteristics, patterns of interaction, priorities for different family functions, and issues associated with life cycle stages and transitions.

Reliable alliances are like a kaleidoscope. A change in one aspect of the family's characteristics, interactions, functions, or life cycle might require professionals and agencies to change accordingly. Just as every turn of the kaleidoscope creates a different pattern, so does every family, consistent with its choices, call forth a different pattern of communication, services, and supports.

This means that flexible professionals and organizations do not have a rigid set of rules for every situation, and they do not act on the basis that "we've always provided services this way, and there's no need for us to change now." Rather, they are creative and follow the family's lead (Jones, Garlow, Turnbull, & Barber, 1996; Schorr & Schorr, 1988). This is basically the way in which the staff in Jason Rocco's "sending" school followed Susan's lead as she sought his inclusion. In schools, as you learned in chapter 2, following families' leads involves moving away from bureaucracy and embracing "adhocracy"—a process emphasizing collaborative partnerships that respond to specific school-based, student-focused priorities and needs (Skrtic, 1991).

Envisioning Great Expectations

To begin to appreciate fully the importance of envisioning great expectations as an aspect of reliable alliances and empowering contexts and as a way to contribute to families' motivation, you should start by being skeptical about special educators' and other professionals' traditional concerns for "being realistic." Shelley Taylor (1989), from her perspective as a social psychologist, has developed a theory of positive illusions in terms of how people adapt to threatening situations. She argues that perception is marked by positive, self-enhancing illusions about the self, the world, and the future rather than by accuracy. Instead of seeing such positive illusions—or, as we call them, great expectations—as representing denial or repression, she suggests that positive illusions are adaptive and promote rather than undermine good mental health.

> Overall, the research evidence indicates that self-enhancement, exaggerated belief and control, and unrealistic optimism typically lead to higher motivation, greater persistence at task, more effective performance, and, ultimately greater success. A chief value of these illusions may be that they help to create self-fulfilling prophecies. They may lead people to try harder in situations that are objectively difficult. Although some failures are certainly inevitable, ultimately the illusions will lead to success more often than will lack of persistence. (Taylor, 1989, p. 64)

Noted editor Norman Cousins (1989), reflecting on his own treatment for cancer, deplored the fact that many professionals were worried about giving people facing threatening situations "false hopes." But these same professionals never realized how frequently they gave "false despair" and how "false despair" can dissuade people from creating any kind of desirable future (Cousins, 1989, p. 100). In describing individuals with cancer who tended to be empowered rather than disempowered in pursuing their recovery, Cousins stated: "They responded with a fierce determination to overcome. They didn't deny the diagnosis. They denied the verdict that is usually associated with it" (Cousins, 1989, p. 83).

What does all of this mean to the field of special education? In today's state-of-the-art services, special educators, social psychologists, and mental health professionals are emphasizing great expectations and positive outcomes for people with exceptionalities (Falvey, Forest, Pearpoint, & Rosenberg, 1994; Seligman, 1990; Snyder, 1994; Turnbull & Turnbull, 1996a). So are parents such as Janet Vohs:

> Families of children with disabilities are not allowed—or at least not encouraged—to have a dream or a vision for their children's future. What the past has given as possible outcomes for people with disabilities is far less than inspiring. If all we have to look forward to is an extension of the past, I should think we would want to avoid the pain of that future as long as possible. But I have a motto: *Vision over visibility*. Having a vision is not just planning for a future we already know how to get to. It is daring to dream about what is possible. (Vohs, 1993, pp. 62–63)

Do you recall the discussion about synergy in chapter 3? As powerful as one's own sense of great expectation can be, even more powerful is a collective and mutually developed vision of great expectations. Remember that Susan Rocco did not decide to go for inclusion until she learned that inclusion is possible and desirable and until she, her friend Cindy, and Jason's teachers created an inclusion alliance. Senge (1990) underscores the importance of collaborative envisioning:

> A shared vision is not an idea. . . . It is rather a force in people's hearts, a force of impressive power. It may be inspired by an idea, but once it goes further—if it is compelling enough to acquire the support of more than one person—then it is no longer an abstraction. It is palpable. People begin to see it as if it is this. Few, if any, forces in human affairs are as powerful as shared vision. (Senge, 1990, p. 206)

Although terms such as *great expectations* and *visions* are not ones that you will typically hear from parents, you are much more likely to hear them talk about hope. As you will recall from the empowerment framework in chapter 3, hope is an element of motivation. Parents typically want professionals to have and express hope about their child's future and their own future—a sense of great expectation, a vision that good things are possible in the future. That is why you should cherish and nurture families' hope and great expectations; as you value and enhance their hope and great expectations, you also become a more empowering professional and a more reliable ally.

Communicating Positively

Positive communication skills are especially important for educators and families. The more accurately you and families communicate thoughts and feelings, the more successful your alliances with them will be, the more you will create an empowering context, and the more the families will be able to act empowerfully. Some individuals, such as Susan Rocco, seem to have a natural ability to communicate well, but most of us must work consciously to develop this ability. Fortunately, professionals and families can learn and apply communication skills to one-on-one and group discussions (Edwards, 1986; Hirsch & Altman, 1986; Kohl, Parrish, Neef, Driessen, & Hallinan, 1988; Lombana, 1983).

Although many communication skills can be taught, some theorists contend that effective communication is an art, not a science (Brammer, 1988). Indeed, there is an art in communication skills that relies heavily on the user's attitudes and personal qualities. We encourage you to master both the science and the art of communication skills and to incorporate these techniques and qualities into your personal style so that they become natural and spontaneous. That requires systematic practice and use of the skills. It also requires cultural and disability sensitivity.

Refining nonverbal communication skills is challenging enough when done within a single cultural context, but it is even more so when you have partnerships with families from cultures different from your own. For example, looking the speaker directly in the eye is typically considered being attentive and polite within an Euro-American culture (Hanson, 1992). But eye-to-eye contact with strangers, people in authority, or elders can be considered disrespectful within an Asian culture and could have been a problem for Susan Rocco if she had not been culturally competent (Chan, 1992).

Moreover, disabilities sometimes interfere with communication skills, so accommodations are necessary. For example, a parent who is deaf and communicates through signs will need an interpreter or professional collaborators who themselves can sign (Luetke-Stahlman, 1993).

In this section, you will learn about nonverbal communication skills, verbal communication skills, influencing skills, and group communication skills. Figure 4–5 highlights the communication skills we will discuss. As you read this section, we encourage you to bear in mind our two cautions about culture and disability accommodations in the section of this chapter titled "Knowing Yourself."

*N*onverbal Communication Skills

Nonverbal communication includes all communication other than the spoken or written word. When most of us communicate verbally, we also communicate nonverbally through the use of gestures, facial expressions, voice volume and intonations, physical proximity to others, and posture. Many of the nonverbal cues that any of us transmit to others are largely beyond our conscious awareness (Hepworth & Larsen, 1982). So if you wish to improve the nature of your interactions with families, you will need to use nonverbal communication skills such as physical attending and listening.

Physical Attending   Physical attending consists of contact, facial expressions, and gestures (Ivey,

---

FIGURE 4–5

Interpersonal Communication Skills

- Nonverbal communication skills
    Physical attending
    Listening

- Verbal communication skills
    Furthering responses
    Paraphrasing
    Response to affect
    Questions
    Summarization

- Influencing skills
    Providing information
    Focusing support attention
    Offering assistance

- Group communication

- Using communication skills in difficult situations

1986). The contact component involves both eye contact and the degree of physical contact, or closeness, between people who are communicating with one another. Because your eyes are a primary vehicle for communicating, maintaining culturally appropriate eye contact is a way of showing your respect for and interest in another person. It is estimated that white middle-class people look away from the listener approximately 50 percent of the time when speaking but make eye contact with the speaker about 80 percent of the time when listening. On the contrary, black Americans have been reported to make greater eye contact when speaking and less eye contact when listening. Navajos use more peripheral vision, believing that direct stares are a way to express hostility and a discipline technique for children when they are being reprimanded (Sue, 1981).

In a similar way, adjusting the physical space between yourself and family members with whom you are communicating may also convey a particular level of interest. Again, cultural considerations come into play.

Hall (1966) has identified four interpersonal distance zones characteristic of Anglo culture: intimate, from contact to 18 inches; personal, from $1\frac{1}{2}$ feet to 4 feet; social, from 4 to 12 feet; and public (lectures and speeches), greater than 12 feet. However, different cultures dictate different distances in personal space. For Latin Americans, Africans, Black Americans, and Indonesians, conversing with a person dictates a much closer stance than normally comfortable for Anglos. A Latin American client may cause a counselor to back away. The client may interpret the counselor's behavior as indicative of aloofness, coldness, or desire not to communicate. On the other hand, the counselor may misinterpret the client's behavior as an attempt to become inappropriately intimate or of being pushy. . . . Eskimos, for example, when talking about intimate aspects of their life, may sit side by side rather than across from one another. (Sue, 1981, p. 41)

As you gain more cultural awareness about the specific traditions of families with whom you interact, observe their interactions with each other and with others and get recommendations from professionals who have worked successfully with them in the past so that you will be able to determine the personal space that is culturally comfortable.

A second component of physical attending is facial expressions. Typically, desirable facial expressions are described as being appropriately varied and animated, occasionally smiling, and reflecting warmth and empathy. On the contrary, having a stiff facial expression, smiling slightly, or pursing the lips is considered undesirable (Hepworth & Larsen, 1982).

Despite these general rules of thumb, you should recognize that some people have facial differences that necessitate accommodations by them and appropriate interpretation of these accommodations by others. Some have no ability to smile, frown, or otherwise express their feelings through their face or eyes. In box 4–2 Sandy Goodwick, who has been an elementary teacher for more than 20 years, describes her own facial difference and her perspectives on the typical identification of desirable and undesirable nonverbal communication traits.

Gestures are a third component of physical attending. Not surprisingly, the meaning of gestures can vary across cultural groups. Some hand gestures mean one thing for one cultural group but a different thing for a different group; some groups may regard "thumbs up" or "V for victory" as vulgar signs, whereas other groups may regard them as entirely positive.

Listening

Listening is the "language of acceptance" and is one of the most essential ingredients of a reliable alliance (Covey, 1990; Gordon, 1970). Unfortunately, true listening rarely occurs naturally or spontaneously. To listen with genuine, undivided attention requires both diligence and practice and

your awareness of different types of listening (Covey, 1990; Gordon, 1970):

- *Ignoring:* not paying attention at all to the person who is talking
- *Pretending:* giving the outward appearance that we are listening but actually thinking about something entirely different or thinking about what we are going to say in response
- *Selective listening:* listening to only parts of what someone is saying based on our own energy, time, interests, or emotions
- *Attentive passive listening:* listening to what the other person is saying but not using nonverbal attending skills, using silence or minimal encouragement for them to continue, or not communicating any acceptance of what they are saying
- *Active listening:* assuming a much more involved and direct role by being animated, making comments, asking questions, and even sharing personal experiences to foster a dialogue
- *Empathetic listening:* standing in the shoes of the person who is talking and seeing the world and their situation as they see it and feel it

Although none of us likes to admit it, we all have ignored, pretended, and selected what we have heard. In addition, we have all used passive and active listening. But empathetic listening will help build reliable alliances. In his description of highly effective people, Covey (1990) describes empathetic listening:

When I say empathetic listening I mean listening with intent to *understand.* I mean *seeking first* to understand, to really understand. It's an entirely different paradigm.

. . . Empathetic listening involves much more than registering, reflecting, or even understanding the words that are said. . . . In empathetic listening, you listen with your ears, but you also, and more importantly, listen with your eyes and with your heart. You listen for feeling, for meaning. You listen for behavior. You use your right brain as well as your left. You sense, you intuit, you feel. (Covey, 1990, pp. 240–241)[1]

Empathy requires you to set aside your own internal frames of reference so that you can understand and experience the world from the other person's point of view, nonjudgmentally and nonevaluatively. When you listen empathetically, you

---

[1]©1989 Fireside/Simon & Schuster, *The Seven Habits of Highly Effective People: Restoring the Character Ethic,* Stephen R. Covey. All rights reserved. Used with permission of Covey Leadership Center, Inc. 1-800-331-7716.

My Face

I was born with absolutely no facial expression—smile, frown, wink, etc. Due to the "wonders" of microscopic surgery, I now can "smile," albeit artificially. . . . It is because of my unique disability, and the seemingly "unknown" difficulties inherent in such a condition that I am writing this letter to you. . . .

"Warmth and concern reflected in facial expression, appropriately varied and animated facial expressions," ". . . . occasional smiles" are all [regarded] as "desirable" traits while "Frozen or rigid facial expressions" is listed as "undesirable." While these characteristics may imply that the practitioner is caring or uncaring, they by themselves are only indicative of facial animation—perhaps a "window" into the mindset or personality of the "practitioner." I, and the others affected by facial "difference," have individually fought a life-long battle of ignorance and stigma—while I ultimately can

accept the fact that families may lack the professional knowledge and skills necessary to "understand" what it is like to have a facial difference, I cannot condone what I perceive as "ignorance" by the "helping profession" any longer. . . . I *resent* having a physical disability categorized as "undesirable."

I have been an elementary school teacher for 20 years. The road to a successful career was not easy—as a sophomore in college, I was called in to the Dean of Students' office. It was suggested that I not go into teaching "because of . . . uh . . . your 'problem,' Sandy." (Which one?— my absolute ignorance in knowing even the *name* of this condition . . . or the accumulation of emotional "garbage" inherent in single-handedly coping with a facial difference). I had, years ago, decided to become a teacher, because I wanted to undo the horrendous experience I had encountered while in elementary

school, via becoming "the world's best teacher." One and a half years later I began student teaching—I went from "excellent" to "barely passing," when I perceived the students were teasing me because I could not smile. . . .

Contrary to the Dean of Students' wishes, I went into teaching (despite the horrific student teaching experience!) and became a well-respected educator. I am completely convinced that neither my students nor their parents or other teachers saw my "frozen or rigid facial expression" as indicative of a frozen personality. While I had not yet fully addressed my myriad of internal emotional baggage related to having a facial difference, I *knew* my lack of facial expression was not, by itself, an insurmountable obstacle in becoming a warm, caring and effective teacher.

Sandy Goodwick
September 1993

---

do not agree or disagree but simply understand what it means to be in the other person's shoes. You convey genuine interest, understanding, and acceptance of the family's feelings and experiences (Perl, 1995). This does not mean that you will necessarily approve of, or agree with, the family's point of view but that you will try to understand the family's situation from the family's point of view—not your own. Remember what Susan Rocco said? "I had come to the understanding that the teachers had a really hard job." That understanding came because Susan cared enough to listen empathetically. "Your best shot," she says, "is to make friends with somebody." What good advice for professionals and families alike!!

Verbal Communication Skills

Although the nonverbal communication skills of physical attending and empathetic listening are effective and essential means for communicating with families, verbal responses are also essential in facilitating communication. Examples of verbal responses include (1) furthering responses, (2) paraphrasing, (3) response to affect, (4) questioning, and (5) summarization.

Furthering Responses   Furthering responses indicate attentive listening and encourage people to continue to speak and examine their thoughts and feelings. There are two types of furthering responses:

1. Minimal encouragers, sometimes referred to as the "grunts and groans" of communication, usually include short but encouraging responses such as "Oh?" "Then?" "Mm-hm," "I see," or "And then?" Minimal encouragers can also be nonverbal and take the form of head nods, facial expressions, and gestures that communicate listening and understanding.

2. Verbal following involves restating the main points or emphasizing a word or phrase contained in what the family member has said, using the language system of the family. Verbal following not only encourages the family member to go on speaking but also provides the professional with a means of checking listening accuracy, as in this example:

Family member: I've had a really rough day.
Professional: Oh? [a minimal encourager]
Family member: Jason woke up with wet sheets and cried all through breakfast. To top it off the bus came early, and I had to send him to school without any lunch.
Professional: You've had a really rough day. [a verbal follow]

Paraphrasing

Paraphrasing involves using your own words to restate the family's message in a clear manner. Paraphrasing emphasizes your restating the cognitive aspects of the message (such as ideas or objects) but not necessarily the affective state of the speaker. Use language as similar to the family's as possible. Paraphrasing responds to both the implicit and explicit meanings of what is said, and its goal is to check for accuracy and make sure that there is a clear understanding of the issues before moving ahead to engage in collaborative problem solving, as in this example:

Family member: Everything seems to be a burden these days, doing the housework, taking care of the kids, paying the bills. I just don't know how much longer I can keep up the pace.
Professional: All your responsibilities really cause a drain on your time and energy.

In this example, you try empathetically to comprehend the situation from the person's perspective and to sense how challenging it is to be spread across so many different tasks and responsibilities. Again, it's not just the words but the frustration, fatigue, and overload that is communicated. In paraphrasing, the task is not just to feed back mechanically a rephrased statement but, through the verbal statement and the

nonverbal communication, to let this person know that you empathize with the tremendous drain on time and energy.

Paraphrasing is an extremely useful technique in clarifying content, tying a number of comments together, highlighting issues by stating them more concisely, checking one's empathetic understanding, and—most important—communicating interest in and understanding of what the family member is saying.

Response to Affect   Response to affect involves the ability to (1) perceive accurately and sensitively the other person's apparent and underlying feelings and (2) communicate understanding of those feelings in language that is attuned to the other person's experience at that moment. You pay attention not only to what is said but also to how it is said. When you use this technique, try to verbalize the family member's feelings and attitudes and use responses that are accurate and match the intensity of the family member's affect. Developing a vocabulary of affective words and phrases can be helpful. Here is an example of response to affect:

Family member: Ever since Elliot was born, my family and friends have put a wall up between me and them. I guess they don't want to do the wrong thing, but what they don't realize is that the worst thing of all is doing nothing and staying away. I have no one to turn to and feel my "resentment gauge" going up by the day. It really hurts me and makes me angry when I've always tried to be there for them, and now when I need them most, they just seem to back away.
Professional: You're feeling very let down by family who you thought would always be there for you.

The purpose of responding to affect is to provide a mirror in which family members can see their feelings and attitudes. This reflection, in turn, helps them move toward greater self-understanding (Benjamin, 1969). Remember Covey's points on empathetic listening—"When you listen with empathy to another person, you give that person psychological air. And after that vital need is met, you can then focus on influencing or problem solving" (Covey, 1990, p. 241)[2]. Finally, response to affect can enable you to

---
[2] ©1989 Fireside/Simon & Schuster, *The Seven Habits of Highly Effective People: Restoring the Character Ethic,* Stephen R. Covey. All rights reserved. Used with permission of Covey Leadership Center, Inc. 1-800-331-7716.

check the accuracy of your own perceptions of the family member's feelings.

Questions   Questions generally fall into two categories: closed-ended and open-ended questions. Closed-ended questions are used mostly to ask for specific factual information. Skillful communicators keep their use of closed-ended questions to a minimum because this type of question limits responses to a few words or a simple yes or no. Moreover, overuse of closed-ended questions also can make an interaction seem like an interrogation. While closed-ended questions can restrict conversation and often yield limited information, they are appropriate when used sparingly and propitiously. Here are some examples of appropriately used closed-ended questions:

- "When did Carlos first start having seizures?"
- "How old is Betty Sue?"
- "Would a ten o'clock meeting be O.K. for you?"

Unlike closed-ended questions, open-ended questions invite family members to share and talk more. Some open-ended questions are unstructured and open the door for family members to talk about whatever is on their mind (for example, "What things seem to be going best for you right now?" or "How can I be of assistance?"). Other open-ended questions are more structured; the professional imposes boundaries on possible responses by focusing the topic (for example, "What are some of the specific methods you've tried to help Matthew behave more appropriately?").

Open-ended questions can be formulated in three general ways (Hepworth & Larsen, 1982):

1. *Asking a question.* "How is Miko getting along with her new wheelchair?"
2. *Giving a polite request.* "Would you please elaborate on your feelings about the new bus route?"
3. *Using an embedded question.* "I'm interested in finding out more about Ansel's toileting program at home."

Open-ended questions generally involve using the words *what* and *how*. We encourage you to be cautious about *why* questions. The word *why* can connote disapproval, displeasure, blame, or condemnation (for example, "Why don't you listen to me?" "Why are you late?") and evoke a negative or defensive response from the person with whom you are speaking (Benjamin, 1969).

We want to express cautions about questioning. The first caution relates to the tendency of educators to phrase questions in a way that focuses on problems, deficits, and concerns:

> We often start our initial contact with phrases like "How can I help you? What are your needs as a family? What kinds of problems are you having with your child? What are your child's most immediate problems?" These words immediately focus attention on what is going wrong and on a relationship based on the professional being in a position of expertise and power. (Winton, 1992, p. 1)

In contrast to this problem-finding approach, we encourage you to use open-ended and problem-solving questions such as the following:

- "What are some of the things that have pleased you most about your child's progress over the last year?"
- "What is one of the best experiences that you have had with a professional? What can we learn from that experience about how we might best work together?"
- "What would an ideal day be like in the life of your family?"
- "Who are some of the people whom you would most like to involve in supporting you and your family?"
- "What is a great expectation that you have for your child's future that we might all share and work toward?"

The second caution is to guard against being intrusive. Families vary in their comfort about having any questions asked at all, believing that most or all questions challenge their competency, invade their privacy, or both. One African-American parent said that she was raised by her parents and she has raised her own children with the firm belief that "what happens in this house stays in this house." She indicated that it was totally foreign to her to go into a conference with educators and be asked questions about what happens in her house and how she raises her children. Our advice: Individualize your communication by respecting family boundaries about what is private and what is public information.

Summarization   Summarization is a recapitulation of what the family member has said, with an emphasis upon the most salient thoughts and feelings. While similar to paraphrasing, summarization is different in one important respect: Summaries are substantially longer. Summarization is particularly useful in recalling the highlights of a previous meeting, tying together confusing, lengthy, or rambling topics, and acknowledging the point at which a topic has become exhausted (Walker & Singer, 1993).

Influencing Skills

The third major category of interpersonal communication skills is influencing skills. Influencing refers to communication aimed at participating in conversation between a parent and professional or among the members of a collaborative team (Ivey, 1986). There are four types of influencing skills: (1) providing information, (2) providing support, (3) focusing attention, and (4) offering assistance (Walker & Singer, 1993).

Providing Information

You learned in chapter 3 about the importance of information as one of the family factors related to empowerment. When families prioritize their needs, they frequently say their greatest need is for relevant information (Bailey, Blasco, & Simeonsson, 1992), particularly about (1) future services, (2) present services, (3) how to teach their child, (4) the nature of their child's disability, and (5) experiences of other parents who have a child with similar needs (Cooper & Allred, 1992). State-of-the-art information enables decisions to be fully informed by capitalizing on the best knowledge available. Families emphasize the importance of information's being free of technical language, hopeful about positive outcomes for their child, presented in their native language, and concisely focused on their priority questions or concerns. Some parents have expressed that they believe that professionals sometimes use jargon as a way of "reminding them who is in charge" (Stonestreet, Johnston, & Acton, 1991, p. 40). In terms of enhancing empowerment, it is especially important when presenting information to do so in a way that does not result in families' feeling that information is being used to persuade or push them into making a decision that they are not ready to make.

> A new, rather officious medical social worker on an Indian reservation attempted to convince the women that their children should receive polio vaccine. In spite of her well-prepared presentation, which included statements like "You don't want them to get polio, do you?", the women did not bring their children to the clinic. They listened politely and sometimes giggled among themselves. Two years later, the social worker learned through another professional that the women had named her "Woman Who Can't Stop Talking." (Yates, 1987, p. 322)

In this situation, the social worker not only barraged the families with information but did not adequately take into account their cultural values of being in harmony with nature and viewing disease, death, and disability as milestones in the natural progression of life. Thus, her attempt to provide information, although well intended, was not delivered in a way that resulted in creating a reliable alliance.

Providing Support

There are many different ways to provide support to families. The two that we will highlight here are providing social support and providing affirming support.

In chapter 3 we discussed social support as a coping strategy (part of the knowledge/skills component of the empowerment framework). People who perceive that they have social support experience less stress and better mental health and feelings of self-efficacy (Barrera, 1986; Cohen & Wills, 1985). A key component of social support is expressing empathy. A mother of three children with muscular dystrophy, two of whom also have mental retardation, writes:

> When we are injured, we need nurturance—whatever age we are. I think one of the dilemmas for the professional . . . is that they have to try to help parents, who may also acutely need nurturance themselves, to give extra care and nurturance to the child. Some of the professionals who worked with us let us know that they understood our pain, and that was often all the care we needed. But sometimes the concern for the child became the total focus, and I felt drained and discouraged. (Weyhing, 1983, p. 127)

One study compared the impact on parental satisfaction when professionals used reassurance, encouragement, and empathy as part of their communication with parents. Empathetic communication was found to lead to the most satisfied response on the part of parents. The study concluded that empathetic support from professionals makes a positive difference in how parents react to professionals (Wasserman, Inui, Barriatua, Carter, & Lippincott, 1984).

The second type of support is affirming support. Affirming support ties to the overall communication principle of affirming and building on family strengths. Providing support through verbal comments gives you an opportunity to express genuine compliments, point out areas of appreciation, and underscore the valuable contribution that families are making to their children. Box 4–3 includes examples of these statements. As you read them, keep in mind that supportive comments should be specific and authentic as well as delivered in a way that expresses respect and appreciation. You might also reflect on the people with whom you interact who are most likely to make supportive statements to you. What do you particularly appreciate and how can you incorporate those same communication skills in your relationships with families?

Anyone can provide support, but often empowered professionals who feel confident about themselves find the most creative and natural ways to affirm others. We encourage you to take every opportunity to let others know what you particularly appreciate about their contributions.

Focusing Attention
Focusing attention has two aspects: (1) making comments to underscore a comment that a family member or another team member has made that may have been overlooked or not adequately addressed in the flow of conversation and (2) making a statement that directs attention to a particular priority issue. For example, if a father expresses several concerns and some of them are addressed and others are not, it can be especially important to pick up on the unaddressed issues to make sure that they do not get pushed to the side. You can support families by specifically acknowledging their comments in meetings.

Can you recall meetings in which you said something and then the next speaker made a totally unrelated comment, as if your contribution were irrelevant? How did lack of acknowledgment of your comment make you feel? Often when this happens, people assume that their contributions are not useful and may stop making them. You can focus attention on the helpfulness of family comments by acknowledging, affirming, and expanding upon what they have said with comments such as the following:

- "What a helpful insight for all of us. What you say about Yolanda's hesitancy to read puts a different light on what she may be communicating to us by that behavior."
- "Your comment underscores why it is so important for us to work together. I hadn't considered that point of view. Thank you for that clarification."

Offering Assistance
When you offer assistance to families, try to do so by presenting options rather than directives. In reflecting on people with whom you regularly communicate, are there some people who routinely provide directives, making statements such as "you should," "you ought to," or "you're really making a mistake if you don't"? When these

---

TOGETHER WE CAN
BOX 4-3

Supporting Families

- "You're so insightful about Danny's moods and can read him like a book. Your insights help us get on his wavelength."

- "It's such a thrill to me to see the way that you and Ramona get such a kick out of eating lunch together. You are always welcome here. Your energy brings a boost to all of us."

- "I look forward to seeing Lucy every day for lots of reasons, but one of them is just to see what new outfit you have

sewed for her. What a talent you have! And Lucy feels like a queen in the dresses that you make."

- "The treats that you sent last week for Jason's birthday were the biggest hit that I have ever seen. How can something be healthy and also taste that great? Any chance you might share the recipe with me?"

- "Because you have been spending many hours on the restructuring committee, it

probably has created lots of challenges in balancing everything you do. I just want to let you know how very much I and other teachers here appreciate your commitment to creating a better school for all students and for all teachers as well. The next time you are at one of those long, drawn-out meetings, I just hope that you will remember how much we appreciate your contributions."

statements are made to you, how do you feel about them and how does that feeling translate to the person who says them to you? Families, like everyone, often resist relationships that are carried out in an authoritarian style. To increase the likelihood that families will accept your offers, try using the comments in box 4–4.

Group Communication

All the communication skills that we have discussed can occur not only in a dyadic relationship between yourself and a family member but also in group discussions. That's one of the points Susan Rocco makes as she describes the group dinners-cum-meetings in Hawaii's tea houses. Whether it is a school-based management council meeting or an IEP conference, skills such as empathetic listening, paraphrasing, providing information, and summarizing can facilitate positive communication and ultimately the relationships between and among participants.

In addition to nonverbal communication skills, verbal communication skills, and influencing skills, another communication option for you is to refine your skills in both facilitating and participating in group problem solving. It is unfortunate that so much time is typically spent in group meetings by having different individuals give reports developed before the meetings instead of incorporating a dynamic and creative problem-solving process (Stonestreet et al., 1991). Although the steps of problem solving can be described in a number of ways, they typically involve those listed in figure 4–6.

The implementation planning form in figure 4–7 provides a structured framework for documenting next steps, the person responsible, resources needed, and time lines. The problem-solving process can be helpful in dealing with minor or major issues, but it is often especially beneficial in times of crisis. For example, if a student has displayed aggressive behavior that has injured another student, there may be an immediate need for all the key stakeholders—family members, teachers, administrators, and related service providers—to meet and develop a comprehensive action plan that has generated a wide range of options and carefully evaluated each one. Because crisis situations often involve heightened risk, danger, or emotional turmoil for the key players, a comprehensive action plan can help everyone move together in a comprehensive, collaborative, and supportive manner.

Using Communication Skills in Difficult Situations

Your knowledge and application of communication skills will provide you with a whole range of options

TOGETHER WE CAN
BOX 4–4

Offering Assistance to Families

- "It sounds as if those evening homework sessions are really painful for everyone. If it would be helpful, I'd certainly be happy to do some brainstorming about some ideas that could possibly result in things' going more smoothly."

- "You are really feeling worried about where Rahul will work after graduation. I remember several parents who expressed that same concern when their sons or daughters were in high school, and now several years after graduation things are working out very well for them. If it sounds like something that might be helpful, I would be happy to invite them to our next meeting. We could get their ideas about what some of our next steps might be."

- "I share your concern that Denise seems to feel so isolated. I'd be happy to give more attention to what we can do here at school to help her connect more with classmates. Maybe those connections could lead to some friendships. Is that an area that you would like to explore together?"

- "If we put our heads together and commit to some hard work on figuring out this assistive technology need, I'll bet we could come up with something that would be useful. I'm willing to give it my best effort if this is a priority for you."

FIGURE 4-6

Steps of Group Problem Solving

- Developing a vision
- Agreeing on a specific goal
- Brainstorming options for addressing the goal
- Evaluating benefits and drawbacks of each option
- Selecting the most appropriate option
- Specifying an implementation plan, including person responsible, resources needed, and time line
- Implementing the plan
- Evaluating how closely the results of action matched the goals
- Modifying the plan and continuing to make progress

for relating to families. Each interaction will be unique and will require its own blend of skills. As a skilled communicator, you will need to choose the communication skills that seem most appropriate for each family in its current situation.

While communication skills are vitally important at any time to build reliable alliances, they are particularly important during times of crisis. This is because families, when in crisis, may respond to you with anger, hostility, fear, or resistance, making meaningful communication between you more difficult to initiate or maintain.

During difficult interactions with families, you may need to use the whole spectrum of communication skills (Hepworth & Larsen, 1982), especially empathetic communication, so that you can stay in touch with families, know how to respond to their sometimes volatile emotions (Covey, 1990; Hepworth & Larsen, 1982), and gauge the effectiveness of your use of empathetic

FIGURE 4-7

Implementation Planning Form

The University of Kansas

Next Steps

In order to reach our goal and to work toward our visions, . . .

	Person Responsible	Resources Needed	Time-Line
starting tomorrow (date:), we will:			
A.			
B.			
C.			
in one month, we will:			
A.			
B.			
C.			
in three months, we will:			
A.			
B.			
C.			

communication by observing the family's response immediately following your interaction.

Family responses that suggest that your use of empathetic communication is beneficial to the family include the following:

- Exploring a problem or staying on the topic
- Expressing pent-up emotions
- Looking within themselves
- Sharing more personally relevant material
- Affirming verbally or nonverbally the validity of your response

On the other hand, if your use of empathetic communication is not particularly helpful to the family, you may see the family engaging in some or all of the following responses:

- Rejecting, either verbally or nonverbally, your response
- Changing the subject
- Ignoring the message
- Becoming more emotionally detached
- Continuing to express anger rather than looking at the relevance of the feelings involved

Your sensitive observations of the family's responses will help you determine the effectiveness of your interactions with the family.

When you are dealing with families in crisis, you may find that other communication skills are helpful, including assertiveness, conflict resolution, negotiation, and ways to diffuse anger. Box 4–5 contains some valuable tips for how to deal with anger.

We also encourage you to remember that crises offer unique opportunities to deepen empowering relationships. Because of heightened vulnerability and the urgency for collaboration, families and professionals can come through a crisis in such a way that their relationship truly bonds. Rather than bemoan a crisis, you can embrace it as a unique opportunity for relationship enhancement.

Another consideration is to realize the positive aspects of anger in motivating people to take action. In chapter 3 you learned about transforming events as a catalyst for energy in the motivation component of the empowerment framework. Often it is anger that leads to transforming events, as outrage is channeled into positive action. Given the critical importance of motivation in the empowerment equation, we encourage you to view each crisis as an opportunity to get things moving in a positive direction, sometimes with a sense of urgency that is hard to establish when all is going well.

Improving Communication Skills

One method to improve your own or someone else's communication abilities is to use audio or video-

---

TIPS

BOX 4–5

Dealing with Anger

Do

- Listen.
- Write down what family members say.
- When they slow down, ask them what else is bothering them.
- Exhaust their list of complaints.
- Ask them to clarify any specific complaints that are too generally stated.
- Show them the list and ask if it is complete.
- Ask them for suggestions about how to solve any of the problems they have listed.
- Write down the suggestions.
- As much as possible, mirror their body posture.
- As they speak more loudly, speak more softly.

Don't

- Argue.
- Defend or become defensive.
- Promise things you can't produce.
- Own problems that belong to others.
- Raise your voice.
- Belittle or minimize the problem.

---

tapes. Although audiotapes are ideal for practicing and evaluating verbal communication skills, videotapes offer the additional advantage of feedback on both verbal and nonverbal behaviors. Ask a friend or colleague to spend 10 to 20 minutes talking over an issue or problem with you. Tape your conversation. As you talk, practice using one or two of the skills we have described. Then review the tape critically, taking note of the positive and not-so-positive contributions you made. Set personal goals for improvement. Ask your friend to provide you with feedback on your performance. As you begin to feel confident about the skills you have practiced, try adding more skills to your repertoire. Over time, and with enough practice, these skills can become a natural and spontaneous part of your communication style.

We also hope that you will practice these skills throughout all your class discussions as well as within any class projects that you are carrying out with families. Improving communication requires a personal commitment of time, effort, and attention and a genuine desire on your part to be the most empowering communicator you can possibly be.

You will recall from chapter 3 our discussion of mobilizing events in peoples' lives in terms of motivating them to take action (Kieffer, 1984). One of the particular impacts of these events comes from the fact that often they are associated with high levels of anger that get channeled toward major systems change.

Warranting Trust and Respect

All the components that we have discussed for building reliable alliances and creating empowering contexts are really prerequisites to the most important element of all—warranting trust and respect. When you have trusting and respectful relationships with families, you can practically ensure that collaboration and empowerment will be enhanced. By the same token, when families trust professionals (and professionals earn families' trust), they create opportunities for all sorts of otherwise unattainable results. It was precisely because Susan Rocco trusted the teachers in Jason's sending school that she was willing to go for his inclusion in a new school with a new teacher.

When you do not have trusting and respectful relationships, no matter how hard you try or how good your instructional ideas are, problems will permeate almost all that you do with families. The bottom line is that trust and respect are absolutely

essential aspects of the reliable alliances that can lead to the empowerment of all team members.

An essential element of a trusting relationship is for all family information to be kept confidential. A parent commented:

> I was horrified when I ran into a friend downtown and she told me that she had heard through the grapevine what my son's teacher had been saying about his behavior. As problematic as his behavior has been, the teacher had even exaggerated to make it sound worse. That's just what happens when people start gossiping. I was so crushed. I went home and vowed to never tell that teacher one more personal thing about my son, myself, or my family. It was all over from that point on.

As you have already learned in chapter 2, the organization of school systems and the strong emphasis on legal compliance sometimes, paradoxically, work against trust and respect rather than in their favor. So what are the ingredients that most enhance trust and respect?

One of the foremost considerations is that trust and respect evolve from establishing power-with and power-from-within rather than power-over relationships with families. As one parent said, professionals need to "come down from their high status and walk with us rather than direct us." That is particularly so for professionals who work with minority families. In discussing the passive participation of low-income minority parents, Harry (1992b) commented:

> When such parents' traditional trust in school authorities is undermined, parents who do not believe that they can challenge school authorities are likely to withdraw from participation. Out of a traditional respect for authority, however, they may continue to defer to professionals, yet fail to cooperate with professional recommendations or even to respond to invitations to participate.

> Parents' behavior may then be interpreted by the professional as a sign of disinterest or apathy. In the light of these observations, it is evident that increasing parental participation is not simply a matter of giving adequate information or providing parents with logistical supports or even being respectful to parents to make them feel more comfortable. The challenge to professionals is to earn the reasoned trust of cultural minority parents through the creation of participation structures that ensure their inclusion rather than their exclusion from the decision-making process. (Harry, 1992b, p. 475)

A recent study of low-income African-American mothers reveals the factors that facilitate or inhibit professionals in moving away from hierarchies and emphasizing partnerships (Kalyanpur & Rao, 1991). The facilitating factors include the following:

- Responding to needs (for example, providing emotional support; providing specific services)
- Establishing rapport (for example, being conversational, interpreting, sharing, and accepting)

The inhibiting factors include the following:

- Being disrespectful
- Focusing on deficits
- Discounting differences

The authors describe the essence of a trusting, respectful relationship and how such a relationship contributes to empowerment:

> Empowerment signifies changing the role of a service provider from that of an expert to that of an ally or friend who enables families to articulate what they need. . . . While the expertise of professionals is an integral aspect of the interaction between parents and professionals, the manner in which the expertise is communicated determines the nature of the relationship. It involves caring, which builds supportive relationships; respect, which builds reciprocity; and the acceptance of differences, which builds trust. . . . Such empathy involves the acceptance and open acknowledgement of the parents' competence, the willingness to interact with them on equal terms, and the adoption of a nonjudgmental stance. (Kalyanpur & Rao, 1991, p. 531)

Summary

To empower families, students with educational exceptionalities, and professionals alike is a daunting task; but it is quite possible—indeed, quite probable—when reliable alliances exist. After all, reliable alliances create an empowering context and thereby contribute to the collaboration that links person factors with context factors.

Building reliable alliances consists of eight elements. Effective professionals—and effective family members like Susan Rocco—understand and apply these elements as they take advantage of the opportunities to be partners with each other:

- They know about families.
- They honor families' cultural diversity and mores.

- They affirm and build on families' strengths.
- They promote families' choices.
- They create great expectations for themselves and students.
- They practice positive interpersonal communication techniques.
- And, as a result of doing all this, they warrant each other's trust and respect.

To create a reliable alliance requires a great deal of empathy—the ability to understand each other's feelings, thoughts, and motives. Practicing the eight techniques helps families such as Susan Rocco's and professionals such as Jason's teachers Cindy and Mrs. Ching develop empathy for each other and become each other's reliable allies.

❦ ❦ ❦ ❦ ❦

As Jason heads into high school, Susan has resolved to "just develop a relationship with Jason's teachers and give them a sense that I am going to be totally supportive and that we are going to work on these goals together and this is going to be so nice for Jason. I really think I'm going to get that cooperation and that support, but I might not if I was just insistent about this, that, or the other thing. I'll have opportunities to invite people to lunch and to talk about people we know in common and just kind of find those common grounds in our lives that are of course going to have some connection to Jason but that are not totally focused around him and his needs. I want them to see me as a regular person and not just a special education parent."

Susan's relationship-building approach is not just a one-on-one strategy. As executive director of a family information network funded by two different state agencies, Susan uses the technique of building reliable alliances in group meetings, too.

"I do a lot of work in this job, where Jason isn't even in the picture in some instances. And after years of serving on committees, I have learned that the ones that really got the work done were the ones where we got along. We enjoyed coming and there wasn't absenteeism, because we had stopped to have a relationship. We brought food to the meetings, or we spent the first 15 minutes talking about each other.

"We just had our annual parents' advocacy group meeting in a lovely pagoda in one of the tea houses, and we had to have two wines before we got the meeting started. Then we had to eat and then we had to chit-chat. By the time we got down to business: boom, boom, no disagreement, creative energy. When you are feeling comfortable and valued, you are safe to express your true needs without feeling someone is shooting you down. You give the other person the benefit of the doubt, because you know them as a person.

"I've learned that is what Jason's life is all about. It's not whether he learns to wipe tables. It's whether or not he has friends. . . . I really believe that if we don't make it pleasurable—you know, the old exchange theory—then Jason's peers will drop him like a hot potato. You know, it's just unrealistic to think folks are going to do it either because they are told to or because it's morally right.

"There has to be a payback. We're having fun; we're getting something out of it; we're having this sense of accomplishment; we're feeling valued. That's what it's all about."

Part Two

Understanding Families

Because this book is about empowerment of and collaboration with families, we describe in part 2 a useful way for understanding families. *Knowing families* is one of the eight obligations of a reliable alliance. We enable you to know families through a family systems perspective. When you regard families as systems, you recognize their interactive and dynamic qualities.

We characterize the family as a system by focusing on family characteristics (chapter 5), the way that family members interact within the family and with people outside the family (chapter 6), the way that a family functions (chapter 7), and the way that a family changes over time (chapter 8).

At the end of part 2, you should be able to describe the family systems perspective through the four components of characteristics, interaction, functions, and life cycle.

Chapter Five

Family Characteristics

*M*arta Cofresi hasn't had it easy. Raising four children is no piece of cake in any circumstances. But being a monolingual immigrant (Spanish only); having twin girls (Roxela and Roxana), each of whom has cerebral palsy; and being a single parent ever since the twins' father abandoned the family just after they were born could get even a lesser person down. But Marta is not a lesser person, and certainly her children aren't either.

Marta and the twins have close friends in school, church, and the community, and great expectations for the future—all because, when Roxela and Roxana were born, Marta declared, "I accept you and I will focus on what you can do. Because of that, people will accept you and focus on what you can do, too."

The first people she helped to accept the twins were their two older siblings, Juan Carlos and Louisa. "The first task was to make them feel no shame because of their sisters," so Marta required Juan Carlos and Louisa to take their sisters out for walks and encouraged the older siblings' friends to visit the twins. And she spent hard-earned money on the twins' clothes because appearance is important. "That is how I introduced the girls to the community."

But Roxela and Roxana had to do their parts, too. A lesson she taught the girls was to "treat others as you like to be treated" and to "accept others as they are." So when one of their peers looks at them or asks why they use crutches or a voice synthesizer, the twins must "tell all the story, be honest."

Moreover, Marta told them, "You can do it, so you can go for it," the "it" being whatever Roxela and Roxana wanted. Constant rewards and encouragement, coupled with Marta's deep faith, sustained the family. "I had to find the answer in God, because God made them that way, so how God would think of them and treat them is how I wanted to be."

Marta has not been alone in her efforts to have Roxela and Roxana lead typical but assisted lives. One of Roxana's 10th-grade teachers, Mr. Arias, played a big role, too. Placed in his vocational tech class, the only girl there, Roxana wanted to drop the course. As she tells it, Mr. Arias made the class "real fun" and "kept insisting, stay in my class, stay in my class." He became her friend, and she stayed there for two years and received an award from him as the student of the year. In her first year in class, she was elected and then reelected president of the local chapter of Vocational Opportunities Clubs of Texas. The Riverside High School chapter has excelled, winning citywide competitions and a second place in a statewide contest.

Because the twins have a believe-in-them network, they believe in themselves. They participate regularly in their IEP conferences. They turn the other cheek when someone makes fun of them; they are friendly and open. They expect to date, to be married, and to have many children. First, however, Roxela and Roxana want to go to the University of Texas at El Paso and study computer science.

Most of all, they want to be role models for their nieces and nephew and their community. As Roxana says, "We want to show them that just because I'm on crutches and their aunt Roxela is in a wheelchair doesn't mean they can't go to us with a problem and tell us, because we'll help."

What more do they need? Roxana answers, "We need more people that believe in us." That is one reason Roxana wants Roxela to be included in general education:

She believes that Roxela will create her own reliable allies in school and the community.

No doubt Marta Cofresi and Mr. Arias believe that, too. And so do Roxela's and Roxana's siblings and many friends. And why shouldn't they? After all, the twins give everyone reason to believe in them.

Traditionally, the word *family* brings to mind the nostalgic picture of a mother, father, and two or three children living together at home. The father works during the week and spends evenings and weekends repairing household goods and fixtures, mowing the yard, and playing with the children. The mother keeps house and nourishes body and soul with home-cooked meals and plenty of love. Grandparents are nearby, ready to take the kids fishing, bake cookies, and dispense wise counsel. On national or religious holidays, all the aunts, uncles, cousins, and grandparents gather for a day of family solidarity and joyous feasting.

The truth is that few American families today fit this nostalgic picture. Indeed, it is doubtful that a "typical" American family ever existed (Hareven, 1982; Zinn & Eitzen, 1993). Many are like the Cofresi family, with only one parent. This chapter focuses on how families differ and how those differences affect and are affected by the child or youth who has an exceptionality—children such as the Cofresi twins.

Families vary in a multitude of ways, as you learned in chapter 4. Let's turn to the family systems framework and study the family characteristics component. In figure 5–1, you will see that family characteristics consist of three dimensions: (1) characteristics of the family, (2) personal characteristics, and (3) special challenges. Characteristics of the family refer to dimensions such as family culture, socioeconomic level, and geographic location. In addition to all these variations in family life, each individual family member also varies in personal characteristics—characteristics of the exceptionality, health status, and coping styles. Finally, many families face special challenges such as poverty, substance abuse, and abuse or neglect of children. Every family is such a mixture of characteristics that it is probably safe to say that every family is idiosyncratic.

Yet the nostalgic image of the "traditional" family continues to cloud professional-family relationships to such an extent that, even today, many home-school programs for families with children with exceptionalities often are best suited for nuclear two-parent, one-worker, middle-class families—a minority today. To individualize for Marta Cofresi and her daughters and for other families, you need to understand their diversities and the three factors that create these diversities: characteristics of the family, members' individual characteristics, and the family's special challenges. The family characteristics section of the family systems framework highlights these three diversity factors, each of which we will discuss.

Whatever a family's characteristics, they do not preclude the family from being motivated or from having or developing the skills to be empowered: Just consider the Cofresi family and how Marta, Roxela, and Roxana have been motivated to "go for it" and have acquired the skills they need to achieve their goals.

Characteristics of the Family

The term *family characteristics* refers to the characteristics of the family as a whole: its size and form, cultural background, socioeconomic status, and geographic location. Each of these characteristics shapes the family's responses to a member's exceptionality, and each is a potential resource for collaboration and family empowerment.

Family Size and Form

Family size and form refers to the number of children, the number of parents, the presence and number of stepparents, the extensiveness of the extended family, and live-in family members who are unrelated by blood or marriage. Larger families may be less distressed by the presence of a child with an exceptionality. Perhaps in large families more people are available to help with the chores and any special adaptations the child needs. A larger number of siblings may absorb parents' expectations for achievement, which otherwise might fall on the shoulders of the only child without an exceptionality (Dyson, 1989; Powell & Gallagher, 1993). Finally, other children may give their parents a frame of reference that reminds them that their child with an exceptionality is more like than unlike his or her brothers and sisters and that all children have various combinations of strengths and needs (Turnbull, Summers, & Brotherson, 1984).

For example, a father of an adolescent daughter with William syndrome noted that the problems of his daughter with a disability are often no greater and perhaps even less difficult than the problems his other children experienced during adolescence.

> Adeliza had been, in many respects, the easiest of our six children. As she was the fourth daughter with two younger brothers, we as parents were "old pros" at raising teenage daughters by the time Adeliza turned 13. She doesn't date and is not as rebellious as our other three daughters. Instead of being another stressful situation, her teenage

Family Systems Framework: Emphasis on Family Characteristics

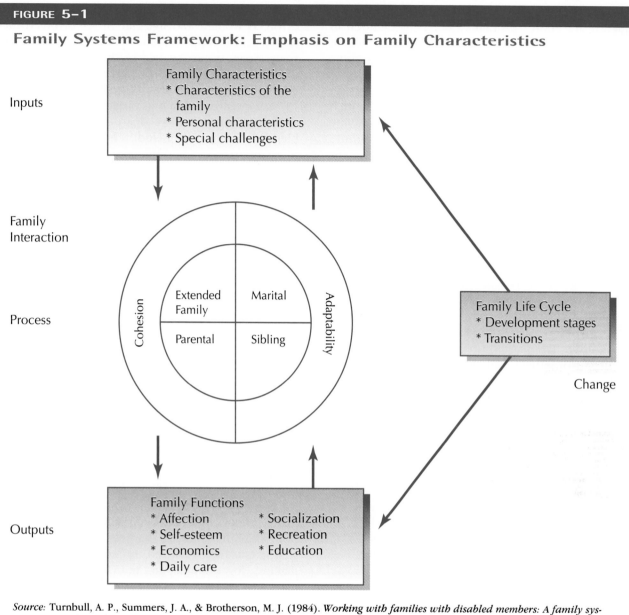

Inputs

Family Characteristics
* Characteristics of the family
* Personal characteristics
* Special challenges

Family Interaction

Process

Cohesion

Extended Family | Marital

Parental | Sibling

Adaptability

Family Life Cycle
* Development stages
* Transitions

Change

Outputs

Family Functions
* Affection   * Socialization
* Self-esteem   * Recreation
* Economics   * Education
* Daily care

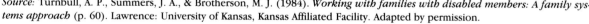

Source: Turnbull, A. P., Summers, J. A., & Brotherson, M. J. (1984). *Working with families with disabled members: A family systems approach* (p. 60). Lawrence: University of Kansas, Kansas Affiliated Facility. Adapted by permission.

years have, in general, been a very positive experience for our entire family.

Similarly, the number of parents (single parent or two parents) may influence a family's reaction to the exceptionality. A supportive husband—even one who does not participate in child care—seems to be an important predictor of a mother's sense of well-being (Crnic & Booth, 1991; Nagy & Ungeser, 1990). In addition, a family usually adapts more positively to a child's exceptionality if it is a two-parent family (Trute & Hauch, 1988).

You are certain to encounter single-parent families (such as the Cofresi family). The U.S. Department of Education (1992) reports that approximately 37 percent of high school students with disabilities live in single-parent families, as contrasted to approximately 30 percent of high school students in general education. A majority of single parents with custody of children are women, but about 15 percent of all children are being raised by single fathers because of divorce, widowing, or adoption (Seligmann, 1992). Single-parent families are disadvantaged when compared to two-parent families because they frequently are poorer (National Center for Children in Poverty, 1995). Because of the special demands of raising a child with an exceptionality, single mothers of children with a disability may have less choice about working than other single mothers (Vadasy, 1986). Thus, single parents must often face the dual responsibilities of raising a child with a disability while also trying to make a living. Far too often, the single parent—indeed, even one of a two-parent family—forgoes work, is underemployed, is part-time employed, or declines job transfers because of child-care demands (National Commission on Childhood Disability, 1995).

Given these pressures, some single parents may have neither the time nor the emotional energy to be heavily involved in their child's education; however, other single parents (like Marta Cofresi) are very active partners of their children's teachers. Some research suggests that children from single-parent homes typically have lower school achievement than peers from two-parent homes (Shreeve, Goetter, Bunn, Norby, Stuekle, Midgely, & de Michele, 1986). This finding also holds for students who have been identified as gifted (Gelbrich & Hare, 1989).

A single parent describes her situation:

> Tired. Lonely. Isolated. This is how it was as a single parent, raising three children, one of whom was disabled. I fell asleep crying, many nights, because I did not have a partner to share the daily responsibilities and problems of raising Katherine. . . . I was both father and mother, trying to meet the emotional needs of all three children, working a forty-hour week, dealing with emergencies, Katherine's therapy schedule, and after-school homework and activities of her brother and sister. (Barnes, 1986, p. 47)

But benefits for single parents include "relief from marital conflict, increased self-esteem derived from one's competency in managing work and family matters, greater autonomy and independence, opportunities for increased self-growth, and closer relationships with children" (Reid, 1985, p. 263).

You probably have noticed that the Cofresi family fits some of the demographics of American families but also defies some of the research findings related to certain families. What makes the Cofresi family different? As Marta observes, the difference comes from within and relates to her and her daughters' motivation—their sense of self-efficacy, perceived control, hope, energy, and persistence.

A different situation—more than two parents—exists when one or both parents in the original family have remarried. Approximately three out of four divorced women and five out of six divorced men remarry, with approximately one-half of all of the remarriages occurring within three years after the divorce. Approximately 40 percent of all the marriages involve stepchildren (Zinn & Eitzen, 1993).

A wide array of family variations and emotional situations exists in reconstituted families. The blended family may include children from two or more marriages. Children may regard their acceptance of a stepparent as a sign of disloyalty to their biological parent (Benson, 1988). They may have to adopt rules and life-styles in two different households or give up adult roles that they may have assumed while the custodial parent was single (Visher & Visher, 1982). Stepparents may be uncertain about their authority over their spouses' children; or with a ready-made family from the first day of marriage, parents may not have the privacy or time to establish their new relationship. Finally, negotiations among all the adults—both former and current spouses—may be required to resolve conflicts concerning the children, including visitation schedules, discipline, life-style, and so on (Sager, Brown, Crohn, Engel, Rodstein, & Walker, 1983; Zinn & Eitzen, 1993). The positive side of a remarried family is that a wide circle of interested family members may be able and willing to support both each other and the person with the exceptionality.

You would do well to be sensitive to possible tensions in a remarried family and accommodate both for the children's academic and behavioral performance and for the implications for family collaboration. If both biological parents and one or more stepparents are involved in educational decision making, for example, an individualized education program conference may range from being an amiable discussion about the child's best interests to a family power struggle where professionals are thrust in the middle.

In your work with families, we encourage you to avoid regarding a reconstituted family—or, for that matter, any family—as "broken," whether it is nuclear, remarried, adoptive, or foster. As the Cofresi family shows, there are simply too many characteristics that affect a family to justify your picking any one characteristic or type of family as the basis for any negative judgment. How wrong it would have been to characterize the Cofresi family as exactly matching some research results solely because Marta is a single parent from a minority culture and has two daughters with disabilities. Strive instead to see the strengths of every family. Every family has them, as Marta and her daughters and son demonstrate. That attitude will help you collaborate with the family and will reinforce the family's motivation and skills for empowerment.

Cultural Background

The U.S. Department of Education describes the racial distribution of youth with disabilities:

> For all disabilities combined, 65 percent are white, 24 percent are black, and 8 percent are Hispanic. In contrast, youth in general (i.e., sophomore cohort of a 1987 Center for Education Statistics sponsored study) are 70 percent white, 12 percent black, and 13 percent Hispanic. Thus, youth with disabilities are twice as likely to be black, substantially less likely to be Hispanic, and only slightly less likely to be white in the total population of youth. (U.S. Department of Education, 1992, p. 15)

Within the group of minority students, numbers of students with limited English proficiency are growing rapidly. The U.S. Department of Education estimates that in 1990 there were approximately 1.9 million students with limited English proficiency in grades kindergarten through 12 (U.S. Department of Education, 1991). Slightly more than three-fourths of these students speak Spanish; but 7 percent speak other European languages, 6 percent speak Southeastern Asian languages, 3 percent speak East Asian languages, and 8 percent speak other languages (U.S. Department of Education, 1993). The number of students with limited English proficiency who have been identified as having disabilities is between one-quarter of 1 million to 1 million (Baca & Cervantes, 1989, cited in U.S. Department of Education, 1993). These students have been identified as being particularly at risk for special education placement (U.S. Department of Education, 1993). To provide an empowering context for family-professional collaboration, special education professionals will need to be multilingual or have access to interpreters (Baca & Almanza, 1991). Perhaps it is too much to expect that they will be of the same culture as the family, as Mr. Arias is with respect to the Cofresi family. That is why most professionals will need to develop multicultural competence.

Chapter 4 introduced cultural aspects of families and suggested a process for increasing your own cultural competence in family-professional collaboration. In this section, concentrate on step 4 in the five-step process depicted in figure 4–2. That step can help you enlarge your cultural-specific and cultural-generic awareness related to exceptionality and family issues by analyzing cultural perspectives on three family factors: (1) individualism versus collectivism, (2) system-centered versus relationship-centered approaches, and (3) a take-charge perspective toward change versus an acceptance perspective toward tradition.

Individualism versus Collectivism

The majority culture in the United States is Euro-American and typically values individualism, self-reliance, early achievement of developmental milestones, and competition with others.

> For example, politicians today still strive to point to humble roots and their climb to a higher status, much like heroes such as Abraham Lincoln. As Althen (1988) related, Americans revere those who do things the biggest, the best, or first. Hence, they are fascinated with sports legends such as Jesse Owens, Jackie Robinson, and Babe Ruth, and aviator heroes such as Charles Lindbergh, Amelia Earhart, and, more recently, the astronauts. (Hanson, 1992, p. 72)

The individualistic perspective is part of special education. Instruction in special education focuses on individual outcomes. Students with disabilities have individualized education programs that target their individual levels of performance and then specify goals and objectives to be achieved. Furthermore, priorities such as self-determination foster autonomy and individual decision making. Similarly, students who are gifted are rewarded in highly individualistic ways by winning contests (for example, national essay contests), achieving National Merit status on the college board examination, and earning admission to prestigious colleges and universities. These educational practices strongly influence families' expectations for their children and their own child-raising practices: Achievement is the coin of the educational realm.

By contrast, some cultures emphasize collectivism—valuing the group more strongly than the individual (Greenfield, 1994; Kim & Choi, 1994). In Marta Cofresi's family, her children without disabilities played important roles in creating friendship networks for their sisters with disabilities; a collective approach to the twins' inclusion came naturally to the Cofresis. Within the African-American culture, group seems to be valued over private gain (Willis, 1992). Similarly, in Asian cultures individuals are viewed "as the product of all generations of the family from the beginning of time" (Chan, 1992, p. 212). Thus, honoring the family's cultural traditions receives utmost importance. The Middle Eastern belief that "children are like canes in the hands of old parents" expresses quite well the collective obligation that family members have to each other (Sharifzadeh, 1992, p. 329).

What is the relevance of individualism and collectivism for collaborating with families? There are two implications, one affecting process and the other affecting curriculum and outcomes. With respect to process, some families from some diverse cultures may regard individualized education programs as contradictory to their orientation of collective, cooperative, and mutually reciprocal priorities. With respect to curriculum, some families may not be interested in their child's accomplishing developmental milestones or specific academic tasks if the accomplishment singles out their child for special acclaim and recognition. Similarly, some families may be far more interested in their sons' and daughters' learning to take care of the home and elderly family members rather than acquiring job skills in a competitive industry.

System-Centered versus Relationship-Centered Approaches
Members of the majority culture typically expect solutions for disability-related problems to be system based—that is, guided by federal and state law and policy and implemented through bureaucratic procedures. This viewpoint emphasizes technological and knowledge-based answers to the challenges posed by exceptionality (Harry & Kalyanpur, 1994). It should not be surprising, therefore, that this value is reflected in the legal underpinnings of special education and that the vast majority of families who participate in policy-reform advocacy are white, middle-, and upper-middle-class families (Turnbull & Turnbull, 1996; Zirpoli, Wieck, Hancox, & Skarnulis, 1994).

By contrast, members of many minority cultures regard personal relationships, not policies and procedures, as the bases of decision making (Correa, 1992).

> It is this personalism that makes it difficult for the Puerto Rican to adjust easily to what Americans call efficiency. For Puerto Ricans, life is a network of personal relationships. They trust people; they rely on people. . . . They do not have that same trust for a system or an organization. Americans, on the other hand, expect the system to work; they have confidence in the organization. . . . Americans become impatient and uneasy when systems do not work. . . . The Latins become uneasy and impatient if the system works too well,

if they feel themselves in a situation where they must rely on impersonal function rather than personal relationships. (Fitzpatrick, 1987, p. 79)

Similarly, the native Hawaiian culture emphasizes not only relationships with other people but also relationships with the community at large, the land, and the spiritual world (Mokuau & Tauili'ili, 1992). And Native American cultures strongly prize relationships with nature, especially those that promote a sense of harmony with nature (Joe & Malach, 1992).

What does this mean for you and your interactions with families? For one thing, bear in mind that the legal and bureaucratic process of referring, evaluating, and individualizing the delivery of special education services (chapters 11 and 12) and advocacy for systems improvement (chapter 15) may be culturally disharmonious for families who approach their child's education from a relationship orientation. You may need to spend significant time establishing genuine relationships in which you and families get to know each other before you and the family start making educational decisions. This has major implications for your time—a rare commodity for many professionals—and your willingness to establish personal familiarity as the basis for trust. Whereas many Euro-American professionals and families may be eager "to get to the bottom line" in a meeting, many culturally diverse families may prefer to spend much more time, especially up-front time, on building relationships.

In addition, people with whom the family already has a reliable alliance can be part of their circle of support in collaborating with you and other professionals. As you have learned, not all encounters need to be dyadic—between an educator and a parent; rather, the families' other trusted "reliable allies"— the members of their own cultural communities and tribes—can make valuable contributions to professional-family collaboration.

Taking-Charge Perspective toward Change versus Acceptance Perspective toward Tradition
Hanson (1992, p. 73) comments on some Euro-American perspectives: "Some valued characteristics of the Anglo-European tradition are taking charge, being assertive, and creating change. Americans believe that individuals, as well as people working together, can 'make a difference' and that change is positive. Related to these notions is the assumption that social and physical environments are under human control or domination." This belief translates into a highly valued action orientation and

frequently results in empowerment's being interpreted as a "taking charge" orientation. Because empowerment can mean many different things in different cultures, you should be cautious about adopting, and asking some families to adopt, Euro-American interpretations of empowerment. We say this while also acknowledging that we have defined empowerment as getting what a person wants and needs (chapter 3) and that we have highlighted the Cofresi family, as well as Hortense and Theresa from chapter 3, as people whose motivation and ability to acquire and apply new skills make them good examples of empowerment. Empowerment for some culturally diverse families may be quite a different concept; you will want to learn what meaning a family gives it and then support the family to act on that meaning.

For example, cultural traditions lead some families to accept the status quo or preserve traditions that have always been part of their cultural heritage. Indeed, some cultures believe that families should persevere without complaint and suffer in silence, and these cultures adopt a fatalistic orientation in which life is presumed to be essentially unalterable and unpredictable. Accepting external conditions and events over which one presumably has little or no control is a way of life for some families (Chan, 1992). But not for all, as the Cofresi family shows.

Reliance on traditionalism has its benefits. This is poignantly expressed from a Native American perspective by Allen Kuetone of the Kiowa tribe:

> Within each of our tribes, there are certain people who are traditionalists. These are the people who hold on to and perpetuate our customs and traditions. They provide those of us who are on the outside, who are in the Bureau of Indian Affairs and other places across the country, with an opportunity to come back and participate. In other words, any time I want to charge my battery, I can go back and enjoy many of these Indian ways; I can participate in them; I can regain a feeling for our traditional values; and I might say that it is the greatest feeling there is. (Morey & Gilliam, 1974, p. 183)

What difference might a taking-charge perspective, in contrast to an acceptance perspective, have on your collaboration with families? Just consider what special educators value: individual developmental gain and outcomes of independence, productivity, and inclusion, always at the maximum accelerated rate. These emphases, however, may be viewed very differently by people who have a traditionalist view. Furthermore, concepts such as supported employment, supported living, and self-determination are all rooted in creating new and innovative opportunities for people with disabilities to experience as much independence as possible; creating those opportunities often requires major family, community, and systems change. For people who tend to "accept the fates," taking risks that involve participating in, much less creating, innovative programs may not be a priority.

We have discussed three ways that cultures may differ, but other variations occur across cultures and even within the same culture. To appreciate within-group cultural variation, reflect on the similarities and differences that you experience with your brothers or sisters, cousins, or other family members. Are you sometimes surprised that people who are members of the same culture and who even share family experiences can have remarkably different values?

Because honoring cultural diversity is essential in all aspects of family-professional collaborations, we will discuss throughout this book how you can collaborate with families who have different cultural traditions. Bear in mind that, whatever a family's stereotypical cultural characteristics may be (that is, whatever they "should" be if they meet all or most of the characteristics of families from the same cultural group), some families, such as the Cofresi family, will defy the stereotype. They will display cultural traits from their own cultural traditions as well as traits from a different cultural tradition. We caution you against pigeonholing a family solely on the basis of certain cultural aspects; that is too simplified an approach, as Marta Cofresi and her twin daughters demonstrate.

Socioeconomic Status

A family's socioeconomic status (SES) includes its income, the level of family members' education, and the social status associated with the occupations of its wage earners. In terms of income, more than two-thirds of high school students with disabilities live in families with household incomes below $25,000, as compared to 55 percent of high school students in general education. As related to family members' educational level, 23 percent of the household heads of secondary students with disabilities have completed at least some college course work, compared to 35 percent of heads of household of high school students in general education (U.S. Department of Education, 1992).

By implication, a higher-SES family arguably has more resources available to address exceptionality issues than a lower-SES family. Indeed, the ability to pay for services and a higher level of education (remember, knowledge is a component of the family empowerment factor) are definite resources. But the equation is not that simple; higher-SES does not guarantee increased collaboration with professionals or family empowerment. Obviously, lower-SES families such as the Cofresi family may also have major resources, such as close families and extensive informal support networks, that are positive forces for collaboration and empowerment. And all families can experience the "within us" elements of empowerment—namely, motivation and knowledge/skills.

Because higher-SES families are often more achievement-oriented, they may consider mental or physical disability to be a severe disappointment and a significant impediment to their child's independence and other types of success. This is what Farber and Ryckman (1965) called the "tragic crisis" for these families: the fundamental dashing of their hopes and aspirations. Lower-SES families, on the other hand, are thought to regard achievement as being less important than values such as family solidarity or happiness (Lee, 1982; Rubin, 1976). To them, a disability arguably represents less of a tragic crisis than a challenge of how to care for the child: a "role organization crisis" (Farber & Ryckman, 1965). These perspectives are the common or conventional wisdom; as such, they are generalizations, do not apply to all families in the same SES groups, and are fraught with the stereotypes, even the stigma, that necessarily accompany them. Some families, such as the Cofresi family, will be the exception to these generalizations.

Another difference between higher- and lower-SES families is that higher-SES families apparently want, and believe they have, a good deal of control of their immediate lives and their futures. Consider the reaction of one father, a professional, to his son's diagnosis of Down syndrome:

> In those first days, my initial reaction was to control. I wanted to understand. I wanted to control the situation by the intellectual process with which I was familiar. But what I learned was not very helpful. . . . While every child's future is uncertain, my son's future seemed hopeless. I could not imagine for him a life so very different from my own. (Isbell, 1983, p. 22)

By contrast, some family researchers theorize that many working-class families may not believe they can control their environment so very few will plan for any child's future, let alone for the future of a child with an exceptionality (Rubin, 1976). According to their theory, while higher-SES families may be more stressed

by an event, such as an exceptionality, that contradicts their belief that they are in control of their lives, lower-SES families may have difficulty considering future options for their child and might be caught unprepared when it is time for their child to enter new programs (for example, finding a long waiting list at an adult service program). Furthermore, their theory holds that lower-SES families may believe that it is useless to try to control a situation or to plan ahead and, accordingly, are relatively passive or inactive participants in educational decision making and transition planning. This theory may hold true for some families, but for others, such as the Cofresi family and still others you will read about in this book, the theory simply doesn't apply. Nor should it: In our experience, a family's SES is not a certain indicator of its motivation or knowledge/skills, of its "empowerment quotient."

To develop professional-family collaboration, you will need to encourage predictable, nonjudgmental, and supportive reliable alliances that convey to all families—regardless of their SES status—that you respect them and recognize their strengths, whatever their characteristics may be. That is your supportive role, a function valued by all families.

Geographic Location

As a result of electronic media and increased mobility in most segments of society, regional differences in family values and forms are becoming less apparent, yet regional patterns remain: Southern hospitality, Yankee stoicism, Midwestern conformity, and Western independence are still attributed to families by family therapists and sociologists (McGill & Pearce, 1982). Rural and urban factors also significantly influence service delivery and family life (Helge, 1991; U.S. Department of Education, 1994).

Geographic location is not a fixed characteristic of families, and indeed some families move in order to find services. A mother of two children with hearing impairments remarked:

> We lived in a small town where they had almost nothing . . . in the schools. We decided that if our children were to get an education, we would have to move; so we started looking at programs all over the country. . . . Finally we settled on Starr King because it had a first-rate oral program. My husband had to quit a good job; we moved to [another town and], he had to search for another job and take a cut in pay. But it was worth it! (Spradley & Spradley, 1978, pp. 214–215)

Military families, migrant farm workers, and others whose jobs require frequent relocations face this problem repeatedly. You would do well to be aware of the anxiety that often accompanies a family's relocation (Luetke-Stahlman, 1991). How can you minimize the anxiety? Communicate with and secure records from the student's previous school. Avoid routine family and medical history questions except when information is missing or when families appear to appreciate the opportunity to retell their story to new professionals. Offer to provide relocated families with tours of facilities, descriptions of programs, and introductions to staff and other families in the program. Try to make their process of settling in a new child and themselves as painless and smooth as possible.

In this description of family characteristics we have emphasized some of the many ways in which families can vary and relevant issues for your consideration. Large or small families, single-parent or blended families, different cultural backgrounds, and the family's geographic location (or relocation)—each of these factors presents unique sets of challenges. Yet the underlying common themes of a good collaborative approach are (1) respect for divergent values, (2) an understanding of some of the many other issues—in addition to their child's exceptionality—the family may be facing, and (3) a creative willingness to capitalize on families' unique strengths and resources.

Personal Characteristics

Family diversity resulting from variations in cultural and other characteristics multiplies as family members present their own idiosyncrasies. For example, the characteristics of a member's exceptionality, each family member's state of mental and physical health, and individual coping styles are all examples of personal characteristics. These personal characteristics can be either strengths or drawbacks for the family as a whole, and each of them—and all of them in the aggregate—affects the family's reaction to an exceptionality and the extent of the family's empowerment.

Characteristics of a Member's Exceptionality

The characteristics of a member's exceptionality will shape a family's reaction to the exceptionality. Characteristics include the nature of the exceptionality (for example, is the student considered gifted?) and the extent or degree of the exceptionality (for example, is the student's disability considered mild

or severe?). Each of these areas raises special issues in regard to a family's reaction.

Nature of the Exceptionality The nature of the exceptionality influences the family's reaction to it. For example, when children have medically complex needs, their families often make many adaptations in family routines in order to provide ongoing care and often have special needs for illness-specific information, special equipment, and financial assistance (Diehl, Moffitt, & Wade, 1991; Jones, Clatterbuck, Barber, Marquis, & Turnbull, 1995; National Commission on Childhood Disability, 1995). The threat of unpredictable seizures can increase worry and protectiveness in parents of children with epilepsy (Pianta & Lothman, 1994; Vining, 1989). Likewise, the primary concerns of parents of children with emotional disorders, attention deficit/hyperactivity disorder (AD/HD), head injury, and autism often relate to behavioral issues and the family's responses to behavioral challenges (Baker, 1994; Bouma & Schweitzer, 1990; Gervasio, 1993; Singer & Nixon, 1996; Turnbull & Ruef, in press).

By the same token, a child with a hearing impairment needs communication accommodations—techniques or equipment for others to understand what the child wants and to make sure the child understands the rest of the family (Tanksley, 1993).

Families who have a child who is gifted may be concerned about their child's being publicly recognized as different, their own capability to support their child's gifts and talents, strategies for promoting positive peer and sibling relationships, and techniques for alleviating family stress associated with students who do not fulfill the educational potential that their giftedness indicates (Carandang, 1992; Friedman & Gallagher, 1991; Raymond & Benbow, 1989; Rimm & Lowe, 1988).

Different exceptionalities can and usually do bring different kinds of challenges for families. Each exceptionality poses its own special needs, including needs to connect and collaborate with specialists and with other families whose members experience the same kind of exceptionality.

But there are more consequences than "special needs" for families. Children and youth with exceptionalities make their own positive contributions (Summers, Behr, & Turnbull, 1988). In box 5–1 you will learn how Mr. Arias, Roxana's teacher, identified and then built on her positive contributions. Indeed, what Mr. Arias did was a two-pronged collaboration. He recognized and affirmed that Roxana had what it takes to be a school leader, and then he collaborated with her and Marta Cofresi in achieving those goals. Empowerment, he knew, is a matter of the family's motivation and skills, coupled with a context that he created. As you read box 5–1, think of the Cofresi family as having empowerment within themselves, of Mr. Arias as the collaborator, and of the programs he sponsored as the empowering context.

Marta Cofresi and Mr. Arias are not the only parents and professionals who see the positive contributions of children with disabilities. Indeed, more than 1,200 birth parents, foster and adopted parents, and legal guardians of children with disabilities have affirmed that their children with disabilities are sources of happiness and fulfillment, strength and family closeness, and opportunities to learn through experiences associated with disabilities. Moreover, they reported stress and well-being levels similar to those of adults in the general population (Behr & Murphy, 1993). Disability does not always involve distress.

> I've had by-pass surgery, three husbands, a son who left for the army and never came back, a pile of bills that never got paid and Colin, who was born with microcephaly. I've had lots of troubles in my life but Colin sure hasn't been one of them.

Troubles with doctors, neighbors, late SSI payments, wheelchairs that won't move, and funny questions I never felt like answering. But never had any trouble with Colin. Churches that never came through, relatives that never came by, one grandbaby I've yet to meet, and heartburn must be since the day I was born. And Colin, he was my sweet-boy. Light my day with that funny smile, and how he'd make up to me when I came to get him in the morning. Why, if it weren't for Colin, I'd have thought life had pulled a dirty trick. (Josetta, mother of Colin, quoted in Blue-Banning, Santelli, Guy, & Wallace, 1994, p. 69)

Extent and Age of Onset of the Exceptionality   The extent or degree of an exceptionality also influences families. You may be tempted to assume that a severe exceptionality has a greater impact, but that assumption is not always valid. The severity of a disability or the extent of giftedness may result in qualitative, not quantitative, differences.

For example, if a child has a severe disability, it may be apparent at birth, causing the parents to deal immediately with the shock. When a disability appears later, such as an emotional disorder or a

MY VOICE
BOX 5–1

The Natural Leader and a Teacher's Response

Fernando Arias understands special education and students' positive contributions from a unique perspective. For three years he himself was in special education, classified as mentally retarded because he could not read or speak English but was monolingual in Spanish.

Perhaps because of that experience and certainly because of his association with the twins, he knows how to highlight their strengths and positive contributions. "Right away upon meeting Roxana, I could tell she was a natural born leader, and she is, she's a leader. She took charge—

what needed to be done she took charge."

Taking charge is a benefit to Mr. Arias. When he has to speak in public, for example, he often becomes nervous; so he asks Roxana to speak for him. "She's able to communicate well with others," he says.

Having seen how influential Marta Cofresi is in including her twins in the family and the community, Mr. Arias follows her example, taking the twins on overnight hiking trips, often accompanied by Mrs. Cofresi as a chaperone for them and the other female students, or to

state vocational education competitions.

As a result of emphasizing what the twins can do and involving them and Marta, Mr. Arias feels a strong bond with Marta and the twins. "We just developed a close bond between all us . . . really, a small family." Whatever Mr. Arias and the twins or the family are doing, especially when they are with their peers, "I try to make that bond stronger amongst each other, because I feel that's very important. Just bonding and becoming good friends, I think that helps anybody out."

Source: Arias, F., Turnbull, A. P., Blue-Banning, M. J., & Pereira, L. (1995, Spring). Personal communication.

learning disability, the parents may feel not so much shock as a sense of relief that their concerns about their child's special needs have been resolved. These families may have to cope with a complex set of mixed emotions. With a learning disability, for example, some may experience confusion and frustration at the discovery that their child, who appears capable in so many ways, indeed has a disability. Others may be relieved to learn that there are reasons for the problems they have observed and yet feel guilty that they did not identify the disability earlier (Walther-Thomas, Hazel, Schumaker, Vernon, & Deshler, 1991). Alternatively, when a disability has a sudden onset, such as a head injury resulting from an adolescent's diving accident, the family is thrust into the world of trauma and rehabilitation units, typically with highly ambiguous prognoses (Cope & Wolfson, 1994; Kreutzer, Serio, & Bergquist, 1994). Families often have to make a series of ongoing readjustments as their child's characteristics fluctuate and permanently change.

In addition, severe exceptionalities are often more apparent than milder disabilities. On the one hand, the obvious disability may excuse a child's inappropriate public behavior. On the other hand, it may cause the family more social stigma and rejection. By contrast, milder exceptionalities may be invisible, leading siblings to worry whether something is wrong with them, too (Powell & Gallagher, 1993). With a severe disability, the family may be able to develop a more definitive understanding of the child's support needs. But with a milder disability, the family may find itself on a roller coaster of expectations, with hopes for the future alternately raised and dashed as the child makes progress or falls back.

Now, consider just how that student's exceptionality can affect professionals' collaboration with the family. Instructional objectives that could help the student and family (such as improved communication, expanded social relationships, or positive behavioral support) probably should be given high priority. For some students and families, learning more about how best to support their son or daughter in being successful with homework or in acquiring more appropriate behavior would be helpful (see chapter 13). Other families might welcome information about services in the community, such as child care or personal care attendant services (see chapter 10). To repeat, the nature and extent or degree of each student's exceptionality have special implications for the family and for how you as a professional can best collaborate with the family. No doubt, the Cofresi twins' disability affects their family, but it also affects how a

professional such as Mr. Arias collaborates with them: He saw Marta's and the twins' motivation and skills and committed himself to augmenting those same traits.

Family Health

People who do not feel well have more difficulty coping with stressful situations. Thus, for example, a mother's health status contributes to the parenting stress in families where there is a child with AD/HD (Anastopoulos, Guevremont, Shelton, & DuPaul, 1992). Conversely, stress produces physiological responses that can make people ill. Some research has found that parents of children with exceptionalities have a higher level of stress than parents who do not have such children and that their stress is associated with additional caregiving responsibilities (Beckman, 1991); other research, however, has not shown that these parents have higher stress levels (Frey, Greenberg, & Fewell, 1989; Harris & McHale, 1989).

Not all family stress is purely disability-related. Some is socially created. Thus, some families of children with exceptionalities experience a wide range of stresses and worries associated with issues such as poverty and racism (Harry, 1992a; Kalyanpur & Rao, 1991). Whether a parent's or a family's stress or health problems are caused by worry about the child's exceptionality or whether their sources lie elsewhere, the result is the same: The parent or family faces greater challenges in taking action to get what the family wants and needs. As we discussed in chapter 4, you can support the family by being flexible in all aspects of providing services and responsive to their preferences, strengths, and needs.

Coping Styles

As we pointed out in chapter 3, Olson and associates (Olson, McCubbin, Barnes, Larsen, Muxen, & Wilson, 1983) developed the following categories of coping styles: passive appraisal, reframing, spiritual support, social support, and professional support. Coping within the Cofresi family consists of the following:

- *Reframing:* looking at the twins' positive contributions instead of their disabilities
- *Spiritual support:* in Marta's words, "I had to find the answer in God, because God made them that way, so how God would think of them and treat them is how I wanted to be"
- *Social support:* support by their friends
- *Professional support:* support from Mr. Arias

Family members vary in their coping capability—in both the number of different coping strategies they use and the quality or effectiveness of each strategy. Within the same family, some members may have strong coping capabilities and others may need much more support because their own capabilities have not yet been developed fully. Think of individual coping metaphorically: "The end of the rope is the end of the rope, regardless of how long the rope is" (Avis, 1985, p. 197). Individual family members have ropes of differing lengths.

Avoid judging one family member in relation to another and wondering why one individual but not another is having such a challenging time coping with what may appear to be a similar situation. Rather than making comparative judgments, remember that the length of everyone's rope varies and depends on all the situations that they are handling in their life at a given time or that they have faced over time. As a collaborator, regard yourself as a "rope lengthener," supporting everyone involved (families, professionals, friends, and community citizens) to lengthen their ropes so that they will be more empowered (more motivated and connected to sources of knowledge/skills) rather than at the end of their rope.

Special Challenges

Families face challenges over and above a child's disability or extraordinary gifts and talents. Examples of special challenges include teenage pregnancy (Muccigrosso, Scavarda, Simpson-Brown, & Thalacker, 1991); having a family member who is incarcerated (National Resource Center for Family Support Programs, 1993); and having HIV/AIDS (Prater, Serna, Sileo, & Katz, 1995). Other special challenges include living in poverty, engaging in substance abuse, and living in a family in which a parent has a disability.

Families in Poverty

Rudimentary and harsh survival problems face families who live in poverty (Lavelle, 1995). Poverty is escalating in the United States. According to the National Center for Children in Poverty (1995), childhood poverty is now at its highest level within the past 10 years and is especially devastating for children under age 6. The number of poor children under 6 years of age grew from 5 to 6 million and the poverty

rate reached 26 percent between 1987 and 1992. As we stated earlier, more families of students in special education have lower socioeconomic levels (household incomes below $25,000) as compared with families of students in general education (U.S. Department of Education, 1992).

Homeless families, generally headed by women, are a subgroup of families in poverty. A study of homeless families in New York City produced a typical demographic profile:

> Almost 100 percent of all families were headed by single women. The majority of these single mothers were younger than 25 years of age with an average of 22. Most of these families have never had a traditional family structure with almost 90 percent reporting never having been married. African-American constituted the largest ethnic group among the families; two-thirds were African-American, roughly one-fourth were Hispanic, and less than seven percent were White or from other ethnic groups. (Homes for the Homeless, 1992, p. 3)

In the book *Rachel and Her Children: Homeless Families in America*, Kozol (1988) tells about the lives of homeless people he has interviewed. One child describes the room in which she lives with her mother and three other children.

> Ever since August we been livin' here. The room is either very hot or freezin' cold. When it be hot outside it's hot in here. When it be cold outside we have no heat. We used to live with my aunt but then it got too crowded there so we moved out. We went to welfare and they sent us to the shelter. Then they shipped us to Manhattan. I'm scared of the elevators. 'Fraid they be stuck. I take the stairs. (Kozol, 1988, p. 62)

Homelessness has devastating effects on children, including an increase in problems of health, peer interactions, transitions, academics, and school attendance (Heflin & Rudy, 1991; Stronge & Tenhouse, 1990). Nonetheless, many families from low socioeconomic backgrounds are vitally interested in special education issues (Harry, 1992a, 1992b). In an in-depth study of 12 Puerto Rican parents from low-income backgrounds, Harry reported the parents' cogent insights about labeling, curriculum and bilingual issues, efficacy of special versus general education placement, and methods for teaching reading. Harry concluded:

> This study shows that the power of parents may be seriously undermined by culturally different ways of understanding. Yet it also shows that poor par-

ents, with little formal education, and a different language and culture, may, through their own analysis of their children's difficulties, have a significant contribution to make to current debates in the field of special education. (Harry, 1992b, p. 38)

In every relationship with families, including those from low-income backgrounds, demonstrate respect, be nonjudgmental, and recognize their unique strengths and their important contributions to their child and family. That is the point that an inner-city mother of an infant makes as she describes the importance of a home visitor's informality and nonintrusive questions:

> She [the previous early intervention specialist] came out to the house when [the child] was 8 months [old], and she said, he has problems, and I said, no, he don't, he's just a baby. . . . She asks me all kinds of stuff like if I have a crib, how many people live here, and she writes it down. She was a nosy lady—nosy, nosy! I kept hiding from her, and finally I moved so they wouldn't bug me. . . . When she [the current specialist] came out, I thought, oh, gee, here we go again. So I asked her, "What's wrong?" and she just says, "Nothing, I just want to know if you need anything." (Summers, Dell'Oliver, Turnbull, Benson, Santelli, Campbell, & Siegel-Causey, 1990, p. 87)

You can provide concrete assistance by helping families connect with community agencies that can assist them to meet their basic needs (see chapter 10).

Families with Substance Abuse

Approximately 14 percent of all adult males and 6 percent of all adult females abuse or depend on alcohol (National Institute on Alcohol Abuse and Addiction, 1990). The use of psychotropic drugs tends to be higher in females (Robbins & Clayton, 1989). Within a group of women who experienced poverty and received Aid to Families with Dependent Children assistance, the prevalence for alcoholism and drug abuse was reported to be between 16 and 21 percent (Sisco & Pearson, 1994). Furthermore, between 13 and 16 percent of pregnant women who use public clinics have tested positively for alcohol, marijuana, cocaine, or opiate drug use in some form (Chasnoff, Landress, & Barrett, 1990). Drug and alcohol abuse are particularly problematic for American Indian and Alaska Native youth (Schinke, Schilling, Kirkham, Gilchrist, Barth, & Blythe, 1986).

Substance abuse involves the use of many different drugs. We will particularly focus on alcohol and cocaine. Children who are exposed to alcohol in utero are at risk for fetal alcohol syndrome. Approximately one to two children per 1,000 are affected annually by this syndrome (Poulsen, 1994). These children typically have decreased growth, a particular pattern of facial malformations, some central nervous system problems, and lower IQ scores than children who have not been exposed to alcohol (Phelps & Grabowski, 1992; Shriver & Piersel, 1994).

Family size and socioeconomic level can make a difference in how a family adjusts to exceptionality and how it interacts with alcohol exposure to determine, at least partially, a child's development and long-term outcomes. For example, children who have been exposed to alcohol who come from smaller families or have fathers with higher levels of education have higher intellectual and achievement scores than peers from larger families or lower-SES families (Sampson, Streissguth, Barr, & Bookstein, 1989). To understand the family, consider not only a family's separate characteristics but also how the characteristics interact.

Cocaine apparently is the most common drug used by women during their child-bearing adult years (Schutter & Brinker, 1992). Although there has not been nearly as much research on the effects of cocaine on children as there has been on the effects of alcohol, infants who have been exposed to cocaine may be at risk for an atypical behavior pattern particularly related to temperament (Patterson, Reid, & Dishion, 1992). They are drowsier and sleep more than infants who have not had drug exposure; their mothers are more passive during play interactions (Gottwald & Thurman, 1994).

In what way should families who experience substance abuse be supported by educational professionals? The bottom line is that highly comprehensive and family-centered services need to be available starting during the neonatal period. Educators will need to collaborate with public health nurses and substance abuse professionals to develop an array of services and supports that can assist parents in getting necessary intervention and that can enhance their child's development. From an empowerment perspective, every dimension of motivation and knowledge/skill factors needs to be addressed, and the context needs to be as empowering as possible. This is equally true when there are other kinds of child abuse and neglect, as we point out in more detail in chapter 10.

Parents with Disabilities

As the rights of people with disabilities expand and they begin to lead more typical lives, the likelihood increases that they will become parents. When a parent has a physical disability, the effects on your relationship with them primarily involve logistics: providing accessible meeting rooms or perhaps communicating through the most accessible and convenient means, such as the telephone.

Parents with visual or hearing impairments rely on their children in many situations. For example, parents with visual impairments may ask their children to read prices in grocery stores and otherwise guide them through daily transactions. They may depend on an older child to provide care for younger siblings, expecting the older child to be like a parent (a member of the parental subsystem [see chapter 6]) and a "little adult." Whether this is detrimental depends, of course, on the individual family and whether parents can also allow the children on whom they depend the time to be "just kids."

The child's role in assisting a parent may require the child to forego some school extracurricular activities or may create conflict with a parent. For example, during the following description of a parent-teacher conference with a mother who has a hearing impairment, the child plays a critical but problematic role:

> We didn't have anybody who had sign language because our district's deaf education teacher was strictly from the oral school. So I asked Jeannie to interpret at our conference, since I knew she was very good at sign language. Unfortunately, what I needed to tell Jeannie's mother was that I had some concerns about her behavior in class. . . . The mother just nodded and smiled. I didn't understand her reaction. . . . It was only later that I discovered that Jeannie had not, to say the least, translated accurately what I was saying!

It's critically important to recognize the strengths of parents with disabilities. Often the disability itself does not interfere with how the family functions. There are also instances when the disability may actually enhance the parent's understanding of the child—for example, when deaf parents raise deaf children.

> Deaf mothers, accustomed to dealing with their own hearing loss, are well aware of and skilled in the use of the visual strategies that facilitate effective communication among deaf children. They are, therefore, unlikely to encounter the sense of powerlessness that overwhelms many hearing parents when confronted with the diagnosis of their child's hearing loss. (Jamieson, 1995, p. 112)

Many myths surround the question of what happens when adults with mental retardation have children. The incidence of mental retardation due to organic or genetic causes does not increase for the child when the parents have mental retardation (Tymchuk, Andron, & Unger, 1987). Poverty, not just parental cognitive limitations, is what puts most children at risk for developmental delays, but support services minimize the risks (Ciotti, 1989; O'Neill, 1985). In addition, parents with mental retardation have fewer or the same number of children as compared to parents without disabilities in the same SES group (Craft & Craft, 1979; Tymchuk et al., 1987). Finally, parents with mental retardation can be, but are not always necessarily, less than adequate parents (Tymchuk, 1990); and most can learn parenting skills when responsive support services are provided (Feldman, Case, Rincover, & Betel, 1989).

The four factors that most inhibit adults with developmental disabilities from seeking help from existing agencies are lack of knowledge of services available, lack of knowledge of how to apply for services, lack of transportation, and lack of necessary skills in locating agency sites. These parents need a broad array of supports, including transportation, housing, parent education services, money management, day care for children, family life education, and counseling (Whitman & Accardo, 1990). School-based comprehensive services (chapter 13) are appropriate responses.

Summary

So many families, so many differences! Yes, that's true, but there are ways you can simplify your work with the Cofresi family and others whose children have disabilities, unusual gifts, or, in the case of Roxela and Roxana Cofresi, both disability and special talents.

What affects families? Clearly, the family's own characteristics—size and form, cultural background, socioeconomic status, and geographic location.

Of course, the personal characteristics of each family member come into play. The nature and severity of the child's exceptionality play important roles but not always in predictable ways. The family's need for support is also influenced by the type and extent of the exceptionality. And the family members' health and coping styles influence family well-being.

Some families face special challenges, and so do the professionals who work with these multiply challenged families. Poverty, substance abuse, and disability in a parent all create unusual circumstances.

Whatever a family's characteristics might be, nearly every family is motivated to help its members, and most families have or can develop skills that help them get what they want. In your work with families, you should regard yourself as a collaborator who, like Mr. Arias, creates or assures that they will have a context in which their motivation and skills will be welcomed. Think of the families as saying, as Marta Cofresi must have said, "It's within us to be empowerful," and then think of yourself as Mr. Arias must have regarded himself, as a person committed to creating an empowering context.

If you were bold enough to be a fortune teller, what fortune would you tell for Marta Cofresi, Roxela, and Roxana? If you did not know them except as a statistic ("single parent, monolingual, twins with disabilities, father left family when twins were born, older siblings, immigrants, not well off financially"), you might describe a scenario quite different from the one that Marta and the twins describe.

What could account for that discrepancy? The answer lies in the family's characteristics. Of course, the nature and severity of the twins' disabilities make a difference, but even more influential are the characteristics of the Cofresi family.

These characteristics are much more than the sum of statistical profiles about the family. At their core, the characteristics have more to do with character than attributes, with courage and attitudes rather than quantifiable facts related to their ethnicity, socioeconomic status, and location.

There is much to learn from Marta Cofresi's early acceptance of her twins' disabilities, the way she molded Juan Carlos, Louisa, and the twins into a single unit of caring, and the way the older siblings and, in time, Roxela and Roxana themselves decided to meet and beat the odds, to use the phrase that Theresa Cooper employs in chapter 3.

One last fact is worth noting: Remember Mr. Arias, who was Roxana's vocational education teacher? He was the professional who insisted that Roxana remain in his class, who developed the trust bond with her that Patty Smith spoke about in chapter 1. He had great expectations for her fixed firmly in his mind, and he collaborated with her and her classmates so she would be a success in school and a person with ambition for higher education. You, like Mr. Arias, can make similar contributions to students and families!

Chapter Six

Family Interaction

Vincent and Joseph Benito, ages 5 and 3, are lucky little guys. Sure, they've both got autism. But they've also got what it takes to combat it: a big—a really big—family.

For starters, there's Nila, their mother, and Joe, their dad. And then there's grandmother Nila and aunt Nancy. And even though he died long before the boys were born, there's granddad Bill, whose teachings ("kill them with kindness," "think the problem through; don't be emotional") guide Nila even now. Finally, there are Nila's friends, her colleagues at the University of South Florida's Florida Mental Health Institute, Florida's Children's Medical Services, and the staff of a local Head Start program in Tampa, Florida.

So when any school administrator or teacher works with the boys, they also work with the whole Benito family, blood and chosen. That doesn't mean that each member of the family duplicates another. Far from it.

Nila describes herself as the planner and organizer; she writes down what she wants to say at the meetings with the educators, she runs it by Joe (who is away on business a couple of weeks each month), she checks off with grandmother Nila, she asks her sister Nancy for input, she tells her friends what she wants to do, and she consults her late father's wisdom. In a way, says Nila, she's like legendary football coach Vince Lombardi: "It's like I'm coaching and setting up all the plays and teaching all the players."

And then there's the team that executes those plays, guided by the quarterback, husband Joe, and consisting of grandmother Nila, aunt Nancy, great-grandmother

Francesca, and the extended family. All of them have been to individual program conferences, all have collaborated with each other, all share Nila's and Joe's concerns and great expectations, all share the pain of persistent problems, and all share the celebrations of the boys' and the family's successes.

That family collaboration helps little Vince and little Joe, but it also "makes us feel stronger" as a family. Feeling that way helps because family members don't always see eye to eye about the boys. They also have some differences in style. "I tend to focus more on the big picture, he [Joe] more on smaller things, so we really complement each other when we meet with professionals," Nila says. But as for their vision of the big picture, they are in agreement: "We have high expectations, we're cautiously optimistic, and we look at our life just as a family in general."

It wasn't that way when Nila decided to go for inclusion after Vincent was subjected to aversive interventions in a preschool he attended before Head Start. She had to persuade Joe, her sister Nancy, and her mother Nila to buy into her vision.

What brought them around? They attended a personal-futures planning meeting that the staff from USF's Individualized Support Program hosted for the Benito family, they acquired information about inclusion from the university staff and Nila, they met the staff at the

Head Start program where inclusion was the norm, and they were exposed to great expectations for inclusion.

So the professionals have to deal with the Benito family as a united family. It's a family that tries to collaborate with the professionals. When possible, Nancy and grandmother Nila attend program planning conferences. Nancy, a nurse, is still skeptical sometimes, but she no longer second-guesses, although she asks her sister hard questions. Grandmother Nila and great-grandmother Francesca give Nila and Joe unconditional emotional support.

Do the professionals partake of the collaboration that permeates the Benito family and friendship circle? Absolutely. The family respects the professionals for what they know, while recognizing that they may not know all the family knows about the boys. Nila says, "We prepare our notes before we meet with them. We show them respect. We give them time to prepare for the boys' presence in school. We are up-front with them and play no games. We follow up with thank-you phone calls and letters. We talk about our boys' autism and the problems it can cause, but we also talk about their strengths and progress. We are very frank and honest. When one of us gets emotional, then another of us leads the conference. It's wonderful when we can all hug—family and professionals—after the conferences are over. When we collaborate as a family, it's a way to show the professionals how to collaborate with us and each other."

In chapter 1, we defined family as two or more people who regard themselves as a family and perform some of the functions that families typically perform. This chapter is about the "two or more people who regard themselves as a family." In other words, it is about family members and their *interactions* within the family and among its members, about their relationships to each other. As the family systems framework shows (the circle within figure 6–1), there are four basic types of interactions or relationships—marital, parental, sibling, and extended family. We display the types of relationships in the inner quadrants of the framework and their qualities in the outer ring, and we describe the qualities as cohesion and adaptability.

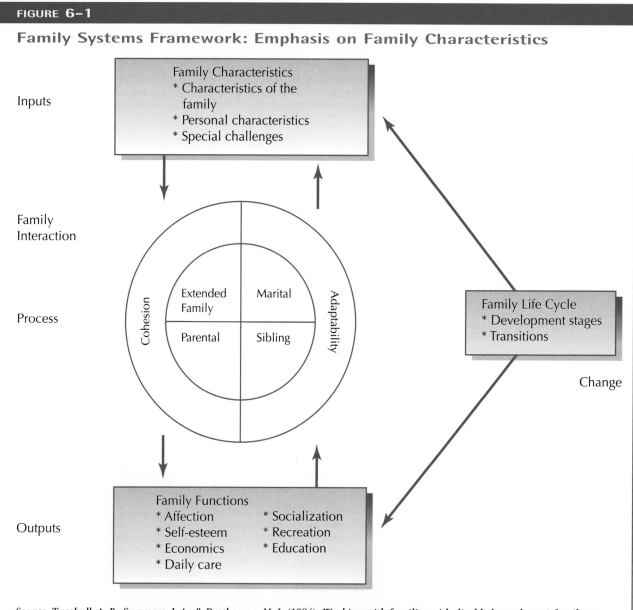

FIGURE 6–1

Family Systems Framework: Emphasis on Family Characteristics

Source: Turnbull, A. P., Summers, J. A., & Brotherson, M. J. (1984). *Working with families with disabled members: A family systems approach* (p. 60). Lawrence: University of Kansas, Kansas Affiliated Facility. Adapted by permission.

Assumptions of Family Systems Theory

One of the most significant recent changes within special education, particularly in early childhood special education, has been the shift from focusing primarily on the child or on the parental subsystem (especially the mother and child subsystem) to focusing more broadly on the whole family. This emphasis on the whole family and on the systemic (systemwide), reverberating impact of input/output through the entire family system brings to mind a mobile:

> In a mobile all the pieces, no matter what size or shape, can be grouped together and balanced by shortening or lengthening the strings attached or rearranging the distance between the pieces. So it is with a family. None of the family members is identical to any other; they are all different and at different levels of growth. As in a mobile, you can't arrange one without thinking of the other. (Satir, 1972, pp. 119–120 copyright © 1972, Reprinted by permission, Science and Behavior Books)

The family systems theory approach provides a framework for understanding what a family is and how it functions (chapters 5 through 8) and shows professionals how to collaborate with families (chapters 9 through 15). Three of the most relevant assumptions of systems theory in general and of family systems theory in particular are (1) the input/output configuration of systems, (2) the concepts of wholeness and subsystems, and (3) the role of boundaries in defining systems (Whitechurch & Constantine, 1993).

Input/Output

The first assumption is that certain characteristics provide input into the system. The system then interacts with these inputs, and the interaction produces output. Systems theory focuses primarily on "what happens to the *input* as it is processed by the system on its way to becoming an *output*" (Broderick & Smith, 1979, p. 114; our emphasis). As you examine the family systems framework (figure 6–1), you will see that the family characteristics you read about in chapter 5 are the inputs into family interaction. The family interaction occurs as families perform roles and interact with each other. The output of these roles and interactions is related to family functions that we discuss in chapter 7. Think of the Benito family and its inputs. They consist of the family's characteristics (for example, a large united family), their members' personal characteristics (such as the boys' autism and each member's coping style), and special challenges (two sons with disabilities).

Wholeness and Subsystems

The second assumption is that the system must be understood as a whole and cannot be understood by examining only its component parts—that is, just one or more of its members (Whitechurch & Constantine, 1993). Simply understanding the child does not mean that you will understand the family, yet understanding the family is necessary to understanding the child. Moreover, many professionals mistakenly assume that they can understand and collaborate with the family if they know only the mother's or the student's perspective.

This is a mistaken assumption because the family consists of the sum of its members' mutual and reciprocal interactions. The aggregation, the combination of interactions, is the sum, the whole family. There are interacting component parts or subsystems: marital, parental, sibling, and extended family relationships. Those are the subsystems in the inner quadrant of figure 6–1. Think of the task that professionals face as they deal with the Benito family: to understand the boys, Vincent and Joe, and then understand and collaborate with all the highly involved family members. It is safe to say that, when a school gets one of the Benito boys, it gets a whole family and needs to become reliable allies with each member.

Boundaries

The third and last assumption is that family subsystems are separated by boundaries and that these boundaries are created by the interaction of family members with each other and by the family unit in its interactions with outside influences. For example, there are boundaries between parents and children and between the children themselves. Likewise, the boundary between the family and the educators with whom they are collaborating may be a different boundary than the one that exists between the family and friends, clergy, other professionals, or tradespeople.

Families vary in the degree to which their boundaries are open or closed to educators or any other nonmember. The openness or closedness of the boundaries affect the degree to which the family will collaborate with educators or others. In the Benitos' case, the boundaries between the professionals and themselves are fairly open, and opportunities for various kinds of partnerships are abundant.

By the same token, the boundaries within a family help to define its members' roles with respect to each other—as parental and extended family subsystems, for example. In some families, extended family members take on parents' roles because the boundary between the two subsystems (extended family and parental) is open. In other families, there might be great resentment if one of the grandparents tries to make suggestions about child rearing. In those families, the boundary between parental and extended family subsystems is closed. In the Benito family, there are open issue-specific boundaries among Nila, Joe, and Nila's sister and mother. A professional who wants effective collaboration with any one member of the family needs to develop a reliable alliance with all Benito family members.

In this chapter, we describe the four family subsystems and the "operating rules" of family systems and subsystems—cohesion and adaptability.

Family Subsystems

Within the traditional nuclear family, there are four major subsystems (see figure 6–1):

1. *Marital subsystem:* marital partner interactions
2. *Parental subsystem:* parent and child interactions
3. *Sibling subsystem:* child and child interactions
4. *Extended family subsystem:* interactions of nuclear family relatives and others who are regarded as relatives

Interactions differ according to the subsystems within each family and according to the membership within each subsystem. For example, a family with only one child has no sibling subsystem. Similarly, single parents do not have a formal marital subsystem that influences the family, but they may have the equivalent if they have a significant partner. Because you may not know exactly who each family considers to be part of the family system, simply ask parents to tell you about "their family" and listen carefully to the people they mention. These people may very well be able to help create broadly based collaborations. In the Benito family, the extended members are so many and so active that it would have been a mistake not to ask Nila whom she considers to be family. Likewise, it probably would be wise to develop partnerships with

all the involved family members, not just Nila, and to infuse the eight obligations of a reliable alliance into each of the partnerships. After all, what happens to one of the Benitos surely will affect all of them.

Marital Partner Interactions (The Marital Subsystem)

The marital subsystem consists of interactions between marital partners or significant others who function as marital partners. The presence of a child or youth with an exceptionality can influence marital relationships and interactions.

Impacts: Negative, Positive, and Mixed

How are marital relationships influenced by the presence of a child with an exceptionality? Are marriages on the whole hurt, unaffected, or improved by the presence of the child? As confusing as it may be, research gives a *yes* answer to each of those questions about marital effects.

Some studies indicate that a child or youth with an exceptionality has a negative impact on the parents' marriage. The role of divorce, marital disharmony, and desertions by husbands have been reported to be disproportionately high in marriages where there is a child or youth with an exceptionality (Gath, 1977; Murphy, 1982; Reed & Reed, 1965). One group of researchers assessed marital harmony in 59 couples soon after the birth of a child with spina bifida and again nearly a decade later (Tew, Payne, & Lawrence, 1974). The researchers maintained contact with these couples as well as with 58 control couples (those who did not have a child with spina bifida). The couples who had a child with spina bifida had lower marital harmony and twice the divorce rate as the control group couples. Thus, it appeared that the birth of a child with spina bifida presented a serious challenge to marital stability and caused many marital needs and activities to be subordinated to the child's needs. As Helen Featherstone (1980), herself the parent of a child with a disability, has noted: "A child's handicap attacks the fabric of a marriage in four ways. It excites powerful emotions in both parents. It acts as a dispiriting symbol of shared failure. It reshapes the organization of the family. It creates fertile ground for conflict" (p. 91).

On the contrary, however, the majority of studies have indicated that the divorce rate is not higher when a family has a child with an exceptionality (Benson & Gross, 1989). Indeed, some husbands and wives report higher levels of marital adjustment, partially because of their shared commitment for their child. Elsie Helsel (1985) reflected this perspective (see box 6–1) when she wrote about her marriage and the contribution to it made by her son, Robin, who has cerebral palsy.

Researchers have validated what Elsie Helsel asserted. Kazak and Marvin (1984) compared marital stress in 56 couples with children with spina bifida and in 53 couples with children without an exceptionality. Their results revealed no significant difference between the groups in terms of total marital satisfaction. In fact, they found that the couples with children with spina bifida actually experienced somewhat higher levels of marital satisfaction. These findings are in direct contrast to the study (Tew et al., 1974) that we discussed previously. According to Kazak and Marvin (1984), their results support the idea that the presence of a child with an exceptionality in some cases may strengthen marital relationships.

Finally, other research has found no difference between families with and without a child with an exceptionality: The child essentially does not affect marriage—positively or negatively. Comparing a matched sample of 60 families with and without children with disabilities, Abbott and Meredith (1986) found no significant differences between the two groups on measures of marital strength, family strength, or personality characteristics. Young and Roopnarine (1994) reported similar findings in their research on families who have preschool children with and without a disability.

Furthermore, research suggests that issues associated with the exceptionality can simultaneously strengthen and impair a couple's relationship (Singer & Nixon, 1996). Consider what you have already learned in chapter 5 about all the different ways that family characteristics can vary. Given these tremendous variations, it should be obvious that many issues within families, not just the child with an exceptionality, influence marital stability.

Marital Satisfaction   Despite the inconsistency in research results related to the positive, negative, neutral, or compound impact of children on marriage, one consistent finding is that higher levels of

MY VOICE   BOX 6–1

Robin's Positive Contributions

Professionals are constantly probing and asking questions concerning how Robin's constant presence and problems affect our marriage. Once again, there are pluses and minuses. I really don't believe any one factor in a marriage can be pinpointed as a strengthener or strainer. There are too many variables affecting a marriage for such a simplistic explanation. The temperament of the individuals; the physical, emotional, and financial strengths; the problem-solving and coping skills; the commitment people bring—all have some bearing on the strain a handicapped child places on a marriage. From my point of view, Robin has added more strength than strain. At least my husband and I are still living together after thirty-seven years of marriage! For one thing, at those points in a marriage when you are contemplating divorce (intellectually, emotionally, or actually), the presence of a child such as Robin is a major deterrent. The focus quickly changes from your own needs, wishes, and desires to our responsibilities, commitment, and the needs of the child. Somehow this helps you work through a problem, and you find another way. I have never bought the argument that the presence of an adult person in a family, handicapped or not, is a disruptive factor. I feel society has lost a mooring with the breakdown of the extended family. Romantic twosomes are great for novels and certain periods of our lives. I do not see such a pattern as essential for a successful marriage. My husband and I will not have a footloose, carefree, romantic retirement lifestyle, but we will have something else—the opportunity to feel needed.

Source: Helsel Family. (1985). The Helsels' story of Robin. In H. R. Turnbull & A. P. Turnbull (Eds.) *Parents speak out: Then and now* (2nd ed.) (pp. 85–86). Englewood Cliffs, NJ: Merrill/Prentice Hall.

marital satisfaction are generally associated with overall family adjustment to a child with an exceptionality (Bristol, Gallagher, & Schopler, 1988; Lichtenstein, 1993). Furthermore, marital harmony is associated with higher levels of self-esteem in brothers and sisters (Rodrigue, Geffkin, & Morgan, 1993). Thus, it appears that a strong marriage makes a difference in overall family well-being. At the same time, a strong marriage is not a prerequisite for positive family outcomes: Many single parents of children with an exceptionality also experience strong family well-being, such as Patty Smith and Marta Cofresi, whom you read about in the opening vignettes of chapters 1 and 5. As partners in marriage, spouses have specific needs for themselves and specific roles to fulfill for their partners (such as affection, socialization, and self-definition). It makes good sense, then, for programs and supports for children and youth with exceptionalities to respect the importance of the marital relationship. Box 6–2 suggests ways you might enhance marital interactions as you form partnerships with families.

There are situations in which couples can benefit from marital counseling or other therapy provided by professionals such as psychiatrists, psychologists, and social workers (Lichtenstein, 1993). If you believe that families with whom you are working might benefit from marital counseling or therapy, discuss your perspectives with the school social worker or counselor, asking for advice on how best to approach the family about the availability of counseling or therapy. In some cases, the social worker or counselor might take the lead and have an initial conversation with a family. One way to help a family is to determine which issues are appropriately handled by teachers and which ones by professionals who specialize in family counseling or therapy and then to make an appropriate referral. Remember that meeting families' needs, providing them with information, and referring them to appropriate services are components of reliable alliances and empowering contexts.

Parent and Child Interactions (The Parental Subsystem)

The parental subsystem consists of interactions between parents and their child or children. Couples experience parenthood in many different ways. Couples can be natural (biological), step, adoptive, foster, or unmarried-couple parents. Some stay married to each other; some divorce. Some remarry; others do not (see chapter 5). Some families are comprised of lesbian, gay, and bisexual members who often must contend with the type of homophobic discrimination that Bonnie Tinker describes in box 6–3. Bonnie laments that educators have blamed her daughter's emotional disorder on Bonnie's sexual orientation and have refused to listen to her and her daughter as they state their perspectives about the reasons for her daughter's emotional challenges.

In this section, we will discuss (1) foster and adoptive families, (2) issues associated with fatherhood, and (3) issues associated with motherhood. All seven opportunities for partnership and the eight obligations of reliable alliances are appropriate for all families and all family members. Partnerships infused with the reliable alliance obligations are inclusive approaches; they exclude no family and no family member.

TIPS   BOX 6–2

Enhancing Marital Interactions

- Encourage parents to consider activities they may wish to engage in separately from their child or children.
- Make information available to couples on child care and companionship services.
- Consider the time and energy implications of homework and home-based teaching on the needs of the couple.
- Seek ways to offer flexible scheduling or alternatives if a planned school activity conflicts with a couple's plans.

Foster and Adoptive Parents Child welfare policies and professionals favor permanency planning, a process for keeping children with their biological families even when the families face special challenges rather than placing the children in foster care or in public or private institutions (Petr, 1994; Taylor, Knoll, Lehr, & Walker, 1989).

There has been an almost 50 percent increase between 1986 and 1991 in the number of children placed into the foster care system (Children's Defense Fund, 1991). A significant proportion of foster children are from minority backgrounds (Briggs, 1994; Steno, 1990). Based on Michigan data from 1985 through 1991, three times as many non-white infants entered the foster care system as white infants (Children's Defense Fund, 1993). Not all of these children have an exceptionality, but many do experience learning, behavioral, and emotional challenges. Sadly, nearly half of all foster children move from one foster home to another in the same year, and most remain permanently in foster care rather than having an opportunity to return to their biological families (Children's Defense Fund, 1991; National Commission on Children, 1991). Despite these findings, foster parents are valuable resources in the lives of children and youth with exceptionalities and can offer greatly needed and valued support. In box 6–4 you will read about the differences that foster families can make. The individual who wrote this was identified in elementary school as having a serious emotional disorder; several years later she also was identified as gifted.

Adoptive families also are valuable resources. Research with mothers who have adopted children with mental retardation shows that adopted families typically experience a high level of well-being (Glidden, 1989; Glidden, Kiphart, Willoughby, & Bush, 1993; Todis & Singer, 1991). For example, one study found that the positive benefits of adopting children with cognitive disabilities range from learning more about disabilities to strengthening one's religious beliefs. By far the greatest benefit was that adoptive parents took pride and pleasure in their child's accomplishments. These parents described more than twice as many benefits as difficulties, and 95 percent of them indicated that, given the opportunity again, they would definitely pursue adoption (Glidden & Pursley, 1989).

Fathers The father-child relationship influences a child's cognitive, personal-social, and sex-role-identification development (Lamb, 1983; Pruett & Litzenberger, 1992; Turbiville, Turnbull, & Turnbull, 1995). Although little information is available about the father's influence when the child has an exceptionality, one study found that children advanced in daily living skills and social competence more successfully when their fathers had positive, not neutral or negative, perceptions of them (Frey, Fewell, & Vadasy, 1989).

MY VOICE

BOX 6–3

Speaking Out on Gay and Lesbian Families

My son spent every day all day long last summer with his friend, a girl whom he has known from infancy. And now her father, a young man who grew up down the street from us and was a "friend" of my spouse's son, has decided that his daughter cannot play at our house. After all of these years of knowing we were gay, he decided to cleanse his family of our imagined sinfulness. And finally, in a burst of anger at me, he told my son that he was not welcome in their house, either. It is like a death for all of us, but there are no support groups for mourning this loss.

Of course, my spouse and I know we were taking a risk when we dared to create our family. We knew we would not be understood nor welcomed by much of the world. We have agonized over the pain homophobia has caused our children. But, we reasoned, life may be hard, but it would be no easier if we lived in violation of the truth of our own reality. In the midst of life's many uncertainties, we knew that we loved each other; and we could not respect ourselves nor abide our lives if we turned away from that fact. We believe it is important to teach our children that life must be lived with integrity, even if this brings hardship.

Bonnie Tinker
Love Makes a Family, Inc.

MY VOICE

My Two Families

Coping Styles

My Biological Family

In general, the higher the level of stress in the family, the more externally active the family members became. My father devoted himself to his work, my mother to luncheons and shopping, my sister to school and social activities.

My Foster Family

My foster family's primary coping style was a reliance on sharing experiences with friends and family, a strong belief that ultimately experiences work out for the good, and a willingness to ask for and accept help in time of need and to provide help and assistance when needed.... A strong spiritual belief system helped to provide strength in meeting difficulties, as did a sense of family unity.

Socialization Needs

My Biological Family

My parents participated in many social activities involving my father's professional organizations and at the country club in which they had membership.

My Foster Family

Many social activities took place within the framework of church activities in which we participated fully. There were often visitors of all ages in the house and these people were incorporated into the ongoing activities on a regular basis. It was always possible to find someone to play with, talk to, or interact with.

Affection Needs

My Biological Family

Overt physical or emotional displays of affection were not highly valued in my biological family.

Achievement was rewarded with a special dinner at times or perhaps an allowance bonus. My parents believed that their relationship should be kept private—I do not remember them touching or hugging. Because of the cycle of abuse, physical contact was something that was very difficult for me, and I fought or ran away more often than not.

My Foster Family

My foster family engaged in frequent displays of affection, with individual and family hugs abounding. We cuddled each other as well as dogs, cats, and others, strayed or in need, who came into the home. Not many people can remember hearing "I love you" for the first time, but I can remember when my mom said it to me.

Other research suggests that fathers of children with exceptionalities may change the relationships they share with their child. For example, researchers who studied father-child interaction found that fathers' play with their children tends to be quite physical and active (Clarke-Stewart, 1978). For children whose disability impairs their ability to interact physically or who have chronic illness or medical conditions that create challenges for robust play, some accommodations in the ways in which fathers and children interact with each other will be necessary. Fathers of gifted students are more involved in quantitative rather than verbal pursuits and are more active with children who are extremely precocious than with those who are modestly gifted (Raymond & Benbow, 1989). With respect to child care, a study that compared fathers of children with disabilities to fathers of children without disabilities found that both groups of fathers devoted two-thirds less time to child care than mothers; the sample in this study was composed entirely of Euro-Americans with middle-income financial resources (Young & Roopnarine, 1994).

A study of the fathers of children who were in kindergarten through third grade reported that fathers of children with and without disabilities spend a comparable amount of time in child care and that fathers of both groups of children assess their level of competence as a parent in a similar way (Turbiville, 1994). Interestingly, fathers of both groups of children reported spending similar amounts of time in school-related activities, but they indicated that they often do not complete the activities that teachers send home. Perhaps the activities suggested by teachers are not consistent with fathers' preferences. The activity these fathers most often shared with their children was watching television; thus, a likely avenue for enhancing father-child interaction may be supporting fathers to be more actively engaged with their children around television shows.

What special considerations need to be taken into account in terms of fathers from minority cultures? There has been a great deal written about the concept of machismo. This concept holds that, in Latino families, there is a traditional gender boundary between the roles of women as nurturers and men as authority figures and breadwinners. This boundary seems to have a diminishing influence given that more females are working and there is greater equality of male and female roles within many Latino families (Ramirez, 1989; Ramirez & Arce, 1981). Carmen Ramirez, a Latino mother of a child with a disability, believes there is an erroneous negative stereotype associated with machismo that anticipates that Latino women are passive. She explains:

> My Mom would always say, "Never let your husband think that you are the key person. Let him know that he's got the forefront, but you're the one that's going to make the difference." That's a culture that I see prevails. . . . I see the character in the Latino woman is to respect other's roles. . . . The Anglo culture misunderstands that and sees the woman as, perhaps, passive when she's not being passive at all. She's just giving him his respect. (Turnbull, 1994, p. 8)

The traditional boundary between women's responsibility for child rearing and homemaking and men's role as breadwinners apparently is prevalent in Middle Eastern cultures. "For example, practices such as Lamaze that engage both men and women in the process of pregnancy and childbirth are not common. Many traditional Middle Eastern men living in the United States may resist in taking part in activities that they regard as belonging to women" (Sharifzadeh, 1992, p. 331).

Because fathers have tended to be the "less apparent parent"(Turbiville, 1994), it may be all the more important for professionals working with them to make an extra effort to take advantage of the seven opportunities for partnerships and infuse into each the eight obligations of a reliable alliance. If a context empowers only one of the parents (or only one of several family members), it will probably fall short of the goal of empowering the entire family unit.

Mothers
Although there is a trend toward more role sharing between fathers and mothers, the fact remains that mothers typically assume the largest part of the responsibility of tending to family needs (Traustadottir, 1991; Wickham-Searl, 1992). Indeed, an in-depth study of 14 mothers shows that mothers who provide care for children with severe disabilities organize their lives around their caring role and provide that care in three ways (Traustadottir, 1991):

1. *Caring for:* taking care of the child—in particular acquiring the specialized knowledge and management procedures that are necessary for the child's development
2. *Caring about:* loving the child as a way of caring
3. *Extended caring:* performing collaborative advocacy roles that address the broader community and societal concerns related to issues of exceptionality

The majority of the mothers were full-time housewives and mothers. The one exception was a mother who combined parenting responsibilities with a professional career in medicine at a large research university. She commented on the pressures that she felt were pushing her to abandon her career and become a full-time caretaker:

> The agency; the care giver; the doctor; the physical, occupational, and speech therapists with whom I came in contact, and with whom I continue to come in contact, assume that I, not my husband, am responsible for this child. But if anything has to be done in order to take care of her, I am the one who is responsible for that. It was assumed by almost everyone that I would give up my career. (Traustadottir, 1991, p. 223)

The mothers also commented on what they perceived to be appropriate father roles: (1) providing financial support, (2) being supportive of the mother's caretaking of the child and family as well as her extended caring role, and (3) discussing with the mother what she learns from investigating services and programs and contributing to joint decision making. Interestingly, in the families where the fathers helped in these roles, the mothers tended to describe the marriage as being good; but when fathers did not support these roles, mothers frequently expressed disappointment and frustration with the extent of fathers' involvement and support. Other research has also documented the importance of fathers' helping with child care; indeed, fathers' greater child-care participation is related to higher marital satisfaction for both parents (Willoughby & Glidden, 1995).

Teenage mothers warrant special considerations. Annually more than 1 million American teenage females become parents. Poverty and fewer educational skills characterize teenage girls who experience pregnancy and who especially need earlier and more comprehensive supports and services for delaying pregnancy and parenting (Children's Defense Fund, 1993). The Black Community Crusade for Children, coordinated by the Children's Defense Fund, reports these data about teenage pregnancy among black teenagers (Black Community Crusade for Children, 1993, p. 113):

- In 1989, Black teens aged 15–19 were more than twice as likely as their White peers to give birth: 115 births per 1000 Black teens, compared with 47 births per 1000 White teens.
- The proportion of births to unmarried teenagers almost tripled between 1969 and 1989. The ratio almost doubled among Blacks and quadrupled among Whites. In 1989 almost two out of three Black infants were born to unmarried mothers.
- Marriage rates among both Blacks and Whites have declined sharply in the past two decades. In 1970 more than one in two young Black women had married; in 1991 fewer than one in five had married.

Teenage mothers are more likely to achieve lower educational levels, have lower-status jobs, and have a greater reliance on public assistance. School-linked comprehensive services can be a responsive support model for teenage mothers (see chapter 13).

In summary, the parental subsystem is complex rather than simple. This is because there are different types of parental units, because each unit is influenced by cultural considerations, and because each member of the parental unit has different needs. As you adopt various strategies to become a reliable ally for each of the people in the parental subsystem, you create an empowering context for the entire family.

Brother and Sister Interactions (The Sibling Subsystem)

The sibling subsystem consists of the interactions between brothers and sisters. Powell and Gallagher (1993) describe siblings as socialization agents who provide the first and perhaps the most intense peer relationships that children experience. By providing a context for social-skills development, these relationships give children the opportunity to experience sharing, companionship, loyalty, rivalry, and other feelings (Powell & Gallagher, 1993).

Although siblings are socialization agents during their younger years, they often are increasingly responsible for providing care and service coordination as their parents age. In fact, research on families whose members with an exceptionality have lived with their parents well into their early and middle

adulthood shows that elderly parents have consistently identified brothers and sisters as the ones whom they expect to take over the parental role once they themselves are no longer able to do so (Seltzer, Krauss, & Janicki, 1994).

Just as a child has multiple impacts on a marriage, so does a brother or sister with an exceptionality have various effects on siblings. Some siblings benefit from the relationship, others experience negative impacts, and others regard it as a neutral experience. Again, because of all the different ways that family life varies, there is no single definitive impact of a family member with an exceptionality on brothers and sisters.

Some studies have found that brothers and sisters have a higher incidence of emotional/behavioral problems (Cornell & Grossberg, 1986; Lavigne & Ryan, 1979; Lobato, Barbour, Hall, & Miller, 1987; McHale & Gamble, 1989; Orsillo, McCaffrey, & Fisher, 1993). Other research has not found significantly greater behavioral problems (Gath & Gumley, 1987; Renzulli & McGreevey, 1986). Indeed, some studies have found these siblings to have fewer behavioral problems than the siblings of children who do not have disabilities (Carr, 1988). In addition, a number of studies have found that brothers and sisters of children with exceptionalities have greater responsibilities for household chores (Stoneman, Brophy, Davis, & Crapps, 1987; Wilson, Blacher, & Baker, 1989); but other research contradicts this finding (Cuskelly & Gunn, 1983; Gath & Gumley, 1987).

Finally, some research indicates that children who have siblings with exceptionalities experience lower self-esteem as compared to children who do not have a sibling with an exceptionality (McHale & Gamble, 1989). Other research, however, indicates no difference in self-esteem or self-concept (an element of "within us" motivation) between children with and without a sibling with an exceptionality (Dyson, Edgar, & Crnic, 1989; Dyson & Fewell, 1989; Lobato et al., 1987). Research also points to a significantly higher level of internal locus of control (perceived control, an element of "within us" motivation) in children who have a sibling with an exceptionality (Burton & Parks, 1994).

Although most research on siblings has focused on the impact of a brother or sister with a disability, sibling effects also occur when one of the children in the family is identified as gifted or talented. Some researchers report that the other siblings feel more jealousy and competition with each other when one is gifted and the other is not or both are gifted

(Grenier, 1985; Pfouts, 1980). Birth order appears to be an important factor given the finding that labeling one child as gifted can create greater sibling problems when the second-born sibling is identified as gifted and fewer problems when the labeled child is first born (Tuttle & Cornell, 1993).

Don Meyer, a national leader in creating support programs for siblings of children with exceptionalities, identifies a number of potential negative sibling impacts (Meyer & Vadasy, 1994). These include overidentification; embarrassment; guilt; isolation, loneliness, and loss; resentment; increased responsibility; and pressure to achieve. On the other hand, Meyer also points out that opportunities and positive contributions can accrue. These include enhanced maturity, self-concept, social competence, insight, tolerance, pride, vocational opportunities, advocacy, and loyalty. A number of these positive contributions are incorporated in the following perspective of a teenager who has an older brother with a developmental disability:

> Because my brother has presented my family so many challenges, we all have had to learn how to seek out help for him and ourselves. I have learned to be an initiator, not a reactor. I have had to be active, not passive; a challenge-seeker, not

fearful. I've seen my family in action and, being part of that action, even though we may not have chosen these challenges, I have learned that I can influence my own destiny. Moreover, I learned the satisfaction of taking charge of my own life. (Turnbull, 1993, pp. 1–2)

"Sibshops" are workshops that provide information and emotional support for brothers and sisters (Meyer & Vadasy, 1994). If your community does not sponsor sibshops, you might collaborate with families, educators, people with disabilities, and other community citizens to start one, using the excellent resource material provided by Don Meyer, sibshops' creator (Meyer & Vadasy, 1994).

Siblings can be valuable collaborators in supporting their brother's or sister's inclusion as well as capitalizing upon the positive contributions of enhanced sensitivity that they have learned from their brother or sister to benefit the inclusion of other students with exceptionalities. Box 6–5 describes the "kid power" potential of sibling collaboration.

Because brothers and sisters of almost any age can play important roles within a family, it behooves professionals to include them in family partnerships. Reflect on the roles that siblings have played in some of the families you have read about, such as Patty and

TOGETHER WE CAN
BOX 6–5

Kid Power

As a fourth grader required to conduct a scientific experiment, the sister of an adolescent brother who has mental retardation and autism taught a lesson to second graders about mental retardation and encouraged those students to have positive attitudes about people with mental retardation (Turnbull & Bronicki, 1986). She collected information from students whom she taught and from students whom she did not teach, in an effort to learn what differences (if any) her instruction made. When her results showed a significant increase in positive attitudes in the class that she taught but no change in her comparison group, she made the

following four conclusions about "kid power" as a collaborative resource:
(a) I'm a kid and I understand the words I used. …Sometimes when adults try to teach kids they use words that are too big, or they use too many words and the kids get all mixed up;
(b) They paid attention because they know me and like me; kids in the second grade respect those in higher grades, they listen to the things they say to them;
(c) I worked hard to present an interesting lesson using a film, book, and discussion;
(d) I was able to tell them about my brother.

Source: Turnbull, A., & Bronicki, G. J. (1986). Changing second graders' attitudes toward people with mental retardation: Using kid power. *Mental Retardation, 24*(1), 44–45.

Jane Smith (chapter 1), Marta Cofresi and her children (chapter 5), and Nila Benito and her sons (this chapter). To be an empowering professional, create a context that can empower all family members.

Extended Family Interactions (The Extended Family Subsystem)

Whom do you consider to be part of your extended family? Think of each person and then add up how many people are in your extended family. Reflect on the role that they have had in your life, beginning when you were a young child until the present time. What factors have either increased or decreased their availability and support?

The answers to these questions may depend upon your particular cultural background. That is because cultures tend to define the composition of extended family and the frequency of contact between the nuclear and extended families. Consider these three examples:

> Elderly persons of Cuban origin are, in comparison with the rest of the Spanish-origin population (and with the total population), more likely to live with their children, probably in a three-generation household. (Perez, 1986, p. 14)

> In many native American Indian families, the child-rearing activities may rest with other family members; in many instances, the grandparents are responsible for the children. Aunts and uncles are also likely to be involved, especially if the family resides on the reservation and not in an urban area. Indian families who live in the city tend to have nuclear households, whereas families on the reservation tend to include extended family members. In fact, in some tribes, the uncles instead of the parents may provide most of the discipline, while grandparents provide most of the spiritual guidance and teaching. (Joe & Malach, 1992, p. 106)

> The concept of "family" in the Anglo-European American United States typically refers to immediate family members such as the mother, father, and children. Other extended family members may or may not live close by, and may or may not participate actively in the "nuclear family." Other members are usually termed "relatives" as opposed to "family." (Hanson, 1992, p. 74)

From the outset, then, ask the parents to define which family members they want to involve with you and other professionals. Only after they identify these extended family members should you try to identify

culturally sensitive ways for creating a reliable alliance. Who are the members of the Benito extended family? To determine who they are and how they participate in the lives of young Vincent and Joe, you first have to ask one or both of their parents.

There is little research about disability issues and extended family members. Vadasy and Fewell (1986) found that mothers of children with visual and auditory sensory losses ranked grandmothers high on the family's support list. More recently, a survey of mothers and fathers of infants and young children in early childhood special education programs reported that the most frequent family supports offered by grandparents include baby-sitting and financial assistance, particularly buying clothes at birthday or other holiday times. When investigating the relationship between paternal and maternal adjustment and grandparent support, results showed that fathers, when compared to mothers, appeared to have higher levels of adjustment when grandparents offered greater levels of support (Sandler, Warren, & Raver, 1995).

Grandparents of children with exceptionalities need information to help them deal with their own feelings and to know how to support the rest of the family (George, 1988; Meyer & Vadasy, 1986; Urwin, 1988). Grandparents' or family members' ideas about people with disabilities may have been formed when they were growing up and may be more traditional than parental views (Meyer & Vadasy, 1986). For example, a Latino mother of a young child with a disability described how her own mother agreed to make a *mandos* (bargain) related to her grandchild with a disability. She made a promise to the Virgin of Guadalupe that she would visit the basilica and wear the colors of the Virgin every day if the Virgin would heal her grandchild. Although the mother did not have this belief in spiritual healing, the child's grandmother clearly did.

Some families have reported that members of the extended family are extremely supportive, understanding, and helpful with a wide range of everyday tasks (Able-Boone, Sandall, Stevens, & Frederick, 1992). This is true for the Benito family: grandmother Nila and aunt Nancy provide emotional support—a sort of "cheerleader and sounding board" contribution all in one. Not all families are as fortunate as the Benitos. In describing their experiences with their child's traumatic brain injury, a parent commented:

> You have your extended family who is there grieving also, and sometimes I think you want to say, "What are you feeling sorry for yourself about?

I'm the one in this situation." You have to deal with their grief when you aren't even through dealing with your own grief, so sometimes it's even more—it's harder to have them around depending on the relationship. (Singer & Nixon, 1996, p. 27)

Literature on African-American families points to the critical role that grandparents play in providing support to teenage mothers and their children. In one study, the average age of the grandmothers was in their early 40s. Although these grandmothers provided extensive support to their teenage daughters and grandchildren, they reported a high level of stress because they were also trying to deal with the roles and responsibilities of middle age and many had young children of their own (Brookes-Gunn & Chase-Lansdale, 1991). These researchers concluded that service programs need to target grandmother supports as a much higher priority. An estimated one-half million grandparents are the primary caregivers for their grandchildren, with African-American grandparents represented nearly twice as often as Euro-Americans (Turner, 1995).

Although there is a strong reliance on extended family support in some minority cultures, do not overgeneralize and assume that every minority family has extended family available to support its needs. For example, despite what some literature reports about the strength of extended family support for Latino families (Vega, 1990), some Latino families report just the opposite situation.

I've got brothers and a half-sister. If I go ask for help, they'll say why do you need help? You've got

money, you go hire somebody or go get somebody or a specialist or whatever. Why do you come to me? What can I help you with? . . . That's the way they are. That's the way I feel with my family. If I had a choice between a brother and a pastor or a president or anything, a stranger, I think I would prefer to go to a stranger than my brother. (Blue-Banning, 1995, p. 11)

Few programs have been developed to support extended family members. Research on a support-group program for grandparents (Vadasy, Fewell, & Meyer, 1986) found that about half the grandparents surveyed had never visited a medical professional (52 percent) or an educational professional (48 percent) regarding their grandchild's exceptionality or specific needs. Fifty-seven percent reported they had doubts that they were doing the right things for their grandchild. Sixty-seven percent understood some of their grandchild's needs, but they wanted many questions answered.

Many extended family members can provide support for the child and the family when some of their needs for knowledge, experience, and skills have been met (Burton, 1988; Gervasio, 1993). Box 6–6 includes some suggestions about how to give extended family members the information and skills that can enable them to support the child and family. Remember, a family's empowerment includes the acquisition of knowledge/skills. So the more you add to members' storehouse of knowledge/skills, the more you augment their empowerment and demonstrate that you are a reliable ally, a person committed to creating an empowering context.

TIPS   BOX 6–6

Enhancing Extended Family Interactions

- Provide parents with information to help them better understand the needs and reactions of extended family members.
- Provide information about exceptionality, the needs of children, and the needs of families that parents can give to extended family members.
- Encourage the development of grandparent or extended-family-member support groups. Those

groups might be facilitated by school social workers, psychologists, PTA volunteers who are grandparents, or extended family members of students with an exceptionality.
- Encourage extended family participation in IEP conferences, classroom visits, school events, and family support programs.
- Provide library materials and resources for extended family members.

Cohesion and Adaptability

We have just described the subsystems—the people who interact in the family. Now it is time to consider *how* they interact—that is, the quality of their relationships. We will start by explaining two elements of interaction—cohesion and adaptability. The degrees of cohesion and adaptability in a family describe the ways that subsystems interact and the nature of boundaries among family subsystems and among family members and nonmembers (Olson, Russell, & Sprenkle, 1980). After describing these two elements, we will discuss the implications for your partnerships with families.

We want to issue a significant caution from the outset. The rules governing family interaction are rooted in one's culture (for example, individualism or collectivism), as you have already learned in chapter 5. There is likely to be tremendous variation in what the families of your students consider appropriate in terms of cohesion and adaptability and what works for them.

Moreover, theory and research about family systems has been conducted mostly by Euro-American researchers with Euro-American research participants (Scott-Jones, 1993). Unfortunately, some professionals fall into the trap of thinking that the level of cohesion and adaptability that is generally appropriate for and acceptable to Euro-American families is the level to which all families should adhere. Cohesion and adaptability can be interpreted only in light of the families' cultures and the other characteristics that you learned about in chapter 5. Indeed, an empowering context is one that honors a family's culture.

Cohesion

You have already learned that one of the basic tenets of family systems theory is that certain boundaries serve as lines of demarcation between people who are inside and outside a subsystem. Often these boundaries are defined by the roles that the subsystem's members play (Minuchin, 1974). For example, the two adult members in a traditional nuclear family may interact with each other in the roles of husband and wife and with their children as father and mother. Boundaries may be open or closed—that is, they may or may not be accessible to interaction with people outside the subsystem. From a Euro-American perspective, subsystems are typically open enough to allow individual autonomy and closed enough to provide support for each family member (Summers, 1987).

These boundaries also help define families' bonding relationships. Thus, family members typically feel closer to each other than to those outside the family or its subsystem relationships (Kantor & Lehr, 1975). This element of family bonding relates to cohesion (Olson, Sprenkle, & Russell, 1979).

Family cohesion refers to family members' close emotional bonding with each other as well as the level of independence they feel within the family system (Olson et al., 1980). Cohesion exists across a continuum, with high disengagement on one end and high enmeshment on the other. One author uses the physical metaphor of "the touching of hands" to describe cohesion in the family:

> The dilemma is how to be close yet separate. When the fingers are intertwined, it at first feels secure and warm. Yet when one partner (or family member) tries to move, it is difficult at best. The squeezing pressure may even be painful. . . . The paradox of every relationship is how to touch and yet not hold on. (Carnes, 1981, pp. 70–71)

Some families may perceive themselves or be perceived by others as not touching enough or as being highly intertwined. Most families, however, operate in the wide swath in the center of the cohesion continuum.

Range of Cohesion When families are highly cohesive, the boundaries among their subsystems are blurred or weak (Minuchin, 1974). Take, for example, a family in which a mother with many physical-care demands for a child who is deaf and blind delegates many of the responsibilities to an older daughter. The daughter may have fewer parent-child and other-sibling interactions because she has been drawn into the parental subsystem; her own needs as a child and a sibling may be overlooked or subordinated.

Siblings frequently do assume additional caretaking roles in families (Stoneman et al., 1987; Wilson et al., 1989). Often this fact is interpreted as problematic for the siblings. Although Euro-American families do distinguish more clearly between parental and sibling roles, that is not necessarily so for families from Asian cultures:

> As the child matures and acquires younger siblings, he or she must further assume selected childrearing responsibilities that augment those of his parents. Older siblings are routinely delegated the responsibility of caring for younger siblings and thus expected to model adult-like behaviors, thereby setting good examples. The eldest son, in particular, is entrusted with the greatest responsi-

bility as the leader among his siblings who must provide them with guidance and support. Like the parent, the older sibling is also periodically expected to sacrifice personal needs in favor of the younger sibling. (Chan, 1992, p. 218)

Your challenge is to interpret the appropriate extent of cohesion and protectiveness according to families' cultural beliefs. What may appear to be overprotection in one culture may be appropriate protection, nurturance, and affection in another. For example, Latino families may find it acceptable for preteens or even adolescents to sit on their mother's lap or for preschoolers to drink from a baby bottle long after Euro-American parents would consider those actions inappropriate (Zuniga, 1992). When you honor families' cultures, you infuse into your partnerships with them a necessary component of the reliable alliances. You thereby create an empowering context.

What happens when families have low degrees of cohesion, even to the point that children with an exceptionality are isolated from the emotional support and friendship of other family members? Limited interaction leaves children without the support, closeness, and assistance needed to develop independence. Disengaged family interactions often are characterized by underinvolvement, few shared interests or friends, excessive privacy, and a great deal of time apart. Few decisions require family input and involvement. For all family members, particularly the member with an exceptionality, such a family situation can be both lonely and difficult.

Disengaged relationships can take place within and between subsystems. For example, disengagement within a subsystem exists when a father denies the fact of the child's exceptionality and withdraws both from parental and marital interactions. Disengagement between subsystems may be found when the members of the extended family subsystem are unable to accept the child, leading to the sharing of increasingly fewer family celebrations.

Again, it is important to view cohesion and relationships within a cultural frame. For example, research shows that children of the Ojibwa tribe who have partially acculturated families are more passive and less responsive than children in either highly traditional or more acculturated families (Boggs, 1965):

The parents of somewhat acculturated children interacted less in the home and appeared less involved with the children. This may be an early symptom of an important component of acculturative stress: Intergenerational conflict. Young people acculturate more rapidly as they attend school and have greater contact with the majority culture. Because of their age, young people may be more open to change than are their parents. Parents feel abandoned and denied in response to their children's greater acculturation. (Yates, 1987, pp. 319–320)

Obviously, you will want to understand the reasons for certain relationships as you work at creating an empowering context, one that is comfortable and personalized for each family because it respects the family's cultural traditions.

An extreme example of a disengaged relationship occurs when adolescents have separated from their parents by leaving home early and living in shelters. More than half of young homeless youths have been identified as having an emotional or behavior disorder, including conduct disorders and depression (Feitel, Margetson, Chamas, & Lipman, 1992). An Australian study indicated that the youths reported that their family life lacked sufficient opportunities for autonomy as well as sufficient care and support. The reaction of the youths was to rebel against the autonomy limitations by leaving the family and thereby separating from family relationships (Schweitzer, Hier, & Terry, 1994). (This information was gathered from the adolescents alone. If information had been gathered from their parents, siblings, or extended family, it may have offered different views on the family interactions. It is difficult to get a clear understanding of family dynamics by getting the viewpoints of only one member.)

The point is that, when family situations may be at an extreme level of cohesion or disengagement, some family members may make an effort to counteract or counterbalance the one extreme by taking an extreme action toward the opposite direction.

Implications of Cohesion   There are two reasons for understanding cohesion in families. First, by recognizing the levels of cohesion both among and within subsystems, you can create a context that supports the family as a whole to meet its needs as well as the child's—that is, to get what it wants (be empowerful).

In the Benito family, for example, there is a great deal of cohesion both among and within subsystems. As Nila herself has noted, the members play different roles, but they play as members of the same team— the Benito family team. Nonetheless, the team's boundaries are quite open to outsiders (people not related by blood or marriage) such as Nila's colleagues at the University of South Florida's Florida Mental Health Institute and the local Head Start program. Indeed, staff at the institute and the Head Start program are collaborators with the family and serve an empowering role for the Benitos as they seek an inclusive education for the two youngsters. The staff creates a context for motivation and knowledge/skills, thus complementing the family's individual and collective empowerment.

Second, by considering the degree of cohesion that exists in a family, you can determine what services and supports may be appropriate, and you can provide or refer the family to those services. For example, you will know to ask whether a particular program encourages a culturally appropriate level of cohesion. Or you will be competent to make appropriate early education recommendations. Mothers involved in early childhood programs are sometimes unintentionally reinforced for establishing highly cohesive relationships with their young children. That is, they are encouraged to spend a lot of time in the classroom, attend mothers' groups, provide home teaching, and transport children to numerous services. When they spend all this time with the child, what happens to their own needs and the needs of other family members? Obviously, you will want to be sensitive to the implications of your professional recommendations on a family's cohesion and disengagement. Knowing a family—the second of the eight obligations of a reliable alliance—is indispensable to creating an empowering context.

*A*daptability

Family adaptability refers to the family's ability to change in response to situational and developmental stress (Olson et al., 1980). In other words, adaptability refers to the family's ability to plan and work out differences when change and stress occur. As with a family's cohesion, its adaptability is influenced by family values and cultural background and can also be viewed on a continuum: At one end are families who are unable or unwilling to change in response to situational or developmental stress; at the other end are families who are constantly changing, so much so that they create significant confusion in the family (Olson et al., 1979). Again, most families fall in the wide swath of balance in the center.

Ranges of Adaptability   At one end of the adaptability continuum, families demonstrate a high degree of control and structure, and their interactions often are governed by many strictly enforced rules. The power hierarchy and roles in these families are firmly delineated, and negotiations are seldom tolerated. Consider the example of a son who sustains a brain injury and accompanying physical disability. The injury requires the family to deal immediately with crisis intervention in the trauma setting (Cope & Wolfson, 1994) and later with many new demanding physical, daily care, economic, and emotional needs in providing both acute and long-term care (Kreutzer, Serio, & Bergquist, 1994; Singer, Glang, & Williams, 1996). If, in the past, meeting child needs was primarily the mother's role, the added demands will likely be more than she is accustomed to or perhaps can handle. If the family has difficulty sharing new responsibilities and roles with the mother and bringing in collaborators from outside the family, the added demands probably will create stress and difficulty for her and all other family members.

In addition to the general reason of knowing families (one of the eight obligations), there are two specific reasons why you need to take into account high degrees of control in the family power hierarchy as you propose educational programs. First, many families adapt their power hierarchies over time to support the child or adolescent in his or her evolving self-determination. As we have noted earlier, self-determination is culturally rooted, with some families placing great value on the increased autonomy of children and youth and other families considering this culturally inappropriate (Turnbull & Turnbull, 1996). As you collaborate with families, you need to be sensitive in negotiating the degree of student decision making that the family considers to be appropriate. Additionally, many family members and professionals, including those in the majority culture, typically keep students with an exceptionality low on the power hierarchy, even into adulthood, treating them like children long after they have ceased to be children. Those families and professionals should consider the full range of options for self-determination before concluding that self-determination is inappropriate.

Second, it is helpful to identify the person or persons (for example, parent, parents, grandmother, or uncle) who have primary control over family decisions and rules. For example, if a teacher asks a mother to implement a home-based language program but does not take into account that the husband has the decision-making power in the family and rejects the program, it is unlikely that the program will be effective. Indeed, if the mother carries out the intervention against her husband's wishes, the program may create marital and parental conflict. As we suggested earlier, you should examine the impact of recommendations for home teaching on every family member, seeking to understand the family's values and goals and working with the family to develop support options that will be consistent with its values and goals and its ability and willingness to adapt.

In contrast, other families demonstrate a low degree of control and structure. Their interactions often are characterized by few rules, and even these are seldom enforced and often changing. Promises and commitments are often unkept, and family members learn that they cannot depend upon one another. Frequently, there is no family leader, negotiations are endless, and roles are unsure and often changing.

All families can experience periods of chaos during stressful life events. But when chaos is a consistent way of life, the consequences can be negative for the family and the student with an exceptionality.

Consider the example of a mother with a son who has attention deficit/hyperactivity disorder (AD/HD). The child has difficulty academically and socially. The mother has a live-in boyfriend who is the family's primary source of financial support. During the last two years, the boyfriend has begun to drink heavily and abuse family members. When the boyfriend begins to fight, existing rules are suddenly harshly interpreted for the child. When the fighting escalates, the rules change; survival is the main concern. Later the remorseful boyfriend becomes extremely indulgent, creating a third set of rules. The instability and chaos continue. Because of his disability, the youngster already experiences difficulty interpreting social cues accurately, and his ever-revolving family life-style only exacerbates his problems.

Implications of Adaptability   Well-functioning families are typically characterized by a balance between the extremes of high or low adaptability (Olson et al., 1980). To support those families who are dissatisfied with their current level of adaptability, you can take three actions that are generally helpful.

First, support families to plan for change. If possible, discuss schedule changes and transitions well in advance of the time they will occur. Ask yourself, "Is this change too sudden or radical for this family's current level of adaptability?" If so, some students and families may benefit from gradual transitions. When a student will be changing classrooms or school buildings, it may be helpful to start with a gradual transition, one day a week, before making the complete transition. If a child needs to learn how to ride the bus and the family is hesitant to make this change, intermediate steps may be reassuring: riding only part of the way, riding with a friend or family member, or bringing the bus driver into the planning team.

Second, encourage families to examine alternatives. Many families who lack adaptability also may not know how to examine alternatives (Shank & Turnbull, 1993). They might benefit from learning a problem-solving process such as the one we described in chapter 4. For example, a single mother might be experiencing a very frustrating morning routine with her four-year-old daughter who has an emotional disorder. The young girl often refuses to dress or be dressed. After generating several alternatives, the mother and teacher agree to send the child to preschool in the morning in her pajamas. This decision improves interactions between mother and child, and after a period of time the dressing-routine procedures the child learns at preschool are put into practice at home.

Remember the role that the staff of the Florida Mental Health Institute and Head Start played in the Benito family's life? It was to support the family to change—to move from education that was essentially segregated and inappropriate to one that is inclusive and appropriate. And it was to support the family to move in that direction by helping them examine alternatives to the unacceptable programs and then advocating for their admission to the more appropriate program. In short, the professional staff offered motivation and skills to the family, participating in the "it's within us" element of empowerment. Then the staff created a context of emotional support, information provision, and advocacy, proving that "it's within our context to be empowering."

Third, if a family may be interested in receiving services from the school counselor, school social worker, or other community professionals who specialize in family counseling or therapy, collaborate with the school counselor or social worker on how to approach the family and suggest these alternatives. By contrast, if a family itself asks you about possible resources, respond by referring members to those resources. Remember, however, that family dynamics are complicated and often require specialization in providing the most appropriate and personalized supports. Knowing when to refer a family to professionals with more family specialization is a critical competency for all professionals in special education.

Summary

The best way of understanding family interactions is to view the family as a system. There are three major assumptions in family systems theory. First, in a family, as in most systems, there are inputs; the family responds to and interacts with the inputs and as a result creates certain outputs in carrying out its family functions.

Second, the family—the system—must be understood as a whole entity; it cannot be understood by examining only its component parts, by understanding only one or more of its members. Simply understanding the child with an exceptionality or the mother does not mean that you will understand the family; indeed, you probably won't. The family consists of subsystems (marital, parental, sibling, and extended); and the child with an exceptionality can have negative, positive, and mixed impacts on each of these subsystems.

Third, family subsystems are separated by boundaries that define the interaction that family members have with each other and with people outside the family. The family's cultural heritage and other characteristics (see chapter 5) affect the family members' interactions and the nature of boundaries.

Finally, two elements of family interaction are cohesion and adaptability. The term *family cohesion* refers to the emotional attachment that family members have toward each other and the level of independence each feels within the family. Some families are extraordinarily cohesive: Their members are enmeshed with each other. Other families are quite the opposite: Their members are disengaged from each other. Although some families are characterized by excessive degrees of closeness or disengagement, most have found—sometimes with the support of professionals such as yourself—a balance between these two extremes.

Similarly, some families are extraordinarily *adaptable*; they seem to have an unlimited ability to change in response to situational and developmental stress. Others, of course, are quite unadaptable; the least amount of stress is unsettling and disruptive. Again, most families strike a happy medium between these two extremes.

As Vincent and Joseph Benito enter elementary school, their family has established its pattern of interactions. Their mother Nila is the planner and organizer; their father Joe is the "deal closer" and final negotiator; their grandmother Nila and great-grandmother Francesca are the cheerleaders; and their aunt Nancy is a listening ear and reliable source of emotional support for their mother Nila. Indeed, the Head Start staff who have been so accommodating to the boys and the University of South Florida family-support staffers who have inspired and guided the Benito family on its way toward great expectations for inclusion have learned three important lessons: The Benito family is influenced by its cultural heritage (it is a large, multigenerational Italian-American family); it is highly (but not problematically) cohesive; and it is adaptable to the challenges that Vincent and Joseph pose because of their autism.

Whatever the Benito family was before it encountered the Head Start and the University of South Florida staff, it now is a family that wants to collaborate with the professionals in Vincent's and Joseph's present and new schools. Indeed, as Nila has said repeatedly, without collaboration within the family and outside it with professionals, Vincent and Joseph would have little, if any, chance of being included in any aspects of general education.

Chapter Seven

Family Functions

*R*ickey Battles makes a big difference to his family—indeed, to his whole community. That's true because, not in spite, of his disabilities. At age 13 1/2, Rickey has scoliosis and wears a brace on his back and one foot; is incontinent because of bladder and colitis problems; has mental retardation, low muscle tone, and epilepsy; and is excitable and sometimes too loud in public.

In Poultney, Vermont, where he, his father Richard, his mother Betty, and his younger brother Michael live and where Richard and Betty run a medium-sized grocery store that Richard's family established a generation ago, Rickey is fully included in his elementary school. He receives a great deal of support from special educators and various therapists, and is the "hit" of a local pet shop where he is volunteering as part of his school/community access program.

Richard and Betty acknowledge that Rickey has brought the family closer together—in a family that was already very affectionate with each other. They know, too, that Rickey has influenced how his schoolmates regard people with disabilities—more welcomingly. And they delight in the fact that Rickey has made fast friends with the workers at the pet shop; his ability to tell traditional New England tall tales endears him to the owners and workers.

Yet Rickey's contributions to the family are accompanied by responsibilities they don't have for his younger brother Michael. Richard and Betty have to be "kind of careful" about what they do with Rickey, always "figuring out and working around things" so Rickey and the family can go to parties. "Rickey's very immature for his

age, and some of the questions he might ask, some of the things he might say, may not be appropriate at the time. So you really have to explain to people what's going on and why, and usually they accept it. You can never tell. You really have to be on your guard every day; you really have to know your child and what's appropriate for him."

And, yes, Rickey's disabilities require his parents to take time off from work to attend to all of Rickey's hygienic and medical needs. But over time Richard and Betty have gotten over their disappointment that Rickey was born with disabilities. Now "we really don't look at it as life with disability. We just look on it as another day with Rickey, as something we deal with. It's normal for us to deal with his disability, we guess."

Rickey's younger brother Michael "wishes that Rickey were more normal so that he could play with him more. Fortunately, we've brought Michael up so he's accepted Rickey very, very well. He knows his limits, he gets a kick out of fooling with him, and he's accepted him very well." So have Rickey's schoolmates, although their teachers have told them that Rickey has special needs and that their role is to pitch in when needed.

The socialization of Rickey's peers has been a joint endeavor between the Battles family and the Poultney educators. There's also the regular weekly meeting involving Rickey's team: his mother Betty, his classroom teacher, the school nurse, and any other educators who want to attend.

There are only two ground rules for the meetings. First, "if they have any concerns or needs, it's all right at the table; and there is a person there who will meet those needs. If not, they'll have to deal with us."

Second, "we don't allow negativism, none at all. We present Rickey in a positive way. If one of us has a problem, we have to state it in a positive way. The rest of us have to ask how we can help meet Rickey's needs."

The bottom line on Rickey? Richard and Betty sum it up as very positive: the affection and closeness that he brings to the family, their sense of self and self-identity, and their and the community's education. Financially, he is a low-cost youngster, in large part because of a nearby

Shriners' Hospital and insurance coverage. Daily care? Well, that's problematic—the constant on-guard attitude and the physical demands he places on them cannot be denied.

But those responsibilities don't weigh heavily on Richard and Betty. "Rickey's participation with the community, his schoolmates, and the teachers gives meaning to his life. He gives something to other people and his giving also gives meaning to our lives. Through Rickey, we give a different perspective, a different tolerance, a different acceptance of other people."

Families exist to meet the individual and collective needs of their members (Caplan, 1976; Leslie, 1979). The tasks that families perform to meet these needs are referred to as *family functions*. There are seven categories of family functions: (1) affection, (2) self-definition, (3) economics, (4) daily care, (5) socialization, (6) recreation, and (7) educational/vocational issues (Turnbull, Summers, & Brotherson, 1984).

The family systems framework calls these *the family's outputs* (see figure 7–1).

We will briefly review each of the seven family functions and discuss some of the their common themes and implications. For each function, a family generally tries to engage in activities that reasonably satisfy its members' needs and show the younger members how to meet the needs and perform the

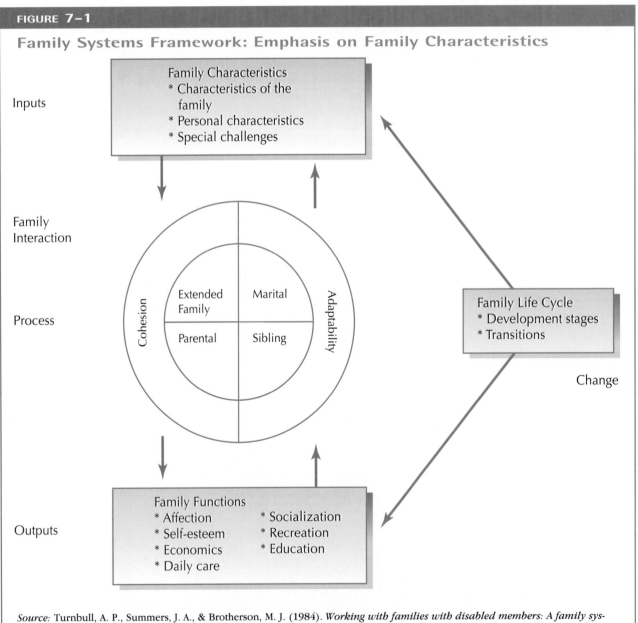

FIGURE 7–1

Family Systems Framework: Emphasis on Family Characteristics

Source: Turnbull, A. P., Summers, J. A., & Brotherson, M. J. (1984). *Working with families with disabled members: A family systems approach* (p. 60). Lawrence: University of Kansas, Kansas Affiliated Facility. Adapted by permission.

functions so that these responsibilities can be transferred from the older to the younger generation (Brotherson, Backus, Summers, & Turnbull, 1986).

As you will learn in chapter 8, family activities and individual family member contributions are strongly influenced by the family's life cycle stage. Additionally, the family's characteristics (chapter 5) and the family's interaction (chapter 6) influence how functions are addressed within the family. Because the family is an interacting system, it is impossible to consider family functions (outputs) without taking the other portions of the family systems framework into account. Likewise, it will be futile to create an empowering context without knowing a family, the way it satisfies these seven functions, and the impact that its cultural traditions have on its functions.

The Impact of Exceptionality on Family Functions

Each category of family functions is distinct; in many ways, however, these functions are interrelated so that problems or benefits in one dimension of family functioning can, and usually do, impact other functions. For example, economic difficulties can have negative impact on family members' social or recreational activities. Likewise, stress or depression related to financial worries can have a negative impact on family affection. On the other hand, a child's positive contributions to household chores (that is, daily care) can enhance self-definition, affection, and recreational outcomes. A benefit or problem related to one family function can have ripple effects on other functions.

Each of the family functions is affected by every family member, including the presence of a family member with an exceptionality. This influence may be positive, negative, or neutral (Barnett & Boyce, 1995; Blacher, 1994; Krauss, 1993; O'Connor, 1995; Summers, Behr, & Turnbull, 1989). In the Battles family, and indeed throughout their community, Rickey's influence is positive. Yes, he needs accommodations in certain of the family's functions, but his needs and the way the family functions to meet them are not especially challenging.

As you read this chapter, consider these two questions: What are the family's and your appropriate priorities for achieving family balance in carrying out family functions, and what cultural traditions and values influence these priorities? Unless you answer these questions as you collaborate with families, you will have a hard time creating an empowering context.

Affection Needs

It is not surprising that studies of successful families have consistently reported that these families emphasize the role of sharing affection (Mellman, Lazarus, & Rivlin, 1990; Summers, 1987a, 1987b). There are many different ways to characterize the dimensions of affection, but especially important are (1) exchanging verbal and physical affection and (2) exchanging unconditional love (Summers, 1987a, 1987b).

Exchanging Verbal and Physical Affection
Much has been written on attachment, particularly between mother and child (Ainsworth, Bell, & Stayton, 1974). From a family systems perspective, attachment between and among all family members is a priority and consists of encouraging those reciprocal interactions between parents and children that deepen their emotional commitments to each other. "Human development occurs in the context of an escalating psychological ping-pong game between two people who are crazy about each other" (Bronfenbrenner, 1990, p. 31).

Cultural influences strongly determine how families deepen their emotional commitments and display affection. For example, Asian families often provide very close physical contact with infants, carrying them even during naps and having infants and toddlers sleep in the same room or bed with their parents and other siblings until they are school age or older (Chan, 1992). Middle Eastern families also are characterized as very affectionate: "Middle Eastern mothers are . . . much more permissive than their Western counterparts in allowing their babies and children to be kissed, held, or hugged" (Sharifzadeh, 1992, pp. 332–333).

A major but natural issue for families is their child's evolution from expressing physical affection within the family to expressing physical affection and sexuality with one or more chosen partners (see chapter 8). Read box 7–1 and consider this issue from the perspective of a 38-year-old woman with a severe learning disability. Especially note how one of the family's cultural heritages—its religion—influences the issue.

Exchanging Unconditional Love
All children have basic needs for acceptance, appreciation, and love. Exchanging unconditional love is an

The Boyfriend Dilemma

I lived at home with my parents until three years ago when I had a chance to move here and work for my cousin. I think Mom and Dad thought I'd always live with them. Sometimes I miss them a lot. I miss their hugs and their encouragement, but I do like being on my own—feeling like a real adult. I have an apartment and a job, but what I'd really like is a husband and a family. I'm Catholic, so having children would mean a lot to me. When I'm feeling lonely I really wish that I was in love. I get depressed sometimes, because I don't think that will ever happen. I'm getting pretty old, and I hardly even know how to meet men or how to act around them. I get really nervous. I've been on about three dates in my entire life. Mom wouldn't let me go out when I was in school. She was afraid that boys would take advantage of me, because I seemed young for my age. When I got out of school, I just didn't meet guys very often. I know that sometimes when I am around guys I act too interested and sometimes I act too shy. They frighten me a lot. I wish I could take a class somewhere on how to find a boyfriend.

---

essential ingredient of family affection, as Harriet Rousso (1984), a social worker with a physical disability, notes:

> In particular, disabled children need to have their bodies, disability and all, accepted, appreciated, and loved. Especially by significant parenting figures. This will solidify the sense of intactness.
>
> For all children, disabled or not, the "gleam in the mother's eye" in response to all aspects of the child's body and self is essential for the development of healthy self-esteem. This includes the parent's ability to show pride and pleasure in the disabled part of the body, as one valid aspect of the child, and to communicate appreciation and respect for the child's unique, often different-looking ways of doing things. . . . Parents too often communicate to their child, directly and indirectly, that the disability should be hidden or altered, if not purged—the child should strive toward appearing as "normal" and nondisabled as possible. This attitude can put the child into an identity crisis, causing him or her to push that feeling of intactness way underground. (Rousso, 1984, pp. 12–13)

Especially related to disability issues, families and professionals alike may need to examine their own values. How much do they, and you, tend to expect a child's achievement, normalcy, success, attractiveness, or progress to be prerequisites for their and your unconditional acceptance, appreciation, or love? Within a family, unconditional love for all family members, whatever their respective characteristics, cannot be taken for granted (Turnbull, 1988a, 1988b). In terms of positive contributions, a number of families have described their child as a major catalyst for enhancing family love.

> Anyone who feels that someone else is a burden has not yet learned to love. Love feels someone else's need above their own. My son, Matthew, was not useless. . . . If he served no other purpose than to give me love, then he served that one and if he served no other purpose than to teach me love, he served that one. (Turnbull & Turnbull, 1986, p. 112)

Need we emphasize that no family role is any more important than the expression of affection? Box 7–2 lists other tips for addressing families' affection needs. The more you express unconditional love for the child, the more likely you are to encourage affection within the family.

Self-Esteem Needs

Families help their members establish who they are and their worth as people, and one member's exceptionality can have an impact on the self-esteem of all. (Self-esteem is closely related to self-efficacy. Remember that self-efficacy is one of the elements of motivation, and motivation is one of the family factor components of empowerment.) For example, new parents may have anticipated raising children with typical abilities. When they are confronted with raising a child who is gifted, they may feel uncertain and even threatened (Dettman & Colangelo, 1980).

Addressing Families' Affection Needs

- Recognize the needs that all family members have for affection. For example, if a parent-child home teaching program each night interferes with a busy family's only opportunities to catch up on the day's events, play games, or snuggle on the couch together, reconsider the plan to achieve a balance in meeting all family needs, not just educational needs.
- Provide materials in a resource library and arrange discussion groups involving resource persons who can help parents and students with an exceptionality gain a better understanding of sexuality and affection. Young adults or adolescents, depending on age, type, and severity of exceptionality, benefit from accurate and sensitive information about sexuality and affection.
- Help parents identify their child's positive contributions to affection as well as other family functions. Encourage family members to discuss what positive contributions each makes. For example, at dinner encourage family members to share at least two things they appreciate about each of the other members. They can also highlight the similarities and differences in each person's list.

Parents of children with disabilities may have self-esteem challenges if they believe their own genetic makeup or their personal misconduct caused the disability. Likewise, their self-esteem may be affected when their infants do not respond readily to soothing or stimulation or when they deal with existential issues of why the child has a disability. Leah Ziskin (1985), mother of a daughter with a severe disability, has commented on the impact that her daughter's birth had on her own self-esteem:

> I remember feeling that I had become a completely different person, I felt that my ego had been wiped out. My superego with all of its guilts had become the most prominent part of my personality, and I had completely lost my self-esteem. Any credits of self-worth that I could give myself from any of my personal endeavors meant nothing. Graduating from college and a first-rate medical school, surviving an internship, practicing medicine, and having two beautiful sons and a good marriage counted for nil. All I knew at this point was that I was the mother of an abnormal and most likely retarded child. (Ziskin, 1985, p. 68)

A different kind of self-esteem challenge occurs for families who have frequently faced multiple challenges and have experienced low levels of self-esteem for almost their entire lives. Many women who experience poverty, especially single mothers, are highly vulnerable to demoralization, depression, and helplessness (Belle, 1990; Knitzer, in press; Parker, Piotrkowsky, Horn, & Greene, in press). Self-esteem is a challenge across the life span in addressing many challenges and is not reserved for exceptionality considerations alone. Nonetheless, some professionals who have reliable alliances with mothers who experience multiple challenges recognize the mothers' strengths. Building on strengths is a way to create an empowering context, and one strength is the mother's persistence.

> In reality, the workers routinely recognized strengths in even the most troubled of the families served. The workers were genuinely respectful and impressed by these families' abilities to endure in the face of events which the workers did not believe they, themselves, could survive. "I see them as survivors. They go through hell and back. They can do things that I couldn't stand. They are strong. If we were suddenly thrown into their situations—well, I would probably die. They don't see that, they don't see it as a strength." In addition to their tenacity, an important strength shared by most of these families was their commitment and sense of identity with their children. For many, their ability to have children was their only source of positive self-esteem. (Summers, McMann, Kitchen, & Peck, 1995, p. 15)

Not surprisingly, a family's self-esteem can depend on whether its members see the connections between their actions and good things that happen as a result of those actions. Note, for example, how a professional treats one of the mothers of the "survivor" group who had not regarded herself as being strong:

> One example of the success is (a mother) who sees something happening. Not only is she getting good things in response to efforts, she is learning not to be helpless. That is helping you get rid of some of that learned helplessness. She hasn't had a lot of things handed to her. So I talk to her. I ask her what was that a result of, can she see that was connected to her efforts? (Summers et al., 1995, p. 20)

Self-esteem is an important issue for not only parents but also young children with exceptionalities. How they come to view themselves—their own healthy development of self-esteem—is influenced by families, educators, peers, and others. A key is ensuring that the exceptionality does not overshadow countless other individual traits, interests, and attributes (Turnbull & Turnbull, 1986). Just consider how Norman Kunc, a family therapist and a person with cerebral palsy, describes how people often see him and how he regards himself (see box 7–3).

One way that the Battles family and their professional collaborators ensure that the shadow of Rickey's exceptionality does not overshadow his other attributes and his life is to focus on his strengths.

Very little research has been done on the self-esteem of children and youth with exceptionalities and the contributions that families make in enhancing their self-esteem (Smith-Horn & Singer, 1996). A number of studies of students with learning disabilities have focused on self-concept, but these studies do not address family factors. Nonetheless, the research is notable. A careful review of 20 studies indicates that, by third grade, students with learning disabilities typically have substantially lower academic self-concepts (Chapman, 1988). They tend to attribute their failures to their own abilities and their successes to factors such as others' help or good luck. Aside from the particular focus on academics, students with learning disabilities had lower—but not significantly lower—general self-concepts than their classmates without exceptionalities.

You might ask, has a program been developed to prepare parents of children with disabilities with the knowledge and skill to enhance their children's self-esteem? Yes. One program for parents of children with physical disabilities and mild cognitive impairments includes six weekly lessons in which parents meet as a group and, through presentations, discussions, and individual and group activities, learn how to help their children develop independence, participate in leisure activities, interact with peers, be

MY VOICE
BOX 7–3

Shadows or Sun on the Sundial

When people first meet me, they tend to see me as 9/10 disability, 1/10 person. What they see as paramount are the things that mark me as "different"—the way I walk, speak, and move. The disability expands in their eyes, throwing a shadow over me and my life in the same way that a shadow on a sundial widens in the afternoon light. My disability is perceived as being more influential than it actually is.

Let me counteract that view for a moment, and describe myself to you—as I see myself. First, I am a white male who grew up in Toronto, Canada. My father is Polish, my mother is English. . . . I like sailing, and used to compete in local and regional races. I'm married to Emma, and live in Port Alberni, British Columbia. I am a step-dad to Jodi, Erinn, and Evan. We live in an old house we

renovated and love. Emma and I have our own business as consultants. We share a passionate interest in social justice and conflict management. I enjoy computers, classical music and Greek food. I play the drums, although not well. I have an uncanny ability to remember phone numbers and jokes. I also have cerebral palsy.

Source: Kunc, N., & Van der Klift, E. (1995). Voice: In spite of my disability. Questions, concerns, beliefs, and practical advice about inclusive education. In J. Thousand & R. Villa (Eds.), *The inclusion puzzle: Fitting the pieces together* (pp. 163–164). Alexandria, VA: Association for Supervision and Curriculum Development. Copyright ©1995 ASCD. Used by permission.

assertive, cope with tough situations, and practice self-advocacy (Todis, Irwin, Singer, & Yovanoff, 1993). As a result of the training, parents' self-esteem increased; children gained self-care skills, completed chores more often, and became more assertive; and the parents became more likely to support their child's request for autonomy and independence. An empowering context (in this situation) was one that provided knowledge and skills.

What are the implications of these self-esteem issues for family and professional collaboration? A family's and student's self-esteem can be influenced by how you affirm their strengths in a genuine way; sadly, many families and students are much more accustomed to having their weaknesses and needs pointed out, not their strengths. You can be an affirmer of strengths. In box 7–4 you will find other tips for addressing families' self-esteem needs.

Economic Needs

Nearly all families need to earn incomes; only a few have the luxury of being supported by unearned income. All families, whatever their sources of income, must decide how to spend the income and methods for handling money.

From reading about family poverty in chapter 5, you know that family resources vary tremendously and that finances affect how families respond to the challenges of their children's exceptionality. Some can and do spend more than others, but that fact alone should not lead you to assume that the families who cannot spend much, or at the level you want them to spend, are not as committed to their children as more affluent families. That is the point that a black single mother makes:

> You've got bummy blacks and bummy whites and you are saying, everybody black is stupid, and you are bums, and you are not good. That's not true. I am a single parent and I am trying to do the best I can with John. I don't send him to school dirty; he don't go hungry. When they need money and stuff for school, I do without. These are white people born with money. They are not struggling. I can't tell you what to do unless I wear your shoes. (Kalyanpur & Rao, 1991, p. 528)

What does research show about the impact of exceptionality on family economics? Data consistently show that families spend more money on their children with disabilities than on their other children; in other words, a child's disability—especially autism, mental retardation, spina bifida, cerebral palsy, and technology dependency—creates excess costs (Aday, Aitken, & Weggener, 1988; Birenbaum & Cohen, 1993; Fujiura, Roccoforte, & Braddock, 1994; Knoll, 1992; Morris, 1987; Worley, Rosenfeld, & Lipscomb, 1991).

Data based on the most recent research show that the largest expense categories for families with children with autism or mental retardation are food (specialized diets), transportation (to service providers), recreation, clothing (specially adapted or tailored), durable consumer items, medical care, specialized services, per-

---

TIPS

BOX 7–4

Addressing Families' Self-Esteem Needs

- Affirm all family members' strengths and positive contributions.
- Underscore links between family members' actions and the positive results that accrue.
- Encourage children and youth with exceptionalities to identify and develop interests that give them pride. One strategy might be to place the student with an exceptionality in the role of helper rather than recipient of help.
- Encourage children and youth with exceptionalities to express their own choices as a strategy to enhance their self-esteem. Encouraging children and youth to choose what is important to them affords them greater control and independence.
- Ensure that children and youth have school opportunities, consistent with their preferences, to establish relationships with friends and mentors who share similar exceptionalities and ones who do not.

Source: Adapted from Stainback, S., Stainback, W., East, K., & Sapon-Shevin, M. (1994). A commentary on inclusion and the development of a positive self-identity by people with disabilities. *Exceptional Children, 60*(6), 486–90.

sonal care, and "other" (Fujiura et al., 1994). The extraordinary costs include adapted clothing, architectural modifications, climate controls and other environmental modifications, consumer electronics, dental or related needs, exercise equipment, furniture, vehicle modifications, wheelchairs or walkers, and other disability-related equipment (Fujiura et al., 1994).

In addition, many families with children with developmental disabilities, chronic health conditions, or technology support needs must administer medications, monitor medical procedures, provide specialized treatments and procedures, and carry out behavioral intervention and other habilitative programs (Aday et al., 1988; Knoll, 1992).

It is not clear which disability creates greater excess costs than another. Data based on 1985–1986 family expenditure patterns showed that families who have children with autism spend more money on them for health care than do families with children who do not have disabilities, and families with children with severe mental retardation spend more on their health care than families with children with autism (Birenbaum & Cohen, 1993). But more recent data show that the excess costs of autism exceed those of cerebral palsy and the costs of cerebral palsy exceed those of mental retardation (Fujiura et al., 1994).

There is another aspect of the costs of exceptionality; some families have "increased consumptive demands" and "decreased productive capacities"—also known as "lost opportunities"—because of their children's disabilities (Aday et al., 1988; Birenbaum & Cohen, 1993). Often families give up new job opportunities because they would have to move away from their present providers and service systems; they take part-time work when they could be employed full time if they did not have to care for their child; they simply leave the workforce altogether to care for their child; they change jobs to get better work hours and at-home care time; they change or refuse to change a job to get or keep medical insurance; or they forego education that would advance their careers (Barnett & Boyce, 1995; Birenbaum & Cohen, 1993; Fujiura et al., 1994; Knoll, 1992).

As a professional committed to providing information so that families can become more empowerful, be prepared to provide families with some general information about the financial benefits to which they might be entitled or to at least refer them to a source from which they can get that information. Generally, the local office of the Social Security Administration is a good source of information and referral; so, too, are state family support programs and Parent Training and Information Centers that you will learn about in chapter 10.

Daily Care Needs

Another basic function of families consists of meeting their members' physical and health needs. This includes the day-to-day tasks of living: cooking, cleaning, laundry, transportation, obtaining health care when needed, and so forth. A substantial portion of family life is devoted to attending to these needs. Daily care is one of the significant outputs of family interaction: Parents, children and youth, and extended family often work together to carry out their roles and responsibilities.

In chapter 6, we discussed issues related to how mothers and fathers distribute household duties. Typically, attending to the daily care needs of family members has been "women's work," and female caring roles often expand when the child has an exceptionality (Traustadottir, 1995). Mothers expressed the commitment to maintain an ordinary family life (Traustadottir, 1995), simply being able to carry out the daily routines of their life without the child's limiting those routines. Rather than assessing the severity of their child's exceptionality according to traditional standards, they more frequently interpreted severity according to the extent of limitations and constraints placed on family life routines.

There are no blanket generalizations concerning the kinds of limitations and constraints that children and youth with exceptionalities place on family living. Again, it all depends upon the nature and characteristics of the exceptionality in relationship to other family characteristics, on family subsystem cohesion and adaptability, and on the ways that professionals collaborate for families' empowerment. In the Battles family's case, they have learned to provide the support that Rickey needs and do not consider it to be a significant imposition on their family routines. In other words, they have developed routines that are compatible with his support needs.

Clearly, a significant factor is the family's level of adaptability, as you learned in chapter 6. Consider two families—one that maintains a very strict schedule and is quite frustrated by any change, another that has a balanced level of adaptability characterized by flexible rules and routines. If these two families had children with identical characteristics, the family with more balanced adaptability probably would have less difficulty in carrying out daily care responsibilities than the family whose roles and routines are strictly implemented.

Research reveals how children with developmental disabilities and chronic medical conditions affect their families with respect to daily care issues (Knoll, 1992):

- Approximately 50 percent of the families gave their child extensive assistance with toileting, bathing, grooming, and medical monitoring.
- Approximately one-fourth indicated that their child needed 24-hour-a-day monitoring.
- Slightly more than half reported that they had experienced some sort of crisis requiring extraordinary intervention within the last month.

These daily care issues can manifest themselves in frequent everyday routines such as sleeping and eating. Consider the situation of the family whose child has a chronic health problem and needs special assistance while eating. His mother explains:

> I can get the most bottle into him if I start before he's totally awake. . . . I guess I spend about 1 1/2 hours in the morning and it's closer to 2 hours at lunch. That's when I get William to eat something besides just milk or formula. . . . He goes to the school in the afternoon, and I'm always late getting him there because it takes so long for him to eat. (Martin, Brady, & Kotarba, 1992, p. 10)

The child's father explains his role:

> I'm not as good as Betty when it comes to feeding William, but by 6:30 she needs a break. She eats her dinner while I feed William. I eat when I get to it. It takes about 2 hours to feed him. . . . I hadn't realized it took so long. I just know it's about 10:00 before I get to the grocery store. (Martin et al., 1992, p. 10)

Although the vast majority of children with exceptionalities do not have such extensive needs, almost every family will create family routines that are consistent with the child's needs and strengths.

Another significant daily care issue for parents of children with medical needs is dealing with the medical equipment, specialized procedures, medical appointments, and insurance paperwork.

> Respiratory therapy 3 times a day normally. When sick or congested, 4–5 times a day, plus medications. She takes 11 different kinds of medicine, including 5 vitamins. Need to monitor stool samples daily—make sure they are solid. The inhalation therapy is not disturbing, but when we're both tired it's no fun—sometimes it's a bother. Takes a half hour—15 minutes on mask, 15 minutes pounding. It depends on her mood—if she's tired at night, she'll sleep through it. Sometimes she'll fight all the way. (Knoll, 1992, p. 26)

Some of the issues of daily care are age-related; as children with exceptionalities grow and develop, most gain an increasing and sometimes wholly independent capacity to carry out these responsibilities. You can teach children and youth daily care skills as part of their IFSP/IEP if those goals are appropriate in light of the student's strengths, preferences, and needs.

Brothers and sisters can also be collaborators. School-age children can be effective in helping their brothers or sisters with exceptionalities carry out and develop basic self-help skills (Swenson-Pierce, Kohl, & Egel, 1987). "Sometimes we ask the older girls to check the batteries in Mary Pat's hearing aid, put in new ones, help her dress or undress, monitor a bath, get her safely down the stairs. They read and sign stories, help out in a thousand other ways" (Luetke-Stahlman, Luetke-Stahlman, & Luetke-Stahlman, 1992, p. 10).

Although some children can create greater daily care needs, others do not. In fact, children with exceptionalities can make many positive contributions to this family function, helping with housekeeping, yard work, laundry, or the needs of younger siblings. As a single mother reported:

> Of my three children, the one with autism is my lifesaver when it comes to housework. He believes that everything has a place and belongs in it. His room would pass any army inspection. He organizes drawers and pulls weeds out of the flower beds. On the other hand, the clutter and mess in the bedrooms of my normal kids is shameful. When I ask for their help, they consider it an infringement on their social life.

Given the increasing number of "latchkey children," including those who have exceptionalities, some schools are teaming with community organizations to provide self-care instruction for parents and children. The goal of these programs is to prepare children in areas such as handling emergencies, preventing accidents and sexual abuse, managing their time, learning leisure skills, and practicing good nutrition. Staying home alone or with other siblings can be particularly challenging for students who experience exceptionalities such as learning disabilities or AD/HD because these impairments might make it more challenging for the children to make quick decisions in threatening circumstances or use their time in a constructive and balanced way. Moreover, students who experience asthma, epilepsy, or diabetes need to know how to respond to an emergency situation, as do brothers and sisters and other people who may be close by and available to provide assistance (Koblinsky & Todd, 1991).

Socialization Needs

Socialization is vital to the overall quality of life for most individuals. Just like everyone else, persons of all ages with exceptionalities need opportunities to experience both the joys and disappointments of reciprocal social relationships. Many families experience stress in meeting the socialization needs of their child or youth with an exceptionality. In a survey of the needs about which families of children and youth with autism, mental retardation, and AD/HD particularly wanted information, the topic of knowing how to help their child make friends received the highest rating (Ruef, 1995).

Similarly, Brotherson (1985) found that, second only to planning for residential options, parents reported that arranging for socialization was their greatest need when they have young adults with mental retardation. As one mother said, "people with disabilities are lonesome, lonesome people" (Brotherson, 1985, p. 119).

Interviews with families of students with challenging behavior revealed the number of comments about the lack of their child's friendships (Turnbull & Ruef, in press):

- George knows a lot of people, but he doesn't hang out with them.
- Danny has no relationships outside his family.
- Jessie has no friends at school. . . . She has only been there a year and a half.
- My dream is that the phone will ring and someone will invite her to play.

Some families and professionals may welcome your encouragement and guidance in this area. Often, even empowered and supportive families and professionals may focus on other important areas of their child's development and unwittingly ignore the social dimensions of their child's life. The reason that social dimensions are underemphasized is that many families and professionals are unsure of how to facilitate relationships. In box 7–5 you will read how two savvy professionals did the job of creating friendships for a student with disabilities.

The Circle of Friends approach has been very successful with many students with disabilities (Falvey, Forest, Pearpoint, & Rosenberg, 1994; Sherwood, 1990). Another extremely helpful resource for preparing families and professionals to facilitate relationships is a guidebook titled *Connecting Students: A Guide to Thoughtful Friendship Facilitation for Educators and Families.* It suggests the following three steps (Schaffner & Buswell, 1992):

1. *Find opportunities.* Bring students together so that they will have an opportunity to know each other.
2. *Make interpretations.* Support the student, to the degree appropriate, and make connections with others in an enhancing way.
3. *Make accommodations.* Adapt the physical environment so that individuals with disabilities have a greater opportunity to participate in a meaningful way.

Recreation Needs

Recreation and the enjoyment of leisure time are important components of life for individuals and families. Recreation includes sports, games, hobbies, or play that can be done outdoors or indoors; as a spectator or a participant; and in an independent, cooperative, or competitive manner (Moon & Bunker, 1987). Naturally, a family's culture influences its views about the role of recreation and leisure. In African-American culture, for example, play is regarded as necessary for promoting children's well-being:

> Play is seen as important for both social (to have friends and fun) and physical (to have a strong body) well-being. In contrast with cultures that push children toward early adulthood, in African-American families there is an attempt to give the child an opportunity to be a child, and to enjoy the care and protection of responsible adults until such time as he or she is maturationally ready for a broader role. (Willis, 1992, p. 139)

Another cultural interpretation of recreational priorities emphasizes not so much the importance of play as it does the appropriate age for children or youth to participate in recreation separately from other family members. A Middle Eastern perspective illuminates this issue:

> Middle Eastern parents, particularly mothers, rarely have social and recreational activities separate from their children. Family gatherings, picnics, cinemas, and, to a lesser extent, sports events are among the most common social events in the Middle East; children are usually included in all of them. Most Middle Eastern boys do not start to have activities of their own until after puberty; for unmarried girls, this may come even later. (Sharifzadeh, 1992, p. 334)

Depending upon the nature of the child's exceptionality, the family's recreational role may be expanded, unaffected, or curtailed. Some children

BOX 7–5

TOGETHER WE CAN

Standing Together

Angel Figueroa and Meili Quiros share two experiences. The first is demographic: They are Puerto Ricans with disabilities living in Hartford, Connecticut. Angel has a learning disability and physical impairments, and Meili has cerebral palsy and mental retardation. The second is strategic: Both have friends, but they came by them quite differently.

In Angel's case, his teacher Luis Delgado not only instructs him but also has found the way for Angel to stay out of trouble and to have a friend—a guy who is street smart where being street smart is important, given the gangs and drugs that permeate their community.

Angel's buddy is Daniel Vasquez, also from Puerto Rico, a guy who has avoided the gangs and drugs. Angel is 13, Daniel is 19, but the age difference that usually separates students in those years makes no difference to them. Daniel cautions Angel not to "look hard" or look menacing when he's around other guys. He coaches him on how to talk with girls. He encourages Angel to let off steam, and in turn he lets out his frustrations with Angel. Together, they enjoy riding bikes, playing basketball, listening to rap music, and com-posing their own songs.

"Of all the friends that I have, I prefer being with [Angel]," says Daniel. "Even though he's younger than my friends, I get along better with him because its like I can do anything. I can say anything. It's okay with him. With my other friends, I gotta watch what I say."

Daniel is quick to point out, "When you live in a project, you find a way to help somebody who needs help. I knew his grandfather. My mom knew their grandmother. It was like we was family. That's the way I see it. Like we were cousins. We stand together."

Standing together isn't something that Meili, 12, and her friend Carolyn, 13, can do—not literally. Meili uses a wheelchair, even when she is competing in the Miss Puerto Rico contest in Hartford. And Carolyn herself is at a disadvantage: She and her mother Agnes are from Guyana, yet they live and work in "Spanish Hartford."

Agnes got to know Meili and her mother Lorna because she works in an agency that provides respite care for Lorna. Agnes became a close friend of Lorna and Meili.

"I do not see Lorna and her family as, well, clients. I see us as a family. That's the way I accepted her from the time I started going to her house. I tell you one thing about Guyanan culture. We are a loving people. Our motto is: Together We Stand. We go beyond friendship."

Standing together means that Agnes told her daughter Carolyn about Meili. Carolyn sought her out at school; the two became instant friends . . . and not just because Carolyn herself understands what it means to be excluded because of her traits—a black African in a brown community.

Carolyn says, "Since the first day I saw Meili, I really liked her. I've been coming [to her home] and we really got to know each other. Now it's like we are family. We visit each other. We talk and we play around. Make stuff. Sing along with tapes. Sometimes I go over and read with her."

Standing together in the streets, as Angel and Daniel do, or standing together at school assemblies, as Meili and Carolyn do—however these youngsters describe it, Luis and Agnes have played their roles as "brokers," as professionals who knew that, in spite of whatever else schools can offer, all kids need friendships.

and youth have special gifts related to sports, athletics, or games (for example, chess or bridge), and a significant portion of family time may be devoted to supporting their interests and involvement. One mother reported:

Because of Susan's reading disability, school has always been very hard for her. She reads now—slowly—but for a long time she never thought she would read at all. To make matters worse, Della and Melinda, her younger sisters, have always been star students—both of them are in the gifted program at their school. Because of these things, I really wanted to find the places where Susan could shine too. When she showed an interest in swimming, I encouraged her. She took swimming lessons at the YWCA and we all started swimming a lot as a family. Now she swims on a team for the city during the summer and next year she's decided to try out for the swim team at her high school. She has a lot of confidence in this area. She swims circles around most of her friends and all of her family! But I'm a lot better swimmer today than I would have been without her influence.

Alternatively, some families' recreation is curtailed because of the nature of their child's exceptionality, the unavailability of community resources, disapproving public reactions to their son or daughter, or general lack of accommodations in making recreation possible. Constraining recreational opportunities can create significant family stress. Families have reported substantial curtailment of activities such as going outside the home, eating in a restaurant, going on a vacation, shopping, and participating in general recreational experiences (Traustadottir, 1995). One mother has noted that she would drive her daughter with autism to the beach but would not get out of the car because of the stares and disapproving looks that her daughter would receive from other people there (Turnbull & Ruef, in press). Similarly, a father has described issues that arise in taking his two-year-old son who is blind to a restaurant:

> We can't just pick up and go out to eat after church, our friends can't understand that. . . . Matthew doesn't sit in a highchair, and he gets overloaded by the noise in a restaurant, he gets afraid. He can't sit for one to two hours; he can't deal with the noise of the dishes, and it's hard to entertain yourself when you can't see. (Martin et al., 1992, p. 11)

Inclusive recreational opportunities help meet the recreational needs of children or youth with exceptionalities (and the family) and provide valuable experiences for their peers. Box 7–6 describes the collaborative process that was used in Iowa City, Iowa, to create an inclusive summer recreational program that responded to the preferences, strengths, and needs of all participants. This sort of collaborative process can develop a similar program in your community, and you can contribute to that effort.

Often families and professionals alike have investigated and sponsored "special populations" recreation programs rather than planning to include children and youth with exceptionalities in typical community opportunities. A mother of a daughter with mental retardation shares how she purposely abandoned special programs in favor of inclusive ones:

> A long time ago I stopped looking at newspaper listings of special programs. . . . Now I just notice what Kathryn might like. All kinds of courses are given by community schools, YMCAs, or churches. Grandparents and teenagers, beginners, or those with some familiarity with the subject—all take the same course. Though there may be beginning, intermediate, or advanced levels, nobody would notice or care if someone took the same course several times. For most of us . . . taking enough time is more important than special techniques. (Bennett, 1985, p. 171)

Too often, schools have minimized educational objectives for leisure and recreation, yet leisure and recreation should be an important part of each child's curriculum (Schleien, Green, & Heyne, 1993). From a family systems perspective, you will want to find out from the families what recreational hobbies and interests they particularly enjoy and where in the community they would especially like to pursue these activities. Then the student's school program can promote the skills the child needs, and the collaborative team will make accommodations for the family and the child's preferences. In addition to strengthening recreational skills, this approach can enhance self-esteem, socialization, and educational achievement. It can also ease the stress of daily care demands and not pose additional economic responsibilities on the family if the community recreational opportunities are available at no charge.

*E*ducation Needs

Across cultures, families generally place a strong emphasis on education. Within the Euro-American culture, education is typically seen as the key to success in employment, financial, and quality-of-life opportunities (Hanson, 1992). A similar Asian perspective appears in this Chinese proverb (Chan, 1992, p. 213):

If you are planning for a year, sow rice;
If you are planning for a decade, plant trees;
If you are planning for a lifetime, educate people.

Minority family members often encounter significant educational and social barriers in attaining equal opportunities for their children (Harry, 1992a, 1992b; Harry, Allen, & McLaughlin, 1995). As a Native American grandparent stated:

TOGETHER WE CAN

BOX 7-6

Hanging Out Inclusively

What do preschool and elementary school students with moderate/severe/profound mental retardation or autism do in the summer in Iowa City, Iowa? They do pretty much what their age peers without disabilities do, thanks to the collaboration of their parents, the parents of children without disabilities, the special educators in the children's schools, and the staff of the local YMCA and city parks and recreation program.

The children—all of them, those with and without disabilities—play table games, have crafts activities, play softball, fish, practice archery, enjoy free play in sandboxes and on playgrounds, and have hotdog roasts. In a word, all the children have "inclusive" summer activities.

That result occurred because a small group of committed parents, professionals, and park and recreation staffers jointly followed an eight-step process to create inclusive recreation:

- They selected the schools where the children with disabilities were enrolled to get the staff, parents, and children involved in the program.
- They surveyed community recreation programs that children without disabilities used.
- They approached the staff of those programs to solicit their participation and offer support.
- They obtained a small grant from the state department of education to pay for staff inservice, planning time, and program enrollment fees.
- They publicized the program to get participants.

- They jointly planned the program and carried it out, making sure that the children with disabilities were in age-appropriate groups, that there were "natural proportions" of those children in each group, and that the special educators served as support personnel for the recreation staff.
- They prepared the children without disabilities by formal means such as brief discussions about disabilities and informal means such as modeling inclusion.
- They carried out the recreation program; and, when the children with disabilities were not in the recreation program, they worked with the children on IEP goals.

The program evaluation was uniformly positive: The children interacted positively with each other, the recreation staff supported the program, the parents of all students—those with and without disabilities—were pleased with it, and the kids themselves had positive attitudes about their peers with disabilities.

A parent of two boys who did not have disabilities who attended the camp commented, "Our sons talked about special kids all of the time. They were the main topic at our supper table. We were pleased because our boys showed so much care. We had our eyes open because they thought of them as kids just like themselves" (Hamre-Nietupski et al., 1992, p. 73).

Source: Adapted from Hamre-Nietupski, S., Krajewski, L., Riehl, R., Sensor, K., Nietupski, J., Moravec, J., McDonald, J., & Cantine-Stull, P. (1992). Enhancing integration during the summer: Combined educational and community recreation options for students with severe disabilities. *Education and Training in Mental Retardation, 27*(1), 68–74.

I had children and grandchildren who are really gifted. At one time they brought home a lot of high marks from school, but they learned that if they were good achievers they would be harassed at school, so they didn't want their peers to know about their good grades. The school talks about this, but they don't know what to do about it.

There should be something we could do to stop this trend and turn these other kids around. Some parents, who have money or were in education and knew their child was gifted, would pull their children out of the school and send them to a white school. (U.S. Department of Education, 1990, p. 5)

Throughout this book, you will learn about families' roles in meeting their children's educational needs. Here, we will emphasize the importance of families maintaining balance in family functions rather than overemphasizing education to the detriment of other functions. In chapter 8, on life cycle, we will describe two educational tasks that many families assume at four different life cycle stages.

Maintaining Balance in Educational Roles

Remember the discussion in chapter 1 of *families as family members*? Sometimes professionals may emphasize the role of parents as teachers or tutors. That emphasis is appropriate if it is consistent with a family's values, priorities, and available time. If it is not, the differences among the focus of school, other service agencies, and home can cause strain or conflict in home-school relationships and impair the development of reliable alliances. Indeed, many parents and students with exceptionalities respond negatively to professional overemphasis on educational/vocational needs. Professionals should remember that educational/vocational needs are only one function that families must address. Maddux and Cummings (1983) warn:

> If academic learning is required in both the home and the school, a child who has difficulty learning gets very little relief. The home ceases to be a haven from scholastic pressures. Imagine how most of us would feel if the most frustrating, least enjoyable, and most difficult thing about our work were waiting for us when we came home each day. (p. 30)

We encourage you to beware of the "fix-it approach" whereby children and youth with exceptionalities are almost continuously placed in quasi-teaching situations by well-intentioned teachers, family, and friends. These perpetual educational efforts to make him or her "better" may have a negative impact on self-esteem, as Harriet Rousso (1984) noted when writing about her mother's approach to her physical therapy:

> Being disabled and being intact at the same time is an extremely difficult notion for non-disabled people to make sense of. I kept thinking of my mother's words: "Why wouldn't you want to walk straight?" Even now, it is hard to explain that I may have wanted to walk straight, but I did not want to lose my sense of myself in the process. Perhaps the best I can say is that my perspective on disability, from the inside out, is different from my mother's, from the outside looking in.

> In our work with congenitally disabled clients, we must always be receptive and respectful of that difference. (Rousso, 1984, p. 12)

Professionals and families need to be keenly aware of a perspective on disability from the inside out. That is one reason why adults with disabilities can be valued mentors, role models, and consultants in assisting professionals, families, and young children with disabilities to gain this vital perspective (Turnbull & Turbiville, 1995).

Encouraging educational achievement is particularly prevalent in the homes of students who have been identified as gifted and talented (Friedman, 1994); and families especially benefit from collaboration with educators, as you will read in box 7–7.

Parents tend to place special emphasis on the particular area of their son's or daughter's special interest and to provide early and continued opportunities for growth and development (Clark & Zimmerman, 1988; Raymond & Benbow, 1989). One study reported that 70 percent of artistically talented students indicated parental support for their artwork and 65 percent had a place to do their art at home (Clark & Zimmerman, 1988). Friedman (1994) warns that many low-income parents of students who are gifted have been found not to place as much emphasis on educational achievement; however, she cautions that the additional attention that these families must devote to issues concerning housing, dangerous neighborhoods, unemployment, and other stressors should not be interpreted to mean that the families do not support their children who are gifted.

Time As a Factor in Meeting Family Functions

We encourage you to review the seven functions that we have just discussed and to imagine yourself as Rickey's parents. If you were Richard or Betty Battles seeking to raise two boys, Rickey and Michael, as well as run the grocery store, participate in the life of your community, have a little time for yourself, and meet the collaboration responsibilities that are required in ensuring that Rickey's great expectations come true, when would you find time to address all seven family functions? Might there be slippage when there were simply not enough hours in the day to go around for all the family functions? In these situations, in what way would you want Rickey's teachers to support you and your family? Would you want them to judge you

BOX 7-7

TOGETHER WE CAN

The Math Prodigy and His Family

Neil Khare is an unusual young man. At the age of 9, he has a dream. It is not just to compete in a national mathematics competition for sixth graders in Washington, DC, but to "win, place, or show." For Neil, his physician parents Pratibha and Narendra, his medical-school brother Rahul, and Mr. McCollough, his mathematics teacher at Pembroke-Hill School in Kansas City, the dream requires an extraordinary degree of concentration and work.

Neil left one school for another with a stronger mathematics program and tolerates the longer commute to that school, usually with his parents as they head to work. Neil has already skipped one grade in school.

Now in the fourth grade for all his academics, he is enrolled in sixth- and seventh-grade math classes.

Three times each week and after school, Mr. McCollough tutors him individually and in a group. His mother, Pratibha, accompanies him in those classes, learns along with him, and does the assignments with him. During the summer between his third- and fourth-grade years, his father Narendra drove him to and from college algebra classes at nearby Johnson County Community College. His brother Rahul and his parents arrange their schedules to transport him to local, regional, and statewide mathematics competitions.

The fact that he has earned first, second, or third-place in those competitions against older students is reinforcing, of course; but Neil's joy, and his family's derivative joy, comes from the thrill of facing and mastering the challenges of advanced mathematics. The fact that Neil's tutor, Mr. McCollough, has become a family friend is an added benefit.

It is worth remembering this: Neil has set these goals for himself. His love of mathematics, his eagerness for the challenges, and his family's and teacher's support happily coincide. The fact that his family's East Indian culture values learning makes Neil's dream all the more appropriate.

---

as "not caring enough about Rickey to meet 100 percent of his needs," or would you hope that they would "cut you some slack," recognizing that you are juggling as many responsibilities in the finite 24-hour day as possible?

Undoubtedly, time is a major issue—if not the major issue—for many families. Just keep in mind that approximately two-thirds of all employed parents with children under 18 report that they do not have enough time to meet their children's needs (Families and Work Institute, 1994), that they often leave their children home unattended, and that they rely on their children to be occupied by watching television. If this is the report from parents, most of whom have children without exceptionalities, what impact on the family do some of the tasks associated with exceptionality have? In box 7–8 you will read the words of Helen Featherstone, mother of a son with a severe disability, who had no unclaimed time in her day or night.

What would you have expected of the Featherstone family if you had been Jody's parents? Or his occupational therapist, teacher, or dentist? What is the balance between meeting the child's disability-related needs and the needs of the entire family?

In a study of family and professional perspectives toward time, parents identified four issues that served as barriers to their efficient and effective use of time—four ways in which the professional context was not empowering (Brotherson & Goldstein, 1992, p 518):

1. The inability of professionals to coordinate their activities among themselves;
2. The overwhelming number of tasks parents were asked by professionals to complete;
3. The lack of local and accessible services; and
4. A lack of flexible and family-centered scheduling of services.

Where Will I Find the Time?

I remember the day when the occupational therapist at Jody's school called with some suggestions from a visiting nurse. Jody has a seizure problem which is controlled with the drug Dilantin. Dilantin can cause the gums to grow over the teeth; the nurse had noticed this overgrowth, and recommended, innocently enough, that [his] teeth be brushed four times a day, for 5 minutes, with an electric toothbrush. The school suggested that they could do this once on school days, and that I should try to do it the other three times a day; this new demand appalled me; Jody is blind, cerebral palsied, and retarded. We do his physical therapy daily and work with him on sounds and communication. We feed him each meal on our laps, bottle him, bathe him, dry him, put him in a body cast to sleep, launder his bed linens daily, and go through a variety of routines designed to minimize his miseries and enhance his joys and his development. (All this in addition to trying to care for and enjoy our other young children and making time for each other and our careers.) Now you tell me that I should spend 15 minutes every day on something that Jody will hate, an activity that will not help him to walk or even defecate, but one that is directed at the health of his gums. This activity is not for a finite time, but forever. It is not guaranteed to help, but "it can't hurt." And it won't make the overgrowth go away but may retard it. Well, it's too much. Where is that 15 minutes going to come from? What am I supposed to give up? Taking the kids to the park? Reading a bedtime story to my eldest? Washing the breakfast dishes? Sorting the laundry? Grading students' papers? Sleeping? Because there is not time in my life that hasn't been spoken for, and for every 15-minute activity that is added one has to be taken away.

Source: Excerpted from *A Difference in the Family* by Helen Featherstone. Copyright © 1980 by Basic® Books, Inc. Reprinted by permission of BasicBooks, a division of HarperCollins Publishers, Inc.

You can make a significant contribution to the quality of family life by helping to remove time barriers and facilitating ways to use time efficiently and effectively. Parent suggestions for effective time use include the following:

> Parents wanted education and therapy for their child to be part of their daily routine and environment. They wanted to work well with professionals to provide care for their children: Time was wasted if activities were learned in artificial settings or if the knowledge of parents was ignored. They wanted professionals to aid their efficiency and effectiveness by using current technology when it is applicable. Further, they wanted to be given more time to develop rapport with professionals. (Brotherson & Goldstein, 1992, p. 515)

One of the greatest lessons that you can derive from understanding family functions is how busy family life is. We encourage you to keep in perspective that educational/vocational issues are one of seven functions; and families may or may not be able to devote the time to educational and vocational issues that you, as an educational professional, might deem desirable. As you pursue your career and your own family life, it is likely that you will experience these same time crunches. Particularly for families who have a child with an exceptionality, it is critical to recognize that they are dealing with lifelong issues, ones that require the endurance of a marathon runner, not a sprinter. Professionals, however, often are tempted to urge the parents to make substantial investments of time over the short term (like a sprinter) to enhance what the child *might* be able to learn. "Parents think of time as daily routine, they also see the care of their child as an ongoing, life long, ever-evolving commitment, not a short-term education or therapeutic contact. This is a significant difference in time orientation that should be highlighted for professional understanding of families" (Brotherson & Goldstein, 1992, p. 523).

Summary

Families exist to meet the individual and collective needs of their members. The tasks they perform to meet those needs are referred to as family functions; in a family systems framework, they are the outputs. There are seven categories of functions or outputs: affection, self-esteem, economics, daily care, socialization, recreation, and education/vocation.

When collaborating with families around these functions, you would do well to bear the following in mind:

- Families' cultures influence the ways they carry out these functions.
- Families may or may not spend the amount or type of time on each function that you predict you would spend if you were they.
- The child with an exceptionality, as well as every family member, influences how the family performs each of these seven functions.

- The child's impact can be both positive and negative and will depend in part on the family's own characteristics (chapter 5), family interactions (chapter 6), and life cycle stages and transitions (chapter 8).
- The family's motivation as well as their knowledge/skills will influence how they carry out their functions and how you can most successfully collaborate with them.
- There are some concrete steps you can take as you collaborate with families to build a reliable alliance around each of these functions.
- Family life is busy, and time is a valuable and limited resource.

Rickey Battles is beating the odds. He's not doing it alone. His family is a powerful resource for him, and each member contributes to meeting his needs in different ways. Similarly, the good citizens of Poultney, Vermont, make a positive difference in his and his family's life, whether they are the owners and customers of the pet shop where he gets his vocational education, his peers who do not have disabilities, or special and general educators and the school nurse.

Whatever Rickey's and his family's needs might be, the ground rule for the Battles family and their collaborators is clear-cut and simple: All of Rickey's needs are put onto the table so the collaboration team can begin to meet them. In meeting his needs, the team also addresses some of the functions that the Battles family, like every other family, performs. Not surprisingly, that approach to collaboration—and indeed Rickey himself—gives meaning to the collaborators' lives. In doing so, the approach meets some of each collaboration team member's needs. In a real sense, what goes around in collaboration comes around: The reciprocity and mutuality within the collaboration team creates a reliable alliance for everyone—Rickey, the Battles family, and every single team member.

Chapter Eight

Family Life Cycle

"*There is certainly denial, that feeling that Jessica is going to get better, always that hope that she is going to get better."*

To listen to Tricia Baccus is to hear that hope. But it also is to hear this: "If the seizures don't kill her, certainly all of the drugs are going to. I imagine one day her liver is just going to get tired and give up. The metabolic disorder only makes Jessica's epilepsy and cognitive impairment more complicated. Jessica's doctor simply told us that she has a degenerative disease and that he doesn't anticipate that she will live past the age of 25."

Now that Jessica is 19 years old, she and her family—mother Tricia, father Craig, younger sisters Melissa and Lara—live time-compressed existences.

Jessica's early years seem so close at hand, even now—the "feeling . . . [that] we never had enough hands to hold onto the kids." Jessica was bright, mischievous, mobile, and filled with humor. But she also had seizures, took medication, had cognitive limitations, and was segregated into an "impaired preschool."

"I worked really hard to be a good mom, because I felt I wasn't adequate. Nothing prepared me for this. The thing I felt most was lack of preparation to be a parent, let alone a parent of a child who was so active and had a disability."

Who helped? Jessica's speech therapist was an early source of help. "She was helpful, because she consistently gave me reassurance that I was O.K. She made us feel we could do this. She never made me feel stupid when I asked her a question. She was the first one who said to me, 'You don't have to be an expert at speech or

any other specialty. It's O.K. That is what I went to school to do. You are an expert at something else.'"

Also helpful were the nurse in a neurologist's office and the Baccus's friends, especially those at their church. Indeed, a turning point for Tricia occurred when Jessica mischievously threw a rock at a friend's car—a car that the struggling medical student, his wife, and their children had scrimped to buy. "Tricia," said Merilee, the friend's wife, "it's just a car, and that's why we have insurance, and we love Jessica, and we love you, and it's not that big a deal."

As Tricia relates it now, Merilee's acceptance of Jessica and her caring for Tricia were unconditional. Tricia repeats—many times a week—what Merilee said then: "Our love should be unconditional. We fail only when we fail to keep trying."

And she says about Merilee, the speech therapist, a school principal, and one of Jessica's teachers: "I have come to realize that sometimes you are called to do something not because of who you are but what you can become, and these people gave me the chance to become."

In doing that, they also gave Jessica a chance to become. Instead of being segregated in junior high school (as she was in preschool and some years of elementary school), Jessica was included. Her principal and her teacher, Amy, recognized her as a unique person, one with a gift for others. "Jessica adored the cheerleaders. I learned from her that when you really like somebody, when you adore them, it's hard for them to not like you back."

The principal and Amy recognized Jessica's gift of adoration and asked the Troy Larson Middle School cheerleaders to consider having her as an honorary cheerleader. "Yes" was the answer, and Jessica was "just thrilled," got a uniform, started to use makeup, and attended practices. When her health began to decline and she was hospitalized, she watched the videotapes that the cheerleaders made just for her.

That kind of reciprocity—Jessica's gift of adoration and the cheerleaders' gift of themselves—made Jessica believe in herself. "Since then, there's been no stopping her. She's decided that she can do things, and we are delighted."

Those things include not just making sure that her lip gloss and blush are on before leaving the house and even dyeing her hair red but also staying overnight at a hotel after the school junior-senior dance.

Jessica is now 19, and the ordinary developmental markers—developing a self-identity, attending to her image, developing a sense of her own sexuality, asserting her independence from her teachers (especially those who want to have more control than she wants to give them), and acquiring mature relationships with peers of both sexes—seem so paradoxical and yet so welcome.

They are paradoxical because, as Tricia says, Jessica's mental abilities have declined. "We now have a daughter who is functioning on the moderate-severe level of mental retardation." She has many seizures and takes 55 pills a day.

And yet they are so welcome. "We can't imagine not having Jessica. She makes us appreciate each day, to take the time to stop and smell the roses. She keeps us focused on what's really important in life. And it's not having money, wealth, or a great education. It's just being happy. It's belonging. It's being accepted."

In anticipation of Jessica's early death, Tricia reflects on the 19 years of Jessica's life and their meaning in light of the family's religious beliefs.

"We think we all existed in heaven before we were born, that we all knew we were going to come to earth. Jessica accepted having this disability; and she came to me and Craig—not because we were special—but because we had potential. She loved us, and she thought that by coming to us she could give us an opportunity to grow."

When the family puts the whole 19 years in perspective, they believe that Jessica "makes our pain a little sharper, makes us more aware of love." "Just to belong" is how Tricia puts it. "Just to belong" has sustained the Baccus family ever since their first encounter with the speech therapist, all through Jessica's early years, and into her adolescence and young adulthood. Or as Jessica said as she was returning home after her last hospitalization and a grave illness, "I'm going home; home is where I belong."

"Yes," says Tricia, "Yes, Jessica, home is where you belong. You have a home. You belong with us, and you are very much a part of us." And always will be—even when the inevitable happens, out of time, unwelcome, and sorrowfully.

In the previous three chapters, we discussed the family system and how it is affected by a member with an exceptionality. The dominant image is one of multilayered complexity. First, families differ in so many ways that we can truly say that every family is unique. Second, every family is an interactive system: Anything that happens to one person reverberates throughout the whole family. Third, every family is busily engaged in a variety of functions designed to fulfill a number of tangible and intangible needs.

A fourth layer of complexity—life cycle changes—affects the family system. The portrait of family characteristics, interactions, and functions is only a snapshot of what should more accurately be portrayed as a full-length motion picture. All families progress through stages and transitions as members are born, grow up, leave home, bring in new members through marriage or other permanent relationships, retire, and die. In addition to expected life cycle changes, families may experience unexpected or sudden changes that drastically alter their lives, such as divorce, separation by military service, immigration, job transfers, unemployment, a windfall inheritance, or natural catastrophes. Whether the change is expected and natural, so that it is "on cycle," or unexpected and unnatural, so that it is "off cycle," the family changes; and as it does, so do its characteristics (chapter 5), its interactions (chapter 6), and its functions (chapter 7). In the family systems framework (figure 8–1), we show how the family system and family life cycle changes relate to each other.

Family Life Cycle Theory

Family life cycle theory seeks to explain how a family changes over time. The theory is that each family experiences certain rather predictable and stable stages. As the family moves from one stage to the next, it enters an interim phase known as *transition*.

For example, families typically experience a birth and child-raising stage. The parents learn to care for the child and understand what parenthood really entails, and the child typically learns how to talk, walk, and explore the environment of home and perhaps preschool (Duvall, 1957; Rodgers & White, 1993).

When, predictably, the child leaves the birth and early childhood stage and enters the childhood stage, the child and the family alike embark on a transition. With that transition come changes in the family's interactions with each other. When the transition is complete—and it may take a while—the family has reached the next stage. It performs tasks and has interactions appropriate to that stage. Thus, as a child such as Jessica Baccus enters adolescence, the family may need, on the one hand, to become more flexible, allowing the teenager more personal freedom (adaptability). On the other hand, the family may need to maintain a family identity for all members, especially the adolescent (cohesion). That's the balancing act that Tricia and Craig Baccus are performing as they watch Jessica growing as an adolescent while simultaneously needing more support and as they also

FIGURE 8-1

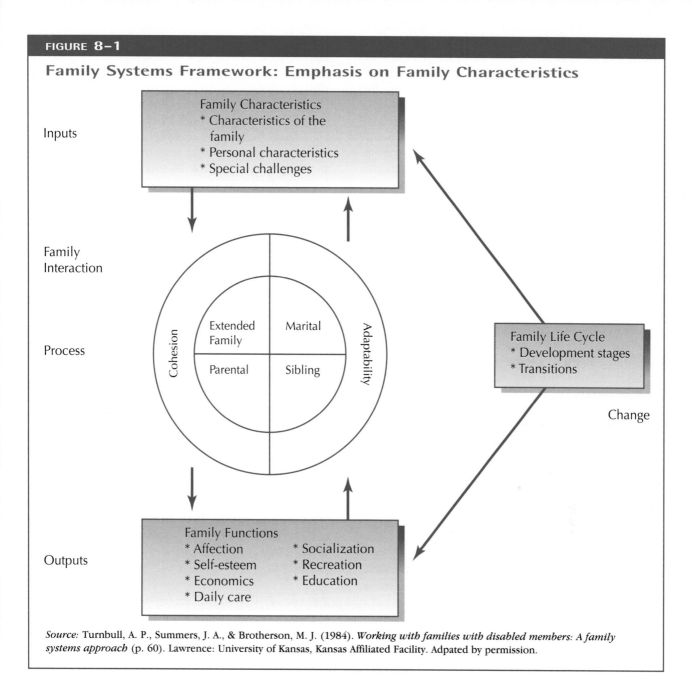

Family Systems Framework: Emphasis on Family Characteristics

Inputs

Family Characteristics
* Characteristics of the family
* Personal characteristics
* Special challenges

Family Interaction

Process

Cohesion

Extended Family | Marital

Parental | Sibling

Adaptability

Family Life Cycle
* Development stages
* Transitions

Change

Outputs

Family Functions
* Affection
* Self-esteem
* Economics
* Daily care
* Socialization
* Recreation
* Education

Source: Turnbull, A. P., Summers, J. A., & Brotherson, M. J. (1984). *Working with families with disabled members: A family systems approach* (p. 60). Lawrence: University of Kansas, Kansas Affiliated Facility. Adapted by permission.

attend to the equally legitimate needs of their two other daughters, Melissa and Lara.

The exact number and character of individual life cycle stages are arbitrary. Theorists have identified as many as 24 and as few as six (Carter & McGoldrick, 1980). Life cycle stages are historically specific. A hundred years ago, when people tended to have large families and shorter life spans, a postparental life stage (when there are no dependent children in the household) was rare (Hareven, 1982).

Life cycle theorists usually regard a family as having three life cycle stages defined by the particular life cycle stages of each member in a family (Terkelson, 1980). For example, the eldest members of a family might be entering old age and facing the task of preparing for their own death and that of their peers, their children may be facing midcareer shifts or the prospect of an empty nest, and their grandchildren may be leaving home and experiencing the first travails of independent adulthood.

To describe family life cycle, however, it is not enough to say that it is the sum of each person's life cycle. A more accurate description is that it encompasses the interactions among all changes in the family (Carter & McGoldrick, 1980). In the example of the three generations, the middle generation may face responsibility for parents with increasing needs while also beginning to let go of their responsibility for their own children. As responsibility shifts, values and approaches to life are transmitted across the generations, thereby preserving the basic identity of the family even while the main characters change (Terkelson, 1980).

A father who was simultaneously caring for his 81-year-old mother, 21-year-old son with a developmental disability, and 13-year-old teenage daughter while also working 50 hours a week commented: "I felt whipsawed. No matter how much I did for one generation, there was always another whose needs cried out to me with such fervor that I felt I couldn't fulfill all of them. In a sense, my mother had become my son, because she had the greater disability and because he was becoming more independent."

Beyond the developmental tasks that the family and individual members must accomplish at each stage, there are the transitions from one stage to another. Transitions are the periods between stages when the family is adjusting its interactional style and roles to meet the needs and challenges of the next developmental stage (Rodgers & White, 1993). Usually transition periods are briefer than the stages to which they relate. But because these shifts may result in confusion and conflict, transitions are almost always times of heightened stress (Neugarten, 1976; Olson, McCubbin, Barnes, Larsen, Muxen, & Wilson, 1983).

Using life cycle theory to understand family change has at least two advantages: (1) It highlights families' similar rhythms over time, and (2) it aids in gaining an understanding of the continuity of family life. But life cycle theory has been criticized for not sufficiently taking into account varying norms across different cultural groups, family forms, and disability-related factors (Alpert, 1981; Rodgers & White, 1993; Turnbull, Summers, & Brotherson, 1986). For example, some ethnic groups place a strong emphasis on close extended families and less value on independence; thus, adults may not leave their parental home to set up a separate household (Harry & Kalyanpur, 1994; Turnbull, A.P., & Turnbull, 1996).

Further, in blended or remarried families, particularly those with older children from a previous marriage, several life cycle stages may occur simultaneously as children from the first marriage approach adulthood and as the new marital partners give birth to new children (Sager, Brown, Crohn, Engel, Rodstein, & Walker, 1983).

Finally, many exceptionality-related issues affect a family. For example, youth like Jessica, whose disabilities cause progressive deterioration, move into the future with less capability than they have experienced at younger ages. For the Baccus family and for other families, the future means longer, but not necessarily easier, lives.

We will concentrate on the four major life cycle stages during which the family is most likely to experience contact with schools: birth and early childhood, childhood, adolescence, and young adulthood. Then we will discuss the general issues of transition from one stage to another and how exceptionality affects and is affected by the family's ability to adjust smoothly to change. As you read, keep in mind the fluidity of the life cycle and the energy and persistence that families need as they run the marathon and face the hurdles of life cycle transitions.

Life Cycle Stages

To illustrate how family functions and their priorities change as the family moves through the life cycle, we will highlight, for each of the selected four stages, two educational issues that many families typically encounter. Thus, we will concentrate on one of the seven family functions—education.

Birth and Early Childhood

For most families, the early childhood years are a period when the family is intensely absorbed with its inner workings (Olson et al., 1983). If the family is not a blended family (in which new marital partners already have children), the childless couple probably has explored the parameters of their relationship, begun to weld the norms of two families of origin into one new unit, and learned how to respond to each other's needs (Duvall, 1957). Now, suddenly, one or more small newcomers arrive on the scene, each dependent on the parents for his or her physical and emotional well-being. While the children are learning to master their bodies and their immediate environment, the parents are facing the task of nurturing their children and meeting their own needs. In addition, a family who has a member with an exceptionality faces a number of educational challenges.

Two of these challenges are (1) discovering and coming to terms with exceptionality and (2) participating in early childhood services.

Discovering and Coming to Terms with Exceptionality

Infants with severe and multiple disabilities, in contrast to those with mild disabilities, typically are identified at birth as having special needs (Batshaw & Perret, 1992). Nowadays, however, early identification can sometimes be made prenatally, even during the first three or four months of pregnancy (Blasco, Blasco, & Zirpoli, 1994). Moreover, emerging new technology related to DNA analysis enables detection of a range of disabling conditions, including some forms of muscular dystrophy, Tay-Sachs disease, phenylketonuria, sickle-cell anemia disease, and cystic fibrosis (D'Alton & DeCherney, 1993; Ostrer, 1989). With such advanced identification, some families make a decision to have an abortion while others use the advanced diagnosis to prepare for the coming birth of a child with special needs (Blasco et al., 1994; Hassed, Miller, Pope, Murphy, Quick, & Curnmiff, 1993).

Regardless of whether the diagnosis happens prenatally, at birth, or during the early years, the professional literature holds that families experience a "grief cycle." The cycle has been likened to stages of dealing with the death of loved ones, and including shock, denial, guilt and anger, shame and depression, and acceptance (Kubler-Ross, 1969; Moses, 1983). This literature, largely based on clinical case studies in the 1960s and 1970s, has concentrated on grief stages experienced by mothers and has been described in later years as sorely lacking in empirical evidence (Blacher, 1984a, 1984b). Nonetheless, you will encounter the literature and the theory behind it, as stated by Ken Moses (1983):

> The grieving process . . . is a feeling process that permits the parent of a developmentally disabled child to separate from dreams and fantasies generated in anticipation of the birth of that child. The inability to successfully separate from such a dream is devastating to both parent and child. If the parent does not generate new dreams that the child can fulfill, then each day the child would be experienced as a disappointment and failure in the eyes of the parent. . . . It is within this context of development that the concept of facilitating grief becomes an important tool in the intervention and habilitation of developmentally disabled children. (Moses, 1983, pp. 27–28)

A new parent gives credence to the grief cycle theory when she describes her feelings:

> Shock, grief, bitter disappointment, fury, horror—my feelings were a mixture of all these after my doctor told me that our new little son, Peter, was born with Down syndrome. I was afraid to have him brought from the nursery. . . . I didn't want to see this monster. But when the nurse brought in this tiny, black-haired baby with up-tilted, almond-shaped eyes, my heart melted. . . . But the grief and fear didn't go away just because we fell in love with our son. They came in great, overwhelming waves. I felt a deep need to cry it out—to cry and cry until I had worked this immense sorrow up from the center of my being and out into the open. . . . I think we should give honest and full expression to our grief. I suspect that when, in our attempts to be brave and face the future we repress our feelings, these feelings of pain and sorrow last longer. All I'm trying to say is that there's a time for weeping and then a time for pushing ahead, and I don't think you can do the second without going through the first. (Vyas, 1983, p. 17)

Although the grief cycle conception is firmly rooted within much of the professional literature and in training programs, we encourage you to consider some alternative perspectives. The first perspective is that the clinical description of parental grief has failed to document how the "grieving" parents were initially told by professionals—and what they were told—about the presence of their child's exceptionality (Lee, 1994). Ruth Johnson, mother of a 15-year-old with Down syndrome, describes how she learned about her son's exceptionality: "About 8 p.m. the doctor came in and said abruptly: 'Read the numbers on the baby's ID bracelet and the one on your wrist. See, it's the same. This baby is yours. This happens to women your age. You may want genetic counseling, and you'll probably want to put it in a home.'"

It is misleading to describe parental reactions without also considering how professionals share the diagnosis. In chapter 11, you will learn about family preferences for learning about the diagnosis. If information were shared in a supportive way and if a family were immediately linked to resources, what difference do you think those approaches might make in family members' emotional reactions? To their hope, sense of self-efficacy, perceived control, and coping skills? Diane Gerst (1991) shares her personal view of the grief process in box 8–1.

Judy O'Halloran, the mother of a son with a disability, counters the grief perspective by describing a "celebration process," a process of reflecting positively and hopefully on the emotions associated with the diagnosis of disability. She suggests that the celebration process moves beyond mere acceptance or

Trevor Is a Citizen, Why Grieve?

I have never had a professional who had high expectations for Trevor tell me I was in denial or that I needed to grieve the loss of my dream. But I have had (more than once) professionals try to get me to accept a lower standard for Trevor by using denial, anger, guilt, and grief to invalidate my opinion and convince me to accept segregation and/or poor services. In the first six months of Trevor's life, I was presented with a grieving process over and over. I experienced stress over the fact that it did not represent what I felt and confusion because other parents felt that it did. I also felt anger with early intervention staff who insisted that *I was grieving* but refusing to acknowledge it.

What would have helped me during the days, weeks and months following my son's diagnosis? First, it would have been helpful if people had seen what I was going through, and helped me to see it, as a crisis, rather than as grief. I've lived through my share of crises, but no one helped me to see that the things

I had learned from previous crises could get me through this one.

It would have been helpful if someone had paid attention to what I was feeling. While judgments were abundant, careful, empathetic, respectful, nonjudgmental listening was in short supply. My feelings were often categorized, but they were not often heard and understood. . . .

And then there was the absence of "congratulations on your new baby" cards, and the "friends" that didn't come to see him. Of all the things that happened, one of the most meaningful for me was a certificate I received from a Congressman, Jack Cera. It said that Trevor was a citizen.

. . . One of the things that helped was a celebration—in spite of the disability, not in ignorance of it—because if the child is not celebrated as he/she is, the parents feel the rejection of a palpable part of the identification crisis.

Having gone through other crises in my life, I can say that

during those my thinking was not discredited or denied. Even though "things had to be worked through," people did not invalidate my ideas or reactions during times of crisis, or dismiss them because I was in an "anger stage." Trevor's a gift, as my other children are. He has never been a source of grief, either now or at his birth. I had indeed been through a crisis and had experienced pain, but he was not the source. He has many times been the consolation.

Added note: Diane wrote down these feelings when Trevor was very young. Today he is a happy, successful student fully included in third grade. Trevor is not only a citizen but also a Boy Scout and a T-ball player. Diane reports that all is well with him, but the crisis more recently has focused on his younger sister who has leukemia. Diane knows how to survive and prevail when she faces crises, and her children are all the consolation.

Source: Gerst, D. (1991). *Trevor is a citizen: Why grieve?* Unpublished manuscript.

---

adaptation. It emphasizes how negative emotions and behaviors can serve as catalysts for energy and persistence (motivation elements of empowerment). She also stresses how the celebration process affirms the positive contributions that children with disabilities make to their families (O'Halloran, 1995).

Not surprisingly, much of the literature about grieving comes from Euro-American professionals and families who are writing about their cultural peers. The initial diagnosis and the impact on families from multicultural perspectives are not yet well

understood. From a Native American orientation, one might expect the following:

When a family member has a disability or illness, traditional ceremonies are conducted to begin the healing process and to protect the individual and the rest of the home from further harm. For that reason, an Indian family may want to complete traditional ceremonies before they seek or become involved in a regime recommended by physicians or other service providers. (Joe & Malach, 1992, p. 106)

Interestingly, developmental milestones also have cultural variations. In a Euro-American culture, a major milestone occurs as the child begins to walk, whereas a first laugh, first hurt, first dance, or ear piercing may have similar priority for some native tribes (Joe & Malach, 1992; Sipes, 1993).

In chapter 11, we will discuss and make suggestions about how to inform families about the presence of an exceptionality and how, in so doing, to foster a reliable alliance by bolstering their motivation (especially self-efficacy, perceived control, and hope). At this point, just remember that discovering the exceptionality and beginning to come to terms with it is a major life cycle task for many families, especially during the early childhood years. (A significant number of students with mild exceptionalities, however, are not identified until they are in elementary school; for their families, discovery and its associated feelings come at a much later time but pose similar challenges.)

Participation in Early Childhood Services

Learning about the exceptionality is only the first of a lifelong series of interactions with professionals. Families with young children whose exceptionalities already have been identified are likely to enter the world of infant stimulation, early intervention, preschool education, and related special services. In their journey through this early childhood stage, they will encounter an early childhood service delivery system that is seeking to be family-centered (Beckman, Newcomb, Frank, Brown, Stepanek, & Barnwell, in press; Murphy, Lee, Turnbull, & Turbiville, 1995; Shelton, Jeppson, & Johnson, 1989). As you read in chapter 2, however, a gap sometimes exists between the family-centered philosophy and practice. This is not to take away from the significant progress that has been made in early childhood services but to underscore the importance of ensuring that your practices are consistent with the espoused philosophy.

How are family-centered services incorporated into early childhood program service delivery? First, the majority of federally funded early childhood programs offer a combined home-center option. Most (75 percent) report that they incorporate a family systems model into services for families, while the others (25 percent) describe services primarily to parents, such as providing training to be their children's teachers.

Ideally, early intervention professionals collaborate with families as they prepare for the marathon ahead—the full life cycle of the family. By supporting families to focus on their long-range needs, these professionals may enable families to enhance their motivation and knowledge/skills and avoid the burnout that can occur when families exert all their efforts during a 100-yard dash in an early intervention program (Turnbull, 1988). Box 8–2 lists tips for assisting families to develop the resilience and pace for attaining their goals over their lifetime marathons.

TIPS
BOX 8-2

Encouraging Success over the Family Marathon

- Meeting the basic needs for food, shelter, health, and security.
- Taking time to reflect on the strengths and limitations of the family.
- Learning to love the child with an exceptionality unconditionally.
- Establishing relationships that will provide the foundation for future support.
- Experiencing and benefiting from the wide range of emotions that accompany having a child with an exceptionality.
- Learning to collaborate to enhance the child's education and development.
- Anticipating the future and learning transitional planning.
- Establishing balance and equity in the family by learning to juggle time and attention among the members.

Source: Adapted from Turnbull, A. P. (1988). The challenge of providing comprehensive support to families. *Education and Training in Mental Retardation, 23*(4), 261–272.

Childhood

Entry into elementary school, a hallmark of childhood, typically widens the horizons of both children and families. For families who have a child with an exceptionality, entry into school may mark their first encounter with many of the issues to which we have devoted whole chapters of this book. For example, the elementary years are a time when many parents acquire—with the support of professionals—(1) a vision for the future and (2) advocacy skills in working for an inclusive education.

Developing a Vision for the Future

Sally Sloop, the mother of Peter, an 8-year-old who has autism, envisions Peter's future when he is 25 years old: "He works where he wants to work, receives a decent paycheck, gets help from the job coach, and is a taxpayer. He has his own apartment and a room-mate or partner so he can continue down life's road without undue loneliness" (Turnbull, Turnbull, Shank, & Leal, 1995, p. 24).

We should not be surprised that parents of children with a disability typically want the same things that almost all parents want for their children: a home, a job to be proud of, friends, happiness, and a chance to contribute to their community (Buswell & Schaffner, 1990; Giangreco, Cloninger, Mueller, Yuan, & Ashworth, 1991).

How do families and professionals develop visions? Visions evolve from great expectations, and they depend on families' hope. In chapter 2, we introduced the concept of vision (Senge, 1990). When professionals initially explain to families that their child has a disability, they can give families hope that families still may accomplish many of their priorities. Professionals can offer themselves as potential allies to achieve the vision, thus enhancing the family's motivation to achieve the vision, and launch the family on a great expectations journey. As the father of a son with autism recounts: "Young people with disabilities can only aspire to what is expected of them. You put them in special education—they learn to wash dishes. You mainstream—they can aspire to live in normal society. We will not allow Jason to use his handicap as an excuse to achieve less than his full potential" (Turnbull, Ruef, & Reeves, p. 32).

Families of elementary students often struggle with the issue of expectations, and often they develop low expectations as a result of wholly negative thinking by professionals, other families, and outdated public attitudes. Professionals such as yourself—and professionals such as the speech therapist and the nurse who had partnerships with the Baccus family when Jessica was very young—play a critical role in igniting family hope (Turnbull & Turnbull, 1985; Turnbull, Turnbull, & Blue-Banning, 1994). So, too, do family and friends. After all, it was Tricia Baccus's friend Merilee who exemplified the hope-giving lesson of unconditional love. Helping families develop positive visions of the future encourages them to push the limits of what is possible. Rather than being trapped by learned helplessness, students, families, friends, and professionals who have great expectations tend to set their sights on what is possible. It is a matter of motivating the family, of providing it with knowledge and skills, and of collaborating as a reliable ally. Where would Jessica Baccus have been educated if her junior high school principal and teacher and her cheerleader friends had not recognized her gifts and had not entertained great expectations for her? Almost surely, Jessica would not have been included in so many aspects of school. Everyone has a role in creating an empowering context, just as they have a role in creating an inclusive education.

Advocating for Inclusive Experiences

Inclusion refers to the practice of educating students with exceptionalities in general education schools and classrooms by using flexible instructional methods and groupings and state-of- the-art individualized methods (Gee, 1996; Thousand, Villa, & Nevin, 1994). Just as perspectives on inclusion vary tremendously among educators and other professionals (Turnbull et al., 1995), so they vary among family members. Many families strongly favor inclusion (Erwin & Soodak, 1995; Guralnick, 1994; Ryndak, Downing, Jacqueline, & Morrison, 1995). Endorsement for inclusion comes from The Arc (1990), the national organization representing individuals with mental retardation and their families, and from other associations of families, professionals, and individuals with disabilities (Turnbull et al., 1995). Here is an excerpt from The Arc's position on education (The Arc, 1990, n.p.):

- All schools should value all students and include them in all aspects of school life.
- Preparation for life in the community best occurs when all students of different backgrounds and abilities learn and socialize together in classrooms and other school settings where all have a chance to achieve and receive instruction designed to develop and enhance accessible living within the community.

- Each student with a disability belongs in an age appropriate classroom with peers who are not disabled.
- Each student has the right to receive individualized education which provides choices, meets the students' needs, and offers the necessary support.

A recent research study shows that 350 educators, administrators, family members, and policymakers from six states generally concur that placement in general education classrooms is an appropriate goal and direction for students with exceptionalities, although they differ in their degree of support for inclusion (Hasazi, Johnston, Liggett, & Schattman, 1994). Different perspectives have resulted in broad state variation in inclusion policy and implementation (Katsiyannis, Conderman, & Franks, 1995).

An important impetus for inclusion has come from parents (such as the Baccus family) who have been initiators (Erwin & Soodak, 1995) and those who have gone on to sue for the implementation of the principle of the least restrictive environment under the Individuals with Disabilities Education Act (Lipton, 1994; Turnbull, H. R., & Turnbull, 1996). One of these cases, *Oberti v. Board of Education of the Borough of Clementon School District* (1992), imposed on schools an affirmative obligation to educate students with disabilities in general education classrooms with the use of supplementary aids and services and to do so before considering more restrictive educational placements. Mr. Oberti, who had the motivation for inclusion but was faced with a context that was noninclusive and certainly not empowering, shares his perspective in box 8–3.

My Voice

BOX 8–3

My Son Rafael Will Succeed

We, the parents of children with disabilities that have had the longest amount of experience working with them from birth, know the way they learn. In my family's case, my son was doing wonderfully, growing and learning in a fully inclusive environment until kindergarten when we hit the brick wall set up by an outdated system. We found that the law is not being taken seriously and that for children with severe cognitive and/or physical disabilities, the path is already written and decided—segregated classes, often very far from their hometown, or if pressed by parents, dumping in the regular class with no supports.

The demands on a child with a disability are not so extraordinary when a group of knowledgeable professionals, together with the parents, have a genuine desire to do what is correct and meet to discuss the abilities, strengths and special needs a child may have as they develop a *fully supported inclusive educational plan*. If that is done instead of "dumping" a child in the regular classroom, and if it is done on an ongoing basis, none of the "robbing" of the rest of the students will occur.

The Individuals with Disabilities Education Act, which proclaims that all children with disabilities have the right to a "free and appropriate eduction" in the "least restrictive environment," is very clear and still, for too many years school bureaucrats have walked all over it.

They feel that based on an IQ score they have the right to label, classify, and ship out children with disabilities to a distant segregated location.

Our son, Rafael A. Oberti, went through six different placements by the time he was seven years old and there would have been many more had we followed the "professionals'" recommendations. Looking back, our only regret is not to have taken charge of the situation sooner than we did. Please remember his name, because he will succeed and he will make a great contribution in this world. Perhaps he already has, certainly in our lives.

Source: Oberti, C. (1993 September). A parent's perspective. *Exceptional Parent*, 18–21. Reprinted with the expressed consent and approval of *Exceptional Parent*, a monthly magazine for parents and families of children with disabilities and special health care needs. Subscription cost is $28 per year for 12 issues. Call 1-800-247-8080. Offices at 120 State Street, Hackensack, NJ 07601.

Alternatively, many parents oppose inclusion and believe that their son or daughter gets more individualized, expert help in special education settings. Several studies have found that parents generally tend to support placement of students with disabilities in general education classrooms, but they are substantially more skeptical in terms of the reintegration of their own child from special education to general education classes (Abramson, Willson, Yoshida, & Hagerty, 1983), preferring special education services to having their child return to the general education classroom (Green & Shinn, 1994). As one parent said, "with the types of problems that he has, he needs one-on-one instruction. He needs someone close by to follow he's comprehending what he's being taught. If he had the self-esteem and the motivation to learn, then he could be in the regular classroom" (Green & Shinn, 1994, p. 274).

Interestingly, other research has pointed out that when children are returned from specialized settings to general education classrooms, parents do tend to report positive perceptions and attribute improvements in academic, behavioral, and social areas to the opportunity to be with age-appropriate classmates (Ryndak et al., 1995).

*A*dolescence

Adolescence is the next life cycle stage in the family's development. Puberty, the beginning of sexual maturity, usually marks the start of adolescence and signals rapid physical and psychological changes and challenges, including (1) development of self-identity, (2) development of a positive body image, (3) adjustment to sexual maturation, (4) emotional independence from parents, (5) increased self-determination, and (6) development of mature relationships with peers of both sexes. All these tasks have implications for the "balance of the family mobile."

Adolescence in general can be stressful for the youth and other family members. Parents may find their authority challenged as adolescents experiment with newfound sexuality or begin to assert their independence. In addition, parents may be facing problems of their own as they enter midlife. In a national study conducted with more than 1,000 families in the general population, parents reported that the life cycle stages of adolescence and young adulthood were the two stages with the highest amount of stresses and strains (Olson et al., 1983).

An exceptionality may either mitigate or compound some of the typical adolescent storms. For example, parents might be confronted with reduced rebellion and conflict because their children may have fewer peers after whom to model such behaviors, fewer opportunities to try alcohol and drugs, or decreased mobility and therefore fewer chances to take dangerous risks. In other cases, adolescence may bring greater isolation, a growing sense of difference, and confusion and fear about emerging sexuality. Some of the educational issues of highest priority during the adolescent stage include (1) sexuality education and (2) self-determination skills.

Sexuality Education   Emerging sexuality often presents family challenges. When the adolescent has an exceptionality, the challenge may be compounded, as it has been for Jessica Baccus and her family. Unlike Tricia Baccus, however, some parents may not even recognize that it is possible for their child to have sexual needs (Brotherson, 1985). In interviews with 24 parents of adults with mental retardation, 88 percent stated that their son or daughter had no needs related to sexuality: Either the parents discouraged it, or they assumed it was beyond their child's comprehension (Brotherson, Backus, Summers, & Turnbull, 1986). In fact, a challenge for many families is to address sexuality education and particularly their special concerns about the risk of sexual abuse.

Sexuality education has been noticeably absent from special or general education curricula in many schools, and families often fail to address their children's sexuality. As one teacher explained: "We see sexual problems among our students all of the time and, although we gossip about them, we do nothing to help students understand their feelings or drive. Really, we avoid getting involved. It's easier for us that way" (Brantlinger, 1992, pp. 9–10).

A professional who provides vocational preparation commented:

> The classic word around here is "redirect"—to be interpreted as "you can't do it here" or "that is not appropriate here." The problem is there is nowhere where sex is appropriate. "Redirect" sounds objective, but it is really oppressive. The administrators talk out of both sides of their mouth. They sound like they are for normalization but, in truth, they're not. At least they're not when it comes to sexual behavior. (Brantlinger, 1992, p. 11)

Educators and parents would do well to include the following topics in a sexuality curriculum: anatomy and physiology, maturation and body changes, birth control, sexually transmitted diseases and their prevention, masturbation, responsibility for sexual behavior, inappropriate sexual behavior and sex offenses, same-sex and opposite-sex activity, psychosocial sexual aspects of behavior and psychosexual development, and marriage and parenthood (Monat-Haller, 1992, p. 42).

There is hardly a parent who does not worry that his or her child—especially one who has a disability—may be a victim of sexual abuse. A study that analyzed patterns of sexual abuse of adults with mental retardation over a five-year period reported that almost three-fourths of the victims were characterized as having mild mental retardation and had an average age of 30. Approximately one-fourth of the abuse incidents occurred in institutions, and another one-fourth occurred in group homes. In the remaining situations, the location of the incidents ranged among the victim's own home, a work setting, or a vehicle. The perpetrator was known to the victim in the vast majority of cases; this also is the case in sexual abuse of people who do not have an exceptionality. Although many families may expect abuse from a stranger or in an unsupervised situation in a public place, the results of this research indicate that sexual abuse is far more likely to occur from a known person in a known place (Furey, 1994). Families and youth need accurate information about the likelihood of sexual abuse; indeed, the skills and knowledge to prevent sexual abuse should be a key topic in sexuality training during the adolescent years.

Moreover, parents justifiably fear that their children will acquire sexually transmitted diseases. Although the Centers for Disease Control do not collect data on the rate of HIV/AIDS infection among individuals with disabilities, infection in this population has been reported to be escalating (Kastner, Nathanson, & Marchetti, 1992). In a survey of 25 community programs that provide services to people with developmental disabilities, 24 expressed a need for the people receiving their services to have the benefit of HIV/AIDS prevention education (Mason & Jaskulski, 1994).

What is a reliable ally—the state-of-the-art professional—to do? Acknowledging families' concerns, offering or referring them to sex education programs, and following tips to prevent child maltreatment of all kinds (chapter 10) are warranted.

Expanding Self-Determination Skills *Self-determination* means choosing how to live one's life consistently with one's own personal values and preferences (Turnbull, Blue-Banning, Anderson, Seaton,

Turnbull, & Dinas, 1996; Turnbull & Turnbull, 1985). Typically, adolescence is a period of increasing autonomy. Although all issues related to family life are culturally rooted, culture plays a special role with respect to self-determination and the appropriate role of children and youth in expressing their preferences and solving their problems. Some cultural norms strongly favor independence, while other cultural norms favor collectivism, familism, and interdependent rather than independent decision-making styles (chapter 5). Honoring families' cultural traditions is one of the eight obligations of reliable alliances.

Cultural norms aside, child development theory (Marvin & Pianta, 1992) and research (Powers, Singer, & Sowers, 1996; Sands & Wehmeyer, 1996) make one fact abundantly clear: Building on a student's interest and direction is a critical aspect of self-determination. Indeed, self-determination competence building, while especially appropriate for the adolescent, is also desirable for very young children, including those in early intervention and preschool services, who should be encouraged to express their choices and act on their preferences. Increasingly, research is documenting the critical role that self-reliance competence during infancy plays in laying the foundation for later self-reliance competence during adolescence and adulthood (Greenspan & Porges, 1984; Marvin & Pianta, 1992).

A comprehensive national survey of adults with mental retardation regarding the extent of their self-determination showed that they have few choices and minimal control over key life decisions, such as selecting roommates, choosing a place to live, or approving people who have major responsibilities and provide support to them (Wehmeyer & Metzler, 1995). Why is this so? Because educational and home environments tend to be overly structured and because, as the severity of the person's disability increases, so do the limitations in choice.

Especially in regard to family issues, there are four obstacles that challenge parents in supporting self-determination: (1) being unclear about the extent of self-determination that is appropriate to expect, (2) being unfamiliar with instructional strategies to encourage the further development of self-determination, (3) having cultural clashes with the expression of self-determination, and (4) dealing with their child's multiple challenges and accordingly relegating self-determination to a lower priority (Powers et al., 1996). In chapter 12 we will discuss ways to support self-determination in culturally relevant ways during IFSP/IEP conferences.

Adulthood

Adulthood is the next life cycle stage and the last one that we will consider in this chapter. Culturally, adulthood can be attained in many ways (for example, leaving parents' homes, marrying, becoming a parent, or entering the armed services); but we characterize adulthood as starting at age 21, which is when school eligibility ends in most states for students with exceptionalities.

Growing up—attaining the status of adulthood—is taken for granted by most adults in our society but cannot be taken for granted by people with disabilities (Ferguson & Ferguson, 1993). There are reasons why this is so. With the move into adulthood comes the responsibility for meeting one's own needs in the seven categories of family functions (chapter 7); but for some adults with disabilities, carrying out these duties is problematic. In addition, the move into adulthood brings opportunities for greater choice and control, but those opportunities may be hard to obtain for people with disabilities. The decisions regarding how to divide independence and responsibility among the young adult, the family, and other support systems can be difficult: Letting go is hard for parents who have had to devote extra attention to meeting the extra needs of children and youth. And it is sometimes hard for professionals, too. Moreover, cultural values strongly influence the concept of growing up and what adulthood means to family relationships. In Euro-American culture, it may mean moving out of the house, but in a Latino culture, it may mean continuing to live with one's parents.

Figure 8–2 highlights three dimensions of adulthood: autonomy, membership, and change (Ferguson & Ferguson, 1993). For most people, especially those of Euro-American culture, moving into adulthood means finding employment and moving away from home. For the young adult, this represents a process of attaining greater independence and responsibility; for the parents, it means a process of letting go of their son or daughter. This stage can be difficult in any family, but it is especially challenging for families with young adults who are exceptional. Two issues facing the individual and his or her family involve (1) identifying postsecondary educational programs and (2) accessing supported employment and supported living opportunities. In both these

---

FIGURE 8–2

Three Dimensions of Adulthood

Autonomy

Autonomy is being one's own person. It is expressed through symbols of:

- *Self-sufficiency*—especially economic self-sufficiency, or having the resources to take care of oneself. Self-sufficiency includes emotional self-sufficiency, or the ability to "make it" on one's own. It makes a shift from economic consumption alone to production and consumption.
- *Self-determination*—assertion of individuality and independence. Self-determination is the ability to assure others that one possesses the rational maturity and personal freedom to make specific choices about how to live one's life.
- *Completeness*—a sense of having "arrived," a shift from future to present tense, no more waiting.

Membership

Membership is community connectedness, collaboration, and sacrifice. It is expressed through symbols of:

- *Citizenship*—activities of collective governance from voting and participating in town meetings to volunteering for political candidates to expressing one's position on issues with money, time, or bumper stickers to recycling to protect the shared environment.
- *Affiliation*—activities of voluntary association, fellowship, celebration, and support from greeting the new family in the neighborhood with a plate of cookies to being an active member of the church, a participant in the local service or garden club, or an entrant in area road races.

Change

Change is adulthood as an ongoing capacity for growth rather than the static outcome of childhood.

Source: Ferguson, P. M., & Ferguson, D. L. (1993). The promise of adulthood. In M. Snell (Ed.), *Instruction of persons with severe disabilities* (4th ed.) (p. 591). Englewood Cliffs, NJ: Merrill/Prentice Hall.

issues, motivation (such as hope and persistence) and knowledge/skills are indispensable and should be provided by the empowering professional.

Identifying Postsecondary Educational Programs and Supports

Planning for a postsecondary education implies selecting a program and finding financial resources. How can you be a reliable ally in this process? Ideally, planning should begin at least two or three years before graduation. Students with postsecondary goals need information and problem-solving skills to evaluate programs at different colleges and universities and compare the capacities of those programs with their own strengths and needs. You should assist students and families in identifying the appropriateness of postsecondary career goals, ensuring that students develop prerequisite skills, and teaching students to complete applications and access services consistent with their support needs. Parents and students alike need advice about scholarship opportunities, loans, and work-study programs. Resource guides in a school or local library and workshops on college planning and academic and financial issues can be helpful resources for family and adolescents.

Students with learning disabilities, sensory impairments, or physical disabilities will need your support in considering a variety of other special needs when selecting a postsecondary institution. Does the college provide special assistance such as tutoring programs for students with learning disabilities or interpreters for students with hearing impairments? Is the campus accessible for wheelchair users? Does the state vocational rehabilitation program provide financial assistance for personal-care attendants while the student is attending college? Is there an office that oversees the provision of reasonable accommodations for students with disabilities? Does the college or university have a published and well-enforced plan for complying with the Americans with Disabilities Act? In other words, is the college the type of empowering context that you yourself try to provide?

Helpful information about postsecondary programs and disability accommodations is available from two national resources. The first is the National Clearinghouse on Postsecondary Education for Individuals with Disabilities at the American Council on Education (1 Dupont Circle, Suite 800, Washington, DC 20063–1193). The clearinghouse publishes annotated resource guides to accommodations in higher education for students with disabilities. The second is the Association on Higher Education and Disability (P.O. Box 21192, Columbus, OH 43221–0192). This association provides a journal, newsletter, and annual conferences. Share resources such as these with families and students with disabilities who are pursuing postsecondary education.

Although families are their children's primary advocates during the elementary and secondary years, colleges expect students themselves to take on this responsibility. One of the best preparations for students' success during postsecondary years is to prepare students and families throughout the elementary and secondary years to assume increasing responsibility to be their own disability and education advocates.

For many students with disabilities, postsecondary education (including junior colleges, technical schools, community colleges, and four-year colleges and universities) has not generally been considered a viable option, even though it may be very appropriate in light of the student's strengths, needs, and future priorities. Although increasing numbers of students with mild disabilities are enrolling in postsecondary education, they are having difficulties completing the program. For example, one study reported that 50 percent of students with learning disabilities who graduated from high school participated in some type of postsecondary program, but only 6.5 percent were still in school one year after they graduated from high school (Sitlington & Frank, 1990). A national survey of postsecondary educational services indicated that community colleges reported a 13.6 percent graduation rate (Bursuck, Rose, Cowen, & Yahaya, 1989). Some student groups have been cited as being particularly underrepresented in postsecondary education, including students with serious emotional disabilities (Koroloff, 1990).

Accessing Supported Employment and Supported Living Options

Given the three dimensions of adulthood specified in figure 8–2, supported adulthood, described by Ferguson and Ferguson (1993), is appropriate for many students with disabilities:

> What is new in the notion of Supported Adulthood is a commitment to participation and affiliation rather than to control and remediation. Support cannot be a predefined service available to any who meet eligibility criteria. The real message of initiatives such as supported employment and supported living should be that all people do not have to be totally independent in terms of skills or fully competitive (or even close) in terms

of productivity to be active, growing, valued adult members of their community. (Ferguson & Ferguson, 1993, p. 599)

Supported employment, one of the two elements of supported adulthood, is not a new concept; federal support for it started in the late 1980s. In supported employment, a person with a disability shares a job with a person who does not have a disability, called a "job coach" because the person without the disability not only shares the job but teaches it to the person with a disability. Both are responsible for doing the job, and the employer pays both at least the minimum wage for at least 20 hours of weekly work. The work must be with people without disabilities; that is, it must be integrated work. Through supported employment, adults with disabilities have opportunities to learn job skills on the job rather than work through a readiness model in sheltered workshops as a prerequisite for getting a real job.

Supported employment is an alternative to sheltered employment. Unfortunately, many families of people with disabilities do not understand the differences between these two models in terms of wages, growth opportunities, and alternatives for support. Many families still prefer the safety and predictability of sheltered workshops to a community work setting (Hill, Seyfarth, Banks, Wehman, & Orelove, 1985). Motivate families toward supported employment by providing them with comprehensive information about its benefits. Consider that (1) families are keys to decision making about future job opportunities and (2) approximately 80 percent of the jobs that were secured by former special educa-

tion students were obtained through a family connection (Hasazi, Gordon, & Roe, 1985). Just as people without exceptionalities access jobs through family and friendship networks (including networks in which you, the professional reliable ally, participate), so do people with exceptionalities. To provide an empowering context and increase parental support for supported employment, apply the tips highlighted in box 8–4.

Supported living is a newer concept than supported employment. Ferguson and Ferguson (1993) describe supported living (as applicable to their son who has multiple disabilities) as follows:

> Simply put, supported living means that Ian should be able to live where he wants, with whom he wants, for as long as he wants, with the ongoing support needed to make that happen (Boles, Horner, & Bellamy, 1988). At a minimum, Ian's home should be the one place he will not have to worry about wheelchair accessibility. Beyond that, however, Ian should have more options than a forced choice of a five- or ten-bed group home. Indeed, supported living means that Ian should be able to find his own place (within his means), whether it be a house, an apartment, a duplex, or a cooperative, with the residential support following him to that location. (Ferguson & Ferguson, 1993, p. 602)

That is an ideal, but what does research say about the reality? Sadly, interviews with parents of young adults with mental retardation and physical disabilities indicate that parents in both groups report most frequently that their greatest need is for the stability

---

TIPS   BOX 8–4

Enhancing Parental Support for Supported Employment

- Obtain information on parents' needs and desires relating to placement.
- Obtain possible job leads from parents and family.
- Keep parents informed of placement activities.
- Review the details of a potential job before proceeding with placement activities.
- Provide specific suggestions for supporting and reinforcing job performance.
- Provide ongoing information about job performance and status.

Source: Sowers, J. (1993). Critical parent roles in supported employment. In G. H. S. Singer & L. K. Irvin (Eds.), *Support for caregiving families: Enabling positive adaptation to disability* (pp. 276–279). Baltimore: Brookes.

and certainty that comes from finding suitable residential options. As one parent says, "work is not high on the hierarchy of Maslow's needs. Survival is most important. Most of all (my daughter) needs a place to live and be happy. The rest is additional" (Brotherson et al., 1986, p. 170).

A national survey revealed that more than 63,000 adults with mental retardation were on waiting lists for residential services in 1988 (The Arc, 1988). Since that time, waiting lists have increased.

Not only families, but also many educators and adult service providers, have limited visions for supported living situations, as indicated by this teacher as she described one of her students: "Realistically down the road, I never see [this student] in an independent status. I see her living with her mom for a long period of time . . . and I don't ever see [her] able to function independently at all! I don't know how she would even handle a group home!" (Gallivan-Fenlon, 1994, p. 15).

Innovative adult agencies are starting exciting supported living options, and some families are pioneering supported living on their own without agency participation (Racino, Walker, O'Connor, & Taylor, 1993).

In box 8–5 you will read how our son J. T. experiences supported living. In chapter 13 we will describe in more detail how his "Action Group" collaborates to design and implement his specific supports.

Having reviewed two educational concerns that many families experience at each of the life cycle stages of early childhood, school age, adolescence, and early adulthood, we remind you that education is only one of the seven family functions that you learned about in chapter 7. Do you now appreciate the challenges that families must face as they deal not only with educational issues but also with challenges associated with each of the other six functions at each new life cycle stage?

And can you now appreciate why Tricia Baccus has to believe in her family; be convinced she can affect what happens to her; and have energy, persistence, and hope? Her words "hope, becoming, and faith" reflect the degree to which she is an empowerful person, just as they reflect the important empowering roles that nurses, school principals, and teachers have played in creating an empowering context for her and her family.

TOGETHER WE CAN BOX 8–5

On My Own

Jay Turnbull (J. T.) lives "on my own," as he likes to describe his adulthood. This is extraordinary, given that he was in segregated special education for all but his last year of public school and "failed" sheltered workshop and group-home living. Why did he fail? Because, by engaging in self-injurious and aggressive behavior in those programs, he gave a very clear message: "This is not how I want to live my life." In a word, J. T. was saying, "I want to live on my own, my way."

Living "on my own" means having two roommates who do not have disabilities and who are (like him) in their mid-20s. J. T. lives in a house that he pays for (with help from his family), takes the city bus to and from work daily, and does clerical work at The University of Kansas. He spends leisure time with friends in activities such as going out to dinner and clubs where he can dance and listen to music and working out at a fitness center. He spends weekends with his parents, sisters, and grandfather and regularly shops in stores where he is well known to the staff and proprietors.

None of this would be possible without the collaboration of a host of people—his parents and sisters, their friends, roommates and their friends, J. T.'s co-workers, and a few professionals. Most important of all are those people to whom J. T. endears himself—the friends he himself makes and who become passionately committed to supporting him.

Life Cycle Transitions

As we noted at the beginning of the chapter, life cycle stages are like plateaus between the peaks and valleys of transitions from one life cycle stage to another, such as from early childhood to elementary school services. Transition times often are the most challenging periods for families. In addition to transitional periods between life cycle stages, there are also transitions as families move from one service system to another. These transitions involve movement from the intensive care nursery to the home and community, preschool to kindergarten, elementary to middle school, middle school to high school, and high school into adulthood (Able-Boone & Stevens, 1994; Brown, Albright, Rogan, York, Solner, Johnson, VanDeventer, & Loomis, 1988; Halvorsen, Doering, Farron-Davis, Usilton, & Sailor, 1989; Lusthaus & Lusthaus, in press; Rosenkoetter, Hains, & Fowler, 1994; Turnbull, Turnbull, Bronicki, Summers, & Roeder-Gordon, 1989). These are the times when you should be particularly careful to be a reliable ally and practice the empowering context techniques that we outlined in chapter 3 and will discuss in chapters 9 through 15.

Two factors tend to reduce the amount of stress most families feel during a transition. First, in every culture the roles of the new stage are fairly well defined. Thus, the transition may be marked by some kind of ritual, such as a wedding, bar mitzvah, graduation, or funeral. These ceremonies serve as signals to the family that their relationships following the event will be changed (Friedman, 1980). The interactions and roles for the new stage are modeled by other families with the same previous or present experiences. Thus, the future is not entirely unknown.

Second, the timing of transitions is also fairly well expected. In Euro-American culture, for example, children are often expected to leave home after they graduate from high school. Likewise, death may be expected and psychologically prepared for as a person reaches old age.

Transitional challenges can, however, be complicated by considerations associated with cultural diversity:

> I think the transition from elementary to intermediate level is really an important transition for young people. We have been looking at this for several years at Zuni and trying to determine what needs to be done to deal with these issues. We see a rise in negative socialization. We see students not being able to pick up the subject matter. And we see teachers not having enough time to teach

because they are coming from a self-contained situation to almost a shot-gun approach with a seven-period schedule and only limited time to concentrate on an area.

> At this transition point kids begin to segregate themselves, whereas in the earlier years kids intermingle more. This is especially true where Native American students are minorities in public schools. As young children they can have friends who are non-Native, but by the time they are older, Native kids seem to gravitate toward the back of the room, as if they had figured out that is their place. So we need to figure out ways to help these kids feel like they belong up front and in the middle as well as in the back. Teachers could influence this by looking at the physical environment in their classrooms and mixing it up a bit more. (Indian Nations at Risk & National Advisory Council on Indian Education, 1990, pp. 15–16)

For families with a member who has an exceptionality, the expected roles as well as the future of the person with an exceptionality may not be clear, and a ritual to mark the change may be absent. Nor may the transition itself, if it does occur, happen at the expected time. Life cycle transitions seem to be much more traumatic and stressful when they occur at other than expected times (Neugarten, 1976; Turnbull et al., 1986). In this section, you will learn about (1) the implications of uncertain futures and (2) off-time transitions.

Uncertainty About the Future

For many individuals with an exceptionality, the future looms like a frightening unknown. Few norms and models of expected behavior may be available for either the child or the family. The common admonition to "take things one day at a time" is particularly apt (and welcomed by a family) not only because there are more than enough responsibilities for the family in the present but also because the future is so ambiguous (Featherstone, 1980). Just reflect about the Baccus family: Tricia, Craig, Jessica, Melissa, and Lara live time-compressed lives, facing Jessica's earlier-than-normal death but trying to put as much joy into their lives as possible.

A sometimes complicating factor associated with transition challenges is that the rituals that serve as "punctuation marks" for transitions for youth without disabilities may be blurred or nonexistent in youth with disabilities. The time when a transition occurs—or should occur—may not be marked with a celebration but with chronic frustration that supports are not in place for transition to the next stage. Thus, not only is the family uncertain about exactly *how* their interactions might change, but they also may have no cues *that* the interactions will change.

You can be an ally of students and families during the transition or "uncertainty" times by working to translate their great expectations into future reality. For example, educators can collaborate with families by creating scenarios of what might happen five years in the future and then pinpoint educational goals and objectives that will best propel the student toward that desirable future. Visits to new classrooms or community jobs, meetings with future teachers and with adults with disabilities and parents of older children with similar exceptionalities can all help to reduce the fear of the future by making it less unknown. Box 8–6 offers some suggestions for easing the transitions into and out of each of the life cycle stages discussed in this chapter.

Off-Time Transitions

Families with a member who has an exceptionality are likely to experience a life cycle transition that occurs at other than its expected time. Transitions are often delayed or fail to occur. For example, a young adult might remain at home with his or her parents well into the parents' elderly years (Seltzer, Krauss, & Janicki, 1994). Although Euro-American culture generally regards this type of living arrangement as an off-time transition, research on elderly parents who have provided care across the decades of their family life indicates that these parents experience positive outcomes. A study of more than 200 aging mothers of adults with mental retardation who were living at home led the researchers to the following conclusion: "Specifically, the women in our sample were substantially healthier and had better morale than did

---

TIPS

BOX 8–6

Enhancing Successful Transistions

Early Childhood

- Begin preparing for the separation of preschool children by periodically leaving the child with others.
- Gather information and visit preschools in the community.
- Encourage participation in Parent to Parent programs. (Veteran parents are matched in one-to-one relationships with parents who are just beginning the transition process.)
- Familiarize parents with possible school (elementary and secondary) programs, career options, or adult programs so they have an idea of future opportunities.

Childhood

- Provide parents with an overview of curricular options.
- Ensure that IEP meetings provide an empowering context for family collaboration.
- Encourage participation in Parent to Parent matches, workshops, or family support groups to discuss transitions with others.

Adolescence

- Assist families and adolescents to identify community leisure-time activities.
- Incorporate into the IEP skills that will be needed in future career and vocational programs.
- Visit or become familiar with a variety of career and living options.
- Develop a mentor relationship with an adult with a similar exceptionality and an individual who has a career that matches the student's strengths and preferences.

Adulthood

- Provide preferred information to families about guardianship, estate planning, wills, and trusts.
- Assist family members in transferring responsibilities to the individual with an exceptionality, other family members, or service providers as appropriate.
- Assist the young adult or family members with career or vocational choices.
- Address the issues and responsibilities of marriage and family for the young adult.

other samples of caregivers for elderly persons and reported no more burden and stress than did other caregivers" (Seltzer & Krauss, 1989, pp. 309–310).

Whereas some transitions are delayed or do not occur, others may occur earlier than the expected time. For instance, researchers have found that placing a child in a living situation outside the home can create a range of emotions including grief as well as relief (Blacher, 1994). Another off-time transition (one that the Baccus family has been obliged to anticipate) occurs at premature death. Illness and death may be expected parts of life for an older person; but when they happen to a child, they are seen as strange and cruel twists of fate.

A brother or sister of a young person who dies may be "the 'silent' family member who seems to be coping well but may be in considerable distress" (Seligman, 1985, p. 276). Lois Wright's two-year-old brother had a rare form of dystrophy and died when she was 12. Lois reflects on the experience:

> Before Gary died, I tried to figure out how I was supposed to respond when he finally did die. Was I supposed to cry? Would people watch me? I periodically wanted Gary to die so Mom would stay home instead of going to the hospital and sometimes so my family could go on weekend trips and vacations. I felt guilty for thinking about the good things that would happen if Gary died.

> After Gary died, I experienced a deep loss and great sorrow. It was much worse than I imagined. I worried about my mom because she was so sad, and I wondered how to act when I went back to school.

> My parents did a good job of helping me through this hard time. They seemed to perceive almost all my feelings and tried to counteract them. They encouraged us kids to talk about how we felt and never rebuked us for expressing those feelings. They made special arrangements for me to visit Gary [at the hospital] and, thus, spend time with my mom. I will always treasure those special moments.

Finally, off-time transitions occur when students who are gifted significantly advance in grade placements, even to the point of leaving secondary schools substantially early to go to college. Although most educators do not generally favor accelerated placement of students into higher grade levels (Southern & Jones, 1991; Tannenbaum, 1986), advancement does occur and can be in the student's and family's best interests. A very unusual example is Michael Kearney, who entered college at age six and graduated several years later. Michael describes his experiences shortly after his college graduation at nine:

> Growing up, I have dealt with teachers who have never knowingly met, much less talked, to someone like me. . . . I remember going to the hallways, looking at the faces of . . . students, and listening to them refer to me as "Doogie Howser." . . . Another issue that I had to deal with while attending college was the chatter of my classmates. They thought that my parents had pushed me; I beg to differ. My parents have done their best to see that I am a well adjusted and a loving human being. For example, when I decided to go to college, they had to deal with the unexpected financial cost of early college attendance. They have been behind me 100 percent.

> I started out, at the age of 6, as a child who thrived on learning and craved a stimulating educational system that would enhance my academic spirit. At the University of South Alabama, I was allowed the freedom to think, act independently, and pursue my educational excellence even though I was only 8. These educators believe that children like myself have the potential to excel in an appropriate education. (Turnbull et al., 1995, p. 389)

Michael's father, Kevin Kearney, adds:

> Now that we look back, most of Michael's accomplishments do seem impossible: reading books at eighteen months, kindergarten at three years old, high school at five years old, high school diploma at six years old, associate's degree in geology at eight years old, and bachelor's degree in anthropology at ten years old. The way we look at it is "Give children all the stimulation and knowledge they want. It can't hurt them." (Turnbull et al., 1995, p. 385)

Regardless of the reason that children make off-time transitions, families deserve your support and assistance—your allegiance in creating a context that helps them get what they want—in dealing with the unexpected.

Summary

Families change; the mere passage of time causes changes in their characteristics (chapter 5), interactions (chapter 6), and functions (chapter 7). The changes over a family's life cycle typically occur during the four stages of birth and early childhood, childhood, adolescence, and adulthood. Sometimes these changes happen "on cycle," sometimes "off cycle." Whenever they occur, the period of time leading up to and just following the change in life cycle stage is the transition time, a period when families usually experience heightened anxiety and stress. In each of these stages, however, you can support the family to take action to get what they want and need—you can be an empowering collaborator—by being especially sensitive to life stages and transitions.

After Jessica Baccus's fourth birthday party had concluded and the streamers, balloons, and torn gift wrappings had been gathered up and put away, Tricia wrote her daughter a letter that reflects on the family life cycle and the meaning of that family's life.

Dear Jessica:

Sweet, sleeping child. So small, so vulnerable. This day has brought to me an aching sense of the passing of time. Just one more day of living, but with one great difference—you are one year older. Jessica, you know by now life is not all pink balloons and streamers. But all in all, life has been pretty good to you. I wish I could promise you it will always go on this way. I can't. I wish I could go ahead of you to guide, warn and protect you . . . "walk out" the hard parts for you. I can't, and even if I could, it wouldn't be right. No, I must free you to live life yourself—whatever that may involve.

Little did Tricia know, a decade ago, what freeing Jessica to live her life would mean: The transition from early childhood to childhood, marked by a fourth birthday, is significantly different than the transition from childhood to adolescence. Lip gloss and overnights have replaced balloons and at-home parties. And a different-than-imagined, a different-than-wanted, future lies ahead: a truncated life. But we can be sure that it will be a family life that is lived with a difference, as Tricia wrote to Jessica after that birthday party: "I may write the lessons [of life for Jessica], but in so many ways you teach me of living and loving." That is a universal lesson: Children and parents are each other's teachers, whatever the life stage and whatever the lesson might have to be.

Part Three

Collaborating for Empowerment

In part 3 you will learn how to collaborate for empowerment. After learning about the contexts for empowerment (chapters 1 and 2), the concept of empowerment (chapters 3 and 4), and family systems perspectives (chapters 5 through 8), you are now ready to become familiar with the seven opportunities for partnerships that form the basis of collaborating for empowerment.

In your work with families, their children, and the schools, you will invariably find opportunities for being a partner with families—for being a collaborator with them. We believe that seven opportunities for being a partner will present themselves to you, no matter what role you have in schools or how that role brings you into contact with families and students.

You always need to communicate with families. Therefore, in chapter 9 we suggest how you can do that collaboratively. Because you will work with families who have great difficulties meeting their basic needs or handling special challenges, such as poverty or child maltreatment, chapter 10 describes how you can enable families to meet their needs and at the same time be their partner. Every student in special education receives an evaluation and then an individualized appropriate special education program, so chapters 11 and 12 describe how these inevitable occurrences also are opportunities for you to be a collaborator. Many families want to work with their children at home, and many children learn not just from school but from their community activities. Thus, chapter 13 describes how you can advance their learning by collaborating with their families at home and in the community. Some families are highly involved with their children's school, often attending school events or serving as volunteers; whenever a family member enters the school building or engages in a school activity, there is another opportunity for you to be a partner, as we show in chapter 14. Finally, parents are by nature advocates for their children; and advocacy, as we explain in chapter 15, is also an activity that generates opportunities for you to be a collaborator.

None of these seven opportunities for partnerships will lead to empowerment unless you enrich them with an affective or attitudinal dimension. We encourage you in each of the chapters in part 3 to meet your obligations to be effective as a partner by being affective in your work with families. We suggest how you can maximize the seven opportunities for partnerships by employing the eight obligations of a reliable alliance introduced in chapter 4.

Chapter Nine

Communicating Among Reliable Allies

"*T*ime is our enemy. Time is our friend." That's not exactly what Sue Manos of Frederick, Maryland, says about her son Nick. But it captures the essence of the approach she and Nick's team of teachers and administrators have used to include him in regular classes.

Nick is 12 and has multiple disabilities, principally cerebral palsy. After spending first grade in a segregated special school, he became the catalyst for inclusion and school teaming during his second through his (present) fifth-grade years.

It took Sue a full year to move Nick from the separate first grade to the integrated second grade. During that year, she told the county board of education that she wanted Nick to be included; then she worked out an inclusion plan with the board, district administrators, school administrators, and general and special educators.

More than that, she convinced the board and Nick's future educators that Nick would benefit from inclusion. She did this by relying on her knowledge of Nick's legal rights, citing research and demonstration models that supported her position, and being both persistent and uncompromising.

"We set the tone by letting them know that we knew what we were entitled to. . . . You know, this is the thing that's kind of sad. It is the fact that they know I persist and that I know what I'm talking about. It keeps the dialogue going. Where I see it die down with other parents is when the parents don't know what they need to know. They're not empowered, and then it's easy for the administrators to just kind of let it die, especially if it's been a difficult issue."

Sue's attitude that Nick is entitled to everything any other student can have, plus being self-taught about rights and techniques, have led Sue to become a "teamer." She and Nick's general and special education teachers, support staff, and administrators have weekly meetings. Sue joins two meetings a month and sits out the other two.

"The benefit of that teaming for the school is that now everyone in my school is comfortable with frequent meetings. . . . They've learned to team. . . . They have this wonderful teaming system for anybody with a child who is included. It requires meeting once a week, getting the entire team together."

Sue is quick to point out that it took her and the school staff four years to get to that point. Some teachers didn't think they had the time or energy for so much planning. But with rearrangement of some schedules, there was indeed time; and with the meetings comes an energy to help Nick and other students. When the team does not meet, Nick begins to spiral down. The team members do not get feedback "on the little things that are crucial."

Naturally, frequent meetings also result in confrontations and disagreements. Paradoxically, however, these meetings have created a reliable alliance involving Sue, Nick, his peers, his teachers (especially those least receptive to his inclusion), and the administrators.

By meeting so often, Sue says, "[I] thought I was destroying the relationships. Oddly, they became stronger than ever. . . . People just needed guidance back into the right direction. . . . They realized how important it was to have me there to provide continuity between home and school."

The team's efforts—sometimes painful, always candid—generated mutual respect. "I gained respect for them in many ways, even as angry or upset as I had been. They also gained some respect for me, just in terms of being able to guide them."

That's at the personal level. Throughout the school, general and special educators who initially opposed the meetings now welcome them. "The school as a whole has benefited in that they now have built in cooperative planning meetings for all children in inclusive education. The really big change for the school was to have this overall attitude of, to make it work we have to team. . . . The school really has become a place where everyone is interested in everyone else's best interest."

Has the teaming made any difference for Nick? Yes, no doubt. Nick is invited to team meetings; this enables him to express his preferences, enhance his self-esteem, and experience a sense of power over his life.

Moreover, there are ways to save time but still be effective for Nick. There are premeeting telephone calls to set an agenda for the meetings, focus on the issues, and handle the smaller, less important aspects of Nick's education and the team's effectiveness as a unit. There are exchanges of daily logs, microcassettes, and a home-school notebook. Nick's peers dictate the log notes into the microcassette and add their own perspectives about Nick's day, and Nick uses a low-tech "cheap talk" (simulated voice) machine. And there are periodic social occasions for Sue and Nick's teachers, when talk about school is completely off limits.

You might think that all these meetings take time and that meeting time is the enemy. On the contrary, Sue's experience is that time can be everyone's friend.

But it took her time to learn that . . . and time for Nick's professional team to learn it, too.

♡ ♡ ♡ ♡ ♡

There are seven opportunities for partnerships between families and professionals (chapters 9 through 15), but none is more important than the partnership that involves ongoing communication. Communication lies at the heart of all the other types of partnerships. It is the initial and indispensable ingredient of the empowering context that we described in the framework discussed in chapter 3 and that we illustrate in figure 9–1.

In figure 9–1 you see that communication is one of your opportunities for creating partnerships and reliable alliances. In communicating with families, you can come to know yourself, know them, honor their cultural diversity, affirm their strengths, promote their choices, envision great expectations, communicate positively, and warrant trust and respect. Your communication is a means by which you can create an empowering context.

More than that, your communication is a way you can affect each family's motivation and knowledge/ skills. When you communicate effectively, you may affect the family's motivation, enabling them to believe in themselves or acquire a greater sense of control. Likewise, you may augment their knowledge and skills by providing them with useful information or augmenting their problem-solving, coping, or communication skills. After all, empowerment is an interactive process: The context factors and the family factors are interactive, and each can strengthen the other.

In this chapter, we will describe how certain strategies and skills can help you be an effective communicator, an effective collaborator, and an empowerful and empowering person.

Communication can be between two people or among more than two (Epstein, 1995; Gelfer, 1991). When two people are together (such as a teacher and a parent) but only one person (the teacher) speaks and does not let the other person (the parent) speak, that is not communication. That kind of interaction is likely to create a frustrated parent and damage any chance for a reliable alliance between these two

people. In the words of one parent, "whenever I go to school, they want to tell me what to do at home. They want to tell me how to raise my kid. They never ask me what I think. They never ask me anything" (Finders & Lewis, 1994, p. 53).

Over the last 20 years, special educators and education agencies have emphasized compliance with legal mandates, investing tremendous time and effort in formal team meetings, formal notices of evaluation and placement, and formal notices of legal rights (as you learned in chapter 2). Given this emphasis on formality, it is paradoxical that parents of children of various ages with various exceptionalities frequently emphasize their preference for informal rather than formal communication (Chapey, Trimarco, Crisel, & Capobianco, 1987; Stephenson, 1992; Turnbull & Winton, 1984; Turnbull, Winton, Blacher, & Salkind, 1983).

Indeed, parents regard "a 'personal touch' as the most enhancing factor in school relations" (Lindle, 1989, p. 13). Families want professionals to relate to them in comfortable, nonhierarchical, positive, and relational ways. They want a reliable alliance with professionals characterized by connection and trust, one like the "Manos connection" in Maryland.

Parents also want frequent interactions with educators. Indeed, teachers who interact more frequently with parents— teachers like those who work with Sue and Nick Manos—tend to view parents as more capable and are more open to parent input (Fuqua, Hegland, & Karas, 1985; Michael, Arnold, Magliocca, & Miller, 1992; Stephenson, 1992).

Collaboration by Communicating Among Reliable Allies

In this section we will discuss (1) identifying and respecting family preferences, (2) written communication strategies, (3) telephone contacts, (4) technology options, and (5) face-to-face interactions.

FIGURE 9–1

Empowerment Framework: Collaborating for Empowerment

Family Factors:
It's Within Us to Be Empowerful

Motivation

Self-efficacy: believing in our capabilities

Perceived control: believing we can apply our capabilities to affect what happens to us

Hope: believing we will get what we want and need

Energy: lighting the fire and keeping it burning

Persistence: putting forth a sustained effort

Knowledge/Skills

Information: being in the know

Problem solving: knowing how to bust the barriers

Coping skills: knowing how to handle what happens to us

Communication skills: being on the sending and receiving ends of expressed needs and wants

Collaborating for Empowerment:
Through Collaboration, We Act Empowerfully

Education Context Factors:
It's Within Us to Make Our Contexts Empowering

Opportunities for Partnerships

Opportunities arise when . . .

Communicating among reliable allies

Meeting families' basic needs

Referring and evaluating for special education

Individualizing for appropriate education

Extending learning in home and community

Attending and volunteering at school

Advocating for systems improvement

Obligations for Reliable Alliances

Reliable alliances consist of . . .

Knowing yourself

Knowing families

Honoring cultural diversity

Affirming family strengths

Promoting family choices

Envisioning great expectations

Communicating positively

Warranting trust and respect

Identifying and Respecting Family Preferences

Although most families prefer informal communication to formal communication, families still vary in their preferences. To determine a family's preferences, you need first to learn about families through a family systems perspective. Then you need to identify the family's communication preferences.

Gaining a Family Systems Perspective You may assume that you need to conduct lengthy interviews with families to know their characteristics, interactions, functions, and life cycle. Fortunately, it will be far easier than you think to gain a systems understanding; and your best approach is to develop a comfortable, trusting, authentic relationship with the family, one that begins informally. The more you genuinely connect with the family, the more members will be eager to share their family story with you and begin to help you fill in the different parts of the family systems framework. Coles (1989), a prominent psychiatrist and humanitarian, describes the advice that was given to him by one of his mentors: "Why don't you chuck the word 'interview.' Call yourself a friend, call your exchanges 'conversations!'" (p. 32).

There is wisdom in this statement. As you develop genuine relationships with families, you will find that you will not need to administer formal assessment instruments, have stiff or professionally controlled interviews, or engage in formal information gathering. The more you think of yourself as a friend or a reliable ally and incorporate the eight obligations of a reliable alliance, the more your exchanges will be conversations. And the more conversations you have, the more likely the information that you gather will be relevant and comprehensive.

One of the catches, however, is that families do not share family stories already organized according to the family systems framework. But in practically every exchange with families, information about that family and its system will crisscross the four components (chapters 5 through 8). For example, what components and subcomponents of the family systems framework do you detect in Armando Sellas's description of his daughter Angelica, who has Down syndrome?

> Our expectations of Angelica have been very, very little different between what we expect from her sister and what we expect from her. We take into account that they are two distinct individuals, and they're each going to have their own identity, but you know we expect Consuelo to do certain things in the way of chores around the house or homework and things like that, then we have the same expectations for Angelica to get up in the morning, make her bed, get freshened up, go to the bathroom, brush her teeth and get ready to go.

What did you learn about sibling interaction, parental expectations, the family function of daily living, or the family cultural characteristics?

Now consider a passage from a different parent:

> I was raised up in my own religion, but then just recently I stopped going. My kids already know God is very important, we were all raised that way. They know right from wrong. They also already know that they are going to experience things, and I sit and tell them "I know this is wrong, because I've done it. You want to smoke a cigarette, I'll buy the pack. You know don't do it behind my back. My daughter, if you're pregnant and you're out there, then come to me and we'll talk about it. Don't keep bringing babies because it's too hard. You want to have sexual intercourse, there's birth control. My son, you want to do drugs, I'll help you find it and then you can go through the experience instead out of freaking out by yourself or something. If you want to talk, we can talk. I'll try to be very open about anything you want to talk about." They want to know what it is to be street smart, and I advise that they learn streets, but be intelligent too. "Stay in school, get an education, because that's the only way you're going to get by in this world."

What do you learn here about family cultural characteristics, family interaction in terms of cohesiveness and adaptability, and life-cycle stages and transitions?

Appendix B is a family systems conversation guide. This guide uses the categories and subcategories of the family systems framework that you read about in chapters 5 through 8. It sets out probes and open-ended questions that you can use in your conversations with families.

We want to point out, however, that families may take the conversation in a very different direction than the sequential questions on the conversation guide. Go with their lead and listen carefully to what they are sharing with you. Even though their conversation may not relate to the next question on the guide, it will likely provide valuable and insightful information. The family systems framework is a listening guide that enables you to recognize relevant information and categorize it into the framework. Keep a portfolio on each family. The portfolio is a single place (folder, file, or packet) for keeping notes of your conversations, copies of correspondence, and information that you can organize into the family systems framework as a way of knowing families—gaining a coherent and personalized understanding. Develop note sheets divided into the categories and subcategories of the family systems framework. Whenever you learn relevant information about a particular component of the framework, make a note in the appropriate place. As the information accumulates, you will increasingly understand and be more empowering for the family.

Although checklists and surveys can also help you collect family information (as we will show in chapter 11), conversations permit information to emerge within the context of open-ended sharing, in contrast to a discussion specifically focused on family needs. The more you establish a reliable alliance with families, the more comfortable they will feel about sharing information informally, frequently, and over time.

Respecting Family Preferences To individualize communication, you need communication skills—verbal, nonverbal, and influencing (as you learned in chapter 4). You are the best judge of which approaches can best help you develop reliable alliances, and we encourage you to evaluate continually your communication effectiveness. Whenever possible, modify the strategies to suit a family's preferences and your personal style. Although individualized strategies require an initial investment of your time and energy, as the teachers of Nick Manos learned when they started working with him and Sue, many will help you to save time and energy in the long run. Indeed, good communication strategies are the means for sharing concerns between yourself and a family such as Sue and Nick and for dealing with problems while they are fresh and before they become more complex. That is the perspective of the Sellas family:

> I'll tell you one thing that we were real surprised by and this is something that we weren't aware of that was happening, but Angelica's pre-kindergarten teacher apparently had some difficulty in dealing with her, and she got Angelica in her class in the middle of the school year. She was the first teacher to receive Angelica in her home school so there was the whole novelty of it. Later on we found out that she had more concerns and more things that she wasn't in agreement with than what she had led us to believe, and I think that if we'd had an opportunity to just be able to meet on a very informal basis, where nothing is official, nothing is recorded, it's not part of the annual review meeting, let's just kind of get together and see where we're at, whether any problems need solving or just kind of come together. I think that

would help people feel a little more relaxed and not so under the gun all of the time. . . . Even though I had asked this of all of Angelica's teachers, I said "Please be honest with me. Don't tell me that she is doing good in class, when you are having trouble, because maybe I can help." That's one of the things I say, if you are a parent you know where I'm coming from, please be honest.

Throughout the remainder of this chapter, we will focus on four communication strategies: (1) written strategies, (2) telephone contacts, (3) technology options, and (4) conferences. Families vary in their resources—whether they can read English or any other language, whether they have a telephone, whether they have access to and an understanding of technology, and whether they have transportation to come to school for a conference. So you will need to adapt your communication strategies to respect the family's preferences and capabilities. Doing that is one way of individualizing the education context factors of empowerment and thus affecting each family's empowerment.

Written Strategies for Communication

There are six major strategies for written communication: (1) handbooks; (2) handouts for specific situations; (3) newsletters; (4) letters, notes, and dialogue journals; (5) progress reports and report cards; and (6) occasional messages.

Handbooks Most school handbooks for families typically outline administrative policies and procedures but do not include information about the various educational options available within the program. For this reason, it may be helpful to develop a supplemental handbook containing information specific to your program, including information about personnel, classroom procedures, classroom supplies, transportation, lunches or snacks, methods of reporting progress and sharing information, and topics unique to your program.

Content aside, what about format? Handbooks are more enjoyable to read when they are concise, attractive, and written in simple and understandable language (Kroth, 1985). If families do not speak English or speak it as a second language, consider having the handbook printed in other languages. Translation services are becoming increasingly available, and sometimes bilingual parents may assist in producing the handbook in different languages. In fact, a San Diego school translates information to reach parents from South America, the Philippines,

Cambodia, Laos, Vietnam, and other countries (National Association of Secondary School Principals, 1994).

Handouts Handouts deal with specific matters such as resources in the community, safety and travel, preparing a child for trips to the dentist and eye doctor, accessible places of leisure and recreation, sources of college scholarships, drug prevention, violence prevention, and summer enrichment programs.

To get families to read the handouts and establish communication with you, consider these issues: What are families' special interests? What are the forthcoming special ethnic occasions and celebrations? How can family strengths be affirmed as you prepare handouts? What tips or ideas from families could go into the handouts? Are any families particularly interested in desktop publishing, and would a family member like to take on the task of helping to prepare handouts?

Also consider individualizing particular portions of the handouts by placing stars next to items that are particularly pertinent to specific families or family members. Ask students to help prepare the handouts by writing, illustrating, or duplicating them; their contributions can be meaningful language arts activities.

Your time and effort in preparing handouts will undoubtedly be appreciated by many families. Often the small, thoughtful gestures show that you care and have their best interests in mind.

Newsletters Newsletters can be enjoyable and useful techniques of communication. They can be developed by an individual teacher and class, an entire grade, an entire school, or families and can include "need to know" information as well as drawings, quotations, and essays written by the students; comic strips; announcements of upcoming special events; students' birth dates; a parent column; horoscopes; updates on ongoing school projects; an advice column; stress-reduction techniques; descriptions of adaptive devices; advertisements for toy swaps; methods of encouraging positive child behaviors; announcements of workshops and seminars; and "bragging" notes. Try to recruit families to help with all steps in publishing the newsletter, thereby affirming that their input is valued and needed. Remember that most people like to see their names in print; by sharing good news about families in the program, you highlight their strengths. Figure 9–2 includes a sample newsletter.

School newspapers that include information about exceptionality issues give a positive message about inclusion and can also address substantive family concerns. Box 9–1 is an example of addressing family concerns. It is a letter written by our daughter Kate for her high school newspaper, expressing her views on using respectful language. This letter emanates from her own sibling experiences.

Not only did Kate express her preferences about respectful language, but she also educated her peers on the important topic of offensive language. In turn, her peers have an opportunity to become more sensitive about disability discrimination.

Articles about homework, teacher profiles, "getting to know you" features, reports about special projects, and parenting tips are often well received by parents. For distribution, some schools have found that it works better to mail newsletters to homes rather than rely on students to take them. Some communities have also found that it works well for the local newspaper to print the entire student newspaper (Loucks, 1992).

Letters, Notes, and Dialogue Journals Letters, notes, and dialogue journals are helpful for exchanging information and strengthening relationships with families. Some professionals and families prefer dialogue journals over notes and letters, which may be more easily lost or misplaced. In addition, dialogue journals offer a record of communication over time and aid in end-of-the-year reports. Try to involve families in deciding how frequently to write, who will write, what kinds of information to exchange, and whether the journal will be open to all family members, not just restricted to parents.

Although dialogue journals typically facilitate conversation between teachers and students (Rueda, 1992; Staton, Shuy, Peyton, & Reed, 1988), they are also useful for educators and families. One recent study indicated that parents tended to report more opinion and personal facts, while teachers gave more attention to directives and evaluations. One parent commented: "I wrote suggestions, but she tended to just tell me what she would do for him the next day" (Ellis, 1993, p. 147). Often the parents focused on academic or behavioral problems, defining the problem and brainstorming ideas, whereas the teachers tended to propose immediate action to resolve the problem. More than half the teachers and parents reported an increase in satisfaction with their communication, noting that the journals provided an opportunity for more frequent and more specific information exchange, leading to better teamwork. As a parent explained, "we could talk about little things more often and not wait for a conference. That way I could work on problems at home, too" (Ellis, 1993, p. 152).

FIGURE 9-2

Sample Newsletter

Young Jayhawks

Volume 5, Number 6   Lois Orth-Lopes, Editor

ACTIVITIES FOR THE WEEK

We have planned large group activities that will help the children to get to know each other, including the songs, "Who Am I" and "Friends." We will also learn a new song, "Sky Bears," and play the bells as we sing.

SHARING TIME ON TUESDAY

Last week, Ryan, Tanya, and Leilani put their sharing things in paper bags and gave clues to the other children. Everybody had a great time guessing. Ryan brought in a photograph of his twin aunts. Tanya shared an animal that she calls Foozy. Leilani showed the children a book that plays music.

This week, Michael, Muhammad, Chad, Annie, and Elizabeth will have a chance to share. Remember to send the sharing item in a paper bag so that the other children can guess what is in the bag.

ARTIST CORNER

The drawing for this week is by Mark. He used felt-tipped markers to make this bear. The original work is on the wall outside our classroom.

THE ZIPPER BEARS

The children have been learning how to zip their coats without any help from their teachers or friends. When they are successful for four days, a zipper bear is hung beside their name on the art wall. Many of the children have been working very hard and will have a zipper bear by their name soon.

In Manuel's daily battle with his zipper on his coat, October 16,1988, Manuel won! His zipper bear proudly hangs on the wall.

PARENTS' NIGHT A SUCCESS

We were very pleased to have so many parents, brothers, sisters, and grandparents come to Parents' Night last Tuesday. It was a nice opportunity for us to get to know you better even though the time was short.

If you were not able to come, or even if you were there and have questions or concerns, please feel free to call. Our number at the office is 864-3831. If it is more convenient, you can call Lois at home (842-7137).

SNACK MEAL

Our cook, Yvonne, prepares a nice variety of snacks for the children each week. The menu for this week is:

Monday:	chex mix, orange juice
Tuesday:	fresh fruit, graham crackers, water
Wednesday:	muffins, apple juice
Thursday:	mixed vegetables, crackers, water
Friday:	crackers with peanut butter, lemonade

Source: Orth-Lopes, L. (Ed.). (1988). *Young Jayhawks.* Lawrence: Assessment Learning Classroom, Edna A. Hill Child Development Laboratory Preschool, Department of Human Development, University of Kansas. Reprinted by permission.

Offensive Language Needs to Stop

The word "retard," unfortunately, has now achieved mainstream status. I have been affected by the word all my life because I have a brother with mental retardation and autism. When I was in elementary school and junior high I was embarrassed about my brother because people always used "retard" so lightly. Now that I am no longer embarrassed, rather, I am proud of him, I had hoped to escape the word. So far at my school, I have been unable to do so.

I frequently hear "You are such a retard!" or "Gosh, I'm so retarded!" when someone has made a mistake or has said something seemingly stupid. Every time I hear the word, I cringe. I think about my brother, my greatest teacher, and know that someone is making a mockery out of his disability.

Often times the speaker does not realize the effect of their words. What happens when lower school students, walking down the hall to class, hear the word spoken by an upper school student? They are going to think that "retard" isn't a bad word. It is. The word itself is obviously derogatory to people with disabilities because it is never used to describe something or someone that is successful or intelligent.

People with mental retardation are not stupid; they are just slower at processing information. J. T., my brother, leads a completely normal life despite his disabilities. He works at the University of Kansas, rides the campus bus to work everyday, and lives in his own house with two graduate students. No one would want to approach him and call him a retard to his face so why is it O.K. to use the term so loosely behind his back? . . .

Some people might say that if they use "retard" or other offensive words in such a way that they don't mean them in a demeaning way, people should not take them offensively. If you know, however, that the words have the potential to demean someone, why use them and intentionally flare up conflict or hurt someone's feelings?

"Retard" is only one example of the offensive language circulating the halls and classrooms. Our vocabulary is filled with stigmatizing words such as "faggot," "chick," and "retard." These words have the potential to deepen the factions already apparent in the human race. They cannot possibly be doing more good than bad, so why use them?

Our school is only a microcosm for the "real" world. We hear these words from our peers and even our role models everyday, but whether or not we choose to use them is solely up to us. This is a major source of conflict for students in high schools and in our everyday society. But does it have to be?

Kate Turnbull
Editor-in-Chief

As much as possible, use dialogue journals to communicate positive information about the student; keep negative comments to a minimum. Negative comments are best given in person, when there is an opportunity for the parents to ask questions and seek clarification. Likewise, reserve sensitive, confidential, or controversial information for private, face-to-face conferences. In a word, do as Sue Manos and Nick's teachers do: Face the problems privately, but by all means face and resolve them.

Report Cards, Grading, and Progress Reports   Report cards are the traditional means of providing families with feedback about how their child is doing in school. A national survey of local school districts to obtain information on their grading policies reported the following results (Polloway, Epstein, Bursuck, Roderique, McGoneghy, & Jayanthi, 1994):

- Approximately two-thirds of the districts have a formal policy. In a majority of them, teachers are required to comply with the policy.
- About two-thirds of the districts that have a general policy on grading also modify the policy for students with disabilities.
- Most policy modifications are based on recommendations by the student's teachers and are incorporated into the report card.
- Percentage cutoffs are the most common stan-

dard benchmarks, followed by criterion-referenced and individually referenced systems.

- More than 99 percent of the school districts communicate with parents regarding grading policies. The most frequent method of communication involves explanations that are included in the school handbook.
- Approximately one-third of the districts use multiple grading systems.

Because more students with disabilities are in general education, grading practices and methods of reporting grades to families take on increased significance. Many students with disabilities are passing general education classes with low grade-point averages (Donahue & Zigmond, 1990). When grading systems are based on percentage cutoffs, students with cognitive disabilities are at a significant disadvantage. Given that grading of students in general education is at the discretion of general educators (Warger, 1983), collaboration among special educators, general educators, and families is necessary for determining grading modifications and methods for reporting student progress. Indeed, communicating grades has been largely neglected within the special education body of research (Rojewski, Pollard, & Meers, 1992).

Another alternative for documenting progress and grading is authentic assessment, particularly portfolio systems (Calfee & Perfumo, 1993). In fact, many teachers use authentic assessment systems for students with disabilities (Bursuck, Polloway, Plante, Epstein, & Jayanthi, 1993; Pike & Salend, 1995).

Progress reports usually provide families with more timely feedback about how their child is doing at school (Smrekar, 1993). These reports can be complex or simple; can be sent home once a day, once a week, or once every few weeks; and can communicate about a single subject or area of development or about many.

Occasional Messages   Finally, you may wish to use occasional messages to inform parents specifically about positive aspects of their child's performance. These messages can take many forms, including mini-diplomas, certificates of recognition, sticker cards, mock telegrams, "happy grams," or "Good News" postcards with a collage of school events on the front and space on the back for a personal message (Loucks, 1992).

*T*elephone Contacts

The telephone can be a convenient and effective means for providing both information and emotional support. Occasional telephone calls to families may even result in improved student performance. An advantage of using the telephone is that 94 percent of all American homes are equipped with telephones, whereas not all parents or other care providers are able to read or write well enough to use printed information as a communication mode (Bowe, 1995). An answering machine at the school central office enables educators to receive messages from parents when it is impossible or inconvenient for school staff to answer the telephone. In-class telephones, although arguably desirable, are atypical: "The Alliance for Public Technology estimates that only 7 percent of American schools have enough electrical outlets to plug anything new into classrooms and that just 4 percent have connections such as phone jacks in the classroom" (Bowe, 1995). As a general rule, telephone conversations with parents should be brief and to the point. Longer, more involved conversations are more effective when conducted in person. Conversing over the telephone poses some disadvantages, such as not being able to see the parents' nonverbal reactions and messages. For this reason, listen carefully and check out your perceptions by asking questions and summarizing. Ask families in advance about convenient times to contact them and also share with them times that it is possible for you to receive telephone calls. Before calling a family member at work, ask whether that person wants to receive telephone calls there. Box 9–2 contains suggestions for use of the telephone.

A telephone tree is an efficient way to get information to several people with little effort (Heward & Orlansky, 1984). You telephone one or two parents with a message; each of them in turn calls two or more parents and so on until all parents have been contacted. This system has the additional advantage of providing parents with opportunities to interact with one another.

Another way to use the telephone is to record daily messages on an automatic answering machine that parents can access. A teacher of a primary class for students with learning disabilities recorded messages such as the following:

> Good evening. The children worked very hard today. We are discussing transportation. They enjoyed talking about the airport and all the different kinds of airplanes. The spelling words for tomorrow are: train, t-r-a-i-n; plane, p-l-a-n-e; truck, t-r-u-c-k; automobile, a-u-t-o-m-o-b-i-l-e; and ship, s-h-i-p. Thank you for calling. (Heward & Chapman, 1981, p. 13)

During the six-week program, the teacher received an average of 18.7 calls per week, compared

BOX 9–2

Using the Telephone

- Treat every message (incoming or outgoing) as an important call.
- Always identify yourself as you place a call or answer one.
- Personalize your conversation at every opportunity by using the caller's name.
- Don't use the telephone for criticism. Criticism is tricky enough even in an eye-to-eye encounter. When the parent must depend completely on your voice, criticism is doubly difficult.
- Be sure to ask parents if you have called at a convenient time. If not, ask them to name a time when they'll be free to talk.
- Jot down in advance what you want to find out from the parent and what you want to tell the parent.
- When taking down information, briefly double-check your notes.

- If it is necessary to leave the line during a call, explain the reason and excuse yourself. When you return, thank the caller for waiting. (On long-distance calls, make every effort to avoid putting a parent on "hold.")
- Always offer the caller or person being called your help or assistance.
- Allow time for parents to ask you their questions.
- Return all calls promptly; the exception, of course, is if you are involved in the classroom with students.
- Give definite information and offer positive information.
- Avoid the use of vague statements that may force the caller to dig for information. Vague statements are irritating and waste time.
- As the conversation ends, thank the caller before you say good-bye.

Source: From the Parent Center of the Albuquerque, New Mexico, Public Schools (1985). Adapted by permission.

with an average of 0.16 calls per week before the program. Students' scores on daily spelling tests improved during the program. A second option for using recorded daily messages is a call-in telephone service ("talk line") that provides developmental guidance, referral, and general information to parents (Fuller, Vandiviere, & Kronberg, 1987).

A common source of telephone information is an office secretary (Stephenson, 1992). Secretaries frequently take messages from families, handle small decision making on their own, call parents when they need to pick up their child, and relay significant information. Collaborate with the school secretary in discussing family preferences for communication, such as whether parents want to be called at work or which parent to call in families in which a divorce or separation has occurred.

Technology Options

Electronic mail (e-mail) may be agreeable to parents who have e-mail access. An e-mail bulletin board system for all parents or a restricted e-mail system for each family may be quite efficient and effective, especially if their child uses a computer with e-mail or Internet and World Wide Web access.

Recently, portable microcassette recording machines have become a popular means of technology-based communication and can be used as Sue and Nick Manos, Nick's teachers, and Nick's peers use them—for "need to know" and "nice to know" information and just for exchanging pleasantries.

Videotape is another medium for communicating with parents. A Georgia survey documented that approximately half the parents of children with disabilities prefer to get information (including student progress reports) through videotape as opposed to other options (Alberto, Mechling, Taber, & Thompson, 1995).

To reduce confusion and lack of clarity, videotapes have served as picture report cards, daily or weekly progress reports to demonstrate newly acquired skills or illustrations of procedures the teachers are asking parents to use in the home for maintenance and generalization of new skills. This option has been especially important for working parents who cannot come into the classroom during school hours. Additionally, support personnel such as the physical therapist, occupational therapist, and speech/language pathologist can provide similar information to assist parents in following up on their suggestions (Alberto et al., 1995, p. 19).

Videotapes can be especially culturally appropriate. Native Americans have long preferred visual pathways for learning new information, a preference that calls for videotapes (Yates, 1987). Videotapes also have been recommended for language-minority families because the reading and writing demands are reduced for those families (Salend & Taylor, 1993).

Face-to-Face Interactions

Face-to-face interactions, one of the most effective and commonly used methods of family-professional communication and the way that Sue Manos and Nick's school team communicate most often and effectively, give families and professionals opportunities to develop a reliable alliance. We will discuss four types of face-to-face interactions: (1) planned meetings, (2) Making Action Plans (MAPs) gatherings, (3) unplanned meetings, and (4) group family meetings.

Planned Meetings   Because of their many potential benefits, meetings should not be limited to the beginning and the end of the school year. Regularly scheduled team meetings can do much to maintain and enhance family partnerships (Heward & Orlansky, 1984).

Sometimes families' cultural values conflict with professional expectations for participation in meetings: "What most people don't understand about the Hispanic community is that you come home and you take care of your husband and your family first. Then if there's time you can go out to your meetings" (Finders & Lewis, 1994, p. 51).

A major cultural barrier for language-minority families is the lack of translation: "It is not easy to have a relative translate for me every time I have an appointment" (Smith & Ryan, 1987, p. 349).

A study that investigated the perspectives of Chinese parents concerning their experiences with service providers concluded:

> The lack of bilingual professionals among provider agencies presented numerous problems for the parents and their children. Translation services were generally not available, and parents had to fend for themselves, using friends and family to translate complex medical and diagnostic concepts. Chinese parents simply could not communicate with professionals, which affected both their access to and use of formal services. What

these parents needed most was a basic, intensive understanding. (Smith & Ryan, 1987, p. 350)

When communicating with language-minority families, explaining ideas or concepts several times, using slight variations in terminology and examples, having more frequent checks for comprehension, and using physical gestures and visual cues can help ensure comprehensible family-professional communication (Gersten & Woodward, 1994).

Even when their cultural diversity is honored, some language-minority families, as well as some majority families, will decline to take an active role in their children's education:

> It's her education, not mine. I've had to teach her to take care of herself. I work nights, so she's had to get up and get herself ready for school. I'm not going to be there all the time. She's got to do it. She's a tough cookie. . . . She's almost an adult, and I get the impression that they want me to walk her through her work and it's not that I don't care either. I really do. I think it's important, but I don't think it's my place. (Finders & Lewis, 1994, p. 52)

Conscientious planning is the key to effective family-professional meetings. In planning a meeting, you will need to consider three major phases: (1) premeeting, (2) meeting, and (3) postmeeting.

Premeeting

Premeeting preparation consists of three steps: (1) notify, (2) plan agenda, and (3) arrange environments (Kroth, 1985).

When notifying parents, give them your rationale for a meeting. Recommend whether you think that just you and the family should meet or whether it would be helpful to invite other team members. Remember that families prefer more frequent, informal contacts. One father suggested, "Save the conferences for the big things" (Lindle, 1989, p. 13).

Many schools schedule regular teacher-parent conference days and send notice of these meetings when they distribute the school calendar at the beginning of the year. Some schedule regular team meetings such as the ones for the "Manos team." Some schools only encourage "as needed" meetings. Opportunities for ongoing communication and collaboration are especially important. Whatever the schedule, be sure to convey to parents in a clear, understandable, and nonthreatening manner the purpose of the meeting, remembering that parents' past experiences with schools and teachers may make them reluctant to attend meetings.

They expect me to go to school so they can tell me my kid is stupid or crazy. They've been telling me that for three years, so why should I go and hear it again? They don't do anything. They just tell me my kid is bad.

See, I've been there. I know. And it scares me. They called me a boy in trouble but I was a troubled boy. Nobody helped me because they liked it when I didn't show up. If I was gone for the semester, fine with them. I dropped out nine times. They wanted me gone. (Finders & Lewis, 1994, p. 51)

Before this father would be comfortable at a meeting, it would be essential for you to establish a reliable alliance with him, probably in a setting other than school, so that he would know that you recognize his strengths, want to affirm his choices, and want to invest your best efforts in supporting his child.

In a workshop designed to help parents and teachers develop communication skills, parents described what they thought and felt when their child's teacher called them for a conference: "I feel worried." "I feel guilty that I haven't done enough to help my child in school." "I feel nervous, I think that Roddy has done something wrong." "I think that Dorene is not doing her work" (Flake-Hobson & Swick, 1984, p. 142). Of the group of 50 parents, not one parent described positive thoughts or feelings when asked to attend a school meeting.

By following up your written notification with a telephone call, you give family members a chance to ask questions and understand why you (and other team members) want to meet with them. You can also inquire about the family's need for child care or transportation assistance. These logistical barriers prevent many families, especially families with restricted financial resources, from participating in meetings (McCarney, 1986). You might be able to persuade other educators at your school, student service clubs, or other community resources to arrange child care and transportation assistance.

To enable families to meet with you without having to make separate child care and transportation arrangements, consider meeting at the family's home if that is convenient for members. Box 9–3 includes tips for making home visits. Or meet at a neighborhood building close to the family's home that is more accessible and convenient than the school.

Teachers just don't understand that I can't come to school at just any old time. I think Judy told you that we don't have a car right now. . . . Andrew catches a different bus than Dawn. He gets there a half an hour before her, and then I have to make sure Judy is home because I got three kids in three different schools. And I feel like the teachers are under pressure, and they're turning it around and putting the pressure on me cause they want me to check up on Judy and I really can't. (Finders & Lewis, 1994, p. 51)

TIPS

BOX 9–3

Making Home Visits

- Talk with family members about the home visit before scheduling the appointment.
- Make home visits only if they are scheduled with the family ahead of time.
- Arrive and leave on time.
- Cancel home visits only when absolutely necessary.
- Dress appropriately and comfortably.
- Respond with sensitivity to offers of food and beverages.
- Expect distractions.
- Bring activities for the child's brothers and sisters.
- Be aware of the environment and alter the visit if your safety or the safety of the family makes you uncomfortable.
- Leave your schedule and where you will be with someone.
- Take a blanket or tablecloth to spread on the floor for your work area.
- Parents make choices during home visits—some choose participation in the visit, some use it for a few minutes of respite. Do not be judgmental of their choices.

Some minority families prefer to "conduct 'business' in everyday settings or in the course of activities such as shopping, meals, visiting, or other 'unrelated' undertakings (Rueda & Martinez, 1992, p. 98). Clearly, there is a wide range of options for conference settings, aside from school or the family's home, such as at locations within the family's natural support systems (Delgado, 1992).

Decide with the family which family members and professionals should attend the meeting and whether the student should attend. Involving the student, when appropriate, in discussion and problem solving (including IEP conferences) can help ensure that decisions are consistent with his or her preferences and interests. Moreover, inviting students presents them with excellent opportunities to learn and practice the decision-making skills that are so important to independent living (Turnbull & Turnbull, 1988). Just be sure to communicate with their family about the cultural appropriateness of their decision-making role (see chapter 12).

Providing families with a list of suggested activities to prepare for the meeting may also reduce their anxiety. Parents who receive a premeeting awareness packet (containing information about what will happen at the meeting and suggestions for preparation) have significantly higher rates of attendance than parents who do not receive premeeting suggestions (Kinloch, 1986).

The second step in premeeting preparation is to prepare an agenda. An agenda (1) helps ensure your own preparation, (2) notifies participants about what topics are to be covered at the conference, and (3) serves as a guide for structure and sequence during the conference. The agenda should be flexible enough to accommodate last-minute additions or changes and should include topics that families have mentioned as important.

Often Euro-American professionals are eager to follow their agenda and to be as time efficient as possible in meetings. But a more indirect approach, in which families and professionals engage in conversation on what they may perceive to be tangential issues as well as share humor and make self-disclosures, may contribute to forming a reliable alliance with Asian, Latino, and Native-American families (Harry & Kalyanpur, 1994).

The third and final step in premeeting preparation is to arrange the physical environment and establish an atmosphere that will enhance communication. Start by deciding where to conduct the meeting (for example, at the family's home, the school, or a neutral location in the community such as the library or community building). Box 9–4 gives you tips on preparing the setting.

Although home visits may mean more distractions (for example, TV or telephone noise or neighbors dropping by), they also provide you with the opportunity to gather a more complete picture of the student's environment and family life and are related to teachers' improved ability to interact with parents (Fuqua et al., 1985).

TIPS   BOX 9–4

Preparing the Setting

- Determine whether it is appropriate to have the meeting at school, in the family's home, or at some other location.
- Make arrangements (if the meeting is at school) for a quiet and private room, one in which the doors can be closed and the windows are not facing out to frequently used areas.
- Gather all necessary materials before the meeting and make arrangements not to be interrupted.
- Be sure that both the temperature and the lighting are comfortable.
- Choose adult-sized chairs and tables.
- Arrange the furniture in a manner that reflects equality. Avoid placing the professional's chair behind a desk or at the head of a table.
- Have tissues, beverages, papers, and pens available for all participants.
- Consider providing coffee and snacks.

In some cases, you may want to consider bringing another person (perhaps a social worker or a school nurse), particularly when the topics to be discussed are apt to cause conflict, when there is a history of misunderstandings between the family and professionals, or when you are concerned about neighborhood safety. This person may serve as a witness to events, a support person, or a mediator in case of serious disagreements.

Recognize that some parents are uncomfortable opening their homes to you and may find home visits intrusive. Families' responses to home visits are often determined by how you characterize why you want to meet at their home.

> When Kristi was first evaluated for a special education program, the school social worker called to say that she was coming to our home for a visit. She did not say why she was coming, and I did not ask. I only knew that social workers normally visit a home to see if it "passes inspection." I cleaned for days, baked cookies and had coffee, tea, and home-made lemonade ready for her visit. The joke was on me. She had only come for a social history. She did not inspect my home or even eat a cookie. How much easier my life would have been if she would have explained to me why she was making her visit.

When you hold meetings at school, you are responsible for preparing the setting. Probably the two most important considerations are privacy and comfort. An atmosphere that is confidential, comfortable, and free of interruptions can elicit open and honest communication. Meetings that are scheduled back-to-back for short periods of time can be major impediments to establishing genuine communication. "Ten minutes is ridiculous, especially when other parents are waiting right outside the door. I need time to tell the teacher about how my child is at home, too" (Lindle, 1989, p. 14).

Meeting

Four major components of parent-professional meetings—such as those that Sue and Nick Manos and their inclusion team practice—are (1) building rapport, (2) obtaining information, (3) providing information, and (4) summarizing and following up (Stephens & Wolf, 1980). The rapport-building phase sets the tone for the remainder of the meeting. *Rapport* is defined as "a condition of mutual understanding, respect, and sustained interest between individuals" (Shertzer & Stone, 1981, p. 187). Your genuine (not forced or artificial) interest in, and acceptance of, the family builds rapport. Reflect on the professionals who provide services to you (such as physicians, counselors, and

(lawyers) with whom you have a genuine rapport. What contributes to that rapport? How long did it take to develop? What could have been done to facilitate it more readily? It is likely that the factors that enhance rapport for you and your professional allies can enhance rapport for you and families. And as you incorporate empathetic reciprocity into your ongoing relationships with families, you will raise the chances of developing rapport that can lead to a genuine reliable alliance. Finally, by knowing, understanding, and accepting yourself and the families and by incorporating all eight reliable alliance obligations presented in chapter 4, you will have a better chance of establishing rapport with families.

The second component of the conference entails obtaining information from the families. Obtaining information provides you with the opportunity to practice many of the nonverbal and verbal communication skills, such as empathetic listening, that we described in chapter 4. Encourage families to share information by asking open-ended questions. When you are unclear about a family member's point of view, ask for clarification or specific examples. Respond empathetically if and when families have difficulty expressing a thought or a feeling. Provide feedback to the family regarding their ideas and, most important, affirm their contributions.

The third component of the conference process, sharing information with families, requires you to use jargon-free language. Jargon limits families' ability to attend to, organize, and understand information (Lavine, 1986).

> Parents are amazed by the vocabulary that interventionists use to describe their children. They are besieged by acronyms that stand for such well-known concepts as retardation and deafness. They wonder why a pronunciation problem is called a phonological disorder. They remain bemused by acronyms such as MET (Multidisciplinary Evaluation Team), IEP (Individual Education Plan), LRE (Least Restrictive Environment), and SPL (Speech-Language). The most articulate parents tell us they believe this jargon is the interventionist's way of reminding them who is in charge. (Stonestreet, Johnston, & Acton, 1991, p. 40)

When sharing information, begin on a positive note, pointing out the student's strong points before mentioning topics that concern you or the family. Provide specific examples by telling anecdotes or giving examples of the student's work. Be aware of and respond to the impact of what you are saying on the family. If they are frowning or appear puzzled, stop for a moment to provide an opportunity for questions or comments. As much as possible, encourage a give-and-take atmosphere for everyone to exchange information and concerns.

The last component of the conference involves summarizing and follow-up activities. Review the high points of the meeting and emphasize next-step activities. Restate who is responsible for carrying out those tasks and the date by which they are to be completed. Discuss and agree on options for follow-up strategies. If another meeting is planned, decide on the time and place. End the meeting on a positive note. Thank the family for their interest and contributions and offer to be available should any relevant questions or issues arise.

Postmeeting

Postmeeting tasks include (1) reviewing the meeting with the student, (2) sharing the outcome of the meeting with other professionals, (3) recording the proceedings, and (4) evaluating your own satisfaction.

If the student did not attend the meeting, it may be appropriate (with family approval) to spend some time talking about what was discussed with the student. Explain the decisions that were made and how they will affect the student's activities. Allow time for questions and respond to any concerns.

It may also be appropriate to share the outcome of the meeting with other professionals who are involved in the student's program. Review the decisions made and any resulting changes in the student's program, thereby ensuring continuity and consistency. Those contacts can be made in person, over the telephone, or through a written report.

Recording major decisions and next steps assures family-professional accountability. Complete the minutes as soon as possible after the meeting adjourns, when the information is still fresh in your mind. Include the time, the location, agenda topics, nature of interactions, decisions, and next steps. Keep a permanent file of each of your meetings so that you can access them at some later date, mark your calendar for agreed-upon follow-up dates, and list the tasks you agreed to complete as a result of the meeting.

A fourth important postmeeting activity is to evaluate what happened, reflecting on how you think things went and seeking reactions, feedback, and suggestions for improvement from other participants. The more you reflect and invite feedback, the more likely it is that you will be able to develop the kind of reliable alliance that will be empowering for all participants.

Making Action Plans (MAPs)   A special type of conference is called Making Action Plans (MAPs), a process frequently used for students with severe disabilities (Falvey, Forest, Pearpoint, & Rosenberg, 1994). In attendance at MAPs gatherings are the student, parents, other family members, student and family friends, educators, and others who have a substantial interest in customizing the student's school and community to be as close to the student's preferences as possible. MAPs gatherings are typically held in comfortable settings—often the student's home or some other community setting that encourages connection and relationships.

Eight key questions form the basis of the MAPs process. The order of the questions might vary, but their purpose is to stimulate a dynamic and open-ended discussion in which people who have a major stake in the student's well-being share their cogent insights and great expectations for the student's future.

In a MAPs gathering, a facilitator is the discussion guide and encourages brainstorming to generate as many creative ideas as possible. As ideas are shared, the facilitator records them on large poster board.

Question 1: *What is a MAPs?* At the beginning of the meeting the facilitator explains the purpose of the process, questions that will be asked, and the general ground rules for open-ended and creative problem solving. The facilitator especially tries to create an upbeat, energized, and relational ambience.

Question 2: *What is the student's history or story?* Typically, the student and family share the background information, highlighting the triumphs and challenges that have been associated with the student's having a preference-based way to live his or her life.

Question 3: *What are your dreams?* It is especially important for students to share their great expectations for the future. Families also should share their dreams and great expectations and supplement what the student is saying if the student cannot or chooses not to communicate with the group members. The key aspect of the MAPs process is to identify these dreams and great expectations as the basis for planning the customized school schedule and extracurricular activities.

Question 4: *What are your nightmares?* Because students with exceptionalities and their families often have major fears that serve as barriers to their working toward great expectations, identifying nightmares lets everyone know what those are so they can put adequate supports into place. Some nightmares cannot be prevented, such as the progressive course of AIDS in a young child, but sharing them can help everyone know issues around which the student will need support.

Question 5: *Who is this person?* The group will use as many adjectives as it takes to get behind the exceptionality label and describe the real or essential aspects of the student's personhood.

Question 6: *What are the person's strengths, gifts, and talents?* Many times teachers, friends, family members, and others can lose sight of the characteristics that the person can bring to bear to achieve the great expectations. So the MAPs meeting takes the time to identify them.

Question 7: *What does the person need?* What will it take to make the student's and family's dreams and great expectations come true? What barriers stand in the way of where the student is at the present time and having the dreams come true? Identifying these needs can serve as the basis for educational programming.

Question 8: *What is the plan of action?* A plan of action includes the specific steps that need to happen to accomplish the dream. The plan of action can involve tasks, time lines, resources, and any other detailed information that will help lead to significant progress.

The MAPs gatherings can help professionals get to know the student and the family and use the information to plan a functional and relevant evaluation (chapter 11) and IFSP/IEP (chapter 12). In addition, the MAPs gatherings can benefit families because the gatherings consist of family members, friends, and professionals (not just families and professionals) and because they are carried out informally and in a familiar and comforting setting—not at school, where meetings tend to be more formal and intimidating for some families. Many aspects of MAPs establish a reliable alliance, adding the personal touch that we have repeatedly emphasized. Moreover, unlike school meetings that primarily describe the student's functioning in school, the MAPs process portrays the student within the full spectrum of his or her life, as exemplified in box 9–5.

Unplanned Conferences

Unplanned meetings inevitably occur at any time and in any place. Parents may unexpectedly drop in at school before, during, and after school hours; you may receive telephone calls at home in the evenings and on weekends; or you may be approached by families with child-related concerns at unlikely places such as a movie theater or a grocery store.

Although it is probably impossible to avoid being caught somewhat off guard at such times, you can prepare for these meetings and the likelihood that parents will express their most intense thoughts and feelings at them (Simpson, 1982). First, decide what is possible for you to do in response to unplanned conferences given the other demands on your time and energy. Talk with other professionals regarding their strategies for handling hard issues at impromptu meetings. You may decide, for example, that telephone calls at home on week nights are acceptable but that conferences at the shopping mall are not. Make a list of options that you consider to be open or closed to consideration at unplanned meetings. Then set your priorities and seek support from the administrator at your school. This support is important both for your own sense of security and in the event that future problems arise concerning these issues. In addition, some administrators wish to be alerted to this information so they can ensure consistency across programs. In addition, seek to maintain appropriate flexibility because sometimes crises or special circumstances will require an immediate meeting that can de-escalate problems.

Of course, you need to inform families of your preferences. Ideally, you should do this at the beginning of the year before any unplanned meetings have had a chance to occur. Communicate your preferences both verbally and in writing to avoid misunderstanding and to allow the families to ask questions. When stating your preferences, be sure to explain your rationale regarding unplanned meetings in noneducational settings: for example, "I want to be able to meet your needs and answer your questions as well and as completely as possible; however, I am not able to do so without sufficient preparation and access to your child's records."

It is always helpful to have well-organized and readily accessible portfolios comprised of files, data sheets, permanent products of the student's work, schedules, graphs, and charts. Other helpful resources include community guides and names, addresses, and phone numbers of other agencies, families, and professionals who may be of assistance to families. Sometimes on-the-spot referral to a school or community-based professional may be more appropriate than attempting to assist a family with a problem that may be more adequately addressed by other professionals. Last, but not least, practice positive communication. Without positive communication skills, even the best-prepared professionals can fail in their attempts to meet the needs of families.

BOX 9–5

TOGETHER WE CAN

MAPping Lee's Inclusion

When Lee Jones, who has Down syndrome, entered middle school in Shawnee Mission, Kansas, his parents, Carolyn and Buddy, had only one concern: that he would be teased or otherwise mistreated. After all, he had been in a small private school with many other students with disabilities. Now he was entering a school that was nearly six times as large as his other school and had many fewer students with disabilities. By the same token, they had a dream: that he would be included socially because he had so many friends in his former school.

"No problem," as the saying goes. One of the school's teachers volunteered to convene a MAPs gathering and start a Circle of Friends for him.

Moreover, Lee's potential for inclusion was high; he has an extraordinarily outgoing personality and is a handsome young man. Indeed, after a week or so in his new school, Lee had already become buddies with four other guys. And his social skills had won him the favor of the principal, the school nurse, his special education teacher, and some general education teachers.

The four classmates and the staff formed the core of Lee's MAPs team, although the boys soon invited three girl classmates to join them. Carolyn and Buddy were somewhat tangential to this Circle of Friends. As Carolyn puts it, the staff and the seven classmates "basically handled everything Lee needed to be included socially." That covered his participation in the school's theater program, the homecoming parade and dance, and the athletic events.

Sometimes Carolyn and Buddy spotted problems in Lee's school program. Rather than inserting themselves into the already well-functioning circle, they spoke off the record with Lee's teacher, who in turn put the problem to the group. Almost invariably, the group, led by the students, solved it.

MAPping for Lee became a matter of knowing what he and his family wanted (social inclusion), what they feared (mistreatment), what Lee's strengths are (amiability and the gift to have others be loyal to him), what he needs (inclusion specialists), and what has to be done to ensure the enviable life that he, Carolyn, and Buddy have envisioned.

And what an enviable life it has been and continues to be. Not only was Lee elected his school's most popular student, but he also has headed off to college—a step that Carolyn, Buddy, Lee, school staff, and other friends charted throughout his senior year by operating a second MAPs gathering.

The biggest surprise is not that Lee is a freshman at Graceland College in Iowa but that his dorm advisor participated in MAPs gatherings and a Circle of Friends in his home town in California and has volunteered to convene one for Lee.

As Carolyn observes, Lee's parents just have to step aside and let the national grassroots movement—the MAPs/Circle of Friends movement—work its way for Lee. "We just let the kids take it from here," she says, acknowledging, as Lee did when he insisted on having a MAPs written into his IEP, that MAPping is indispensable for him and them.

Group Family Meetings Sometimes, group meetings with families will be especially appropriate (see chapter 14). Almost all schools have orientation meetings at the beginning of the school year; throughout the year they also may have open houses in which families come and learn about their child's daily schedule. Although it is difficult to connect with families individually at such large meetings, group meetings provide significant quantities of information to a large number of people at one time and give families an opportunity to meet each other. Typically, attendance is optional, although a high school in Denver sent parents of incoming ninth graders a letter suggesting that they were required to participate in the orientation meeting and at least one parenting workshop during the school year. Students whose parents complied with this expectation received extra academic credit toward graduation (National Association of Secondary School Principals, 1994, p. 3).

Linking Our Themes

Review of Major Themes and Frameworks

Having discussed the type of partnership that we call communicating among reliable allies, we now invite you to put that partnership into a larger context. That context is the one we call collaborating for empowerment, represented in figure 9–1 and discussed in chapters 3 and 4.

As you see from figure 9–1 and as you read in chapters 3 and 4, empowerment occurs when the family factors of motivation and knowledge/skills connect with the education context factors of opportunities for partnerships and obligations for reliable alliances. Your first step in creating the empowering context is to communicate using the techniques we discussed in this chapter.

To create an empowering context, you need to infuse the eight obligations for reliable alliances (listed under education context factors in the second column of figure 9–1) into your communication partnership. As you communicate (or have any other interaction with families), you will want to know yourself and know the families with whom you are communicating. Likewise, as you communicate, you will want to honor their cultural diversity, affirm their strengths, promote their choices, jointly envision great expectations, communicate positively, and thereby warrant their trust and respect.

In the rest of this chapter, we will show how you can create a reliable alliance through communication and how the communication partnership has many positive effects on the family's motivation and knowledge/skills. Indeed, as we conclude each of the chapters that follow this one, we will show you how you can infuse the eight obligations of a reliable alliance into the type of partnership we discuss in that chapter and thereby have a powerful influence on the family's motivation and knowledge/skills.

Creating a Reliable Alliance

How do you infuse each of the eight obligations of a reliable alliance into your communication partnership? Look at figure 9–3. On the left side of the figure, we list each of the eight obligations. Across from each obligation, we present an issue that may face you as you try to carry it out. In the last two columns after each obligation, we describe one action that you should *not* take—a disempowering action—and one action that you *might* take—an empowering action (personalized for each family situation). Altogether, figure 9–3 links each of the eight obligations of a reliable alliance to an issue that families may face and to a negative/disempowering action and a positive/empowering action. The obligation of *knowing families* separately identifies family characteristics, interaction, functions, and life cycle to aid you in taking a family systems approach.

Strengthening Family Factors

Now, how do you know that the empowering context, the one you create by communicating among reliable allies and that you have infused with the eight obligations for a reliable alliance, has a positive effect on the family's own empowerment? How can you have any confidence that your communications and empowering context make a difference to a family's motivation and knowledge/skills? Frankly, you may never know exactly what difference you make; but in figure 9–4 we illustrate how you can make a difference, through communication, on the five elements of a family's motivation and the four elements of a family's knowledge/skills.

One final note: Remember that, as you enhance families' empowerment, you will likely enhance your own and your colleagues' as well. That's one of the key points of chapter 3.

Summary

Positive communication is the single most important key to developing a partnership between families and professionals. This is so because communication lies at the heart of all other forms of partnership and is an indispensable ingredient of the empowering context that we described in chapters 2 and 3. It also is a way to practice the eight obligations of a reliable alliance that we discussed in chapter 4.

On the whole, families prefer informal and frequent communication with professionals over formal and infrequent communication. To be an effective communicator, you will need to apply what you learned about family systems; this means identifying families' preferences. You also will need to know and practice specific communication strategies—written, telephone, and technology-based. In addition, you

FIGURE 9–3

Creating a Reliable Alliance: Disempowering and Empowering Actions

Obligations	Issues	Disempowering Actions	Empowering Actions
Knowing yourself	You feel frustrated when you talk with parents who concentrate on barriers rather than solutions.	Tell parents that you wish they would not be so negative.	Listen about the barriers, empathize, and break their and your actions down into small, manageable steps.
Knowing families			
Family characteristics	Parents tell you that they are going to be busy on the night of the school open house, but you sense that, really, they are not comfortable coming to the school.	Tell parents that they will be letting their child and you down if they don't come.	Invite the parents to come to the school at another time, such as when their child is performing in a music program or otherwise demonstrating a strength of which everyone can be proud.
Family interaction	The family does not have a telephone or transportation and the adults are unable to read because one is legally blind and the other functionally illiterate.	Assume that you will not be able to communicate with the family except through conferences at school.	Ask the family what has worked best in the past when getting information from the school. Inquire about any neighbors, friends, or family members who have a telephone and would be willing to relay messages or read documents aloud.
Family functions	Both parents are work-oriented young professionals who frequently use e-mail at their businesses or home.	Tell them that it would not be fair to use e-mail with them if other families do not have access to it.	Ask the parents if they would be interested in communicating with you by e-mail and make arrangements at your school to send and receive the e-mail messages.
Family life cycle	The family has just moved to a new community, and neither the student nor parents know anyone at their child's new middle school.	Assume that the parents may be interested in coming to the school open house next year; leave them on their own to make connections in the new community and school.	Call the parents, issue a special invitation to come to the school open house, and arrange with another family to meet the new parents and student and introduce them to others.
Honoring cultural diversity	The school handbook is available only in English, yet the parents speak Mandarin.	Tell the parents that maybe their child or some friends can translate parts of the handbook for them.	Talk with your administrator about translating the handbook into Mandarin or securing someone to explain it to them.
Affirming & building on family strengths	A father is an accomplished photographer and particularly enjoys using his home video camera to record family activities.	Tell the father that it is impracticable for him to videotape his child at school, especially interacting with other children.	Ask the father if he would be willing to get other families' consent to tape classroom activities and make the tape available to families.

FIGURE **9-3** CONTINUED

Creating a Reliable Alliance: Disempowering and Empowering Actions

Obligations	Issues	Disempowering Actions	Empowering Actions
Promoting family choices	A parent asks if a conference can be arranged before school to accommodate her work schedule.	Tell the parent it is against teacher-union policy.	Ask the parent if it would be possible to talk on the telephone early in the school day rather than to meet at school.
Envisioning great expectations	A group of parents ask you to explore the use of e-mail in communicating with families.	Dismiss their request as too far-fetched because of limited computer access.	Form a committee of families and educators to contact computer companies about the possibility of being a model site for technology demonstrations.
Using interpersonal communication skills	You are participating in a conference with parents who are extremely angry that their gifted child is making poor grades and believe that it is your fault.	Tell the parents that they have not provided proper supervision for homework and that the poor grades are their fault.	Listen empathetically and ask if they would be willing to brainstorm options that would involve them and you collaborating to promote their child's progress.
Warranting trust and respect	The school administration asks parents to contribute to a fund to pay for the classroom newspaper, but the parents do not have money to contribute.	Tell them they'll not be able to get the newspaper, since they have to "pay their own way."	Identify a non-monetary way for them to contribute to the class; tell them their classroom contribution represents their donation; keep everything confidential.

FIGURE **9-4**

Strengthening Family Factors Through an Empowering Context: Communicating Among Reliable Allies

Motivation	Enhancing Actions You Can Take	Knowledge/Skills	Enhancing Actions You Can Take
Self-efficacy	Emphasize student and family strengths in a dialogue journal and phone calls.	Information	Provide a thorough description of grading policies and procedures.
Perceived control	Ask families their communication preferences and incorporate those preferences into all communication.	Problem-solving	Hold a MAPs gathering and determine the elements of an ideal day; collaborate to put those elements into place.
Persistence	Schedule sufficient meetings to ensure that all necessary problems are resolved.	Coping skills	Empathetically listen when families need social support.
Energy	Initiate communication as soon as problems occur rather than waiting for problems to escalate.	Communication skills	Model refined verbal and nonverbal skills.
Hope	Communicate the positive gains you expect the student to accomplish by the end of the school year.		

will need skills for planning, carrying out, and following up on face-to-face interactions. Most of all, you will need to recognize that families want to be and can become your reliable allies.

For them to become your allies, so that you and they can collaborate for empowerment, you will want to create an empowering context and infuse into it the eight obligations of reliable alliances: know yourself, know families (use the family systems perspective), honor their cultural diversity, affirm their strengths, promote their choices, jointly envision great expectations, communicate positively, and warrant their respect and trust.

Finally, you will want to link what you know and your own actions with families' motivation and skills/knowledge. When you do all this, you create an empowering context and enable families to become more empowerful; in short, you collaborate for empowerment.

In Frederick, Maryland, Sue Manos, Nick, his peers, and the entire team of educators involved in his inclusion can count on each other, through thick and thin, to support each other and Nick as he gets an inclusive education. It took a long time—four years, to be precise—before Sue and Nick and the school's teachers and administrators became "communicators." These have been years marked by painful but always candid conversations and by joyous times as well.

The result of the communication, which the school's staff thought would take too much time and energy, benefits the staff, Sue, Nick, and a host of other included students and their families.

To make Nick's education work, they all had to become reliable allies and work at communicating effectively with each other. The alternative would have been unacceptable because it would have meant that Nick probably would not have benefited from inclusion, Sue would have been treated as an outsider and possibly frustrated in getting what she wanted for Nick, and the professionals themselves would not have grown in their capacities and attitudes toward all students. The communication that each person practiced also empowered each person. In Frederick, "team Manos" has demonstrated that communication is mutually empowering.

Chapter Ten

Meeting Families' Basic Needs

Kurt Baxter is only 12 years old, but what an impact he and his parents, Lorrie and Garry, have had worldwide. Kurt is a kid with a rare condition. In his case, it's Rubinstein-Taybi syndrome (RTS), a condition that causes mental retardation, respiratory and mobility impairments, and limitations in speech and vision. Throughout the whole world, there are only about 530 reported cases like his. Yet from the Baxter home in Cedar, Kansas, (population 30, a "suburb" of Smith Center, population 2,500), there has sprung up an international network of RTS families—a network whose links are strengthened by Parent to Parent activities all across the United States.

When Kurt was diagnosed, Lorrie and Garry began to track down other families whose children have Rubinstein-Taybi syndrome. They found a physician in Cincinnati, Ohio, (Dr. Jack Rubinstein), who in turn connected them with other families through their physicians. The Kansas-Ohio connection produced some family-to-family networking. So did a letter that was published in Exceptional Parent, a magazine for families affected by disability. Indeed, as of late 1995, about 260 families belong to the National Rubinstein-Taybi Syndrome Parent Group. Its headquarters? Cedar, Kansas.

At first, just six families were inside the Baxter alliance. Then, as the Baxters corresponded with them, as physicians began to refer newly diagnosed children and families to each other and to other families, and as the magazine article began to circulate around the country, the Baxters organized the national support group. They corresponded with families in the United States and far-flung places such as Austria and Israel, and with Dr. Rubinstein's help organized the first Rubinstein-Taybi syndrome national and international conference in 1993.

Let's move, now, from Kansas to the hub city of the south, Atlanta. There Kathleen Judd, an early member of the Georgia Parent to Parent movement, operates NPPSIS, the National Parent to Parent Support and Information System. NPPSIS has a single goal: to link families of children with special health care needs and rare disorders to each other. This modest goal (!!) works remarkably well, judging by what has happened with the Baxters and two other families.

In a suburb of Elberton, Georgia, about 100 miles east of Atlanta, live Nancy and Barry Lunsford, parents of Kerri (age 14, who has Rubinstein-Taybi syndrome), Sandy (18), and Robin (16).

In northern New Hampshire live Nancy and Larry Ward and their daughter Bethany, age 12, who has the same syndrome.

What possible connection do the Baxters of Kansas, the Lunsfords of Georgia, and the Wards of New Hampshire have with each other except that their children have Rubinstein-Taybi syndrome? The answer: They are almost like family to each other. Here's how that has come about, via Kathleen Judd.

On learning that the Wards of New Hampshire wanted to be matched with another family facing similar challenges, and having known about the Baxters and how they supported the Lunsfords, Kathleen telephoned the Lunsfords and asked (not in so many words), "How about it? How about contacting the Wards and seeing if you can help them out? After all, you have gotten help from the Baxters. So what comes around goes around, yes?"

Nearly simultaneously, the New Hampshire Parent to Parent organization told the Wards about the Lunsfords and suggested that Nancy of New Hampshire call Nancy of Georgia.

It's not quite clear who first called whom. But soon, Nancy of Georgia was in contact with Nancy of New Hampshire. Telephone calls, letters, pictures—all worked their ways up and down the East Coast.

Before long, Larry of New Hampshire called Barry of Georgia; the two men talked and talked and talked. When Larry (of the north) said to Barry (of the south) that his family had a vacation coming up soon and would the Georgians mind if the Yankees drove south for the spring week, the answer was "Of course not. Come on down." The result? A friendship, an alliance.

And so it is that, with Kurt Baxter's birth in the Kansas wheatland and through the pioneering medical research of Dr. Taybi and Dr. Rubinstein and their abilities to link with other physicians and families, there has developed a highly specialized family support system, a model of family and professional collaboration.

Does it really make any difference? Ask the Baxters, and they will answer, "Yes. We needed information. Other families shared information with us, and they gave us hope. So when it came our turn, we had to make sure that other families knew that they were not alone in this world."

Ask the Lunsfords, and their Nancy will say, "Yes. We talked with two other families in Georgia and the Baxters. We learned how they handled their situations. What the other families go through, we go through. They know where we're coming from. The other families gave us hope, so we wanted to give it to others."

And ask the Wards, and their Nancy will say, "Yes. It's like meeting family you didn't know you had." Her experience was like the Lunsfords' in the sense that the Baxters and their connections gave them information and hope. But the "good connection" that the Wards

achieved with the Lunsfords extends beyond the mothers (the two Nancys) and the fathers (Barry and Larry). Now Bethany and Kerri—and their older sisters, too—have connections with each other.

Nearly every day of her busy life, Kathleen Judd probably indulges in a broad smile of satisfaction—or she should—for she has linked the needy to the giving in a chain of continuous contribution.

And in his fifth-grade class in the Smith Center middle school, Kurt Baxter—unaware of his gift in motivating Lorrie and Garry and of Dr. Rubinstein's gift of providing them with the knowledge and skills to support other families—benefits from an inclusive education program. Strange how inclusive his life has been—if you include the Lunsfords and Wards and nearly 300 other families who experience Rubinstein-Taybi syndrome as part of his family's reliable alliance.

The partnership of attending to families' basic needs involves supporting families to meet their emotional, informational, financial, safety, and health needs. Figure 10–1 highlights this partnership opportunity.

Some educators may wonder if it is appropriate for them to direct their time and attention to families' basic needs, believing that their primary role is to teach the student. The answer is yes, and the rationale is fairly simple: The more you support families to address their critical personal and family needs, the more likely it is that they will devote time and energy to their child's educational needs. You already know from a family systems perspective that families attend to many simultaneous functions, and each demands their time and attention. Their child's education is only one of seven functions. When they have major unmet needs in some of those functions (perhaps inadequate economic resources to purchase food, shelter, and medical expenses) or in education (such as understanding the nature of their child's exceptionality), then your assistance and support to fulfill those needs can enhance their child's education.

Collaborating to Meet Families' Basic Needs

You can collaborate with families to meet their basic needs by (1) helping them access social and emotional support, (2) guiding them to the information they need, (3) linking them with family support services, and (4) addressing the issues associated with abuse or neglect of their children.

Accessing Social and Emotional Support

By referring to the empowerment framework (figure 10–1) and recalling chapter 3, you already know the importance of the coping skill of social support. Informal neighborhood groups, extended family networks, friends, coworkers, and religious groups are examples of typical social support networks. Many studies have shown that social support is linked to reducing stress and improving emotional well-being (Beckman & Pokomi, 1988; Crnic, Greenberg, Ragozin, Robinson, & Basham, 1983; Dunst, Trivette, & Cross, 1986).

Social support networks can provide a variety of assistance, including emotional, informational, and material support. Emotional support provides the family with psychological resources; referral and information provides families with knowledge and services; and material support provides tangible items such as money, food, or physical objects (Schradle & Dougher, 1985).

Unfortunately, families of children with disabilities often have smaller social support networks than other families, and they often tend to get their support

FIGURE 10–1

Empowerment Framework: Collaborating for Empowerment

Family Factors:
It's Within Us to Be Empowerful

Collaborating for Empowerment:
Through Collaboration, We Act Empowerfully

Education Context Factors:
It's Within Us to Make Our Contexts Empowering

Family Factors: It's Within Us to Be Empowerful

Motivation

Self-efficacy: believing in our capabilities

Perceived control: believing we can apply our capabilities to affect what happens to us

Hope: believing we will get what we want and need

Energy: lighting the fire and keeping it burning

Persistence: putting forth a sustained effort

Knowledge/Skills

Information: being in the know

Problem solving: knowing how to bust the barriers

Coping skills: knowing how to handle what happens to us

Communication skills: being on the sending and receiving ends of expressed needs and wants

Education Context Factors: It's Within Us to Make Our Contexts Empowering

Opportunities for Partnerships

Opportunities arise when . . . .

Communicating among reliable allies

Meeting families' basic needs

Referring and evaluating for special education

Individualizing for appropriate education

Extending learning in home and community

Attending and volunteering at school

Advocating for systems improvement

Obligations for Reliable Alliances

Reliable alliances consist of . . . .

Knowing yourself

Knowing families

Honoring cultural diversity

Affirming family strengths

Promoting family choices

Envisioning great expectations

Communicating positively

Warranting trust and respect

from nuclear and extended family members (Herman & Thompson, 1995; Kazak & Marvin, 1984). Families from low socioeconomic backgrounds also are more likely to have smaller social support resources (Taylor, 1988). Yet when families do have access to social support, they often report greater satisfaction as parents and more positive interactions with their children (Crnic et al., 1983; Dunst et al., 1986).

One way to enable families to find social support is to connect them with other families who share similar experiences (Herman & Thompson, 1995), as the Baxters have done through their Rubinstein-Taybi syndrome network.

> Family and friends fell by the wayside in a fantastic pattern of despair . . . like a chain of dominoes. Many of these friends were professionals that I had the utmost confidence in. Pillars of strength and guidance drifted away like straws in the wind. . . . I knew then that from that day forward my whole life must change if [my son] were to survive. His vulnerability frightened me. I knew what I must do. I could no longer go it alone. I needed other mothers, other fathers to relate to. (Pizzo, 1983, p. 25)

Like the Lunsfords, Wards, and so many others, this parent wants to talk to others who have already walked in similar shoes down similar paths. Especially during the early childhood years, parents of sons and daughters with exceptionalities frequently express a desire to be linked with other families whose children have similar needs (Summers, Dell'Oliver, Turnbull, Benson, Santelli, Campbell, & Siegel-Causey, 1990). Making these connections is part of the self-help movement in which people who face similar experiences offer each other (1) a psychological sense of community, (2) an ideology for interpreting their experiences, (3) an opportunity for catharsis with others who understand the experience firsthand, (4) role models, (5) an opportunity to learn practical and tested coping strategies, and (6) access to a network of people for social relationships (Levine & Perkins, 1987). The self-help movement offers both group and one-to-one support.

Group Support
Support groups for families whose children have exceptionalities often are organized around some base of commonality, such as parents of very young children; children with a similar exceptionality; parents from a similar ethnic background; and family member roles such as groups for mothers, fathers, or grandparents (Affleck, Tennen, Rowe, Rosscher, & Walker, 1989; Burton, 1988; Koroloff & Friesen, 1991; Krauss, Upshur, Shonkoff, & Hauser-Cram, 1993; Shapiro & Simonsen, 1994;

Vadasy, Fewell, Meyer, & Greenberg, 1985). The national Rubinstein-Taybi syndrome network is an example of group support. What difference do these groups make?

> Empirical studies of the effects of parent group participation have produced inconsistent findings. On the one hand, there is evidence that parent groups are associated with benefits for some participants, especially those who feel a need of support and who have the skills to interact effectively in a group setting. On the other hand, there is evidence that parent groups may have equivocal or even adverse effects on some participants, especially those who have fewer needs for additional support. For parents of children with disabilities, we have little knowledge about the characteristics of those who participate in such groups or about the effects of participation on their functioning. (Krauss et al., 1993, p. 10)

In chapter 1, you learned about some of the benefits and drawbacks of parent organizations from the perspective of families. Clearly, because family systems are diverse, no one type of support has uniform effects. Thus, your role is to individualize your efforts in meeting families' basic needs and in all other opportunities for partnerships.

One-to-One Support
A widespread and popular type of support goes by the name of Parent to Parent. Parent to Parent programs establish one-to-one matches between a trained "veteran parent"—someone who has experience as a parent of a child with a disability—and a "referred parent," who is dealing with an issue for the first time. The veteran parent provides emotional and informational support to the referred parent in personalized ways (Santelli, Turnbull, Lerner, & Marquis, 1993; Santelli, Turnbull, Marquis, & Lerner, 1993; Smith, 1993).

Parent to Parent programs started nearly 20 years ago in Omaha, Nebraska. Fran Porter, the young mother of a child with Down syndrome, realizing how much help she had received from parents of children who had "been there" and how many of her own experiences she had to offer, teamed with a social worker, Shirley Dean, to create a program that would foster one-to-one connections between parents. She named the model program Pilot Parents, symbolizing a pilot tugboat that goes out of a rocky and dangerous harbor to guide an incoming boat safely to shore. She envisioned that the veteran parent would be the pilot for the new parents in guiding them to supportive harbors. As the Omaha program grew, it hired its first paid director, Patricia McGill Smith, who was featured in the chapter 1 vignette. From that modest start has grown, informally and spontaneously, a national grassroots movement, Parent to Parent (Santelli, Turnbull, Lerner, & Marquis, 1993; Santelli, Turnbull, Marquis, & Lerner, 1993; Smith, 1993).

Local Programs

In 1994 and 1995, nearly 30,000 parents were served by approximately 550 Parent to Parent programs. Typically, the programs serve parents without regard for the type of disability their children have, are developed and run by volunteer parents in low-budget ways, and match a veteran parent who has successfully faced a certain challenge with a parent who is just beginning to deal with that challenge. The greatest percentage of programs serve between 13 and 25 referred parents, are less than six years old, and operate in a community of more than 100,000 people (Santelli, Turnbull, Marquis, & Lerner, 1993; Santelli, Turnbull, Lerner, & Marquis, 1993). At the heart of the Parent to Parent program is the one-to-one match of someone to listen and understand. The match is typically made on the basis of six factors: (1) a similar disability, (2) a family facing similar problems, (3) a veteran parent who can respond within 24 hours, (4) children with disabilities who are close to the same age, (5) families who live close by, and (6) families who have a similar family structure. In approximately three-fourths of the local programs, the veteran parent receives specific training in the communication, listening, and problem-solving skills needed to be an effective supporting parent. In approximately 80 percent of the matches, the relationship lasts for longer than one month. In about one-third of the situations, the relationship lasts for more than six months. In addition to providing emotional support, the one-to-one match is often a source of information about disability and community resources, a source of a referral to other agencies, a provider of advocacy training, and a source of group activities for individual and family participation.

The greatest percentage of those who participate in Parent to Parent are Caucasian (88 percent). The majority of families are two-parent households (90 percent), and approximately one-third of the families have annual incomes over $50,000. The largest single age group of children of referred parents includes those from birth to age 2 (40 percent), and the single largest age range of children of veteran parents is 6- to 11-year-olds (43 percent). Approximately two-thirds of the children have a moderate or severe disability. In about two-thirds of the matches, contact is made within the first week; and 86 percent of the first contacts are made by telephone.

The Parent to Parent match usually occurs just after the initial diagnosis that the child has a disability, typically within the neonatal intensive care unit of the hospital or shortly after the family leaves the hospital and begins to explore community services and supports.

> Parent to Parent has been my life-line. When I first heard the diagnosis, I was devastated. Well-meaning doctors and nurses, as well as friends and families, simply did not understand. It was only when I finally connected with another parent through the Parent to Parent program that I could begin to hope for a future for us all. My veteran parent was gently there for me whenever I needed her.

Most parents who are matched during the child's early years testify to the value of such early support, as this typical statement indicates:

> When our son with Down syndrome was born three years ago, my husband and I were shocked and devastated. We called our Parent to Parent program, which supplied us with invaluable information, as well as sending us a "support couple" to talk with. It was important to us to meet with the couple—not just the mother—since my husband takes as much responsibility for caring for our children as I do. Also important was that we were matched with a couple whose child had also had been through open heart surgery (our son had major defects). The couple that our Parent to Parent program sent us were such warm, optimistic, "normal" people, they gave us hope. About a year later, my husband and I were trained by our program to be support parents. The Parent to Parent office has many requests for visits from both father and mother. My husband was one of very few men willing to go through formal training. I have also found that support for non-English speaking families is hard to come by. It has been satisfying to me to be able to serve the Spanish-speaking community.

As this mother describes, many referred parents take on veteran parent roles as they share their insights and practical know-how with new parents. Because it is true that "to teach is to learn twice," veteran parents have not only the benefit of knowing that they are helping others but also an opportunity to reinforce their own learning.

Statewide Programs

Because local programs need support and coordination, statewide Parent to Parent programs exist in 22 states. These statewide programs provide technical assistance to local programs and make matches on a statewide basis when a local match is not available. Statewide program models represent a continuum of services from highly centralized to highly decentralized.

National Programs

Sometimes families need specialized support for rare disabilities and health care needs but cannot find the support in their local community or through a statewide network. The National Parent To Parent Support and Information System (NPPSIS) is a resource for them. This is the program you read about in the vignette, the one that Kathleen Judd operates in Atlanta. NPPSIS has a data base of thousands of veteran parents and matches people whose children have extremely rare conditions.

NPPSIS also provides information to educators and physicians about disabilities and helps connect them to state and local resources and national family organizations. Parents can call the NPPSIS toll-free number (800-651-1151), but professionals are encouraged to use the toll number (706-632-8822).

What options exist if you are in a community that does not have a Parent to Parent program and you perceive that families might want one? You might convene a group of potential veteran parents and committed professionals to brainstorm about the possibility of starting a new local program. Box 10–1 includes tips for beginning a local program. You can also arrange for individualized matches among parents of children with disabilities and giftedness when no programs are available.

*A*cquiring Information

As you learned in chapter 3, information is a significant element of a family's knowledge and skill and, in turn, their empowerment. Most studies about the information needs and priorities of families have

---

TIPS   BOX 10–1

Starting a Parent to Parent Program

- The most important first step is to identify a small group of parents who are interested in developing a Parent to Parent program. Parent leadership, energy, and commitment are keys to the program's success. Professionals can be important guides and offer a newly developing program many important resources.

- Decide whether your program is going to be entirely staffed by volunteers or sponsored by a service provider agency, disability organization, existing parent group, or other group. If you take the volunteer route, you may find it useful to ask people in the community for advice and assistance. Also consider asking banks, religious organizations, libraries, and other places to donate space for your meetings or office needs. If you decide to get support from sponsors, you could ask for space, donated initial costs, professional staff availability for training help, referrals, and assistance with fundraising.

- Established Parent to Parent programs offer excellent information and training materials.

The Beach Center on Families and Disability at the University of Kansas has a list of these programs. It also has program-related materials and can provide technical assistance. Call (913) 864-7600 for further information.

- Establish a system to connect parents. You will need a local telephone number, preferably available at all times, that potential program parents can call. Use an answering machine if necessary. Appoint someone to coordinate incoming referrals and establish matches.

- Develop a record-keeping system for keeping track of referrals and matches.

- Let people know about you. Use flyers, brochures, word of mouth, parent speeches, radio, newspapers, doctor offices—anything you can to promote the program.

- Consider optional support activities, such as ongoing consultation for veteran parents, informational group activities, social gatherings, advocacy training, and instruction for others in the community.

Source: Beach Center on Families and Disability, University of Kansas, Lawrence.

gathered data from Euro-American families; but one study interviewed more than 500 families of infants and toddlers from Hispanic, Native American, and Euro-American families to determine parents' needs for information and where they find it (Sontag & Schacht, 1994). More than anything else, these parents needed information about service availability. They also needed information about parenting, services to which their children have a legal right, their child's educational needs, expectations for children at different ages, and their child's disability. The parents reported that physicians were their most frequent sources of information. Although 75 percent of the parents indicated that they were told about their child's problem when they began receiving services, almost two-thirds indicated that they had received confusing, incomplete, or inaccurate information. Slightly more than two-thirds expressed that they had to find out many things on their own or by chance.

- Native American and Hispanic parents reported a greater need than Euro-American parents to receive information about accessing services.
- Native American parents indicated a preference for information on legal rights more frequently than Hispanic and Euro-American parents.
- A greater percentage of Native American parents identified doctors and public health nurses as sources of information than the other two ethnic groups.
- Native American and Hispanic parents were more likely to select therapists as a source of information and hospitals as a place for obtaining information than were Euro-American parents, but Euro-American parents reported agencies other than hospitals and doctors more frequently than did the other two groups.
- Native American parents reported significantly more often than Hispanic and Euro-American parents that they were not told why a service could not be provided.
- Euro-American and Native American parents were more likely than Hispanic parents to report that they had been told what could be done for their child.

Parents from diverse cultural groups, particularly those whose primary language is not English, clearly need and want more information. Yet the vast majority of printed information is geared to middle- and upper-middle-class Euro-American parents. What are your options for providing information to families so that all of them can become more empowered? You could, by chance, happen upon a family like the Baxters and start a national network. But that would be rare, so you need to rely on many other avenues of information, including (1) Parent Training and Information Centers, (2) clearinghouses, (3) family organizations, (4) books and magazines, (5) technology, and (6) adults with exceptionalities.

Parent Training and Information Centers

Recognizing that parents need training and information to help their children develop to their fullest potential and to secure their rights under federal and state laws, Congress began to authorize and fund parent coalitions in the late 1960s. Currently there are 71 Parent Training and Information Centers (PTIs) funded by the U.S. Department of Special Education, Office of Special Education and Rehabilitative Services. Each state has at least one PTI, and there are also centers in Palau and Puerto Rico. (See appendix A for a list of PTIs.) By law, the majority of PTI governing board members must be parents of individuals with disabilities, and each PTI must have private, nonprofit status. By tradition, PTIs typically employ parents as directors and staff members.

State PTI Programs

As we have noted, there is at least one PTI in every state. We encourage you to contact the PTI in your state to learn what services it offers. You yourself may want to take advantage of these services for your own continuing education, and you certainly will want to alert families about PTI activities. In box 10–2 you can read about what a difference the Kansas PTI, called Families Together, has made for Denise Poston, the mother of a young boy with autism.

By law, PTI projects support parents to do the following:

- Better understand the nature and needs of the disabling conditions of their children;
- Provide follow-up support for their children's educational programs;
- Communicate more effectively with special and general educators, administrators, related services personnel, and other relevant professionals;
- Participate fully in decision-making processes, including the development of the child or youth's individualized education program (IEP);
- Obtain information about the programs, services, and resources available at the national, state, and local levels to their children and the degree to which the programs, services, and resources are appropriate to the needs of their children;

BOX 10–2

From Parent Advocacy to a Professional Career

According to its director, Patty Gerdel, the Kansas PTI, Families Together, offers "the security of belonging to a group of caring individuals with similar goals, challenges, and needs."

Families Together offers more than the security of group membership, however important that is. It sponsors regularly scheduled statewide and regional workshops on the rights of children with disabilities and the strategies their parents can use to advocate for their children. It also monitors the activities of the state's legislature and attends nearly every meeting of any disability-related study commission or legislative committee in Kansas. And it activates a statewide political action network and informs state legislators and members of Congress about what children and adults with disabilities and their families need.

One aspect of collective security, then, is advocacy. Patty is fond of reminding parents about "the power of one" and that one passionately committed person can make a huge difference. Another part is training and networking to meet families' other needs, including those related to the brothers and sisters of the child with a disability.

Denise Poston was a major on active duty with the U.S. Army at Fort Leavenworth, Kansas, when she learned (significantly, from other families) about the PTI's "sibling workshops." She had been attending a training session about students' special education rights and IEP content when families began to comment about the great amount of time they spend advocating for their children with disabilities, attending not-so-fruitful IEP meetings, and feeling that they are neglecting their other children.

The mother of a 6-year-old boy who has autism and a 5-year-old son who has no disabilities, Denise was in the market for information about siblings. She wondered, "Could Families Together help me be more effective in balancing the needs of two sons and a career?" At a sibling workshop, she learned that the answer is a resounding yes. She also learned that Families Together would welcome her as a trainer and help her develop skills to be one.

Denise became a volunteer Families Together trainer. "Getting involved with Families Together has helped me as a parent, broadened my perspective about disability, and widened my circle of reliable allies," she says.

That circle of allies now includes professionals because, within a year after becoming a trainer for Families Together, Denise resigned her commission (after 18 years of service) and enrolled as a doctoral student at the University of Kansas's Beach Center, studying about families, public policy, and disabilities, all in preparation for her second career.

Meeting families' basic needs by advocating for them, offering workshops that address the issues involving their children's education, and offering other kinds of information and networking—that is what Families Together means by "collective security." But creating and maintaining collective security also means raising a new generation of family leaders, people like Denise Poston. Already Denise is a "power of one" person; Families Together has a lot to do with that.

- Understand the provisions for educating infants, toddlers, children, and youth with disabilities under the Individuals with Disabilities Education Act.

In 1994, 36 PTIs provided 163,780 people with direct, person-to-person services and sent newsletters and other mailings to many more parents. Of those receiving PTI services, 46 percent were parents (including 25,000 minority parents), and 54 percent were educators and other service providers. Of the parents who received PTI services, the greatest representation of disabilities was in the areas of attention deficit/hyperactivity disorder (AD/HD), learning disabilities, mental retardation, and emotional disabilities (Center for Resource Management, 1995).

Regional and Focus Centers

To ensure that state PTIs have access to other PTIs and to provide them with consulting and other technical assistance, the national PTI network has created four regional PTI centers:

- *West Regional Center—PAVE* (Washington Parents Are Vital in Education), Tacoma, Washington
- *Midwest Regional Center—PACER Center* (Parent Advocacy Coalition for Educational Rights), Minneapolis, Minnesota
- *South Regional Center—ECAC* (Exceptional Children's Assistance Center), Davidson, North Carolina
- *Northeast Regional Center—Parent Information Center,* Concord, New Hampshire

Each regional center is administered by a state PTI that provides technical assistance and conferences for all PTIs within the region.

In addition, the PTI network has designated three centers to focus expertly on three topics of national significance:

- *Inclusion:* PEAK Parent Center, Colorado Springs, Colorado
- *Assistive technology:* Parents Let's Unite for Kids (PLUK), Billings, Montana
- *Early childhood services:* Pilot Parent Partnerships, Phoenix, Arizona

Like the regional PTI centers, the focus centers are administered by a state PTI but provide technical assistance to all other PTIs nationwide and to professional groups as well. They may serve as valuable resources for you.

Special Projects

The PTI network has two types of special projects: (1) Experimental Parent Training and Information Centers, and (2) the Supported Employment, Parents, Transition, and Technical Assistance Project.

Experimental Projects provide information and training for ethnic and cultural minority families. When these centers were first authorized by Congress in 1990, there were five of them. In early 1996, there are 16 of them, serving more than 150,000 parents in more than 50 urban and rural areas. These parents are African-American, Korean, Vietnamese, Latino, Caucasian, and Native American. You have already learned in chapter 3 about one of these programs, Loving Your Disabled Child, where Theresa Cooper and Hortense Walker provide an empowering context for African-American families.

In the summer of 1995, directors of many of the Experimental Projects met to consider how best to protect and strengthen these community-based projects and serve the families associated with them. Recognizing that each project could benefit from the experience of the others, the group formed a new consortium, Grassroots: A National Multicultural Consortium of Community Parent Resource Centers.

The unifying concept of Grassroots is that the best solutions to social problems grow from the bottom to the top; accordingly, Grassroots' priorities include promoting leadership within underserved communities and linking the various centers, through the consortium, to each other. Grassroots' publication, *Tapestry,* highlights the activities and successful strategies of these community-based organizations.

The Supported Employment, Parents, Transition, and Technical Assistance Project is located at the PACER Center in Minnesota. This project provides training and resource materials for families whose sons and daughters are graduating from high school and technical assistance for other PTIs concerning resource materials, evaluation and record keeping, referral to consultants, and training. Their materials are extremely helpful for educators as well as families.

National Network

Congress also has authorized a national program of PTI technical assistance, Technical Assistance for Parent Programs (TAPP) Network, located in Boston, Massachusetts, and directed by Martha Ziegler. Glenn Gabbard, who is featured in the vignette in chapter 2, is a TAPP leader. TAPP's activities include centralized coordination and support of regional and topical content-focus centers, peer support and training, individualized technical assistance plans, and national policy advocacy. TAPP services are directed to regional and state PTIs, which will be your primary source of contact and support for the families with whom you collaborate.

Clearinghouses Clearinghouses of information for families and professionals receive federal funding to distribute information. Two different types of clearinghouses funded by the U.S. Department of Education are the National Information Center for Handicapped Children and Youth (NICHCY) and the Beach Center on Families and Disability. The addresses for these centers appear in appendix A.

NICHCY prepares and disseminates free information about children and youth with disabilities and disability-related issues. It has six different kinds of services: (1) personal responses to questions about disability issues, such as specific disabilities, early intervention, special education, family issues, transition, legal issues, and multicultural issues; (2) referrals to state and national disability groups, advocacy organizations, parent associations, and professional groups; (3) information searches of NICHCY's data bases and library; (4) free publications, such as fact sheets about disabilities and legal guides; (5) technical assistance to parent and professional groups; and (6) materials in disability-accessible formats and in Spanish.

The Beach Center on Families and Disability at the University of Kansas (which is the center we direct) conducts research and training to enhance families' empowerment and disseminates information to families, individuals with disabilities, policymakers, and the general public. The Beach Center's information for families covers a broad array of topics, including Parent to Parent support, IFSP/IEPs, child abuse and neglect, fathers and their support needs, family support, and family-centered service delivery. Families find especially useful the center's one-page "How To" and "What Research Says" fact sheets, free newsletter, videos, and resource guides. Some of the materials are available in Spanish.

Family Organizations
Kathleen Judd, NPPSIS director, estimates that there are more than 2,000 family organizations nationally and that many also have state and local groups. One such organization is the Rubinstein-Taybi Syndrome Parent Group, operating out of the Baxter home in Kansas. Family organizations vary in size, activities, and operating budgets. Most focus on specific disabilities: Some of those are large-population categories of disabilities such as mental retardation; others are concerned with a particular rare syndrome.

One of the largest family organizations is The Arc (formerly the Association for Retarded Citizens of the United States). In chapter 1, you read about The Arc's critical role in advocating for individuals with mental retardation and their families and in stimulating state-of-the-art programs and support systems. The Arc's newspaper is free to The Arc's nearly 200,000 members and costs $15.00 per year for nonmembers. Its semimonthly *Government Report* reviews the latest federal legislation, activities in Congress and the courts, and activities of various federal agencies. *Advocates' Voice* is a newsletter for individuals interested in self-advocacy. It is written at a low reading level, so it can be used very appropriately as part of a high school curriculum in preparing students with cognitive challenges in self-advocacy skills. The Arc

also produces one-page fact sheets, pamphlets, manuals, videotapes, and posters on a wide range of topics, including HIV/AIDS prevention, the Americans with Disabilities Act, and assistive technology devices. All these materials are useful to families and employers, volunteers, community citizens, and teachers.

Books and Magazines
Many books for families have been written by professionals and family members themselves. The Beach Center's resource directory, *Resources for Families and People Who Work with Families,* annotates many of these books and tells where to get them.

Disability information is not systematically incorporated into popular magazines, although there has been an increase in coverage in the last several years. A recent review of popular magazine articles on learning disabilities identified 71 articles in 31 popular publications from January 1980 to December 1990 (Rankin & Phillips, 1995).

A magazine that is specifically aimed at parents who have a child with an exceptionality is *Exceptional Parent.* Published since 1971, the magazine offers practical information about the day-to-day issues of living and working with a child with a disability or special health care need. Regular features include Search and Respond (in which parents and professionals interact about specific questions), Fathers' Voices, Ask the Doctor, Media, and New Products.

Television and Radio
Increasingly, regular programming and specialized segments on television and radio highlight family and exceptionality issues. A number of regular TV shows routinely incorporate people with exceptionalities, including "Sesame Street." Canada has even implemented the Disability Network, which has had a market share of 11 percent or more than 1 million viewers for the past five years.

Radio stations are also beginning to incorporate disability news and have special programs related to disability. For example, a radio station in Arizona currently has a call-in talk show about disability that is broadcast for two hours one evening each week.

Technology
Technology vastly expands families' access to information. The National Rehabilitation Information Center (NARIC) and ABLEDATA Data Base of Assistive Technology (800-346-2742) will conduct computer searches for families concerning products and devices, disability organizations, and funding opportunities. NARIC has more than 20,000

products on its service list, and users can call the electronic bulletin boards to search the data base, get messages, and download fact sheets. (At this time the computer dial is 301-589-3563.) Another option for accessing the data base is through CD-ROM. NARIC has a directory of national information sources on disabilities, including 42 data bases, 700 organizations, and more than 100 resource directories.

Computer list servers provide new and immediate access to information for families. All list servers have unique characteristics. For example, a recent check of the autism list server revealed 30 to 40 daily messages on topics such as teenagers, toilet training, the use of aversive intervention, inclusive education, research possibilities, sign language, and siblings.

Another technology resource is operated by the U.S. Department of Education, Office of Educational Research and Innovation (OERI). Its National Library of Education maintains an electronic repository of education information and provides public access through electronic networks. You can call 202-219-1547 or access the library through e-mail at gopheradm@inet.ed.gov.

Adults with Exceptionalities

Adults with exceptionalities have long valued the empowerment that comes through peer counseling—connecting with another individual with a similar exceptionality for the purpose of providing information and emotional support (Brown, 1992). As in the Parent to Parent approach, an adult with an exceptionality can provide peer counseling and information to other adults and to children and youth with disabilities and their families (Turnbull & Turnbull, 1993). In box 10–3 Vicki Turbiville, a member of the Beach Center's staff who has expertise in early intervention and family studies, shares her perspectives (as an adult with a physical disability) about the potential contribution that adults with disabilities can make to young children with disabilities and their families.

Children and youth with exceptionalities and their families can get valuable information from adults with exceptionalities, who have "insider" knowledge. Consider adults in your own community as possible mentors, guides, and sources of information and advocacy. You can contact them through a local or state independent living center, which is a community advocacy program for adults with disabilities.

Now what can you do; what steps should you take? Consider all the information sources available. Familiarize yourself with them. Create your own library and make it available to families. Work with the school librarian, other educators, and community librarians to develop school and community resource libraries for families. In addition, the more you develop your computer expertise, the more you will be able to communicate readily with a number of major clearinghouses and list servers that can help you get the information that you and families need. Just remember that knowledge is power, and power is at the heart of empowerment.

Linking Families to Family Support Services

During the past decade, public policy has increasingly favored home and community care for children with disabilities. Home and community care creates a number of basic needs for families. Why have home and community become the nation's policy?

Reasons for Family Support Policies

These are some of the key factors guiding family support policies (Agosta & Bradley, 1985; Knoll, Covert, Osuch, O'Connor, Agosta, & Blaney, 1990; Turnbull, Garlow, & Barber, 1991):

- Deinstitutionalization of people from state institutions and efforts to prevent their institutionalization in the first place have effectively closed down many out-of-home placements.
- Programs increasingly include children with disabilities in the schools' general education facilities and programs, thus making their education a community concern.
- More children with severe disabilities are living, and more of them are living longer.
- More mothers or other caregivers are working outside the home.
- More families are smaller than in past decades, and more are single-parent families; fewer families have help from extended family members as family and individual mobility increase.
- Taxpayers and policymakers have been concerned about holding down the costs of institutional and medical care.
- There are many benefits to families, children, and the public when children are cared for in homes and communities.
- Families have wanted to have more control over their lives; they have begun to resist professional decision making and to be empowered by making and carrying out their own decisions about the services they will or will not use.

Federal Programs

To carry out a home and community policy, the federal government has created several important programs of direct aid to

Peers Empowering Peers

Talking to other parents when you are a new parent or to an upper classman when you are a freshman can be helpful. And children who have disabilities also have a powerful resource—we who are adults and have disabilities.

I contracted polio in 1949 when I was 3 1/2 years old. We lived in rural Iowa and were miles from anyone who knew much about polio or any disability for that matter. Although this was a time of polio epidemics, no other child in my community of 800 had polio or any other comparable disability. Once in a while, when we went to Des Moines, I would see an adult who had a disability. But most people who had disabilities were kept at home, and there was little accommodation to provide cognitive or physical access to public places or services. At a fairly young age, 10 or 11, I remember being concerned about whether I would be able to use my crutches and braces as I got older. When I finally spotted a young adult of 20 or so who was using them, I was reassured that they were usable by older people. This search for a model has continued throughout my life (although my definition of who is old has changed as I've gotten older). Recently, I saw a woman in an airport who appeared to be in her mid-60s using crutches and braces. She's my "older" model today. I hope I see her again in about 20 years!

Everyone needs a role model, including kids who have disabilities—maybe *especially* kids who have disabilities. When a child without a disability is growing up, the parents have a reasonable idea of how their child should be when grown. Having a child who has a disability is usually a new experience for everyone in the family, and it is sometimes difficult to envision an enviable life for the child. An adult who has a disability and "has a life" can help everyone see the future and move toward it.

When you're a child or especially an adolescent (with apologies to Kermit the Frog), it isn't always "easy to be green." I remember one of my best summers was spent at the National Foundation for Infantile Paralysis in Warm Springs, Georgia. Everyone there had had polio and used a wheelchair or crutches or braces. We all had a wonderful summer being "just like everyone else." This is not to argue against inclusion. It is to suggest that students who have disabilities should have an opportunity to be included with all children, including others who have disabilities. They also need to have an opportunity to learn from adults who have disabilities and to see us in responsible and desirable positions. Then they will develop one kind of vision for the future and the knowledge needed to achieve that vision.

Just as children who have disabilities can learn from adults who have disabilities, so can those who provide services to these children learn from us. I remember talking to a parent recently about her 5-year-old who was entering kindergarten. Her daughter has cerebral palsy and uses a variety of means of mobility, including a walker and a power wheelchair. The occupational and physical therapists were not concerned that the classroom was going to be too crowded to accommodate the daughter's power chair; they wanted her to have to use the walker. I said that it was going to be most important that the child have functional mobility in the kindergarten classroom. The other kids would be moving fast; her mobility has to be adequate to permit her to move with her classmates. She was slow and awkward with the walker; the room had to be accessible for her to use the power chair. Not every event has to be an opportunity to achieve a therapeutic goal. Service providers need to remember that individuals who have disabilities have lives to lead, not just goals and objectives to accomplish. Adults with disabilities know this firsthand and can help identify the important outcomes for the children.

Getting information directly from us also affirms our own skills and abilities. We all value competence and helpfulness. When you ask for help or information from an adult with a disability, you are affirming our contribution to the well-being of others and our place in the community.

Vicki Turbiville

families. The Supplemental Security Income (SSI) program is among the most important federal responses. The SSI program provides cash ($460 on average per month in 1995) to families so they can pay for the basic necessities for maintaining their children at home, cover the additional costs of caring for and raising their children, enhance the children's opportunities to develop, and offset the family's lost income (National Commission on Childhood Disability, 1995). Only those families who are below the federal poverty level and have children with severe disabilities are eligible, and they must apply through local offices of the Social Security Administration.

The federal government also provides a series of other benefits, including home- and community-based medical or related services for children with severe disabilities. This program is called the Medicaid program or Title XIX, referring to the portion of the Social Security Act that authorizes the program (National Commission on Childhood Disability, 1995). Again, the Social Security Administration operates this program.

Moreover, Congress passed the Support for Families of Children with Disabilities Act of 1994, authorizing federal aid to the states so they can (1) support families in their efforts to raise their children in the family home, (2) strengthen the family as the child's primary caregiver, (3) prevent inappropriate and unwanted out-of-home placement and maintain family unity, and (4) reunite families whose children with disabilities have been placed outside their homes. Unfortunately, Congress has not appropriated any money for the states. Thus, the act is essentially an empty financial vessel, although it is a significant policy direction.

State Programs   Because federal responses have been insufficient to meet families' basic needs, families have advocated for—and nearly half the states have adopted—family support policies and programs (Bradley, Knoll, & Agosta, 1993; Singer, Powers, & Olson, 1996; Turnbull, Garlow, & Barber, 1991; Walker, 1995). The purposes of state family support laws and programs are essentially the same as the federal family support law. The eligible families are typically those whose children have developmental disabilities, although some states include children with emotional disorders. The families are "means tested" and have to show that they are financially needy (Bergman & Singer, 1996; Garlow, Turnbull, & Schnase, 1991).

To empower families to make and carry out the decisions they think are best for them, some states pay cash to the families; this is the federal government's approach under the SSI program. Others give the families a voucher that they can redeem for services. Some provide both cash and a voucher. Families may use the cash or vouchers to secure a wide range of services. Typically, states fund the following (Agosta & Melda, 1995; Bergman & Singer, 1996; Bradley et al., 1993; Garlow, Turnbull, & Schnase, 1991):

- Case management and service coordination
- Respite care and day care
- Other care services (for example, homemaker services)
- Medically related services (for example, home health care services; medical and dental care not paid for by other sources; and therapeutic, habilitative, and nursing services)
- Assistive technology and related services (for example, vehicle and home adaptations and modifications)
- Parent education and support services (for example, parent education, counseling services, crisis intervention, estate and transition planning services)
- Services for the child that are not paid for by other sources (for example, personal care attendants, specialized nutrition and clothing, communication services, and self-advocacy training)

Family support programs are usually administered by the state's human resources or social/rehabilitation agency and have local councils. The local councils not only determine which families are eligible for the services but also assist them in developing and carrying out an individualized family support plan. A helpful contact for finding state-specific resources is your Parent Training and Information Center (see appendix A).

On the whole, families approve of these services, and the services themselves are effective in carrying out the purposes for which they were created (Friesen & Wahlers, 1993; Herman & Thompson, 1995; Human Services Research Institute, 1995). Because families have the power to define their needs and spend the cash to satisfy the needs, they believe that they experience less stress and have an improved quality of life (Herman, 1994). Families also report an increased capability for maintaining their child at home, assisting in the child's development, and compensating to a degree for their lost income because they care for their child instead of taking a job (Agosta & Melda, 1995; Friesen & Wahlers, 1993; Herman & Thompson, 1995). Box 10–4 includes quotations from families in Iowa, Illinois, and Louisiana who participate in their states' family support programs and describe what those programs mean to them.

When you begin to collaborate with a family whose child has a severe disability and who is financially needy, you may well find that they cannot meet some of their basic needs for food, shelter, clothing, medical attention, and care for themselves and especially their child. Those are precisely the families that the federal SSI program and the states' family support programs were designed to assist.

Meeting the families' basic needs means linking the families with the state and federal programs or, if a state does not have a family support program, advocating for one. When you take either or both of these steps, you create an opportunity to be a partner in meeting families' basic needs. And in doing so, you also affect the families' own motivation (especially their perceived control and hope) and their knowledge and skills (acquiring information and problem solving). The bottom line is that linking families to federal SSI or Medicaid programs and to state family support programs is being an empowerment agent.

Addressing Issues of Abuse and Neglect

There is a fourth way you can support families to meet their basic needs. It is to collaborate with them to prevent them from abusing or neglecting their child or to intervene if they have already maltreated their child.

Definitions Abuse and neglect consist of physical or mental injury, sexual abuse or exploitation, negligent treatment, or maltreatment that harms or threatens a child's health or welfare (Child Abuse Prevention and Treatment Act, 1992). The term *maltreatment* refers to physical, emotional, and sexual abuse and neglect; and because it includes specific types of improper treatment, it is the term we use here. It also is the term that the research community uses to include all types of improper treatment.

Abuse generally is nonaccidental and intentional infliction of pain and includes physical acts that result in injury, sexual molestation and exploitation, and emotional abuse (verbal attacks that impair the child's emotional development and diminish the child's sense of self-worth). Neglect generally is the failure to provide the child with basic necessities such as food, shelter, and education (Turnbull, Buchele-Ash, & Mitchell, 1994).

Maltreatment usually occurs within a pattern of similar acts; repetition usually is an essential element of maltreatment. This means that single instances usually are excluded, and infrequent blowups within a family usually do not cause abuse and usually are not evidence of neglect. But a severe, especially violent single instance can, of course, cause great harm and by itself constitute maltreatment.

Not surprisingly, each element of the definition, such as "physical injury" or "sexual exploitation," has its own definitions, not just in the federal law but also in state laws. To find out how your state law defines

MY VOICE
BOX 10–4

What Family Support Means to Us

- Having a child who is quadriplegic is very expensive. I am a single mother and this money helps us get through everyday living.
- [We appreciate] the fact that we are able to spend the money on our child without being told what to buy. We feel that we are being trusted to meet the needs of our child.
- It is like a breath of fresh air to a drowning person.
- It is the only program that has been willing to help us financially and recognize our needs.
- The extra money helps us to keep our child at home.
- Our family member was able to get high-quality hearing aids that we would not have been able to afford.
- It gave us an opportunity to build a ramp which increased our child's safety and lessened physical stress on us.

Source: Agosta, J., & Melda, K. (1995). *Supplemental Security Income for children.* Boston, MA, and Salem, OR: Human Services Research Institute.

abuse and neglect, ask your school social worker, counselor, nurse, or principal; the local district or county attorney; or your state attorney general.

Incidence   Children with disabilities seem to be at greater risk for being maltreated by their families and other caregivers, including professionals, than other children. A recent report by the National Center on Child Abuse and Neglect (1993) reports the following:

- Children with disabilities experienced maltreatment at a rate 1.7 times higher than did children without disabilities.
- Children who have disabilities experienced emotional maltreatment at a rate 2.8 times more often than did children without disabilities.
- The incidence of physical abuse among maltreated children with disabilities was 9 per 1,000, or 2.1 times the rate for maltreated children who did not have disabilities.
- Among maltreated children with disabilities, the incidence of sexual abuse was 3.5 per 1,000, or 1.8 times the rate for sexually abused children who did not have disabilities.
- Among maltreated children with disabilities, the incidence of physical neglect was 12 per 1,000, or 1.6 times the rate for maltreated children without disabilities.

Pathways   There are several pathways that put children with disabilities at greater risk of maltreatment than other children (Ammerman, 1989). When two or more of these pathways intersect, children's risk of maltreatment increases. Thus, the context in which the child lives is extremely important (Garbarino & Kostelny, 1992).

It is essential for you to know families (one of the obligations of a reliable alliance) and the pathways that may lead them to maltreat their child. The family systems framework will key you into each family's situation and help you identify some of those pathways. Certain pathways are related to the family's characteristics and include the following (Ammerman, 1989; Garbarino & Kostelny, 1992; Sobsey, 1994):

- *Family form.* One example is divorce.
- *Cultural background.* For example, some cultures tolerate physical punishment.
- *Socioeconomic status.* For example, poverty can cause stress; stress can cause abuse.
- *Geographic location.* For example, isolation can be a pathway to maltreatment.

- *The nature of exceptionality.* A child who is noncompliant can trigger abuse; a nonverbal child can hardly say what ails him or her and thus can become neglected.
- *The family's own health.* Declining health in a family member may contribute to neglect of other members.
- *Coping styles.* Poor problem-solving skills or frequent expressions of anger can be accompanied by violence to family members.

Characteristics of the child also are important in determining whether the child is on a risk pathway. A child who was born prematurely, has low birth weight or medical complications at birth, has a chronic illness or disabilities, is unable to "read" caregivers' moods and does not know when to desist difficult behaviors, or is a girl in the case of sexual abuse, clearly is at risk for maltreatment (Ammerman, 1989; Lutzker, Campbell, Newman, & Harrold, 1989).

Identification   Symptoms of abuse include bruises and injuries that the child cannot or will not explain or that the child explains implausibly. Injuries on parts of the child's body that are not usually damaged by a fall (such as the child's back or thighs) may indicate maltreatment. Signs of neglect include unkempt appearance, poor hygiene, malnutrition, and developmental delays. Sexual molestation often results in tissue damage and evidence of sexually transmitted diseases (Ammerman & Baladerian, 1993).

You probably will not be able to detect some of these symptoms. For example, unless you are a nurse, other health care provider, provider of related services such as catheterization, or a staff member in an infants and toddlers program, you will not detect tissue damage to the child's sexual organs. But you may be able to detect others easily.

It is usually helpful to construct a history of the child's time with you. Look for sudden changes in the child's behavior, regression to earlier developmental stages, enuresis (involuntary urination), withdrawal, aggressiveness, or deterioration in academic or other performance. Ask yourself whether the child has become especially shy, hypervigilant, or resistant to being touched. Be curious about whether the child has become particularly anxious or distressed in the presence of a caregiver (Ammerman & Baladerian, 1993).

Detecting maltreatment in children with disabilities is very difficult. The children may have little or no ability to communicate or report abuse or neglect; they may be unwilling to just "say no, go, and report"—the three strategies that most professionals teach children who do not have disabilities.

Also, their very disabilities may make some children more injury-prone than others. Children with visual impairments may bump into objects more frequently than others; children with seizure disorders or physical impairments may fall down regularly; children with hyperactivity are more prone to accidental injuries than other children (Ammerman & Baladerian, 1993). So injury-proneness may lead you to overlook maltreatment or make you more apt to suspect that maltreatment has occurred.

Finally, some children with disabilities are in the classic double bind of depending on the person who maltreats them to help them meet their basic needs and yet having to put up with the maltreatment because they cannot find another caregiver: "I knew I needed this person [my caregiver] to get me up out of bed and keep me alive and do my breathing treatments. This person became my life line but was also my abuser" (National Symposium on Abuse and Neglect of Children with Disabilites, 1995).

Reporting

What should you do if you suspect that a child has been maltreated? First, make sure that your suspicions are based on facts and that you have reasonable grounds for your concern. Second, follow your school's procedures for reporting within the school. You may be required to report what you know and reasonably suspect to the school social worker, counselor, nurse, or principal depending on school procedures. Third, call the local or state child protection agency; if you do not know what agency to call, then contact your school social worker, counselor, or principal or call your local district or county attorney. Remember, every state requires people who have any child care responsibilities to report maltreatment. If you do not report it, you may violate the reporting law and be subject to civil or criminal punishment. Finally, do not try to intervene on your own; the techniques for preventing and intervening almost invariably require collaborative and interdisciplinary responses.

Prevention

When you and your colleagues do intervene, begin by focusing on the child. If the child has a disability, the suggestions in box 10–5 are particularly useful and supported by research, but they also can apply to a child who does not have a disability.

Then spread your prevention efforts to the family (or other caregivers) who put the child at risk. Begin by trying to increase a family's capacities to withstand the forces that contribute to maltreatment. Recognize the family's strengths and build on them; and remember that maltreatment often occurs because the child's, the family's, and the community's characteristics intersect in ways that can lead to maltreatment (Turnbull et al., 1994).

Be sure to assemble a collaborative team, as the suggestions in box 10–6 point out. Work with your school social worker, counselor, or principal to get support in forming a collaborative team. Almost always, effective intervention requires people with different expertise and resources (Turnbull et al., 1994).

TIPS

BOX 10–5

Preventing Maltreatment by Working with the Child

- Help to decrease behaviors that are difficult to handle and facilitate more appropriate and adaptive behaviors through the use of positive behavioral support (discussed in chapter 13).
- Provide sexuality education that includes self-protection behaviors and assertiveness training. This one measure is particularly important because most programs train compliance by the child with a disability. Rather than allowing children to make their own choices or assert their own rights of assertiveness during appropriate situations, their goals are usually set up to develop compliance.
- Provide developmentally appropriate communication techniques so the child has an effective ability to "say no, go, and tell."
- Provide individual rights education.
- Provide social skills training.

Source: National Symposium on Abuse and Neglect of Children with Disabilities. (1995). *Abuse and neglect of children with disabilities: Report and Recommendations.* Lawrence, KS: Universtiy of Kansas, Beach Center on Families and Disability and Erikson Institute of Chicago.

Preventing Maltreatment by Working with the Family

- Provide opportunities to increase parenting skills. (This includes fathers. Most training programs are targeted toward mothers only.)
- Link parents to other families for support to reduce the factor of isolation.
- Provide social and other informal positive supports.
- Provide information on positive parental responsiveness to their child.
- Increase parental awareness of resources.
- Ensure parental involvement in child-serving programs.
- Teach nonviolent strategies for handling aggressive behaviors.
- Teach nonviolent discipline techniques.

- Enhance parental coping strategies.
- Arrange for home health visitors trained in detecting child maltreatment to visit families' homes following the birth of a new baby for up to one month and thereafter as needed.
- Facilitate intervention at birth to help ensure parent-child attachment and newborn care techniques.
- Provide community resource referrals to families who have substance abuse problems.
- Provide the support needed by parents when they themselves have a disability.
- Carefully select caregivers when the child is removed from the natural home.

Source: National Symposium on Abuse and Neglect of Children with Disabilities. (1995). *Abuse and neglect of children with disabilities: Report and Recommendations.* Lawrence, KS: Universtiy of Kansas, Beach Center on Families and Disability and Erikson Institute of Chicago.

The cardinal rule in intervention is to protect the child. To do this, it may be necessary to remove the child from the family's home, often immediately, and secure foster placement. Then a thorough, interdisciplinary assessment of the causes and nature of maltreatment must precede any intervention. Thereafter, the principal goal is supporting family members to be more effective in parenting the child and managing the child's behaviors and their own (assuming the child is to stay in the family home).

Teachers and other school personnel face a dilemma when confronted with maltreatment, their obligation to report it, and their desire to collaborate with a family. In box 10–7 you will read about how one of those professionals deals with this dilemma.

Although some professionals will want to use psychotherapeutic strategies and counseling, these often do not bring about significant changes in parents' behavior (Kempe & Kempe, 1978). Instead, collaborative interventions seem to work better if they are offered over a sustained period of time and in the place (such as the home) where the maltreatment has occurred (Lutzker, 1984; Lutzker & Newman, 1986). Sometimes treatment is one-on-one; sometimes it consists of involving the perpetrator in parent training, support groups (help lines, respite care, visiting nurses, or neighborhood programs), and other

multiparticipant activities.

It is by no means easy to propose or carry out intervention strategies. The child may be out of the home. Parents may be under court order to engage in treatment but lack the intrinsic motivation to benefit from it. Parents may also deny the fact of maltreatment, be reluctant to reveal information that relates to maltreatment and reasons for it, and be unable or unwilling to establish a reliable alliance or trusting relationship with a treatment provider (Walker, 1988; Kelly, 1983).

Nevertheless, you can be an effective professional in dealing with child maltreatment and a family. The key is to remember that you are a collaborator with the family, a collaborator against maltreatment.

Linking Our Themes

What action should you take to meet families' basic needs that is consistent with the empowerment framework? You can create a reliable alliance by meeting families' basic needs and by infusing into that alliance the eight obligations that enrich it. Your actions will create an empowering context, and that context in turn will have a positive effect on a family's own empowerment.

BOX 10–7

TOGETHER WE CAN

Reporting Maltreatment

Iva Goodwin is the social worker at a school for students with severe and multiple disabilities in Wichita, Kansas. Donna Swall is a child protective services worker in Douglas County, Kansas. The families with whom they work come from all walks of life and represent a broad spectrum of socioeconomic and racial-ethnic-cultural differences. Among them, there are those families who abuse or neglect their children.

State law requires Iva to report suspected maltreatment, just as it requires Donna to act on those reports. How do they report and investigate and, at the same time, recognize that families have strengths and that it is in their and their child's interests to regard Iva and Donna as reliable allies?

Iva starts by trying to earn families' trust, using their strengths as the basis of her relationship with them. Providing them with supports as soon as their children enter the school, educating them about what the school and other agencies can do to help them raise their child and meet their other needs, inviting personnel from outside the school to attend IEP meetings and showing families how these personnel can support them, developing interagency collaborative

teams, and showing families how to access the service provider system—these are the preventive measures Iva takes for all families.

Likewise, Donna recognizes that, while her first duty is to protect the child, she often can accomplish that if she offers to help the family. To stay connected with the families, she practices good listening skills, not only expressing her confidence in family members but also making it clear that she recognizes their frustrations. Undergirding Donna's work is her presumption that families are trying to do the best they can for their children and that they want to be good parents.

When the time comes for Iva to comply with state law and file a maltreatment report, she meets her legal obligation, telling the families that reporting is mandatory and that they should regard child protective services intervention as a source of help, not of criticism or blame.

Similarly, when Donna initiates an intervention, she makes it clear that she is offering a service, not a form of punishment. "Proactive" characterizes her approach, not "reactive."

Some families accept these explanations. Others do not. The trust that Iva has tried to

earn—by preventive steps—sometimes survives her telling the families that she will report. Sometimes it doesn't. In Donna's case, the same is true: Some families accept the services gladly. When they have a child with a disability, their feelings of guilt may make them more accepting of the offer of help.

When families do not accept Iva's offer, it is largely because the families themselves have been hard to reach in the first place. Either they are not connected with the schools or any other agency or people in their communities, or they are not experienced in developing relationships, or they are inaccessible (having no telephone and not allowing Iva or her colleagues to visit them).

Iva's advice: Build the trust, recognize it takes a long time, work especially hard with disconnected or isolated families, and build on strengths. When the time comes to report, then comply with the law and say that child protective services are sources of help, not blame.

Donna's advice: Be especially sensitive to families' reactions, and work especially hard at the staying-connected tips.

Creating a Reliable Alliance

In figure 10–2 we show how you can create a reliable alliance by meeting families' basic needs.

Strengthening Family Factors

Remembering that the way in which you meet families' basic needs creates an empowering context, you should be able to recognize how that context, in turn, affects a family's motivation and knowledge/skills. In figure 10–3 we illustrate the link between your actions (the context factors) and the family's empowerment (the family factors). This link occurs through collaboration: Through collaboration we act empowerfully.

FIGURE 10–2

Creating a Reliable Alliance: Disempowering and Empowering Actions

Obligations	Issues	Disempowering Actions	Empowering Actions
Knowing yourself	You feel very angry and frustrated at parents who belittle their child with a learning disability.	At a conference tell them that it's imperative that they stop "putting down" their child.	Discuss learning disabilities with the parents and problem-solve on information resources that would enable them to better understand their child's challenges.
Knowing families Family characteristics	The parents, who have mental retardation, are extremely fearful that their children will be put into foster care.	Assume that parents with mental retardation cannot be capable parents and urge the parents to consider foster care.	Brainstorm with the parents about the community resources available to them, parenting information, and support; make referrals in light of their preferences, strengths, and needs.
Family interactions	The child's challenging behavior creates major frustrations for all family members.	Tell the parents that this is something that they should expect, given that their child has autism, and that they will need to learn to live with it.	If the family agrees, post a request on the autism list server describing the specific situation and asking for tips and advice that has worked for other families.
Family functions	Both parents are unemployed and are financially unable to provide for their child with cerebral palsy.	Tell the parents that you are very worried about their child and wish that they could do more to provide for him or her.	Give the family a description and contact information for the state's family support program; put them in touch with other families who have participated.
Family life cycle	The family is very worried about their daughter with epilepsy transitioning to a large middle school and facing adolescent issues.	Tell parents to "take a day at a time" and everything will be fine.	Tell the parents about a transition workshop that the PTI is sponsoring and ask if they would be interested.
Honoring cultural diversity	A parent wants her child with mental retardation to learn Spanish as well as English, but the language pathologist says that two languages will be too confusing.	Advise the parents to be realistic about the fact that their child will be lucky to learn English.	Network to locate the most current information on bilingual education for children with disabilities. Review information with parents and plan next steps.

FIGURE 10-2 CONTINUED

Creating a Reliable Alliance: Disempowering and Empowering Actions

Obligations	Issues	Disempowering Actions	Empowering Actions
Affirming and building on family strengths	Parents of a child with spina bifida who is in an early intervention program believe that their child will have no future.	Warn the parents that they'd better make sure that their marriage is not torn apart by the child.	Suggest to the parents that they contact the local Parent to Parent program to be matched with parents of older children with spina bifida.
Promoting family choices	A family has just been informed that their child has AD/HD and invited to an IEP conference; they do not have any relevant information.	Send the parents a list of their legal rights even though you know the information is practically incomprehensible.	Ask the family about their preferences for information and review a range of resources with them. Respond to their priorities.
Envisioning great expectations	Parents of a daughter with a rare syndrome lament that they feel isolated and resentful when they hear parents of typical kids sharing their "trials and tribulations."	Suggest that they will probably have similar feelings for the rest of their lives.	Provide information about NPPSIS and the toll-free number. Suggest that parents could possibly be matched with a family whose child has the same syndrome.
Using interpersonal communication skills	Parents walk out of a conference when one of the participants says their adolescent daughter is too "available" to young men; they refuse to return telephone calls.	When you see them at a shopping mall, say, "Sex is part of life. Get information about it now, or become grandparents later."	Write the parents an empathetic letter and state your own discomfort with how the topic was addressed. Offer to meet with them, listen to their perspectives, and respond to their priorities.
Warranting trust and respect	A student comes to school with unexplained bruises and cuts. He has a communication impairment and will not or cannot explain why he is so frequently injured.	Call the parents, accuse them of abuse, and threaten to call the police if their son ever shows any more signs of maltreatment.	Talk with the school social worker and get her to join you in gathering more information; filing a report if appropriate; and informing the parents.

Summary

Collaborating with families to meet their basic needs may not seem to be the same as educating their children, but it nonetheless is an important role for all educators. The reason is simple: The more you and other educators support families to address their critical, basic, personal, and family needs, the more likely it is that they will devote time and energy to their child's educational needs . . . and, of course, the more likely it is that you and they will develop an empowered and empowering relationship.

There are four ways you can assist families in meeting their basic needs. First, you can enable them to access social and emotional support, particularly through Parent to Parent networks. Second, you can help them acquire information, providing a broad array of viable options. Third, you can link families to family support services such as SSI and those available from state-operated family support programs. Fourth, you can assist families who are on one of several pathways toward abuse and neglect.

FIGURE **10-3**

Strengthening Family Factors Through an Empowering Context: Meeting Families' Basic Needs

Motivation	What You Can Do	Knowledge/Skills	What You Can Do
Self-efficacy	Encourage parents to serve as veteran parents in Parent to Parent programs to share their expertise and support with others.	Information	Provide information on scholarship opportunities for enrichment and postsecondary programs to all interested families.
Perceived control	Ask families facing transition what type of information on future options would be helpful and respond in their order and priority.	Problem solving	If a parent wants to discuss it, brainstorm about community resources that can help him or her escape domestic violence.
Energy	Encourage families who experience abuse and neglect to take breaks from child care responsibility by linking with respite care programs.	Communication skills	Affirm families' positive communication skills, and let parents know how much you recognize and appreciate their skills.
Persistence	If parents get turned down for family support services, encourage them to reapply and to continue making their needs known to program administrators.	Coping skills	Encourage parents who engage in abuse to develop skills in disciplining their children that will enable them to avoid abusive interactions.
Hope	If you are in a state that does not have a family support program, share your vision with other families and professionals that such a program could be started through collaborative efforts and take action.		

In all that you do, you can create a reliable alliance and take actions that empower families; remember, your job is to create a context that is empowering of the family's motivation and knowledge/skills.

Kurt Baxter, Kerri Lunsford, and Bethany Ward and their families have more in common with each other than the fact that the three youngsters have a rare disease. Their other common ground is the "goes around, comes around" factor: When they help others ("what goes around"), they eventually benefit ("comes around"). From Cedar, Kansas, to Elberton, Georgia, to Laconia, New Hampshire, and in thousands of communities all across the United States, families—mothers, fathers, children and youth with exceptionalities, and brothers and sisters—provide emotional support and information to each other through Parent to Parent networks. True, these networks are no substitute for solidly funded, family-friendly, professionally operated service systems; but as necessary as such service systems are, they are not wholly sufficient. What sustains families? Nancy Ward makes a revealing point: When the Wards found the Lunsfords, it was like finding family they didn't know existed.

Chapter Eleven

Referring and Evaluating for Special Education

*T*he way Pam and Mark Gorian figure it, they shouldn't have had to fight to get their son Ryne evaluated. As Pam puts it, "we saw one boy at home, and the schools saw another at school."

What Pam and Mark saw was a youngster with memory and math problems; a boy whom they thought had dyslexia or attention-deficit/hyperactivity disorder (AD/HD). What the school in Connecticut saw was a "lazy little boy," one whom they refused to evaluate despite Pam's four-year campaign for an evaluation.

It was not that the schools didn't have some indications that Ryne might need help. He was struggling, every year, just to pass. He was always behind, always on the "low end" of his peers; and he was the topic of numerous teacher meetings. In kindergarten, they thought he had a hearing loss, despite medical judgment to the contrary. In first grade, they thought he was a troubled kid but not one who had a disability. In second grade, they denied that he had a learning disability or AD/HD, but they admitted he needed summer school because he had failed some courses. "I was very taken aback. I was, like, well, where did this come from, you haven't called me and said that he was having any difficulties. I haven't seen anything different than what I've seen. How can you suddenly tell me that this child is going to fail second grade, and he has to go to summer school?" In third grade, teachers finally got around to pulling Ryne out of math for a half-hour of special help, although they still insisted that they would not evaluate him for AD/HD. Not surprisingly, Ryne struggled through each grade, his frustration, anger, and withdrawal escalating every year.

Pam and Mark, however, are people of action, the children of families who served in the Marine Corps, as Mark himself did. More than that, they are well connected and used their friendships strategically. Mark is employed by a nearby school district, and Pam has a cousin in a neighboring state who is a school principal. When they made their concerns about Ryne and the schools known to their allies, they got a straightforward message: "You've got the right to have him evaluated. Don't let the schools get away with not evaluating him."

Ryne's evaluation occurred at the beginning of his fourth-grade year but not without more struggle. Pam and Mark describe their efforts to help Ryne with his homework as a nightmare—he wouldn't and couldn't do it. Pam's efforts to help were seemingly futile because no one at his school had told her how she could help him learn. At last, Ryne's special education teacher convened a meeting of his family and his two general education teachers. The teachers reached this consensus: Ryne has many of the characteristics of AD/HD; but because he is not a troublemaker or loud and disruptive, and is a quiet kid who just reverts into himself, he is being shuffled along, passed through the grades, and passed over for evaluation.

Armed with the knowledge of his rights that they acquired from their out-of-school allies and the information that his home-district teachers gave them, Pam and Mark secured an evaluation from a well-known neurologist. His report: "I can't believe it. Ryne has been screaming for help, and no one has given it to him." His prescription: Ritalin to treat the AD/HD. His bill: to Pam and Mark, although they knew the school was required to pay for the diagnosis. The upshot: the school planning and placement team conceded that Ryne has both AD/HD and a specific learning disability (LD).

Pam concedes that none of these activities would have occurred except for Ryne's special education consultant, Mrs. Nilen. "I would be lost without her. She made it all possible," says Pam. She recalled that Mrs. Nilen had advocated against the principal to get an evaluation for Ryne, convened the teachers to discuss Ryne, endured reprimands from the school district for referring this student for special education evaluation and services, took the time to go far above and beyond the elements of her job description, and stayed in regular contact with Pam and Mark.

Ask Pam to give the bottom line on her collaboration with Mrs. Nilen, and she says, "If it weren't for her, I would be lost, because I wouldn't have somebody who I felt comfortable with contacting all the time. She's going to be honest with me, no matter what." Mrs. Nilen put Pam and Mark on the right path as they negotiate the special education maze and figure it out for themselves.

As Ryne progresses through the fifth grade, Pam and Mark shudder in anticipation of his entry into the middle school next year. There, they and Ryne will encounter new professionals, a new system, and different kinds of student behaviors, including all the problems related to gangs and the trouble they can bring to a shy youngster.

"We get very tired of being the one to contact the educators. Why are we always the ones who have to hound professionals and hound them and hound them again? We know we have to make the waves, to fight, to trust our instincts. We trust Mrs. Nilen completely. But *we're no longer naive. We're more involved. We're watchdogs. We don't assume the schools know what to do and will always do what they should for Ryne. We are aware, now; we have self-confidence."*

So Pam, Mark, and Ryne will not only survive; they will prevail. But did they really have to be motivated by Ryne's failure and their own frustration, by their *distrust of the schools? Did so many years have to pass before the schools gave Ryne the help he needed, before they finally stopped talking about his problems and acted on them? Why must Pam and Mark be so persistent all the time? And where might they find another person like Mrs. Nilen who warrants their trust and respect?*

Evaluation is the gateway to special education, and referral is the path to the evaluation gate. In this chapter, we will describe both IDEA's requirements and today's best practices related to referral and evaluation; and we will explain how partnership in the referral-evaluation process can empower students, families, and professionals. Figure 11–1 depicts the empowerment model; the shaded portion pertains to referral and evaluation partnerships.

The term *referral* refers to the formal request for an evaluation of a student. Here's how IDEA defines *evaluation:*

> procedures used . . . to determine whether a child has a disability and the nature and extent of the special education and related services that the child needs. The term means procedures used selectively with an individual child and does not include basic tests administered to or procedures used with all children in a school, grade, or class. (34 C.F.R. Sec. 300.500)

Collaboration in Referring and Evaluating for Special Education

Traditionally, partnerships in referral and evaluation refer to professional-to-professional interaction: General or special educators collaborate with each other and with school psychologists, counselors, social workers, and related service providers to refer or evaluate or both. Also traditionally, families are on the edges of professional decision making related to referral and evaluation (Mehan, 1993; Ware, 1994). Certainly, in Ryne Gorian's case the partnership occurred only after his parents applied a great deal of pressure; even then, they were somewhat peripheral to his school-based evaluation.

The immediate outcome of partnerships in referral and evaluation is a better understanding of the student's strengths, great expectations, preferences, and needs. That understanding is the foundation for the student's IFSP/IEP; for developing partnerships among student, family, and educators as they implement the IFSP/IEP; and for assuring that the student has long-term outcomes of independence, contribution, inclusion, and empowerment.

To show you how partnerships in referral and evaluation merge IDEA requirements, best practices, and your eight obligations for reliable alliances, we refer you to figure 11–2, which outlines eight steps in the process of referral and evaluation. We will describe each of the steps of that process in this chapter. Take note: States differ in their requirements for referring and evaluating students for gifted education. Sixty percent of states require programs for students who are gifted, but the requirements vary to some extent. Forty-three states have policies related to initial screening to identify students who are gifted (Coleman, Gallagher, & Foster, 1994). If you work with students who are gifted, you need to identify and follow local and state policies.

Coordinating the Referral and Evaluation Process

The entity with overall responsibility for referral and evaluation is the school-based special services team, called the planning and placement team at Ryne Gorian's school. (This team goes by different names in different schools.) Typically, this team consists of special services personnel (that is, teachers, psychologists, social workers, counselors, and therapists) and administrators.

Whatever these professionals can contribute, they typically lack the insights that come from living daily and closely with the students they are evaluating. Pam and Mark Gorian certainly saw a different Ryne from the one the schools saw: There is a world of difference

FIGURE 11–1

Empowerment Framework: Collaborating for Empowerment

Family Factors:
It's Within Us to Be Empowerful

Collaborating for Empowerment:
Through Collaboration, We Act Empowerfully

Education Context Factors:
It's Within Us to Make Our Contexts Empowering

Motivation	**Knowledge/Skills**	**Opportunities for Partnerships**	**Obligations for Reliable Alliances**
		Opportunities arise when . . .	*Reliable alliances consist of . . .*
Self-efficacy: believing in our capabilities	*Information:* being in the know	Communicating among reliable allies	Knowing yourself
Perceived control: believing we can apply our capabilities to affect what happens to us	*Problem solving:* knowing how to bust the barriers	Meeting families' basic needs	Knowing families
Hope: believing we will get what we want and need	*Coping skills:* knowing how to handle what happens to us	Referring and evaluating for special education	Honoring cultural diversity
Energy: lighting the fire and keeping it burning	*Communication skills:* being on the sending and receiving ends of expressed needs and wants	Individualizing for appropriate education	Affirming family strengths
Persistence: putting forth a sustained effort		Extending learning in home and community	Promoting family choices
		Attending and volunteering at school	Envisioning great expectations
		Advocating for systems improvement	Communicating positively
			Warranting trust and respect

FIGURE 11–2

Referral and Evaluation Process

Responsible Agent	Function	Activities
Special services team	Coordinating the referral and evaluation process	Develop an organizational plan. Appoint committees. Assure compliance with law and regulations. Intervene when obstacles prevent other committees from carrying out assignments. Work with other service agencies.
School-based professionals or family members	Implementing prereferral intervention	Make contact with early intervention programs to coordinate referral. Provide consultation assistance to teacher considering referral. Discuss concerns with parents.
Special services team	Initiating and reviewing the referral	Determine if a referral is necessary. If so, complete and submit referral form. Examine available information. Review questions generated by team. Determine need for evaluation. Appoint multidisciplinary evaluation team. Discuss concerns with parents.
Special services team	Providing notice; obtaining consent	Inform parents of rights and of proposed actions. Obtain parental consent for evaluation.
Multidisciplinary evaluation team	Collecting evaluation information	Assign responsibilities for obtaining evaluation (consulting members named). Match options for family collaboration with family preferences. Share information on each team member's resources, priorities, and concerns. Schedule and complete evaluation. Receive evaluation summaries. Review evaluation summaries for appropriateness and completeness. Document any biasing factors during evaluation.
Special services team Multidisciplinary evaluation team	Analyzing evaluation information	Score and interpret meaning of evaluation results. Analyze and synthesize all evaluations.
Special services team	Discussing evaluation results with family	Inform family of meeting and invite members to attend. Examine all available information and evaluations. Discuss all obtained information. Document needs related to program planning. Provide family with a written summary of evaluation results.
Special services team	Informing family of the IFSP/IEP conference	Invite family to attend IFSP/IEP conference. Provide family with material to prepare them for the IFSP/IEP process.

Source: Adapted from Strickland, B., & Turnbull, A. P. (1990). *Developing and implementing individualized education programs* (3rd ed.) (p.50) Englewood Cliffs, NJ: Merrill/Prentice Hall. Copyright© 1990 by Merrill Publishing Company. Adapted by permission.

between having two disabilities and being lazy. So although it is rare for schools to include parents on the special services team, they can provide valuable information. Parental contribution can occur if a school (1) pays a parent coordinator at the school or district level to be a permanent member of the team, (2) pays parents of children to serve rotating terms, (3) invites the parents of the student being evaluated to attend meetings whenever the team discusses the student, or (4) combines any of these steps. In addition, adults with a disability who know firsthand about the impact of labeling, the benefits and drawbacks of special and general education, and ways to accommodate to the community can assist the team in connecting the student's evaluation to the student's IEP and an appropriate education.

Implementing Prereferral Intervention

Prereferral intervention occurs before a formal referral for evaluation. Its primary purpose is to analyze the student's strengths and needs and then provide additional individualized assistance without providing special education. When Ryne's school finally gave him a half-hour of "pull out" help in math, they were providing prereferral intervention; they had not yet formally evaluated him for special education.

The frequency of prereferral intervention increased dramatically in the mid-1980s. By the close of that decade, state educational agencies typically recommended or required some type of prereferral intervention with students (Carter & Sugai, 1989). Referral rates for formal evaluation dropped when general and special education teachers collaborated in modifying instruction according to individualized student needs (Fuchs, Fuchs, & Bahr, 1990; Fuchs, Fuchs, Bahr, & Stecker, 1990; Graden, Casey, & Bonstrom, 1985; Graden, Casey, & Christenson, 1985). Most prereferral practices involve professional collaboration and typically do not include active family and student participation in problem solving (Sindelar, Griffin, Smith, & Watanabe, 1992). In chapter 13 we show how family-professional collaboration in helping children be successful with homework and addressing issues associated with challenging behavior can be effective prereferral intervention strategies.

A different approach to preventing formal referral is the heterogeneous school and collaborative consultation model (Pugach & Seidl, 1995; Pugach & Wesson, 1995; Thousand, Villa, & Nevin, 1994; Villa, Thousand, Stainback, & Stainback, 1992). In these schools, special and general educators adapt stu-

dents' instruction within general education classrooms to meet the needs of all learners. They begin with the assumption that all students belong in the general education classroom and that intensive intervention is not primarily for the purpose of preventing evaluation for and placement in separate special education programs but for enhancing the student's success in the classroom.

Initiating and Reviewing the Referral

Referral is a formal request to evaluate a student to determine whether he or she has a disability and, if so, the nature and extent of the student's special education and related services. Parents, other family members, community professionals, or school professionals may initiate a request for referral.

When does referral occur? It usually occurs after prereferral intervention, but not always. Typically, children with severe congenital disabilities are identified during their infancy and increasingly are enrolled in early intervention and preschool programs. Their referral frequently comes from early childhood professionals. But children identified as having an educational exceptionality during school years typically have milder exceptionalities, experience a later onset of an exceptionality (such as a learning disability or AD/HD), or live where there is no comprehensive preschool identification program. Ryne Gorian exemplifies this later onset and delayed evaluation that many students and families experience. Students who are gifted are usually identified after they enter school, although preschool identification is increasingly desirable (Sandel, McCallister, & Nash, 1993). Their parents often have some indication that their son or daughter has unusual abilities or potential achievement.

Why does referral occur? It happens because educators or others suspect that a student may need special education. Often the student is performing significantly below expectation levels, as shown by classwork, homework, tests, and teacher observations. Referral also occurs because the school system itself may be ineffective—class size, teachers' lack of knowledge of education methodologies, and inappropriate instructional materials may lead staff to think that the student has special needs.

Traditionally, educators have assumed that the problem lies within the student; however, progressive educational programs recognize that problems may be attributed as much to the educational context as to the student's strengths, preferences, great expectations, and needs. Thus, rather than removing the student

Referring and Evaluating for Special Education **203**

from general education, the intervention expands the supplementary aids and services provided in the general education classroom. This is how Ryne's school dealt with him.

Many schools have checklists that can help you identify or document your concerns and forms to complete when you ask for an evaluation, whether for a student with a disability or one who seems exceptionally capable. IDEA does not set out time lines or processes for referring students between ages 5 and 21 (Part B of IDEA), but there are special regulations regarding infants and toddlers (Part H of IDEA).

The infant and toddler regulations require states to identify and locate eligible infants and toddlers (that is, child find) and to develop procedures for evaluation and services by hospitals, physicians, parents, day-care programs, local educational agencies, public health facilities, other social service agencies, and other health care providers. Referrals must be made two working days after a child has been identified as potentially needing or being eligible for early intervention. Once the referral is made, the evaluation and assessment activities and the development of an IFSP—Individualized Family Service Plan—must be completed within 45 days. Your state infant and toddler coordinator can provide you with a description of the state's child-find program and the procedures developed for the primary referral sources. (The state Department of Education can provide you with the name of and contact information for your state infant and toddler coordinator.)

Although IDEA does not require parental consent for referral of students between ages 5 and 21, some states and local educational agencies do. Even if consent is not required where you work, communicate early on and certainly during preevaluation with parents about your concerns that their child may need special help. By communicating, you enhance parents' understanding of their son's or daughter's current level of performance and grade-level expectations and why more extensive evaluation and intervention is desirable.

A survey of more than 100 parents of students with learning disabilities at the elementary, junior high, and high school levels indicated that many parents, like Pam and Mark Gorian, were relieved when their child received special assistance:

> The most painful parental response had to do with the difficulty in getting the child appropriate help, the school's denial of parental suspicions of problems, and the "time wasted" between when the parent raised the possibility of the child's needing special help and when the child actually began to

receive it. (Malekoff, Johnson, & Klappersack, 1991, p. 421)

Other parents, however, may object to a more formal referral and evaluation process: "My family is doing whatever we can to keep our adopted son's disability hidden from the school, knowing that once the disability is labeled . . . the expectations that will arise will not at all be positive" (National Council on Disability, 1995, p. 32).

The more you communicate with honesty and frequency, with a genuine interest in the student and family, and with sincere great expectations, the more families probably will see how the referral process can benefit their sons and daughters. Remember Pam and Mark Gorian's trust and respect for Mrs. Nilen because she is honest with them and genuinely has Ryne's, not the school district's, interests as her paramount concern. If, however, families strongly object to referral, try to understand why. Then, in the spirit of partnership, try to see the situation from their point of view. They may be absolutely correct that referral would not be in the student's best interest. The bottom line is that partnership frees you from being limited by only your own perspective and enables you to benefit from family perspectives about referral for evaluation.

The school's special services team is responsible for reviewing the information on the referral form and deciding how to address the concerns stated there. The team may gather more information about the nature and results of prereferral intervention, wait several months on the suspicion that the problem is temporary, provide remedial education rather than evaluate the student for special education (as the schools did for Ryne), or decide to pursue a multidisciplinary evaluation. Under IDEA, the team must inform parents if it proposes or refuses to evaluate the student, the reasons for its decision, and its plans for responding to the concerns that initially triggered the referral. IDEA also requires the local education agency to tell parents where they may obtain an independent evaluation, as you will learn later in this chapter.

Providing Notice and Obtaining Consent

Typically, one member of the special services team is responsible for communicating with the family throughout the entire process (see figure 11–2), including the step of providing notice and obtaining consent. This person, often referred to as the service coordinator, may be the one who has already established a reliable alliance with the parents, who has had the most frequent contact with them or is likely to have such contact, whose values or communication style are most complementary to the parents', or has enough time to work with the family and team members. The service coordinator is the hub of communication and ongoing support for the family, guiding the family through the referral and evaluation process and having a significant role in the IFSP/IEP conference, as you will learn in chapter 12. Service coordinators also ensure that necessary special education services are provided and that the services and supports are coordinated for the benefit of all team members (Friesen & Poertner, 1995; Turbiville, Turnbull, Garland, & Lee, 1996).

Providing Notice IDEA requires schools to provide a written and timely notice to parents in their native language when the schools propose or refuse to initiate or change the student's identification, evaluation, or educational placement or the provision of a free, appropriate public education to the student (including an infant or toddler). The notice must set forth the following:

1. A full explanation of all the procedural safeguards available to the parent
2. A description of the proposed or refused action, an explanation of why the school proposes or refuses to take the action, and a description of any options it considered and the reasons why it rejected those options
3. A description of each evaluation procedure, test, record, or report it used as a basis for its proposal or refusal
4. A description of any other factors that are relevant to its proposal or refusal

The term *procedural safeguards* refers to parents' legal rights. As we noted in chapter 10, an excellent resource for you to get information on parents' legal rights, written in family-friendly ways, is the Parent Training and Information Center in your state (see Appendix A). You and the families you serve also can attend Parent Training and Information Center workshops on legal rights.

The special services team typically sends parents a written statement of their rights. Review your school's statement of rights to determine whether you believe it is comprehensible to the families with whom you work. Share it with several parents with varying degrees of education and invite their suggestions for eliminating jargon and enhancing its clarity and relevance. If it is unclear to you and your colleagues or other parents, you may well conclude that it is a poor example of communication and hardly a good way to build partnerships.

The notice must describe the school's proposed course of action, rationale, and alternatives. At this point, the proposed action is to evaluate the student to determine whether he or she has an exceptionality and the nature and extent of special education necessary. Even if school staff members have already explained the reasons to the parents, they must state them in writing and explain why they rejected other possible options in favor of a full-fledged evaluation. It is a good practice to summarize the information on the referral form and to include the team's concerns and reasons.

The school's notice also must describe the assessment procedures, data, and other information the special service team used in deciding to seek an evaluation. It is a good practice to summarize information from the prereferral intervention or from the team's discussion and include the names and especially the purposes of the tests the team plans to administer. The purposes of each test will probably be more meaningful to most parents than the actual names, but you should give both the names and purposes.

Finally, the notice must describe any relevant information the team considered in its decision to pursue an evaluation, including the student's academic performance, health status, peer relationships, or other relevant information.

The requirements for notice serve at least two purposes. First, a notice can help equalize the power relationship between professionals and families— moving from a power-over to a power-with and power-from-within approach. Second, the notice can relieve some of the anxiety that families naturally feel about the school's authority and the student's education.

Sometimes a notice does not enable professionals and families to communicate with each other because it is written to satisfy legal requirements and tends to be stated in terms that lawyers or school administrators use with each other. In those instances, it is a good practice to supplement the written notice with face-to-face explanations and a clearly written notice.

Some parents will not respond to notices. There may be many reasons for their lack of response, and you should seek to determine why parents do not respond. Follow a "touch-base" policy of telephoning, making a home visit, or consulting with other professionals involved with the family. The more you build a reliable alliance and communicate in an open way, warranting trust and respect, the more likely it is that families will respond to the notices that you send. If they do not respond, reflect on how you might personalize your communication and encourage them to respond.

Obtaining Consent

To protect parents' and their children's rights and to secure their participation in evaluation, IDEA requires parental consent for the first special education evaluation and placement. Your local or state education agency may also require parental consent for subsequent evaluations. Under IDEA, *consent* means the following:

1. The parent has been fully informed of all information relevant to the evaluation in his or her native language or other mode of communication.
2. The parent understands and agrees in writing to the evaluation and knows what student records (if any) will be released and to whom.
3. The parent understands that the consent is voluntary and may be revoked at any time.

It is a good practice to communicate clearly, even repeatedly, the reasons explaining why an evaluation and specially designed instruction would benefit the student. If you believe that evaluation and placement will not benefit the student, it is also good practice and ethically right to state your viewpoints. Parents who refuse to give consent may be exactly right in their perspectives that their son or daughter may be harmed rather than helped by the evaluation and placement.

If parents refuse to consent when their consent is required, they and the school must first attempt to resolve the conflict by complying with any applicable state law, such as mediation. If they still cannot agree, the school may initiate a due process hearing, which is a mini-trial before an independent "judge" called a hearing officer. If the hearing officer rules in the school's favor, the school may evaluate or place the student and notify the parents of its actions. Although school administrators are responsible for deciding whether to seek a hearing, teachers and related services staff should consult with them and be consulted by them. If the hearing officer rules in favor of the parents, the school will not be able to move forward with the evaluation unless the school successfully appeals the decision.

Supplementing Written Notices and Consent Forms

Although the notice to parents and their consent must be in writing, any or all face-to-face explanations can be advantageous, so: (1) Send parents the written notice and consent form to review and then schedule a follow-up meeting to discuss the need for an evaluation and answer any questions, (2) give the notice and consent form to the parents and review the written information with them, or (3) share information with parents orally and then follow up the meeting with a written notice and consent form. Ask parents which option they would prefer. A face-to-face meeting with parents can be helpful in developing a reliable alliance.

When holding a face-to-face meeting with parents, you or an evaluation team member should (1) inform parents of your desire to have a meeting and state your rationale, (2) provide a thorough explanation of what will happen at the meeting, and (3) give parents information in a format of their choice so they can prepare for their role in the meeting. (We discussed ways to have successful conferences in chapter 10.)

Collecting Evaluation Information

Figure 11–3 describes legal requirements for nondiscriminatory evaluation. The special services committee is responsible for appointing a multidisciplinary team to conduct the evaluation. IDEA requires the team to include at least one teacher or other specialist with knowledge in the area of the suspected exceptionality. There is no explicit requirement that family members be involved in collecting evaluation information. As you have learned from reading about Pam, Mark, and Ryne Gorian, however, the more you involve families in the evaluation process, the more you can learn about the student and the more you can provide an appropriate education. If you plan to work with students who are gifted, comply with any local and state requirements related to the evaluation for gifted education.

Family members like Pam and Mark Gorian can provide valuable information from a unique perspective, but professionals do not regularly seek it (Halpern, 1982). Apparently, parents such as the Gorians have to take the initiative to share their perspectives (National Council on Disability, 1995).

Harriet Rose, the mother of a young adult with cerebral palsy, has described her desperate attempt to get professionals to accept her opinions regarding her daughter:

> How could I convince them my daughter was bright and capable of learning? What could I say to keep them from brushing my opinions aside because I was "just a mother"? I decided I was going to have to take an aggressive approach in order to keep from being ignored.
>
> I whisked Nancy inside the center in her wheelchair, gave my interviewer a smashing smile and

FIGURE 11–3

IDEA Evaluation Requirements

1. Types of tests or other evaluation materials:
   - Must be tailored to assess specific areas of the student's educational needs and not merely result in a single score.
   - Must be validated for the specific purposes for which the tests are used.

2. Administration of the tests or other assessment procedures:
   - Must be by a multidisciplinary team or group of persons, including at least one teacher or other specialist who has knowledge in the area of suspected disability.
   - Must be selected and administered so as to best ensure that, when administered to a student with impairments in sensory, manual, or speaking skills, the results accurately reflect the student's aptitude or achievement level or whatever factors they purport to measure; and must not reflect the student's impairments in sensory, manual, or speaking skills unless those skills are the factors that the test or procedures themselves purport to measure.
   - Must be administered in the student's native language or other mode of communication (e.g., Braille or signing for students with visual or hearing impairments).
   - Must be administered by trained personnel in conformance with instructions by the producer of the tests or material.

3. Number of tests:
   - Must include more than one, since no single procedure may be used as the sole basis of evaluation.

4. Breadth of the evaluation:
   - Must assess in all areas related to the suspected disability including health, vision, hearing, social and emotional status, general intelligence, academic performance, communicative status, and motor abilities.
   - Must, with respect to infants and toddlers, include the child's unique strengths and needs and the services appropriate to meet those needs (in the developmental areas of cognitive, physical, communication, social or emotional, and adoptive development); and the resources, priorities, and concerns of the families (if the family chooses to discuss them) and the supports and services necessary to enhance the family's capacity to meet the developmental needs of their infant or toddler.

5. Timing of the evaluation:
   - Must occur before initial placement in a program providing special education and related services. Must ensure re-evaluation every three years or more frequently if conditions warrant or if requested by student's parent or teacher.

6. Parental consent and notice:
   - Must ensure parents are fully informed and that they provide written consent prior to the initial evaluation.
   - Must include a full explanation of all due process rights, a description of what the educational agency proposes or refuses to do, a description of each evaluation procedure that was used, and a description of any other factors that influenced the educational agencies' decisions.

7. Interpretation of the evaluation information:
   - Must draw upon and carefully consider a wide variety of information sources including aptitude and achievement tests, teacher recommendations, physical status, social or cultural background, and adaptive behavior.
   - Must be made by a group of persons.

Source: Turnbull, A. P., Turnbull, H. R., Shank, M., & Leal, D. (1995). *Exceptional lives: Special education in today's schools.* Englewood Cliffs, NJ: Merrill/Prentice Hall.

---

proceeded to tell her more than she really needed to know about Nancy, using all the technical and medical jargon I had learned over the previous 10 years. I also mentioned, very casually, that I had earned my master's degree in special education and had taught school before Nancy was born. All of which was a bare-faced lie.

At first I felt a little guilty about what I had done. It really wasn't fair for me to take out my previous frustrations on those perfectly innocent professionals. But on the other hand, it was sad to think that my opinion as a pseudoprofessional was valued so much more than my opinions as a mother had ever been.

Family Participation in Collecting Evaluation Information

How can you create a partnership with families in evaluation and avoid creating a context in which families resort to desperate communication attempts? Invite families to choose any one or more of these options: (1) sharing their family story; (2) expressing their preferences and great expectations and describing their child's strengths and needs; (3) assisting professionals in administering assessments; (4) collaborating with professionals in constructing authentic assessments; and (5) especially in the case of infant and toddler evaluation, sharing their own priorities, resources, and concerns.

Sharing Their Family Story

The first alternative involves having the family share their family story. Listening to family stories helps you know families—one of your obligations for creating a reliable alliance. As we have said in previous chapters, often the most relevant information evolves from informal conversations in which families share in an open-ended way their hopes, worries, successes, and questions as a basis for planning the evaluation. The conversation guide in Appendix B furnishes probes for conversing with families and eliciting their family story in ways consistent with the family systems framework.

Expressing Preferences, Great Expectations, Strengths, and Needs

The second alternative provides the student and family with an opportunity to share their preferences, great expectations, and perspectives on the student's strengths and needs. Students and families can convey their likes and dislikes related to homework (a bone of school-family contention for Ryne Gorian's family), school subjects, hobbies, peer relationships, future aspirations, and any other relevant information. As you know from the empowerment model in chapter 3, perceived control is a critically important family factor in the empowerment process. When information about student and family preferences is available at the outset of the evaluation process, members of the multidisciplinary team can ensure that assessments take these preferences into account.

Likewise, students and families can be encouraged to share their great expectations for the future

and give their own perspectives on student strengths and needs related to their schoolwork and other school-related issues, such as getting along with others, paying attention, and completing homework (Van Reusen, Bos, Schumaker, & Deshler, 1994). Professionals can support students and families in sharing this information directly, using probe questions and actively listening.

Administering Assessments

The third alternative involves collaborating with families in administering assessments. Although some assessment procedures have standardized instructions for administration, others are more flexible and can be adapted for family participation. Family members may join the professional who is administering the assessment, as audiologist David Luterman describes in box 11–1.

Consider the perspectives of the parent of a child with an impairment. Would you prefer to participate in the assessment and discover the exact nature of your child's disability through your own observation and collaboration, or would you prefer to sit in the waiting room and receive the verdict from an expert? The more you collaborate with families in collecting evaluation information, the more likely you are to have accurate information and to develop a reliable alliance with them. That is certainly what Mrs. Nilen demonstrated as she sided with the Gorians; it is what other professionals in Ryne's school should have known all along, but did not.

Maitreyi Das, a professional in the Indian government, was studying in the United States when her daughter (Moeena) was diagnosed as having a hearing impairment. Listen to what she said about working with David Luterman (the audiologist quoted in box 11–1):

> David Luterman became the guru that we, as Indians, are apt to seek out. The difference between him and an Indian guru, who directs and orders, was that he developed *our* capacity to decide for Moeena. In those hopeless, strained moments, he instilled hope and confidence. His team of teachers, students, and parents were our support group and fulfilled the role our extended family would have if we had been in India. Perhaps the most enduring contribution this group made was its information sharing, which enabled and empowered all the parents to become advocates for their children with hearing impairments. (Das, 1995, pp. 5–6)

Constructing Authentic Assessments

The fourth alternative is for schools to rely more heavily on authentic assessments and for families to participate

Collaborating in Evaluation

After the parents have shared their concerns and their story, I enlist them as co-workers. I say something to them like, "I may be an expert on testing of hearing, but you are certainly an expert on this child; I need your help." This begins the process of empowering parents. As co-workers, we all enter the testing booth. I also bring in other family members who have accompanied the parents, including grandparents and siblings . . . I proceed to start testing the child, usually giving one parent the audiogram to fill out. In this way the information they need is being incorporated into what they are doing and seeing. The audiogram becomes much more meaningful to them because they are using it. . . .

I never overruled the parents' opinion. Although I might hold to my opinion that the child does have a hearing loss, I never impose it on the parents—they lose too much power if I did this and would not be fully invested in the child's habilitation program. . . .

Active parental involvement in the diagnostic process not only diminishes the denial mechanism, but also strengthens the bond between the audiologist and the parent. Parents have reported to me how glad they were that I was there helping them through the painful process. I was seen as an ally rather than an adversary. . . .

Another benefit of having the parents as co-diagnosticians is that they are also being educated about the audiological process. . . . Participating parents not only understand audiograms better, but they also obtain an idea of what this child can and cannot hear in the home environment, information that becomes very useful for them in the habilitation process.

Source: Luterman, D. (1991). Counseling and the diagnostic process. In *Counseling the communicatively disordered* (pp. 80–82). Austin, TX: Pro-Ed.

actively in that process (as we also suggested in chapter 9). In contrast to traditional assessments that primarily rely on norm-referenced tests, authentic assessments provide opportunities for students to demonstrate their mastery of skills and knowledge in real-life situations. Authentic assessments include essays, hands-on science problems, open-ended problems, computer simulations of real-world problems, artistic productions, and portfolios of student work (McLaughlin & Warren, 1994, p. 8). Because authentic assessments assure a close link between typical experiences and school instruction and assessment, there is a much greater role for family partnership (Flood & Lapp, 1989; Menchetti & Bombay, 1994).

For example, all parents, but especially minority parents, can nominate their children as gifted and organize a portfolio of work that best represents the student's gifts and talents (Hadaway & Marek-Schroer, 1992). An early childhood program associated with Columbia University sends parents pocket-sized "Let Me Tell You about My Child" cards, written in the parents' primary language, with a letter encouraging them to jot down notes and share infor-mation about their child's interests and activities. In this way, family input presents a more well-rounded picture of the child's development, and the method itself encourages communication focused on the child's strengths.

> Although children identified as potentially gifted . . . are high in potential, not all of their home or school experiences have been positive. We have been surprised by the extent to which some parents have initially denied that their children are in any way capable of academic achievement and also by the change in the behavior of both the parents and the children when more positive assessments of the children start to emerge. (Wright & Boyland, 1993, p. 208)

Sharing Priorities, Resources, and Concerns

The last alternative applies particularly to parents of infants and toddlers, but it is good practice for students of any age. Families of infants and toddlers have the option, as specified by IDEA, to discuss their resources, priorities, and concerns related to enhancing the development of their child. The purpose of this provision is to plan services and supports that can promote family well-being related to the child's development. This identification of resources, priorities, and concerns must be (1) voluntary; (2) carried out by personnel trained to use appropriate methods and procedures; (3) based on a personal interview; and (4) done by incorporating the family's own description of their resources, priorities, and concerns.

Compared to other areas of family research, the area of family assessment has generated a significant body of literature (Bailey & Henderson, 1993; Garshelis & McConnell, 1993; Henderson, Aydlett, & Bailey, 1993; McGrew, 1992; Sexton, Snyder, Rheams, Barron-Sharp, & Perez, 1991). We prefer to steer away from the term *family assessment* and instead describe this process of gathering family information as the identification of family resources, priorities, and concerns. We think the term *identification* is more likely to create partnerships than the term *assessment*. Assume that you are a parent who has just learned that your infant has a significant disability and is being referred to an early intervention program. When you find out about the process of obtaining services from the early intervention program, do you want to hear that a family assessment will be administered to you and your family? Or do you prefer to hear you and your family will have an opportunity, if you choose, to share your own perspectives about what resources are available to support your child, your priorities for supporting your child and your family over the next year or so, and the concerns or worries that you have for the present and future? Which terminology is likely to enhance your own motivation for participating in the process? Which terminology is likely to be a catalyst for you to form a reliable alliance with early intervention staff? We prefer nonclinical over clinical language.

We concur with the benefit of providing families with the opportunity, if they so choose, to share their resources, priorities, and concerns at the *outset* of the evaluation process so that family perspectives can guide the nature and extent of information that is collected. Think what a difference it would have made early on for Ryne (who struggled to pass his first few years of school) and his parents, Pam and Mark, to have had a chance to describe Ryne to an empathetic team. Ryne might have acquired a different sense of his own worth. He and his parents might have avoided intrafamily conflicts over his homework. His school's special services team might have intervened earlier, preventing the sadly wasted years of his elementary education. Finally, an enduring alliance between Ryne, Pam, and Mark, on the one hand, and the school staff, on the other, could have been developed.

Furthermore, we think it is important at this stage to start formulating the collaborative team that will administer the evaluation and be involved in developing and implementing the IFSP/IEP. The major value of collaboration is that it brings together people whose collective resources can be the basis for planning an evaluation that will enable team members to implement individualized appropriate special education. After all, the basis of evaluation should be to address the resources, priorities, and concerns of team members in a way that most effectively builds on each collaborator's unique resources. Thus, we recommend not only that families have an opportunity to share resources, priorities, and concerns but that this same opportunity be extended to all team members (as we will discuss in more detail in chapter 12).

During the evaluation phase, every interaction with a family can help identify its resources, priorities, and concerns. As you learned in chapters 4 and 9, communication is the key to all interactions; and you can continually evolve a family's systems understanding by listening and organizing what you hear using the family systems framework. Again, as you develop a reliable alliance with the family, they will increasingly trust you and share more and more information on resources, priorities, and concerns with you.

In addition to open-ended and conversational sharing, offer families the option of completing checklists. A number of these have been developed at the early childhood level, including the Family Needs Survey (Bailey & Simeonsson, 1988), How Can We Help (Child Development Resources, 1989), and the Family Needs Scale (Dunst, Cooper, Weeldreyer, Snyder, & Chase, 1988). These checklists provide an opportunity for families to rate the extent to which the items, almost all of them related to needs, apply to their family situation. These scales are not nearly as focused on family resources that the family members have to offer as they are on family needs. The Family Need Survey (Bailey & Simeonsson, 1988) enables families to share their needs with professionals. Approximately 60 percent of mothers reported that they would prefer to share information through conversations, whereas 60 percent of fathers preferred the written survey. Guidelines to keep in mind when using surveys include the following (Bailey & Henderson, 1993):

1. Families should have the choice of whether or not to share family information.
2. Items need to be worded in a way so that they are not deficit-oriented or judgmental.

3. Open-ended formats need to supplement a written survey.
4. Because family preferences vary, family members should be given a choice about how they share information.

The service coordinator should also identify other key people who have ongoing relationships with and commitments to the child. Thus, the team can consider a broader spectrum of perspectives on resources, priorities, and concerns. This is a very different process than is typical nowadays. In programs for infants and toddlers, typically only families share this information. In programs at the elementary and secondary levels, this step of the process is typically omitted; and evaluation becomes a "canned" process of administering a package of assessment instruments rather than ensuring that the team and the family will reflect on the nature of the individual and collective resources, priorities, and concerns and use that information to enhance the student's education.

Each of the five ways for involving families in collecting evaluation information can contribute to developing partnerships while they also produce a much richer understanding of the student. Rather than having a mere "snapshot" of the child's skills and abilities on a given day, the team has a panoramic "motion picture" of the student's and family's lives and is more likely to individualize supports and services and make a meaningful and sustainable difference in family members' lives.

Right of Parents to Obtain Independent Evaluations

Under IDEA, parents have the right to obtain an independent evaluation that the school must take into account in the evaluation process. This right to an independent evaluation applies even if the school's evaluation has already been completed. The school must provide parents with information about where they can obtain an independent evaluation. Indeed, the school must pay for the evaluation, unless it can prove through a due process hearing that its own evaluation was appropriate.

Why would parents seek an independent evaluation? They may be concerned about the appropriateness, accuracy, completeness, or timeliness of the agency's evaluation; or they may be concerned about the implications of the evaluation. Or like Pam and Mark Gorian, they might be convinced that their child has a disability, be blocked by the schools in determining whether or not the child receives an evaluation, and basically not trust the schools to evaluate their child. In either case, it is important for profes-

sionals, with parental consent, to communicate their findings and recommendations to each other (Hepner & Silverstein, 1988). Unfortunately, that type of collaboration does not always occur, as a father recounts: "We invited one of the evaluators, who had a Ph.D., at our expense to come to Dubuque to observe Alex in a school setting. . . . We were told later that the independent evaluation was considered, when honestly, it was ignored" (testimony by Greg Omori, in National Council on Disability, 1995, p. 46)

Analyzing Evaluation Information

The multidisciplinary team must (1) determine whether the student qualifies for special education and (2) if so, develop a profile of the student's strengths and needs for the purpose of determining the nature and extent of special education. Under IDEA, the team achieves this goal by (1) scoring and interpreting the results of each evaluation instrument or procedure and (2) analyzing and synthesizing all the separate evaluations to obtain an overall composite of the student's performance. The first task typically is done individually or collaboratively by team members who administered the evaluation procedures, and the second typically takes place at a full-team meeting.

Family-professional partnerships for analyzing evaluation information are rare. Many professionals assume that the scoring, analysis, and synthesis of evaluation procedures require technical expertise that most families do not have. Family members can, however, be partners in collecting, documenting, and interpreting evaluation procedures, as in box 11–1, which recounted the audiological assessment in which the parents and other family members were co-diagnosticians. True, some assessment procedures, such as an IQ test, are standardized and may be administered and scored only by people with special training. But many assessment procedures, such as the audiological examination, can be carried out collaboratively with family members.

Some families participate in the analysis of evaluation information, but others prefer to not be involved. Some families appreciate being present at any discussion related to their child's possible identification for special education, perhaps because they perceive that the best way to ensure that their perspective is considered is to be part of the decision-making process from its beginning and at all later points. Others will opt out of the process. Particularly for them, but indeed for all families, the interpretations should not be considered final until they are reviewed and commented on by the families. Thus, lack of family involvement at this stage should lead to only tentative interpretations. If you want partnerships, respect the families' perspectives and insights and be careful about reaching conclusions without their involvement.

Discussing Evaluation Results with Parents

This section will discuss five aspects related to discussing evaluation results with parents: (1) notifying parents, (2) taking the families' perspective, (3) fostering a reliable alliance, (4) considering the student's role in discussing evaluation results, and (5) following an agenda for discussing results.

Notifying Parents   IDEA requires the schools to notify parents any time the schools propose or refuse to change a student's identification, evaluation, educational placement, or the provision of a free, appropriate education. Consequently, written notification (or a written summary) of evaluation results must follow the initial evaluation.

The mandatory three-year reevaluations do not require written notice, but it is always good practice to summarize the results in writing and give a copy of the summary to the family. Full disclosure frequently enhances family trust and increases the probability of their making informed decisions. In addition, because evaluation information can be highly technical and written explanations may not be fully informative, it is good practice to explain the results face to face. These discussions can elicit family perspectives that can be extremely helpful in validating or dispelling tentative interpretations. Parents can share information about their son's or daughter's special needs, confirm whether the performance described by professionals is typical, and make connections between the current and previous evaluations completed by persons outside the school (such as pediatricians and preschool teachers).

One option for interpreting evaluation findings for families is to convene a conference with the parents; another is to review the evaluation during the IEP conference. The advantages of a separate conference, particularly for the initial evaluation, is that it allows more time to discuss findings in depth and enables the family to assimilate evaluation information before immediately making program and placement decisions. On the other hand, the advantage of incorporating the discussion of evaluation results into the IFSP/IEP conference is that it eliminates an additional

meeting. It is a good practice to invite parents to a separate conference to discuss the initial and all subsequent reevaluations. It is practically impossible to do justice to reviewing and discussing a formal evaluation and planning the IFSP/IEP in one meeting. Further, most families and professionals have a hard time simultaneously receiving and then immediately translating evaluation information into decisions about goals, objectives, placement, and related services.

Taking the Families' Perspectives   What are families' perspectives about receiving evaluation results? Family perspectives widely vary, and it is impossible to make hard-and-fast generalizations. As you already know, some families will be relieved to get an accurate diagnosis—for example, the Gorians. Other families experience despair over the diagnosis. Regardless of the similarity of the exceptionality, the reactions to the evaluation process vary widely.

How do families respond to evaluation results? From relief to pain, the gamut of their responses is long and varied. However sensitively you convey the information, many families, particularly those who strongly value academic achievement and success, will be sorely disappointed by the confirmation of a disability. Many parents want hopeful information. That kind of information can enhance families' motivation, just as negative expectations can dispel families' hope:

> My frustration is with professionals in the field who say "she'll plateau"; she'll "like to do only routine things"; "don't expect too much"; "she's already doing better than I ever expected," etc., etc. . . . These individuals are very dangerous in the predictor's status quo that individuals [with disabilities] all fit in a neat nutshell. In fact, I often see them no differently than those who characterize a race, those of a specific religion, those of a specific sport, etc. The thing that is very troubling is that these are young graduates in special education and those who have lots of contacts with parents.

Some parents may feel that, in some ways, they have contributed to their child's exceptionality or that they should have attended to it earlier. They may worry about their child's future and fear that their child's and family's challenges will necessarily and inevitably escalate. They may doubt the credibility or expertise of the evaluation team. And some will need more time than others to come to grips with the reality of the evaluation results.

> Fourteen years ago, when my son was in junior high, I remember walking into the room with five

teachers, a guidance counselor, a vice principal, a psychologist, a social worker and a learning consultant. I was told that my child was a behavior problem, dyslexic, hyperactive and a general "pain in the neck." He was always clowning and disrupting classes. This child was the light of my life, yet no one had anything positive to say about him. No one suggested that his clowning was a need to cover for his feelings of inadequacy. No one realized that it is easier to let others think he was funny than reveal that he couldn't do the work. I looked up and saw the eyes of all ten people upon me. I felt that each of them had not only judged my son but was judging me as a parent. I was a working mother, which elicits some guilt under any circumstances, but in this situation, I believed they were questioning why I was working when my son had problems. I felt guilty, inadequate, angry, frustrated, and most of all helpless. (Halperin, 1989, p. 6)

Other families, like the Gorians, will feel justified and relieved. Justified because they, unlike the schools, believed all along that their children had real needs, that they were not just lazy or uncooperative students. Relieved because at last they have an evaluation that can lead to an effective intervention, whether that be a regimen of medication (like Ritalin for Ryne Gorian) or a program of special education (such as Ryne also receives).

Consider family perspectives about labeling. Parents' opinions range widely. Some object to labels as demeaning to their children:

My young son . . . must learn, build his own self-esteem, and learn his valuable role in society. He doesn't need to be singled out by receiving a label and all these self-fulfilling prophecies that attach themselves to that label . . . so please advocate . . . for changes that will stop the identification, segregation, and isolation of students with disabilities. (Testimony by Fran Maiuri, in National Council on Disability, 1995, p. 32)

Other parents believe that a noncategorical, non-labeling approach will reduce the services and supports their children need:

We also have concerns about proposed changes in disability categories which may result in denial of services for some students with disabilities or may result in dumping them in regular classes without appropriate support services. (Testimony by Charlotte Des Jardins, in National Council on Disability, 1995, p. 33)

Still other parents favor new disability categories, believing that their children will get better services when their special needs are more specifically identified:

I would like to speak about these children that we like to call children with neurobiological disorders. Our children are very stigmatized when they are served under the category of SED [serious emotional disturbance]. . . . As their parents, many times, when we go to try to work with the schools, our advice and our input is discounted because we are seen as the cause of their disturbance. . . . The families that we represent would like to see a change in the SED category, to truly talk about what's going on in the brains and central nervous systems of children with special learning needs . . . because research has shown that many of the behaviors and the learning needs of children are generated because of . . . the brain dysfunction, and so we would like to see that reflected in the law. (Testimony of Sara Gonzales, in National Council on Disability, 1995, pp. 49–50)

Not surprisingly, different cultures ascribe different connotations to standard terminology. For example, a Puerto Rican mother described the distinction, from her cultural and language perspective, between *retarded* and *handicapped:*

For me, retarded is crazy; in Spanish that's "retardado." For me, the word "handicapped" means a person who is incapacitated, like mentally, or missing a leg, or who is blind or deaf, who cannot work and cannot do anything . . . a person who is invalid, useless. . . . But for Americans, it is a different thing—for them "handicapped" is everybody! (Harry, 1992, p. 31)

Paradoxically, the state and local education agencies that offer noncategorical services and do not assign labels based on evaluation results can create confusion by using ambiguous language:

The disposition for 5-year-old Tyrone indicated that his disability category was "04" (speech and language impaired) and that he would continue in his present placement of "Level III services" until the new academic year, at which time he would be moved to a "Level IV" (more restrictive) placement. At the end of the meeting, after the disposition was signed, the mother, . . . asked the professional team what Level IV meant, and was told it meant that the child would have more hours of service, which meant a smaller class and more one-to-one attention. When we asked the mother in an interview what she thought the other "04" designation on the record meant, she replied: "I think that's what they call Level IV: it means 4 hours of special education a week." (Harry, Allen, & McLaughlin, 1995, p. 369)

The similarity in the two types of codes, and the fact that the 04 code was never explained, led the mother to confuse the two and thereby remain unaware that her child had been assigned a categorical code. Although the professionals had assigned the diagnostic category of mental retardation to the child, they did not communicate that fact to the mother. Thus, in an attempt to be noncategorical, they increased their power-over approach by communicating to the mother in a code that she did not fully understand.

Another issue relates to cultural challenges and language. Consider the situation of 59 Chinese families (most of whom had low income and all but one of whom used Chinese as their primary language) who reported to a researcher how they received evaluation information. Sixty percent of them said that none of the professionals involved in the diagnosis of their child spoke Chinese: "It was hard for us to understand because we were confused. We did not know how to start or who to turn to. We felt alone and helpless" (Smith & Ryne, 1987, pp. 347–348). When asked to describe their feelings about the initial evaluation of their child, parents reported "confusion, anger, guilt, shame, and being upset, overwhelmed, heart-broken, sorry, depressed, helpless, worried, and embarrassed" (Smith & Ryne, 1987, p. 348). They continued (p. 348):

- I was afraid that my in-laws would blame me for producing a problem child. They felt that I brought them bad luck with my first son.

- My husband at first could not understand why

my son would not speak, then, slowly he began to feel I didn't bring him up properly.

How can you be helpful to these and other culturally different families? You should use positive communication skills in a way that honors cultural diversity. In all your communication with families, particularly those from culturally diverse backgrounds, there is no time when your sensitivity, personalization, and respect is more important than when you are sharing evaluation information. Beth Harry and her colleagues, national leaders in developing culturally sensitive services, provide tips in box 11–2 for assessing students from diverse cultures.

Fostering a Reliable Alliance An early intervention professional on a Native American reservation has described far better than we can the importance of a reliable alliance in pursuing infant assessment:

I felt that the families were a little bit reluctant. [Even though] I'm a member of their own tribe, . . . they still considered me an intruder of some type, because a lot of other times when programs came in, they felt there were too many people hounding them or hovering over them and wanting them to do this or do that, but as I explained to them, I'm also the parent of a child with disabilities, and that made it a little bit easier. I share their culture and beliefs, and I encourage them to use traditional medicines, never doubting that, and that always comes first, but at the same

---

TIPS

BOX 11–2

Assessing Students from Diverse Cultures

- Include parents in the assessment process by inviting them to observe and/or participate in all assessment procedures, following their lead in identifying which family members to involve, and arranging meetings at convenient times and places.
- Provide extended time for explaining assessment results to parents who hold very different values and beliefs about the meaning of disability.
- Provide an independent person who is

familiar with the family's culture to interpret during conferences and encourage families to bring friends or advocates who share their cultural beliefs with them to the conference.
- Ensure that children are assessed in their native language.
- Consider using alternative assessment approaches, such as authentic assessment, that will best enable students to demonstrate their capabilities, strengths, and needs.

Source: Adapted from Harry, B., Grenot-Scheyer, M., Smith-Lewis, M., Park, H., Xin, F., & Schwartz, I. (1995). Developing culturally inclusive services for individuals with severe disabilities. *Journal of the Association for Persons with Severe Handicaps, 20*(2), 99–109.

time, getting them to believe that in reality, too, there is something different. And that's how I've gained a lot of the parents' trust. (Testimony of Norberta Sarracino, in National Council on Disability, 1995, p. 38)

You can build a reliable alliance by responding to parents' questions, clearly describing and giving concrete examples of their child's performance, demonstrating a genuine interest and commitment to their child's success, and highlighting their child's strengths and abilities. In chapter 4, we emphasized the importance of empathetic listening, expressions of empathy, and empathetic reciprocity in building reliable alliances. Especially when parents are dealing with evaluation information, display empathy in all your communications. Linda Mitchell, a parent and speech-language pathologist whose son experiences a developmental disability, characterizes the critically important role of empathy:

> I don't want someone to feel sorry for me. Sorrow sets me up to grieve for a loss, but I don't feel that my son, John, is any kind of a loss. He is truly a source of great happiness and a huge contributor to our family. Empathy says I feel for you because I care about you. Sympathy says I feel sorry for you. Empathy connects, sympathy disconnects. If you want to really begin to build a relationship with me, empathize with me, and then help me move on.

How can families learn to trust? Families learn to trust when professionals learn and practice ways to warrant their trust—as when Mrs. Nilen bucked the school system and insisted on prereferral and then an evaluation for Ryne Gorian. Many professionals still think their main role is to interpret evaluation results for parents, but that role can involve one-way communication—professionals' telling parents how their child is performing. On the contrary, the conference's other and more valuable function is for professionals and families (and others whom they invite— including, when families and professionals agree, the child) to discuss the evaluation findings and reach the most complete understanding possible of the student's instructional needs. Some parents prefer to be passive recipients of information, while others want to be actively involved in making evaluation decisions. It is best for you to honor those preferences.

Sometimes professionals are frustrated by parents who do not immediately accept the evaluation results. But by taking into account the parents' perspectives, you may realize how much they love their child and how strong their parental need is to "stack the deck" in their child's favor. Your support and patience will pay off in the end.

Some parents seek additional information, perhaps from one specialist and then another, in a search for answers to their questions. These parents have been unkindly labeled "shoppers" who have failed to accept their child's exceptionality (Blacher, 1984). But like the Gorians, they may be seeking full and complete information so that they can make the best decision. Alternatively, they may be investigating the fullest-possible range of professional resources so that they will be able to make an informed decision about the professional team with whom they might be able to form a genuine reliable alliance. Unfortunately, some professionals interpret families' desire to get a second opinion or question evaluation results as a personal challenge to their expertise. Any family who needs or wants additional information or resources related to evaluation deserves immediate referrals. Your own communication—affirming their strengths in taking action rather than criticizing their refusal to accept the diagnosis—will be a catalyst for their further empowerment.

Considering the Student's Role in Discussing Evaluation Results Sharing evaluation results with children and youth can enable them to make decisions about themselves, provide them with accurate estimates about their abilities, and contribute to building their esteem (Sattler, 1988). A student can be involved in conferences at many different levels (Teglasi, 1985). First, the parents may share the evaluation results and recommendations with their son or daughter. Second, the student may participate at the end of a conference held initially only with the parents. Third, one or more members of the evaluation team may hold a separate conference with the parents and the student. Separate conferences also can be followed by a joint conference where the results are reviewed on the student's level. This approach may prevent the student from becoming overpowered by the presence of many adults. Finally, students can participate in the regular evaluation team meeting. If this option is chosen, it is necessary to prepare the student in advance and ensure that the discussion at the conference is clear to the student and affirms the student's strengths as well as discusses needs. It does not matter which approach is used as long as you are sensitive to the family's and student's preferences and needs about how to receive evaluation information.

Following an Agenda for Discussing Results There are at least three goals of the conference, and they require a careful agenda:

(1) ensuring a clear understanding of the student's strengths, preferences, great expectations, and needs; (2) empathetically supporting families in the emotional adjustment to the evaluation information; and (3) interpreting and communicating information to facilitate an appropriate education for the student and mutual empowerment for the student and all team participants (Teglasi, 1985). One broad way of structuring the agenda is to include these four components (Rockowitz & Davidson, 1979):

1. Initial proceedings
2. Presentation of findings
3. Recommendations
4. Summary

Initial Proceedings

Whatever the agenda, families should have the opportunity, according to their preferences, to provide their own input and to react to and reflect upon others' input. For example, during the initial proceedings it is important for families to describe their perspectives of their son's or daughter's functioning. Their comments will give you clues to their current level of understanding. Perhaps you can incorporate some key words they use (such as "lagging behind") in subsequent explanations.

Presentation of Findings

It will be helpful to be as concrete and specific as you can, following these four suggestions (Hirsch, 1981):

1. Introduce the skill being discussed and include examples.
2. State the student's current level of functioning with the skill and how it compares to chronological age peers.
3. Give examples of skills the child can and cannot perform.
4. Address the importance of any discrepancy between age and achievement and how the discrepancy may affect the student's development now or in the future.

You also should incorporate the communication skills that you learned in chapters 4 and 9. Many families have had multiple clues that problems exist, and they usually appreciate direct yet sensitive communication—for example, using jargon-free language, offering suggestions for follow-up reading material, and conveying the clear message that you have the child's and family's interests in mind.

The evaluation team should present a composite of the student's strengths, preferences, great expectations, and needs, not just list a string of separate and isolated discipline-specific reports. The family is dealing with the whole child—not a child segmented into discrete parts.

> Specialists see [my daughter] from their own point of view. I guess the hardest thing is that I want answers. I wanted them to say she is going to make it or she isn't going to make it. I guess the hardest thing is not getting answers and everyone looking at their particular area and no one giving me the whole picture. Everyone is just looking at one area and forgetting she is a whole child.

The evaluation conference should seek to do more than present a composite; it should also stimulate discussion and assist in addressing the priorities and concerns of family participants and other team members.

> Feedback of test results inevitably affects the way in which a family conceives their child's problem. It may serve to answer questions the family has already framed, such as "is he able to perform his schoolwork?" It may also serve to introduce whole new viewpoints from which to see a certain behavior. That is, a child whom the parents see as "bad" or "disobedient" may be reframed by the consultant as "disabled." One who is seen as "lazy" may be reframed as "depressed." The main purpose of "reframing" a child's problem is to "construct a workable reality" (Liebman, 1975) for the family. That is, to state the problem in a way that permits a solution. (Fulmer, Cohen, & Monaco, 1985, pp. 145–146)

Different families will have different reframing schedules. Most will need time to integrate the evaluation information fully and develop new perceptions about their child. Switzer (1985) describes a cognitive problem-solving seminar she offered for parents of children who recently received the diagnosis of learning disabilities. The purpose was to provide them with factual knowledge, decrease their feelings of anxiety, and increase their receptivity to remediation. She reported a positive evaluation by families. Interestingly, parents recommended that such a seminar be delayed for two months after diagnosis so that they could have the needed distance before being ready to learn about disability-related information.

The evaluation team should discuss the student's performance and the type of exceptionality, particularly at the initial evaluation conference. Categorical labels are often painful for parents to hear—although, again, some parents are relieved to have a name to call the condition that has created so many concerns for them. Thus, merely discussing labels (without the significance of the label) can create tension for families and professionals alike.

Many professionals have difficulty discussing mental retardation in a straightforward manner. These professionals are usually extremely sensitive to the social stigma associated with mental retardation and/or to the parents' distress, . . . usually this phenomenon is seen among young professionals, but occasionally even experienced professionals have identified so closely with the parents that to cause them pain is extremely difficult. When professionals are uncomfortable with mental retardation, they have been observed to ramble around the topic and "forget" that the term has not been used, become dysfluent and almost incoherent as they approach the use of the term, or to report that they had to "force" themselves to say it. Unfortunately, these reactions on the part of the professionals usually increase the stress and tension felt by the parents. (Shea, 1984, p. 275)

Professionals should explain that mental retardation actually means that the child has slower-than-average development. Because many families may associate mental retardation with negative societal stereotypes, team members should talk about the different degrees of mental retardation and the positive outcomes that many individuals at all levels of mental retardation are experiencing when they have access to state-of-the-art services. They should offer to connect the parents with local or regional parent organizations (such as a PTI, Parent to Parent, or disability-specific groups of the type you read about in chapter 10) so that they can talk with other parents whose children also experience mental retardation, learn about services, and get emotional support.

Recommendations

After discussing evaluation results, professionals have to make recommendations. The more that parents have been partners in the evaluation process, the more likely it is that they will generate and follow through on professionals' and their own recommendations. Traditionally, evaluation conferences have been characterized by professionals' agreeing in advance about their recommendations and then presenting them to families. A partnership model, however, encourages families and professionals to reflect collaboratively on the evaluation information and generate recommendations for action. The recommendations should enhance the student's appropriate education.

Many evaluation conferences tend to do nothing more than recommend that the student be placed in a special education program. They do not describe the specially designed instruction, placement, and related services that will benefit the student. Given that the purpose of evaluation is to lead to an appropriate education, recommendations logically must provide families, teachers, and related service providers with detailed information about how best to promote preferences, build on strengths, and remediate needs. Parents are most apt to carry out recommendations in the following cases (Teglasi, 1985, pp. 419–420):

- They perceive their child's needs and strengths in a manner similar to the professionals'.
- Both parents attend the conference, particularly if there are two or more conferences.
- The professionals are precise and clear in their presentations.
- Families perceive professionals as caring.

To assure that all recommendations are implemented, it is helpful to recommend a specific plan of action, specifying who is responsible for following through on each recommendation, when those people will begin and finish their duties, the necessary resources for the job, and how people will know the work has been done. This plan can help make sure that team members and parents alike act in an empowered way—taking action in light of the conference recommendations. It also is useful to engage in continuous reflection in subsequent evaluation or IFSP/IEP conferences about the extent to which a reliable alliance has been developed and how team members interact with each other and with families.

Finally, two major outcomes should result from discussing evaluation results. First, the team and the family should determine that the student does not qualify for special education; they find other ways to address the referral concerns; and parents then receive the legally required notice that the student does not qualify for special education. Or second, the team and family determine that the student is eligible for special education (that is, specially designed instruction), all or some of which may be delivered in the general education class. Special education should not be equated with separate placements only. When students are identified as eligible for special education, the next step is to arrange for a conference to develop an individualized program.

Informing Parents of the Individualized Program Conference

In chapter 12, we will discuss in detail IDEA's requirements for an individualized program for every child, ages birth through 21, who receives special education. At this point, we simply call your attention to the IDEA requirement that schools must take steps to ensure that the child's parents are present or are given the opportunity to participate in each meeting related to their child's individualized program. This means that schools must (1) notify (in writing or orally) the parents about the meeting early enough to allow them to make arrangements to attend; (2) indicate the purpose, the time, and the location as well as the persons who will attend; and (3) schedule the conference at a mutually agreed-upon time and place.

Linking Our Themes

Building a Reliable Alliance

By now, you should realize that the eight reliable alliance obligations can be infused into every partnership opportunity. Just as you have already learned about infusing these obligations into the partnerships of communicating among reliable allies (chapter 9) and meeting families' basic needs (chapter 10), so

you can learn to infuse obligations into the partnership opportunity of referring and evaluating for special education. Figure 11–4 provides an example of issues related to each of the eight obligations as well as disempowering and empowering actions that you can take.

Strengthening Family Factors

Ultimately, the empowering context that you help create can provide an opportunity for students to flourish in their educational outcomes and an opportunity for families to enhance their motivation and knowledge/skills. It bears repeating that a family's empowerment can contribute to mutual empowerment; thus, as you contribute to enhancing families' empowerment, it is likely that the synergy created will have the outcome of also enhancing your own empowerment. How can you enhance families' empowerment through the process of referring and evaluating students for special education? Figure 11–5 provides some examples.

FIGURE 11–4

Creating a Reliable Alliance: Referring and Evaluating for Special Education

Obligations	Issues	Disempowering Actions	Empowering Actions
Knowing yourself	You feel highly frustrated with students who have behavior disorders, and you have a tendency to want their parents to know how much they disrupt your class.	Recount to the parents a litany of all the irritations that you have experienced with their son.	Identify the student's strengths and let the student and family know that you appreciate those strengths. Stop dwelling on frustrations and irritations.
Knowing families Family characteristics	A Vietnamese family with whom you have scheduled an evaluation conference does not speak English.	Ask the student to come to the conference and interpret for his parents.	In advance of the conference, confirm with family members their need for an interpreter. Ask whether they would like to recommend a specific interpreter. If possible, act on their recommendation in getting the interpreter of their choice.

FIGURE **11-4** CONTINUED

Creating a Reliable Alliance: Referring and Evaluating for Special Education

Obligations	Issues	Disempowering Actions	Empowering Actions
Family interaction	Divorced parents attend a meeting to devise jointly prereferral strategies. They argue with each other, and the father abruptly leaves in the middle of the conference.	Tell the mother that it will be impossible for you to communicate with them until they can work out a way to be in a conference without experiencing such conflict.	When it is obvious that stress is escalating, ask the parents if they would like to reschedule the meeting. After the father leaves, solicit the mother's preferences for next steps. Telephone the father after the meeting and solicit his preferred next steps.
Family functions	A family does not understand its legal rights and is totally confused by the formal notice and consent form. Family members are extremely overextended with multiple challenges.	Send the parents a notice of a workshop on legal rights as well as the school district's legal rights handbook.	Ask the family members what you and other educators can do that would be the most supportive to them given the multiple challenges that they are facing. Offer to give them explanations in a time-efficient fashion.
Family life cycle	Family members of a gifted girl in your class are distressed that their daughter wants to pursue a career in mathematics rather than be a homemaker, which is the traditional role for women in their culture.	Reprimand the family members for not having a stronger feminist orientation toward the education of their daughter.	Invite family members to share with you their visions of their daughter's future and seek to understand their values about women's roles and career options. Invite the student to do the same.
Honoring cultural diversity	Asian family members tell you that they believe their son's learning disability is a punishment to them for not adequately honoring their ancestors.	Tell the family to discount nonscientific interpretations as groundless and foolish.	Listen empathetically to the family's perspectives and ask members what information or support you could provide that they might find helpful.
Affirming and building on family strengths	A mother with AIDS comes to a diagnostic conference to hear the latest educational report on her child, who also has AIDS.	Tell the mother that nothing would make you feel as guilty as giving AIDS to your child.	Share with the mother one or more things that she has done that has made a positive difference in the child's educational progress and tell her you appreciate her efforts.

FIGURE 11–4 CONTINUED

Creating a Reliable Alliance: Referring and Evaluating for Special Education

Obligations	Issues	Disempowering Actions	Empowering Actions
Promoting family choices	Parents are highly dissatisfied with the evaluation that you believe has been done very appropriately. They request an independent evaluation, but you do not believe one is needed.	Defend the school's evaluation and tell the parents that their request is unwarranted.	Encourage the parents to discuss with you their concerns and ask them to describe an evaluation process that they would find satisfactory. Inform them of the process for initiating an independent evaluation.
Envisioning great expectations	Parents have just received the diagnosis that their infant is legally blind.	Encourage the parents to be realistic and to recognize that it is too much of a burden for community preschools to adapt their programs.	Ask the parents what information would be especially helpful for them as they consider their next steps. Let them know that you look forward to collaborating with them and watching their child grow and develop. Tell them that you are available to help make their dreams for their child come true.
Using interpersonal communication skills	In the evaluation conference, the parents seem to want to "kill the messenger." They are angry at the professionals for "creating" their child's problem.	Point out to the parents that they have displaced anger and that you and other professionals are doing all that you know how to do to help them.	Listen empathetically to the parents' perspective and reflect on whether any of the communication used in the conference could unintentionally come across as representing a "we-they" orientation.
Warranting trust and respect	In your noncategorical program, parents ask you what "functional placement" means. You know that the professional interpretation is "severe disability," but the school district forbids you to use that classification.	Tell parents that "functional placement" really does not have a meaning, and that the professionals do not associate any kind of diagnostic label with it.	Explain to parents the rationale for noncategorical programming and share your own values. Also tell them that sometimes noncategorical labels have other connotations, and honestly share those connotations with them.

FIGURE 11–5

Strengthening Family Factors Through an Empowering Context: Referring and Evaluating for Special Education

Motivation	What You Can Do	Knowledge/Skills	What You Can Do
Self-efficacy	Emphasize to parents how helpful their ideas on instructional accommodations have been in enhancing the success of the prereferral process.	Information	Provide information to families in their preferred language and/or at their preferred reading level to ensure that they gain a meaningful understanding of evaluation results.
Perceived control	Brainstorm with family members about the roles that they would like to have in collecting and interpreting evaluation results.	Problem solving	When evaluation results are mixed and even conflictual, brainstorm with families on their interpretations and plan a strategy to gain a clearer picture of the student's strengths, great expectations, preferences, and needs.
Persistence	Encourage parents to pursue an independent evaluation if they are dissatisfied with the school's evaluation.	Coping skills	Encourage parents to share their disappointment over their child's lack of progress and brainstorm with them about what kind of support would be helpful in addressing their emotional and information needs.
Energy	When parents share their priorities, resources, and concerns, emphasize the importance of their taking time for themselves and enhancing their own wellness to the greatest degree possible.	Communication skills	Point out to parents how their questions about the evaluation report end up pinpointing ambiguous areas and clarifying information for all team members. Encourage them to keep asking such excellent questions.
Hope	As evaluation results are interpreted, consistently point out hopeful indications that the student is progressing and that educational challenges are being resolved.		

Summary

The steps in the referral and evaluation process and the activities associated with them for school-age children are summarized in figure 11–2. The process is long, with many component parts: (1) coordinating the referral and evaluation process, (2) implementing prereferral intervention, (3) initiating and reviewing the referral, (4) providing notice and obtaining consent, (5) collecting evaluation information, (6) analyzing evaluation information, (7) discussing evaluation results with the family, and (8) informing the family of the IFSP/IEP conferences. When you accomplish referral and evaluation soundly and humanely, you build a relationship of trust and collaboration among families and other professionals. It is upon this strong foundation that you can develop the student's individualized program.

Ryne Gorian is in his last year of elementary school. To put it another way, his mother Pam and father Mark are in their last year of a reliable alliance with Mrs. Nilen. Their "high comfort zone" with her and her willingness to be honest with them, whether about Ryne or the school district, has come about because she and the Gorians had a single focus: Ryne. They were also willing to buck the system, together.

What will empower the Gorians as Ryne moves from elementary to middle school? Obviously, empowerment has to come from many sources and in many ways:

- Finding another "Mrs. Nilen"
- Having Ryne's present team work with the special education team in the middle school to plan and implement his individualized education program
- Reevaluating him as necessary
- Relying on outsiders such as the professionals Mark knows at his place of employment and Pam knows in special education in another state

- Knowing Ryne's and his family's rights and knowing how to get schools to implement them
- Bringing Ryne into the decision-making process involving his own education and life
- Giving each other a sense that, like the Marines, they are "can do" people
- Looking back on the obstacles they have surmounted and being hopeful that they can be victorious if they have to go to battle again

Evaluation is, after all, a make-or-break opportunity for students, their families, and professionals. It is a time when a right course can be set or, sadly, a wrong course fixed that later must be corrected.

For Pam, Mark, and Ryne, there has been no one person who set the right course or corrected the wrong one; but certainly Mrs. Nilen has been an indispensable and reliable member of their crew.

Chapter Twelve

Individualizing for Appropriate Education

Jordan Ackerson's education is, in many ways, a model of how schools should collaborate with a family to educate a young student with autism or any other exceptionality. Yet in so many other ways, it is a model of what should not happen.

When Jordan received his formal diagnosis of autism at the age of 2½, his mother, Lisa Lieberman, and his father, Craig Ackerson, had already determined that he had autism.

They had compared his behaviors to the characteristics of autism as set forth in the Diagnostic Standards Manual *(3rd edition) of the American Psychiatric Association. To convince physicians and others about his behaviors and to corroborate their own written observations about him, they had videotaped his behaviors at home. When they presented their evidence to the professionals who evaluated him, they received a quick confirmation: This beautiful young boy has autism. More than that, Lisa and Craig gave one very strong message: They are always ready and able to collaborate with professionals.*

When Jordan entered preschool, professionals reinforced their readiness, encouraging Lisa and Craig to develop their own plans for his individualized education. Lisa and Craig dutifully prepared a list of goals, objectives, curricular methodologies, and services for Jordan. After presenting their proposed individualized plan to his preschool staff, they and the staff negotiated their differences and agreed to the program.

Lisa notes, "We always had a vision of full participation in Jordan's program planning. With staff encour-

agement, we proposed the program that we thought would benefit him most and the staff responded, as our colleagues. To prepare ourselves to be their partners, we studied and availed ourselves of training on individualizing for Jordan. So we had tremendous power to influence the professionals working with him."

At least, they did for a while—until, after two years in early intervention and two in kindergarten, Jordan entered first grade. That's when things began to change.

The advance preparation of a jointly developed individualized program that was typical of Jordan's preschool and kindergarten years simply was not the norm in first grade. Making it clear that the school team was in charge of his education, the principal designated only one staff member as the family's point of contact, forbade other teachers or staff to talk with them, and reprimanded teachers who went outside that chain of communication. Lisa was less welcome into Jordan's classroom and found that she had to develop behind-the-scenes communication links with other teachers. Team members began to skip regularly scheduled meetings with Lisa and Craig to discuss Jordan's education, impairing parent-school and intraschool communication. And his teacher began to exclude from "her classroom" the professionals who knew Jordan best and could help her the most.

The friendliness that had characterized parent-teacher meetings when Jordan was in preschool and kindergarten was absent. Gone were the easy exchanges of ideas, chapters, articles, and materials. Gone were Lisa and Craig's comfortable giving and the staff's relaxed receiving of food at the meetings. Gone was the family's opportunity to develop an individualized program and present it to the staff for reaction and improvement. Gone, too, was Lisa and Craig's vision that they would be full partners with Jordan's professional team.

Now Lisa and Craig began to face the marathon of Jordan's disability, his exaggerated perseverance in closing doors, turning lights off and on, opening and shutting drawers, and trying to control his environment. Clearly, they concluded, he is unhappy at school. Are we beginning to see him regress? they wondered.

They also began to face another challenge. Craig began to experience the debilitating effects of his own multiple sclerosis. Together, he and Lisa experienced fear of an unknown future and sensed isolation, frustration, disappointment, and sadness surrounding their lost dreams and abilities.

Simultaneously, Lisa and Craig encountered, for the first time, professionals who stated, point-blank, that Jordan would not be able to keep up with nondisabled peers.

Indeed, when Lisa and Craig met with the school's learning specialist to discuss a possible change of Jordan's placement in first grade because he had begun to regress at school and home, they confronted the ultimate in professional dominance. Told by the school's learning specialist that any change of Jordan's placement was a decision for the school's multidisciplinary team, Lisa and Craig sent a letter of protest to the school's principal:

"Though we well understand and honor the need for that team to convene to discuss options, it is inconceivable *that anyone could make a final placement decision about our son without the input of his assistant, who spends so many hours with him, and without his parents' direct participation in the final decision-making process."*

What happened, Lisa and Craig are wondering? What has gone wrong and how can we get back to the partnership we had before first grade?

Whenever you develop and implement an individualized program for any student, you have a ready-made opportunity to be a partner and create a reliable alliance with the student and the family. Figure 12–1 highlights this opportunity.

Evaluating students is of little value unless educators then provide them with an appropriate education. The cornerstone of an appropriate education for students ages 3 through 21 is the Individualized Education Program (IEP) and, when students turn 14, the Individualized Transition Program (ITP) that becomes part of their IEP. For students ages birth through 3, the cornerstone is the Individualized Family Service Plan (IFSP). Every student who receives special education (ages 3 through 21) or early intervention services (birth through 2) must have an IEP or IFSP as appropriate. The legal requirements and research related to IFSP/IEP partnerships provide you with many opportunities for forming reliable alliances related to individualizing for a child's appropriate education.

Legal Requirements

Because there are differences in IEP and IFSP legal requirements, we will review them separately.

Individualized Education Program (IEP)

The IEP is a written document setting forth the nature of the student's specially designed instruction. The IEP must contain the following components:

- The student's present levels of educational performance
- Annual goals and short-term instructional objectives in each area requiring specially designed instruction
- Specific educational services (also referred to as related services) that will be provided and the extent to which the student will be able to participate in general education programs
- Projected date for the beginning and the anticipated duration of those services

- Appropriate objective criteria and evaluation procedures
- Schedules for determining, on at least an annual basis, whether the instructional objectives are being met
- Statement of needed transition services (coordinated activities for postsecondary education, vocational training, integrated employment, adult education, adult services, independent living, or community participation) and the responsibilities of the school or other agencies starting at least when the student is age 16 and younger, if appropriate or required by state law

The coordinated set of activities that provide the basis of transition services (from high school to adulthood) must take the student's needs, preferences, and interests into account. The transition activities must also include instruction, community experiences, employment and other postschool adult objectives, and (if appropriate) instruction in daily living skills and a functional vocational evaluation.

The IEP must be reviewed and, if appropriate, revised annually; it may be reviewed and revised more often if warranted in the judgment of professionals or parents. If a public school enrolls a student in a private school at public expense, the public and private schools must jointly develop an IEP and ensure that it is carried out. If a student's parents enroll the student in a private school at their expense, the local education agency must see to it that the student has access to special education and related services.

The participants in IEP meetings must include the following individuals:

- A representative of the school who is qualified to provide or supervise the provision of special education
- The student's teacher (or teachers)
- One or both of the student's parents
- The student, when appropriate
- Other individuals at the discretion of the parents or school district

FIGURE 12–1

Empowerment Framework: Collaborating for Empowerment

Collaborating for Empowerment:
Through Collaboration, We Act Empowerfully

Family Factors:
It's Within Us to Be Empowerful

Education Context Factors:
It's Within Us to Make Our Contexts Empowering

Family Factors

Motivation

Self-efficacy: believing in our capabilities

Perceived control: believing we can apply our capabilities to affect what happens to us

Hope: believing we will get what we want and need

Energy: lighting the fire and keeping it burning

Persistence: putting forth a sustained effort

Knowledge/Skills

Information: being in the know

Problem solving: knowing how to bust the barriers

Coping skills: knowing how to handle what happens to us

Communication skills: being on the sending and receiving ends of expressed needs and wants

Education Context Factors

Opportunities for Partnerships

Opportunities arise when . . .

Communicating among reliable allies

Meeting families' basic needs

Referring and evaluating for special education

Individualizing for appropriate education

Extending learning in home and community

Attending and volunteering at school

Advocating for systems improvement

Obligations for Reliable Alliances

Reliable alliances consist of . . .

Knowing yourself

Knowing families

Honoring cultural diversity

Affirming family strengths

Promoting family choices

Envisioning great expectations

Communicating positively

Warranting trust and respect

- For students evaluated for the first time, either a member of the evaluation team or another individual who is knowledgeable about the evaluation procedures used with the student and the results

The IEP has been characterized as a written commitment of agency resources, a management tool to ensure that the student's needs are being addressed, a compliance/monitoring document for determining if the student is receiving an appropriate education, an evaluation device for gauging the student's progress, and a communication vehicle between parents and school personnel (U.S. Department of Education, 1981).

As Jordan Lieberman's IEP is developed and implemented, his parents, Lisa and Craig, are very much involved with the professionals who serve him; this is exactly what IDEA enables and intends. Given IDEA's purposes, educators must take steps to assure that a student's parents have a chance to attend the IEP conference. These steps include advance notice of the meeting, mutually convenient scheduling, and interpreters for parents who are deaf or non-English speaking. If parents are unable to attend, they may still participate through individual or conference telephone calls.

IEP meetings may be held without parents present only if schools have unsuccessfully attempted to have the parents participate. Educators must document their efforts to secure parent participation through records of telephone calls, copies of letters to or from the parents, and the results of visits to the parents' home or place(s) of work.

Students may attend the IEP meeting if appropriate—that is, if they are over the age of majority or, if younger, if their parents and teachers agree to their attendance or federal or state law give them a right to attend. Students' right to attend the IEP conference affirms that students frequently can contribute to the meeting by ensuring that (1) the student's perspective is taken into account and (2) the other participants focus on the student's strengths, needs, preferences, and great expectations, not on what they themselves want or find convenient. Similar to families and professionals, students can become more empowered through collaborative decision making. When the student attains the age of 16 and acquires an individualized transition program, and even before then under some state laws, the student has the legal right to have his or her preferences for postsecondary outcomes taken into account.

Individualized Family Service Plan (IFSP)

Like the IEP, the IFSP is a written document; but it specifies the services for infants and toddlers, ages birth to 3 (that is, birth through 2), and their families. Whereas the IEP focuses on the needs of the individual student, the IFSP focuses on services and supports for the family as well and has the dual goals of enhancing the child's development while simultaneously enhancing the family's capacity to meet the child's special needs. Accordingly, the IFSP must contain the following:

- A statement of the child's present levels of physical, cognitive, communicative, social or emotional, and adaptive development based on professionally acceptable objective criteria
- With the family's agreement, a statement of the family's resources, priorities, and concerns related to enhancing their child's development
- A statement of major outcomes for the child and family and the criteria, procedures, and time lines for determining the degree of their progress and whether modifications or revisions of outcomes or services are necessary
- A statement of specific early intervention services necessary to meet the child's and the family's unique needs, including the frequency, intensity, location, and method of service delivery; the location of services, including the natural environment; and payment arrangements
- To the extent appropriate, a statement of medical and other services that the child needs but that are not required to be provided under this legislation and, if necessary, a statement of the steps to be taken to secure those services through public or private resources
- A statement of the projected dates for beginning the services and their duration
- The name of the service coordinator who will be responsible for IFSP implementation and coordination with other agencies and persons
- A statement of steps to be taken to support the child's transition from early intervention services to preschool or other services, including discussions with and training of the child's parents regarding future placements and other matters relating to the child's transition

The IFSP uses the term *family,* whereas the IEP uses the term *parent.* This difference reflects the evolving recognition within the field of special education of the importance of a family systems perspective. Accordingly, the participants in the initial and in each annual IFSP meeting must include the following:

- The child's parent or parents
- Other family members as requested by the parent(s) if it is feasible to include them
- The service coordinator
- A person(s) directly involved in conducting the child and family evaluations and assessments
- As appropriate, persons who will provide services to the child or family

If a required person is not available to attend the meeting, other means for participation must be used, such as telephone conference calls, attendance by a knowledgeable representative, or pertinent records made available at the meeting. All meetings must be scheduled at times and places convenient to the family. The family's native language or other mode of communication must be used. The meetings must be arranged to allow the families enough time to plan to attend.

The initial meeting to develop the IFSP must take place within 45 days after the child or family is referred for early intervention services. Thereafter, periodic review is available in two ways: (1) Every six months the IFSP must be reviewed for progress and appropriate revision by a meeting or other means agreeable to the participants, and (2) annually a meeting must be held to evaluate the IFSP and revise it as appropriate.

Early intervention services may begin before evaluation and assessment if the parents agree. In that event, an interim IFSP is developed (naming the service coordinator and demonstrating that the services are needed immediately by the child and family), and the evaluation and assessment must be completed within the 45-day period.

Review of Research on IEP/IFSP Partnerships

The Office of Special Education Programs within the U.S. Department of Education has clarified the expectations for family and professional partnerships:

> The IEP meeting serves as a communication vehicle between parents and school personnel, and enables them as equal participants to jointly decide what the child's needs are, what services will be provided to meet those needs, and what the anticipated outcomes will be. (*Federal Register*, 1981, p. 5462)

Note the language in this policy interpretation— "equal participants" and "jointly decide." The federal expectation is that there will be a collaborative process, characterized by having a reliable alliance, to make decisions concerning "services" and "anticipated outcomes." This expectation of collaboration is, not surprisingly, exactly the same one that Lisa Lieberman and Craig Ackerman have for their son Jordan.

How has this expectation been incorporated into educational practices? Sadly, but typically, there is a great shortcoming: The expectation of partnership is usually unfulfilled. Lisa and Craig's preschool experiences are the exception rather than the rule.

One of the earliest research studies was conducted within the first several years after schools began to implement IDEA (Goldstein, Strickland, Turnbull, & Curry, 1980). The researchers observed IEP conferences of 14 elementary students with mild disabilities and analyzed the topics of discussion and the frequency of contributions by each conference participant. After each conference, all participants completed a questionnaire to rate their satisfaction with their role in the conference and the decisions made. The researchers reached the following conclusions:

- Parental contributions (mothers in 12 of 14 conferences) accounted for less than 25 percent of the total conference contributions.
- The mean length of conferences was 36 minutes.
- The most frequently discussed topics were the student's curriculum, behavior, and performance.
- The topics of placement, related services, legal rights and responsibilities, individual responsibility for implementing goals and objectives, the child's health, future contacts among parents and professionals, and future plans for the child were each discussed (on average) less than once per conference.
- Parents, resource teachers, classroom teachers, and principals were overwhelmingly positive.
- Overall, these conferences consisted of the resource teacher's describing a previously developed IEP to the student's mother.

Eight years later, other researchers evaluated 26 conferences of students with learning disabilities (Vaughn, Bos, Harrell, & Lasky, 1988), determining the length, composition, parental participation, and parental attitudes of each. They reported the following:

- On average, 6.5 participants met for 41 minutes.
- Parent interactions accounted for only 14.8 percent of the conference time, or 6.5 minutes.

- More than one-fourth of the parents thought the term *learning disability* meant that their child was slow. To 12 percent, the term implied that their child had a physical problem. Some merely responded, "Learning disabled is what my child is" (Vaughn et al., 1988, p. 86). Twenty-three percent had no or an unrelated explanation.
- Nearly two-thirds (59 percent) of the parents were positive and appreciative of the meeting. Some mentioned being nervous and cautious, while others said they felt confused and overwhelmed. In spite of these descriptions, 65 percent believed that all their questions had been answered.

A third study focused on the IFSP rather than the IEP. The researcher, who observed 25 IFSP conferences and conducted 50 interviews with parents and professionals to examine their overall satisfaction with the IFSP process (Able-Boone, 1993), reported the following:

- The average number of conference participants was 6, with 24 mothers and only 3 fathers attending.
- All conferences were held during the work week during typical working hours, but one was held at 5:30 P.M.
- The average conference lasted for one hour.
- Professionals spoke more often than parents.
- Only four of the conferences focused on family-centered outcomes such as respite care, parent support groups, and counseling services.
- Parents and professionals reported equally high satisfaction with the conferences.
- The typical conference focused primarily on child development rather than on the child within the context of the family.

One of the most recent IEP studies reported data on 24 families whose children were in special education. Twelve families participated for three years, six for the first year only, and six for the second and third years only (Harry, Allen, & McLaughlin, 1995). Over a three-year period, the researchers interviewed families, observed conferences, and reported the following:

- Although 16 out of 18 parents attended the IEP conference during the first year, only 11 of 18 attended in the third year. Parents' reasons for not attending included conflicts with work schedules, late notice of the meeting, the routine nature of the meeting in which they felt their input was discounted, and the fact that the school tended to send papers home for signa-

tures whether or not parents attended.
- Six parents indicated that they were able to influence decisions in the conference.
- The length of a conference ranged from 20 to 30 minutes. (In one school, conferences were always terminated at the end of 30 minutes regardless of whether they were complete. Parents were advised that they could continue discussions with the teacher after the meeting.)
- The main activity was securing parents' signatures on IEP documents rather than encouraging genuine participation in the meeting.
- Extensive special education jargon was evident in all meetings.

The researchers commented:

As professionals identify with the culture of the school bureaucracy, most become entrenched in a "we-they" posture by which parents are seen as potential adversaries rather than allies. . . . In this study, professional role identification seemed to become the dominant ethic driving how most educators, regardless of race, interacted with parents. (Harry et al., 1995, p. 374)

Although we have highlighted only these four studies, Smith (1990) has summarized the entire body of IEP research and has categorized IEP implementation into three phases:

- *Normative phase.* During the early years of IDEA implementation, research focused on explaining the IEP components and the expectations for implementation (Abeson & Weintraub, 1977; Morissey & Safer, 1977; Turnbull, Strickland, & Hammer, 1978).
- *Analytic phase.* Here, research focused on the implementation of the IEP (similar to the four studies reported earlier in the chapter), particularly related to assumptions of IEP development, special education teacher perceptions, parent involvement, team approach, and general education teacher participation (Gerber, Banbury, Miller, & Griffin, 1986; Goldstein & Turnbull, 1982; Lewis, Busch, Proger, & Juska, 1981; Lynch & Stein, 1982; Nadler & Shore, 1980; Pyecha, Cox, Dewitt, Drummond, Jaffe, Kalt, Lane, & Pelosi, 1980). More recently there has been an analytic phase of IFSP research (DeGangi, Royeen, & Wietlisbach, 1992; Minke & Scott, 1993).
- *Technology-reaction phase.* This phase of research has focused on computer-managed instructional systems to reduce time and

paperwork hassles associated with the IEP. During this phase of research, the shift of attention moved from the quality of the process to the logistical management of the process (Davis, 1985; Enell & Barrick, 1983; Ryan & Rucker, 1986).

Based on this extensive literature review, Smith concluded:

After more than a decade of implementation, research, and subsequent recommendations for improvement, substantive IEP change has not ensued. In consequence, we may have been ignoring "specially designed instruction" for special needs students, and thus, the very students the law was designed to protect and educate with their individual needs in mind. (Smith, 1990, p. 11)

During the time the reported research on IEPs was being conducted, the major debate in the field focused on the Regular Education Initiative and then on the implementation of inclusive education (chapter 2). Limited attention has been directed at educational outcomes and whether special education programs (IEPs) were preparing students to achieve independence, inclusion, and productivity as adults.

In some states, students who are gifted have a right (under state law) to an IEP. The parents of students who are gifted may have a less positive attitude about the IEP process than parents of students classified as having a disability (Lewis et al., 1981).

That [IEP process, including the IEP meeting,] was about as much of nothing as one could imagine. They, at that time and I'm afraid still now, had the same goal plan for every student; they really did not know how to run a program although there were some very talented teachers working with gifted. The meeting merely consisted of reporting the score (99+ on the Wechsler) and passing around a form which everyone at the table signed.

In 1994, the National Council on Disability took testimony in ten states from families and individuals with disabilities concerning their perspectives about IEPs. The following quotations illustrate this grassroots testimony:

In regard to the IEP process itself, I wish it stood for Individual Encouragement to Parents. . . . In many ways this Public Law has become our enemy. Educators are being consumed by accountability and the IEP process itself. . . . The IEP process is so labor-intensive that it actually drives us away from the child instead of closer to the child. It has become a burden to our professionals. You may have five to eight professionals on a team and not

one of those people really possess a true trusting relationship with the parents. Not one sees that big picture of this child's life, because they are caught up in the accountability, they are caught up in time, which also becomes their enemy. (Testimony by Kathy Davis, in National Council on Disability, 1995, pp. 56–57)

I felt a very small and incidental part of this procedure, and at times I've felt I left with a feeling that my daughter really wasn't getting her full share or placement of services. (Testimony by Diana Sullivan, in National Council on Disability, 1995, p. 108)

The dominant theme of all the research and testimony is that schools try to comply with legal mandates and procedures but do not make an effort to foster empowerment through collaboration. There is scant evidence that the motivation and knowledge/skills of family and professional participants in the process is enhanced or that an empowering context has been developed—one characterized by the eight obligations of a reliable alliance. Finally, there is little evidence that a collaborative process bridges the individual factors (motivation and knowledge/skills) and the context factors associated with collaborating for empowerment in individualizing for appropriate education. It is entirely possible, however, to develop and implement IFSPs/IEPs in an empowerful way.

The key, as Lisa Lieberman points out, includes parents' and professionals' getting to know each other, emphasizing what each does that is helpful, supporting each other in their respective roles, meeting often, planning collaboratively, and then implementing the individualized program rigorously. Most of all, we agree with Lisa when she says that developing a sense of entitlement about deserving help and then being ready to seek and receive it, and to offer it, creates the empowerment that otherwise may not flow from the individualized program process. As box 12–1 shows, this is an achievable result. (The box highlights the IFSP process but can be just as easily adapted to the IEP process, and should be.)

The IEP process has tended to be a disempowering experience for most participants. Although research generally indicates that the IFSP process comes closer than the IEP process to creating a reliable alliance, generally it still falls short of being a reliable alliance that fosters collaboration leading to empowerment. By moving from a disempowering to an empowering partnership with families as you and they individualize for appropriate education, you can be part of the team that supports students' success.

A Family-Friendly IFSP

Developing a family-friendly IFSP—or, for that matter, an IEP—is never a hurried matter; you can't hurry and listen at the same time. Making the process and goals family-friendly, however, can create collaboration between professionals and families. This Beach Center model of collaboration, in turn, can empower all of the participants, in the sense that each gets some of what each wants.

For Leslie Jones, her husband David, and her daughter Natalie (who has multiple disabilities and significant health problems), the collaboration begins when they tell, and professionals empathetically listen to, the Jones family story—their background, concerns, people to whom and places where they are most connected. Developing a "to do" list—services that respond to the Jones family and Natalie's specific needs, preferences, and great expectations that become outcome-based goals—is the second stage.

Both the first and second stages are designed for the family and professionals to "get onto the same wavelengths" and even develop an interim IFSP. There follows an evaluation of Natalie; a discussion with Leslie and David about the evaluation results and their implications for Leslie, David, Natalie, and her sisters; the development of the

IFSP; and the delivery of services to Natalie and her family.

Leslie describes the unhurried and whole-family approach of the Beach Center's family-friendly IFSP as "very sensitive to the well-being of the family as a whole and to the individual family members. No one is overlooked. Natalie's needs were balanced with the family's needs, recognizing that the family must be strong to meet her needs adequately. We talked a lot about me and whether I felt I could handle the work demanded by the various potential programs in her service plan."

Two problems emerged. The first one was getting Natalie dressed every day for preschool while also dressing and spending time with her sisters. The second problem was transporting Natalie directly to preschool rather than making her sit on a school bus for a long time, something that would be hard on her physically.

The Joneses' friends—whom they had invited to the IFSP meeting—and the professionals voluntarily developed a simple solution. They would help with both tasks, splitting the responsibilities among themselves.

Rather than being a "heavy weight" like other IFSPs that "created demands" on Leslie—demands for her time, energy, planning, and money—the family-friendly approach "looked

at ways to provide services for Natalie without interrupting everything that was happening at home. This way, our needs were met, as well as Natalie's."

Most of all, the family-friendly process and services changed the Joneses' perspectives, helping them to "think about our relationship with Natalie and to view her as a part of the larger community . . . as someone who has a place in the community."

"Now that we realize that Natalie can give as well as receive in these relationships, we do not feel hopelessly indebted to others who help in Natalie's care. We recognize that they benefit from this 'togetherness,' just as much as we do. This new attitude toward our circle of friends has relieved our fear, and we are more willing to ask others to help. Now our approach is to encourage others to see our vision and to become part of the team effort."

[The Beach Center publication *Handbook for the Development of a Family-Friendly IFSP* (Turbiville, Lee, Turnbull, & Murphy, 1993) describes this process; its *Parent Handbook for Individualized Family Service Plans* (Turbiville, 1995) includes suggestions for families as they prepare for IFSP meetings. Both are available from the Beach Center; see Appendix A for the Center's address.]

Source: Turnbull, A. P., Turbiville, V., Jones, L. & Lee, I. (1992, Summer). A family-responsive approach to the development of the individualized family service plan. *OSERS News in Print*, pp. 12–15.

Opportunities for Collaboration

The IFSP/IEP conference should consist of the following eight components:

1. Preparing in advance
2. Connecting and getting started
3. Sharing visions and great expectations
4. Reviewing formal evaluation and current levels of performance
5. Sharing resources, priorities, and concerns
6. Developing goals and objectives (or outcomes)
7. Specifying placement and related services
8. Summarizing and concluding

Before reading about each component of the IFSP/IEP process and our suggestions for collaborating with families, study our summary of these suggestions in box 12–2.

Preparing in Advance

In far too many situations, families and educators do not adequately prepare for IFSP/IEP conferences. Indeed, the primary work for the conference usually starts once everyone sits down. This is much too late. As you prepare for the conference, implement the suggestions we made in chapter 4 regarding a reliable alliance. Start communicating with families from the outset, in ways consistent with what you have already learned in chapters 4 and 9 about communication skills and strategies. By using a family systems perspective, you will contribute to meaningful IFSP/IEP preconference preparation. Indeed, when you work with families such as the Lieberman-Ackerman family, knowing that Craig has a disability, that his son Jordan also has one, and that Lisa is concerned about the impact of both those facts on their family and herself is helpful as you try to collaborate with the family; that kind of knowledge about family characteristics comes from using the family systems approach.

Even before a conference, you can refer families who are interested to Parent to Parent and Parent Training and Information Centers so they may obtain the emotional and informational support they may need to come to conferences in a more confident and empowered manner. For students who are initially evaluated for special education, the way that you and other educators carry out the referral and evaluation process will also significantly contribute to preconference preparation. The more you collaborate with families and respect their preferences in the referral

and evaluation process, the more likely it is that a reliable alliance will be well under way before the IFSP/IEP meeting is even scheduled.

If you will pause to take stock of what you have already learned, everything that we have discussed up to this point can become part of your preconference preparation. But you should also consider four other issues: (1) designating a service coordinator, (2) inviting participants, (3) taking care of logistical considerations, and (4) attending to advance preparation.

Designating a Service Coordinator You have already learned about the important role of a service coordinator in supporting families throughout the prereferral, referral, and evaluation process. A service coordinator can be similarly useful during the IFSP/IEP process. The service coordinator's primary responsibility at this stage is to ensure that preconference preparation is adequately carried out and guided by students' and families' strengths, preferences, great expectations, and needs. The service coordinator can and should continue as the primary team facilitator throughout IFSP/IEP implementation. Some families, such as Lisa Lieberman and Craig Ackerson's, may find that the service coordinator blocks their access to and communication with other professionals. That is not good practice. If anything, the coordinator should *ensure* access and communication.

Inviting Participants To determine families' preferences, discuss their preferences with them in a conference or over the telephone or ask for advice from professionals who have worked successfully with a family in the past (such as teachers) or who have a positive current relationship (such as a social worker or a public health nurse). Find out families' preferences concerning the family members, friends, and professionals who should attend the conference, convenient times and places for scheduling, whether assistance with transportation or child care would be helpful, and the kinds of information they would like to have in advance. Give them a chance to have evaluation reports, a summary of the student's strengths and needs in each subject area, information on legal rights, descriptions of various placement options and related services, draft goals and objectives from the professionals' perspective, options of extracurricular activities, and information on transition services. Gather this information early enough so you can carry through on it in making the necessary arrangements.

Collaborating with Parents in IFSP/IEP Conferences

Preparing in Advance

- Appoint a service coordinator to organize the conference.
- Make sure the evaluation has included all relevant areas, is complete, and has clearly synthesized results.
- Ask the family about their preferences regarding the conference.
- Discuss the conference with the student and consider his or her preferences for participation.
- Decide who should attend the conference and include the student if appropriate.
- Arrange a convenient time and location for the conference.
- Assist the family with logistical needs such as transportation and child care.
- Inform the family (in straightforward, jargon-free language) verbally and/or in writing about the following:
  - Purpose of the conference
  - Time and location of conference
  - Names and roles of participants
- Give the family the information they want before the conference.
- Encourage and arrange for the student, family members, and their advocates to visit educational placements for the student before the conference.
- Encourage the student and family members to talk with each other about the conference.
- Encourage the family to share information and discuss concerns with all participants.
- Review the student's previous IFSP/IEP and ensure that school records document the extent to which each of the goals and objectives (or outcomes) have been accomplished.
- Identify the factors that have most contributed to the attainment of those results and the factors that have been the most significant barriers.
- Request an informal meeting with any teachers or related service providers who will not attend the conference. Document and report their perspectives at the conference.
- Consider whether providing snacks would be appropriate and possible. If so, make necessary arrangements.
- Prepare an agenda to cover the remaining components of the conference.

Connecting and Getting Started

- Greet the student, family, and their advocates.
- Share informal conversation in a comfortable and relaxed way.
- Serve snacks, if available.
- Share an experience about the student that was particularly positive or one that reflects the student's best work.
- Provide a list of all participants or use name tags if there are several people who have not met before.
- Introduce each participant, briefly describing his or her role in the conference.
- State the purpose of the conference. Review the agenda and ask if additional issues need to be covered.
- Ask the participants how long they can stay and offer to schedule a follow-up conference if necessary to complete the agenda.
- Ask if family members want you to clarify their legal rights. If so, do so.

Sharing Visions and Great Expectations

- If a MAP process has been completed, share the results with everyone.
- If a MAP process has not been completed, consider incorporating it into the conference.
- Encourage the student and family to share their great expectations for the future. Then encourage all committee members to share their visions of the most desirable future for the student, based on the student's preferences, strengths, and needs.
- Affirm the excitement about the great expectations and the connection between the goals and objectives (or outcomes) that are planned at the conference and the achievement of those great expectations.

Reviewing Formal Evaluation and Current Levels of Performance

- Give family members a written copy of all evaluation results.
- Avoid educational jargon as much as possible and clarify any terms that seem to puzzle the family, student, or their advocates.
- If a separate evaluation conference has not been scheduled, discuss the evaluation procedures and tests and the results of each.
- Invite families and other conference participants to agree or disagree with the evaluation results and to state their reasons.

BOX 12–2

Collaborating with Parents in IFSP/IEP Conferences

- Discuss the meaning and implications of the results in terms of the student's appropriate education, preferences, strengths, great expectations, and needs.
- Review the student's developmental progress and current levels of performance in each subject area or domain.
- Ask families if they agree or disagree with the stated progress and performance levels.
- Strive to resolve any disagreement among participants.
- Proceed with the IFSP/IEP only after all participants agree about the student's current levels of performance.

Sharing Resources, Priorities, and Concerns
- Taking into account the student's and family's strengths, preferences, great expectations, and needs, encourage each participant to identify the particular resources, expertise, and strengths that they (and absent professionals) can bring to bear.
- Ask participants to share their priorities and reach consensus on the most important issues.
- Encourage all participants to express their concerns about their own roles in supporting the student, especially in areas where they feel they will need support or assistance.
- Plan how all participants can share expertise and resources to create the most comprehensive support system possible in addressing priorities and responding to concerns.

Developing Goals and Objectives (or Outcomes)
- Generate appropriate goals and objectives for all subject areas requiring specially designed instruction consistent with stated great expectations and priorities.
- Discuss goals and objectives for the student's future educational and career options based on great expectations.
- Identify goals and objectives to expand the positive contributions the student can make to family, friends, and community.
- Prioritize all goals and objectives in light of student and family preferences, great expectations, strengths, and needs.
- Clarify who—student, family, professionals—is responsible for reaching the objectives and ensuring their generalization or mastery.
- Determine evaluation criteria, procedures, and schedules for goals and objectives.

- Explain that the IFSP/IEP is not a guarantee that the student will attain the goals and objectives but that it represents a good-faith effort among all participants to work toward the goals and objectives.

Determining Placement and Related Services
- Discuss the benefits and drawbacks of less restrictive, more inclusive placement options. Consider the resources that all committee members can bring to bear, especially supplementary aids and related services, in inclusive settings.
- Select a placement option that enables the student to receive appropriate individualized instruction and to develop a sense of belonging with peers without exceptionalities.
- Agree on a tentative placement until the student and family can visit and confirm its appropriateness.
- Specify the supplementary aids and related services that the student will receive to ensure the appropriateness of the educational placement.
- If the student is to be placed in a special education program, state why supplementary aids and related services are not capable of assisting the student within a general education setting.
- Document and record the time line for providing the supplementary aids and related services that will enable the student to make the transition to the general education setting.
- Discuss the benefits and drawbacks of types, schedules, and modes of providing related services that the student needs.
- Specify the dates for initiating related services and the anticipated duration.
- Share the names and qualifications of all personnel who will provide instruction and related services.

Concluding the Conference
- Assign follow-up responsibility for any task requiring attention.
- Summarize orally and on paper the major decisions and follow-up responsibilities of all participants.
- Set a tentative date for reviewing IFSP/IEP implementation.
- Identify preferred options for ongoing communication among all participants.
- Express appreciation to all team members for their collaborative decision making.
- Affirm the value of a reliable alliance and cite specific examples of how having an alliance enhanced the quality of decision making.

Most IFSP/IEP conferences have been composed of three to five professionals and a mother (Able-Boone, 1993; Campbell, Strickland, & La Forme, 1992; Goldstein et al., 1980; Vacc, Vallecorsa, Parker, Bonner, Lester, Richardson, & Yates, 1985). From a family systems perspective, take stock of which family members may want to participate—fathers, grandparents, brothers and sisters, cousins, live-in significant others, godparents, or other people within the family's culture who have family-like relationships. In addition to family members, friends of the student or family, people who are in strategic positions to foster community inclusion (such as soccer coaches, scout leaders, and religious education teachers), and people who can be mentors in supporting the student to explore preferences for hobbies or careers (such as musicians, business leaders, and mechanics) are all potential participants who can enhance the quality of a student's education (Turbiville, Turnbull, Garland, & Lee, 1996). Encourage families to identify the people whom they have typically included in IFSP/IEP conferences and the ones who may have unique resources and expertise to offer their son or daughter.

A key component of empowerment is making choices, including students' making choices about their own participation in conferences. Under IDEA, all students may participate in IEP meetings "when-ever appropriate"; and students who are 16 and older must have their preferences and interests taken into account when developing transition services. The legal presumption is that the transition-age student will participate.

The majority of students in special education still are not participating in the development of their IEPs (Van Reusen & Bos, 1994). Some students have described experiences that prevent them from wanting to participate again in the future:

> When I go to them meetings, I get really frustrated because it seems like if you do something wrong you know, which everybody does, they exaggerate it. I mean you tell them the basic what happened, but they like exaggerate it. Teachers are good at that. They should be salesmen. (Morningstar, Turnbull, & Turnbull, 1995)

An approach for enhancing student participation is an educational planning strategy referred to as I-PLAN (Van Reusen, Bos, Schumaker, & Deshler, 1987). The five steps of this planning process are illustrated in box 12–3. The I-PLAN steps involve working with students and parents in advance, teaching them how to complete the student inventory, and using those inventories as a basis for generating goals. Students make more contributions and generate more IEP goals with this training than without it (Van

---

TIPS

I-PLAN to Enhance Student Participation

- The first step is the *Inventory* step. This provides the student an opportunity to list his or her perceived strengths, areas that need improvement, goals and choices for learning. The information is listed on an Inventory sheet, which the student can take to a conference. The student uses the remaining steps of the strategy for communicating during the conference.

- The second step, *Provide Your Inventory Information*, focuses on knowing how and when to provide information during a conference.

- The third step, *Listen and Respond*, includes procedures for effectively listening and knowing how and when to respond to statements and questions made by other individuals at the conference.

- The fourth step, *Ask Questions*, enables the student to know how and when to ask questions.

- The fifth and final step, *Name Your Goals*, requires the student to name the goals that were agreed upon before the end of the conference.

Source: Van Reusen, A. K. (1993). Learning disabled adolescents and motivation. In *Their World* (pp. 28–31). New York: National Center for Learning Disabilities (p. 697A). Reprinted with the permission of the National Center for Learning Disabilities, 381 Park Avenue South, New York, NY 10016.

Reusen, Deshler, & Schumaker, 1989; Van Reusen & Bos, 1990). Furthermore, conferences have more positive communication, especially in affirming students' strengths (Van Reusen & Bos, 1994).

As we have pointed out before, it is critically important to recognize cultural values associated with special education practices, including practices such as student participation in IEP conferences. Some cultures value child and adolescent autonomy more than others. A Taiwanese mother of a high school student who is gifted described her frustration at the IEP conference when the professionals were more concerned with having her daughter express her preferences than with giving the mother an opportunity to express her own opinions:

> When my daughter, Jean, was in junior high school, the gifted education counselor, she never asked me and then she never gave me eye contact. During the meeting she only asked my daughter what she wanted to do in the next year, and she didn't ask me. After she asked my daughter, then she give me the papers and say, "Okay, sign your name." That was really frustrating.

A Hispanic mother concurred with this view when she added her comments:

> We felt the same, and I think that basically the cultural differences are not being considered in these IEP meetings. And here in the United States it is like you always ask the child first, and for us it's very important for us as a parent to participate. And so the way that they handle those IEP meetings is like the American people, and they're not considering Chinese or Hispanic or any other culture. I know that it's not on their mind, but it really hurts our feelings. . . . We tell our children more what to do, what's wrong, what's right, and maybe we don't develop that independence . . . and maybe we start doing that after they turn 19 or 20. When we came to the United States five years ago, my children felt that difference in their education from school and home. They didn't understand very well what was going on; why we were one way at home (in asserting parental authority) and the teachers treated them in a different way (offering them more choices).

Clearly you need to consider the cultural appropriateness of involving students in conferences; when it is appropriate to do so, then support students to develop participation skills, using strategies such as the I-PLAN. Honoring cultural diversity, which includes determining the appropriateness of self-determination, is one of the eight objectives of establishing a reliable alliance.

Taking Care of Logistical Considerations

A third task takes into account logistical considerations such as scheduling, committee size, transportation, and child care. We discussed these same logistical considerations in chapter 9 as they pertained to other school conferences, and the tips we suggested there also apply here.

The more you work with families on these issues from the outset, the more families will be able to participate meaningfully. Addressing the logistical barriers can foster creative school-community partnerships as when employers provide time off from work for parents and community groups assist with transportation and child-care needs.

Some parents prefer a minimum number of people at the conference, and others prefer that everyone who has a stake in the quality of the child's education attend. Marion (1979) warned that "the single greatest deterrent to minority parent participation is that they might feel overwhelmed when they walk into a meeting and see all the school people are lined up against them" (p. 9). He suggests having in attendance only those people who are most familiar with the child. Other professionals should be on call to join the meeting upon request.

By contrast, a survey of 243 parents (whose ethnicity was not identified) in Colorado showed that the presence of large numbers of professionals at conferences did not make it difficult for parents to ask questions and did not prevent good discussions. Indeed, some parents view the large numbers as evidence of concern and interest (Witt, Miller, McIntyre, & Smith, 1984). The more people present, the greater the breadth of expertise and the chance of including all persons who have responsibility for implementing the IFSP/IEP. The benefit of smaller conferences is that they can be less intimidating and more focused. Thus, the number of people at conferences affects different families in different ways.

Time is a major logistical issue requiring systematic and creative problem solving. Many professionals feel harried by what seem to be overwhelming time requirements needed to complete IFSP/IEP-related paperwork.

> I cannot ask my wife and children to put up with me, depressed and tense for months each spring because I must finish my testing, must begin testing with the new kids we've identified, must get the reports in on time, must complete reams of papers (the law says so, and tells me how much time I have to do it), and can't teach. When I am in class, I am tense and harried because the testing isn't getting done on time. I don't have any time to

plan, to diagnose, to remediate, and I can't get on top. (Katzen, 1980, p. 582)

One research study underscores that, compared to five other variables, allowing enough time for the conference was the most important variable associated with parent satisfaction (Witt et al., 1984). Clearly, the place to cut time corners is not during the conference itself. To address time barriers, some schools hire a permanent floating substitute to free teachers to attend to IFSP/IEP-related tasks, hire aides or use volunteers to provide educators with additional release time, assign specific times each week for staff collaboration, and set aside one day in each grading period as a collaboration day in which no other activities can be scheduled (West, 1990).

Attending to Advance Preparation

Box 12–2 includes suggestions for work to complete in advance of IFSP/IEP meetings. Consider exchanging advance information, such as tentative or draft goals and objectives. Families frequently find it helpful to reflect in advance on information—such as current levels of performance, goals, objectives, placement, and related services—so they can feel confident about agreeing or disagreeing with professionals' opinions and recommendations. Other families, such as Lisa Lieberman and Craig Ackerson's, may find it empowering to draft their own version of an IFSP/IEP and then have professionals respond to it. By exchanging information in advance, families and professionals alike can use the conference time to clarify issues and make decisions. Without advance information, participants are likely to spend most of their time reviewing information and generating ideas and rushing to decisions. When families prefer to not receive advance written information, two meetings—one to review information and one to make instrumental decisions—are useful, taking into account both personal preference and time efficiency.

Planning in advance also can eliminate or minimize cultural differences between families and professionals. A sometimes-overlooked component of cultural difference is a family's religious beliefs, as one teacher noted:

Sam's expression was wide-eyed when the psychologist who was to test him walked through the door. Sam was not going to perform well for this man, I could tell. I was teaching in a private Christian school, and Sam's parents were fundamentalist Christians. The psychologist was dressed, to put it kindly, casually and very differently from the dress code we had at our school. . . . I have found that some of the people who take pride in

their tolerance can be the most close-minded and provincial. A simple phone call to Sam's administrator, myself, or his parents to ask what might prove offensive to the family's religious beliefs would have established a better rapport with all concerned and provided Sam with an opportunity to perform to his capacity during assessment.

Connecting and Getting Started

The initial conference proceedings can set a "reliable alliance ambience" for the entire meeting—one of welcoming, valuing, trusting, respecting, listening to, and collaborating with families to enhance the student's appropriate education. Lisa Lieberman and Craig Ackerson suggest that families and professionals try to look behind each other's roles and see each other as individuals who can help meet one another's needs. That's good advice and was easy for Lisa and Craig to carry out when Jordan was in a non-controlling, nonfearful preschool and kindergarten. How else might each member of the team welcome, value, trust, respect, listen to, and collaborate with each other? People working with people—not people in roles working with other people in other roles—is an ingredient of an appropriate education and mutual empowerment. Many factors can help family members believe that professionals have a power-with/power-from-within orientation toward them rather than a power-over orientation.

In a study of 145 special education teachers in six states, only slightly more than half of the teachers valued parents' participation. Seventy-one percent of them agreed to an option to waive parents' rights to attend and instead give decision-making authority to professionals. Moreover, 44 percent of the teachers regarded the IEP conference as little more than a formality. A parent commented about the differential power structure, saying: "One group has power and the other doesn't. I think the ultimate lack of power is to have a child who has special needs" (Ferguson, 1984, p. 44).

To equalize power and move from a professionally dominated process to a reliable alliance, try to create a warm and relaxed atmosphere in which all committee members use the positive communication skills that we discussed in chapter 4. Betsy Santelli, a parent of two daughters enrolled in a gifted program, described the importance of informal sharing:

Although anxious at first about what our roles might be, Jim and I were delighted to find a real willingness and genuine interest on the part of the staffing team to learn from us about Maren and

Tami's unique and special qualities as well as those of our family. Before any assessment results were shared or questions were asked, time was allowed for informal sharing among all of us as people—not professionals, not parents—just people. Those few minutes helped set the stage for the comfortable sharing of information that followed and continues to this day.

Researchers have assessed the impact of interpersonal communication by measuring the effect of a school counselor's serving as a parent advocate (Goldstein & Turnbull, 1982). The counselors were asked to engage in five communication skills: (1) introduce parents, (2) clarify jargon, (3) ask questions, (4) reinforce parental contributions, and (5) summarize decisions at the end of the conference. Significantly more parent contributions occurred in conferences in which a parent advocate was present (using the five communication skills) than in the control group that lacked a parent advocate.

Regrettably, some parents believe that school personnel blame them for their child's disability. Indeed, parents' satisfaction with conferences depends to a large degree on professionals' behavior in attributing blame to sources other than the parents (Witt et al., 1984). As we stated in chapter 1, you need to be particularly sensitive to direct comments or innuendoes that families might interpret as blaming them for their child's special needs. In addition, you should affirm the positive contributions that parents make to their son or daughter. Empathetic reciprocity will be one of your best guides during the initial portion of the conference and throughout the whole conference. Ask yourself, How would I want to be treated at this conference? How would I want others to support me? To what extent would I be feeling secure or vulnerable? What could others do to minimize my vulnerability and maximize my empowerment? By taking this perspective, you can make substantial progress toward establishing a reliable alliance. If you invest time and energy in genuinely connecting with families, conveying to them your authentic interest in their son or daughter and them, and expressing your unconditional regard and respect for their opinions and suggestions, you will do more toward having a successful IFSP/IEP conference than anything else you could do. Remember, far too many professionals have erred on the side of formal compliance with legal mandates and have failed to build a reliable alliance (Harry et al., 1995). To build a reliable alliance, positive interpersonal communication practices are an indispensable obligation.

Sharing Visions and Great Expectations

In chapter 9 you learned about the MAPs process as a technique for providing an open-ended, intimate, and personalized view of the student and family. If the family has already completed a MAPs process, the initial portion of the IFSP/IEP meeting is an appropriate time to review that information with the group. If the family has not had an opportunity to engage in a MAPs process, you might want to incorporate that into the initial conference proceedings, recognizing that you will not be able to complete that activity as well as the full IFSP/IEP all at one occasion. When Lisa Lieberman and Craig Ackerson begin to look far down the road in Jordan's life, they see that, as much as anything, he will need and can contribute to a Circle of Friends. Soon they will begin to put that vision to paper, working out a MAPs or similar process as part of Jordan's IEP process.

If the family and professionals decide to forego the MAPs process, they still need to set aside time for sharing visions and great expectations. Sharing visions and great expectations can generate enthusiasm and motivation for the future. Moreover, when people—family members and professionals alike—share their great expectations, they reveal a good deal about themselves and let others get to know them. Typically, people get more excited and have higher levels of motivation when they are working for something that genuinely sparks their hopes and dreams. Within the empowerment framework, great expectations are a way to enhance the individuals' motivation.

Figure 12–2 includes a framework for families to start writing down their vision for their child. Of course, students, educators, and other IFSP/IEP members can join in this process. As everyone's visions become more concrete, the next step is to identify the goals or outcomes that will most likely transform the vision to a reality.

Reviewing Formal Evaluation and Current Levels of Performance

The IEP must include the student's current levels of performance. This information derives directly from the evaluation and provides the foundation for the student's IFSP/IEP and appropriate education. Two options are available. First, the IFSP/IEP conference can be used to review formal evaluation results and develop the IFSP/IEP. Second, a separate meeting (before the IFSP/IEP conference) can be held only to

FIGURE 12–2

My Vision for My Child as a Young Adult

1. Home Environment—I envision my child will
   a. live in:
   b. live with:
   c. be able to:
2. Work Environment—I envision my child will
   a. work in:
   b. be employed as:
   c. be able to (responsibilities):
3. Community Environment—I envision my child will participate in
   a. places:
   b. activities:
   c. social events:

4. I hope that my child will develop relationships/friendships with:

   _____

5. I would also like my child to:

   _____

6. I think that my child will probably need the following supports and/or environmental modifications:

   _____

   _____

Source: Parker, D., with Moore, C. (1991). *Achieving inclusion through the IEP process: A handbook for parents.* Hanover MD: Maryland Coalition for Integrated Education.

review evaluation results. (We discussed both options in chapter 11.) The decision about when to report evaluation results should be based on family and professional preferences. (We made many of the suggestions included in box 12–2 in chapter 11.)

Sharing Resources, Priorities, and Concerns

The referral and evaluation process can be a time for families, teachers, related service providers, friends, and other interested people (such as physicians) to identify their respective resources, priorities, and concerns. As we pointed out in chapter 11, the process of identifying and agreeing to share resources, priorities, and concerns should start during the evaluation process and continue during the IFSP/IEP conference. The goal is to link the evaluation information to educational outcomes.

Thus, at the IFSP/IEP conference, after reviewing the evaluation and performance information, review each participant's resources, priorities, and concerns, making sure that sufficient information is available to decide about goals, objectives, placement, and related services. (As we said in chapter 11, IFSP regulations specify that families should have the opportunity to share their resources, priorities, and concerns. We certainly endorse this option for families; but we also believe that collaboration best occurs when all participants share their resources, priorities, and concerns.)

The participants should begin by focusing on their resources—the special contributions that they can make in best supporting the student. Remember the definition of collaboration: the opportunity to pool *diverse resources* in the problem-solving process. Each professional on the team brings different resources and strengths to the IFSP/IEP process. Only by sharing their unique resources can they combine these resources to benefit the student and each other.

Next, team members should identify their priorities based on their great expectations and the student's current levels of performance. Discuss priorities at the outset, before identifying goals and objectives, to help ensure that goals and objectives reflect individual and collective priorities.

Finally, the team should discuss concerns—what worries them; the student's most significant needs; how the school can enhance the student's educational outcomes; and whether resources are available within the group or from other people within the family, school, or community to accomplish the agreed-upon outcomes. For example, a general educator who has concerns about individualizing the curriculum for a student with a learning disability can collaborate with a special education consulting teacher. Teachers who are fearful about having students who are supported by medical technology can receive instruction and support from parents, the school nurse, and other specialists on how to maintain the medical equipment and attend to the student's special needs (Clatterbuck & Turnbull, 1996).

By discussing resources and concerns, the team can match some people's concerns with other resources. Remember that collaboration means that individual members are not stuck with their concerns to address alone.

Developing Goals and Objectives (or Outcomes)

Goals and objectives are the heart of the IEP; they are the substance of a student's educational program. All participants must address the central issue: What are the most important goals and objectives (or outcomes) for this student based on the student's as well as the family's current and future strengths, needs, preferences, and great expectations? Identify the criteria that are most important to the family, student, and professional team members for determining appropriate goals and objectives. These criteria should include the following:

- Student needs and strengths
- Student and family preferences and great expectations
- Likelihood that the goal and objective will promote successful participation in inclusive settings
- Connection to career and other postsecondary outcomes
- Age-appropriateness

Add to or modify these criteria based on professional and family recommendations. Conference participants can rank draft goals and objectives and then discuss the rankings and select priority goals and objectives. Consider nonacademic and extracurricular opportunities, not just academic skills, as goals and objectives.

> Tony is a 17-year-old student with autism. His major needs relate to independent living and career education. Considering his many deficits, it would be easy to identify more than enough goals and objectives for the year in these two areas alone. But Tony also has a special interest and talent in music. He believes that "music is magic." Music was identified as an important subject to include on Tony's IEP. One of the objectives was to teach Tony to play a guitar. As the year progressed, the music program and the guitar—as contrasted to the independent living and career-education programs—provided the spark for Tony to turn off the alarm clock and get out of bed every morning.

Make the goals and objectives sufficiently specific so that the team can monitor the student's progress.

> Regarding IEPs more often than not parents are presented with what is more or less a completed IEP at their planning placement team meeting. . . . The goals and objectives are generally very, very vague, nonspecific and often don't have an appropriate way to evaluate whether the child is making progress in his or her program. (Testimony by Laura Glomb, in National Council on Disability, 1995, p. 57)

We have been discussing IEP goals and objectives, but what about IFSP *outcomes?* Some people regard goals, objectives, and outcomes as relatively synonymous. Others regard outcomes as more likely to be stated in the language of the family in terms of what changes they want to see rather than being stated in the format of a behavioral objective. For example, this might be a "professionally stated" behavioral objective:

> The siblings will attend a siblings support group for at least 80% of the meetings in order to gain a developmentally appropriate understanding of Down syndrome.

But a "family-stated" outcome might be worded like this:

> We want some assistance in knowing how to help our other children understand why their little sister is slow, so they can answer the questions of their friends at school. (McGonigel, Kaufmann, & Johnson, 1991, p. 58)

Unlike the IEP, the IFSP must state outcomes for both the child and the family (if the family agrees to having outcomes stated), whereas IEP goals and objectives focus only on the student. An early IFSP study noted that the majority of family outcomes were primarily written by staff and stated what a parent was responsible for doing—for example, "parent will attend scheduled classes" (Bailey, Winton, Rouse, & Turnbull, 1990). Remember, the purpose of family outcomes is not for staff to assign duties to families but for the early intervention programs to provide supports and services to families and their infants and toddlers. Figure 12–3 includes a framework for thinking about outcomes: child outcomes that are primarily child- or family-related and family outcomes that are primarily child-related but also address the family's general well-being.

To state and implement outcomes related to the family's general well-being, early intervention programs will need to collaborate with other professionals and agencies. (In chapter 13, we discuss comprehensive school-linked services, which is one model for supporting diverse family priorities and

FIGURE 12-3

Framework for Distinguishing Child and Family Outcomes

Component	Child Outcomes	Family Outcomes
Child-related	Child intervention related to physical, cognitive communication, social or emotional development, and adaptive skills	Family intervention to help family life be easier—respite care, assistive technology, sibling support
Family-related	Child intervention to help family life be easier—eating, sleeping, behavior	Family intervention focused on general family needs (which will likely have positive spin-off effects on child)—marital counseling, financial support, GED education

Source: Adapted from "Issues in Developing the IFSP: A Framework for Establishing Family Outcomes" by P. J. Beckman and M. M. Bristol, 1991, *Topics in Early Childhood Special Education*, 11, pp. 19-31. Copyright © 1991 by PRO-ED, Inc. Reprinted by permis-

needs.) There are differences between the outcomes that educators and related service providers are prepared to address and the ones that require special expertise or training from social workers, psychologists, and counselors to ensure that appropriate services are offered.

The more you create a reliable alliance with families, the more they will trust you, share their concerns, and brainstorm about the most appropriate child and family outcomes. Being guided by the eight obligations for establishing reliable alliances, honor the family's cultural diversity, affirm their strengths, and build on their choices as you develop family outcomes (Beckman & Bristol, 1991).

Specifying Placement and Related Services

Few aspects of educational decision making are more important than placement and related services, for placement and related services that are specified on the student's IFSP/IEP must be made available, and those that are not stated need not be made available.

Families who are unfamiliar with placement options have a right to a specific description of the various options available. Yet based on observations of 34 conferences, a team of researchers concluded that the concept of least restrictive placement was neither explicitly stated nor used as a basis for making placement decisions in any of the conferences (Ysseldyke, Algozzine, & Mitchell, 1982). The authors observed: "In general, teams presented data, and then someone on the team recommended a placement. The efficacy of the placement was seldom discussed" (p. 311). Consistent with this finding, a parent advocate recently commented:

> I've been to 57 IEP meetings. Not once, not ever once, did the school offer regular class placement as a placement for a child. Beyond that, they never offered, never discussed, never considered what kinds of supports, modifications, options would be necessary for a child to succeed in a regular class environment. Children are placed within existing programs, they're placed categorically and/or into existing programs. (Testimony by Laura Glomb, in National Council on Disability, 1995, p. 59)

In addition, a survey of parents of children who are deaf and enrolled in residential schools revealed that about two-thirds of the parents had been given information about residential schools, but almost half of those who had received information had not received information on any other educational option (Bernstein & Martin, 1992). Approximately one-third of the parents who were surveyed were not satisfied with the information that they had received about placement. Consistent with this research, some parents feel that they do not have real choices about less restrictive options:

> One parent was told from an administrator, "[Your son] can either go to his neighborhood school, where he will be teased and humiliated, or he can continue to go to the segregated school, where he will have the opportunity to be class president and captain of the basketball team." (Testimony by E. J. Jorgensen, in National Council on Disability, 1995, p. 84)

You have already learned about the Regular Education Initiative and inclusion movement in chapter 2, and you have learned about parent perspectives on inclusion in chapter 8. Sadly, many parents receive an explicit or implicit message that their children will be a burden to their teachers and classmates (Barber & Brophy, 1993). One such parent, Carmen Ramirez, shares her experiences in box 12–4.

Carmen and Alfredo Ramirez did "go for it" by winning a major lawsuit to compel their school district to include Danny in general education. This lawsuit—*Daniel R.R. v. State Board of Education*—is cited in chapter 15. Listen to what Charles Fields, Danny's general education language arts teacher, says five years later about teaching him:

> The definitive nature of teaching is to be accepting of anybody who is willing to learn and if you have that person there, you are supposed to have the talents and creativity in order to produce some

type of objective where that person can grow from it. . . . One of the things I try to stress is the process of learning, and I have to utilize my resources. I don't try to do it all myself. I work with other teachers, and we get together and we modify lesson plans. If I have a particular problem, I go to the person who's the expert on that problem. . . .

Danny just belongs, because he wants to belong . . . . You know he's not combative; he's not a behavioral problem. He's hard not to like. . . . I can see ideas in his eyes. Danny has his dreams, I'm sure he does. You know, even though he can't express them right now, we need to get as many people involved as we can to make his dreams come true.

Carmen and Alfredo's description of their reaction to teachers who do not want Danny in their classes underscores how important it is for teachers to *welcome* students into general education placements, not just to ensure that special education supports and

MY VOICE
BOX 12–4

Who Wants Danny?

The discrimination I felt was rich to poor, but racist also. I wondered if it would ever end. First, because I was poor and brown and of Mexican descent, and then because I had a child with a disability. With Danny, I felt like I was being discriminated against all over again. One of the things that stands out in my mind is our not being allowed to belong we were called "dirty Mexican greasers."

When Danny was in pre-kindergarten, we saw that the kids were separated. They had an early childhood classroom next to the pre-kindergarten classroom—the kids were the same age but one class was for kids with disabilities and the other one was for typical kids. I'd come home and I'd tell Alfredo, "You know, this isn't right. I mean the other kids—they get to eat in the cafeteria and go out on

the playground, and Danny's class doesn't. I want that for Danny. When he turns 4, I want that for him."

So then we asked for Danny to be included, and they were very offended. The school people were very offended. How dare we ask that. You don't do that. I mean, "Don't you see we're giving you all the best here with these kids, and you got the best teacher and whatever. We're sorry, but we don't think it's best for him."

The special education teacher, when she found out that she was going to have a child with Down syndrome in her classroom, did not want him there, because her classroom was for "high-functioning kids." She told me, "I've never taught kids with Down syndrome and this is for kids that function very high, and I think your son is going to end up at that

other school that's three miles from here. That's the one that takes the kids with severe challenges."

Well, it ended up being that Danny got in her class, but, not because we pushed it, but because of the IQ scoring. She didn't like it at all. So we had trouble with her, because she was always dragging her feet in educating him, because it was going to be all this work. I remember I would get so frustrated and I would tell Alfredo, "What is so wrong with even special education? They're supposed to be so prepared and so perfect and so wonderful, and they don't want Danny. Who's going to want him?" So for us, he was being rejected from both sides. What the hell, let's go for it!

Carmen Ramirez, 1994

services are provided. Families yearn to hear that their children are wanted, and they are alienated from professionals who describe their children as being a burden to teachers and classmates. "The teacher that honestly believes that a child is an asset to the class and is a privilege to teach communicates much to that child, and sets an example for the rest of the class to value all people" (Testimony by Gayle Underdown, in National Council on Disability, 1995, p. 82).

Danny's teacher, Charles Fields, underscores an important point: He doesn't have all the answers himself, but his success depends on collaboration with others to help to make Danny's dreams come true. When discussing placement options, everyone should try to draw upon the resources that each other participant can offer. Concentrate on mutual support to implement the IFSP/IEP. Remember that the goal is mutual empowerment for all.

The Maryland Coalition for Integrated Education has developed an IEP-based process for family-professional collaboration aimed at fostering "meaningful participation and inclusion in the life of a typical school" (Parker, 1991, p. 2). The process has two parts: (1) laying the groundwork for decision making and (2) achieving inclusion through the IEP process. The manual outlines specific steps and then provides worksheets for families to carry out the steps. Figure 12–2, "My Vision for My Child As a Young Adult," is from this manual.

As you learned in chapter 8, families vary in their support for inclusion (York & Tundidor, 1995): "I have some serious concerns about the current movement to adopt inclusionary practices as a single, universal concept to meet the needs of deaf and hard of hearing" (Testimony by Timothy Jaech, in National Council on Disability, 1995, p. 92). Parents of deaf children often cite "the lack of language education in many integrated settings, isolation from peers because of communication barriers, and underdeveloped self-esteem due to a lack of role models" (National Council on Disability, 1995, p. 94).

The National Council on Disability recognizes the legitimacy of different family perspectives on placement but underscores the need for systemic school reform in developing greater capacity for individualization through high quality support services:

> There will be situations where parents will want substantially separate placements, usually because school districts have not offered appropriate supports within the regular school environment. Other times, parents might require such placements based on the nature of their child's disability (e.g., deafness). At this point in history, such requests might be appropriate. However, this

should not obstruct the overall process of rebuilding special education as a high-quality support service available in every public school building in America. The problem at present is not a lack of options to segregate students with disabilities from their peers; rather, it is a lack of options to include students with disabilities in the ongoing lives of their schools and communities. (National Council on Disability, 1995, p. 98)

Figure 12–4 includes some of the Council's recommendations regarding IEP development and placement in the least restrictive environment. Advocate to implement these recommendations, especially with respect to items 2 and 3.

In addition to the placement decision, the other critical decision in the IFSP/IEP addresses related services. IDEA defines related services as developmental, corrective, or other supportive services that are necessary for students with disabilities to benefit from special education. Related services for students ages 3 through 21 are audiology, counseling services, early identification, medical diagnostic services, occupational therapy, parent counseling and training, physical therapy, psychological services, recreation, school health services, social work services, speech pathology, and transportation. In addition, the IEP/IFSP should specify any assistive technology services and devices that the child needs.

Additional related services specified for infants and toddlers include family training, counseling, and home visits; certain health services, limited medical services, vision services, and nursing services; service coordination; and services related to special instruction. The special instruction skills include learning environments and activities designed to promote the child's skill acquisition; curriculum planning related to IFSP outcomes; provision of information, skills, and support to families; and working with children to enhance their development.

If related service providers cannot attend IFSP/IEP meetings, the committee should secure their written recommendations or generate recommendations but not finalize this portion of the IFSP/IEP until they have an opportunity to respond.

Many parents and professionals are concerned about the unavailability of necessary related services. In a survey of parents of students who are ventilator-assisted, parents reported that they were most satisfied with the schools' success in the areas of academics, health care, and socialization but most dissatisfied with the provision of related services (Jones, Clatterbuck, Marquis, Turnbull, & Moberly, in press). Parents wanted more therapy than the schools

Recommendations of the National Council on Disability Regarding Placement in the Least Restrictive Alternative

1. The requirement that State and local education agencies must provide a continuum of services should be replaced with a requirement that State and local education agencies must provide an "array of support services designed to maximize the student's participation in regular education environments and activities." While it may be necessary to maintain many of the current features of the "continuum" as a transition to a "supports and services" orientation takes place, and it may be the case that a relatively small number of students might continue in substantially separate placements (e.g., deaf students), the requirement that a wide array of supports and services be available in regular school buildings will better address the intent of IDEA and other legislation in eventually reducing the number of more restrictive placements.

2. Removal of a student with a disability from the regular education environment should be documented with a written report attached to the student's IEP. The written report should include: a statement of the supplementary aids and services considered, but rejected, by the IEP team; a statement of the reasons why the supplementary aids and services are not capable of assisting the child within the regular education setting; and a statement as to when appropriate supplementary aids and services will be made available to transition the student back to the regular education environment.

3. The IEP for any child with a disability who is to remain in the regular education setting should list necessary aids and services with the same specificity as the listing of necessary related services, including the time and frequency of delivery of such aids and services.

Source: From National Council on Disability. (1995). *Improving the implementation of the Individuals with Disabilities Education Act: Making schools work for all of America's children.* Washington, DC: Author.

were providing, and they had expectations different from the schools' concerning school responsibility for providing related services.

The IFSP/IEP must specify the nature of the services to be provided and the amount of time devoted to each. Committee members may choose among a variety of service delivery models, including consultation to general education teachers, provision of therapy within general education classrooms, and pull-out services—that is, working with students in a one-to-one arrangement or in small groups (Rainforth, York, & Macdonald, 1992). School systems also can develop cooperative agreements with private related service providers or other school districts.

A key consideration for families is to ensure that the related services are provided at no cost to parents (Rogers, 1994). When the IFSP/IEP committee agrees that a related service is necessary, the school is responsible for the full cost of the related service even if the school does not provide it and must obtain it from a private agency. In some instances, related services might be reimbursable by the family's insurance provider. Many insurance policies provide coverage for medically related services such as physical therapy, occupational therapy, and speech therapy. Parents' insurance may be

used to pay for related services, at the parents' option. The school district may not require parents to use their insurance to pay for related services. If, however, parents choose to obtain related services that are not part of the IFSP/IEP, they are responsible for paying for them and should use any available insurance.

A student's educational needs should be the only basis for determining which services are needed and the amount of service. If you find yourself in conferences in which school personnel are trying to avoid their responsibility for related services, we encourage you to ask yourself, What would you want school personnel to do if you were the student's parents? The bottom line for you to remember is that the student's needs are the primary consideration, not the availability or cost of related services.

Summarizing and Concluding

The concluding portion of the conference should synthesize recommendations and develop an action plan for follow-up responsibility as specified in box 12–2. As the conference concludes, it is especially important for the participants to acknowledge and affirm the value of the family's and each other's contributions, express great expectations for ongoing collaboration in implementing the IEP or IFSP, and encourage the family to contact the other members with any follow-up questions or suggestions. The suggestions in box 12–2 will help the team reach closure and identify next steps. A goal is to end the conference with the recognition that the reliable alliance is stronger and that there is an enhanced appreciation for the likelihood of getting what is wanted and needed (empowerment) through collaboration.

Linking Our Themes

Creating a Reliable Alliance

By now you are becoming well prepared to infuse the eight obligations of a reliable alliance into each part-

nership opportunity. As you collaborate with families to individualize for an appropriate education, we encourage you to do what you have learned to do on all previous opportunities for partnerships: to develop the values, knowledge, and skills to build a reliable alliance with families. Figure 12–5 summarizes tips for how you can do just that.

Strengthening Family Factors

In the four previous chapters on developing partnerships with families, you have learned a myriad of ways to enhance family empowerment. In the partnership opportunity that we have focused on in this chapter—individualizing for appropriate education—you will have numerous additional opportunities to contribute to family empowerment. To stimulate your thinking, study figure 12–6.

FIGURE 12–5

Creating a Reliable Alliance: Disempowering and Empowering Actions

Obligations	Issues	Disempowering Actions	Empowering Actions
Knowing yourself	You realize you do not have sufficient time to listen to families.	Ask only close-ended questions that can be answered quickly.	Work with other school personnel to create innovative options for release time.
Knowing families			
Family Characteristics	Parents have a low educational level and find the IFSP/IEP process confusing and intimidating.	Tell the parents that it really isn't important for them to attend the conference.	Contact the PTI, ask about available resources, and brainstorm options with the parents.
Family interactions	A grandparent and mother (who has a history of chronic drug abuse) attend the conference; the grandmother criticizes her daughter and preempts her contributions.	Assume that a mother with a history of drug abuse probably does not care about her child and is not capable of making worthwhile contributions.	Reflect on the mother's strengths and let her know the positive things that she is doing or can do. Affirm the grandmother's strengths and express your desire to work together as a team.
Family functions	The parents' major priority is facilitating friendships for their child with multiple disabilities. They are very worried and sad that their child has no friends.	Inform the parents that the IFSP/IEP focuses only on pre-academic and academic skills.	Have all IFSP/IEP committee members share visions, goals, objectives, and strategies for increasing the child's social connections.

FIGURE **12-5** CONTINUED

Creating a Reliable Alliance: Disempowering and Empowering Actions

Obligations	Issues	Disempowering Actions	Empowering Actions
Family life cycle	The parents of a toddler who is reaching her third birthday are worried about leaving a specialized early intervention program and entering the early childhood program at the neighborhood public school.	Inform the parents that they'll never have it so good again and suggest that they be realistic about inclusion.	Arrange to visit preschool classrooms with the parents and share impressions about the benefits and drawbacks of each in terms of the child's preferences, great expectations, strengths, and needs.
Honoring cultural diversity	You need to develop an IEP with parents who are deaf.	Hold the IEP meeting and have the student sign for his parents.	Ask the parents in advance whom they would prefer to have as an interpreter; make necessary arrangements.
Affirming and building on family strengths	You are developing an IFSP with parents whom you believe emotionally neglect their toddler.	Scold parents in the conference for being the cause of their child's low self-esteem.	Highlight one or more positive contributions that the parents make to their child; alert them to community resources (including Parent to Parent) that provide parenting support and information.
Promoting family choices	A family wants an adolescent with mental retardation to attend a community college; you and other team members do not think it is a feasible transition goal.	Ignore family members' preferences and talk with them only about vocational training.	Contact community colleges and find out about their admission policies and accommodations for persons with disabilities.
Envisioning great expectations	A gifted student says her goal is to get a scholarship to Harvard.	Discourage the student by emphasizing the excess expense that the scholarship is unlikely to cover.	Collaborate with the student and family to research scholarship options; locate a community mentor who graduated from Harvard to provide admissions advice.
Using interpersonal comunication skills	You are working with parents who have had past negative professional interactions; they're angry.	Tell parents that you are not the one who committed past mistakes, and you do not appreciate their taking it out on you.	Listen empathetically to their experiences; invite suggestions on making the IEP conference as supportive as possible.
Warranting trust and respect	A family shares concerns during the IEP conference about their child's sexuality.	Confront the student and probe for more information.	Obtain sexuality information, curriculum guides, and community resources and review them with the family and student.

FIGURE 12-6

Strengthening Family Factors Through an Empowering Context: Individualizing for Appropriate Education

Motivation	What Team Members Can Do	Knowledge/Skills	What Team Members Can Do
Self-efficacy	Point out to participants their contributions in IFSP/IEP conferences that are especially helpful to other team members.	Information	Brainstorm about services after high school and encourage participants to visit future options before making career-education decisions.
Perceived control	Listen to each participant's preferences regarding goals, objectives, placement, and related services and ensure that their priorities are incorporated into the IFSP/IEP.	Problem solving	Brainstorm about helpful supplementary aids and related services in inclusive settings.
Hope	Incorporate great expectations into the IFSP/IEP discussion and ensure that goals and objectives are providing the foundation for accomplishing great expectations.	Coping skills	Encourage participants to network with others who have had empowering IFSP/IEP meetings and to get their suggestions.
Energy	Ensure that IFSP/IEP meetings are energizing rather than draining by having comfortable communication, highlighting progress, serving snacks, and respecting participants' time frames.	Communication skills	Encourage the facilitator to summarize the most important next steps that should be taken based the participants' consensus.
Persistence	If any participant is dissatisfied with the recommended plan for related services, do not finalize the IFSP/IEP until exploring satisfactory options.		

Summary

It is by no means easy to individualize for a student's appropriate education, but neither is it terribly difficult. First, there is the team's commitment—commitment to the student, to the concept of teaming and collaboration, and to bringing the eight opportunities for a reliable alliance to bear on the opportunity to develop a partnership through individualizing. Within this commitment, there is a strong affective element. Lisa Lieberman and Craig Ackerson refer to this element as "getting behind people's roles." We call it "getting to know families"—and letting families get to know you. That's part and parcel of collaboration for empowerment.

Second, there is the team's adherence to process—following the logical steps of preparing; connecting and getting started; sharing visions and great expectations; reviewing the nondiscriminatory evaluation and using it as a springboard to delivering services; sharing resources, priorities, and concerns; developing goals and objectives; specifying placement and related services; and summarizing and concluding.

Is it possible to create a reliable alliance while individualizing for an appropriate education? Yes, of course, it is, as we have suggested. Is it possible to strengthen a family, to make it more empowerful, while following the process? Yes, and we have shown how you can do just that. Predictably, individualizing for the student also involves individualizing for the team members. Some will want to be part of the team; others will not.

When Jordan was placed into a typical first-grade classroom, Lisa found that the full-time paraprofessional assigned to him was also expected to be a classroom aide; she is doing a good job of keeping him as her first priority and balancing the many demands on her. The speech-language therapist, inclusion specialist, and learning specialist who work with Jordan also are committed to collaboration.

What is disconcerting, however, is that not all members of the school faculty are equally committed to Jordan's individualized and inclusive program. Lisa is quick to point out that ensuring that the professionals implement Jordan's IEP may mean that she will have to choose her battles. Having to engage in a battle is not necessary if there can be collaboration. But battling seems inevitable unless the recalcitrant professionals begin to understand that power-with and power-from-within approaches can benefit them, too.

Giving up some control and sharing roles may come easier to some than to others. It doesn't seem right to Lisa and Craig—and indeed it makes them sad—that Jordan's success will be achieved in spite of the staff members who are unwilling to collaborate. A good guess is that it makes some other school team members feel just the same way. When, they might all wonder, will everyone finally understand that, with collaboration, nearly everything is possible?

Chapter Thirteen

Extending Learning into Home and Community

Scefenia Hill has discovered that schools are more than just buildings and programs where her children can learn. They also are contexts where she can find information and emotional support and where she can even get new pairs of shoes for her five children. It's all a matter of community outreach.

Scefenia's five children include Allen (age 5), three older children (in elementary school), and the oldest (in junior high school). Allen attended a preschool located in the neighborhood elementary school.

Because her husband commutes from their home in Lawrence to work and attend college in Kansas City, some 40 miles away, Scefenia often is the only adult in the family available to work with her children's teachers. Shouldering that kind of responsibility poses some unique problems. For example, when 4-year-old Allen was excluded from a local preschool because its staff could not handle his acting-out behaviors, Scefenia would have been stumped about what to do . . . would have been except for the School-Linked Community Services Project, a joint venture of the local school district and the University of Kansas (KU).

Operating out of the elementary school where three of Scefenia's children were enrolled, project staffers Julie Sergeant and Teresa Kopsa learned that Allen had been dismissed from preschool and why. They began to communicate with the preschool about that situation, with good results. Suspecting that Allen might have a disability or be at risk for developing one, the preschool staff then contacted Scefenia and explained that she could have Allen evaluated for free at KU. The staff also explained the advantages and disadvantages of an evaluation, and that they could arrange for the evaluation (if that is what she wanted).

Scefenia did indeed want Allen to be evaluated, but most of all she wanted him to be included in day care and school and to benefit from them. There was one big problem: She lacked access to the KU system and transportation to the evaluators there.

No problem, said Julie and Teresa. We'll arrange for the evaluation, and we'll even drive him and you to and from the evaluation. Indeed, we'll advocate for him to be included in the university's early intervention program and, if we're successful, we'll help you arrange transportation on a permanent basis. And that's exactly what happened.

The evaluators determined that Allen has an emotional disorder. With that information in hand, questions followed: How can we secure a successful transition into kindergarten? What kind of program would benefit him most? What school would be most suitable for him—the neighborhood school or a more distant one where the staff were more expert and the resources richer?

Those questions were not ones that Scefenia was prepared to answer on her own. Nor were the staff meetings between the KU teachers and the public school elementary teachers the sort of meetings that Scefenia felt comfortable attending on her own.

Her reliable allies, providing her with information, emotional support, and physical presence at two meetings, were Julie and Teresa. Five KU and school professionals, Scefenia and her husband, and Julie and Teresa met twice, developed an individualized plan for Allen, agreed on his placement in the resource-rich school, and arranged for his transportation to it.

More than that, when Allen's teachers at his new school proposed, after he had attended for several weeks, to change his placement because he was acting out so much, Scefenia turned once again to Julie and Teresa for help. They had taken notes of the meetings involving Allen's family and the schools; the notes showed that Allen's teachers had promised to provide him with full-day kindergarten services as part of an intensive intervention. When they proposed to provide only half-day services, Julie and Teresa were able to remind them of their commitment.

Allies, Scefenia learned, do more than help hold people accountable. They also help a family meet its very basic needs, such as having funds to buy shoes for the children. Scefenia had transferred jobs, from the local police department to a federal-loan processing company; the transfer had impaired her earnings for a while. Her husband had enrolled in a junior college some 40 miles away; he was paying tuition and incurring transportation costs. And winter was on its way.

At New York Elementary School, where Allen's siblings are enrolled and where the outreach project has its offices, the students and parents have access to a fund to help families. One aspect of the fund is the clothing voucher program. When Scefenia called the "parent room" at the school after she let Julie and Teresa know that her children needed shoes, it was not long before the vouchers were in her hands and her children were wearing new shoes.

Allies don't draw boundaries. And school-linked community service projects don't, either. As Julie and Teresa make clear, their project acts to make goals come true—the goals of supporting families by following families' preferences and needs and of doing that through collaboration among families, students, school, and community.

The partnership of extending students' learning into their homes and communities involves building links among the many activities and environments in which students participate. Figure 13–1 reminds you how the partnership focus of this chapter—extending learning into home and community—relates to the overall empowerment process.

Given the special challenges of giftedness or disability, it makes sense for students to benefit from integrated and comprehensive opportunities for learning in school, home, and community. Their progress in achieving educational outcomes should not depend wholly on their six-hour school day. This is particularly true for students with cognitive challenges because they usually have difficulty generalizing what they learn at school to home and community settings. (In chapter 7, we emphasized the importance of collaborating with recreational and leisure-time service providers, and in chapter 8 we emphasized giving students opportunities for a variety of job experiences. Both chapters relate to extending learning beyond school.)

Collaborating to Extend Learning into Home and Community

Four opportunities to extend learning, which are the focus of this chapter, involve (1) school-linked comprehensive services, (2) homework, (3) inclusion for students with behavior problems, and (4) Group Action Planning.

School-linked Comprehensive Services

School-linked comprehensive services (also referred to as family-focused services or comprehensive school-based services) coordinate and deliver comprehensive services to the child and family, including (1) governmental (education, social services, mental health, juvenile justice), (2) community (child care, recreation, special interests), and (3) private (volunteer organizations such as Big Brother/Big Sister, scouts, and special interest clubs). They use a single point of contact, make

funding arrangements cohesive, and thereby increase the likelihood that children and their families will achieve desired outcomes. In Lawrence, Kansas, for example, school-linked services have helped Scefenia Hill and her family handle the challenges of inclusion in a governmental program (public kindergarten), access to community services (the KU early intervention program), and private services (the clothing voucher program). As we said in chapter 2, the school-linked comprehensive services model has been a significant element of school reform, especially in general education (Crowson & Boyd, 1993; Kagan & Neville, 1993a, 1993b). Moreover, the status of American families makes this model especially compelling. The following bulleted facts are from *The State of America's Children Yearbook 1995* (Washington, DC: Children's Defense Fund, 1995, pp. 21, 28, 49, 55, 64, 75, and 82) and are used by permission of the publisher:

- Young families with children have suffered an economic freefall over the past two decades. Half of the nation's six million young families lived on less than $18,420 in 1992.
- More than 9.4 million children were without health insurance in 1993, an increase of more than 800,000 from 1992.
- Millions of poor children who benefit from free or reduced-price school lunches are not being served by the school breakfast or summer food service programs.
- Guns claimed the lives of more than 5,000 children in 1992. Tens of thousands more were injured or scarred emotionally by gun violence.
- One in four homeless persons is a child younger than 18.
- High poverty neighborhoods lack the supports and resources to help families foster their children's healthy development.
- Only three in five teen mothers received early prenatal care in 1992; one in 10 received late or no prenatal care.
- Illegal drug and alcohol use increased among teens between 1992 and 1993.

FIGURE 13–1

Empowerment Framework: Collaborating for Empowerment

Family Factors:
It's Within Us to Be Empowerful

Collaborating for Empowerment:
Through Collaboration, We Act Empowerfully

Education Context Factors:
It's Within Us to Make Our Contexts Empowering

Motivation	Knowledge/Skills	Opportunities for Partnerships — *Opportunities arise when . . .*	Obligations for Reliable Alliances — *Reliable alliances consist of . . .*
Self-efficacy: believing in our capabilities	*Information:* being in the know	Communicating among reliable allies	Knowing yourself
Perceived control: believing we can apply our capabilities to affect what happens to us	*Problem solving:* knowing how to bust the barriers	Meeting families' basic needs	Knowing families
			Honoring cultural diversity
Hope: believing we will get what we want and need	*Coping skills:* knowing how to handle what happens to us	Referring and evaluating for special education	Affirming family strengths
Energy: lighting the fire and keeping it burning	*Communication skills:* being on the sending and receiving ends of expressed needs and wants	Individualizing for appropriate education	Promoting family choices
			Envisioning great expectations
Persistence: putting forth a sustained effort		Extending learning in home and community	Communicating positively
		Attending and volunteering at school	Warranting trust and respect
		Advocating for systems improvement	

Extending Learning into Home and Community 253

To combat these problems, school-linked comprehensive services consolidate community services and supports. For example, at the Watts/Jordan School-Based Clinic at Jordan High School in Los Angeles, physical and mental health services include a year-round clinic that provides immunizations, treatment for common illnesses, referral and follow-up for serious illnesses, health education regarding pregnancy and sexually transmitted diseases, and mental health counseling. A 10-day violence prevention curriculum is mandatory for all ninth-grade students, and prisoners visit the school to talk with the students about violence prevention. Entertainment options, such as movies and outings to sporting events, museums, and parks, are available for students who maintain passing grades (Sheffield, 1994).

Similarly, at the Fienberg-Fisher Elementary School in Miami Beach, Florida, there are service links among schools, police, the chamber of commerce, the mayor's office, a local university, health services, and volunteer agencies (Alameda, 1993–1994). The school serves a community whose families represent 46 nationalities, approximately 80 percent of whom are Latino. During its first two years of operation, the school-linked comprehensive services program developed a family bill of rights, made home visits to families, developed the Homework Club for after-school tutoring, provided meals for senior citizens, provided housing and transportation assistance, mobilized the parent Absenteeism Home Intervention Team to support children in walking to school and to serve as volunteer "lice busters," and supported parents to develop the Resource Information and Referral Network (RAIN). Parent volunteers, referred to as RAINMAKERS, assist families in problem solving and accessing community services such as Medicaid and food stamps. The RAINMAKERS receive 40 hours of training and a small stipend of $40 weekly for eight hours of work per week.

School-linked comprehensive services also are making a difference at Community Elementary School No. 11 in the southwest Bronx in New York City (Brown, 1993–1994). The neighborhood is located in one of the poorest congressional districts in the United States and has three times the citywide average number of children per square mile. In 1991, the school's MOSAIC (Maximizing Opportunity, Service & Action in the Community) Center began to offer the following free activities to the school's 3,000 members and their families:

> classes in GED, conversational English, Afro-Brazilian dance and aerobics, nutrition, and art and crafts; support groups and parent education; a youth education/training program, test preparation for training and jobs, and a Job Bank; AIDS prevention training for women; an after-school program with hot meals; a food cooperative; a chorus; and a competitive cheerleading team. Other special activities at MOSAIC have included sponsoring a City Volunteer Corps team, Summer Youth Employment Program registration and work team, a community garden, holiday celebrations, and award ceremonies for children and volunteers. (Brown, 1993–1994, p. 39)

Starting in 1991, New York City began its Beacons initiative in each of the city's 32 community school districts. Under the Beacons program, a single agency coordinates an advisory council comprised of neighborhood youth, parents, school personnel, community school boards, and local service providers. These councils have increased the hours that schools are open by 300 percent, including evenings, weekends, vacations, and holidays. Box 13–1 depicts Beacons' day and evening activities. In the words of one Beacon's parent:

> When you put up a flyer for a program, people may look at it and then continue on. But when the program is right there—in the school where they bring their children every day—it's easier to learn about the center's services. . . . Weekend programs are especially important since they allow working parents to get errands done knowing their children are safe. (Brown, 1993–1994, p. 40)

School-linked comprehensive services do not take hold in the community immediately, as Sonia Sanchez, assistant director of one of the Beacon programs, noted about developing reliable alliances:

> Community residents in our underserved neighborhoods are used to having new programs come in and then leave. They are not apt to trust a new program immediately, and it will take a great deal of effort to gain the trust. But if your staff gets out there in the neighborhood and explains the center's services truthfully—not making promises they can't keep—progress will be made. (Brown, 1993–1994, p. 40)

As we indicated, school-linked comprehensive services have primarily been developed in general rather than special education. A somewhat similar model in special education is referred to as wraparound services and has primarily been used with children and youth who experience emotional and behavioral disorders (Burchard, Burchard, Sewell, & VanDenBerg, 1993; Eber, Wilson, Notier, & Pendell,

TOGETHER WE CAN

BOX 13-1

What's Going on in Beacons?

Activities at Beacon Centers throughout New York City

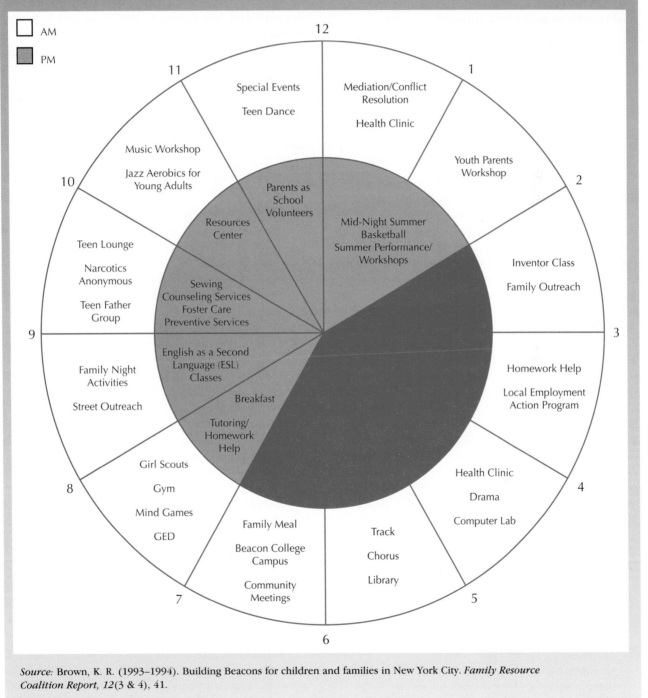

☐ AM

▨ PM

12

Special Events
Teen Dance

Mediation/Conflict Resolution
Health Clinic

11

Music Workshop
Jazz Aerobics for Young Adults

1

Youth Parents Workshop

10

Parents as School Volunteers

Resources Center

Mid-Night Summer Basketball
Summer Performance/ Workshops

2

Teen Lounge
Narcotics Anonymous
Teen Father Group

Sewing
Counseling Services
Foster Care
Preventive Services

Inventor Class
Family Outreach

9

English as a Second Language (ESL) Classes

3

Family Night Activities
Street Outreach

Breakfast

Homework Help
Local Employment Action Program

Tutoring/ Homework Help

Girl Scouts
Gym
Mind Games
GED

Family Meal
Beacon College Campus
Community Meetings

Track
Chorus
Library

Health Clinic
Drama
Computer Lab

8

4

7

5

6

Source: Brown, K. R. (1993–1994). Building Beacons for children and families in New York City. *Family Resource Coalition Report, 12*(3 & 4), 41.

1994). One of the first programs to use wraparound services is a Chicago child welfare agency, Kaleidoscope, which is a joint effort to combine education, mental health, corrections, child welfare, and family services (Goetz, 1994). More than 20 years ago the agency began to develop alternatives for children and youth with emotional and behavioral disorders who have been institutionalized and are returning to the community. Kaleidoscope's executive director, Karl Dennis, describes the services:

> All good services should include a wrap-around component. . . . All too often, services are not flexible, due to an allegiance to a particular model of service delivery or because funding sources allow only limited interventions. Wrap-around intervention dictates that "whatever works" should be the model and that unconditional care or never giving up on the child should be the philosophy. (Goetz, 1994, pp. 20–21)

Moving wraparound services from child welfare, school districts are beginning to adopt this approach, especially in facilitating inclusion of students with emotional and behavioral disorders. In the La Grange Area Department of Special Education outside of Chicago, the school-based wraparound model offers creative and personalized services by (1) having social workers serve as family service facilitators to broker services within the school and outside the school in the community; (2) having mobile team teachers provide support to special and general education teachers to allow planning time and co-teaching; (3) having teacher assistants who can move around the school, increase information sharing among team members, and coordinate a peer support plan; and (4) facilitating the involvement of students in sports and extracurricular activities (Eber, 1994). Due to the extremely high percentage of students with serious emotional and behavior disorders who are in restricted settings (Koyanagi & Gaines, 1993), have experienced failing grades (Chesapeake Institute, 1994), and have disappointing adult outcomes with postsecondary education and employment (McLaughlin, Leone, Warren, & Schofield, 1994), the need for coordinated, integrated, and comprehensive services for this population of students is especially critical. Although different terms are used (wraparound services and school-linked comprehensive services), the bottom line of both these service models is service integration:

> An ultimate goal of service integration is to have a single, comprehensive individual service plan for a child and his or her family. The plan will identify

the goals or outcomes to be achieved, the services to be provided in reaching these goals, and the agencies or persons responsible for delivering these services. This integrated plan is a working document that guides the activities of all providers and family members. All individuals and agencies are accountable to this plan. (McLaughlin et al., 1994, p. 53)

Service integration can take many forms. For Scefenia Hill, her youngest son Allen, and her other children, integration occurred when a university/public school joint collaboration successfully addressed Allen's needs and Scefenia's preferences, merging the university's capacities with the school system's and the family's in order to benefit the family as a whole and Allen in particular.

What differences do school-linked comprehensive services make? Research evidence is still preliminary, but national research conference participants reached consensus on the following points (U.S. Department of Education & American Education Research Association, 1995, pp. 15–16):

- School-linked comprehensive services are not new, but their diversity and rapid growth are.
- Reliable, validated information about school-linked comprehensive services is scanty at best; and new evaluation approaches that are culturally sensitive, family-centered, and sufficiently long term to measure results, are needed.
- What is known about school-linked collaborative services tends to be positive in that the most successful collaborative services are cost-effective, empowering, culturally sensitive, and well integrated into communities.
- The purpose of school-linked collaborative services is to make existing services more flexible and create among them a mutual vision about the well-being of children, youth, and families.
- Leadership for school-linked collaborative services is essential, yet many of the leaders do not have a background in collaborative efforts and often do not have sufficient time for professional development.
- School-linked collaborative services are built on fragile, insufficient, and inconsistent financial foundations. Moreover, different funding sources often lead to "turf" problems and barriers to collaboration.

Like family support services (chapter 10), school-linked comprehensive services expand the array of services and supports for families and children, emphasizing a power-with and power-from-within approach as contrasted to a power-over orientation (Kagan & Neville, 1993a, 1993b; Melaville & Blank, 1993; Sailor, 1996). There are, however, important fundamental differences between family support and school-linked services, as figure 13–2 shows.

*H*omework

Traditionally, homework has been one of the activities that families, students, and schools have shared most usually and most often. In a study of the involvement of parents of gifted and talented children, the type of involvement (of 27 possible involvement options) practiced by the highest percentage of parents—59 percent in New York City and 49 percent in Cleveland—was checking and signing homework (Chapley, Trimarco, Crisci, & Capobianco, 1986–1987). As you learned in chapter 2, school reform efforts to ensure excellence by raising curriculum standards have raised expectations for homework as a strategy to enhance student performance (U.S. Department of Education, 1990). Nonetheless, special education teacher training programs seem to disregard the positive outcomes of homework in building a home-school partnership. A review of five

of the most commonly used curriculum and methods texts for special education teachers reported that only one discusses homework (Epstein, Polloway, Foley, & Patton, 1993).

Does homework have a positive effect on the academic achievement of students? It is difficult to answer this question definitely, given the current research base. Some people suggest that homework is primarily beneficial at the secondary level (Cooper, 1989a, 1989b), but others suggest that homework is beneficial across elementary and secondary education (Wahlberg, Paschal, & Weinstein, 1985).

Generally, homework does have a desirable effect on school achievement for students with mild disabilities; there has been only limited research on the role of homework for students with severe disabilities, particularly those who are in inclusive settings (Epstein et al., 1993). Often students with exceptionalities have more problems with homework than classmates who do not have special needs (Epstein et al., 1993; Gajria & Salend, 1995; Polloway, Epstein, & Foley, 1992; Salend & Schiff, 1989). For example, adolescents with behavior disorders have far more significant homework problems (for example, failing to bring home assignment materials, denying they

---

FIGURE 13–2

Differences Between Family Support and School–Linked Comprehensive Services

Family Support Programs	School-Linked Services
1. Programs are initiated through the disability service system.	1. Services are initiated through general education reform.
2. Eligibility requirements focus on disability categories, particularly developmental disability.	2. Services are available to students with and without exceptionalities.
3. Services often begin with legislation and the creation of new programs for service delivery.	3. Services begin by coordinating existing programs through already-funded bureaucracies and programs.
4. Primary service component is the availability of cash subsidies.	4. Primary service component is a program option rather than cash.
5. Primary emphasis is on serving the family as a whole, including the child.	5. Primary emphasis is on serving the child, and services are provided to the family in order to benefit the child.

Source: Adapted from Kagan, F. L., & Neville, P. R. (1993–1994). Family support and school-linked services: Variations on a theme. *Family Resource Coalition Report, 3 & 4,* 4–6.

have homework, producing sloppier homework, responding poorly when told by parents to correct homework) than their classmates without disabilities (Soderlund, Bursuck, Polloway, & Foley, 1995). Moreover, 50 percent of teachers of students with learning disabilities have reported that they do not discuss, review, and regularly grade homework assignments (Salend & Schiff, 1989).

In this section we will discuss (1) family concerns about homework and (2) suggestions for homework collaboration.

Family Concerns about Homework

Parents of students with mild disabilities often raise the following concerns (Kay, Fitzgerald, Paradee, & Mellencamp, 1994):

- They feel inadequate to help their children with homework.
- They want more information about the classroom teacher's expectations and approach to homework.
- They want homework to be individualized and to respect student and family needs.
- They prefer experiential homework related to life skills.
- They want comprehensive, two-way communication.

Parents Feel Inadequate

Parents may feel inadequate for three reasons: (1) changes in instructional methods since they were students, (2) a lack of information about what is being taught at school, and (3) their belief that specialized training is needed for them to be able to help their children.

If I could actually see once in a while how they're teaching him, then it might spill over into how I could do it at home. . . . When it comes to teaching my child, I feel like times have changed since I was in school, and I hate to teach him wrong. (Kay et al., 1994, p. 555)

Parents Want More Information about a Teacher's Homework Expectations

Parents' concerns center around (1) end-of-the-year expectations, (2) a teacher's expectations for parents' roles and contributions, and (3) ensuring consistency and structure between home and school. Their ambiguity about expectations causes them to worry that they will do the wrong thing.

Last year with my son I was told by the teacher that I could help him with math. This year I don't know if I can help with math so I am very hesitant to help or correct. I want to show him the right way, but how much should I be helping or pushing him? I need clarification from the teacher on what she expects. (Kay et al., 1994, p. 555)

Homework Assignments Should Respect Family Needs

Box 13–2 includes diary entries of a parent, Connie, who has a family that includes three sons: David (eighth grade), Fred (fourth grade), and Ethan (third grade). The log entries focus on issues associated with Fred's homework. At age 10, Fred was receiving services for students who have an IQ of 76 or less or whose performance falls $1\frac{1}{2}$ standard deviations below the norm on standardized aptitude and achievement tests. He spent 80 percent of his time in a general education fourth-grade classroom and

MY VOICE
BOX 13–2

Homework Concerns

9/10: [He had four subjects for homework.] Fred didn't want to read today. The math seemed way over his head, even after I tried to explain it. I still feel that Fred brings home some inappropriate homework for his level. I think this is discouraging for him.

9/24: I am feeling swamped with the homework. Even though each subject takes a reasonable amount of time, I feel the total time spent on homework is too much....I wonder how other fourth grade parents feel.

9/30: Fred seems to be forgetting homework lately. I can't seem to figure out if he is really forgetting it, or if he is sick of doing it and is doing this on purpose.

Source: From "Making Homework Work at Home: The Parent's Perspective" by P. J. Kay, M. Fitzgerald, C. Paradee, and A. Mellencamp, 1994, *Journal of Learning Disabilities, 27*, pp. 550–561. Copyright ©1994 by PRO-ED, Inc. Reprinted by permission.

received direct special education services within the classroom in a small group setting and reading instruction in a resource room. His homework was assigned by his general classroom teacher.

Consider Connie's perspectives. What would your response be to these homework issues? What kind of partnership would you want to establish with the teacher to alleviate some of these concerns? Think back to chapters 6 and 7 on family interaction and functions. What impact do homework and stress associated with homework have on parental and sibling interactions? What spillover might there be to marital and extended family interactions? What impact does this situation have on family functions? If Connie spends more time on the family function of education by assisting Fred with his homework, what is the impact on other family functions? Has the teacher tried to individualize homework assignments, considering that what may be easy for one student is difficult for another?

Parents Prefer Experiential Homework Related to Life Skills

Parents prefer hands-on, practical homework that involves project activities rather than paper-and-pencil tasks. Contrast Connie's perspectives in box 13–2 with her perspectives about the benefit of experiential homework, described in box 13–3.

Compare both "My Voice" figures. What differences are evident in Fred's motivation? What differences are evident in the family support available to Fred? One thing that is particularly interesting to note is the number of times that "I" is used in box 13–2 and the number of times that "Fred" is used in box 13–3. In which instance do both Fred and Connie appear to be more empowered?

Parents Want Communication

Parents like many of the communication strategies you learned about in chapter 9, including telephone calls, written notes, and dialogue journals (which they find useful because journals have specific information about homework assignments).

Suggestions for Homework Collaboration

Educators and families have communication problems pertaining to homework (Epstein, 1987; Jayanthi, Sawyer, Nelson, Bursuck, & Epstein, 1995). Yet there are at least five ways to enhance homework collaboration (Jayanthi et al., 1995):

- Create more opportunities for parents, general education teachers, and special education teachers to communicate with each other.
- Provide increased information on a regular basis in individualized formats.
- Overcome attitudinal and ability barriers through positive communication.
- Minimize family responsibility for homework.
- Provide a potpourri of ideas to improve practice.

MY VOICE
BOX 13-3

Experiential Homework

9/8: [Dad helped him with social studies.] He had to cut and glue pieces on the map and study it. Fred really enjoys working on his map. It is usually the first homework he does each night and he looks back and relocates each country he has done before.

2/1: Fred had a great day! He finished his project before anyone else. He made an animal of the rain forest out of papier-mâché and then had to tell about the animal.

5/14: [Fred spent $1\frac{1}{2}$ hours making a miniature of his bedroom, based on a book that the classroom teacher was reading to the class.] Fred really enjoyed creating his bedroom. We brainstormed together how the bedroom should look and what materials to use. It was one of the best homework assignments I have seen this year.

5/17: Fred came home excited, because Mrs. K. really liked the bedroom. She had the whole class go over to his desk to admire it. It made his whole day.

Source: From "Making Homework Work at Home: The Parent's Perspective" by P. J. Kay, M. Fitzgerald, C. Paradee, and A. Mellencamp, 1994, *Journal of Learning Disabilities, 27,* pp. 550–561. Copyright ©1994 by PRO-ED, Inc. Reprinted by permission.

Create Communication Opportunities

Lack of time and communication opportunities present major challenges for both families and educators. Box 13–4 includes tips for overcoming challenges and incorporates what you learned in chapter 9 about communication strategies.

As you review box 13–4, consider what you learned in chapter 9 and the suggestion about answering machines. Listen to what a single mother says about how helpful an answering machine might be in exchanging information related to homework:

> I am a single parent. I work all day long. By the time I ever get home, the teachers are gone. Why couldn't there be some sort of an answering machine at the school, so [that I could] dial this number to leave a message for the math teachers [and] dial this number for the English teachers. Answering machines are cheap. I have an answering machine. [The teachers] could probably answer me back and that might solve [these communication problems]. (Jayanthi et al., 1995, p. 217)

The point is that the communication skills and strategies we discussed in chapter 9 can enhance homework collaboration.

Providing Increased Information on a Regular Basis in Individualized Formats

Many families would like to have more information about the best way to contact teachers:

> I have a very hard time catching these teachers. I would like to know at the beginning of the year what are the break hours for each teacher, I could call them during that time period instead of [the officer workers] always telling me [that the teacher] is in class. (Jayanthi et al., 1995, p. 217)

Here are some suggestions for providing increased information (Jayanthi et al., 1995):

- Provide parents with teachers' names and their preferred times and methods for being contacted.
- Increase communication among all teachers to avoid homework overload and increase the likelihood of consistent homework modifications.
- Ensure that general education teachers have access to information on student preferences, strengths, and needs related to accommodation.
- Ask families and educators to share their expectations with each other and agree on the consequences for incomplete homework.

Overcome Attitudes and Ability Barriers through Positive Communication

The issue here is how to make home-school communication positive and support the student to be responsible for doing homework. Although research has not documented that homework enhances academic achievement of elementary students, it does seem to develop students' study habits (Cooper, 1989a, 1989b). In this respect, the student's role of being accountable takes on special significance. To enhance collaboration related to a student's attitudinal and ability barriers:

- Ensure positive communication among families, general educators, and special educators on the contribution each makes to increasing a student's completion of homework.
- Put students into this communication loop and encourage and reward them to take more responsibility for keeping track of their own homework.

Create Options for Minimizing Family Responsibility for Homework

Sometimes it may be advantageous to consider options for a student to complete homework outside the family setting, as one special education teacher pointed out:

> I have a situation where the mom cannot read and the girl wants to do her homework. She cannot help, so I modify her assignments. If I have a parent that either cannot read or chooses not to read, I take the responsibility on myself and modify things, so that the child can feel successful, feel like they are doing homework. (Jayanthi et al., 1995, p. 221)

Another teacher emphasized the importance of considering community resources: "Another thing might be having copies of major assignments, research projects, and all of that in your local library, so that the parents have a way to see those, because the libraries are open until 10 o'clock at night" (Jayanthi et al., 1995, p. 221).

Other options include the following (Jayanthi et al., 1995):

- Teachers provide less homework, particularly on weekends.
- Schools provide more supervised study halls and after-school sessions to support students in doing their homework.
- Peer tutoring and support programs enable classmates to help each other.

TIPS

BOX 13-4

Time and Opportunity

Recommendations:	Parents said:	General education teachers (GED) said:	Special education teachers (SPED) said:
Use technology for improving:			
• Parent/student access to homework.	Put assignments on audiotape so that parents can access them by phone.	Use homework hotlines, answering machines, and computer networks.	Use homework hotlines, PCs in homes linked to school's computer.
• Exchange of messages between home and school.	Use answering machines and electronic mail.	Use electronic mail.	Provide a telephone in every classroom, FAX machines in homes.
• Parent access to student performance.		Provide computer-generated progress reports for parents.	
Change teacher schedules, office locations to facilitate communication.		Have SPED and GED offices near each other to facilitate informal, short, and frequent meetings. Schedule common planning periods for GED and SPED and/or add additional period to school day.	SPED offices should be accessible to GED. Schedule common planning times for GED and SPED. Give teachers a communication period in addition to a planning period.
Provide opportunities for communication in the evening.	Hold conferences in the evenings for working parents.		Hold conferences in the evenings to facilitate parent attendance.
Provide release time or additional pay for teachers.		Provide release time regularly for teachers to communicate with each other, with parents, and with students. Pay teachers to come early or on Saturdays.	Provide release time to teachers via substitutes or pay stipends for additional time.
Provide more staff time (other than teachers).		Ask aides and guidance counselors to monitor students in mainstream classes and communicate with parents.	Provide an aide in every mainstream class to improve communication. Increase clerical help for SPED.
Other.	Call teachers early in the morning so that they can call back the same day.	Limit number of mainstreamed students in any given class. Establish drop-in times for parents without phones, and utilize occasions and locations outside of school to communicate (e.g., home visits, neighborhood coffees, extracurricular activities).	Ask SPED to meet with their students at least one class period daily. Give special support to GED with 5 or more mainstreamed students.

Source: From "Recommendations for Homework-Communication Problems" by M. Jayanthi, V. Sawyer, J. S. Nelson, W. D. Bursuck, & M. H. Epstein, 1995, *Remedial and Special Education, 16*, pp. 212–225. Copyright ©1995 by PRO-ED, Inc. Reprinted by permission.

- Senior citizens volunteer to be in study hall or after-school sessions as homework aides.

Provide a Potpourri of Ideas to Improve Practice

Here is a broad range of other ideas (Jayanthi et al., 1995):

- Encourage families to designate a study area and regular study time at home.
- Develop a regular routine for giving assignments and be consistent about when and how information is given (for example, assignments always written on the board in the same place and at the same time).
- Develop a schoolwide policy on homework and consider providing incentives to teachers who create individualized adaptations.
- Ensure that homework expectations and modifications are discussed in the IEP meeting and incorporated into the IEP document.

When students have special learning challenges and needs, consider the impact on the parent-child relationship of expecting a parent to help the child with homework or teach specific objectives at home. Some parents may experience stress when working with their child at home, and this pressure may escalate when the child with a disability is in a general education rather than special education setting.

There are comparable concerns with early childhood services. Working with children on developmental outcomes (often called home teaching instead of homework) still requires families to devote substantial time to accomplishing educational objectives. Judy O'Halloran looks back on the time when her son Casey was in early intervention: "I could get really angry thinking about how early intervention intruded into our lives. Until he was eight, Casey never had a bath that wasn't an educational experience" (Turnbull, 1993, p. 2).

In chapter 7 we discussed the importance of the family's role in supporting the child to develop positive self-esteem. Simply stated, you should be cautious about the downside of home teaching and homework: Home can be a second school.

For example, one research study reported that mothers' teaching interaction with their children with learning disabilities tends to be more adult-centered and does not incorporate much encouragement or negotiation. The students apparently participated in learning tasks out of a sense of obligation rather than internal motivation. When compared to students who did not have disabilities and who were working with their mothers, the students with learning disabilities did not cooperate as much (Lyytinen, Rasku-Puttonen, Poikkeus, Laakso, & Ahonen, 1994).

What are the possible implications for the mother-child relationship? Given that students with disabilities often experience learning challenges, interactions based on parent teaching may not be as satisfying and may be more stressful than those between parents and children with typical learning characteristics. Clearly, individual variations exist: Some parents do extremely well when working with their child at home, and others find it highly stressful. To create a responsive context around homework issues, you will need to individualize your approach for each family.

Inclusion for Students with Problem Behaviors

Students with problem behaviors present certain idiosyncratic challenges:

- Students with problem behaviors are least likely to be successful in general education settings (Horner, Diemer, & Brazeau, 1992; SRI International, 1990; U.S. Department of Education, 1992).
- Students' problem behaviors are the key factors contributing to teacher attrition among special and general education teachers (Billingsley, 1993; Billingsley & Cross, 1991).
- Teachers have identified support related to problem behaviors as a critical staff development need (Bulgatz & O'Neill, 1994; Horner et al., 1992).

Supporting these students in home and community settings is also an area where more collaboration is needed. There are problems, represented by Scefenia's efforts on behalf of her son Allen, in simply getting an evaluation, translating its findings into an appropriate program, and ensuring that the program is carried out. There are additional problems when families face economic difficulties, as Scefenia did. Sadly, Scefenia is not alone in needing a collaborative team to support Allen's education in a community setting and his development in his home. Seventeen families, each of whom has a child with severe problem behaviors, characterized problem behaviors into two major categories—dangerous and difficult behaviors (Turnbull & Ruef, in press). Within those two categories, they described challenges related to their son's or daughter's behavior and challenges related to their own and others' perceptions about the dangerous and difficult behavior (such as fear, worry, concern, embarrassment, and annoyance).

Figure 13–3 summarizes family perspectives on how they characterize problem behavior.

Interestingly, even though the behavior problems were often episodic, family fear and worry about their occurrence frequently resulted in families' restricting their activity every day, throughout the day, to ensure that the behavior would not occur. Clearly, the extent of actual observable behavior does not correspond fully with the impact on the family in terms of worrying about the behavior in schools, home, and community settings. Rather, it is families' perception of problem behavior that impairs their activities. This suggests that community members should know more about students' needs and appropriate interventions (Koegel, Koegel, & Dunlap, 1996). One parent said:

> Parents are overloaded with responsibilities. I don't even think educating the community will happen if it is left up to the parents. It is possible that I might be able to get it done here on my own. It would make more sense for schools to address these problems as a transition issue. . . . It's a job in and of itself. . . . We need to have a team whose job it is to educate the local social services personnel, the local medical community, the local retailers. It's too big of a job for most lay people or families. (Turnbull & Ruef, in press)

Positive behavioral support is an effective intervention for students with problem behaviors. It is a value- and data-based approach that views the "problem" as typically residing in the failure to provide personalized and comprehensive supports and services. Its goal is not a single-shot intervention directed at the student but the development of a system for supporting the student to "get a life" in the school, home, and community by achieving comprehensive life-style changes (Risley, 1995; Turnbull & Turnbull, 1996):

> The positive/nonaversive approach focuses on the lifestyle of the individual, in addition to the frequency, duration, and intensity of the challenging behaviors (Horner, Dunlap, & Koegel, 1988). Behavioral support should result in durable, generalized changes in how an individual behaves, and these changes should affect an individual's access to community settings, social contacts, and to a greater array of preferred events. Among the most important issues for technology of behavioral support is recognition that the standard scores assessing "success" are changing. (Horner, Dunlap, Koegel, Carr, Sailor, Anderson, Albin, & O'Neill, 1990, p. 127)

In the previous extract, note Horner and associates' emphasis on outcomes related to community

---

FIGURE 13–3

Families' Definition of Problem Behavior

	Dangerous Behaviors	Difficult Behaviors
Observable Behaviors	"He broke the windshield out of the car recently—this is one of his high skill areas."	"When I am around him it is constant noise. He talks or squawks. By afternoon I am frazzled."
Family Perceptions	Fear/Worry: "Our greatest fear is that she will do something so awful that she will be locked up. We live in fear of that."	Concern/Embarrassment/Annoyance: "I am always thinking about his behavior. It is always in the back of my mind anytime we bring him anywhere."
Others' Perceptions	Fear/Worry: Teacher fears that the child will tear earring out of a classmate's ear.	Concern/Embarrassment/Annoyance: "One time I took George to the supermarket, and he kind of jumped up and down and rocked and hummed. He was laughing a lot, and a woman gave me a look. She wouldn't dare say anything, but she gave me a look almost to say, 'Why would you bring a boy like that in here?' She didn't have to say anything. Her look told it all."

Source: Turnbull, A. P., & Ruef, M. (in press). Family perspectives on problem behavior. *Mental Retardation.*

settings, social contacts, and preferred events. Supporting individuals with problem behavior and their families to "get a life" involves personalized supports to foster interdependence (friendship and other social contacts), inclusion (supported education, supported employment, and supported living), contribution (community participation and productivity), and choice (Turnbull & Turnbull, 1996). There are eight major features of positive behavioral support (Horner et al., 1990):

- Creating a vision for inclusion
- Completing a functional assessment (the function or purpose that the behavior serves for the individual)
- Organizing the environment
- Teaching new skills
- Rewarding positive behavior
- Anticipating the most dangerous situation
- Ensuring a cultural fit
- Monitoring for improvement

The Family Connection, an interuniversity collaboration involving the University of Kansas and the Research and Training Center on Positive Behavioral Support headquartered at the University of Oregon, has synthesized research literature on positive behavioral support and provides an array of relevant and easily comprehensible products for families, community members, friends, and practitioners. If you would like to have information about these products, you can contact the Family Connection at the Beach Center address in appendix A. Box 13–5 describes how we have used positive behavioral support with our son, J. T., a young man (in his late 20s) with mental retardation and autism.

Group Action Planning

Group Action Planning (the strategy we use with J. T.; see box 13–5) is a form of person-centered planning that involves creating great expectations for the future, establishing an interdependent group of committed people, and engaging in creative problem solving in order to accomplish great expectations (Turnbull & Turnbull, 1996; Turnbull, Turnbull, &

FIGURE 13–4

Comparison of Traditional and Person–Centered Planning Approaches

IEP Conferences—Traditional Planning	Group Action Planning—Person-Centered Planning
Professionally directed, unequal ratio of professionals to family members and friends	Approximately equal proportion of participants from the groups of friends, community citizens, family members, and professionals
Structured, formal process	Reflective, creative process that focuses on divergent problem solving
Regulated by mandated paperwork for monitoring compliance	Not mandated or regulated; facilitated by an individual skilled in collaborative communication
Held in professional setting (e.g., conference room)	Held in an informal setting, most often the home of family or friends
Serious atmosphere in which the focus of attention is on the student's developmental needs	Relational, fun, affirming atmosphere in which the strengths, capabilities, contributions, and dreams are the focus of attention
Meets once or twice a year	Meets regularly (usually monthly) to accomplish next steps
Developmental assessment and outcomes guide the process	Visions and relationships guide the process
Professionals and agencies are primarily responsible for implementing programs to accomplish developmental outcomes	Group members form a reliable alliance with every member, assuming responsibility for transforming visions to reality

Source: Turnbull, A. P., Turnbull, H. R., & Blue-Banning, M. J. (1994). Enhancing inclusion of infants and toddlers with disabilities and their families: A theoretical and programmatic analysis. *Infants and Young Children*, 7(2), 1–14. Copyright © 1994 Aspen Publishers, Inc.

BOX 13-5

TOGETHER WE CAN

Positive Behavioral Support

For nearly a decade, our son, J. T., had inexplicably, but only occasionally, pulled the pony-tailed hair of young women. His aggressiveness had restricted him and us in many respects; when he seemed "on the cusp" or in the iron grip of these aggressive moods, we had to closely monitor and even restrict his movement throughout the community and at his job, fearing a horrible-to contemplate scenario of criminal prosecution. Fortunately, because we used positive behavioral support, J. T. has not been aggressive at all during the last several years.

We began by trying to "stand in his shoes" and see the world from his perspective. We began to understand his aggression as insecurity and unhappiness, not hostility; and we focused on what in his world was contributing to his insecurity and unhappiness. J. T.'s vision bolstered our own—to create a life-style that J. T. truly wanted to live, a life filled with music, places to go, things to do,

and people with whom to share it all.

To organize J. T.'s environment, we withdrew him from a group home and sheltered workshop (where he had been self-injurious and aggressive to others) and planned a consistent and predictable schedule full of rich, rewarding, socially connected, and J. T.-preferred activities. We adapted his world so it would bring him the greatest sense of control and pleasure.

We taught him new skills, such as expressing in words what he wants or what troubles him, taking a "cool down" or "deep breathing" break if he gets tense, and learning to give himself verbal feedback. ("Don't talk about hair.")

We learned to identify and respond immediately to the first signals of insecurity and unhappiness. We try to anticipate the most dangerous situation and have even prepared a "script" that we role-play with members of J. T.'s Action Group. So when we

think he might be "on the cusp," we rehearse what we are going to do and intervene before he can act out.

To get a good cultural fit, we all make clear to each other what J. T.'s values are—interdependence with others, self-directedness, predictability, and a chance to contribute. If anyone does not "buy in," they are free to opt out.

Finally, keeping track of the number of times that J. T. engages in problem behavior is simple, because with intensive environmental support this behavior hardly ever happens. Instead, we reflect *continually* on how we are implementing each feature of his positive behavioral support plan. His roommates and job coach exchange a notebook every day to share relevant information on how things are going; and his Action Group convenes on a biweekly basis to review, address issues, and celebrate his and the group's progress.

Blue-Banning, 1994). You have already learned about the Making Action Plans (MAPs) process in chapter 9; Group Action Planning is an extension of MAPs and gives special attention to implementing the vision that is created in MAPs gatherings. Other person-centered approaches include Personal Futures Planning (Mount & Zwernik, 1988) and Essential Lifestyles Planning (Smull & Harrison, 1992). Although both Group Action Planning and IFSP/IEP approaches focus on long-term goals and short-term objectives, they are radically different, as figure 13–4 illustrates.

Significant life-style changes are necessary before great expectations can be achieved. Within a life cycle

perspective (as you learned in chapter 8), these changes are particularly necessary at transition times, when children, youth, young adults, and their families are moving from one service system to another (such as early intervention to preschool or high school to employment) or from one school to another (such as middle school to high school). When Scefenia Hill had to solve the problem posed by Allen's expulsion from day care and the potential that his behaviors would become problematic over the long term and that his transition would be difficult, she found her support in a group of professionals. Would an Action Group be useful to Scefenia and her family? Probably. Who will suggest it? Who will convene it? Is that a role for a school-linked comprehensive services program? Probably. Although all transitions are times of special challenge, the transition from high school to adulthood can be particularly problematic because so many new supports and services need to be put into place. That's when Group Action Planning may be especially useful.

Action Groups consist of family members, professionals, and friends who are especially committed to the individual and can be strategically helpful. Figure 13–5 lists people who might be Action Group members for a student in transition from high school to adulthood.

Typically, Action Groups might start with four to six people, but it is not unusual for 12 to 15 people

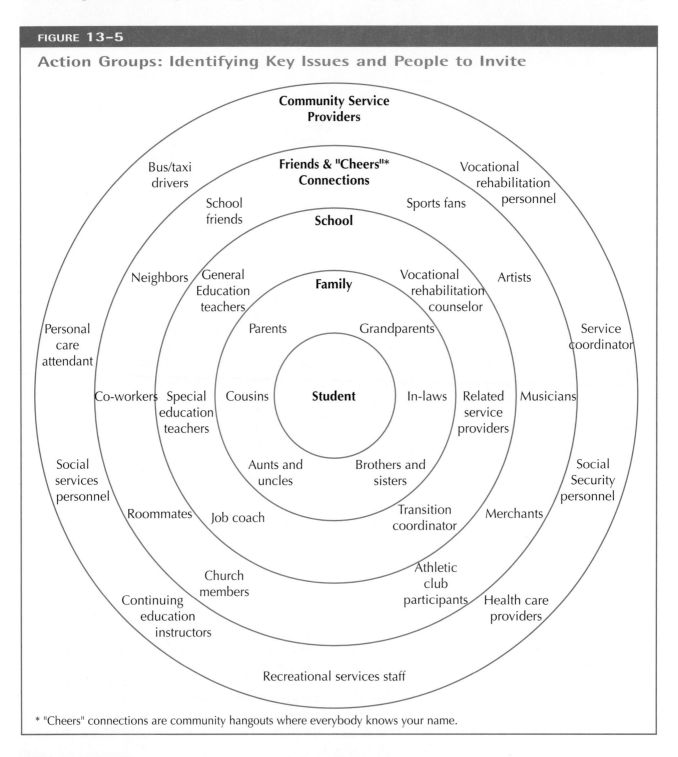

FIGURE 13–5

Action Groups: Identifying Key Issues and People to Invite

* "Cheers" connections are community hangouts where everybody knows your name.

to be involved within 12 to 24 months after an Action Group begins. Because Action Group gatherings tend to be especially enjoyable and are characterized by a strong sense of social connectedness and mutual empowerment, people who get involved tend to stick with their commitment over a long period of time. The Group Action Planning process consists of the five components described in box 13–6.

How can Group Action Planning contribute to empowerment? Box 13–7 includes our perspective of how Group Action Planning has benefited our son, J. T.

You may be wondering how Group Action Planning can be tied to the IFSP/IEP process. In a sense, Group Action Planning is the same as an *ideal* IFSP/IEP conference process. Once Group Action Planning gets underway, the resulting reliable alliance can be carried over into IFSP/IEP planning. Although some merger can occur, we recommend Group Action Planning as a process to be carried on

---

TIPS

BOX 13-6

Implementing the Five Components of the Group Action Planning Process

1. Invite Support.
- Before you ask anyone to join the group, determine where to meet. Someone's home could be ideal because you want a casual setting so people will be at ease. Or use a restaurant, community building, or other accessible, comfortable place. Find a convenient day and time. Then invite people.
- Explain to potential members what Group Action Planning is, why they would be a welcome addition, and that they do not have to make a definite commitment to the group before coming to a meeting. You only want them to experience the Group Action Planning meeting.
- Before you have an actual meeting, choose a facilitator—someone who can listen well, connect well with people, make others feel valued, set a comfortable discussion pace, maintain a positive tone, keep comments relevant, identify key points, summarize discussions, and assign tasks (if needed).

2. Create Connections.
- Leave ample time before and after the meeting for members to visit.
- Offer food.
- Be alert to each other's special days and recognize those days (such as birthdays or other anniversaries).

3. Share Great Expectations.
- Think big. Everyone needs to have a dream for his or her future.

- Think of the ideal job, home, friends, recreation, etc.
- Think "what if" and "why not." Push the limits of possibility.

4. Solve Problems.
- Treat problems as questions.
- Brainstorm to solve problems—that is, answer questions.
- Address one specific problem at a time.
- Seek quantity, not quality, of ideas.
- Encourage everyone to speak up. Expand on each other's ideas.
- Discourage negative and critical remarks.
- Decide on the best ideas; discard the impracticable or nearly impossible ones.
- Discuss each idea's possibilities and problems; then pick the strongest.
- Develop an action plan specifying next steps, persons responsible, and time lines.

5. Celebrate Success.
- Get together once in a while for pure enjoyment. Consider watching a sporting event, having a backyard cookout, or doing whatever you can do to have fun and feel positive about the group's successes.
- Have food and drink and let members know how much their support is appreciated.

The Beach Center has materials on Group Action Planning (See appendix A for address). These materials include fact sheets, a manual, and a videotape.

Group Action Planning for J. T.

J. T.'s Action Group has made *all* the difference in his life and ours, and in the lives of the group members. For J. T., it provides social, emotional, daily-living support and instruction. Friendships, comfort, affection, and help in doing and learning the tasks of everyday life flow generously from its members. The group assures us and his sisters that, no matter where we are or what happens to us, group members will stick by J. T. through thick and thin. His Action Group, not some government program, is his real social security and safety net, although both are needed. Finally, J. T.'s Action Group benefits its members; friendships develop and endure as group members empower J. T. and themselves. Those friendships, in turn, help satisfy the needs and preferences of the group members. The Action Group is an empowering context for all who come to it. The constant and clarion phrase, one that every member voices to J. T. and each other, is this: "How can I respond?"

---

primarily outside of school, even though it has the strong participation of educators, because it differs from the school-based, curriculum/placement-focused process that is typical of schools.

Do educators have the time to participate in Action Groups that meet on a monthly basis? Clearly, it would not be possible for them to have an Action Group for every student. But in our experience and judging from the comments we have received from educators and families throughout the United States who use Group Action Planning, many educators look forward to Action Groups because they tend to be enjoyable, socially connected, and mutually empowering. As one teacher (who wanted to remain anonymous) commented:

> When I'm at Action Group meetings, I'm reminded of why I went into the field of special education in the first place. Sometimes in the hectic pace of day-to-day responsibilities in dealing with all of the system rules and regulations, its easy to forget what this field is really all about. Sitting there and looking around the room, it does my heart good to get flooded with feelings that what my work is really all about is making sure students and families have the best life possible.

Group Action Planning creates a context of belonging and reciprocity among Action Group members. This is one of its goals and benefits. Even though individuals originally decide to join an Action Group to provide emotional, social, and problem-solving support to the individual with an exceptionality, the Action Group can foster reciprocal relationships (Turnbull et al., 1994). Mike Ruef, a member of J. T.'s Action Group, said:

As Americans, we are raised to be independent and self-sufficient. What we often don't realize (in my case I was over 35 before I realized it) is that we need each other; we need community. While I know some members of J. T.'s GAP [Group Action Planning] better than I know others, I have the feeling that I can go to any of them for help, because we are all on the same wavelength. These people are my safety net, my reliable alliance. Although I have been a contributor, GAP has never felt like an "obligation." Rather, it enriches me and has become an essential part of my life.

Linking Our Themes

Creating a Reliable Alliance

By now, you know how important it is to infuse the eight obligations of a reliable alliance into all your partnership opportunities. Figure 13–6 provides suggestions for how best to create this reliable alliance. Review the figure carefully and generate additional ideas for empowering actions that you can take and disempowering actions to avoid.

Strengthening Family Factors

Your own actions in creating an empowering context can enhance family motivation as well as the motivation of yourself and all team members. As you reflect on figure 13–7, we encourage you to make the link in your own thinking and actions between what you do and the impact that it has on others.

FIGURE 13-6

Creating a Reliable Alliance: Emphasis on Extending Learning into Home and Community

Obligations	Issues	Disempowering Actions	Empowering Actions
Knowing yourself	You are interested in Group Action Planning, but you know that you have a tendency to overcommit yourself and then experience stress because you are so busy.	Even though it's not feasible, commit to starting Action Groups for six students.	Commit to starting an Action Group for one student and encourage a colleague or friend who may be a potential facilitator of another group to join you. After she has learned the process, encourage her to start a group for another student.
Knowing families			
Family characteristics	A family who has just recently moved to the community where you teach is interested in starting an Action Group but doesn't know anyone to invite.	Suggest to the family that they wait until they meet people and have a social network from which to draw.	Facilitate a MAPs gathering to learn more about the student and family. Brainstorm with the family about community resources to consider (such as Big Brother/Big Sister Programs, religious organizations, community recreation programs).
Family interaction	A mother's partner (who is gay) is interested in helping the student in your class with homework, but she doesn't know the best way to go about it.	Ignore the partner because of your own values related to gay life-styles.	Set up a dialogue journal to send notes home with homework suggestions.
Family functions	A student in your class has asthma and is getting inadequate medical care; the family has no money or health insurance.	Send a note home and suggest to family members that they need to take their child to the doctor.	Contact the coordinator of school-linked services who is at another school in your district and ask how a student in your school might be able to get services.
Family life cycle	Parents refuse to allow their teenager to go out during evenings or weekends because they are afraid of the problem behavior that might occur.	Consider out-of-school issues to be outside of the realm of your professional responsibility.	Facilitate friendships at school with peers, support them in using positive behavioral support with the student, and encourage them to include the student in evening and weekend activities.
Honoring cultural diversity	A family who has been contacted to be involved in school-linked services will not answer the door when someone makes a home visit, fearing loss of family identity.	Decide that the family has "lost its chance" and drop them from a list of potential participants.	Arrange for someone from the family members' own cultural group to make contact with them and recognize that building a trusting relationship may take significant time and effort.

FIGURE **13-6** CONTINUED

Creating a Reliable Alliance: Emphasis on Extending Learning into Home and Community

Obligations	Issues	Disempowering Actions	Empowering Actions
Affirming and building on family strengths	A parent of one of your students is particularly successful in modifying homework assignments and making homework sessions motivating and enjoyable.	When she makes suggestions, ignore them because you are the expert and you do not want her to think that she can influence school actions.	Brainstorm with her to elicit as many ideas as possible that you can incorporate into homework modifications and arrange for her to share her ideas with other families.
Promoting family choices	Parents of a student with AD/HD are worried about the problems that their child is having during after-school hours when they both are working and there is no one to provide child care.	Tell them that you strongly encourage them to take action before there is a serious problem with neighbors or others who live close by.	Provide them with information on the comprehensive school-linked services program and ask if they would like to receive information on community resources for after-school child care.
Envisioning great expectations	Parents have requested that their child with a serious problem behavior be fully included.	Tell the parents that full inclusion is out of the question and that if the student doesn't improve he will likely be transferred to a special school.	Get information from the Family Connection about schools engaging in model inclusionary practices for students with serious problem behavior; contact the organization to find out what it is doing to make inclusion work.
Using interpersonal communication skills	In an Action Group, the father of a student in your class repeatedly criticizes her for being overweight.	Tell the father that you think his comments are rude and that he is contributing to a negative atmosphere within the meetings.	Invite the father to share what he perceives to be his daughter's strengths and needs as well as his concerns about her. Brainstorm with him about ways that his concerns can be addressed in a constructive manner.
Warranting trust and respect	Family members share with you that they feel very embarrassed when they are in public and their child with problem behavior goes up to strangers and makes inappropriate remarks.	Tell the family that you are not embarrassed, and they should not be either.	Listen empathetically to what they are saying and ask what they think would be helpful in becoming more comfortable; ask if they have ever had the opportunity to talk with other families who face similar situations.

Summary

It is by now common knowledge that children are full-time learners; they need not be six-hour students, restricted to schools as the only source of their development.

Extending children's learning into their homes and communities can occur incidentally, almost accidentally. A haphazard approach will produce haphazard results. Because children with disabilities,

FIGURE 13-7

Strengthening Individual Factors: Emphasis on Extending Learning into Home and Community

Motivation	What You Can Do	Knowledge/Skills	What You Can Do
Self-efficacy	Encourage parents who have been particularly successful with their own Action Group to consider being facilitators for a family who needs the support of an Action Group.	Information	Provide families with information on Action Groups and ask them to consider whether they would be interested in starting one.
Perceived control	Encourage family members to suggest the amount of homework they believe is reasonable for their son to complete on a regular basis.	Problem solving	Problem-solve with families about the triggers of their child's problem behavior and make environmental adaptations to eliminate or reduce those triggers.
Persistence	When episodes of problem behavior occur, remind the parents how much progress has been made and how you will be a reliable ally with them until the problem behavior is practically nonexistent.	Coping skills	Encourage families to help their child develop time-management skills for completing homework assignments. Provide concrete and practical tips.
Energy	Ask the parents how school-linked comprehensive services can help relieve them of anxiety about providing for their son or daughter and give them a break from assuming so much logistical and emotional responsibilty.	Communication skills	Use an answering machine at home and school to leave messages about homework completion. Let families know how much you appreciate their feedback and suggestions.
Hope	Encourage families who live in a violent neighborhood and are receiving school-linked services on violence prevention to maintain hope that their neighborhood can become a safety rather than danger zone.		

more than other students, need systematic approaches to learning in order to help them generalize what they learn and make their learning durable over time, schools and families have developed several approaches to extending their learning.

School-linked comprehensive services provide a single point of access to the wide variety of services that children with disabilities (and other children) and their families need. They consolidate services and then ensure that the services are permeated throughout the community.

Homework need not be onerous for students or their families, but it often is. Collaboration between schools and families can make homework beneficial; here, the key is for schools and families to be sensitive to each other's, and the student's, needs and preferences. Indeed, when schools and parents col-

laborate around homework, they develop the habit and techniques of collaborating around other issues and challenges.

One of those challenges is finding ways to develop positive approaches to problem behaviors. Dangerous or difficult behaviors jeopardize the student's opportunities to be included in school and community; they also create great stress for families. Supporting a person who has problem behaviors requires schools and families to collaborate to "create a life" for the student, blending school, home, and community into a holistic and supportive environment that involves a rich mix of social contacts and preferred events.

Finally, Group Action Planning puts into effect an action-oriented process whereby families, the students with disabilities, family friends, and professionals collaborate to arrange the student's environment so that it satisfies the student's needs and preferences. It is a five-step process that converts the "great expectations" visioning of other future-planning techniques into a regularized, sometimes daily, set of activities engaged in by all members of the group.

Scefenia Hill and Allen are now navigating through their first year of public school education—the kindergarten year. Scefenia says that Allen seems to have little problem with the academics. Instead, his problem is coping with all the rules and regulations that teachers impose, sustaining his energy to engage in a full day of kindergarten, and mustering enough spirit to go to school daily when he would rather not attend at all.

Fortunately, Scefenia and Allen benefit from a collaborative school-linked community services program—the one operated jointly by the Lawrence, Kansas, schools and the University of Kansas. This program provides practical support (such as transportation and access to summer programs) and emotional support (such as having allies at meetings with school staff members).

Can Scefenia and Allen hope to extend his learning into home and community through homework? Yes, and they need not wait until he begins to have more difficult academic challenges. Homework can be whatever behavioral interventions would provide Allen with positive behavioral support.

And here's the wonderful part: Scefenia and Allen don't have to go it alone. Through collaboration with Julie Sergeant and Teresa Kopsa, they can create a Group Action Plan, assembling the professional allies at the school-linked program and at Allen's school and inviting their family friends.

Indeed, they already are on their way to doing just that. Julie and Teresa act not just as professional educators; they also do what friends do—find transportation and help get shoes.

Often, a little structure is all that people such as Scefenia, Allen, Julie, and Teresa need in order to do what comes naturally to them. The structure can be school-linked services, homework, or Group Action Planning. With a framework, doing what comes naturally then comes more easily.

Chapter Fourteen

Attending and Volunteering at School

*I*f you were to put Pat Boyd and John and Jane Hoyt into the same room and ask only one question–"What do you truly have in common?"–the most correct answer would not be "Andrew, Nick, and Grace Hoyt." That would be correct enough: Pat taught Andrew (now 16), is teaching Nick (14), and will teach Grace (11) in the gifted-talented program at Central Junior High School in Lawrence, Kansas.

But the most correct answer would be "We are restoring parents' rights to be involved in their children's education."

Pat believes something has gone wrong in American schools. "The schools have removed families from teaching. We haven't built on the overlapping environments of home and school. We have set ourselves up as the experts. We have treated parents as phenomena to be set aside, as people whom we have to deal with, reluctantly."

To counterbalance what has gone wrong, Pat has her own creed about schools, professionals, and families. It goes something like this:

"Parents and teachers are invested partners, invested in each other and the children. Teachers are not giving families anything new. We are returning to them what was taken from them. Parents, the school belongs to you."

As director of the Excalibur Choir and a teacher in the gifted-talented program at Central, Pat puts that creed into effect in the most remarkable way. When Andrew and then Nick expressed an interest in participating in Excalibur, they, together with John and Jane, met the creed head on.

Pat told the boys that they had to keep a certain grade-point average, that they had to attend 7:00 A.M. rehearsals (with no "if/and/buts" about it), and that they had to help raise money for the choir's activities. "Raising the standard," the Hoyts noted, "created an instant positive peer group for the boys, because the discipline thinned the ranks of the uncommitted kids."

Pat's creed did more than raise the standards for the students. It set a high one for their parents, too.

"Pat invited us to participate in Excalibur. Well, 'invite' is not exactly it. Truth be told, she expected our participation."

To participate meant that parents and students set the agenda for the choir's performances and decided how to raise money and to which local charity it should be donated.

"Partnership with Pat is a myriad of little instances," Jane and John say. It consists of her knowing the names of all the children in the choir and their parents' names, too. It entails understanding how and why family members respond to their children in certain ways. It means being interested in the details of the family's life. It means singing at the weddings and funerals. It means treating families such as the Hoyts as competent and trustworthy people.

Ask Pat how she goes about her work, and she replies, "I am passionate about investing in the families.

I am honest with them. I give parents tasks to do. I ask them to write the home-school handbook. I get families into the art rooms and photography dark rooms, and on the stage with their kids. I give them something tactile to do. I help families, their kids, and the school work along-side each other. We get to see each other as people, not as role-holders. We reduce the remoteness between us. I ask upper-grade parents to guide lower-grade parents. Teachers guide families. Families guide us. We bring each other along."

Bringing each other along has a curious effect on families. "We become real to our children and their friends, and they become real to us." Becoming real occurs because John and Jane are disc jockeys at the winter formal, invite their children's friends to learn how to garden, show them how to weave, make uniforms for them, help them build mazes for their science projects, teach them dance steps from the 1960s, and push them around school in their wheelchairs. "Pat articulates and practices what we feel inside, that we are part of our children's education," say the Hoyts.

Pat's parent-empowerment approach means the Hoyts get to become friends with other families. "There is a community that wants us. That is healing. It is restorative. We see our children are happier than we were. The pain of our school years vanishes, and we have a peace about our own pasts. It's all because we have had the opportunity to be involved. It is because we are valued and respected as co-educators. She expected our participation, and she demanded it. That's how we came to trust each other. We are part of a trusting community . . .

a community that begins with Pat and extends to our children, their friends, and their friends' families."

Ask Pat about a trusting community, and she says that "we" is its central word. But "we" and community can't exist where authority is the value that drives the schools and where "we" has a unilateral meaning, referring only to educators who have and want to keep authority.

"We" is a trilateral "we." It consists of the students, their families, and the teachers. "We" comes alive because of the highly participatory experiences of co-educating children and each other—writing handbooks, developing photos, and singing together.

When the parents cleaned out a room at Central, painted it, and designated it as "our place," they engaged in the tactile act of empowering themselves: they invited themselves into school.

Who found the unused room? Yes, it was Pat Boyd. And who filled it up? Yes, it was eager families like the Hoyts and creative teachers like Pat. Filling up a place, a room—that's a metaphor for co-educating each other, for mutual empowerment.

You have already learned about five opportunities for partnerships. This chapter will present a sixth opportunity—attending and volunteering at school. Figure 14–1 highlights this opportunity within the empowerment framework.

Collaboration in Attending and Volunteering at School

What special issues arise if and when parents of children with exceptionalities attend and volunteer at their children's schools?

The answer depends on the school and its staff—that is, on the context. For Jane and John Hoyt, the issue is meeting Pat Boyd and her creed head on—invitations, expectations, and demands for their participation and co-education. For families whose children have disabilities or are gifted, the issue depends on the degree to which their children are being educated in inclusive settings. When parents attend functions at special schools attended only by other students with similar special needs or talents, the context differs greatly from that of a typical elementary, middle, or secondary school. Given that the vast majority of students with exceptionalities do not attend special schools and that students with disabilities or special gifts/talents are in the minority in nearly all schools, their families will find themselves in the minority of parents who do attend inclusive school events.

Two research studies have focused on the interactions of parents of children with and without exceptionalities in inclusive settings, and both of these studies report on families whose children are at the preschool level. One study in an integrated preschool indicated that there is limited interaction between families whose children have disabilities and those whose children do not have disabilities (Blacher & Turnbull, 1983). A later study that investigated patterns of friendship and acquaintance among families in an integrated day-care program found that families of children with disabilities were more likely to become friends with families of other children with disabilities and were not as satisfied with their relationships with families whose children do not have disabilities (Bailey & Winton, 1989). How might a school facilitate intermingling among families? How might a school accomplish the co-education of its students and create a trusting community, such as the one that Pat Boyd accomplishes through her parent-empowerment efforts and the Excalibur Choir at Central Junior High School?

Professionals can create partnerships around families' (1) attending school events, (2) contributing to classroom instruction, (3) contributing to other school tasks, (4) attending classes of their own, and (5) participating in the parent-teacher organization.

Attending School Events

Many schools have been creative in arranging a broad array of school events that attract families' interest and participation (Stouffer, 1992; Wheeler, 1992). In our discussion, we will focus first on families' attending general school events. Then we will address issues associated with families attending extracurricular activities in which their children participate.

Attending General School Events Schools typically offer various options for parents to attend general school events, such as book fairs, school car-

FIGURE 14–1

Empowerment Framework: Collaborating for Empowerment

Family Factors:
It's Within Us to Be Empowerful

Collaborating for Empowerment:
Through Collaboration, We Act Empowerfully

Education Context Factors:
It's Within Us to Make Our Contexts Empowering

Family Factors

Motivation	Knowledge/Skills
Self-efficacy: believing in our capabilities	*Information:* being in the know
Perceived control: believing we can apply our capabilities to affect what happens to us	*Problem solving:* knowing how to bust the barriers
Hope: believing we will get what we want and need	*Coping skills:* knowing how to handle what happens to us
Energy: lighting the fire and keeping it burning	*Communication skills:* being on the sending and receiving ends of expressed needs and wants
Persistence: putting forth a sustained effort	

Education Context Factors

Opportunities for Partnerships	Obligations for Reliable Alliances
Opportunities arise when . . .	*Reliable alliances consist of . . .*
Communicating among reliable allies	Knowing yourself
Meeting families' basic needs	Knowing families
Referring and evaluating for special education	Honoring cultural diversity
Individualizing for appropriate education	Affirming family strengths
Extending learning in home and community	Promoting family choices
Attending and volunteering at school	Envisioning great expectations
Advocating for systems improvement	Communicating positively
	Warranting trust and respect

nivals, and seasonal parties. Probably the most typical school event is the open house at the beginning of the school year, when families may learn about their child's educational program. In schools that offer a departmentalized curriculum, families frequently follow their child's schedule from class to class, having an opportunity to listen to each teacher describe the curriculum and to ask questions. One of the particular issues to keep in mind for students with exceptionalities in inclusive settings is that some of the families' questions may differ from those of families whose children do not have special needs. For example, parents of a child with challenging behavior might attend their child's classes and worry about the teachers' frustration related to their child's behavior as well as about the frustration of other parents because their child's behavior is disrupting the class. On the other hand, parents of students who are gifted may listen to an overview of the year's curriculum knowing that their son or daughter mastered similar materials several years earlier.

Be sensitive to families' exceptionality-specific issues and concerns and develop approaches to respond to them. In meeting with a group of families, it is extremely difficult to address individual concerns; however, let families know that you will be available to meet with them separately at a later time to address specifically their individual issues.

A second issue to consider when families of children with exceptionalities attend general school events is that they may not know many of the other families. Often, families come to know other families because their own children are friends with children of other families. Have you noticed that families of students who are friends sit together at school events and experience a sense of having more in common with each other than with other families in the school? Indeed, many students with exceptionalities, particularly significant disabilities, often have fewer close friends and even acquaintances. Just as they often feel on the periphery of student life, their isolation makes them feel on the periphery of family life at general school events. To welcome families into the school, increase the social relationships and friendships that their children experience. As schools welcome and include children and youth with exceptionalities in schools, their families may have the similar experience of being welcome and included in the school at large. At general school events, introduce the families of students with exceptionalities to others and highlight their children's positive contributions to peers.

Attending Extracurricular Activity Events

Parents have their most frequent contact with schools by attending school plays, sports events, or concerts (Harris, Kagay, & Ross, 1987). But it is likely that families of students with disabilities are underrepresented in attending such activities because many of their children have not had the same opportunities to participate in extracurricular events as their classmates who do not have disabilities (Falvey, Coots, & Terry-Gage, 1992; Harris, 1994).

There are many reasons that explain why this is so, including (1) an overemphasis on academic goals to the exclusion of other important student outcomes, (2) an assumption that students with exceptionalities will not be able to compete or participate successfully, (3) the placement of special classes in schools where the students in the special class do not match the age ranges of the students without exceptionalities and the resulting extracurricular activities are not as appropriate for the students with exceptionalities, and (4) schools' failure to have the necessary supplementary supports and services to enhance the student's success in extracurricular activities.

In our own family experience, it was not until our son, J. T., was in his last year of high school (at the age of 20–21) that he had his first opportunity to participate in an inclusive sports activity. He served as a manager for the school's football team, so our attendance at football games was a regular Friday night activity. Box 14–1 describes the collaboration that J. T.'s teacher and others at his school practiced to include him and us in school activities.

Why not earn a letter, not as a manager of the football team, but as a player? You may assume that some students with disabilities are not able to compete as players, but additional supports can help make that possible. For example, David Cain, a high school student with a severe emotional and behavioral disability, has had an incredibly successful experience as a member of his high school's football team. After spending most of his elementary and middle school years in a state residential facility, David came back home to live with his family and attend his local school. Although he very much wanted to participate in football, people feared that his unpredictable behavior and quick temper would escalate in a competitive contact sport such as football. To make football a successful experience for him, the local mental health center hired a paraprofessional who served as an assistant football coach, recognizing that it is far more economical to hire a paraprofessional than to pay $60,000 to $100,000 per year to keep a student in a state residential facility.

J. T.'s Letter Jacket

When Walt Whitman High School opened its doors for the fall 1987 semester, there walked, rolled, and was pushed into the building a much different group of students than ever before had attended the Bethesda, Maryland, school. For the first time, Whitman was including students with disabilities among its student body. Now, instead of just the college-bound sons and daughters of members of Congress and diplomats, lawyers and lobbyists, physicians and physicists, Whitman counted among its number students for whom supported employment and supported living were appropriate goals.

Among that group of students was J. T., our 20-year-old son. And as lead teacher of the two special education classes, there was Mary Morningstar. Mary's first goal for J. T. was his placement among the most high-status students in school—the football players, cheerleaders, pom-pom girls, and band members.

She figured that if J. T. could demonstrate his abilities as an assistant manager of the football team, he would meet all these youngsters and their families, show that he and his classmates belonged, and create a network of friends. Just as important, she calculated that if J. T. could do all that and also pick up the first-period roll from each classroom, he would have a positive impact on her colleagues on the faculty.

Mary's gamble paid off, big time. J. T. handed out towels to every player at every game, whether they needed a towel or not. His loyalty to the team, his insistence on traveling on the team bus to away games, and his school spirit and friendliness with the supporting crew of cheerleaders and musicians all opened up a world of inclusion for him.

Little did anyone know how much J. T. was included, and how successful he and Mary had been, until the fall sports banquet in mid-December. The banquet proceeded rather predictably, with a few speeches and the awarding of letters, "player of the week" mugs, and certificates to the junior varsity players and managers.

When, however, it came time for the varsity awards to be given, J. T.'s name was the first one called. "Jay Turnbull, assistant manager, has been with us for only one year, but he has made a significant contribution to our program. J. T., come up for your letter."

As J. T. walked toward the elevated platform where the coaches, school board members, and superintendent and principal sat, his awkward gait was faster than usual. His pride in himself was evident. So evident that, instead of allowing the letter to be handed down to him, he tried to mount the platform. Seeing that he was determined to stand with the dignitaries, some of them pulled him up, and players at nearby tables pushed him up.

Standing on the platform, he now received his letter. In his typical fashion, he patted himself on the back. Only then did the parents, players, and supporting crew notice, "That's J. T. up there. That's that young man with the towels."

The usual polite applause turned into a crescendo, peaked, abated, and rose again. That night, J. T. got more applause than any other player or manager, coach or volunteer.

A few minutes later, J. T., now seated at his table with his beaming parents and Mary Morningstar, had an unexpected visitor. The mother of the team's quarterback came to him, a jacket in her hand.

"J. T., all of us want you to know how much we appreciated your help. It will be a long while before you get your own letter jacket. So here's my son's. We want you to wear it until you get your own. You belong, and we want everyone to know that."

With this one simple gesture, J. T. was more than included; he was welcomed. Not by the players and supporting crew: They had already taken him in. No, he was welcomed by the parents of those academically elite young people. And we ourselves confirmed the direction for J. T.: inclusion now, inclusion forever…whatever it takes, however long it takes, with whoever will be our reliable allies. There has been no substitute for that evening, and no other event in J. T.'s eight years thereafter has made us prouder of him and Mary, who, by the way, now is our colleague at the Beach Center.

When David demonstrated inappropriate behavior during practices or games, the assistant coach immediately responded by providing him with the supports to redirect his behavior appropriately. Participating on the team was a major ticket to acceptance for David in terms of establishing a network of friends and status among his classmates as a school contributor. Likewise, his football participation is a major source of family pride and a catalyst for his family's developing a vision of greater hope for his future (Barbetta, 1995).

On the other hand, families can participate in a wide range of extracurricular activities—whatever their children's exceptionalities. The Excalibur Choir at Central Junior High includes students who have physical disabilities and who are blind; it also includes their parents—sometimes as singers, always as contributors in one way or another. And because Pat Boyd insists on good grades and regular attendance, it includes students who are competent, disciplined, and committed.

You can create an empowering context for families to attend school events by including students with exceptionalities as full members of extracurricular activities. When children participate in events, it is far more likely that their family members will take an interest in the event, attend the special functions associated with the event, and experience for themselves a feeling of genuine membership in the school community. To enhance extracurricular involvement, supplementary aids and services may be necessary, just as they are for a student's academic program. Indeed, the curriculum adaptations that enable students to participate in regular physical education programs also can enable them to engage in extracurricular sports activities (Block, 1994). Box 14–2 includes tips for increasing successful participation of students in extracurricular activities.

As you attend extracurricular activities, note the extent to which parents of students with exceptionalities sit with parents of other children, have conversations with them, and generally become part of the school community. Introduce them to other families. Ask the "experienced" families to mentor the new ones, as Pat Boyd asks the upper-grade families to set examples for and bring along the lower-grade families at Central Junior High. Work and hope to build a trusting and inclusive community, as Pat and the families have. But keep in mind that parents of children with exceptionalities receive support from each other (Santelli, Turnbull, Marquis, & Lerner, 1995). Predictably, parents of children with exceptionalities may prefer to spend time with each other and not at all perceive an undesired separation from other parents.

TIPS

BOX 14–2

Including Students with Exceptionalities in Extracurricular Activities

- Identify activities based on the student's preferences and strengths. Involve the sponsor, coach, or teacher of the extracurricular activities in collaborative decision making to share a vision of the student's participation and develop a plan for supplementary aids and services.

- Consider the appropriateness of providing peer support.

- If necessary, provide additional training and skill development to help ensure that the student has the expertise and capability for meaningful participation.

- Encourage the parents to make friends with other parents whose children are participating and to be an active contributor to the group effort.

- Encourage the parents to initiate invitations to the other children who participate in the activities to have additional time for companionship outside of school activities.

- Encourage the parents to contribute to the extracurricular activity by providing transportation, snacks, supervision, fundraising, or other needed support.

- Incorporate the student's experience into academic subjects such as writing a story during language arts about the extracurricular activity or integrating it into other subject areas as appropriate.

Contributing to Classroom Instruction

Families have expertise that can enhance the breadth and depth of classroom instruction. Frequently, educators have concerns about how much time it takes to individualize instruction and attend to their many instructional responsibilities. Families can contribute to classroom instruction by developing instructional materials, adaptive equipment, or games; copying and collating instructional materials; grading papers; tutoring individual students during or after class; and serving as instructional aides (Vatterott, 1994). As instructional aides, families can participate on field trips, volunteer to come into the classroom and serve in the capacity somewhat similar to a paraprofessional's, and make guest presentations to classes in their particular area of expertise. Jane Hoyt teaches her children's schoolmates about weaving and gardening, and John teaches them about renovating houses and doing the "twist and shout" dances of 30 years earlier. Individualizing for students means individualizing for the participation of their families.

Within the special education field, volunteering in the classroom has been more prevalent during early childhood services (Stayton & Karnes, 1994) as contrasted to elementary and secondary years. One of the most prominent examples of parents as classroom instructors within the early childhood special education field is the Regional Intervention Program, which started in Nashville, Tennessee, and has been expanded to communities throughout the United States and several other countries (Timm, 1993). The Regional Intervention Program incorporates parents of young children with behavioral disorders and developmental delays as the primary teachers of their children as well as trainers of other parents and evaluators of program effectiveness. This program model provides extensive training for parents in behavioral intervention, with all parents being expected to acquire skills enabling them to be effective teachers of their own children and other children in the program.

A useful approach for securing parents to contribute to classroom instruction is a model that takes a "funds-of-knowledge perspective" (Moll, 1992,

---

FIGURE 14–2

A Sample of Household Funds of Knowledge

Agriculture and Mining	Economics	Household Management	Material & Scientific Knowledge	Medicine	Religion
Ranching and farming	Market values	Budgets	Construction	Contemporary medicine	Catechism
Horsemanship (cowboys)	Appraising	Child care	Carpentry	Drugs	Baptisms
Animal husbandry	Renting and selling	Cooking	Roofing	First aid procedures	Bible studies
Soil and irrigation systems	Loans	Appliance repair	Masonry	Anatomy	Moral knowledge and ethics
Crop planting	Labor laws		Painting	Midwifery	
Hunting, tracking dressing	Building codes		Design and architecture		
	Consumer knowledge			Folk medicine	
Mining	Accounting		Repair	Herbal knowledge	
Timbering	Sales		Airplane	Folk cures	
Minerals			Automobile	Folk veterinary cures	
Blasting			Tractor		
Equipment operation and maintenance			House maintenance		

Source: From p. 22 of Moll, L. C. (1992). Bilingual classroom studies and community analysis: Some recent trends. *Educational Researcher, 21*(2), 20–24. Copyright 1992 by the American Educational Research Association. Reprinted by permission of the publisher.

p. 21). Figure 14–2 describes a sample of the household funds of knowledge of just one class.

By interviewing families and asking about the resources and expertise they might share to supplement the teacher's curriculum (Moll, 1992), teachers become aware of the wealth of knowledge and information from which they can draw. A particular strength of this approach is that it builds on families' cultural values, traditions, and diversities (Gallimore, Weisner, Kaufman, & Bernheimer, 1989).

An excellent example of using a fund-of-knowledge approach is Jo-Anne Wilson Keenan's first- and second-grade classroom (Keenan, Willett, & Solsken, 1993). Before Jo-Anne used a funds-of-knowledge approach, parents of her students typically only attended open houses, parent-teacher conferences,

and special performances. To change the school so it would support families, rather than expecting the families to change to support the school, Jo-Anne invited one of her student's families to participate in classroom instruction. Her story and its lessons appear in box 14–3.

The student body in this school was approximately 75 percent Puerto Rican and African-American students and 25 percent Euro-American students. Many of them were regarded as "at risk," and 86 percent qualified for free or reduced-fee school lunches. Within Jo-Anne's class of 24, 20 students had a family member who visited the class at least once. Like Jimmy Pérez, these parents had a wealth of valuable information to share, especially about multicultural traditions.

TOGETHER WE CAN
BOX 14–3

"Professor" Jimmy Pérez

Jimmy Pérez is an unlikely candidate to be a "courtesy professor" or co-teacher at his daughter's school. But Jimmy is an unusual man, and the teacher, Jo-Anne Wilson Keenan, is an unusual teacher.

As the school year was coming to a close, Blanca Pedraza, her father Jimmy, and her mother Evelyn had not yet visited school together. That's curious, thought Jo-Anne, because Evelyn had come into school the year before, albeit briefly, and seemed to support Blanca to learn to read and write (despite her disability). Did Blanca's parents care about her?

The answer was an unequivocal *yes*. When they appeared at school for the dress rehearsal for the spring performance, Jo-Anne told Jimmy, "I'd love to have your

family come in and spend time in the classroom. It would mean a lot to Blanca if you'd come. Many of the families have joined us. You could tell about some things your family does together. You could show us some of your photographs. What are your hobbies?"

An hour later, Jimmy entered his daughter's classroom, a portfolio of his artwork under his arm. To an increasingly admiring crowd of students, he displayed the cartoons he had drawn and told why he draws. "Drawing is like your feelings. You know, you're feeling sad, you're feeling happy, you're feeling bad; you know, some things come out the way you feel."

There soon appeared another facet of Jimmy—his career as a martial artist. Over a 13-year

period of study, he had earned three black belts. He spoke with spiritual respect for this ancient art, telling how the art form blends mind, body, and spirit into a disciplined whole, stressing that the students should never use the martial arts for aggression, and debunking the cartoon ninjas as inaccurate caricatures.

Discipline, Jimmy said, is the key to painting and to martial arts. That lesson—from a gentle and immensely talented man—showed again how valuable parents are as teachers. He was the expert that day, the person to whom the students turned for approval and assistance. His was an important lesson, not just that discipline is necessary for all endeavors, but that parents can be great allies for their children's teachers.

Source: Adapted from Keenan, J. W., Willett, J., & Solsken, J. (1993). Focus on research. Constructing an urban village: School/home collaboration in a multicultural classroom. *Language Arts, 70,* 204–214. Copyright 1993 by the National Council of Teachers of English. Used with permission.

The visitors brought into the classroom the languages and cultures of the diverse community served by the school. The children heard each of these—Spanish, Polish, Arabic, Hebrew, Italian, French, and various dialects of English spoken; and they learned about the different ways that families lived, ate, worked, played, and celebrated. (Keenan et al., 1993, p. 205)

Jo-Anne offers some tips in box 14–4 about how to incorporate the funds-of-knowledge approach.

Jo-Anne highlights the reciprocal benefits to herself and the families as they create a reliable alliance with each other. In terms of teacher benefits, she comments:

English is the predominant language in our classroom, but home languages include Spanish and Polish. Home cultures are Polish, Puerto Rican, Irish American, Italian American, and African American. Since many of the students are Puerto Rican, I have recently been attempting to read in Spanish, and I employ the assistance of my students and their families in doing so. The children and their parents seem to enjoy helping me. They can also help us to understand whether or not information found in our books is authentic to their upbringing and culture. (Keenan et al., 1993, p. 211)

In terms of family benefits, she comments:

In almost every family visit, especially those of low-income and minority families, there have been signs that the parents did not expect to be seen as capable teachers of children. They did not expect the cultural knowledge and practices of their families to be valued in the classroom, and they did not expect to be treated as partners in the education of their own children and children of other cultural backgrounds. It is hard for a "village" to raise a child well unless each member of the community is an equal among equals. (Keenan et al., 1993, p. 212)

Reflect on what it means to view families as an equal among equals and how that view contributes to the motivation and knowledge/skills components of their own empowerment. What impact might being a valued classroom contributor have on Mr. Pérez's self-efficacy, perceived control, hope, information, and communication skills?

Finally, what difference does such a collaborative instructional partnership have on the reliable alliance that you might have with families? This is one of the benefits that Jo-Anne pointed out:

The most satisfying part of the families' visits to our classroom is that they lead to a greater appreciation and understanding of each other as people, and this understanding generates an intimate level of communication that was unattainable in the past. Just before Miriam's mother left, she apologized for not having been able to come in the previous week. She then told me about a tragedy that had befallen the family. I told her that we had expe-

TIPS

BOX 14-4

Families' Contributions to Classroom Instruction

- Inviting parents to become curriculum partners allows us to discover the often unsuspected knowledge and teaching capabilities of parents and to tap them as valuable resources for classroom learning.

- Collaborating with parents requires that we confront our own fears of difference and open our classrooms to discussions of topics that may raise tensions among the values of different individuals, groups, and institutions.

- In co-teaching with parents, the curriculum often emerges in the give and take of what may appear to be noninstructional conversation, as the children make connections to the visitor, the teacher, school subjects, and each other through stories.

- Constructing equitable relations with parents and students requires that we acknowledge our limitations, share our vulnerabilities, and take the risk of letting them teach us about their languages and cultures.

Source: Keenan, J. W., Willett, J., & Solsken, J. (1993). Focus on research. Constructing an urban village: School/home collaboration in a multicultural classroom. *Language Arts, 70,* 204-214. Copyright 1993 by the National Council of Teachers of English. Used with permission.

rienced a similar sorrow in my family. We spent the next few minutes sharing details and consoling each other. The stories of our families have become common ground in my classroom. The support we give each other once we share the joys and sorrows of those stories is the common bond of our community. (Keenan et al., 1993, p. 211)

Describing the "trusting community" that they entered through the Excalibur Choir and the parent-empowerment project that Pat Boyd directs, the Hoyts recalled that, when one of their children was involved in a minor incident with the local police, they confided their concerns to not only Pat but also other families. Alarmed that they would be so candid about something that most families would hide, some of their friends asked, in effect, how they could be so open. The answer: We can trust each other because we have come to know each other through the choir and other activities.

That common ground is the basis of experiencing the synergistic communities we discussed in chapter 3. Once synergy among participants is present, it is very likely that there will be mutual empowerment for all.

Contributing to Other School Tasks

Families can make meaningful contributions to other school tasks. They can be involved in activities as volunteers, committee members, and full- or part-time employees. Their noninstructional volunteer activities can include activities that enliven everyone (such as John Hoyt's being a disc jockey or Jane Hoyt's being a member of the school choir), or they can include typical ones such as substituting for teachers during lunch duty, bus duty, or planning time; collecting money and student forms associated with various school activities; handling lunch money; organizing the library; raising money; or engaging in a broad range of other activities (Vatterott, 1994).

Many schools have organized family resource centers within the school building where families may come to learn about volunteer activities and meet other families. Pat Boyd and the families at Central Junior High School have their own room, a physical and symbolic presence as co-educators. Similarly, Kosciuszko Middle School in Milwaukee established a room where parents can meet, make phone calls, and engage in problem solving. An average of 5 to 15 parents stop by the room each week. They are supported by a school staff member, three parents who are paid $6.00 an hour for 16 hours of work each week, and a network of

volunteers. During the 1992–1993 school year, an average of 10 to 15 parents volunteered at school each week for a total of 1,400 volunteer hours (Lynn, 1994).

Families of students with disabilities often have extensive expertise related to exceptionality-specific issues. They can be extremely helpful in providing information for educators about the nature of a child's exceptionality and specific ways that the child needs to be supported. They can also provide assistance with supplementary aids and services such as providing sign-language interpretation for school plays and musical performances (Luetke-Stahlman, Luetke-Stahlman, & Luetke-Stahlman, 1992).

School districts find it helpful to have one or more parent coordinators who can identify family preferences, provide a broad range of opportunities, and offer networking support to make such volunteer efforts especially beneficial (Rich, 1993). Working collaboratively with parent coordinators or other educators and families, you can identify the full range of noninstructional responsibilities that you will have as an educator. Consider the ones where you would especially appreciate family assistance. Work with others to coordinate family contributions in a systemic way. If the administration of the school where you teach is not interested in setting up a systemic program, consider how the families of your students might collaborate to accomplish various school tasks. In building on the preferences, interests, and time availability of parents and other family members, you might discover a whole reservoir of assistance that would be empowering not only for you but for them as well. That is Professor Jimmy Pérez's lesson to you.

Attending Classes of Their Own

Closely related to school-linked comprehensive services (which you learned about in chapter 13) are the opportunities that many schools provide for parents to come to school to participate in classes of their own. For example, at Paul Robeson High School in Chicago, computer training and stress-reduction classes are available to families, as is a class entitled Strategy to Empower Parents and Students. A group of parents who received computer instruction became interested in writing and printing a school newsletter, which in turn improved home-school communication. Parents also have the opportunity to participate in classes to learn to write proposals, and several of the proposals were funded to benefit the school. Another class teaches families how to obtain community services. All these classes invited parents to come to the school to expand their own information and problem-solving skills (Lynn, 1994). On a less formal basis, families can be co-learners with their children, becoming involved—as Pat Boyd insists they must—in learning the rudiments and refinements of photography, all the way from loading a camera, to framing and composing the photograph, to developing the negatives, to displaying the finished product.

In terms of exceptionality-specific issues, families may be interested in attending workshops on topics such as legal rights, planning for life after high school, augmentative communication, and inclusion. Workshops on helping children develop talents, take tests, and improve behavior are also popular among families of general education students (Dauber & Epstein, 1993) and probably also would be of interest to many families of students with exceptionalities.

How can you find people to lead the workshops? Using a collaborative approach, survey possible speakers in terms of their unique expertise and resources. Create a pool of collaborators from among school staff members, families of students, and community citizens who have special interests in contributing to the life of the school. A useful resource on exceptionality-specific information is the Parent Training and Information Program (see appendix A) and other exceptionality-related programs in your communities, such as Parent to Parent programs and parent support groups.

Participating in the Parent-Teacher Organization

Started in 1897 as the National Congress of Mothers, the PTA now has a membership of approximately 6.8 million members in more than 27,700 local units in each of the 50 states (Moles, 1993). In a survey of more than 1,000 teachers and 2,000 parents, approximately two-thirds of the parents reported attending a PTA or similar meeting at least once annually (Harris et al., 1987). PTAs have not traditionally taken a strong role in exceptionality-related issues, but this is certainly an area that could be expanded within individual PTA units, as Candace Cortiella explains in box 14–5.

The national PTA encourages local chapters to form committees for exceptional children. These committees can provide current information on the needs of students who receive special education and network with organizations such as the Council for Exceptional Children and other exceptionality-specific organizations, including those representing children who have disabilities as well as those who are gifted and talented.

PTAs have developed excellent materials on topics related to enhancing self-esteem, expanding student participation in volunteer activities, participating in cultural arts, and becoming more knowledgeable on topics such as HIV/AIDS and drugs and alcohol. A helpful addition to the PTA portfolio of materials would be information on enhancing the success of inclusion and exceptionality-specific information. The more that parents of students with and without exceptionalities become informed about best practices in special education, the more they are apt to support inclusion of students with special needs.

A Comprehensive Program

Many schools that genuinely embrace families' attendance and volunteer efforts at school apply some or all five of the options we described. To illustrate how a range of different options can be merged within a single school, we will highlight the model developed by Professor James Comer at Yale University. The Comer model encourages collaboration options integrated into the life of the school, not as just adjunct programs to the school (Comer & Haynes, 1991).

Comprising the Comer model are the following three mechanisms:

1. *School Planning and Management Team.* This team represents families, professional staff, and all nonprofessional support staff to carry out the three management operations of (a) developing and implementing a comprehensive school plan including a focus on school climate and academics, (b) staff development to implement the plan, and (c) evaluation and modification of the school program as needed. The major goals include creating a sense of direction and providing a sense of program ownership and purpose to all stakeholders.
2. *Mental Health Team.* This team focuses on students' developmental and behavioral needs and shares knowledge/skills related to child development and teacher/administrator relationships. The team's goal is to address difficult issues as soon as they appear and to prevent problematic issues from escalating.
3. *Parent Program.* This program supports the social program of the school and gives less emphasis to its academic program.

Across all three programs, the operating guidelines include "a 'no-fault' problem-solving approach;

The PTA and Disability Issues

For Candace Cortiella, being a member of the district-wide coordinating council of local PTAs is rather like swimming upstream: The tide is unfavorable, but the goal is important.

The tide is unfavorable because, in Fairfax County, Virginia, the numbers alone make it hard for her to be an advocate for students such as her 14-year-old daughter Sara, who has a learning disability.

To begin with, there are only 20,000 students in special education out of a total district population of 145,000. The parents of these 20,000 students have their hands full just being parents and advocating for their own children, much less participating in the hundreds of local PTAs within the 14th largest school district in the country. Moreover, when the parents do have time to participate in parent-professional associations, they typically do so within disability-specific groups.

Next, the Fairfax school administrators seem to play fast and loose with the numbers—the costs of educating students with disabilities, the numbers included in special education, and so on. Candace describes their presentation of data as "deceiving." Just getting a handle on the facts is a challenge.

Finally, so many parents of children without disabilities reflect the "slow build-up of resentment against special education." They believe that special education is draining off money from the education of their children in general education.

"What those parents don't grasp," says Candace, is that "special education is general education for students with disabilities. It's not a frill, like intensive French instruction for second graders. And they don't get the point we are making about our children going to neighborhood schools. The administration is against that for our children, but favors it for other kids; and the parents simply parrot the administration. It's a matter of segrega-

tion or integration, in my view."

"My job as a member of the coordinating council," says Candace, "is to advocate for and defend special education, to remind the PTAs that our children have rights, to evaluate and comment on the district's special and general education budgets, and to shape national and local PTA policy about such things as school discipline."

Where does Candace get her allies in these unfavorable waters? "Of course, the parents of children with disabilities are allies. So are the special educators. And to a surprising degree so are the general educators. Sometimes, the parents of students who do not have disabilities are allies, but only sometimes and only some of them. After all, if the administration put our children outside the neighborhood schools and the PTAs are based at the neighborhood schools, why should we expect much support from general education teachers and parents?"

---

consensus decision making based on child development principles; and collaborative management that does not paralyze the school principal" (Comer & Haynes, 1991, p. 273).

The Parent Program has three levels. Level 1 includes five or six parents who are elected by other parents to represent them on the School Planning and Management Team. Working with other stakeholders on the Management Team, parent representatives contribute a strong community perspective and an important link to other parents. When parents expressed interest in learning more about how to access community services, the School Planning and

Management Team planned a "Share Night," enabling community service providers to discuss their services with families. A large number of parents attended, primarily because the program directly responded to their top priority. Many families experience difficulty in school participation because of work schedules; therefore, the principal contacted employers, sought their collaboration in supporting families to attend school meetings, and received it.

Level 2 involves encouraging parents to attend and volunteer in school activities. Parents and staff work together in establishing the school calendar and participating in school events such as assemblies, parties, field trips, and athletic programs. Extending the volunteer work of families, a "Parent Assistant in the Classroom" program was developed so that parents were paid minimum wage for 10 hours of work each week, with arrangements made so that deductions were not made from their welfare checks. On top of the 10 hours of paid work, parents frequently volunteered an additional 20 to 30 hours a week. Tips for carrying out level 2 activities are included in box 14–6.

> They were not assigned the clean-up or "dirty work" in the classroom or school; rather, they helped carry out the academic and social program of the classroom, assisted on field trips, and supported desirable behaviors of students within the school. Between 8 and 12 classroom parents, one in each class, became the core of the parent organization within the school. When they invited two friends each to help sponsor a school activity, 30–50 parents were then involved. (Comer & Haynes, 1991, p. 274)

Level 3 involvement is characterized by parents' attending the general activities of the school. Over a four-year period, as this program was implemented, attendance went from 15 to 30 parents at an activity such as a Christmas program to 400 parents. Approximately 250 parents, representing a student body of 300 students (with a majority of these being single parents), regularly attended most school activities. Program leaders placed special emphasis on student performances so that parents could take pride in their children's participation. These leaders also communicated positive news to parents. The program developers commented:

> Recently we visited one of the lowest-income schools in New Haven unannounced, on a warm fall day. Over 100 parents from the three housing projects in the area had arrived to pick up their children. Many of the teachers were visiting with the parents, discussing both school and home happenings. Such interaction is possible when parents view school as a good place, the product of a process that integrates the parent program with the overall program of the school. (Comer & Haynes, 1991, p. 276)

Do you remember our discussion in chapter 2 about the general education reform movement and site-based management? There, we also described the Comer model and included a vignette on a principal, Dwight Fleming, at a Comer school in Connecticut.

TIPS BOX 14–6

Encouraging Parents to Attend and Volunteer at School

- Before inviting or hiring parents to serve in schools, ensure that there is a broad agreement among staff, and do so only after the governance and management mechanism is in place.
- Be sure that the organizational structure and climate are sufficiently developed to accommodate parents.
- Check the rules and regulations regarding the hiring of parents to ensure that there is no conflict with union guidelines or local, state, and federal requirements.
- Carefully screen and train parents before involving them as paid workers in schools.

- Involve staff in the selection or orientation of parents as paid workers or free-time volunteers in the school.
- Have clearly defined roles and activities for parents to perform to avoid confusion and conflict.
- Take all steps necessary to safeguard the confidentiality of student, teacher, and parent information.
- Establish reasonable procedures for ongoing assessment of parent involvement at this level, including a mechanism for providing feedback to parents.

Source: Comer, J. P., & Haynes, N. M. (1991). Parent involment in schools: An ecological approach. *Elementary School Journal,* 91(3), 275. Copyright © 1991 by The University of Chicago. All Rights Reserved.

Reread box 2–1 and reflect on the important role of the school principal in setting the tone for parents' attending and volunteering at school. Reflect also on Pat Boyd, John and Jane Hoyt, the three Hoyt children, and Excalibur Choir. Like Dwight Fleming in New Haven, Pat Boyd in Lawrence, Kansas, sets the tone for the families and students. The tone is simple: "This school belongs to you." So she goes beyond inviting the families and students to participate. She expects it. And the families and students become co-educators and co-empowerers.

Linking Our Themes

Creating a Reliable Alliance

You know by now the significance of infusing the eight obligations for reliable alliances into the partnership opportunity of families attending and volunteering at school. Throughout the chapter, we have emphasized ways that you can do just that. Figure 14–3 highlights examples of this infusion.

FIGURE 14–3

Creating a Reliable Alliance: Emphasis on Attending and Volunteering at School

Obligations	Issues	Disempowering Actions	Empowering Actions
Knowing yourself	You would like to invite a parent in your classroom to volunteer, but she speaks Russian and you don't know how to bridge the language barrier.	Rationalize that the parent would probably not have time to participate anyway.	Locate the people in your district with the strongest bilingual expertise and invite their collaboration in learning how best to approach this parent.
Knowing families			
Family characteristics	The parent of one of your students has a chronic mental illness, and you are hesitant to include her as a classroom volunteer.	You ask the student if he thinks his mother is up to coming to school.	You call the mother, invite her perspectives on the kinds of school activities that would be especially meaningful to her, and make arrangements to respond to her priorities.
Family interactions	A grandmother of one of your students has the predominant decision-making role in the family.	You assume that it would usurp the parents' role to invite the grandmother to chaperon a field trip.	Share your idea to include the grandmother with the parents and solicit their reactions.
Family functions	A mother of one of your students is a computer executive and seems to always work overtime when school events occur.	Write the mother a note and tell her that she is neglecting her child.	Share your vision of how technology could be incorporated into your instruction and invite the mother to share her expertise with you and other school colleagues in options for expanding technology.
Family life cycle	Parents of a student with a severe disability are very anxious about their daughter's transition from junior high to high school.	Encourage them to consider having their daughter stay another year in your class so that they will not have to deal with the transition.	Six to nine months before the transition, ask if they would like to attend an open house at the high school so that they can begin to get a picture of what it will be like and what kinds of plans need to be made. Accompany them to the open house.

FIGURE 14–3 CONTINUED

Creating a Reliable Alliance: Emphasis on Attending and Volunteering at School

Obligations	Issues	Disempowering Actions	Empowering Actions
Honoring cultural diversity	All PTA materials are in English, but the family of one of your students speaks Hindi.	Encourage the parents to come to the meetings anyway because it might help them learn English more quickly.	Find an interpreter who speaks Hindi who could accompany the parents to the meetings and provide simultaneous translation.
Affirming and building on family strengths	A father has gone far beyond the call of duty in the number of volunteer hours that he has contributed to the school.	Suggest to the father he back off some and encourage his wife to be more involved.	Create a special award for parent contributions and present a certificate to this father at an assembly program.
Promoting family choices	A parent is interested in starting a grandparent volunteer day, which has never been done in your school before.	Tell the parent that she will need to prepare a written proposal and submit it to the district office.	Arrange a collaborative meeting with the school principal and other key school leaders and invite them to support this mother in implementing her idea.
Envisioning great expectations	Parents would like to set up a family resource center within the school, but there is no available space.	Tell the families that it simply is not feasible given space limitations.	Convene a group of educators and PTA leaders and brainstorm about how space might be rearranged to free up a location for the family resource center.
Using interpersonal communication skills	A parent volunteering in your classroom expresses concern to you about how you discipline students.	Tell the parent that you are the professional and that it is not her place to make suggestions about classroom discipline.	Encourage the parent to share examples with you and brainstorm with her about the pros and cons of your approach versus other approaches that you might take.
Warranting trust and respect	You encourage parents to allow their son to try out for the wrestling team, but the parents are afraid he will be hurt and ridiculed.	Concede that wrestling team participation is probably unrealistic.	Listen empathetically to the parents' concerns, brainstorm a plan for addressing their concerns, and consider ways that their son could be involved in extracurricular activities even though some risks must be addressed.

Strengthening Family Factors

Just as with every other partnership opportunity, families, professionals, and all who participate in collaborative decision making have opportunities to expand individual and collective empowerment. Figure 14–4 illustrates specific ways that attending and volunteering at school can enhance motivation and knowledge/skills components in the empowerment equation.

FIGURE 14–4

Strengthening Family Factors Through an Empowering Context: Emphasis on Attending and Volunteering at School

Motivation	What You Can Do	Knowledge/Skills	What You Can Do
Self-efficacy	Provide feedback to parents on how helpful their instructional contributions are in expanding learning opportunities for the students.	Information	When parents are volunteers in the classroom, provide them with information on how to respond most effectively to challenging behavior.
Perceived control	Invite parents to prioritize the ways that they would like to attend and volunteer at school and create opportunities based on their preferences.	Problem solving	Meet with highly involved parents to have them come up with new ways to attract the interest of parents who have not attended or volunteered at school in the past.
Persistence	Provide encouragement to parents who plan PTA activities when few parents participate.	Coping skills	Invite parents' ideas in resolving student conflicts that arise during field trips when parents are chaperoning.
Energy	Help create a family resource center in the school for parents to relax, have coffee, and provide support to each other.	Communication skills	Provide opportunities for parents to present to the class and develop more self-confidence in making group presentations.
Hope	Consider all of the extracurricular opportunities in which a student and parents could participate and brainstorm with parents about the benefits that could accrue.		

Summary

Attending and volunteering at school can take five different but mutually compatible forms: attending school events, contributing to classroom instruction, contributing to other school tasks, attending classes for families alone, and participating in parent-teacher organizations. Because these are not and should not be mutually exclusive activities, schools are using comprehensive approaches (such as the model that James Comer at Yale University developed and that Dwight Fleming in New Haven is practicing) or they can do as Pat Boyd does in Lawrence, Kansas.

Talking to Pat Boyd, one learns that she has been teaching for almost 20 years. You might expect some sense of fatigue, some slight hint of burnout. But you won't find it.

To listen to Pat is to hear not just the language of family participation, co-education, and empowerment. It is to detect, easily and early on, her fierce and passionate commitment to returning the schools and educa-

tion to the families. "Invested partners" is the phrase that she uses over and over again: invested in the same sense that she is, which is deeply and permanently; and partners in the same sense that she is a partner, one who is reciprocal with families and students alike.

Listening to the Hoyts, one learns that their own school experiences were less than ideal. Jane describes her education as isolated—not just in the geographic sense that her homes in southern Minnesota and mountainous Colorado were isolated but in the sense that she herself was a loner in school. John talks freely about growing up in the wealthy suburbs in lower Connecticut, about being afraid to do anything in a community of "expert throat cutters," and about not being able to find his own niche when he was sent off to boarding school.

That was then—some 30 years ago. Now Jane and John speak in much different words about their involvement in school, in the Excalibur Choir and the empowerment approach that Pat Boyd directs. Jane uses the word healing and attributes that turnaround to her opportunity to be involved. John uses the word restorative and is clearly delighted that he is "valued as a parent and co-educator, a respected collaborator" with Jane, Pat, and his three children.

"It's a trust thing," they say, "we're members of a trusting community." It's quite clear whom they trust—Pat, each other, their children, and other families. And it's quite clear whom Pat trusts—the Hoyts and other families, too.

With trust comes power—the educator's power to return education to the families and the families' power to accept that responsibility.

Chapter Fifteen

Advocating for Systems Improvement

There's a paradox in the lives of Delfy and James Roach. The paradox is this: Being destructive is being constructive. At least sometimes that's the case.

It certainly was the case when James—who has been diagnosed with a bipolar disorder called manic depression—was expelled from special education when he was in the second grade. The trigger for his expulsion was his behavior: Placed in a time-out room because he acted out so much, he simply destroyed the room.

When Delfy asked how long he would be out of school, she was told, "Until we fix the room."

"How long will that take?" she asked.

"We aren't sure."

What would happen in the meanwhile? James would get one hour a day of homebound instruction, four days a week.

"That was not acceptable. I was a full-time working person, I'm a single parent, my husband committed suicide several years before, and that's when my advocacy started. I found a support group and learned that James had a right to an appropriate public education and the supports to be successful in school."

So Delfy began her advocacy career because James destroyed the time-out room. That makes sense, Delfy reasons. "I came in fighting at that time, and I think I made a few enemies then, but I didn't know what else to do at the time. I was so upset that they had totally destroyed James. Here was a kid who had been doing okay in the program he was in before. Now we were talking hospitalization, because his disorders are so severe. I guess what's so depressing about that and so

agonizing is that I knew that hospitalization wasn't the answer for him. I truly felt like I was up against the wall and could go no other place except to come out fighting. So I did."

Delfy hasn't stopped fighting, but now she fights not just for James but for other families whose children have severe emotional problems. "My advocacy has been a process," from being helped by Parents for Behaviorally Different Children, a statewide parent-directed advocacy program in New Mexico, to being its executive director. "I didn't want other families to have to go through what I had to go through."

Delfy's statewide advocacy is for parents like her whose children have emotional challenges, especially for parents who, like her, are members of a minority group.

As part of her advocacy, Delfy was instrumental in changing New Mexico's laws governing parents' decisions to hospitalize their children. Parents and children needed services not available in schools or community mental health centers, so hospitalization or outpatient services were needed. Civil rights advocates opposed easier hospitalization, while providers and parents wanted easier hospitalization.

"As parents, we took a lot of abuse at those meetings. There was so much blaming going on—people saying that the reason the kids are the way they are is because of the parents. People said that there's nothing wrong

with the kids; it's the parents, and they should be hospitalized, not the kids."

So not only do Delfy and others have to bear the stigma of mental illness, but they have to do so as a cultural minority. The schools do not print forms in Spanish. The Spanish-speaking parents have a cultural heritage of respecting the teachers and not asking questions of people in authority. "You just accept what is being given you."

Acceptance is not only natural but necessary for those families who are illegal immigrants. They fear the immigration services and believe the schools will "use retribution and have them or their child deported."

So advocacy for the Spanish-speaking minority means holding conferences in only Spanish, in their communities, in collaboration with their community leaders, and at times when their religious holidays or fiestas are not in process. It means teaching them about their rights and accepting that they will use the medicine man (the Curandero) or the witch doctor (the Brujo), not just the teachers, therapists, or physicians that schools or the state hire.

But advocacy means a whole lot more than that. It also means, more fundamentally, helping people change their centuries-old cultural habits.

And when school restructuring is the issue, it means recognizing that the schools will restructure themselves without consulting with the families in advance. "Right now, we aren't exactly involved in the restructuring the schools are doing around inclusion. We were invited to hear the reform after it was already done, so the school people could run it by us.

"Principals normally don't want our children in there (in school, much less in inclusive programs). I don't think they want kids with disabilities. Period. But especially kids with behaviors."

So advocacy means reaching the families in family-friendly and culturally appropriate ways, letting them know their rights, and constantly monitoring the principals and the whole school.

It means showing respect for the educators. "We don't need to bash or blame professionals for everything. We're going to have to come together and work in the best interest of our kids. Professionals are going to need the commitment

the families have." It means asking the professionals to ask themselves a simple but difficult question: "If this were my family, what would I want to see happen?"

After all, as Delfy says, "Our kids are with us for a lifetime. The professionals may be in our kids' lives and our families' lives for an hour a week for a whole year, but we are with our kids the rest of our lives. They need to understand and respect that."

The seventh and last partnership opportunity is advocating to improve school systems. We present the empowerment framework in figure 15–1 with the last partnership opportunity—advocating for systems improvement—shaded.

As you advocate for systems improvement, you will have opportunities to implement all the seven opportunities for partnerships.

Collaboration in Advocating for Systems Improvement

This chapter focuses on (1) becoming an advocate, (2) advocating for change through school reform, (3) advocating for change in parental participation, and (4) advocating for change through legislative and judicial processes.

Becoming an Advocate

Have you ever had to stand up for something you believed in? Of course, you have. Sometime, some place in your family, school or college, workplace, or military service, you have asserted your interests or those of another person. What you did then is a form of advocacy. It is a very natural behavior of families and professionals, but that does not mean it is easy to be an advocate.

Definition   Advocacy is defined as taking one's own or another's perspective to obtain a result not otherwise available. Advocacy is closely aligned to empowerment; and as you know, empowerment means taking action to get what you want and need. Advocacy is a strategy for taking action. It consists of presenting, supporting, or defending a position.

Advocacy can be for yourself (self-advocacy) or for another (representational advocacy).

For example, a student who is engaged in supported employment may not want to learn a particular job or have a particular job coach; and the student, by words or behavior, communicates that choice. This is self-advocacy. In a curious way, James Roach's destructive behaviors were a form of self-advocacy: He was saying he wanted out of the time-out confinement. Alternatively, parents who challenge the curriculum or placement that a school proposes for their child engage in representational advocacy (on their child's behalf). Delfy Roach engaged in representational advocacy when she "came out fighting" for her son James and for other parents of children with emotional challenges. Finally, advocacy is purposeful; it seeks a particular outcome from a situation in which at least one person perceives that a change is needed. Accordingly, when Delfy sought more appropriate education for James and different civil commitment laws, she was advocating—purposefully arguing for change.

Places, Issues, and Orientations for Advocacy   Advocacy occurs in many different places. It occurs when a school-based team meets with a student's family to develop an IEP. In that case, the place probably is a conference room at the school, the issue concerns the student's rights under the Individuals with Disabilities Education Act, and the people are professionally and family oriented. Advocacy can occur in a hearing before a judge in a lawsuit between a student's parents and the local school system. In that case, the place will be a courtroom, the issue is legal, and the people are rights-and-duties oriented. It can occur when a group of parents present their concerns to a local or state

FIGURE 15-1

Empowerment Framework: Collaborating for Empowerment

Family Factors:
It's Within Us to Be Empowerful

Motivation

Self-efficacy: believing in our capabilities

Perceived control: believing we can apply our capabilities to affect what happens to us

Hope: believing we will get what we want and need

Energy: lighting the fire and keeping it burning

Persistence: putting forth a sustained effort

Knowledge/Skills

Information: being in the know

Problem solving: knowing how to bust the barriers

Coping skills: knowing how to handle what happens to us

Communication skills: being on the sending and receiving ends of expressed needs and wants

Collaborating for Empowerment:
Through Collaboration, We Act Empowerfully

Education Context Factors:
It's Within Us to Make Our Contexts Empowering

Opportunities for Partnerships

Opportunities arise when . . .

Communicating among reliable allies

Meeting families' basic needs

Referring and evaluating for special education

Individualizing for appropriate education

Extending learning in home and community

Attending and volunteering at school

Advocating for systems improvement

Obligations for Reliable Alliances

Reliable alliances consist of . . .

Knowing yourself

Knowing families

Honoring cultural diversity

Affirming family strengths

Promoting family choices

Envisioning great expectations

Communicating positively

Warranting trust and respect

superintendent of education. In that case, the venue will be an office; the issue concerns the development or implementation of special or general education policies; and the people have a policy, political, and family orientation. Likewise, advocacy can occur when parents and professionals testify before a state or congressional committee. In that case, the venue is a legislative committee room; the issue is the development or implementation of state or federal law; and the people have a policy, political, family, and professional orientation. Delfy Roach has engaged in each of these types of advocacy. Like many other family members, she has found that she cannot limit her advocacy to simply one place, one issue, and one forum.

So advocacy involves all kinds of people (including students, parents or other family members, professionals, lawyers, judges, policymakers, and bureaucrats) who struggle with all kinds of issues (such as professional, student-related, family-related, legal, policy, and fiscal) in all kinds of places (schools, offices, courtrooms, committee rooms, and so on). Advocacy involves *you*.

When you identify barriers that are blocking you, other educators, students, and families from getting what you and they want and need, your role is to be an advocate—taking action to eliminate those barriers and to produce a more empowering educational context. You do not have to be stuck with the status quo or work around problems that could be solved if someone would take the initiative to solve them. As a professional, it is your duty to advocate to improve the capacity of school systems to empower students and families.

Sources and Levels of Advocacy   Advocacy can occur at the federal/national, state, regional, or local levels. It can be as high-profile as Patricia McGill Smith's work as executive director of the National Parent Network on Disability (chapter 1 vignette), a job that requires her to be an advocate for families and the national, state, and local family organizations to which they belong. It can be as low-profile as the work of one parent advocating in an IFSP/IEP conference for her child's rights under IDEA. It can be somewhere in between, as the following cases illustrate:

- The volunteer president of a state family organization for students with learning disabilities testifies before a state legislative committee.
- You poll your professional colleagues and families to determine the extent of their concern about the unavailability of sufficient supplementary aides and services to include students successfully in general education classrooms.

- People such as Delfy Roach work simultaneously at the local and state levels.

Sometimes there is the expectation that families of children with exceptionalities should be advocates for their own child and for others. As we have discussed throughout this book, many families embrace the role of advocacy and eagerly work for systems improvement. But even families who embrace this role often tire of the laborious job of advocacy and retaliatory issues:

> When you have to advocate for your child, you pay a high price for that in many ways. It's very stressful on the family. . . . Because of the kind of advocacy work that I've had to do . . . I'm not able to teach anywhere locally. I actually teach school in Texas, which is a 30-mile drive in the time difference away from my home. . . . My son suffers from bipolar disorder and numerous other difficulties. That illness itself is stressful, but when you have a vindictive, harassing, retaliatory school district to deal with, it makes your life completely miserable . . . that's what I've had to deal with. (testimony of Edris Klucher, quoted in National Council on Disability, 1995, p. 124)

Parents' advocacy burden would be significantly lessened for them if every single educator saw him or herself as an advocate. Mark A. Mlawer, a professional who works for inclusive education, shares his perspective on advocacy expectations for families and professionals in box 15–1. He reminds us that the expectation that every parent should be an advocate may be inconsistent with what some parents want (Mlawer, 1993; Turnbull & Turnbull, 1982).

Monitoring and Advisory Committees
Often advocacy occurs when a group of individuals is responsible for monitoring or advising educators. These groups perform various types of functions, but the most usual are to assure themselves, families and students, and educators that the educational agency is delivering the services in the manner required by law or good professional practice.

Monitoring involves inspecting the educational agency's records; holding hearings; interviewing families, students, and agency employees; and seeking peer review from wholly disinterested individuals or associations. In a very real sense, this work is more than quality control; it is advocacy for the people for whom the services are intended.

Monitoring teams, often constituted by the state education agency or sometimes by the U.S. Department of Education, may come into your school

Advocacy Expectations for Families and Professionals

The answer, therefore, to the question "Who should fight?" is: professionals. Those of us who enter the special education and disability "fields" by choice rather than necessity, those of us who ask for the duties and responsibilities of working on behalf of students with disabilities, are those with the obligations of advocacy. No matter what our job, advocacy must be part of it.

It is impossible to avoid one implication of this point of view: by engaging in advocacy, special education and disability professionals risk making their employers angry and may even risk their jobs. While the risks are usually overestimated, it cannot be denied that they exist. Nevertheless, it is time to accept that working on behalf of students with disabilities entails risks; and as with many other professions, one should not

enter this profession without accepting its values and all the risks that living in accordance with those values entails. And, in fact, some special education and disability professionals—particularly some classroom teachers—take these risks and have for some time. Parents will be spared the burdens of advocacy when others, especially more of those in administrative positions, join these courageous professionals.

Moreover, in order to truly empower parents, programs must be developed that are capable of engaging in advocacy along with and on behalf of parents; programs that are available regardless of income; programs that are well publicized and easy to access; and programs that have available a corps of independent, uncompromised special educators to serve as experts on behalf of students. Only by

creating a true balance of power between parents and school systems, not just between some middle- and upper-class parents and school systems, will *all* parents be given the opportunity of empowerment. "Empowerment" without real power is an empty concept, a cruel sham that results in disempowerment for many....

We can best assist children and youth with disabilities if we stop pushing their parents to become advocates and simply allow them to be parents. But this will only happen if we expand the ranks of, and access to, qualified advocates, and start doing our jobs as professionals; this can begin once we accept the responsibilities our roles entail, and once funding priorities are set based upon the real needs of parents and families, rather than upon what we wish those needs were.

Source: Mlawer, M. A. (1993). Who should fight? *Journal on Disability Policy Studies, 4*(1), 112–114.

---

system and carry out the monitoring roles that we just described. Present to them the strengths and needs of the program; do not try to emphasize only strengths and minimize some of the real needs that exist. As you develop collaborative relationships with other educators and administrators, the goal of that collaboration should be to provide the highest-quality program possible, not merely to put an unjustified favorable light on something that needs improvement. Remember that the purpose of the special education program is to enhance educational outcomes for students and provide support to families. By keeping focused on this goal, you can participate in the monitoring process in an ethical and honest way.

Another form of advocacy occurs when a group of individuals is constituted as an advisory com-

mittee for a state or local education agency or other provider. The role of the advisory committee is to give advice to the educational agency that created it. The advisory committee seeks to improve the quality of service delivery according to good professional standards. Many school districts have a special education advisory committee composed of families, teachers, and administrators, whose role is to review the special education program and make recommendations for improvement. As inclusive school practices are being implemented, some school districts are eliminating a separate special education advisory committee and having an educational advisory committee whose responsibility includes the education of students with and without exceptionalities.

Of course, some school districts are uncommitted to parent participation in school reform; they are like the district where James Roach goes to school and thus create a situation in which the students' families have yet another advocacy challenge. That new challenge is to advocate for a fair process for school reform. If families can open up the process, then they confront the challenge of advocating for more appropriate and inclusive special education.

In all these kinds of advocacy, an individual's role is not necessarily advocacy; but advocacy is almost always unavoidable. This is because most monitoring and advisory committees will find one or more ways in which the educational agency can improve its services and make one or more recommendations on how the agency can do its job better.

The risk for both professionals and families in any of these groups is that they will be co-opted by the educational agency and persuaded to be the advocate for the agency against students and families. The issue of dual allegiance arises and requires you and other professionals to be very clear about your loyalties: Are you loyal to protecting the educational agency or to ensuring an appropriate education for students?

Advocacy, Collaboration, and Empowerment

Advocacy can and should be a collaborative undertaking between families and professionals. That is an idealized view. In reality, when parents and professionals clash, as they often do, collaboration withers away and adversarial, even irreparable, relationships take its place.

There are many reasons to avoid adversarial relationships between yourself and families. Adversarial relationships cause lingering hard feelings and great emotional and financial costs (especially to a family); they also risk retaliation against the student (Fiedler, 1985; McGinley, 1987). Moreover, adversarial positions create a "win-lose" world, an environment in which one side must gain and the other must lose. In that environment, collaboration is nearly impossible.

Recognizing that adversarial positions have great limitations, many people now advocate for a form of alternative dispute resolution involving mediation (Fisher & Ury, 1991). A "win-win" approach to advocacy emphasizes "enlarging the pie" so that everyone gains and no one loses much or at all. The advocate—whether a student, parent, teacher, or bureaucrat—who takes the "win-win" approach, who wants to "get to yes" (Fisher & Ury, 1991), stands a much better chance of having a long-term collaboration and a mutually empowering context than does one who approaches advocacy as an adversarial confrontation.

When all stakeholders have something to gain, the nature of the services—their effectiveness in supporting families and educating students—seems to improve (Allen & Petr, 1996; Clatterbuck & Turnbull, 1996; Jones, Garlow, Turnbull, & Barber, 1996).

Unfortunately, advocacy is not always collaborative, and mediation is not always successful. Sometimes parents or professionals, or both, need to develop other ways for securing systems change. For Delfy Roach, the solution was to join the New Mexico organization Parents for Behaviorally Different Children and later to rise to its executive directorship. But not everyone wants to do what Delfy did, nor can everyone follow her path. They have to find other vehicles for systems change.

One popular approach to systems advocacy involves a program called Partners in Policy. Developed by the Minnesota Governor's Planning Council on Developmental Disabilities, this program provides information, training, and resources to the parents of children, youth, and adults with disabilities and to adults with disabilities. The program has been immensely successful in developing a cadre of well-informed and skillful advocates for disability policies, programs, and funding, both in Minnesota and in other states where it has been replicated (Zirpoli, Wieck, Hancox, & Skarnulis, 1994). Graduates of the program have increased contact with national, state, and local elected and appointed officials; they have testified at public hearings, made presentations at state and national conferences, appeared on TV and radio shows, been appointed to state and local disability-policy committees, and published articles and letters in newspapers or professional journals. Clearly, when family members and adults with disabilities are motivated and then gain the knowledge/skills to be effective advocates, they collaborate in systems change. Although seemingly designed as a strategy for systems change, the Partners in Policy program also is a vehicle for personal empowerment.

Similarly, Parent Training and Information Centers (which you learned about in chapter 10) provide advocacy training for families. In Kansas, for example, the Parent Training and Information Center called Families Together provides training to families about their children's rights to an education and the families' rights to various health and family support services. It also mobilizes families to write letters, make telephone calls, send faxes, and make personal contacts with their state and national representatives, advocating for or against policy changes.

The Parent Training and Information Centers are not the only family-advocacy groups. In nearly every state, disability-specific associations that are affiliated with national organizations (such as United Cerebral Palsy Associations and state and local chapters of The Arc) regularly engage in systems advocacy. One of the most effective—and newest—of those organizations is the Federation for Children's Mental Health (which we described in chapter 1). Its local chapters, such as Delfy Roach's Parents for Behaviorally Different Children in New Mexico and Keys for Networking in Kansas, have played a major role in the welfare-reform debates of the late 1990s. Indeed, Keys for Networking collaborated with the Kansas National Guard and the Judge David Bazelon Center for Mental Health Law (based in Washington, DC) to make a videotape about families whose children have disabilities. The videotape enabled families to describe the negative impact that cuts in the children's Supplemental Security Income (SSI) program would have on them; and the videotape, shown to senators and representatives from Kansas and other states, provided powerful testimony and was influential in keeping the SSI program from being thoroughly decimated by Congress in 1995.

When you or the families you work with want to push for system change or resist policies that would impair a present system of services, you can go to the Parent Training and Information Centers or other family-advocacy associations. They are effective agents for empowerment, providing motivation, knowledge/skills, and reliable alliances among many different but equally interested stakeholders.

Advocating for Change through School Reform

Overview   In chapter 2 you learned about the highlights of general and special education school reform over the last 20 years. Figure 2–7 summarizes the major phases of general and special education school reform and shows how those two reform movements are converging into a new era of collaboration and empowerment.

You also read about Goals 2000: Educate America Act, passed in March 1994, which established the eight National Education Goals included in figure 15–2.

FIGURE 15–2

National Education Goals

Ready to Learn
By the year 2000, all children in the United States will start school ready to learn.

School Completion
By the year 2000, the high school graduation rate will increase to at least 90 percent.

Student Achievement and Citizenship
By the year 2000, all students will leave grades 4, 8, and 12 having demonstrated competency in challenging subject matter including English, mathematics, science, foreign languages, civics and government, economics, arts, history, and geography; and every school in the United States will ensure that all students learn to use their minds well, so they may be prepared for responsible citizenship, further learning, and productive employment in our nation's modern economy.

Mathematics and Science
By the year 2000, U.S. students will be the first in the world in mathematics and science achievement.

Adult Literacy and Lifelong Learning
By the year 2000, every adult American will be literate and will possess the knowledge and skills nec-

essary to compete in a global economy and exercise the rights and responsibilities of citizenship.

Safe, Disciplined, and Drug-Free Schools
By the year 2000, every school in the United States will be free of drugs, violence, and the unauthorized presence of firearms and alcohol and will offer a disciplined environment conducive to learning.

Teacher Education and Professional Development
By the year 2000, members of the nation's teaching force will have access to programs for the continued improvement of their skills and the opportunity to acquire the knowledge and skills needed to instruct and prepare all American students for the next century.

Parental Partcipation
By the year 2000, every school will promote partnerships that will increase parental involvement and participation in promoting the social, emotional, and academic growth of children.

The National Education Goals derive from the grave concern of many professionals, parents, and citizens at large that educational quality has declined to unacceptable levels and that bold and ambitious new efforts are needed to advocate for systems change. Figure 15–3 includes a summary of the 1993 National Education Goals Report providing data on educational concerns.

Empowerment is at the heart of the process for achieving these goals. School, family, and community participants taking action to get what they need and want—namely, higher standards and achievement for all students. An underlying theme of the National Education Goals is great expectations for all:

> All students can learn at significantly higher levels, given the proper tools and resources. Yet our system sorts children almost from the beginning of grade school into advanced vs. slow tracks. We test children against a bell-shaped curve—essentially against each other—rather than against any standard of what it is they need to know and be able to do to get jobs or maintain a high standard of living. . . .
>
> To turn this around, we need a revolution in our thinking. We must shape a system of teaching and learning based on the philosophy that all students can learn at higher levels—that achievement is as much a function of expectations and effort as it is of innate ability.
>
> Perhaps the greatest barrier of all to achieving equity is that we have not made clear to our students what it is they need to know and be able to do to be successful. If we have not thought through this clearly and cannot articulate it, then we are guaranteeing that our system cannot be held accountable for providing a high-quality and equitable education for all children. (U.S. Department of Education, 1995, p. 14)

The National Education Goals set high standards for all students, emphasizing these three:

1. *Content standards:* defining the knowledge, skills, and understandings that students should accomplish in the broad range of subject areas
2. *Performance standards:* defining the levels of student achievement in the subject matter that must be met to exemplify proficiency
3. *Opportunity-to-learn standards:* defining the conditions in schools that will enable all students to achieve the content and to perform at an acceptable proficiency level

The emphasis on standards shores up educational accountability for all stakeholders. For students with exceptionalities, these standards need to form the basis of their IEP development and implementation and be a vehicle for translating great expectations into outcomes to be attained by high school graduation:

> Standards replace the guesswork. They say to employers: This is what you can expect from our graduating students. They say to parents: This is what your son or daughter needs to accomplish if he or she wants to go to college or get a good job after school. And they say to concerned citizens: This is how your public school dollar is being invested. This is how we will hold ourselves accountable to results, how we are achieving the National Education Goals. (U.S. Department of Education, 1995, p. 15)

Roles in Advocating for Change   A collaborative process among all stakeholders is at the heart of implementing the National Education Goals (Buswell, 1993; Buswell & Schaffner, 1994). That was the point Glenn Gabbard made in the beginning of chapter 2. And it is just what Delfy Roach sought, but did not find, in her school district in New Mexico. The U.S. Department of Education (1995) recommends the steps listed in box 15–2 as methods to address the National Education Goals within schools and communities. You will recognize these steps as the key steps of the problem-solving process that you learned about in chapter 4. Once you master the basic steps of the problem-solving process, you can apply them to almost any problem, whether it be at the individual-student level or the system level.

Discuss the National Education Goals with your principal and find out about the planning process within your school and community. Many schools are appointing a school improvement team that brings together stakeholders for collaborative planning and implementation. If you are interested, request to become a member of the school improvement team. The more you participate actively in the change process, the more empowered you are likely to be (Prestby, Wandersman, Florin, Rich, & Chavis, 1990).

How are families of students with exceptionalities participating in the school reform process? Recent research answers the question from the perspectives of parents (of students with disabilities) who are members of school improvement teams (Wade, 1994).

1. *Do school improvement teams make important decisions?* Approximately half the participants stated that no important decisions had been made by their school improvement team.

FIGURE 15-3

Summary of 1993 Goals Report Findings

The conclusion from the 1993 National Education Goals Report is that at no stage in a learner's life—before school, during the traditional school years, or as adults—are Americans doing as well as they should, or can be.

Despite modest gains, our progress is wholly inadequate if we are to meet the national education goals by the year 2000.

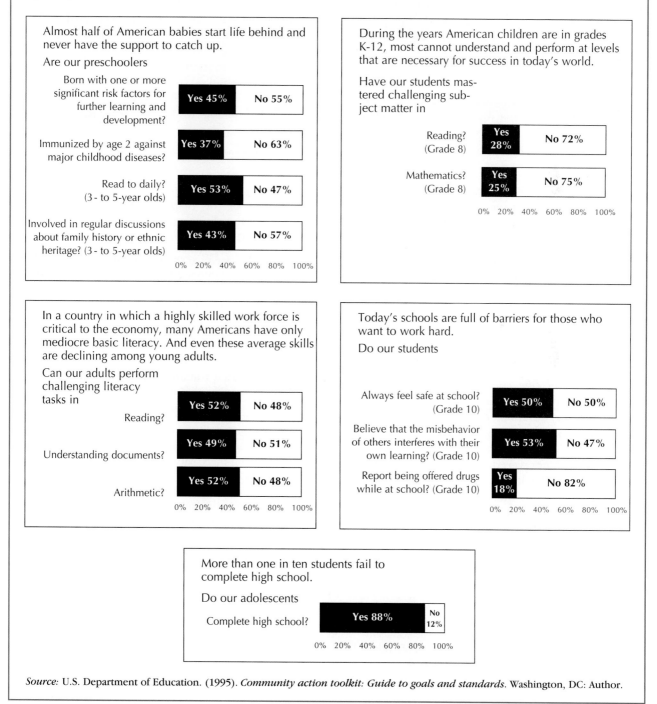

Almost half of American babies start life behind and never have the support to catch up.

Are our preschoolers

Born with one or more significant risk factors for further learning and development? — Yes 45% / No 55%

Immunized by age 2 against major childhood diseases? — Yes 37% / No 63%

Read to daily? (3- to 5-year olds) — Yes 53% / No 47%

Involved in regular discussions about family history or ethnic heritage? (3- to 5-year olds) — Yes 43% / No 57%

0% 20% 40% 60% 80% 100%

During the years American children are in grades K-12, most cannot understand and perform at levels that are necessary for success in today's world.

Have our students mastered challenging subject matter in

Reading? (Grade 8) — Yes 28% / No 72%

Mathematics? (Grade 8) — Yes 25% / No 75%

0% 20% 40% 60% 80% 100%

In a country in which a highly skilled work force is critical to the economy, many Americans have only mediocre basic literacy. And even these average skills are declining among young adults.

Can our adults perform challenging literacy tasks in

Reading? — Yes 52% / No 48%

Understanding documents? — Yes 49% / No 51%

Arithmetic? — Yes 52% / No 48%

0% 20% 40% 60% 80% 100%

Today's schools are full of barriers for those who want to work hard.

Do our students

Always feel safe at school? (Grade 10) — Yes 50% / No 50%

Believe that the misbehavior of others interferes with their own learning? (Grade 10) — Yes 53% / No 47%

Report being offered drugs while at school? (Grade 10) — Yes 18% / No 82%

0% 20% 40% 60% 80% 100%

More than one in ten students fail to complete high school.

Do our adolescents

Complete high school? — Yes 88% / No 12%

0% 20% 40% 60% 80% 100%

Source: U.S. Department of Education. (1995). *Community action toolkit: Guide to goals and standards.* Washington, DC: Author.

Essential Steps in the Goals Process

- Adopt the National Education Goals or similar goals that reflect high expectations for all and cover the entire breadth of focus from pre-natal care to lifelong learning.
- Assess current strengths and weaknesses and build a strong accountability system to measure and report regularly on progress toward the goals over time.
- Set specific performance benchmarks to mark progress along the way and guide the change process.

- Identify the barriers to and opportunities for goal attainment in the many systems that support teaching and learning.
- Create and mount strategies to overcome the barriers, seize the opportunities, and meet the performance benchmarks.
- Make a long-term commitment to continuously re-evaluate your accomplishments and shortcomings in meeting the community goals and be willing to modify your strategy as needed.

Decisions focused on curriculum, technology, physical plant, and parent involvement. Two different opinions about progress represent the range of perspectives:

We're talking about the six weeks we spent on getting the extra bulletin board for the teacher's lounge so that they could get communication. That was the biggest waste of time.

I have only been here one year, but my experience has been that the school improvement committee has an incredible amount of power. (Wade, 1994, p. 7)

2. *Do they feel like empowered members of the team?* Slightly more than half of the participants (53 percent) described themselves as being equal members of the team, but slightly fewer than half (47 percent) stated that they were not equal members. Empowered members attributed their equal role to the leadership of the principal (context factor) or to their own personal attributes (family factors related to motivation and knowledge/skills). Contrasting perspectives include the following:

It's almost like you're part of the family when you go in and sit down and talk.

[At] my school it's the principal. They don't start anything until the queen bee comes in, and nothing can be finalized until she is there. [If] she comes in late or doesn't come that just sets the whole thing off for the entire school. (Wade, 1994, p. 9)

3. *Do school improvement teams deal with issues concerning disability? Do decisions made*

directly affect children with disabilities? Three-fourths of the respondents indicated that the needs of students with a disability were not a concern of the school improvement team.

We're not per se at the top of the list and maybe not really mentioned, you know, in the meeting because I think they are probably looking at the majority. (Wade, 1994, p. 13)

4. *What type of training and information do participants receive? What type of training and information do they and others need?* Participants who had attended training believed that it was beneficial and indicated that more training and advanced planning would be helpful.

There needs to be a method developed where I get the same information everybody else does. My son is right there with a backpack that goes home everyday, but no one is able to figure out how to get the same information to me that the staff have. This lends to the feeling of this is "just a parent" so it isn't important. (Wade, 1994, p. 14)

Discussion of important issues that might lead to school improvement was families' most favorable perspective about the process; their least favorable perspectives related to providing adequate training for parent involvement activities and addressing the needs of students with disabilities.

These data show that school improvement teams, in attempting to address the needs of all students in the school, may advertently or inadvertently overlook the needs of students with exceptionalities. As a professional with a special interest in this area, you should advocate for school improvement teams to solicit and consider family and professional perspectives related to exceptionality. In other words, do not abandon Delfy Roach and other families by keeping them on the outside of school reform discussions. If you do, you will simply perpetuate the power-over posture that impairs collaboration and empowerment.

The second major concern relates to providing adequate preparation for families. Consider family factors in the empowerment framework, especially the knowledge/skills component. You and other educators, in carrying out the partnership of advocating for systems improvement, should provide opportunities for families to expand their information, problem-solving skills, coping skills, and communication skills related to school reform issues. When you create that kind of empowering context, there is every reason to be optimistic about families' contribution to the accomplishment of the National Education Goals. Box 15–3 includes tips to help families enhance their meaningful participation in school reform efforts, including school improvement teams.

Advocating for Change in Parental Participation

The National Education Goal related to parental participation (see figure 15–2) has three objectives:

1. Every state will develop policies to assist local schools and local educational agencies to establish programs for increasing partnerships that respond to the varying needs of parents in the home, including parents of children who are disadvantaged or bilingual and parents of children with disabilities.
2. Every school will actively engage parents and families in a partnership that supports the academic work of children at home and shared educational decision making at school.
3. Parents and families will help to ensure that schools are adequately supported and will hold schools and teachers to high standards of accountability.

What are the key themes of these objectives? What have you learned that can prepare you, as an educational professional, to implement these objectives? We hope that you note the strong emphasis on *increasing partnerships*. You have learned a great deal about partnerships—seven different opportunities for partnerships, with each one infused with the eight obligations for a reliable alliance. Advocating for systems improvement related to the National Education Goal of increasing parental participation means that you can be an advocate within your school to carry out these partnerships yourself and help create a plan for your

---

TIPS   BOX 15–3

Enhancing Family Participation in School Reform and School Improvement Teams

- Become familiar with the groups in your school and district that are studying school reform issues and join the one that interests you most.
- Look at education reform broadly rather than with a narrow, specialized focus that might serve only one group of students.
- Learn the issues.
- Ask students for feedback as new practices are implemented in their schools.
- Locate and build allies in your school, school district, or state with people who have vision,

who are informed about quality education, and who are open to exploring new ideas.
- Assist people to view students with disabilities as whole children who happen to have particular challenges.
- Provide key decision makers with information and reading material on educational issues.
- Encourage ongoing training for a wide variety of participants, a key to successful school reform.
- Talk with university leaders in the community and state.
- Understand the process of change.

Source: Buswell, B., & Schaffner, B. (1994). Parents in school reform. *Coalition Quarterly (published by the Federation for Children with Special Needs), 12*(1), 16–19.

entire school and even entire school district in implementing the seven opportunities for partnerships and eight obligations for a reliable alliance. As Delfy Roach was working to reform her state's hospitalization laws, she found that some professionals were her partners and others were not. Those who were her partners had a very clear understanding of the difficulties that she and other families face in raising a child who has emotional disabilities and is also a minority citizen. They had infused into their alliances with the families their understanding of the families and the cultural traditions the families followed, affirming their strengths, promoting their choices, and warranting the families' trust and respect.

Joyce Epstein (1995) has proposed a process for creating change in implementing school-family-community partnerships. She suggests creating a partnership action team in each school to plan and implement a comprehensive partnership program. This team must have strong support from state and district administrative leaders. It might be a subgroup of the school improvement team, which has responsibility for implementing all six National Education Goals. The partnership action team has the responsibility of focusing specifically on the goal related to parental participation. There are five implementation steps to apply:

1. *Create a partnership action team.* Epstein suggests that the team be composed of at least one administrator, one member from the community, three teachers from different grade levels, and three parents of children in different grade levels. Nonprofessional staff, including custodians and cafeteria workers, can also be included. We would add the caveat that the number of parent representatives might be increased and should include families of typically developing children, children with disabilities, and children who are gifted and talented. A chairperson or facilitator of the action team needs to be strong in the family factors associated with empowerment—five elements of motivation and four elements of knowledge/skills. An empowered leader can be a critical factor in the overall success of the partnership action team.

   One method of organization is to have a subcommittee for each of the seven opportunities for partnerships. The subcommittee membership should represent the broad range of stakeholders.

2. *Obtain funds and other support.* Epstein (1995) suggests that partnership action teams have at least $1,000 per year for three to five years, with additional summer supplements, to invest in staff development, demonstration programs, consultants, and special materials. Another key aspect of support is having sufficient release time so that careful thinking can be invested in the process of developing and implementing action plans for each of the opportunities for partnerships.

3. *Identify starting points.* Conducting a self-assessment of present strengths, needed changes, expectations, and a sense of community can provide a starting point for specifying goals, objectives, and time lines for implementation. Figure 15–4 includes a list of questions that can serve as the basis for planning (Epstein, 1995).

   Strategies for assessing the school's current level of performance related to school-family-community partnerships include interviews, focus groups, questionnaires, panel discussions, and self-assessments.

4. *Develop a three-year plan.* Epstein (1995) suggests developing a three-year plan of the specific action steps for implementing partnerships. After the three-year general plan is developed, the subcommittees can develop a more detailed one-year plan. This one-year plan should specify the activities, time line, persons responsible, resources needed, cost, and method of evaluation. These plans need to be presented to all stakeholders (for example, school faculty, families of students in the school, and community) through school newsletters; stakeholder assemblies; and the community's local radio, television, and newspapers.

5. *Continue planning and working.* The partnership action team should recommend a plan for close monitoring of the implementation of each annual plan and ensure that the monitoring process provides opportunities for troubleshooting, refinement, and a review of evaluation results. As each one-year plan is implemented, subcommittees should develop more detailed plans for the second and third years. As the hard work of implementation goes forward, the partnership action team should celebrate its success and recognize people who have been key contributors. At the end of three years, it will probably be necessary to develop another three-year plan for ongoing implementation and refinement.

Progress in partnerships is incremental, including more families each year in ways that benefit more

FIGURE 15-4

Identifying Starting Points

- *Present strengths.* Which practices of school, family, and community partnerships are now working well for the school as a whole? For individual grade levels? For which types of involvement?

- *Needed changes.* Ideally, how do we want school, family, and community partnerships to work at this school three years from now? Which present practices should continue, and which should change? To reach school goals, what new practices are needed for each of the major types of involvement?

- *Expectations.* What do teachers expect of families? What do families expect of teachers and other school personnel? What do students expect their families to do to help them negotiate school life? What do students expect their teachers to do to keep their families informed and involved?

- *Sense of community.* Which families are we now reaching, and which are we not yet reaching? Who are the "hard-to-reach" families? What might be done to communicate with and engage these families in their children's education? Are current partnership practices coordinated to include all families as a school community? Or are families whose children receive special services (e.g., Title I, special education, bilingual education) separated from families?

- *Links to goals.* How might family and community connections assist the school in helping more students reach higher goals and achieve greater success? Which practices of school, family, and community partnerships would directly connect to particular goals?

Source: Epstein, J. L. (1995, May). School/family/community partnerships: Caring for the children we share. *Phi Delta Kappan*, p. 709.

students. Like reading or math programs, assessment programs, sports programs, or other school investments, partnership programs take time to develop, must be periodically reviewed, and should be continuously improved. The schools in our projects have shown that three years is a minimum time needed for an action team to complete a number of activities on each type of involvement and to establish its work as a productive and permanent structure in a school. (Epstein, 1995, p. 710)

You can and should be a key contributor to the development of regularized opportunities for partnerships in the school where you are employed and be a key advocate for empowered family involvement. To do this, you will need to enhance your own development on the family factors of empowerment and then contribute to the process of creating an empowering context for systemic planning to take place. As plans are developed and implemented and partnerships begin to flourish, you probably will find that you are part of the synergistic community we discussed in chapter 2. When the energy of all participants contributes to a coordinated and comprehensive planning process, the whole becomes greater than the sum of the parts, and empowerment for all becomes the reality.

Advocating for Change through Legislative and Judicial Processes

National Influence   Nowhere is the advocacy role more obvious than with respect to the federal special education law known as the Individuals with Disabilities Education Act (Turnbull & Turnbull, 1996). When, between 1972 and 1975, Congress was first considering whether or not to help the states educate students with disabilities, its members discovered just how effective families can be.

With direction from a national coalition of family-run disability advocacy organizations and professional groups such as the Council for Exceptional Children, parents mounted a highly organized grassroots advocacy effort. Families visited their representatives in their Washington, DC, and local offices. They invited legislators to tour the schools where children and youth with disabilities were educated and to see also the institutions where other children and youth were deprived of an education and any meaningful treatment. Parents were witnesses at congressional hearings held throughout the country and in Washington, DC. They pleaded with state representatives, governors, and school officials to join their cause in getting federal money to educate students.

They skillfully used the media to publicize their cause and elicit public support. And most important of all, they secured the strategic help of passionately committed insiders—members of Congress or members' staff as well as appointees to high positions in the administrations of Presidents Nixon and Ford (Turnbull & Turnbull, 1996).

Even today, families and their advocacy organizations, in collaboration with some (but not all) professional organizations, are using the same strategies that their predecessors used 20 years earlier. Few things are so constant and effective as families' systems advocacy. This is because many families are highly motivated to create favorable policies and programs and because they have the knowledge/skills to be effective.

State/Local Influence

It should not come as a surprise that families such as Delfy Roach's also engage in systems change advocacy at the state and local levels. After all, most service delivery systems are operated by state and local government agencies or by private agencies under the supervision of state and local governments.

A sterling example of effective state-level advocacy during the early to mid 1990s relates to family support laws and programs. We described family support in chapter 10; it is a program that provides cash, vouchers, or both to families of children with developmental or emotional disabilities. During the late 1980s and early 1990s, families, assisted by researchers and policy analysts, developed a grassroots movement to secure family support laws. This movement was organized nationally but carried out locally; its targets were governors, state representatives, and state bureaucrats. It was, without doubt, enormously successful: The number of states with family support laws increased over a period of five years or so from a handful to more than half the states (Bergman & Singer, 1996; Powers, 1996; Yuan, Baker-McCue, & Witkin, 1996). In the family support advocacy movement, there is a recurring theme: the collaboration among families, professionals, and other interested individuals and organizations for systems change. This is the same kind of collaboration that produced the reforms in New Mexico's mental health laws that Delfy Roach and other families and professionals wanted.

Influencing Policy through the Courts

Finally, families have advocated for systems change by suing state or local educational agencies for more appropriate and more inclusive education for children with disabilities. To a very large degree they have been successful.

As early as 1972, parents and their skilled civil-rights lawyers persuaded federal courts in Pennsylvania and the District of Columbia that their children have a constitutional right to go to school (*Mills v. DC Board of Education*, 1972; *PARC v. Commonwealth*, 1971, 1972). Armed with these victories, the parents then persuaded Congress to put some teeth behind that right to education; the result of their advocacy was, of course, the Individuals with Disabilities Education Act.

When state and local educational agencies were reluctant or unable to discharge their duty to educate children with disabilities, parents sued. Sometimes they got what they wanted, such as clean intermittent catheterization (*Irving Independent School District v. Tatro*, 1984). Sometimes they did not get what they wanted (such as an interpreter) but instead benefited from a decision holding that the state and local agencies must provide some benefit to the students and cannot get away with simply opening the schoolhouse doors and admitting them to the building (*Board of Education v. Rowley*, 1982).

Over time, parents became increasingly dissatisfied with the schools' refusal to comply with the doctrine of least restrictive placements. Impelled by the Regular Education Initiative and later the full inclusion doctrine (chapter 2), families sued for and won the rights to have their children included in the same schools and same academic and extracurricular programs as children who do not have disabilities (*Board of Education v. Holland*, 1994; *Daniel R. R. v. State Board of Education*, 1989; *Greer v. Rome City School District*, 1990; *Oberti v. Board of Education*, 1992; *Roncker v. Walters*, 1983). You may want to reread box 8–3, which features Carlos Oberti talking about his fight for his son's inclusion.

When the United States Supreme Court interprets IDEA, its decision is binding throughout the country. When a federal court of appeals or trial court interprets IDEA, its opinion is binding on all educational agencies within its jurisdiction. Clearly, then, a victorious lawsuit can have systemwide implications. It sets into motion change for the one student whose rights were defined by the court. Additionally, it generates systemwide changes because many other students now have acquired the same rights as the child in the lawsuit.

Because many parents cannot afford to hire a lawyer and because system change often requires lawsuits, Congress has created two programs of legal services. The first system is called Protection and Advocacy and is responsible for advocating for families or individuals with developmental disabilities or mental illness. Much of the work of Protection and Advocacy agencies deals with the rights of students under IDEA. Each state has a Protection and Advocacy agency; contact your governor's office to find out its address and telephone number.

The second system is organized under the Legal Services Corporation, a public corporation created by Congress for the purpose of providing legal aid to poor or low-income families. Every state has one or more Legal Services Offices; most large cities have an office. Contact the administrative offices of the state bar association or state supreme court or check the local telephone directory (white or yellow pages) for the listings for the local or regional legal services corporation.

In most states, the Parent Training and Information Center should know the name, address, and location of the Protection and Advocacy and Legal Services Corporation offices or should be able to help you find low-cost legal aid (such as aid usually provided under the auspices of state or county bar associations). In addition, those bar associations should be able to help families locate lawyers who

will do pro bono work. The term *pro bono* is short for *pro bono publico* and means "for the public good." A lawyer or firm that does pro bono work usually charges a reduced fee or no fee at all if it takes a case that it determines will be in the public interest. That kind of case is usually one that will achieve systemwide changes.

Linking Our Themes

Creating a Reliable Alliance

The eight obligations of a reliable alliance need to be infused into the partnership opportunity of advocating for systems improvement in the same way that you infuse them into the six other opportunities for partnerships. By this point, this infusion should seem like second nature for you. Figure 15–5 highlights issues that are likely to arise and disempowering and empowering options that you have in creating the reliable alliance obligations.

FIGURE 15–5

Creating a Reliable Alliance: Emphasis on Advocating for Systems Improvement

Obligations	Issues	Disempowering Actions	Empowering Actions
Knowing yourself	As a new teacher you think you might be "out-of-place" to express your interest in being a member of the school improvement team.	Decide to wait several years until you have more credability before you let others know of your interest in systems improvement.	Ask the principal to bring you up to date on how the school is implementing the National Education Goals and express your interest in being an active participant in the process.
Knowing families			
Family characteristics	A father from a lower socioeconomic background has a special commitment to partnerships and could represent a whole segment of families who do not currently have a voice in school planning.	Conclude that this father would likely not be able to hold his own in serving on the partnership action team and recommend a parent who is a university professor in his place.	Advocate for the father to be a parent representative on the team. Stress the importance of parents from all backgrounds being represented.
Family interactions	A mother of one of your students is so involved in organizing a letter-writing campaign to influence state policy that she is unavailable to help her child with homework assignments. Her child is falling further and further behind.	Suggest to the mother that her child's progress needs to take precedence over her advocacy efforts and that it is not fair to neglect him.	Brainstorm with the mother about how she might be able to get others to help with the letter-writing campaign so that she will not have so much to do herself. Also, consider who else might be available to help with homework.

FIGURE 15–5 CONTINUED

Creating a Reliable Alliance: Emphasis on Advocating for Systems Improvement

Obligations	Issues	Disempowering Actions	Empowering Actions
Family functions	Parents of one of your students want to know about the latest court cases on inclusion, but they don't have access to this information and don't know where to get it.	Conclude that sharing information about court cases is just encouraging parents to sue you. Tell them there is nothing that you can do to help.	Encourage parents to contact the Parent Training and Information Center to gather the latest information on inclusion court cases.
Family life cycle	Parents of one of the students who is graduating from your high school class are very frustrated by only having a sheltered workshop as a post-secondary option. Your director of special education encourages them to be realistic about their son's potential.	Accept what the director of special education says so that you can be sure to protect your job.	Convene a meeting of high school teachers and families and invite people to share great expectations of the kinds of services they would like to have after high school. Develop an action plan for professionals taking more responsibility to advocate for appropriate services.
Honoring cultural diversity	As you review the roster of members of the school improvement team, you realize that all are Euro-American.	Assume that the principal knew what she was doing when these appointments were made and that it is none of your business to make any suggestions.	Reflect on possible school, family, or community participants from culturally diverse backgrounds. Make recommendations to the principal of additional participants representing diverse backgrounds.
Affirming and building on family strengths	A parent of a student in your class is an attorney who has a particular interest in disability policy.	Assume that it is better for parents of students in your classroom not to know much about disability policy because they may start making too many unreasonable demands on you.	Ask the parent who is a lawyer if he would be willing to provide an update to all parents in your classroom of the process the state uses to monitor IDEA implementation and how they might be able to contribute to the process.
Promoting family choices	A parent of one of your students suggests activities that the school might undertake to improve the IEP process.	Acknowledge that the parent has a good idea but dismiss it because it would require change in the procedures that the school has always followed.	Give the parent the name or the person who is in charge of the partnership action team subcommittee related to individualizing education. Encourage the parent to meet with the subcommittee and share her good idea.
Envisioning great expectations	You develop your own vision for how the opportunities for partnerships might permeate every professional and family in your school.	Assume that you are only responsible for yourself and that all you can do is to take care of your own classroom.	Share your vision with professional colleagues and families and encourage them to start a partnership action team.

FIGURE **15–5** CONTINUED

Creating a Reliable Alliance: Emphasis on Advocating for Systems Improvement

Obligations	Issues	Disempowering Actions	Empowering Actions
Using interpersonal communication skills	During meetings of the school improvement team, you notice that the principal dominates the discussion and cuts off family contributions.	Assume that the principal has the prerogative to dominate decision making.	Discuss with the principal the fact that you have heard many good ideas raised by families in private conversations and brainstorm about what might be done to ensure that these ideas come up at the school improvement team meetings.
Warranting trust and respect	You are intimidated by parents of one of your students who are making adversarial threats.	When parents try to schedule a meeting, tell them that you do not have any available time.	Listen empathetically to the parents' concerns and consider ways that their concerns can be taken into account by the school improvement team and by your own advocacy efforts.

Strengthening Family Factors

Your partnerships with families can make all the difference in either enhancing or detracting from their motivation and knowledge/skills related to empowerment. Figure 15–6 suggests how your actions can make a meaningful difference in family empowerment as well as the empowerment of yourself and your professional colleagues.

Summary

Advocacy simply means taking one's own or another's perspective to obtain a result not otherwise available. Standing up for one's own rights and interests (self-advocacy) or for the rights and interests of another (representational advocacy) occurs at the local, regional, state, and national levels. Indeed, many families have to engage in local advocacy at one time or another, and many who have become advocates for change at the local level have also become advocates at the state or national level.

Advocacy seeks to make a difference not only in the education of a single student but also in the way a school system educates all students; this is *systems advocacy*. Many parents welcome the chance to be single-student or even systems change advocates; others do not care to be advocates.

Advocacy can involve collaboration with professionals; often, it is most effective if does involve collaboration. And advocacy often involves efforts to change laws or win lawsuits.

The agencies that seem most helpful to families and their professional allies are the Partners in Policy programs, the Parent Training and Information Centers, disability-specific organizations at the national/state/local levels, Protection and Advocacy agencies, Legal Services Corporation law firms, and pro bono lawyers.

The national emphasis on school reform gives parents a chance to advocate for the effective implementation of the National Education Goals. Many schools have created school improvement teams, comprised of a full range of stakeholders, to collaborate for educational improvement. In many school improvement teams, issues associated with students who have exceptionalities have taken a back burner to other issues that have priority with typically developing students. One of your roles can be to ensure that family and professional perspectives related to exceptionality get meaningfully incorporated into the school reform planning process.

FIGURE 15–6

Strengthening Family Factors Through an Empowering Context: Emphasis on Advocating for Systems Improvement

Motivation	What You Can Do	Knowledge/Skills	What You Can Do
Self-efficacy	Provide feedback to parents on partnership action teams to reinforce their contributions. Cite specific examples of how they help the team be effective.	Information	Keep families informed of proposed changes in national and state legislation and contact information for how they can make their viewpoints known to key policymakers.
Perceived control	When many changes are needed to ensure an appropriate education for the student, identify families' priorities and advocate for those priorities to be addressed first.	Problem solving	Ensure that the partnership action teams incorporate a systematic problem solving process so that detailed action plans are developed and implemented.
Energy	Help identify empowerful professionals and families to serve on the school improvement team so the full responsibility will not fall on a few individuals.	Communication skills	Emphasize to families how important it is to be assertive in school improvement team meetings to make sure that issues associated with special education are included on the agenda.
Persistence	If initial efforts fail to influence appropriate state and local policies, encourage advocates to keep working until the goal is reached.	Coping skills	Encourage families who are heavily involved in advocacy to work closely with others who have similar interests so that mutual support can be shared.
Hope	When funds are being cut back at the national and state levels, emphasize the importance of advocacy and the possibility that the cuts might be restored.		

Of the eight National Education Goals, one focuses on parent participation. We suggested a process that your school can follow in creating partnership action teams to plan for the effective implementation of all seven opportunities for partnerships.

Finally, many families (and professionals) have meaningfully advocated for systems change through the legislative process at national and state levels and through judicial processes. We encourage you to recognize all avenues for policy change and to participate in the process of developing and refining policy related to the education of students with exceptionalities.

The street wisdom that Delfy Roach offers shows just how effective she can be—or any parent could be—as an advocate. Yes, she had to come out fighting against school administrators; and yes, she had to do the same when seeking reform of the state's mental health laws.

One reason that Delfy seems to have prevailed is that she is a smart advocate. She enlisted the assistance of professionals, and she was attuned to and honored the cultural customs of the people she represented.

Delfy would be the first to admit that overcoming the stigma of mental disability and the disadvantage of membership in a cultural minority is not easy. But her motivation was high; after all, what the schools were doing to her son James was utterly unacceptable. Moreover, her belief in herself and in her ability to affect what happens to her and her dogged persistence converted the transforming event—James's expulsion—into a bundle of energy.

Targeting that energy was simple enough: Delfy learned what James's rights were, devised strategies to solve the challenges facing him and her, and became a successful advocate.

There is, however, more to Delfy's advocacy than the individual and representational advocacy she does for James and other students and families. Knowing that "our kids are with us for a lifetime" and asking profes-sionals to "understand and respect that" guides Delfy into a different kind of advocacy—a less confrontational type.

She asks professionals to ask themselves, "If this were my family, what would I want to see happen?" In asking them to consider that question, Delfy does more than appeal to their empathy; she creates a common thread of humanity and ties them to her life.

Advocates can, after all, be just as hard and tough as Delfy and just as compassionate. She refuses to "bash or blame" professionals. And she is strategic, linking a mother's passionate commitment to her son to a profes-sional's dedication to that same person and to the imag-ined child who might be born to that professional.

Is Delfy a good advocate? No doubt, she is. And that's because, after all is said and done, she is fiercely motivated and knowledgeable.

Appendices

A. Names and Addresses

B. Conversation Guide

Appendix A

Names and Addresses

Please feel free to contact us at this address:

Beach Center on Families and Disability
and
The Family Connection
3111 Haworth Hall
University of Kansas
Lawrence, Kansas 66045
Beach Center general telephone number: (913) 864-7600
The Family Connection telephone number: (800) 854-4938

The following names and addresses may also be useful.

Statewide Parent to Parent Programs

ARIZONA

Pilot Parent Partnerships
4750 Black Canyon Highway,
    Suite 101
Phoenix, AZ 85017-3621

ARKANSAS

Parent to Parent
2000 Main
Little Rock, AR 72206

CALIFORNIA

Parents Helping Parents
3041 Olcott Street
Santa Clara, CA 95054-3222

CONNECTICUT

**Parent to Parent Network of
Connecticut
The Family Center**
181 East Cedar Street
Newington, CT 06111

FLORIDA

**Family Network on Disabilities
of Florida**
5510 Gray Street, Suite 220
Tampa, FL 33609

GEORGIA

Parent to Parent of Georgia
2900 Woodcock Boulevard,
    Suite 240
Atlanta, GA 30341

INDIANA

**Indiana Parent Information
Network**
4755 Kingsway Drive, Suite 105
Indianapolis, IN 46205

IOWA

Iowa Pilot Parents (IEPC)
33 North 12th Street,
P.O. Box 1151
Fort Dodge, IA 50501

KANSAS

Families Together
501 SW Jackson, Suite 400
Topeka, KS 66603

KENTUCKY

**Parent Information Network
of Kentucky**
1887 Rutherford Avenue
Louisville, KY 40205-1856

MICHIGAN

**Family Support Network of
Michigan**
1200 6th Street, 9th Floor, N.
    Tower
Detroit, MI 48226

NEW HAMPSHIRE

**Parent to Parent of New
Hampshire**
117 Mascoma Street, Box 622
Lebanon, NH 03766

NEW MEXICO

**Parents Reaching Out (PRO)
Project ADOBE**
1000A Main Street, NW
Los Lunas, NM 87037

NEW YORK

**Parent to Parent of New York
State**
Balltown and Consaul Roads
Schenectady, NY 12304

NORTH CAROLINA

**Family Support Network of
North Carolina**
CB #7340, Chase Hall
University of North Carolina
Chapel Hill, NC 27699-7340

OHIO

Family Information Network
246 N. High Street, 5th Floor
Columbus, OH 43266-0118

PENNSYLVANIA

**Parent to Parent Network of
Pennsylvania**
4446 Dunmore Drive
Harrisburg, PA 17112

SOUTH CAROLINA

**Family Connection of South
Carolina**
2712 Middleburg Drive,
Suite 103-B
Columbia, SC 29204

TENNESSEE

Parent to Parent
312 8th Avenue North
Tennessee Tower, 10th Floor
Nashville, TN 37247

UTAH

HOPE-A Parent Network
2290 East 4500 South, Suite 110
Salt Lake City, UT 84117

VERMONT

Parent to Parent of Vermont
1 Main Street
69 Champlain Mill
Winooski, VT 05404

VIRGINIA

**Parent to Parent—Family and
Children's Services**
1518 Willow Lawn Drive
Richmond, VA 23230

WASHINGTON

**Parent to Parent Support
Program**
10550 Lake City Way NE, Suite A
Seattle, WA 98125

Parent Training and Information Centers

ALABAMA

**Special Education Action
Committee (SEAC)**
P.O. Box 161274
Mobile, AL 36616-2274

ALASKA

**Alaska PARENTS Resource
Center**
540 W. International Airport Road,
Suite 200
Anchorage, AK 99518

ARIZONA

Pilot Parent Partnerships
4750 N. Black Canyon Highway,
Suite 101
Phoenix, AZ 85017-3621

ARKANSAS

Arkansas Disability Coalition
10002 West Markham, Suite B7
Little Rock, AR 72205

FOCUS
305 W. Jefferson Ave
Jonesboro, AR 72401

CALIFORNIA

TASK
100 W. Cerritos Avenue
Anaheim, CA 92805-6546

**Northern California Coalition
for Parent Training and
Information (NCC)
Parents Helping Parents**
3041 Olcott Street
Santa Clara, CA 95054-3222

DREDF
2212 6th Street
Berkeley, CA 94710

**MATRIX, A Parent Network and
Resource Center**
555 Northgate Drive, Suite A
San Rafael, CA 94903

Exceptional Parents Unlimited
4120 N. 1st Street
Fresno, CA 93726

COLORADO

PEAK Parent Center
6055 Lehman Dr., Suite 101
Colorado Springs, CO 80918

CONNECTICUT

**Connecticut Parent Advisor
Center (CPAC)**
5 Church Lane, Suite 4
P.O. Box 579
East Lyme, CT 06333

DELAWARE

PIC of Delaware
700 Barksdale Road, Suite 3
Newark, DE 19711

DISTRICT OF COLUMBIA

COPE
300 I Street NE, Suite 209
Washington, DC 20002

FLORIDA

Family Network on Disabilities
5510 Gray Street, Suite 220
Tampa, FL 33609

GEORGIA

Parents Educating Parents
Georgia ARC
2860 East Point Street, Suite 200
East Point, GA 30344

HAWAII

**AWARE/Learning Disabilities
Association of Hawaii (LSAH)**
200 N. Vineyard Boulevard, Suite
310
Honolulu, HI 96817

IDAHO

**Idaho Parents Unlimited
Parent Education Resource
Center**
4696 Overland Road, Suite 478
Boise, ID 83705

ILLINOIS

**Family Resource Center on
Disabilities (FRCD)**
20 E. Jackson Boulevard, Room
900
Chicago, IL 60604

Designs for Change
6 N. Michigan Avenue, Suite 1600
Chicago, IL 60602

National Center for Latinos with Disabilities
1921 South Blue Island
Chicago, IL 60608

INDIANA

Indiana Resource Center for Families with Special Needs (IN*SOURCE)
809 North Michigan
South Bend, IN 46601

IOWA

Iowa Pilot Parents (IEPC)
33 North 12th Street,
P.O. Box 1151
Fort Dodge, IA 50501

KANSAS

Families Together
501 SW Jackson, Suite 400
Topeka, KS 66603

KENTUCKY

Kentucky Special Parent Involvement Network (KY-SPIN)
2210 Goldsmith Lane, Suite 118
Louisville, KY 40218

LOUISIANA

Program of Families Helping Families of Greater New Orleans: Project PROMPT
4323 Division Street, Suite 110
Metairie, LA 70124-3179

MAINE

Special-Needs Parent Information Network (SPIN)
P.O. Box 2067
Augusta, ME 04330-2067

MARYLAND

Parents Place of Maryland
7257 Parkway Drive, Suite 210
Hanover, MD 21076

Parents Place of Western Maryland
23 East Frederick Street
Walkersville, MD 21793

MASSACHUSETTS

Federation for Children with Special Needs
95 Berkeley Street, Suite 104
Boston, MA 02116

MICHIGAN

Parents are Experts: Parents Training Parents Project
23077 Greenfield Road, Suite 205
Southfield, MI 48075-3744

Citizens Alliance to Uphold Special Education (CAUSE)
3303 W. Saginaw Street, Suite F1
Lansing, MI 48917-2303

MINNESOTA

PACER Center
4826 Chicago Avenue, South
Minneapolis, MN 55417-1098

MISSISSIPPI

Parent Partners
3111 N. State Street
Jackson, MS 39216

Project Empower
P.O. Box 851
Greenville, MS 38702-0851

MISSOURI

Missouri Parents Act (MPACT)
1901 Windriker Drive
Jefferson City, MO 65101

MPACT—St. Louis Office
8631 Delmar, Suite 300
St. Louis, MO 63124

MPACT—Kansas City Office
3100 Main, Suite 303
Kansas City, MO 64111

PEARS (Parent Education and Advocacy Resource Support Project)
MPACT—Kansas City Office
3100 Main, Suite 303
Kansas City, MO 64111

MONTANA

Parents Let's Unite for Kids (PLUK)
1500 North 30th Street, Room 267
Billings, MT 59101-0298

NEBRASKA

Nebraska Parents' Center
3610 Dodge Street, Suite 102
Omaha, NE 68131

NEVADA

Nevada Parent Training Information Center
4970 Arvil Road, Suite 110
Las Vegas, NV 89118

Northern PEP
1359 Kim Place
Minden, NV 89423

NEW HAMPSHIRE

Parent Information Center
151A Manchester Street
P.O. Box 1422
Concord, NH 03302-1422

NEW JERSEY

Statewide Parent Advocacy Network (SPAN)
516 North Avenue East, Suite 2
Westfield, NJ 07090-1446

NEW MEXICO

EPICS Project
S.W. Communication Resources
P.O. Box 788
2000 Camino del Pueblo
Bernalillo, NM 87004

Parents Reaching Out (PRO) Project ADOBE
1000A Main Street, NW
Los Lunas, NM 87031

NEW YORK

Parent Network Center (PNC)
250 Delaware Avenue, Suite 3
Buffalo, NY 14202-1515

Advocates for Children of New York
24–16 Bridge Plaza South
Long Island City, NY 11101

Resources for Children with Special Needs
200 Park Avenue South, Suite 816
New York, NY 10003

Sinergia
15 W. 65th Street, 6th Floor
New York, NY 10023

NORTH CAROLINA

Exceptional Children's Assistance Center (ECAC)
P.O. Box 16
Davidson, NC 28036

Parents Project
300 Enola Road
Morganton, NC 28655

NORTH DAKOTA

Pathfinder Family Center
1600 2nd Avenue, SW
Minot, ND 58701

Native American Experimental Parent Training and Information Center
Arrowhead Shopping Center
16th Street and 2nd Avenue, SW
Minot, ND 58701

Child Advocacy Center
1821 Summit Road, Suite 303
Cincinnati, OH 45237

Ohio Coalition for the Education of Handicapped Children (OCEHC)
165 W. Center Street, Suite 302
Marion, OH 43302-3741

Parents Reaching Out in Oklahoma Project (PRO-OK)
1917 South Harvard Avenue
Oklahoma City, OK 73128

Oregon COPE Project
999 Locust Street, NE Box B
Salem, OR 97303

Parents Union for Public Schools
311 S. Juniper Street, Suite 602
Philadelpha, PA 19107

Parent Education Network
333 E. 7th Avenue
York, PA 17404

Asociacion De Padres Pro-Bienstar de Ninos con Impedimentos de PR
Box 21301
San Juan, PR 00928-1301

Rhode Island Parent Information Center (RIPIN)
500 Prospect Street
Pawtucket, RI 02860

PRO-PARENTS
2712 Middleburg Drive,
   Suite 102
Columbia, SC 29204

South Dakota Parent Connection
3701 W. 49th, Suite 200B
Sioux Falls, SD 57106

Support and Training for Exceptional Parents (STEP)
1104 Tusculum Boulevard,
   Suite 401
Greenville, TN 37745

Partners Resource Network PATH
Longfellow Drive, Suite B
Beaumont, TX 77706-4889

Special Kids (SKI)
6202 Belmark
P.O. Box 61628
Houston, TX 77208-1628

Project PODER
2300 W. Commerce, Suite 205
San Antonio, TX 78207

Utah Parent Center (UPC)
2290 East 4500 South, Suite 110
Salt Lake City, UT 84117

Vermont Parent Information Center (VPIC)
Chace Mill
1 Mill Street, Suite A7
Burlington, VT 05401

Parent Educational Advocacy Training Center (PEATC)
10340 Democracy Lane,
   Suite 206
Fairfax, VA 22030

VI FIND
67th Street Sugar Estate
P.O. Box 11670
St. Thomas, USVI 00801

Washington PAVE
6316 South 12th Street
Tacoma, WA 98465-1900

PAVE/STOMP Specialized Training of Military Parents
12208 Pacific Highway, SW
Tacoma, WA 98499

West Virginia PTI (WVPTI)
104 East Main Street, Suite 3-B
Clarksburg, WV 26301

Parent Education Project of Wisconsin (PEP-WI)
2195 South 60th Street
West Allis, WI 53219-1568

Wyoming PIC
5 North Lobban
Buffalo, WY 82834

Grassroots

COFFO
P.O. Box 900368
Homestead, FL 33090

IPEST
Martha's Vineyard
108 Lake Street
P.O. Box 4081
Vineyard Haven, MA 02586

Loving Your Disabled Child (LYDC)
4715 Crenshaw Boulevard
Los Angeles, CA 90043

Mentor Parent Program
Route 257, Salem Road
P.O. Box 718
Seneca, PA 16346

Oglala Sioux Tribe
Public Safety Commission
Box 300
Pine Ridge, SD 57770

Parent Advocate for Disabled
332 W. Alverez Avenue
Clewiston, FL 33440

Parent Empowerment Project
4255 Fifth Avenue, SW
Naples, FL 33999

Parents of Watts
10828 Lou Dillon Avenue
Los Angeles, CA 90059

Parent Power
1118 142nd Street
Tacoma, WA 98444

Pyramid Parent Training Project
3132 Napolean Avenue
New Orleans, LA 70125

Special Kids (SKI)
P.O. Box 61728
Houston, TX 77208

United We Stand
c/o Francis of Paola Preschool
201 Conselyea Street
Brooklyn, NY 11206

UPBEATT
9950 Fielding
Detroit, MI 48228

Vietnamese Parents of Disabled Children (VPDC)
314 Gina Drive
Carson, CA 90745-3617

VI FIND
67th Street Sugar Estate
P.O. Box 11670
St. Thomas, USVI 00801

Appendix B

Conversation Guide

Family Characteristics

Characteristics of the Family

- Who are the members of your family? Which ones live together in your home? Which ones are interested in supporting _____ 's education?

- We all have certain cultural characteristics that especially influence our families. These might be related to the part of the country where we grew up, our jobs, religion, race, or the financial resources that we have. For me, I've always considered one of the major cultural influences on my family to be _____. How do you characterize your family's culture?

- What are the most important things that parents should teach their children? What are the most important things that schools should teach children?

- Has there been any particular type of advice handed down through the generations of your family about how people ought to live their life? What is it and do you think it has implications for _____ 's educational program?

- What particular concerns do you have about financial resources that are important for the school to take into account?

- What is one of the major strengths of your family?

- Is there a particular challenge or struggle that your family is having now that might influence _____ 's educational program?

Personal Characteristics

- I'm eager to get to know _____. Tell me about _____ 's typical day and especially about the things that he or she most likes and dislikes about the day.

- What are things that seem to be going especially well for _____?

- What are some of the particular challenges that _____ is facing now?

- So much of _____ 's day is spent in school. What's your view of how things are going at school?

- How does _____ 's exceptionality influence schoolwork as well as relationships with classmates?

- How would you characterize the nature of _____ 's exceptionality? What have others told you about it that you especially agree or disagree with?

- What do you most enjoy about _____ ?

- How does _____ contribute to the family in a positive way?

- What are the issues that seem to pose the greatest family challenges?

- We all have different ways of dealing with problems when they arise. As you think back over the last 6 to 12 months and the problems that various members of your family have faced, what are some of the things that you and other family members do that particularly help you not only to survive but prevail?

- What are some of the less effective ways that you have tried to solve problems?

- Are there any particular health concerns of family members that influence your daily and weekly routines?

- Who are the people most available to participate in school activities and help _____ at home in his or her educational goals?

Special Challenges

- All families face times when things seem to be a bit easier and other times when things seem to be more difficult. Are there any particular challenges that your family is now facing that impact the time, energy, and resources that you can invest in _____ 's educational program?

- On a long-term basis, are there family issues or circumstances that make life more challenging? Do you feel comfortable sharing these with me?

Family Interaction

Marital Interactions

- What is your current marital status?

- How would you describe _____ 's impact on your marriage?

- Has there been a time in the past when _____ 's educational program somehow created marital strain? How could we work together to make sure to avoid such situations in the future?

- What are the strengths or interests of each person who will be involved that we should take into account in communicating with you?

- Are there any custody issues associated with your separation or divorce about which the school needs to be aware?

- If there is joint custody, what are your preferences about who should receive communication from the school and participate in conferences?

Parental Interactions

- How do you and your spouse share parental roles? Given this pattern, what are your preferences for how you participate this year in _____ 's educational program?

- Sometimes in families there are adults who take on some parental responsibilities even though they are not an actual parent. Are there people like that involved with _____ ? How might we best involve them in his or her educational program?

- What do you find to be the most and least enjoyable aspects of interacting with _____ ? Given those aspects, how can we best ensure that we respect your preferences as we offer a menu of educational activities for the home?

- Over time, has there been a fairly consistent pattern for your parental responsibilities or has this changed because of some kind of special circumstances?

- Are there any basic parental needs that you have that staff could support you in addressing?

Sibling Interactions

- What are the most and least enjoyable ways that your other children interact with _____ ?

- In what ways might _____ 's brothers or sisters provide educational support?

- What challenges are your other children experiencing that are taking a large amount of time, energy, and resources right now?

- What approach is right in terms of spreading your time and attention across all your children's interests? Do you think any of your children feel that _____ 's exceptionality has taken undue time and attention from them? Which ones think that? Why?

- What do you think about the idea of having _____ 's brothers and sisters attend conferences to plan his or her educational program?

Extended Family Interactions

- Who is in your extended family? How often do you see them?

- In what ways have extended family members provided you with support and assistance in raising _____ ?

- Do you think your extended family members would be interested in having additional information about how they might best support _____ ? What information would be helpful and what would be the best way to share it with them?

- Would you like us to extend an invitation to your extended family to participate in educational conferences or school events?

Family Functions

Affection

- In what ways does _____ particularly appreciate having affection expressed?

- How important do you think it is to express affection to _____ and your other children?

- Are there other people outside of the family on whom _____ depends for affection?

Self-Esteem

- Standing in _____ 's shoes, how do you think _____ sees him or herself in terms of personal strengths and weaknesses?

- What are your family beliefs about how best to help your family members feel good about themselves?

- What have been some school experiences in the past that have particularly helped _____ feel good about him or herself?

- What have been some school experiences in the past that have had a very negative impact on _____ 's self-esteem?

- What do you think are the most significant ways that we can work together to support _____ to develop a stronger sense of capability and contribution?

Economics

- To what extent do family economics influence the kind of support that you can provide to _____ ?

- Has _____ required more or fewer economic resources than other family members?

- Are you interested in _____ 's learning job skills so that he or she might get a part-time job after school or during the summer to contribute to family income?

- Because of _____ 's exceptionality, have there been special family responsibilities for dealing with insurance or other reimbursement programs?

Daily Care

- What is a typical day like in your family?

- What are the most challenging aspects of the day?

- Do you have time built in throughout the day for relaxation and rest?

- As a family, how do you divide the daily tasks related to meeting each individual's needs?

- What kinds of chores does _____ assume and in what ways might we work together to teach him or her skills that make the family's daily routine easier?

*R*ecreation

- As a family, what do you do for fun?

- In what way does _____ 's exceptionality influence family recreation and leisure?

- What recreation or leisure skills might _____ learn at school that would make family recreation and leisure more enjoyable?

*S*ocialization

- Who are the people that _____ hangs out with when he or she is not at school?

- What are your perspectives on _____ 's friendship network? What do you think would be an ideal friendship network for _____ ?

- In what way do you think _____ 's exceptionality has influenced his or her opportunities for friends?

- How would you characterize the extent to which your family friends support _____ ?

*E*ducation/Vocation

- Of all the educators who have worked with _____ in the past, could you tell me about an individual who had an especially good relationship with him or her and you? What can we learn from that situation that we can incorporate into the school year?

- Now, don't give me a name but just describe a situation in the past that was really difficult when an educator was not especially helpful at all to _____ and your family. What can we learn from that situation to make sure that we don't repeat any of it?

- What do you see _____ doing after graduating from high school in terms of where he or she works and lives? Does _____ have the same vision for him or herself?

- In what ways do you most enjoy participating with _____ in his or her educational program?

- There are many different ways that we could communicate throughout the school year, such as through home visits, school conferences, telephone calls, notes, or exchanging a notebook back and forth. What are your preferences for communication? What do you think will work best for you and your family?

- In terms of _____ 's vocational development, are there family members or friends who might be especially good resources in helping to create job training situations? How might we best capitalize upon their contributions?

Family Life Cycle

Early Childhood

- Tell me about _____ 's early years. What stands out in terms of some of your happiest memories? What about your most problematic memories?

- Did you find out during the early years that _____ has an exceptionality? If so, how did you find out? Looking back, in what ways would you like to have improved the manner in which it was communicated to you?

- Did _____ participate in an early childhood program? What were your views of the program?

School Age

- What would you say have been the highs and lows of _____ 's educational experiences?

- If you found out about _____ 's exceptionality during school years, what was that process like? Looking back, how would you have improved it?

- In what way do you think _____ is or has been best prepared for his or her future by school experiences?

- Try to create a picture in your mind of an ideal situation for _____ when he or she is an adult. Describe that situation to me. What are your great expectations for his or her future?

Adolescence

- When you look to the future, what are your great expectations for _____ 's life? What are your greatest concerns?

- As you look ahead to adolescence, what do you anticipate to be the easiest and most difficult aspect?

- Now that _____ is a teenager, how would you describe the highs and lows of adolescence?

- How does _____ 's adolescence compare with his or her brothers and sisters?

- What do you see as the priorities that need to be addressed in school to best prepare _____ for life as an adult?

Early Adult Years

- When you look to the future, what are your great expectations for _____ 's life? What are your greatest concerns?

- Where do you see _____ living and working and what role do you anticipate having in supporting his or her success?

- How do you see that your family life might change after _____ graduates from high school?

References

Chapter 1 HISTORICAL AND CURRENT ROLES OF FAMILIES AND PARENTS

Avis, D. W. (1985). Deinstitutionalization jet lag. In H. R. Turnbull & A. P. Turnbull (Eds.), *Parents speak out: Then and now* (2nd ed.) (pp. 185–200). Englewood Cliffs, NJ: Merrill/Prentice Hall.

Baker, B. L., with Ambrose, S. A., & Anderson, S. R. (1989) Parent training and developmental disabilities [Special issue]. *Monographs of the American Association on Mental Retardation, 13.*

Barr, M. W. (1913). *Mental defectives: Their history, treatment, and training.* Philadelphia: Blakiston.

Baumeister, A. A., Kupstas, F. D., & Woodley-Zanthos, P. (1993). *The new morbidity: Recommendations for actions and an updated guide to state planning for the prevention of mental retardation and related disabilities associated with socioeconomic conditions.* Washington, DC: U.S. Department of Health and Human Services.

Beckman, A. A., & Brent, R. L. (1986). Mechanism of known environmental teratogens: Drugs and chemicals. *Clinics in Perinatology, 13,* 649–687.

Bennett, J. M. (1985). Company, halt! In H. R. Turnbull & A. P. Turnbull (Eds.), *Parents speak out: Then and now* (2nd ed.) (pp. 159–173). Englewood Cliffs, NJ: Merrill/Prentice Hall.

Benson, H., & Turnbull, A. P. (1986). Approaching families from an individualized perspective. In R. H. Horner, L. M. Voeltz, & H. D. Fredericks (Eds.), *Education of learners with severe handicaps: Exemplary service strategies* (pp. 127–157). Baltimore: Brookes.

Bettelheim, B. (1950). *Love is not enough.* Glencoe, NY: Free Press.

Bettelheim, B. (1967). *The empty fortress: Infantile autism and the birth of the self.* London: Collier-Macmillan.

Boggs, E. M. (1985). Who is putting whose head in the sand? (Or in the clouds, as the case may be). In H. R. Turnbull & A. P. Turnbull (Eds.), *Parents speak out: Then and now* (2nd ed.) (pp. 39–55). Englewood Cliffs, NJ: Merrill/Prentice Hall.

Bricker, W. A., & Bricker D. D. (1976). The infant, toddler, and preschool research and intervention project. In T. D. Tjossem (Ed.), *Intervention strategies for high risk infants and young children* (pp. 545–572). Baltimore: University Park Press.

Buck v. Bell, 274 U.S. 200 (1927).

Buyse, M. L. (1990). *Birth defects encyclopedia.* Dover, MA: Center for Birth Defects Information Services.

Caplan, P. J., & Hall-McCorquodale, I. (1985). Mother-blaming in major clinical journals. *American Journal of Orthopsychiatry, 55*(3), 345–353.

Carter, E. A., & McGoldrick, M. (Eds.). (1980). *The family life cycle: A framework for family therapy.* New York: Gardner.

Chilman, C. S. (1973). Programs for disadvantaged parents: Some major trends and related research. In H. H. Ricciuti & M. Caldwell (Eds.), *Review of child development research* (Vol. 3) (pp. 403–465). Chicago: University of Chicago Press.

Coleman, M. R., Gallagher, J., & Foster, A. (1994). *Updated report on state policies related to the identification of gifted students* [Report]. Chapel Hill: University of North Carolina, Gifted Education Policy Studies Program.

Conlon, C. J. (1992). New threats to development: Alcohol, cocaine, and AIDS. In M. L. Batshaw & Y. M. Perret (Eds.), *Children and disabilities: A medical primer* (3rd ed.) (pp. 111–136). Baltimore: Brookes.

Cooper, C. S., & Allred, K. W. (1992). A comparison of mothers' versus fathers' needs for support in caring for a young child with special needs. *Infant-Toddler Intervention, 2*(2), 205–221.

Coulter, D. L. (1987). The neurology of mental retardation. In F. J. Menolascino & J. A. Stark (Eds.), *Preventative and curative intervention in mental retardation* (pp. 113–154). Baltimore: Brookes.

Education for All Handicapped Children Act (P.L. 94-142) 1975, amending Education of the Handicapped Act, renamed Individuals with Disabilities Education Act, as amended by P.L. 98-199, P.L 99-457, P.L. 100-630, & P.L. 100-476, 20 U.S.C., Secs. 1400–1485.

Ferguson, P. M. (1994). *Abandoned to their fate: Social policy and practice toward severely retarded people in America, 1820–1920*. Philadelphia: Temple University Press.

Friesen, B. J., & Koroloff, N. M. (1990). Family-centered services: Implications for mental health administration and research. *Journal of Mental Health Administration, 17*(1), 13–25.

Gallagher, J. J., & Gallagher, G. G. (1985). Family adaptation to a handicapped child and assorted professionals. In H. R. Turnbull & A. P. Turnbull (Eds.), *Parents speak out: Then and now* (2nd ed.) (pp. 233–244). Englewood Cliffs, NJ: Merrill/Prentice Hall.

Goddard, H. H. (1912). *The Kallikak family: A study in the heredity of feeblemindedness*. New York: Macmillan.

Goldenberg, I., & Goldenberg, H. (1980). *Family therapy: An overview*. Monterey, CA: Brooks/Cole.

Goldenson, L. H. (1965, March). *Remarks on the occasion of United Cerebral Palsy Associations' 15th anniversary*. Paper presented at the 15th annual meeting of the United Cerebral Palsy Associations, Los Angeles.

Goldstein, S., Strickland, B., Turnbull, A. P., & Curry, L. (1980). An observational analysis of the IEP conference. *Exceptional Children, 46*(4), 278–286.

Haller, E. J., & Millman, J. (1987). *A survey of Arc members* [Internal report]. Arlington, TX: The Arc.

Harry, B., & Kalyanpur, M. (1994). Cultural underpinnings of special education: Implications for professional interactions with culturally diverse families. *Disability & Society, 9*(2), 145–165.

Harry, B., Allen, N., & McLaughlin, M. (1995). Communication versus compliance: African-American parents' involvement in special education. *Exceptional Children, 61*(4), 364–377.

Hunt, J. (Ed.). (1972). *Human intelligence*. New Brunswick, NJ: Transaction Books.

Kanner, L. (1949). Problems of nosology and psychodynamica of early infantile autism. *American Journal of Orthopsychiatry, 19*, 416–426.

Karnes, M. B., & Teska, J. A. (1980). Toward successful parent involvement in programs for handicapped children. In J. J. Gallagher (Ed.), *New directions for exceptional children: Parents and families of handicapped children* (Vol. 4) (pp. 85–109). San Francisco: Jossey-Bass.

Kirk, S. A. (1984). Introspection and prophecy. In B. Blatt & R. J. Morris (Eds.), *Perspectives in special education: Personal orientations* (pp. 25–55). Glenview, IL: Scott, Foresman.

Knoll, J. (1992). Being a family: The family experience of raising a child with a disability or chronic illness. In V. J. Bradley, J. Knoll, & J. M. Agosta (Eds.), *Emerging issues in family support* (pp. 9–56). Washington, DC: American Association on Mental Retardation.

Kolstoe, O. P. (1970). *Teaching educable mentally retarded children*. New York: Holt, Rinehart, & Winston.

Lucito, L. J. (1963). Gifted children. In L. M. Dunn (Ed.), *Exceptional children in the schools* (pp. 179–238). New York: Holt, Rinehart, & Winston.

Lynch, E. W., & Stein, R. (1982). Perspectives on parent participation in special education. *Exceptional Education Quarterly, 3*(2), 56–63.

MacMurphy. H. (1916). The relation of feeblemindedness to other social problems. *Journal of Psycho-Asthenics, 21*, 58–63.

Malekoff, A., Johnson, H., & Klappersack, B. (1991) Parent-professional collaboration on behalf of children with learning disabilities. *Families in Society: The Journal of Contemporary Human Services, 72*, 416–424.

Marcus, L. M. (1977). Patterns of coping in families of psychotic children. *American Journal of Orthopsychiatry, 47*(3), 388–399.

Minuchin, S. (1974). *Families and family therapy*. Cambridge, MA: Harvard University Press.

Morgan, S. B. (1988). The autistic child and family functioning: A developmental-family systems perspective. *Journal of Autism and Developmental Disorders, 18*(2), 263–281.

National Society for Autistic Children, Board of Directors and Professional Advisory Board. (1977). *A short definition of autism*. Albany, NY: Author.

Oliver, J. M., Cole, N. H., & Hollingsworth, H. (1991). Learning disabilities as functions of familial learning problems and developmental problems. *Exceptional Children, 57*(5), 427–440.

Orton, S. T. (1930). Familial occurrence of disorders in the acquisition of language. *Eugenics, 3*, 140–147.

Patterson, J. M. (1991). A family systems perspective for working with youth with disability. *Pediatrician, 18*, 129–141.

Pennsylvania Association for Retarded Citizens (PARC) v. Commonwealth of Pennsylvania, 334 F. Supp. 1257, 343 F. Supp. 279 (E. D. Pa. 1971, 1972).

Poulsen, M. K. (1994). The development of policy recommendations to address individual and family needs of infants and young children affected by family substance abuse. *Topics in Early Childhood Special Education, 14*(2), 275–291.

Powers, L. E., Singer, G. H. S., & Sowers, J. (Eds.). (1996). *On the road to autonomy: Promoting self-competence among children and youth with disabilities*. Baltimore: Brookes.

Robbins, F. R., Dunlap, G., & Plienis, A. J. (1991). Family characteristics, family training, and the progress of young children with autism. *Journal of Early Intervention, 15*(2), 173–184.

Rosenberg, M. S., Reppucci, N. D., & Linney, J. A. (1983). Issues in the implementation of human service programs: Examples from a parent training project for high-risk families. *Analysis and Intervention in Developmental Disabilities, 3*, 215–225.

Sands, D., & Wehmeyer, M. (Eds.). (1996). *Self-determination across the life span: Theory and practice*. Baltimore: Brookes.

Scheerenberger, R. C. (1983). *A history of mental retardation*. Baltimore: Brookes.

Shank, M. S., & Turnbull, A. P. (1993). Cooperative family problem solving: An intervention for single-parent families of children with disabilities. In G. H. S. Singer & L. E. Powers (Eds.), *Families, disability, and empowerment: Active coping skills and strategies for family interventions* (pp. 231–254). Baltimore: Brookes.

Shearer, M. S., & Shearer, D. E. (1977). Parent involvement. In J. B. Jordan, A. H. Hayden, M. B. Karnes, & M. M. Wood (Eds.), *Early childhood education for exceptional children* (pp. 208–235). Reston, VA: Council for Exceptional Children.

Terman, L. (1916). *The measurement of intelligence*. Cambridge, MA: Riverside.

Thomas, C. J. (1905). Congenital "word-blindness" and its treatment. *Ophthalmoscope, 3,* 380–385.

Turbiville, V. P., Turnbull, A. P., & Turnbull, H. R. (1995). Fathers and family-centered early intervention. *Infants & Young Children, 7*(4), 12–19.

Turbiville, V. P., Turnbull, A. P., Garland, C. W., & Lee, I. M. (1996). Development and implementation of IFSPs and IEPs: Opportunities for empowerment. In S. L. Odom & M. E. McLean (Eds.), *Early intervention/early childhood special education: Recommended practices* (pp. 77–100). Austin, TX: Pro-Ed.

Turnbull, A. P., Blue-Banning, M. J., Anderson, E. L., Turnbull, H. R., Seaton, K. A., & Dinas, P. A. (1996). Enhancing self-determination through Group Action Planning: A holistic emphasis. In D. Sands & M. Wehmeyer (Eds.), *Self-determination across the life span: Theory and practice* (pp. 237–256). Baltimore: Brookes.

Turnbull, A. P., Brotherson, M. J., & Summers, J. A. (1985). The impact of deinstitutionalization on families: A family systems approach. In R. H. Bruininks (Ed.), *Living and learning in the least restrictive environment* (pp. 115–152). Baltimore: Brookes.

Turnbull, A. P., & Summers, J. A. (1987). From parent involvement to family support: Evolution to revolution. In S. M. Pueschel, C. Tingey, J. W. Rynders, A. C. Crocker, & D. M. Crutcher (Eds.), *New perspectives on Down syndrome* (pp. 289–306). Baltimore: Brookes.

Turnbull, A. P., Summers, J. A., & Brotherson, M. J. (1984). *Working with families with disabled members: A family systems approach*. Lawrence: University of Kansas, Kansas University Affiliated Facility.

Turnbull, A. P., & Turnbull, H. R. (1996). Self-determination within a culturally responsive family systems perspective: Balancing the family mobile. In L. E. Powers, G. H. S. Singer, & J. Sowers (Eds.), *On the road to autonomy: Promoting self-competence among children and youth with disabilities* (pp. 195–220). Baltimore: Brookes.

Turnbull, A. P., Turnbull, H. R., Shank, M., & Leal, D. (1995). *Exceptional lives: Special education in today's schools*. Englewood Cliffs, NJ: Merrill/Prentice Hall.

Turnbull, H. R. (1994). *Free appropriate public education: The law and children with disabilities* (4th ed.). Denver: Love.

Turnbull, H. R., Turnbull, A. P., & Wheat, M. (1982). Assumptions about parental participation: A legislative history. *Exceptional Education Quarterly, 3*(2), 1–8.

Warren, F. (1985). A society that is going to kill your children. In H. R. Turnbull & A. P. Turnbull (Eds.), *Parents speak out: Then and now* (2nd ed.) (pp. 201–232). Englewood Cliffs, NJ: Merrill/Prentice Hall.

Weicker, L. (1985). Sonny and public policy. In H. R. Turnbull & A. P. Turnbull (Eds.), *Parents speak out: Then and now* (2nd ed.) (pp. 281–287). Englewood Cliffs, NJ: Merrill/Prentice Hall.

Werner, E. E., & Smith, R. S. (1992). *Overcoming the odds: High risk children from birth to adulthood*. Ithaca, NY: Cornell University Press.

Winton, P. J., & DiVenere, N. (1995). Family-professional partnerships in early intervention personnel preparation guidelines and strategies. *Topics in Early Childhood Special Education, 15*(3), 295–312.

Zigler, E., & Muenchow, S. (1992). *Head Start: The inside story of America's most successful educational experiment*. New York: Basic Books.

Chapter 2 SCHOOLS AS SYSTEMS: THE CONTEXT FOR FAMILY-PROFESSIONAL COLLABORATION

Bailey, D. B., Buysse, V., Edmondson, R., & Smith, T. (1992). Creating family-centered services in early intervention: Perceptions of professionals in four states. *Exceptional Children, 58,* 298–309.

Beckman, P. J., Robinson, C. C., Rosenberg, S., & Filer, J. (in press). Family involvement in early intervention: The evolution of family-centered services. In L. J. Johnson, R. J. Gallagher, M. J. LaMontagne, J. B. Jordan, J. J. Gallagher, P. L. Hutinger, & M. B. Karnes (Eds.), *Early intervention for children and their families: Providing services from birth to three*. Baltimore: Brookes.

Comer, J. P. (1986). Parent participation in the schools. *Phi Delta Kappan, 67*(6), 442–446.

Comer, J. P., & Haynes, N. M. (1991). Parent involvement in schools: An ecological approach. *Elementary School Journal, 91*(3), 271–277.

Dolan, L., & Haxby, B. (1995). *Removing barriers to learning: Factors that affect participation and dropout in parent interventions* (Report No. 27). Baltimore: Johns Hopkins University, Center on Families,

Communities, Schools, and Children's Learning.

Dunst, C. J., Johnson, C., Trivette, C. M., & Hamby, D. (1991). Family-oriented early intervention policies and practices: Family-centered or not? *Exceptional Children, 58*(2), 115–126.

Education for All Handicapped Children Act (P. L. 94-142) 1975, amending Education of the Handicapped Act, renamed Individuals with Disabilities Education Act, as amended by P.L. 98-199, P.L. 99-457, P.L. 100-630, & P.L. 100-476, 20 U.S.C., Secs. 1400–1485.

Epstein, J. L. (1987). Toward a theory of family-school connections: Teacher practice and parent involvement. In K. Hurrelman, F. Kaufman, & F. Losel (Eds.), *Social intervention: Potential and constraints* (pp. 121–136). New York: DeGruyter.

Epstein, J. L. (1992). School and family partnerships. *Encyclopedia of Educational Research* (Vol. 6) (pp. 1139–1151). New York: Macmillan.

Epstein, J. L. (1994). Theory to practice: School and family partnerships lead to school improvement and student success. In C. L. Fagnano & B. Z. Werber (Eds.), *School, family, and community interaction: A view from the firing lines* (pp. 39–52). Boulder, CO: Westview.

Epstein, J. L. (1995, May). School/family/community partnerships: Caring for the children we share. *Phi Delta Kappan,* 701–712.

Epstein, J. L., & Connors, L. J. (1994a). *School and family partnerships in the middle grades*. Unpublished manuscript, Johns Hopkins University, Center on Families, Communities, and Schools.

Epstein, J. L., & Connors, L. J. (1994b). *Trust fund: School, family, and community partnerships in high schools* (Report No. 24). Boston: Boston University, Center on Families, Communities, Schools, and Children's Learning.

Goldstein, S., Strickland, B., Turnbull, A. P., & Curry, L. (1980). An observational analysis of the IEP conference. *Exceptional Children, 46*(4), 278–286.

Green, S. K., & Shinn, M. R. (1994). Parent attitudes about special education and reintegration: What is the role of student outcomes? *Exceptional Children, 61*(3), 269–281.

Gruber, J., & Trivette, E. J. (1987). Can we empower others? The paradox of empowerment in the governing of an alternative public school. *American Journal of Community Psychology, 15*(3), 353–371.

Hallahan, D. P., Keller, C. E., McKinney, J. D., Lloyd, J. W., & Bryan, T. C. (1988). Examining the research base of the Regular Education Initiative: Efficacy studies and the adaptive learning environments model. *Journal of Learning Disabilities, 21*, 29–35.

Harry, B. (1992a). *Cultural diversity, families, and the special education system: Communication and empowerment*. New York: Teachers College Press.

Harry, B. (1992b). An ethnographic study of cross-cultural communication with Puerto Rican-American families in the special education system. *American Educational Research Journal, 29*(3), 471–494.

Harry, B., Allen, N., & McLaughlin, M. (1995). Communication versus compliance: African-American parents' involvement in special education. *Exceptional Children, 61*(4), 364–377.

Harry, B., & Kalyanpur, M. (1994). Cultural underpinnings of special education: Implications for professional interactions with culturally diverse families. *Disability and Society, 9*(2), 145–165.

Jenkins, J. R., Pious, C. G., & Peterson, D. L. (1988). Categorical programs for remedial and handicapped students: Issues of validity. *Exceptional Children, 55,* 147–158.

Kagan, S. L., with Neville, P. R. (1993). *Integrating services for children and families: Understanding the past to shape the future*. New Haven, CT: Yale University Press.

Katz, L., & Scarpati, S. (1995). A cultural interpretation of early intervention teams and the IFSP: Parent and professional perceptions of roles and responsibilities. *Infant-Toddler Intervention, 5*(2), 177–192.

Kauffman, J. M., Gerber, M. M., & Semmel, M. I. (1988). Arguable assumptions underlying the Regular Education Initiative. *Journal of Learning Disabilities, 21*, 6–11.

Koyanagi, C., & Gaines, S. (1993). *All systems failure: An examination of the results of neglecting the needs of children with serious emotional disturbance*. Alexandria, VA: National Mental Health Association.

Lindle, J. C. (1989, October). What do parents want from principals? *Educational Leadership*, 12–14.

Lortie, D. C. (1975). *Schoolteacher: A sociological study*. Chicago: University of Chicago Press.

McBride, S. L., Brotherson, M. J., Joanning, H., Whiddon, D., & Demmit, A. (1993). Implementation of family-centered services: Perceptions of families and professionals. *Journal of Early Intervention, 17*, 414–430.

McLaughlin, M. (1996). School restructuring. In National Council on Disability, *Improving the implementation of the Individuals with Disabilities Education Act: Making schools work for all of America's children. Supplement* (pp. 635–660). Washington, DC: National Council on Disability.

Meyer, J. W., & Rowan, B. (1978). The structure of educational organizations. In M. W. Meyer (Ed.), *Environments and organizations* (pp. 78–109). San Francisco: Jossey-Bass.

Minke, K. (1991). The development of individualized family service plans in three early intervention programs: A data-based construction. *Dissertation Abstracts International, 52*(06), 2077A. (University Microfilms No. 9134817)

Murphy, D. L., Lee, I. M., Turnbull, A. P., & Turbiville, V. (1995). The family-centered program rating scale: An instrument for program evaluation and change. *Journal of Early Intervention, 19*(1), 24–42.

National Commission on Excellence in Education. (1983). *A nation at risk: The imperative for educational reform*. Washington, DC: U.S. Government Printing Office.

National Council on Disability. (1995). *Improving the implementation of the Individuals with Disabilities Education Act: Making schools work for all of America's children*. Washington, DC: Author.

Peraino, J. M. (1992). Post-21 follow-up studies: How do special education graduates fare? In P. Wehman (Ed.), *Life beyond the classroom: Transition strategies for young people with disabilities* (pp. 21–70). Baltimore: Brookes.

Pugach, M., & Lilly, S. M. (1984). Reconceptualizing support services for classroom teachers: Implications for teacher education. *Journal of Teacher Education, 35*, 48–55.

Sailor, W. (1991). Special education in the restructured school. *Remedial and Special Education, 12*(6), 8–22.

Sailor, W. (1994). Services integration: Parent empowerment through school/community partnerships. *Coalition Quarterly, 11*(3), 11–13.

Schumaker, J. B., & Deshler, D. D. (1987). Implementing the regular education initiative in secondary schools. *Journal of Learning Disabilities, 21*(1), 36–42.

Sen. Rep. 103-85, 103rd Cong., 1st Sess.

Shelton, T. L., Jeppson, E. S., & Johnson, B. H. (1989). *Family-centered care for children with special health care needs*. Washington, DC: Association for the Care of Children's Health.

Skrtic, T. M. (1991). *Behind special education: A critical analysis of professional culture and school organization*. Denver, CO: Love.

Sonnenschein, P. (1984). Parents and professionals: An uneasy relationship. In M. L. Henniger & E. M. Nesselroad (Eds.), *Working with parents of handicapped children: A book of readings for school personnel* (pp. 129–139). Lanham, MD: University Press of America.

Stainback, W., & Stainback, S. (Eds.). (1990). *Support networks for inclusive schooling: Interdependent integrated education*. Baltimore: Brookes.

Summers, J. A., Dell'Oliver, C., Turnbull, A. P., Benson, H. A., Santelli, E., Campbell, M., & Siegel-Causey, E. (1990). Examining the Individualized Family Service Plan process: What are family and practitioner preferences? *Topics in Early Childhood Special Education, 10*(1), 78–99.

Turnbull, A. P., & Summers, J. A. (1987). From parent involvement to family support: Evolution to revolution. In S. M. Pueschel, C. Tingey, J. W. Rynders, A. C. Crocker, & D. M. Crutcher (Eds.), *New perspectives on Down syndrome* (pp. 289–306). Baltimore: Brookes.

Turnbull, A. P., Turnbull, H. R., Shank, M., & Leal, D. (1995). *Exceptional lives: Special education in today's schools*. Englewood Cliffs, NJ: Merrill/Prentice Hall.

Wagner, M., D'Amico, R., Marder, C., Newman, L., & Blackorby, J. (1993). *What happens next? Trends in postschool outcomes of youth with disabilities: The second comprehensive report from the National Longitudinal Transition Study of Special Education Students*. Menlo Park, CA: SRI International.

Wagner, M., Newman, L., D'Amico, R., Jay, E. D., Butler-Nalin, P., Marder, C., & Cox, R. (1991). *Youth with disabilities: How are they doing? The first comprehensive report from the National Longitudinal Transition Study of Special Education Students*. Menlo Park, CA: SRI International.

Wang, M. C., Reynolds, M. C., & Wahlberg, H. J. (1986). Rethinking special education. *Educational Leadership, 44*(1), 26–31.

Ware, L. P. (1994). Contextual barriers to collaboration. *Journal of Educational and Psychological Consultation, 5*(4), 339–357.

Wright, R., Saleeby, D., Watts, T. D., & Lecca, P. J. (1983). *Transcultural perspectives in the human services: Organizational issues and trends*. Springfield, IL: Thomas.

Zipperlen, H., & O'Brien, J. (1994). *Cultivating thinking hearts: Letters from the Lifesharing Safeguards Project*. Kimberton, PA: Camphill Village, Kimberton Hills.

Chapter 3 EMPOWERMENT

Allen, R., & Petr, C. G. (1996). Toward developing standards and measurements for family-centered practice in family support programs. In G. H. S. Singer, L. E. Powers, & A. L. Olson (Eds.), *Redefining family support: Innovations in public-private partnerships* (pp. 57–86). Baltimore: Brookes.

Ashton, P. A., & Webb, R. B. (1986). *Making a difference: Teachers' sense of efficacy and student achievement*. White Plains, NY: Longman.

Bailey, D. B., Blasco, P. M., & Simeonsson, R. J. (1992). Needs expressed by mothers and fathers of young children with disabilities. *American Journal on Mental Rehabilitation, 97*(1), 1–10.

Bandura, A. (1977). Self-efficacy: Toward a unifying theory of psychological change. *Psychological Review, 84*, 91–215.

Bandura, A. (1982). Self-efficacy mechanism in human agency. *American Psychologist, 37*(2), 122–147.

Beckman, P. J. (1991). Comparison of mothers' and fathers' perceptions of the effect of young children with and without disabilities. *American Journal on Mental Retardation, 95*(5), 585–595.

Behr, S. K. (1989). *Underlying dimensions of the construct of positive contributions that individuals with disabilities make to their families: A factor analytic study*. Unpublished doctoral dissertation, University of Kansas, Lawrence.

Blue-Banning, M. J., Santelli, B., Guy, B., & Wallace, E. (1994). *Cognitive coping project: Coping with the challenges of disability*. Lawrence: University of Kansas, Beach Center on Families and Disability.

Boyce, S. (1992, April). Coping well with the labellers of Down syndrome. *Down Syndrome News*, 37.

Cochran, M. (1992). Parent empowerment: Developing a conceptual framework. *Family Science Review, 5*(1 & 2), 3–21.

Cochran, M., & Dean, C. (1991). Home-school relations and the empowerment process. *Elementary School Journal, 91*(3), 261–269.

Cooper, C. S., & Allred, K. W. (1992). A comparison of mothers' versus fathers' needs for support in caring for a young child with special needs. *Infant-Toddler Intervention, 2*(2), 205–221.

Cornell Empowerment Group. (1989). Empowerment through family support. *Networking Bulletin: Empowerment and Family Support, 1*(1), 1–3.

Covey, S. R. (1990). *The seven habits of highly effective people: Restoring the character ethic*. New York: Fireside/Simon & Schuster.

Craig, J. H., & Craig, M. (1974). *Synergic power: Beyond domination and permissiveness*. Berkeley, CA: Proactive.

DiBella-McCarthy, H., McDaniel, E., & Miller, R. (1995). How efficacious are you? *Teaching Exceptional Children, 27*(3), 68–72.

Donahue-Kilburg, G. (1992). *Family-centered early intervention for communication disorders: Prevention and treatment*. Gaithersburg, MD: Aspen.

Dunst, C. J., Trivette, C. M., & Deal, A. G. (1988). *Enabling and empowering families: Principles and guidelines for practice*. Cambridge, MA: Brookline.

Dunst, C. J., Trivette, C. M., Gordon, N. M., & Pletcher, L. L. (1989). Building and mobilizing informal support networks. In G. H. S. Singer & L. K. Irvin (Eds.), *Support for care-giving families: Enabling positive adaptation to disability* (pp. 121–142). Baltimore: Brookes.

Dunst, C. J., Trivette, C. M., Gordon, N. J., & Starnes, L. (1993). Family-centered case management practices: Characteristics and consequences. In G. H. S. Singer & L. E. Powers (Eds.), *Families, disability, and empowerment: Active coping skills and strategies for family interventions* (pp. 89–118). Baltimore: Brookes.

Dunst, C. J., Trivette, C. M., & LaPointe, N. (1992). Toward clarification of the meaning and key elements of empowerment. *Family Studies Review, 5*(1 & 2), 111–130.

Fewell, R. R. (1986). Supports from religious organizations and personal beliefs. In R. R. Fewell & P. F. Vadasy (Eds.), *Families of handicapped children: Needs and supports across the life span* (pp. 297–316). Austin, TX: Pro-Ed.

Fine, M. (1990). Facilitating home-school relationships: A family-oriented approach to collaborative consultation. *Journal of Educational and Psychological Consultation, 1*(2), 169–187.

Florin, P., & Wandersman, A. (1984). Cognitive social learning and participation in community development. *American Journal of Community Psychology, 12*, 689–708.

Friesen, B. J., Koren, P. E., & Koroloff, N. M. (1992). How parents view professional behaviors: A cross-professional analysis. *Journal of Child and Family Studies, 1*(2), 209–231.

Garlow, J. E., Turnbull, H. R., & Schnase, D. (1991). Model Family and Disability Support Act of 1991. *Kansas Law Review, 39*(3), 783–816.

Gowen, J. W., Christy, D. S., & Sparling, J. (1993). Informational needs of parents of young children with special needs. *Journal of Early Intervention, 17*(2), 194–210.

Hadadian, A., & Merbler, J. (1995). Parents of infants and toddlers with special needs: Sharing views of desired services. *Infant-Toddler Intervention, 5*(2), 141–152.

Heller, K. (1990). Social and community interventions. *Annual Review of Psychology, 41,* 141–168.

Hoover-Dempsey, K. V., Bassler, D. C., & Brissie, J. S. (1992). Explorations in parent-school relations. *Journal of Educational Research, 85*(5), 287–294.

Johnson, L. J., & Pugach, M. C. (1991). Peer collaboration: Accommodating students with mild learning and behavioral problems. *Exceptional Children, 57,* 454–461.

Jones, T. M., Garlow, J., Turnbull, H. R., & Barber, P. A. (1996). Best practices: Empowerment in a family support program: Program, professional, and policy issues. In G. H. S. Singer, L. E. Powers, & A. L. Olson (Eds.), *Redefining family support: Innovations in public-private partnerships* (pp. 87–114). Baltimore: Brookes.

Jones, T. M., Ross, M. E., & Marquis, J. G. (1995). *The Psychological Empowerment Scale: Preliminary investigations of reliability and validity*. Unpublished manuscript.

Katz, R. (1984). Empowerment and synergy: Expanding the community's healing resources. *Prevention in Human Services, 3*(2 & 3), 201–226.

Kieffer, C. H. (1984). Citizen empowerment: A developmental perspective. *Prevention in Human Services, 3*(2 & 3), 9–36.

Knackendoffel, E. A., Robinson, S. M., Deshler, D. D., & Schumaker, J. B. (1992). *Collaborative problem solving: A step-by-step guide to creating educational solutions*. Lawrence, KS: Edge Enterprises.

Knoll, J., Covert, S., Osuch, R., O'Connor, S., Agosta, J., Blaney, B., & Bradley, V. (1990). *Family support services in the United States: An end of decade status report* [Summary report]. Cambridge, MA: Human Services Research Institute.

Lonsdale, G. (1978). Family life with a handicapped child: The parents speak. *Child Care, Health, and Development, 4*, 99–120.

Olson, D. H., McCubbin, H. I., Barnes, H., Larsen, A., Muxen, M., & Wilson, M. (1983). *Families: What makes them work*. Beverly Hills, CA: Sage.

Ozer, E., & Bandura, A. (1990). Mechanisms governing empowerment effects: A self-efficacy analysis. *Journal of Personality and Social Psychology, 58*(3), 472–486.

Rappaport, J. (1981). In praise of paradox: A social policy of empowerment over prevention. *American Journal of Community Psychology, 9*(1), 1–25.

Seligman, M. E. P. (1990). *Learned optimism: How to change your mind and your life*. New York: Pocket Books.

Shank, M., & Turnbull, A. P. (1993). Cooperative family problem solving: An intervention for single-parent families with a child who has a disability. In G. H. S. Singer & L. E. Powers (Eds.), *Families, disability, and empowerment: Active coping skills and strategies for family interventions* (pp. 231–254). Baltimore: Brookes.

Singer, G. H. S., & Nixon, C. (1996). A report on the concerns of parents of children with acquired brain injury. In G. H. S. Singer, A. Glang, & J. Williams (Eds.), *Children with acquired brain injury: Educating and supporting families* (pp. 23–52). Baltimore: Brookes.

Snyder, C. R. (1994). *The psychology of hope: You can get there from here*. New York: Free Press.

Swift, C., & G. Levin. (1987). Empowerment: An emerging mental health technology. *Journal of Primary Prevention, 8*(1 & 2), 71–94.

Summers, J. A., Behr, S. K., & Turnbull, A. P. (1988). Positive adaptation and coping strengths of families who have children with disabilities. In G. H. S. Singer & L. K. Irvin (Eds.), *Support for caregiving families: Enabling positive adaptation to disability* (pp. 27–40). Baltimore: Brookes.

Turbiville, V. P., Turnbull, A. P., Garland, C. W., & Lee, I. M. (1996). Development and implementation of IFSPs and IEPs: Opportunities for empowerment. In S. L. Odom & M. E. McLean (Eds.), *Early intervention/early childhood special education: Recommended practices* (pp. 77–100). Austin, TX: Pro-Ed.

Turnbull, A. P. (1988). The challenge of providing comprehensive support to families. *Education and Training in Mental Retardation, 23*(4), 261–272.

Turnbull, A. P., Blue-Banning, M. J., Behr, S. K., & Kearns, G. (1986). Family research and intervention: A value and ethical examination. In P. R. Dobecki & R. M. Zaner (Eds.), *Ethics of dealing with persons with severe handicaps: Toward a research agenda* (pp. 119–140). Baltimore: Brookes.

Turnbull, A. P., & Friesen, B. J. (1995, April). *Forging collaborative partnerships with families in the study of disability*. Paper presented at Participation Action Research and the Family, a conference sponsored by the National Institute on Disability and Rehabilitation Research, Washington, DC.

Turnbull, A. P., Patterson, J. M., Behr, S. K., Murphy, D. L., Marquis, J. G., & Blue-Banning, M. J. (1993). *Cognitive coping, families, and disability*. Baltimore: Brookes.

Turnbull, A. P., & Ruef, M. (in press, a). Family perspectives on problem behavior. *Mental Retardation*.

Turnbull, A. P., & Ruef, M. (in press, b). Family perspectives on inclusive lifestyle issues for individuals with problem behavior. *Exceptional Children*.

Turnbull, A. P., & Turnbull, H. R. (1993). Enhancing beneficial linkages across the lifespan. *Disability Studies Quarterly, 13*(4), 34–36.

Turnbull, H. R., Garlow, J. A., & Barber, P. A. (1991). A policy analysis of family support for families with members with disabilities. *Kansas Law Review, 39*(3), 739–782.

Turnbull, H. R., & Turnbull, A. P. (1985). *Parents speak out: Then and now* (2nd ed.). Englewood Cliffs, NJ: Merrill/Prentice Hall.

Weisner, T. S., Belzer, L., & Stolze, L. (1991). Religion and families of children with developmental delays. *American Journal on Mental Retardation, 95*(6), 647–662.

Weiss, H. (1989). New state initiatives for family support and education programs: Challenges and opportunities. *Family Resource Coalition Report, 1*, 18–19.

Zimmerman, M. A. (1990). Toward a theory of learned hopefulness: A structural model analysis of participation and empowerment. *Journal of Research in Personality, 24*, 71–86.

Zimmerman, M. A. (1992). *The measurement of psychological empowerment: Issues and strategies*. Unpublished paper, University of Michigan, Ann Arbor.

Zimmerman, M. A. (in press). Further explorations in empowerment theory: An empirical analysis of psychological empowerment. *American Journal of Community Psychology*.

Zimmerman, M. A., & Rappaport, J. (1988). Citizen participation, perceived control, and psychological empowerment. *American Journal of Community Psychology, 16*(5), 725–731.

Chapter 4 Building Reliable Alliances

Allen, R., & Petr, C. G. (1996). Toward developing standards and measurements for family-centered practice in family support programs. In G. H. S. Singer, L. E. Powers, & A. L. Olson (Eds.), *Redefining family support: Innovations in public-private partnerships* (pp. 57–86). Baltimore: Brookes.

Anderson, P. P., & Fenichel, E. S. (1989). *Serving culturally diverse families of infants and toddlers with dis-*

abilities. Arlington, VA: National Center for Clinical Infant Programs.

Bailey, D. B., Blasco, P. M., & Simeonsson, R. J. (1992). Needs expressed by mothers and fathers of young children with disabilities. *American Journal on Mental Retardation, 97*(1), 1–10.

Barrera, M. (1986). Distinctions between social supports concepts, measures, and models. *American Journal of Community Psychology, 14*(4), 413–445.

Benjamin, A. (1969). *The helping interview*. Boston: Houghton Mifflin.

Brammer, L. (1988). *The helping relationship*. Englewood Cliffs, NJ: Prentice Hall.

Bruder, M. B., Anderson, R., Schultz, G., & Caldera, M. (1991). Ninos especiales program: A culturally sensitive early intervention model. *Journal of Early Intervention, 15*(3), 268–277.

Chan, S. (1992). Families with Asian roots. In E. W. Lynch & M. J. Hanson (Eds.), *Developing cross-cultural competence: A guide for working with young children and their families* (pp. 181–258). Baltimore: Brookes.

Cohen, S., & Wills, T. A. (1985). Stress, social support, and the buffering hypothesis. *Psychological Bulletin, 98*, 310–357.

Commission on the Education of the Deaf. (1988). *Toward equality: Education of the deaf*. Washington, DC: U.S. Government Printing Office.

Cooper, C. S., & Allred, K. W. (1992). A comparison of mothers' versus fathers' needs for support in caring for a young child with special needs. *Infant-Toddler Intervention, 2*(2), 205–221.

Cousins, N. (1989). *Head first: The biology of hope*. New York: Dutton.

Covey, S. R. (1990). *The seven habits of highly effective people: Restoring the character ethic*. New York: Fireside/Simon & Schuster.

Crago, M. B., & Eriks-Brophy, A. A. (1993). Feeling right: Approaches to a family's culture. *Volta Review, 95*(5), 123–129.

Csikszentmihalyi, M. (1992, February). *Family influences on the development of creative motivation*. Paper presented at the second annual Esther Katz Rosen Symposium on the Psychological Development of Gifted Children, University of Kansas, Lawrence.

Dunst, C. J., Trivette, C. M., & Deal, A. G. (Eds.). (1994). *Supporting and strengthening families: Vol. 1. Methods, strategies, and practices*. Cambridge, MA: Brookline.

Edwards, M. (1986). Effects of training and self-evaluation upon special educators' communication and interaction skills when discussing emotion-laden information with parents of handicapped infants (Doctoral dissertation, University of Idaho). *Dissertation Abstracts International, 47*, 2996A.

Falvey, M. A., Forest, M., Pearpoint, J., & Rosenberg, R. (1994). Building connections. In J. S. Thousand, R. A. Villa, & A. I. Nevin (Eds.), *Creativity and collaborative learning: A practical guide to empowering students and teachers* (pp. 347–368). Baltimore: Brookes.

Friedman, R. C. (1994). Upstream helping for low-income families of gifted students: Challenges and opportunities. *Journal of Educational and Psychological Consultation, 5*(4), 321–338.

Gordon, T. (1970). *Parent effectiveness training*. New York: Wyden.

Hall, E. T. (1966). *The hidden dimension*. Garden City, NY: Doubleday.

Hall, E. (1976). *Beyond culture*. Garden City, NY: Anchor.

Hanson, M. J. (1992). Families with Anglo-European roots. In E. W. Lynch & M. J. Hanson (Eds.), *Developing cross-cultural competence: A guide for working with young children and their families* (pp. 65–87). Baltimore: Brookes.

Harry, B. (1992a). Developing cultural self-awareness: The first step in values clarification for early interventionists. *Topics in Early Childhood Special Education, 12*(3), 333–350.

Harry, B. (1992b). An ethnographic study of cross-cultural communication with Puerto Rican-American families in the special education system. *American Educational Research Journal, 29*(3), 471–494.

Harry, B. (1992c). Making sense of disability: Low-income, Puerto Rican parents' theories of the problem. *Exceptional Children, 59*(1), 27–40.

Hepworth, D. H., & Larsen, J. A. (1982). *Direct social work practice: Theory and skills*. Homewood, IL: Dorsey.

Hirsch, G., & Altman, K. (1986). Training graduate students in parent conference skills. *Applied Research in Mental Retardation, 7*(3), 371–385.

Ivey, A. P. (1986). *Developmental therapy: Theory into practice*. San Francisco: Jossey-Bass.

Jones, T. M., Garlow, J., Turnbull, H. R., & Barber, P. A. (1996). Best practices: Empowerment in a family support program: Program, professional, and policy issues. In G. H. S. Singer, L. E. Powers, & A. L. Olson (Eds.), *Redefining family support: Innovations in public-private partnerships* (pp. 87–114). Baltimore: Brookes.

Kalyanpur, M., & Rao, S. S. (1991). Empowering low-income black families of handicapped children. *American Journal of Orthopsychiatry, 61*(4), 523–532.

Kieffer, C. H. (1984). Citizen empowerment: A developmental perspective. *Prevention in Human Services, 3*(2 & 3), 9–36.

Knoll, J. (1992). Being a family: The experience of raising a child with a disability or chronic illness. In V. J. Bradley, J. Knoll, & J. M. Agosta (Eds.), *Emerging issues in family support* (pp. 9–56). *Monographs of the American Association on Mental Retardation, 18*.

Kohl, M. A., Parrish, J. M., Neef, N. A., Driessen, J. R., & Hallinan, P. C. (1988). Communication skills training for parents: Experimental and social validation. *Journal of Applied Behavior Analysis, 21*(1), 21–30.

Lombana. J. H. (1983). *Home-school partnerships: Guidelines and strategies for educators*. New York: Grune & Stratton.

Luetke-Stalhman, B. (1993). Basic interpreting strategies for parents. *Perspectives, 12*(1), 12–14.

Marion, R. (1979). Minority parent involvement in the IEP process: A systematic model approach. *Focus on Exceptional Children, 10*(8), 1–16.

O'Connor, S. (1995). We're all one family: The positive construction of people with disabilities by family members. In S. J. Taylor, R. Bogdon, & Z. M. Lutfiyya (Eds.), *The variety of community experience: Qualitative studies of family and community life* (pp. 67–78). Baltimore: Brookes.

Perl, J. (1995, Fall). Improving relationship skills for parent conferences. *Teaching Exceptional Children*, pp. 29–31.

Ruiz, R. A., & Padilla, A. M. (1977). Counseling Latinos. *Personnel and Guidance Journal, 55*, 401–408.

Schorr, L. B., & Schorr, D. (1988). *Within our reach: Breaking the cycle of disadvantage*. New York: Doubleday.

Seligman, M. E. P. (1990). *Learned optimism: How to change your mind and your life*. New York: Pocket Books.

Seligman, M., & Darling, R. B. (1989). *Ordinary families, special children: A systems approach to childhood disability*. New York: Guilford.

Senge, P. M. (1990). *The fifth discipline: The art and practice of the learning organization*. New York: Doubleday.

Skrtic, T. M. (1991). *Behind special education: A critical analysis of professional culture and school organization*. Denver, CO: Love.

Snow, C. E., Barnes, W. S., Chandler, J., Goodman, I. F., & Hemphill, L. (1991). *Unfulfilled expectations: Home and school influences on literacy*. Cambridge, MA: Harvard University Press.

Snyder, C. R. (1994). *The psychology of hope: You can get there from here*. New York: Free Press/Macmillan.

Stonestreet, R. H., Johnston, R. G., & Acton, S. J. (1991). Guidelines for real partnerships with parents. *Infant-Toddler Intervention, 1*(1), 37–46.

Sue, D. W. (1981). Barriers to effective cross-cultural counseling. In D. W. Sue, E. H. Richardson, R. A. Ruiz, & E. J. Smith (Eds.), *Counseling the culturally different: Theory and practice* (pp. 27–47). New York: Wiley.

Summers, J. A., Dell'Oliver, C., Turnbull, A. P., Benson, H. A., Santelli, E., Campbell, M., & Siegel-Causey, E. (1990). Examining the Individualized Family Service Plan process: What are family and practitioner preferences? *Topics in Early Childhood Special Education, 10*(1), 78–99.

Taylor, S. E. (1989). *Positive illusions: Creative self-deception and the healthy mind*. New York: Basic Books.

Turnbull, A. P., Turbiville, V., Turnbull, H. R., & Gabbard, G. (1993, September). *Fathers' roles in intervention programs for children at special risks: Disabled, chronically ill, and children living in poverty*. Paper presented at the National Research Council, National Academy of Sciences, Washington, DC.

Turnbull, A. P., & Turnbull, H. R. (1996a). Group Action Planning as a strategy for providing comprehensive family support. In L. K. Koegel, R. L. Koegel, & G. Dunlap (Eds.), *Community, school, family, and social inclusion through positive behavioral support* (pp. 99–114). Baltimore: Brookes.

Turnbull, A. P., & Turnbull, H. R. (1996b). Self-determination within a culturally responsive family systems perspective: Balancing the family mobile. In L. E. Powers, G. H. S. Singer, & J. Sowers (Eds.), *On the Road to autonomy: Promoting self-competence among children and youth with disabilities* (pp. 195–220). Baltimore: Brookes.

Turnbull, A. P., Turnbull, H. R., Shank, M., & Leal, D. (1995). *Exceptional lives: Special education in today's schools*. Englewood Cliffs, NJ: Merrill/Prentice Hall.

Vohs, J. (1993). On belonging: A place to stand, a gift to give. In A. P. Turnbull, J. M. Patterson, S. K. Behr, D. L. Murphy, J. G. Marquis, & M. J. Blue-Banning (Eds.), *Cognitive coping, families, and disability* (pp. 51–66). Baltimore: Brookes.

Walker, B., & Singer, G. H. S. (1993). Improving collaborative communication between professionals and parents. In G. H. S. Singer & L. E. Powers (Eds.), *Families, disability, and empowerment: Active coping skills and strategies for family interventions* (pp. 285–316). Baltimore: Brookes.

Wasserman, R. C., Inui, T. S., Barriatua, R. D., Carter, W. B., & Lippincott, P. (1984). Pediatric clinicians' support for parents makes a difference: An outcome-based analysis of clinician-parent interaction. *Pediatrics, 74*(6), 1047–1053.

Webster, E. J. (1977). *Counseling with parents of handicapped children: Guidelines for improving communication*. New York: Grune & Stratton.

Weyhing, M. C. (1983). Parental reactions to handicapped children and familial adjustments to routines of care. In J. A. Mulick & S. M. Pueschel (Eds.), *Parent-professional partnerships in developmental disabilities* (pp. 125–138). Cambridge, MA: Ware.

Winton, P. J. (1992). Family-centered intervention: Words can make a difference. *Focus, 1*(2), 1–5.

Yates, A. (1987). Current status and future directions of research on the American Indian child. *American Journal of Psychiatry, 144*(9), 1135–1142.

Althen, G. (1988). *American ways: A guide for foreigners in the United States*. Yarmouth, ME: Intercultural Press.

Anastopoulos, A. D., Guevremont, D. C., Shelton, T. L., & DuPaul, G. J. (1992). Parenting stress among families of children with attention deficit hyperactivity disorder. *Journal of Abnormal Child Psychology, 20*, 503–520.

Avis, D. W. (1985). Deinstitutionalization jetlag. In H. R. Turnbull & A. P. Turnbull (Eds.), *Parents speak out: Then and now* (pp. 181–191). Englewood Cliffs, NJ: Merrill/Prentice Hall.

Baca, L. M., & Almanza, E. (1991). *Language minority students and disabilities*. Reston, VA: Council for Exceptional Children.

Baker, D. B. (1994). Parenting stress and ADHD: A comparison of mothers and fathers. *Journal of Emotional and Behavioral Disorders, 2*(1), 46–50.

Barnes, K. (1986). Surviving as a single parent. *Exceptional Parent, 16*(3), 47–49.

Beckman, P. J. (1991). Comparison of mothers' and fathers' perceptions of the effect of young children with and without disabilities. *American Journal of Mental Retardation, 95*(5), 585–595.

Behr, S. K., & Murphy, D. L. (1993). Research progress and promise: The role of perceptions in cognitive adaptation to disability. In A. P. Turnbull, J. M. Patterson, S. K. Behr, D. L. Murphy, J. G. Marquis, & M. J. Blue-Banning (Eds.), *Cognitive coping, families, and disability* (pp. 151–163). Baltimore: Brookes.

Benson, H. A. (1988). The changing American family and students at risk. *Behavior in Our Schools, 3*(1), 7–12.

Blue-Banning, M. J., Santelli, B., Guy, B., & Wallace, E. (1994). *Cognitive coping project: Coping with the challenges of disability*. Lawrence: University of Kansas, Beach Center on Families and Disability.

Bouma, R., & Schweitzer, R. (1990). The impact of chronic childhood illness on family stress: A comparison between autism and cystic fibrosis. *Journal of Clinical Psychology, 46*(6), 722–730.

Carandang, L. A. (1992). Family dynamics of the gifted. *Gifted Education International, 8*(2), 117–120.

Chan, S. (1992). Families with Asian roots. In E. W. Lynch & M. J. Hanson (Eds.), *Developing cross-cultural competence: A guide for working with young children and their families* (pp. 181–258). Baltimore: Brookes.

Chasnoff, I., Landress, H., & Barrett, M. (1990). The prevalence of illicit-drug or alcohol abuse during pregnancy and discrepancies in mandatory reporting in Pinnellas County, Florida. *New England Journal of Medicine, 322*, 1202–1206.

Ciotti, P. (1989, May 9). Growing up different: When the retarded become parents, perhaps their children know best how it works. *Los Angeles Times*, pp. V–1, V–4, V–10.

Cope, D. N., & Wolfson, B. (1994). Crisis intervention with the family in the trauma setting. *Journal of Head Trauma Rehabilitation, 9*(1), 67–81.

Correa, V. I. (1992). Cultural accessibility of services for culturally diverse clients with disabilities and their families. *Rural Special Education Quarterly, 11*(2), 6–12.

Craft, A., & Craft, J. (1979). *Handicapped married couples*. London: Routledge & Kegan Paul.

Crnic, K., & Booth, C. (1991). Mothers' and fathers' perceptions of daily hassles of parenting across early childhood. *Journal of Marriage and the Family, 53*, 1042–1050.

Diehl, S. F., Moffitt, K. A., & Wade, S. M. (1991). Focus group interview with parents of children with medically complex needs: An intimate look at their perceptions and feelings. *Children's Health Care, 20*(3), 170–178.

Dyson, L. L. (1989). Adjustment of siblings of handicapped children: A comparison. *Journal of Pediatric Psychology, 14*, 215–229.

Farber, B., & Ryckman, D. B. (1965). Effects of severely mentally retarded children on family relationships. *Mental Retardation Abstracts, 2*, 1–17.

Feldman, M. A., Case, L., Rincover, A., & Betel, J. (1989). Parent Education Project III: Increasing affection and responsivity in developmentally handicapped mothers: Component analysis, generalization, and effects on child language. *Journal of Applied Behavior Analysis, 22*, 211–222.

Fitzpatrick, J. P. (1987). *Puerto Rican Americans: The meaning of migration to the mainland*. Englewood Cliffs, NJ: Prentice Hall.

Frey, K. S., Greenberg, M. T., & Fewell, R. F. (1989). Stress and coping among parents of handicapped children: A multidimensional approach. *American Journal of Mental Retardation, 94*(3), 240–249.

Friedman, R. C., & Gallagher, T. (1991). The family with a gifted child. In M. J. Fine (Ed.), *Collaboration with parents of exceptional children* (pp. 257–276). Brandon, VT: Clinical Psychology Publishing.

Gelbrich, J. A., & Hare, E. K. (1989). The effects of single parenthood on school achievement in a gifted population. *Gifted Child Quarterly, 33*(3), 115–117.

Gervasio, A. H. (1993). How TBI affects the family. *TBI Transmit, 4*(1), 1–3.

Gottwald, S. R., & Thurman, S. K. (1994). The effects of prenatal cocaine exposure on mother-infant interaction and infant arousal in the newborn period. *Topics in Early Childhood Special Education, 14*(2), 217–231.

Greenfield, P. M. (1994). Independence and interdependence as developmental scripts: Implications for theory, research, and practice. In P. M. Greenfield & R. R. Cocking (Eds.), *Cross-cultural roots of minority child development* (pp. 1–37). Hillsdale, NJ: Erlbaum.

Hanson, M. J. (1992). Families with Anglo-European roots. In E. W. Lynch & M. J. Hanson (Eds.), *Developing cross-cultural competence: A guide for working with young children and their families* (pp. 65–88). Baltimore: Brookes.

Hareven, T. K. (1982). American families in transition: Perspectives on change. In F. Walsh (Ed.), *Normal family processes* (pp. 446–466). New York: Guilford.

Harris, V. S., & McHale, S. M. (1989). Family life problems, daily caregiving activities, and psychological well-being of mothers of mentally retarded children. *American Journal on Mental Retardation, 94,* 231–239.

Harry, B. (1992a). *Cultural diversity, families, and the special education system.* New York: Teachers College Press.

Harry, B. (1992b). Making sense of disability: Low-income, Puerto Rican parents' theories of the problem. *Exceptional Children, 59*(1), 27–40.

Harry, B., & Kalyanpur, M. (1994). Cultural underpinnings of special education: Implications for professional interactions with culturally diverse families. *Disability and Society, 9*(2), 145–165.

Heflin, L. J., & Rudy, K. (1991). *Homeless and in need of special education.* Reston, VA: Council for Exceptional Children.

Helge, D. (1991). *Rural, exceptional, at risk.* Reston, VA: Council for Exceptional Children.

Homes for the Homeless. (1992). *Who are homeless families? A profile of homelessness in New York City* [Report]. New York: Author.

Isbell, H. (1983). He looked the way a baby should look. In T. Dougan, L. Isbell, & P. Vyas (Eds.), *We have been there: Families share the joys and struggles of living with mental retardation* (pp. 19–23). Nashville, TN: Abingdon.

Jamieson, J. R. (1995). Interactions between mothers and children who are deaf. *Journal of Early Intervention, 19*(2), 108–117.

Joe, J. R., & Malach, R. S. (1992). Families with Native American roots. In E. W. Lynch & M. J. Hanson (Eds.), *Developing cross-cultural competence: A guide for working with young children and their families* (pp. 89–119). Baltimore: Brookes.

Jones, D. E., Clatterbuck, C. C., Barber, P., Marquis, J., & Turnbull, H. R. (1995). *Educational placements for children who are ventilator assisted.* Lawrence: University of Kansas, Beach Center on Families and Disability.

Kalyanpur, M., & Rao, S. S. (1991). Empowering low-income black families of handicapped children. *American Journal of Orthopsychiatry, 61*(4), 523–532.

Kim, U., & Choi, S. H. (1994). Individualism, collectivism, and child development: A Korean perspective. In P. M. Greenfield & R. R. Cocking (Eds.), *Cross-cultural roots of minority child development* (pp. 226–257). Hillsdale, NJ: Erlbaum.

Kozol, J. (1988). *Rachel and her children: Homeless families in America.* New York: Fawcett Columbine.

Kreutzer, J. S., Serio, C. D., & Bergquist, S. (1994). Family needs after brain injury: A quantitative analysis. *Journal of Head Trauma Rehabilitation, 9*(3), 104–115.

Lavelle, R. (1995). *America's new war on poverty: A reader for action* [Companion to the public television series *America's war on poverty*]. San Francisco: KQED Books.

Lee, G. R. (1982). *Family structure and interaction: A comparative analysis.* Minneapolis: University of Minnesota Press.

Luetke-Stahlman, B. (1991). Moving with a deaf child in the family. *Perspectives, 9*(5), 8–10.

McGill, D., & Pearce, J. K. (1982). British families. In M. McGoldrick, J. K. Pearce, & J. Giordano (Eds.), *Ethnicity in family therapy* (pp. 457–482). New York: Guilford.

Mokuau, N., & Tauili'ili, P. (1992). Families with native Hawaiian and Pacific Island roots. In E. W. Lynch & M. J. Hanson (Eds.), *Developing cross-cultural competence: A guide for working with young children and their families* (pp. 301–318). Baltimore: Brookes.

Morey, S. M., & Gilliam, O. L. (1974). *Respect for life: Traditional upbringing of American Indian children.* Garden City, NY: Waldorf.

Muccigrosso, L., Scavarda, M., Simpson-Brown, R., & Thalacker, B. E. (1991). *Double jeopardy: Pregnant and parenting youth in special education.* Reston, VA: Council for Exceptional Children.

Nagy, S., & Ungerer, J. (1990). The adaptation of mothers and fathers to children with cystic fibrosis: A comparison. *Children's Health Care, 19*(3), 147–154.

National Center for Children in Poverty. (1995). Number of poor children under six increased from 5 to 6 million, 1987–1992. *National Center for Children in Poverty News and Issues, 5*(1), 1–2.

National Commission on Childhood Disability. (1995, November). *Supplemental security income for children with disabilities: Report to Congress of the National Commission on Childhood Disability.* Washington, DC: Author.

National Institute on Alcohol Abuse and Addiction. (1990). *Seventh special report to the U.S. Congress.* Washington, DC: U.S. Government Printing Office.

National Resource Center for Family Support Programs. (1993). *Family support programs and incarcerated parents* [Fact sheet]. Chicago: Family Resource Coalition.

Olson, D. H., McCubbin, H. I., Barnes, H., Larsen, A., Muxen, M., & Wilson, M. (1983). *Families: What makes them work?* Beverly Hills, CA: Sage.

O'Neill, A. M. (1985). Normal and bright children of mentally retarded parents: The Huck Finn syndrome. *Child Psychiatry and Human Development, 15,* 255–268.

Patterson, G. R., Reid, J. B., & Dishion, T. J. (1992). *Antisocial boys.* Eugene, OR: Castalia.

Phelps, L., & Grabowski, J. (1992). Fetal alcohol syndrome: Diagnostic features and psychoeducational risk factors. *School Psychology Quarterly, 7*(2), 112–128.

Pianta, R. C., & Lothman, D. J. (1994). Predicting behavior problems in children with epilepsy: Child factors, disease factors, family stress, and child-mother interactions. *Child Development, 65*, 1415–1428.

Poulsen, M. K. (1994). The development of policy recommendations to address individual and family needs of infants and young children affected by family substance abuse. *Topics in Early Childhood Special Education, 14*(2), 275–291.

Powell, T. H., & Gallagher, P. A. (1993). *Brothers and sisters: A special part of exceptional families* (2nd ed.). Baltimore: Brookes.

Prater, M. A., Serna, L. A., Sileo, T. W., & Katz, A. R. (1995). HIV disease: Implications for special educators. *Remedial and Special Education, 16*(2), 68–78.

Raymond, C. L., & Benbow, C. P. (1989). Educational encouragement by parents: Its relationship to precocity and gender. *Gifted Child Quarterly, 33*(4), 144–151.

Reid, W. J. (1985). *Family problem solving*. New York: Columbia University Press.

Rimm, S., & Lowe, B. (1988). Family environments of underachieving gifted students. *Gifted Child Quarterly, 32*(4), 353–359.

Robbins, C., & Clayton, R. R. (1989). Gender-related differences in psychoactive drug use among older adults. *Journal of Drug Issues, 19*(2), 207–219.

Rubin, L. B. (1976). *Worlds of pain: Life in the working-class family*. New York: Basic Books.

Sager, C. J., Brown. H. S., Crohn, H., Engel, T., Rodstein, E., & Walker, L. (1983). *Treating the remarried family*. New York: Brunner/Mazel.

Sampson, P. D., Streissguth, A. P., Barr, H. M., & Bookstein, F. L. (1989). Neurobehavioral effects of prenatal alcohol. Part 2: Partial least squares analysis. *Neurotoxicology and Teratology, 11*, 477–491.

Schinke, S. P., Schilling, R. F., Kirkham, M. A., Gilchrist, L. D., Barth, R. P., & Blythe, B. (1986). Stress management skills for parents. *Journal of Child and Adolescent Psychotherapy, 3*(4), 293–298.

Schutter, L. S., & Brinker, R. P. (1992). Conjuring a new category of disability from prenatal cocaine exposure: Are the infants unique biological or caretaking casualties? *Topics in Early Childhood Special Education, 11*(4), 84–111.

Seligmann, J. (1992, December 14). It's not like Mr. Mom. *Newsweek, 120*(24), 70–73.

Sharifzadeh, V. S. (1992). Families with Middle Eastern roots. In E. W. Lynch & M. J. Hanson (Eds.), *Developing cross-cultural competence: A guide for working with young children and their families* (pp. 319–352). Baltimore: Brookes.

Shreeve, W., Goetter, W. G. J., Bunn, A., Norby, J. R., Stueckle, A. F., Midgely, T. K., & de Michele, B. (1986). Single parents and students' achievements—A national tragedy. *Early Child Development and Care, 23*, 175–184.

Shriver, M. D., & Piersel, W. (1994). The long-term effects of intrauterine drug exposure: Review of recent research and implications for early childhood special education. *Topics in Early Childhood Special Education, 14*(2), 161–183.

Singer, G. H. S., & Nixon, C. (1996). Parents describe their experience with a child's traumatic brain injury. In G. H. S. Singer, A. Glang, & J. Williams (Eds.), *Families and children with acquired brain injury* (pp. 23–52). Baltimore: Brookes.

Sisco, C. B., & Pearson, C. L. (1994). Prevalence of alcoholism and drug abuse among female AFDC recipients. *Health and Social Work, 19*(1), 75–77.

Spradley, T. S., & Spradley, J. P. (1978). *Deaf like me*. New York: Random House.

Stronge, J. H., & Tenhouse, C. (1990). *Educating homeless children: Issues and answers*. Bloomington, IN: Phi Delta Kappa Educational Foundation.

Summers, J. A., Behr, S. K., & Turnbull, A. P. (1989). Positive adaptation and coping strengths of families who have children with disabilities. In G. H. S. Singer & L. K. Irvin (Eds.), *Support for caregiving families: Enabling positive adaptation to disability* (pp. 27–40). Baltimore: Brookes.

Summers, J. A., Dell'Oliver, C., Turnbull, A. P., Benson, H., Santelli, B., Campbell, M., & Siegel-Causey, E. (1990). Examining the individualized family service plan process: What are family preferences? *Topics in Early Childhood Special Education, 10*(1), 78–99.

Tanksley, C. K. (1993). Interactions between mothers and normal-hearing or hearing-impaired children. *Volta Review, 95*, 33–47.

Trute, B., & Hauch, C. (1988). Building on family strength: A study of families with positive adjustment to the birth of a developmentally disabled child. *Journal of Marital and Family Therapy, 14*(2), 185–193.

Turnbull, A. P., & Ruef, M. (in press). Family perspectives on inclusive lifestyle issues for individuals with problem behavior. *Exceptional Children*.

Turnbull, A. P., Summers, J. A., & Brotherson, M.J. (1984). *Working with families with disabled members: A family systems approach*. Lawrence: University of Kansas, Kansas University Affiliated Facility.

Turnbull, A. P., & Turnbull, H. R. (1996). Self-determination within a culturally responsive family systems perspective. In L. E. Powers, G. H. S. Singer, & J. Powers (Eds.), *On the road to autonomy: Promoting self-competence among children and youth with disabilities* (pp. 195–220). Baltimore: Brookes.

Tymchuk, A. J. (1990). Parents with mental retardation: A national strategy. *Journal of Disability Policy Studies, 1*(4), 43–55.

Tymchuk, A. J., Andron, L., & Unger, O. (1987). Parents with mental handicaps and adequate child care—A review. *Mental Handicaps, 15*, 49–54.

U.S. Department of Education. (1991). *The condition of bilingual education in the nation: A report to Congress and the president*. Washington, DC: Author.

U.S. Department of Education. (1992). *To assure the free appropriate public education of all children with disabilities: Fourteenth annual report to Congress on the implementation of the Individuals with Disabilities Education Act*. Washington, DC: Author.

U.S. Department of Education. (1993). *To assure the free appropriate public education of all children with disabilities: Fifteenth annual report to Congress on the implementation of the Individuals with Disabilities Education Act*. Washington, DC: Author.

U.S. Department of Education. (1994). *The condition of education in rural schools*. Washington, DC: Author.

Vadasy, P. F. (1986). Single mothers: A social phenomenon and population in need. In R. R. Fewell & P. F. Vadasy (Eds.), *Families of handicapped children: Needs and supports across the life span* (pp. 221–249). Austin, TX: Pro-Ed.

Vining, E. P. G. (1989). Educational, social, and life-long effects of epilepsy. *Pediatric Clinics of North America, 36*, 449–461.

Visher, J. S., & Visher, E. B. (1982). Stepfamilies and step-parenting. In E. Walsh (Ed.), *Normal family processes* (pp. 331–353). New York: Guilford.

Walther-Thomas, C., Hazel, J. S., Schumaker, J. B., Vernon, S., & Deshler, D. D. (1991). A program for families with children with learning disabilities. In M. J. Fine (Ed.), *Collaborative involvement with parents of exceptional children.* (pp. 239–256). Brandon, VT: Clinical Psychology Publishing.

Whitman, B. Y., & Accardo, P. J. (Eds.). (1990). *When a parent is mentally retarded*. Baltimore: Brookes.

Willis, W. (1992). Families with African American roots. In E. W. Lynch & M. J. Hanson (Eds.), *Developing cross-cultural competence: A guide for working with young children and their families* (pp. 121–150). Baltimore: Brookes.

Zinn, M. B., & Eitzen, D. S. (1993). *Diversity in families* (3rd ed.). New York: HarperCollins.

Zirpoli, T. J., Wieck, C., Hancox, D., & Skarnulis, E. R. (1994). Partners in policymaking: The first five years. *Mental Retardation, 32*(6), 422–425.

Chapter 6 Family Interaction

Abbott, D. A., & Meredith, W. H. (1986). Strengths of parents with retarded children. *Family Relations, 35*, 371–375.

Able-Boone, H., Sandall, S. R., Stevens, E., & Frederick, L. (1992). Family support resources and needs: How early intervention can make a difference. *Infant-Toddler Intervention, 2*(2), 93–102.

Benson, B. A., & Gross, A. M. (1989). The effect of a congenitally handicapped child upon the marital dyad: A review of the literature. *Clinical Psychology Review, 9*(6), 747–758.

Black Community Crusade for Children. (1993). *Progress and peril: Black children in America*. Washington, DC: Children's Defense Fund.

Blue-Banning, M. J. (1995). [Unpublished raw data.] Lawrence: University of Kansas, Beach Center on Families and Disability.

Boggs, S. T. (1965). An interactional study of Ojibwa socialization. *American Sociological Review, 21*, 191–198.

Briggs, H. E. (1994). Promoting adoptions by foster parents through an inner-city organization. *Research on Social Work Practice, 4*(4), 497–509.

Bristol, M. M., Gallagher, J. J., & Schopler, E. (1988). Mothers and fathers of young developmentally disabled and nondisabled boys: Adaptation and spousal support. *Developmental Psychology, 24*(3), 441–451.

Broderick, C., & Smith, J. (1979). The general systems approach to the family. In W. R. Burr, R. Hill, F. I. Nye, & I. L. Reiss (Eds.), *Contemporary theories about the family* (vol. 2) (pp. 112–129). New York: Free Press.

Brookes-Gunn, J., & Chase-Lansdale, P. L. (1991). Children having children: Effects on the family system. *Pediatric Annals, 20*(9), 467–481.

Burton, S. L. (1988). *Serving the needs of grandparents and siblings of the handicapped in rural America: A preservice/inservice curriculum module for preparation of rural special educators*. Bellingham: Western Washington University, National Rural Development Institute.

Burton, S. L., & Parks, A. L. (1994). College-aged siblings of individuals with disabilities. *Social Work Research, 18*(3), 178–185.

Carnes, P. (1981). *Family development I: Understanding us*. Minneapolis, MN: Interpersonal Communications Programs.

Carr, J. (1988). Six-weeks to twenty-one years old: A longitudinal study of children with Down's syndrome and their families. *Journal of Child Psychology and Psychiatry, 29*(4), 407–431.

Chan, S. (1992). Families with Asian roots. In E. W. Lynch & M. J. Hanson (Eds.), *Developing cross-cultural competence: A guide for working with young children and their families* (pp. 181–257). Baltimore: Brookes.

Children's Defense Fund. (1991). *The state of America's children: 1991*. Washington, DC: Author.

Children's Defense Fund. (1993). *The state of America's children: 1993*. Washington, DC: Author.

Clarke-Stewart, K. A. (1978). And daddy makes three: The father's impact on mother and young child. *Child Development, 49*, 466–478.

Cope, D. N., & Wolfson, B. (1994). Crisis intervention with the family in the trauma setting. *Journal of Head*

Trauma Rehabilitation, 9(1), 67–81.

Cornell, D. G., & Grossberg, I. N. (1987). Family environment and personality adjustment in gifted program children. *Gifted Child Quarterly, 31*, 59–64.

Cuskelly, M., & Gunn, P. (1993). Maternal reports of behavior of siblings of children with Down syndrome. *American Journal on Mental Retardation, 97*(5), 521–529.

Dyson, L., Edgar, E., & Crnic, K. (1989). Psychological predictors of adjustment by siblings of developmentally disabled children. *American Journal on Mental Retardation, 94*(3), 292–302.

Dyson, L., & Fewell, R. R. (1989). The self-concept of siblings of handicapped children: A comparison. *Journal of Early Intervention, 13*(3), 230–238.

Featherstone, H. (1980). *A difference in the family: Living with a disabled child*. New York: Basic Books.

Feitel, B., Margetson, N., Chamas, J., & Lipman, C. (1992). Psychosocial background and behavioural and emotional disorders of homeless and runaway youth. *Hospital and Community Psychiatry, 43*(2), 155–159.

Frey, K. S., Fewell, R. R., & Vadasy, P. F. (1989). Parental adjustment and changes in child outcome among families of young handicapped children. *Topics in Early Childhood Special Education, 8*(4), 38–57.

Gath, A. (1977). The impact of an abnormal child upon the parents. *British Journal of Psychiatry, 130*, 405–410.

Gath, A., & Gumley, D. (1987). Retarded children and their siblings. *Journal of Child Psychology and Psychiatry, 28*, 715–730.

George, J. D. (1988). Therapeutic intervention for grandparents and extended family of children with developmental delays. *Mental Retardation, 26*(6), 369–375.

Gervasio, A. H. (1993). How TBI affects the family. *TBI Transmit, 4*(1), 1–3.

Glidden, L. M. (1989). *Parents for children, children for parents: The adoption alternative*. Washington, DC: American Association on Mental Retardation.

Glidden, L. M., Kiphart, M. J., Willoughby, J. C., & Bush, B. A. (1993). Family functioning when rearing children with developmental disabilities. In A. P. Turnbull, J. M. Patterson, S. K. Behr, D. L. Murphy, J. G. Marquis, & M. J. Blue-Banning (Eds.), *Cognitive coping, families, and disability* (pp. 173–182). Baltimore: Brookes.

Glidden, L. M., & Pursley, J. T. (1989). Longitudinal comparisons of families who have adopted children with mental retardation. *American Journal of Mental Retardation, 94*(3), 272–277.

Grenier, M. E. (1985). Gifted children and other siblings. *Gifted Child Quarterly, 29*, 164–167.

Hanson, M. J. (1992). Families with Anglo-European roots. In E. W. Lynch & M. J. Hanson (Eds.), *Developing cross-cultural competence: A guide for working with young children and their families* (pp. 65–88). Baltimore: Brookes.

Helsel Family. (1985). The Helsels' story of Robin. In H. R. Turnbull & A. P. Turnbull (Eds.), *Parents speak out:*

Then and now (2nd ed.) (pp. 81–100). Englewood Cliffs, NJ: Merrill/Prentice Hall.

Joe, J. R., & Malach, R. S. (1992). Families with Native American roots. In E. W. Lynch & M. J. Hanson (Eds.), *Developing cross-cultural competence: A guide for working with young children and their families* (pp. 89–120). Baltimore: Brookes.

Kantor, D., & Lehr, W. (1975). *Inside the family: Toward a theory of family process*. San Francisco: Jossey-Bass.

Kazak, A. E., & Marvin, R. S. (1984). Differences, difficulties and adaptation: Stress and social networks in families with a handicapped child. *Family Relations, 33*, 67–77.

Kreutzer, J. S., Serio, C. D., & Bergquist, S. (1994). Family needs after brain injury: A quantitative analysis. *Journal of Head Trauma Rehabilitation, 9*(3), 104–115.

Lamb, M. (1983). Fathers of exceptional children. In M. Seligman (Ed.), *The family with a handicapped child* (pp. 125–146). New York: Grune & Stratton.

LaVigne, J. V., & Ryan, M. (1979). Psychological adjustment of siblings of children with chronic illness. *Pediatrics, 15*, 616–627.

Lichtenstein, J. (1993). Help for troubled marriages. In G. H. S. Singer & L. E. Powers (Eds.), *Families, disability, and empowerment* (pp. 259–283). Baltimore: Brookes.

Lobato, D., Barbour, L., Hall, L. J., & Miller, C. T. (1987). Psychosocial characteristics of preschool siblings of handicapped and nonhandicapped children. *Journal of Abnormal Child Psychology, 15*, 329–338.

McHale, S. M., & Gamble, W. C. (1989). Sibling relationships of children with disabled and nondisabled brothers and sisters. *Developmental Psychology, 25*(3), 421–429.

Meyer, D. J., & Vadasy, P. F. (1986). *Grandparent workshops: How to organize workshops for grandparents of children with handicaps*. Seattle: University of Washington Press.

Meyer, D. J., & Vadasy, P. F. (1994). *Sibshops: Workshops for siblings of children with special needs*. Baltimore: Brookes.

Minuchin, S. (1974). *Families and family therapy*. Cambridge, MA: Harvard University Press.

Murphy, A. T. (1982). The family with a handicapped child: A review of the literature. *Developmental and Behavioral Pediatrics, 3*(2), 73–82.

National Commission on Children. (1991). *Beyond rhetoric: A new American agenda for children and families*. Washington, DC: U.S. Government Printing Office.

Olson, D. H., Russell, C. S., & Sprenkle, D. H. (1980). Circumplex model of marital and family systems II: Empirical studies and clinical intervention. *Advances in Family Intervention Assessment and Theory, 1*, 129–179.

Olson, D. H., Sprenkle, D. H., & Russell, C. S. (1979). Circumplex model of marital and family systems I: Cohesion and adaptability dimensions, family types, and clinical applications. *Family Process, 18*, 3–28.

Orsillo, S. M., McCaffrey, R. J., & Fisher, J. M. (1993). Siblings of head-injured individuals: A population at risk. *Journal of Head Trauma Rehabilitation, 8*(1), 102–115.

Perez, L. (1986). Immigrant economic adjustment and family organization: The Cuban success story reexamined. *International Migration Review, 20*, 4–20.

Petr, C. G. (1994, April). Crises that threaten out-of-home placement of children with emotional and behavioral disorders. *Families in Society: The Journal of Contemporary Human Services, 75*(4), 195–203.

Pfouts, J. H. (1980). Birth order, age spacing, I.Q. differences, and family relations. *Journal of Marriage and the Family, 42*, 517–521.

Powell, T. H., & Gallagher, P. A. (1993). *Brothers and sisters—A special part of exceptional families* (2nd ed.). Baltimore: Brookes.

Pruett, K., & Litzenberger, B. (1992). Latency development in children of primary nurturing fathers. In A. J. Solnit, P. B. Neubauer, & A. S. Dowling (Eds.), *The psychoanalytic study of children* (Vol. 47) (pp. 85–101). New Haven, CT: Yale University Press.

Ramirez, O. (1989). Mexican American children and adolescents. In J. T. Gibbs, L. Nahme Huang, & Associates (Eds.), *Children of color* (pp. 24–25). San Francisco: Jossey-Bass.

Raymond, C. L., & Benbow, C. P. (1989). Educational encouragement by parents: Its relationship to precocity and gender. *Gifted Child Quarterly, 33*(4), 144–151.

Reed, E. W., & Reed, S. C. (1965). *Mental retardation: A family study*. Philadelphia: Saunders.

Renzulli, J. S., & McGreevey, A. M. (1986). Twins included and not included in special programs for the gifted. *Roeper Review, 9*, 120–127.

Rodrigue, J. R., Geffkin, G. R., & Morgan, S. B. (1993). Perceived competence and behavioral adjustment of siblings of children with autism. *Journal of Autism and Developmental Disorders, 23*(4), 665–674.

Sandler, A. G., Warren, S. H., & Raver, S. A. (1995). Grandparents as a source of support for parents of children with disabilities: A brief report. *Mental Retardation, 33*(4), 248–250.

Satir, V. (1972). *Peoplemaking*. Palo Alto, CA: Science and Behavior Books.

Schweitzer, R. D., Hier, S. J., & Terry, D. (1994). Parental bonding, family systems, and environmental predictors of adolescent homelessness. *Journal of Emotional and Behavioral Disorders, 2*(1), 39–45.

Scott-Jones, N. (1993). Families as educators in a pluralistic society. In N. F. Chavkin (Ed.), *Families and schools in a pluralistic society* (pp. 245–254). Albany: State University of New York Press.

Seltzer, M. M., Krauss, M. W., & Janicki, M. P. (Eds.). (1994). *Life course perspectives on adulthood and old age*. Washington, DC: American Association on Mental Retardation.

Shank, M. S., & Turnbull, A. P. (1993). Cooperative family problem solving: An intervention for single-parent families of children with disabilities. In G. H. S. Singer & L. E. Powers (Eds.), *Families, disability, and empowerment: Active coping skills and strategies for family interventions* (pp. 231–254). Baltimore: Brookes.

Sharifzadeh, V. S. (1992). Families with Middle Eastern roots. In E. W. Lynch & M. J. Hanson (Eds.), *Developing cross-cultural competence: A guide for working with young children and their families* (pp. 319–354). Baltimore: Brookes.

Singer, G. H. S., Glang, A., & Williams, J. (Eds.). (1996). *Children with acquired brain injury: Educating and supporting families*. Baltimore: Brookes.

Singer, G. H. S., & Nixon, C. (1996). A report on the concerns of parents of children with acquired brain injury. In G. H. S. Singer, A. Glang, & J. Williams (Eds.), *Children with acquired brain injury: Educating and supporting families* (pp. 23–52). Baltimore: Brookes.

Steno, S. M. (1990). The elusive continuum of child welfare services: Implication for minority children and youths. *Child Welfare, 69*, 551–562.

Stoneman, Z., Brophy, G. H., Davis, C. H., & Crapps, J. M. (1987). Mentally retarded children and their older same-sex siblings: Naturalistic in-home observations. *American Journal on Mental Retardation, 92*, 290–298.

Summers, J. A. (1987). *Defining successful family life in families with and without disabilities: A qualitative study*. Unpublished doctoral dissertation, University of Kansas.

Taylor, S. J., Knoll, J. A., Lehr, S., & Walker, P. M. (1989). Families for all children: Value-based services for children with disabilities and their families. In G. H. S. Singer & L. K. Irvin (Eds.), *Support for caregiving families: Enabling positive adaptation to disability* (pp. 27–40). Baltimore: Brookes.

Tew, B. J., Payne, E. H., & Lawrence, K. M. (1974). Must a family with a handicapped child be a handicapped family? *Developmental Medicine and Child Neurology, 18*, Suppl. 32, 95–98.

Todis, B., & Singer, G. (1991). Stress and stress management in families with adopted children who have severe disabilities. *Journal of the Association for Persons with Severe Handicaps, 16*(1), 3–13.

Traustadottir, R. (1991). Mothers who care: Gender, disability, and family life. *Journal of Family Issues, 12*(2), 211–228.

Turbiville, V. P. (1994). *Fathers, their children, and disability*. Unpublished doctoral dissertation, University of Kansas, Lawrence.

Turbiville, V. P., Turnbull, A. P., & Turnbull, H. R. (1995). Fathers and family-centered early intervention. *Infants and Young Children, 7*(4), 12–19.

Turnbull, A. P. R. (1993). [Unpublished college essay.]

Turnbull, A. P. (1994). [Unpublished raw data.] Lawrence: University of Kansas, Beach Center on Families and Disability.

Turnbull, A., & Bronicki, G. J. (1986). Changing second graders' attitudes toward people with mental retardation: Using kid power. *Mental Retardation, 24*(1), 44–45.

Turnbull, A. P., & Turnbull, H. R. (1996). Self-determination within a culturally responsive family systems perspective: Balancing the family mobile. In L. E. Powers, G. H. S. Singer, & J. Sowers (Eds.), *On the road to autonomy: Promoting self-competence among children and youth with disabilities* (pp. 195–220). Baltimore: Brookes.

Turner, L. (1995). Grandparent-caregivers: Their challenges and how to help. *Family Resource Coalition Report, 14*(1 & 2), 6–7.

Tuttle, D. H., & Cornell, D. G. (1993). Maternal labeling of gifted children: Effects on the sibling relationship. *Exceptional Children, 59*(5), 402–410.

Urwin, C. A. (1988). AIDS in children: A family concern. *Family Relations, 37*, 154–159.

Vadasy, P. F., & Fewell, R. R. (1986). Mothers of deaf-blind children. In R. R. Fewell & P. F. Vadasy (Eds.), *Families of handicapped children* (pp. 121–148). Austin, TX: Pro-Ed.

Vadasy, P. F., Fewell, R. R., & Meyer, D. J. (1986). Grandparents of children with special needs: Insights into their experiences and concerns. *Journal of the Division for Early Childhood, 10*(1), 36–44.

Vega, W. A. (1990). Hispanic families in the 1980s: A decade of research. *Journal of Marriage and the Family, 52*(4), 1015–1025.

Wickham-Searl, P. (1992). Mothers with a mission. In P. M. Ferguson, D. L. Ferguson, & S. J. Taylor (Eds.), *Interpreting disability: A qualitative reader* (pp. 251–274). New York: Teachers College Press.

Whitechurch, G. G., & Constantine, L. L. (1993). Systems theory. In P. G. Boss, W. J. Doherty, R. LaRossa, W. R. Schumm, & S. K. Steinmetz (Eds.), *Sourcebook of family theories and methods: A contextual approach* (pp. 325–352). New York: Plenum.

Willoughby, J. C., & Glidden, L. M. (1995). Fathers helping out: Shared child care and marital satisfaction of parents of children with disabilities. *American Journal on Mental Retardation, 99*(4), 399–406.

Wilson, J., Blacher, J., & Baker, B. L. (1989). Siblings of children with severe handicaps. *Mental Retardation, 27*, 167–173.

Yates, A. (1987). Current status and future directions of research on the American Indian child. *American Journal of Psychiatry, 144*(9), 1135–1142.

Young, D. M., & Roopnarine, J. L. (1994). Fathers' childcare involvement with children with and without disabilities. *Topics in Early Childhood Special Education, 14*(4), 488–502.

Zuniga, M. E. (1992). Families with Latino roots. In E. W. Lynch & M. J. Hanson (Eds.), *Developing cross-cultural competence: A guide for working with young children and their families* (pp. 151–180). Baltimore: Brookes.

Chapter 7 FAMILY FUNCTIONS

Aday, L. A., Aitken, M. J., & Weggener, D. H. (1988). *Pediatric homecare: Results of a national evaluation of programs for ventilator assisted children.* Chicago: Pluribus Press and the Center for Health Administration Studies, University of Chicago.

Ainsworth, M. D. S., Bell, S. M., & Stayton, D. (1974). Infant-mother attachment and social developing. In M. P. Richards (Ed.), *The introduction of the child into a social world.* London: Cambridge University Press.

Barnett, W. S., & Boyce, G. C. (1995). Effects of children with Down syndrome on parents' activities. *American Journal on Mental Retardation, 100*(2), 115–127.

Belle, D. (1990). Poverty and women's mental health. *American Psychologist, 45*(3), 385–389.

Bennett, J. M. (1985). Company, halt! In H. R. Turnbull & A. P. Turnbull (Eds.), *Parents speak out: Then and now* (2nd ed.) (pp. 159–173). Englewood Cliffs, NJ: Merrill/Prentice Hall.

Birenbaum, A., & Cohen, H. J. (1993). On the importance of helping families: Policy implications from a national study. *Mental Retardation, 31*(2), 67–74.

Blacher, J. (1994). Placement and its consequences for families with children who have mental retardation. In J. Blacher (Ed.), *When there's no place like home: Options for children living apart from their natural families* (pp. 211–212). Baltimore: Brookes.

Bronfenbrenner, U. (1990). Discovering what families do. In D. Blankenhorn, S. B. Ayme, & J. B. Elshtain (Eds.), *Rebuilding the nest: A new commitment to the American family* (pp. 27–38). Milwaukee: Family Service American.

Brotherson, M. J. (1985). *Parents self report of future planning and its relationship to family functioning and family stress with sons and daughters who are disabled.* Unpublished doctoral dissertation, University of Kansas, Lawrence.

Brotherson, M. J., Backus, L., Summers, J. A., & Turnbull, A. P. (1986). Transition to adulthood. In J. A. Summers (Ed.), *The right to grow up: Introduction to developmentally disabled adults* (pp. 17–44). Baltimore: Brookes.

Brotherson, M. J., & Goldstein, B. L. (1992). Time as a resource and constraint for parents of young children with disabilities: Implications for early intervention services. *Topics in Early Childhood Special Education, 12*(4), 508–527.

Caplan, G. (1976). The family as a support system. In G. Caplan & M. Killilea (Eds.), *Support systems and mutual help: Multidisciplinary explorations* (pp. 19–36). New York: Grune & Stratton.

Chan, S. (1992). Families with Asian roots. In E. W. Lynch & M. J. Hanson (Eds.), *Developing cross-cultural competence: A guide for working with young children and their families* (pp. 181–258). Baltimore: Brookes.

Chapman, J. W. (1988). Learning disabled children's self-concepts. *Review of Educational Research, 58*(3), 347–371.

Clark, G. A., & Zimmerman, E. D. (1988). Views of self, family background, and school: Interviews with artistically talented students. *Gifted Child Quarterly, 32*(4), 340–346.

Dettman, D. F., & Colangelo, N. (1980). A functional model for counseling parents of gifted students. *Gifted Child Quarterly, 24*(4), 158–161.

Falvey, M. A., Forest, M., Pearpoint, J., & Rosenberg, R. L. (1994). Building connections. In J. S. Thousand, R. A. Villa, & A. I. Nevin (Eds.), *Creativity and collaborative learning: A practical guide to empowering students and teachers* (pp. 347–368). Baltimore: Brookes.

Families and Work Institute. (1994). *Employers, families, and education: Facilitating family involvement in learning.* New York: Author.

Friedman, R. C. (1994). Upstream helping for low-income families of gifted students: Challenges and opportunities. *Journal of Educational and Psychological Consultation, 5*(4), 321–338.

Fujiura, G. T., Roccoforte, J. A., & Braddock, D. (1994). Costs of family care for adults with mental retardation and related developmental disabilities. *American Journal on Mental Retardation, 99*(3), 250–261.

Hanson, M. J. (1992). Families with Anglo-European roots. In E. W. Lynch & M. J. Hanson (Eds.), *Developing cross-cultural competence: A guide for working with young children and their families* (pp. 65–87). Baltimore: Brookes.

Harry, B. (1992a). *Cultural diversity, families, and the special education system: Communication and empowerment.* New York: Teachers College Press.

Harry, B. (1992b). An ethnographic study of cross-cultural communication with Puerto Rican-American families in the special education system. *American Educational Research Journal, 29*(3), 471–494.

Harry, B., Allen, N., & McLaughlin, M. (1995). Communication versus compliance: African-American parents' involvement in special education. *Exceptional Children, 61*(4), 364–377.

Kalyanpur, M., & Rao, S. S. (1991). Empowering low-income black families of handicapped children. *American Journal of Orthopsychiatry, 61*(4), 523–532.

Knitzer, J. (in press). Meeting the mental health needs of young children and families: Service needs, challenges, and opportunities. In B. Stroul (Ed.), *Systems of care for children and adolescents with serious emotional disturbances: From theory to reality.* Baltimore: Brookes.

Knoll, J. (1992). Being a family: The family experience of raising a child with a disability or chronic illness. In V. J. Bradley, J. Knoll, & J. M. Agosta (Eds.), *Emerging issues in family support* (pp. 9–56). Washington, DC: American Association on Mental Retardation.

Koblinsky, S. A., & Todd, C. M. (1991, Spring). Teaching self-care skills. *Teaching Exceptional Children,* pp. 40–44.

Krauss, M. W. (1993). Child-related and parenting stress: Similarities and differences between mothers and fathers of children with disabilities. *American Journal on Mental Retardation, 97*(4), 393–404.

Leslie, G. R. (1979). The nature of the family. In G. R. Leslie (Ed.), *The family in social context* (4th ed.) (pp. 3–23). New York: Oxford University Press.

Luetke-Stahlman, B., Luetke-Stahlman, B., & Luetke-Stahlman, H. (1992). Yes, siblings can help. *Perspectives, 10*(5), 9–11.

Maddux, C. D., & Cummings, R. E. (1983). Parental home tutoring: Aids and cautions. *Exceptional Parent, 13*(4), 30–33.

Martin, S. S., Brady, M. P., & Kotarba, J. A. (1992). Families with chronically ill young children: The unsinkable family. *Remedial and Special Education, 13*(2), 6–15.

Mellman, M., Lazarus, E., & Rivlin, A. (1990). Family time, family values. In D. Blankenhorn, S. Bayme, & J. B. Elshtain (Eds.), *Rebuilding the nest: A new commitment to the American family* (pp. 73–92). Milwaukee, WI: Family Service America.

Moon, M. S., & Bunker, L. (1987). Recreation and motor skills programming. In M. E. Snell (Ed.), *Systematic instruction of persons with severe handicaps* (pp. 214–244). Englewood Cliffs, NJ: Merrill/Prentice Hall.

Morris, M. W. (1987). Health care: Who pays the bills? *Exceptional Parent, 17,* 38–39.

National Commission on Childhood Disability. (1995). *Supplemental security income for children with disabilities: Report to Congress of the National Commission on Childhood Disability.* Washington, DC: Author.

O'Connor, S. (1995). We're all one family: The positive construction of people with disabilities by family members. In S. J. Taylor, R. Bogdan, & Z. M. Lutfiyya (Eds.), *The variety of community experience: Qualitative studies of family and community life* (pp. 67–78). Baltimore: Brookes.

Parker, F. L., Piotrkowsky, C., Horn, W. F., & Greene, S. (in press). The challenge for Head Start: Realizing its vision as a two-generation program. In S. Smith (Ed.), *Two-generation programs for families in poverty: A new intervention strategy*. Norwood, NJ: Ablex.

Raymond, C. L., & Benbow, C. P. (1989). Educational encouragement by parents: Its relationship to precocity and gender. *Gifted Child Quarterly, 33*(4), 144–151.

Rousso, H. (1984). Fostering healthy self-esteem. *Exceptional Parent, 8*(14), 9–14.

Ruef, M. (1995). *Informational priorities of parents regarding the challenging behaviors of their sons and daughters: Results of a national survey*. Unpublished manuscript, Beach Center on Families and Disability, University of Kansas.

Schaffner, C. B., & Buswell, B. E. (1992). *Connecting students: A guide to thoughtful friendship facilitation for educators and families*. Colorado Springs: PEAK Parent Center.

Schleien, S. J., Green, F. P., & Heyne, L. A. (1993). Integrated community recreation. In M. E. Snell (Ed.), *Instruction of students with severe disabilities* (4th ed.) (pp. 526–555). Englewood Cliffs, NJ: Merrill/Prentice Hall.

Sharifzadeh, V. S. (1992). Families with Middle Eastern roots. In E. W. Lynch & M. J. Hanson (Eds.), *Developing cross-cultural competence: A guide for working with young children and their families* (pp. 319–352). Baltimore: Brookes.

Sherwood, S. K. (1990). A circle of friends in a 1st grade classroom. *Educational Leadership, 48*(3), 41.

Smith-Horn, B., & Singer, G. H. S. (1996). Self-esteem and learning disabilities: An exploration of theories of the self. In L. E. Powers, G. H. S. Singer, & J. A. Sowers (Eds.), *On the road to autonomy: Promoting self-competence in children and youth with disabilities* (pp. 135–154). Baltimore: Brookes.

Summers, J. A. (1987a). *Defining successful family life in families with and without children with disabilities: A qualitative study*. Unpublished doctoral dissertation, University of Kansas, Lawrence.

Summers, J. A. (1987b). Family adjustment: Issues in research on families with developmentally disabled children. In V. B. Van Hasselt, P. S. Strain, & M. Hersen (Eds.), *Handbook of developmental disabilities* (pp. 79–90). New York: Pergamon.

Summers, J. A., Behr, S. K., & Turnbull, A. P. (1989). Positive adaptation and coping strengths of fami-lies who have children with disabilities. In G. H. S. Singer & L. K. Irvin (Eds.), *Support for caregiving families: Enabling positive adaptation to disability* (pp. 27–40). Baltimore: Brookes.

Summers, J. A., McMann, O. T., Kitchen, A., & Peck, L. (1995). *A qualitative study to identify best practices in serving families with multiple challenges: Using direct line staff as researchers*. Unpublished manuscript.

Swenson-Pierce, A., Kohl, F. L., & Egel, A. L. (1987). Siblings as home trainers: A strategy for teaching domestic skills to children. *Journal of the Association for Persons with Severe Handicaps, 12*(1), 53–60.

Todis, B., Irvin, L. K., Singer, G. H. S., & Yovanoff, P. (1993). The self-esteem parent program: Quantitative and qualitative evaluation of a cognitive-behavioral intervention. In G. H. S Singer & L. K. Irvin (Eds.), *Support for caregiving families: Enabling positive adaptation to disability* (pp. 203–229). Baltimore: Brookes.

Traustadottir, R. (1995). A mother's work is never done: Constructing a "normal" life. In S. J. Taylor, R. Bogdan, & Z. M. Lutfiyya (Eds.), *The variety of community experience: Qualitative studies of family and community life* (pp. 47–65). Baltimore: Brookes.

Turnbull, A. P. (1988a). The challenge of providing comprehensive support to families. *Education and Training in Mental Retardation, 23*(4), 261–272.

Turnbull, A. P (1988b). A life span perspective. *Family Resource Coalition Report, 7*(2), 13.

Turnbull, A. P., Summers, J. A., & Brotherson, M. J. (1984). *Working with families with disabled members: A family systems approach*. Lawrence: University of Kansas, Kansas University Affiliated Facility.

Turnbull, A. P., & Ruef, M. (in press). Family perspectives on inclusive lifestyle issues for individuals with problem behavior. *Exceptional Children*.

Turnbull, A. P., & Turbiville, V. P. (1995). Why must inclusion be such a challenge? *Journal of Early Intervention, 19*(3), 200–202.

Turnbull, A. P., & Turnbull, H. R. (1986). Stepping back from early intervention: An ethical perspective. *Journal of the Division for Early Childhood, 10*, 106–117.

Turnbull, A. P., & Turnbull, H. R. (1988). Toward great expectations for vocational opportunities: Family-professional partnerships. *Mental Retardation, 26*(6), 337–342.

U.S. Department of Education. (1990, January 9). Reading and writing proficiency remains low. *Daily Education News*, pp. 1–7.

Willis, W. (1992). Families with African American roots. In E. W. Lynch & M. J. Hanson (Eds.), *Developing cross-cultural competence: A guide for working with young children and their families* (pp. 121–150). Baltimore: Brookes.

Worley, G., Rosenfeld, L. R., & Lipscomb, J. (1991). Financial counseling for families of children with chronic disabilities. *Developmental Medicine and Child Neurology, 33*, 679–689.

Ziskin, L. (1985). The story of Jennie. In H. R. Turnbull & A. P. Turnbull (Eds.), *Parents speak out: Then and now* (2nd ed.) (pp. 65–74). Englewood Cliffs, NJ: Merrill/Prentice Hall.

Chapter 8 FAMILY LIFE CYCLE

Able-Boone, H., & Stevens, E. (1994). After the intensive care nursery experience: Families' perceptions of their well-being. *Children's Health Care, 23*(2), 99–114.

Abramson, M., Willson, V., Yoshida, R. K., & Hagerty, G. (1983). Parents' perceptions of their learning disabled child's educational performance. *Learning Disability Quarterly, 6*(2), 184–194.

Alpert, J. L. (1981). Theoretical perspectives on the family life cycle. *Counseling Psychologist, 9*(4), 25–34.

The Arc. (1988, September). *A status report on waiting lists for community services* [Fact sheet]. Arlington, TX: Author.

The Arc. (1990, November). *Position statement on education*. Arlington, TX: Author.

Batshaw, M. L., & Perret, Y. M. (1992). *Children with handicaps: A medical primer* (3rd ed.). Baltimore: Brookes.

Beckman, P. D., Newcomb, S., Frank, N., Brown, L., Stepanek, J., & Barnwell, D. (in press). Preparing professionals to work with families on early intervention teams. In D. Bricker & A. Widerstrom (Eds.), *Preparing personnel to work with infants, young children, and their families: A team approach*. Baltimore: Brookes.

Blacher, J. (1984a). Sequential stages of adjustment to the birth of a child with handicaps: Fact or artifact? *Mental Retardation, 22*, 55–68.

Blacher, J. (Ed.). (1984b). *Severely handicapped young children and their families: Research in review*. New York: Academic Press.

Blacher, J. (1994). Placement and its consequences for families with children who have mental retardation. In J. Blacher (Ed.), *When there's no place like home: Options for children living apart from their natural families* (pp. 211–212). Baltimore: Brookes.

Blasco, P. M., Blasco, P. A., & Zirpoli, T. J. (1994). Prenatal diagnosis: Current procedures and implications for early interventionists working with families. *Infants and Young Children, 7*(2), 33–42.

Boles, S., Horner, R. H., & Bellamy, G. T. (1988). Implementing transition: Programs for supported living. In B. L. Ludlow, A. P. Turnbull, & R. Luckasson (Eds.), *Transitions to adult life for people with mental retardation: Principles and practices* (pp. 101–117). Baltimore: Brookes.

Brantlinger, E. (1992). Professionals' attitudes toward the sterilization of people with disabilities. *Journal of the Association for Persons with Severe Handicaps, 17*(1), 4–18.

Brotherson, M. J. (1985). *Parents self report of future planning and its relationship to family functioning and family stress with sons and daughters who are disabled*. Unpublished doctoral dissertation, University of Kansas, Lawrence.

Brotherson, M. J., Backus, L., Summers, J. A. & Turnbull, A. P. (1986). Transition to adulthood. In J. A. Summers (Ed.), *The right to grow up: Introduction to developmentally disabled adults* (pp. 17–44). Baltimore: Brookes.

Brown, L., Albright, K. Z., Rogan, P., York, J., Solner, A. U., Johnson, F., VanDeventer, P., & Loomis, R. (1988). An integrated curriculum model for transition. In B. L. Ludlow, A. P. Turnbull, & R. Luckasson (Eds.), *Transitions to adult life for people with mental retardation: Principles and practices* (pp. 67–84). Baltimore: Brookes.

Bursuck, W. D., Rose, E., Cowen, S., & Yahaya, A. (1989). Nationwide survey of postsecondary education services for students with learning disabilities. *Exceptional Children, 56*, 236–245.

Buswell, B. E., & Schaffner, C. B. (1990). Families supporting inclusive schooling. In W. Stainback & S. Stainback (Eds.), *Support networks for inclusive schooling: interdependent integrated education* (pp. 219–230). Baltimore: Brookes.

Carter, E. A., & McGoldrick, M. (Eds.). (1980). *The family life cycle: A framework for family therapy*. New York: Gardner.

D'Alton, M. E., & DeCherney, A. H. (1993). Prenatal diagnosis. *New England Journal of Medicine, 328*(2), 114–120.

Duvall, E. (1957). *Family development*. Philadelphia: Lippincott.

Erwin, E. J., & Soodak, L. C. (1995). I never knew I could stand up to the system: Families' perspectives on pursuing inclusive education. *Journal of the Association for Persons with Severe Handicaps, 20*(2), 136–146.

Featherstone, H. (1980). *A difference in the family: Living with a disabled child*. New York: Basic Books.

Ferguson, P. M., & Ferguson, D. L. (1993). The promise of adulthood. In M. Snell (Ed.), *Instruction of persons with severe disabilities* (4th ed.) (pp. 588–607). Englewood Cliffs, NJ: Merrill/Prentice Hall.

Friedman, E. H. (1980). Systems and ceremonies: A family view of rites of passage. In E. A. Carter & M. McGoldrick (Eds.), *The family life cycle: A framework for family therapy* (pp. 429–460). New York: Gardner.

Furey, E. M. (1994). Sexual abuse of adults with mental retardation: Who and where. *Mental Retardation, 32*(3), 173–180.

Gallivan-Fenlon, A. (1994). "Their senior year": Family and service provider perspectives on the transition from school to adult life for young adults with disabilities. *Journal of the Association for Persons with Severe Handicaps, 19*(1), 11–23.

Gee, K. (1996). Least restrictive environment: Elementary and middle school. In National Council on Disability, *Improving the implementation of the Individuals with Disabilities Education Act: Making schools work for all of America's children. Supplement* (pp. 395–426). Washington, DC: National Council on Disability.

Gerst, D. (1991). *Trevor is a citizen: Why grieve?* Unpublished manuscript.

Giangreco, M. F., Cloninger, C. J., Mueller, P. H., Yuan, S., & Ashworth, S. (1991). Perspectives of parents whose children have dual sensory impairments. *Journal of the Association for Persons with Severe Handicaps, 16*(1), 14–24.

Green, S. K., & Shinn, M. R. (1994). Parent attitudes about special education and reintegration: What is the role of student outcomes? *Exceptional Children, 61*(3), 269–281.

Greenspan, S., & Porges, S. (1984). Psychopathology in infancy and early childhood: Clinical perspectives on the organization of sensory and affective-thematic experience. *Child Development, 55*, 49–70.

Guralnick, M. J. (1994). Mothers' perceptions of the benefits and drawbacks of early childhood mainstreaming. *Journal of Early Intervention, 18*(2), 168–183.

Halvorsen, A. T., Doering, K., Farron-Davis, F., Usilton, R., & Sailor, W. (1989). The role of parents and family members in planning severely disabled students' transitions from school. In G. H. S. Singer & L. K. Irvin (Eds.), *Support for caregiving families* (pp. 253–268). Baltimore: Brookes.

Hareven, T. K. (1982). American families in transition: Perspectives on change. In F. Walsh (Ed.), *Normal family processes* (pp. 446–466). New York: Guilford.

Harry, B., & Kalyanpur, M. (1994). Cultural underpinnings of special education: Implications for professional interactions with culturally diverse families. *Disability and Society, 9*(2), 145–165.

Hasazi, S., Gordon, L., & Roe, C. (1985). Factors associated with the employment status of handicapped youth exiting from high school from 1979 to 1983. *Exceptional Children, 51*(6), 455–469.

Hasazi, S. B., Johnston, A. P., Liggett, A., & Schattman, R. (1994). A qualitative policy study of the least restrictive environment provision of the Individuals with Disabilities Education Act. *Exceptional Children, 60*(6), 491–507.

Hassed, S. J., Miller, C. H., Pope, S. K., Murphy, P., Quick, J. G., & Curnmiff, C. (1993). Perinatal lethal conditions: The effects of diagnosis on decision making. *Obstetrics and Gynecology, 82*, 37–42.

Hill, J., Seyfarth, J., Banks, P., Wehman, P., & Orelove, F. (1985). Parent/guardian attitudes toward the working conditions of their mentally retarded children. *Exceptional Children, 54*(1), 9–24.

Indian Nations at Risk & National Advisory Council on Indian Education. (1990, October). *Joint issues sessions proceedings summary: Education of exceptional children.* National Indian Education Association 22nd Annual Conference, San Diego. (ERIC Document Reproduction Service No. ED 341 529)

Joe, J. R., & Malach, R. S. (1992). Families with Native American roots. In E. W. Lynch & M. J. Hanson (Eds.), *Developing cross-cultural competence: A guide for working with young children and their families* (pp. 89–120). Baltimore: Brookes.

Kastner, T. A., Nathanson, R., & Marchetti, A. (1992). Epidemiology of HIV infection in adults with developmental disabilities. In A. C. Crocker, H. J. Cohen, & T. A. Kastner (Eds.), *HIV infection and developmental disabilities: A resource for service providers* (pp. 127–132). Baltimore: Brookes.

Katsiyannis, A., Conderman, G., & Franks, D. J. (1995). State practices on inclusion: A national review. *Remedial and Special Education, 16*(5), 279–287.

Koroloff, N. M. (1990). Moving out: Transition policies for youth with serious emotional disabilities. *Journal of Mental Health Administration, 17*(1), 78–86.

Kubler-Ross, E. (1969). *On death and dying.* New York: Macmillan.

Lee, I. M. (1994, June). *Collaboration: What do families and physicians want?* Paper presented at the international conference on the Family on the Threshold of the 21st Century: Trends and Implications, Jerusalem.

Lipton, D. (1994). The "full inclusion" court cases: 1989–1994. *National Center on Educational Restructuring and Inclusion Bulletin, 1*(2), 1–8.

Lusthaus, E., & Lusthaus, C. (in press). Teachers, parents, and students in inclusive education: Working together throughout the high school years. In J. Andrews (Ed.), *Teaching students with diverse needs: Secondary classrooms.* Toronto: Nelson Canada.

Marvin, R. S., & Pianta, R. C. (1992). A relationship-based approach to self-reliance in young children with motor impairments. *Infants and Young Children, 4*(4), 33–45.

Mason, C. Y., & Jaskulski, T. (1994). HIV/AIDS prevention and education. In M. Agran, N. E. Marchand-Martella, & R. C. Martella (Eds.), *Promoting health and safety: Skills for independent living* (pp. 161–192). Baltimore: Brookes.

Monat-Haller, R. K. (1992). *Understanding and expressing sexuality: Responsible choices for individuals with developmental disabilities.* Baltimore: Brookes.

Moses, K. I. (1983). The impact of initial diagnosis: Mobilizing family resources. In J. A. Mulick & S. M. Pueschel (Eds.), *Parent-professional partnerships in developmental disability services* (pp. 11–34). Cambridge, MA: Ware.

Murphy, D. L., Lee, I. M., Turnbull, A. P., & Turbiville, V. (1995). The family-centered program rating scale: An instrument for program evaluation and change. *Journal of Early Intervention, 19*(1), 24–42.

Neugarten, B. (1976). Adaptations and the life cycle. *Counseling Psychologist, 6*(1), 16–20.

Oberti v. Board of Education, 789 F. Supp. 1322 (D. N. J., 1992).

O'Halloran, J. M. (1995). The celebration process [Fact sheet]. *In Parent articles 2* (pp. 195–96). Phoenix, AZ: Communication Skill Builders/The Psychological Corporation.

Olson, D. H., McCubbin, H. I., Barnes, H., Larsen, A., Muxen, M., & Wilson, M. (1983). *Families: What makes them work?* Beverly Hills, CA: Sage.

Ostrer, H. (1989). Prenatal diagnosis of genetic disorders by DNA analysis. *Pediatric Annals, 18*, 701–713.

Powers, L. E., Singer, G. H. S., & Sowers, J. A. (1996). *On the road to autonomy: Promoting self-competence among children and youth with disabilities.* Baltimore: Brookes.

Racino, J. A., Walker, P., O'Connor, S., & Taylor, S. J. (Eds.). (1993). *Housing, support, and community: Choices and strategies for adults with disabilities.* Baltimore: Brookes.

Rodgers, R. H., & White, J. M. (1993). Family development theory. In P. J. Boss, W. J. Doherty, R. LaRossa, W. R. Schumm, & S. K. Steinmetz (Eds.), *Sources of family theories and methods: A contextual approach* (pp. 225–254). New York: Plenum.

Rosenkoetter, S. E., Hains, A. H., & Fowler, S. A. (1994). *Bridging early services for children with special needs and their families: A practical guide for transition planning.* Baltimore: Brookes.

Ryndak, D. L., Downing, J. E., Jacqueline, L. R., & Morrison, A. P. (1995). Parents' perceptions after inclusion of their children with moderate or severe disabilities. *Journal of the Association for Persons with Severe Handicaps, 20*(2), 147–157.

Sager, C. J., Brown. H. S., Crohn, H., Engel, T., Rodstein, E., & Walker, L. (1983). *Treating the remarried family.* New York: Brunner/Mazel.

Sands, D., & Wehmeyer, M. (Eds.). (1996). *Self-determination across the life span: Theory and practice.* Baltimore: Brookes.

Seligman, M. (1985). Handicapped children and their families. *Journal of Counseling and Development, 64*, 274–277.

Seltzer, M. M., & Krauss, M. W. (1989). Aging parents with adult mentally retarded children: Family risk factors and sources of support. *American Journal of Mental Retardation, 94*(3), 303–312.

Seltzer, M. M., Krauss, M. W., & Janicki, M. P. (Eds.). (1994). *Life course perspectives on adulthood and old age.* Washington, DC: American Association on Mental Retardation.

Senge, P. M. (1990). *The fifth discipline: The art and practice of the learning organization.* New York: Doubleday.

Shelton, T. L., Jeppson, E. S., & Johnson, B. H. (1989). *Family-centered care for children with special health care needs.* Washington, DC: Association for the Care of Children's Health.

Sipes, D. S. B. (1993). Cultural values and American Indian families. In N. F. Chavkin (Ed.), *Families and schools in a pluralistic society* (pp. 157–174). Albany: State University of New York Press.

Sitlington, P., & Frank, A. (1990). Are adolescents with learning disabilities successfully crossing the bridge to adult life? *Learning Disability Quarterly, 13*, 97–111.

Southern, W. T., & Jones, E. (1991). *The academic acceleration of gifted children.* New York: Teachers College Press.

Tannenbaum, A. J. (1986). The enrichment matrix model. In J. S. Renzulli (Ed.), *Systems and models for developing programs for the gifted and talented* (pp. 391–428). Mansfield Center, CT: Creative Learning.

Terkelson, K. G. (1980). Toward a theory of family life cycle. In E. Carter & M. McGoldrick (Eds.), *The family life cycle: A framework of family therapy* (pp. 21–52). New York: Gardner.

Thousand, J. S., Villa, R. A., & Nevin, A. I. (1994). *Creativity and collaborative learning: A practical guide to empowering students and teachers.* Baltimore: Brookes.

Turnbull, A. P. (1988, December). The challenge of providing comprehensive support to families. *Education and Training in Mental Retardation, 23*(4), 261–272.

Turnbull, A. P., Ruef, M., & Reeves, C. (1995). *Family perspectives on inclusive lifestyle issues for individuals with problem behavior.* Lawrence, KS: University of Kansas, Beach Center on Families and Disability/The Family Connection.

Turnbull, A. P., Blue-Banning, M. J., Anderson, E. K., Seaton, K. A., Turnbull, H. R., & Dinas, P. A. (1996). Enhancing self-determination through Group Action Planning: A holistic emphasis. In D. Sands & M. Wehmeyer (Eds.), *Self-determination across the life span: Theory and practice* (pp. 232–256) Baltimore: Brookes.

Turnbull, A. P., Summers, J. A., & Brotherson, M. J. (1986). Family life cycle: Theoretical and empirical implications and future directions for families with mentally retarded members. In J. J. Gallagher & P. M. Vietze (Eds.), *Families of handicapped persons: Research, programs, and policy issues* (pp. 25–44). Baltimore: Brookes.

Turnbull, A. P., & Turnbull, H. R. (1985). Developing independence. *Journal of Adolescent Health Care, 6*(2), 108–119.

Turnbull, A. P., & Turnbull, H. R. (1996). Self-determination within a culturally responsive family systems perspective: Balancing the family mobile. In L. E. Powers, G. H. S. Singer, & J. A. Sowers (Eds.), *On the road to autonomy: Promoting self-competence among children and youth with disabilities* (pp. 195–220). Baltimore: Brookes.

Turnbull, A. P., Turnbull, H. R., & Blue-Banning, M. J. (1994). Enhancing inclusion of infants and toddlers with disabilities and their families: A theoretical and programmatic analysis. *Infants and Young Children, 7*(2), 1–14.

Turnbull, A. P., Turnbull, H. R., Shank, M., & Leal, D. (1995). *Exceptional lives: Special education in today's schools.* Englewood Cliffs, NJ: Merrill/Prentice Hall.

Turnbull, H. R., & Turnbull, A. P. (1996). Lessons for early care and education from the disability rights movement. In S. L. Kagan & N. Cohen (Eds.), *American early care and education.* San Francisco: Jossey-Bass.

Turnbull, H. R., Turnbull, A. P., Bronicki, G., Summers, J. A., & Roeder-Gordon, C. (1989). *Disability and the family: A guide to adulthood.* Baltimore: Brookes.

Vyas, P. (1983). Getting on with it. In T. Dougan, L. Isbell, & P. Vyas (Eds.), *We have been there* (pp. 17–19). Nashville, TN: Abingdon.

Wehmeyer, M. L., & Metzler, C. A. (1995). How self-determined are people with mental retardation? The national consumer survey. *Mental Retardation, 33*(2), 111–119.

Chapter 9 COMMUNICATING AMONG RELIABLE ALLIES

Alberto, P. A., Mechling, L., Taber, T. A., & Thompson, J. (1995, Spring). Using videotape to communicate with parents of students with severe disabilities. *Teaching Exceptional Children,* pp. 18–21.

Bowe, F. G. (1995). *Birth to five: Early childhood special education.* New York: Delmar.

Bursuck, W., Polloway, E. A., Plante, L., Epstein, M. H., & Jayanthi, M. (1993). *Report card grading and adaptations: A national survey of practices.* Unpublished manuscript.

Calfee, R. C., & Perfumo, P. (1993). Student portfolios: Opportunities for a revolution in assessment. *Journal of Reading, 36*(7), 532–537.

Chapey, G. D., Trimarco, T. A., Crisel, P., & Capobianco, M. (1987). School-parent partnerships in gifted education: From paper to reality. *Educational Research Quarterly, 11*(3), 37–46.

Coles, R. (1989). *The call of stories.* Boston: Houghton Mifflin.

Delgado, M. (1992). *The Puerto Rican community and natural support systems: Implications for the education of children* (Report No. 10). Boston: Boston University, School of Social Work, Center on Families, Communities, Schools, and Children's Learning.

Donahue, K., & Zigmond, N. (1990). Academic grades of ninth-grade urban learning disabled students and low-achieving peers. *Exceptionality, 1,* 17–27.

Ellis, C. L. (1993). *Dialogue journal communication between parent and teacher to describe a parent involvement program.* Unpublished doctoral dissertation, University of Kansas, Lawrence.

Epstein, J. L. (1995, May). School/family/community partnerships: Caring for the children we share. *Phi Delta Kappan,* pp. 701–712.

Falvey, M. A., Forest, M., Pearpoint, J., & Rosenberg, R. (1994). Building connections. In J. S. Thousand, R. A. Villa, & A. I. Nevin (Eds.), *Creativity and collaborative learning: A practical guide to empowering students and teachers* (pp. 347–368). Baltimore: Brookes.

Finders, M., & Lewis, C. (1994, May). Why some parents don't come to school. *Educational Leadership,* pp. 50–54.

Flake-Hobson, C., & Swick, K. J. (1984). Communication strategies for parents and teachers, or how to say what you mean. In M. L. Henniger & E. M. Nesselroad (Eds.), *Working with parents of handicapped children: A book of readings for school personnel* (pp. 141–149). Lanham, MD: University Press of America.

Fuller, C., Vandiviere, P., & Kronberg, C. (1987). TALKLINE: An evaluation of a call-in telephone source for parents. *Journal of the Division for Early Childhood, 11*(3), 265–270.

Fuqua, R. W., Hegland, S. M., & Karas, S. C. (1985). Processes influencing linkages between preschool handicap classrooms and homes. *Exceptional Children, 51*(4), 307–314.

Gelfer, J. I. (1991, Spring). Teacher-parent partnerships: Enhancing communications. *Childhood Education,* pp. 164–166.

Gersten, R., & Woodward, J. (1994). The language-minority student and special education: Issues, trends, and paradoxes. *Exceptional Children, 60*(4), 310–322.

Harry, B., & Kalyanpur, M. (1994). Cultural underpinnings of special education: Implications for professional interactions with culturally diverse families. *Disability and Society, 9*(2), 145–165.

Heward, W. L., & Chapman, J. E. (1981). Improving parent-teacher communication through recorded telephone messages: Systematic replication in a special education classroom. *Journal of Special Education Technology, 4,* 11–19.

Heward, W. L., & Orlansky, M.D. (1984). *Exceptional children* (2nd ed.). Englewood Cliffs, NJ: Merrill/Prentice Hall.

Kinloch, D. (1986). *An investigation of the impact of a preparation strategy on teachers perceptions of parent participation in the IEP review conferences of learning disabled and educable mentally retarded students.* Unpublished doctoral dissertation, University of Missouri, Columbia.

Kroth, R. L. (1985). *Communicating with parents of exceptional children: Improving parent-teacher relationships* (2nd ed.). Denver, CO: Love.

Lavine, J. (1986). De-mystifying professional evaluations. *Academic Therapy, 21*(5), 615–617.

Lindle, J. C. (1989, October). What do parents want from principals? *Educational Leadership,* pp. 12–14.

Loucks, H. (1992). Increased parent/family involvement: Ten ideas that work. *National Association of Secondary School Principals Bulletin, 76,* 19–23.

McCarney, S. B. (1986, February). Preferred types of communication indicated by parents and teachers of emotionally disturbed students. *Behavior Disorders*, pp. 118–123.

Michael, M. G., Arnold, K. D., Magliocca, L. A., & Miller, S. (1992). Influences on teachers' attitudes of the parents' role as collaborator. *Remedial and Special Education, 13*(2), 24–30, 39.

National Association of Secondary School Principals (NASSP). (1994). Building parent involvement. *NASSP Practitioner, 20*(5), 1–4.

Pike, K., & Salend, S. J. (1995, Fall). Authentic assessment strategies: Alternatives to norm-referenced testing. *Teaching Exceptional Children*, pp. 15–20.

Polloway, E. A., Epstein, M. H., Bursuck, W. D., Roderique, T. W., McConeghy, J. L., & Jayanthi, M. (1994). Classroom grading: A national survey of policies. *Remedial and Special Education, 15*(3), 162–170.

Rojewski, J. W., Pollard, R. R., & Meers, G. D. (1992). Grading secondary vocational education students with disabilities: A national perspective. *Exceptional Children, 59*(1), 68–76.

Rueda, R. S. (1992). Characteristics of teacher-student discourses in computer-based dialogue journals: A descriptive study. *Learning Disability Quarterly, 15*, 187–206.

Rueda, R., & Martinez, I. (1992). Fiesta Educativa: One community's approach to parent training in developmental disabilities for Latino families. *Journal of the Association for Persons with Severe Handicaps, 17*(2), 95–103.

Salend, S. J., & Taylor, L. (1993). Working with families: A cross-cultural perspective. *Remedial and Special Education, 14*(5), 25–32, 39.

Shertzer, B., & Stone, S. C. (1981). *Fundamentals of guidance* (4th ed.). Boston: Houghton Mifflin.

Simpson, R. L. (1982). *Conferencing parents of exceptional children*. Rockville, MD: Aspen.

Smith, M. J., & Ryan, A. S. (1987). Chinese-American families of children with developmental disabilities: An exploratory study of reactions to service providers. *Mental Retardation, 25*(6), 345–350.

Smrekar, C. E. (1993). Rethinking family-school interactions: A prologue to linking schools and social services. *Education and Urban Society, 25*(2), 175–186.

Staton, J., Shuy, R. W., Peyton, J. K., & Reed, L. (1988). *Dialogue journal communication: Classroom, linguistic, social, and cognitive views*. Norwood, NJ: Ablex.

Stephens, T. M., & Wolf, J. S. (1980). *Effective skills in parent/teacher conferencing*. Columbus: Ohio State University, National Center for Educational Materials and Media for the Handicapped.

Stephenson, J. (1992). The perspectives of mothers whose children are in special day classes for learning disabilities. *Journal of Learning Disabilities, 25*(8), 539–543.

Stonestreet, R. H., Johnston, R. G., & Acton, S. J. (1991). Guidelines for real partnerships with parents. *Infant-Toddler Intervention, 1*(1), 37–46.

Turnbull, A. P. (1994). [Unpublished raw data]. Lawrence: University of Kansas, Beach Center on Families and Disability.

Turnbull, A. P., & Turnbull, H. R. (1988). Toward great expectations for vocational opportunities: Family-professional partnerships. *Mental Retardation, 26*(6), 337–342.

Turnbull, A. P., & Winton, P. J. (1984). Parent involvement policy and practice: Current research and implications for families of young severely handicapped children. In J. Blacher (Ed.), *Severely handicapped children and their families: Research in review* (pp. 377–397). New York: Academic Press.

Turnbull, A. P., Winton, P. J., Blacher, J. B., & Salkind, N. (1983). Mainstreaming in the kindergarten classroom: Perspectives of parents of handicapped and nonhandicapped children. *Journal of the Division of Early Childhood, 6*, 14–20.

Warger, C. L. (1983). An analysis of curriculum and grading forms used by regular secondary teachers. In P. L. Reed (Ed.), *Mainstreaming in secondary schools: Focus on research* (pp. 1–8). (ERIC Document Reproduction Service No. ED 242721)

Yates, A. (1987). Current status and future directions of research on the American Indian child. *American Journal of Psychiatry, 144*(9), 1135–1142.

Chapter 10 MEETING FAMILIES' BASIC NEEDS

Affleck, G., Tennen, H., Rowe, J., Rocsher, B., & Walker, L. (1989). Effects of formal support on mothers' adaptation to the hospital-to-home transition of high-risk infants: The benefits and costs of helping. *Child Development, 60*, 488–501.

Agosta, J. M., & Bradley, V. J. (Eds.). (1985). *Family care for persons with developmental disabilities: A growing commitment*. Cambridge, MA: Human Services Research Institute.

Agosta, J., & Melda, K. (1995). *Supplemental security income for children*. Boston: Human Services Research Institute.

Ammerman, R. T. (1989). Child abuse and neglect. In M. Hersen (Ed.), *Innovations in child behavior therapy* (pp. 353–394). New York: Springer.

Ammerman, R. T., & Baladerian, N. J. (1993). *Maltreatment of children with disabilities* [Invited Working Paper No. 860]. Chicago: National Committee for the Prevention of Child Abuse.

Beckman, P. J., & Pokomi, J. L. (1988). A longitudinal study of families of preterm infants: Changes in stress and support over the first two years. *Journal of Special Education, 22*, 55–65.

Bergman, A. I., & Singer, G. H. S. (1996). The thinking behind the new public policy. In G. H. S. Singer, L. E. Powers, & A. L. Olson (Eds.), *Redefining family support: Innovations in public- private partnerships* (pp. 435–464). Baltimore: Brookes.

Bradley, V., Knoll, J., & Agosta, J. (1993). *Emerging issues in family support* (Monograph No. 18). Washington, DC: American Association on Mental Retardation.

Brown, D. S. (1992, Fall). Empowerment through peer counseling. *Office of Special Education and Rehabilitative Services News in Print*, pp. 27–29.

Burton, S. L. (1988). *Serving the needs of grandparents and siblings of the handicapped in rural America: A preservice/inservice curriculum module for preparation of rural special educators*. Bellingham: Western Washington University, National Rural Development Institute.

Center for Resource Management. (1995). *Summary of data from annual PTI reports FY'95* [Report]. South Hampton, NH: Author.

Child Abuse Prevention and Treatment Act, 42 U.S.C. 5106 (Supp. 1992).

Crnic, K. A., Greenberg, M. T., Ragozin, A. S., Robinson, N. M., & Basham, R. (1983). Effects of stress and social support on mothers and premature and full-term infants. *Child Development, 54,* 209–217.

Dunst, C. J., Trivette, C. M., & Cross, A. H. (1986). Mediating influences of social support: Personal, family, and child outcomes. *American Journal of Mental Deficiency, 90,* 403–417.

Friesen, B. J., & Wahlers, D. (1993). Respect and real help: Family support and children's mental health. *Journal of Emotional and Behavioral Problems, 2*(4), 12–15.

Garbarino, J., & Kostelny, K. (1992). *Neighborhood-based programs* [Manuscript prepared for U.S. Advisory Board on Child Abuse and Neglect]. Chicago: Erikson Institute.

Garlow, J. E., Turnbull, H. R., & Schnase, D. (1991). Model disability and family support act of 1991. *Kansas Law Review, 39*(3), 783–816.

Herman, S. E. (1994). Cash subsidy program: Family satisfaction and need. *Mental Retardation, 32*(6), 416–421.

Herman, S. E., & Thompson, L. (1995). Families' perceptions of their resources for caring for children with developmental disabilities. *Mental Retardation, 33*(2), 73–83.

Human Services Research Institute. (1995, May). *Supplemental security income for children with disabilities: An exploration of child and family needs and the relative merits of the cash benefit-program*. Salem, OR: Author.

Kazak, A. E., & Marvin, R. S. (1984). Differences, difficulties, and adaptations: Stress and social networks in families with a handicapped child. *Family Relations, 33,* 67–77.

Kelly, J. A. (1983). *Treating child abusive families: Intervention based on skills-training principles*. New York: Plenum.

Kempe, R. S., & Kempe, C. H. (1978). *Child abuse*. Cambridge, MA: Harvard University Press.

Knoll, J., Covert, S., Osuch, R., O'Connor, S., Agosta, J., & Blaney, B. (1990). *Family supports services: An end of decade status report*. Cambridge, MA: Human Services Research Institute.

Koroloff, N. M., & Friesen, B. J. (1991). Support groups for parents of children with emotional disorders: A comparison of members and nonmembers. *Community Mental Health Journal, 27*(4), 265–279.

Krauss, M. W., Upshur, C. C., Shonkoff, J. P., & Hauser-Cram, P. (1993). The impact of parent groups on mothers of infants with disabilities. *Journal of Early Intervention, 17*(1), 8–20.

Levine, M., & Perkins, D. V. (1987). *Principles of community psychology*. Oxford: Oxford University Press.

Lutzker, J. R. (1984). Project 12-ways: Treating child abuse and neglect from an ecobehavioral perspective. In R. F. Dangel & R. A. Polster (Eds.), *Parent training: Foundations of research and practice* (pp. 260–297). New York: Guilford.

Lutzker, J. R., Campbell, R. V., Newman, M. R., & Harrold, M. (1989). Ecobehavioral interventions for abusive, neglectful, and high-risk families. In G. H. S. Singer & L. K. Irvin (Eds.), *Support for caregiving families* (pp. 313–326). Baltimore: Brookes.

Lutzker, J. R., & Newman, M. R. (1986). Child abuse and neglect: Community problem, community solutions. *Education and Treatment of Children, 9,* 344–354.

National Center on Child Abuse and Neglect. (1993). *A report on the maltreatment of children with disabilities* [Report No. 20-10030]. Washington, DC: U.S. Department of Health and Human Services.

National Commission on Childhood Disability. (1995). *Supplemental security income for children with disabilities: Report to Congress of the National Commission on Childhood Disability*. Washington, DC: Author.

National Symposium on Abuse and Neglect of Children with Disabilities. (1995). *Abuse and neglect of children with disabilities: Report and recommendations*. Lawrence: University of Kansas, Beach Center on Families and Disability/Erikson Institute of Chicago.

Pizzo, P. (1983). *Parent to parent*. Boston: Beacon.

Rankin, J. L., & Phillips, S. (1995, Spring). Learning disabilities in the popular press: Suggestions for educators. *Teaching Exceptional Children*, pp. 35–39.

Santelli, B., Turnbull, A. P., Lerner, E., & Marquis, J. G. (1993). Parent to parent programs: A unique form of mutual support for families of persons with disabilities. In G. H. S. Singer & L .E. Powers (Eds.), *Families, disability, and empowerment* (pp. 27–66). Baltimore: Brookes.

Santelli, B., Turnbull, A. P., Marquis, J. G., & Lerner, E. (1993). Parent-to-parent programs: Ongoing support for parents of young adults with special needs. *Journal of Vocational Rehabilitation, 3*(2), 25–37.

Schradle, S. B., & Dougher, M. J. (1985). Social support as a mediator of stress: Theoretical and empirical issues. *Clinical Psychology Review, 5,* 641–661.

Shapiro, J., & Simonsen, D. (1994). Educational/support group for Latino families of children with Down syndrome. *Mental Retardation, 32*(6), 403–415.

Singer, G. H. S., Powers, L. E., & Olson, A. (1996). *Redefining family support: Innovations in public/private partnerships.* Baltimore: Brookes.

Smith, P. M. (1993). Opening many, many doors: Parent-to-parent support. In P. J. Beckman & G. B. Boyes (Eds.), *Deciphering the system: A guide for families of young children with disabilities* (pp. 129–142). Cambridge, MA: Brookline.

Sobsey, D. (1994). *Violence and abuse in the lives of people with disabilities.* Baltimore: Brookes.

Sontag, J. C., & Schacht, R. (1994). An ethnic comparison of parent participation and information needs in early intervention. *Exceptional Children, 60*(5), 422–433.

Summers, J. A., Dell'Oliver, C., Turnbull, A. P., Benson, H. A., Santelli, B., Campbell, M., & Siegel-Causey, E. (1990). Examining the individualized family service plan process: What are family and practitioner preferences? *Topics in Early Childhood Special Education, 10*(1), 78–99.

Taylor, R. J. (1988). Aging and supportive relationships among Black Americans. In J. Jackson (Ed.), *The Black American elderly: Research on physical and psychosocial health* (pp. 259–281). New York: Springer-Verlag.

Turnbull, H. R., Buchele-Ash, A., & Mitchell, L. (1994). *Abuse and neglect of children with disabilities: A policy analysis prepared for the National Symposium on Abuse and Neglect of Children with Disabilities.* Lawrence: University of Kansas, Beach Center on Families and Disability.

Turnbull, H. R., Garlow, J. E., & Barber, P. A. (1991). A policy analysis of family support for families with members with disabilities. *Kansas Law Review, 39*(3), 739–782.

Turnbull, A. P., & Turnbull, H. R. (1993). Enhancing beneficial linkages across the life span. *Disabilities Studies Quarterly, 13*(4), 34–36.

Vadasy, P. F., Fewell, R. R., Meyer, D. J., & Greenberg, M. T. (1985). Supporting fathers of handicapped young children: Preliminary findings of program effects. *Analysis and Intervention in Developmental Disabilities, 5,* 125–137.

Walker, J. L. (1988). Young American Indian children. *Teaching Exceptional Children, 20*(4), 50–51.

Walker, P. (1995, April). *Selected issues in family support: A compilation of materials and resources.* Syracuse, NY: Syracuse University, Research and Training Center on Community Integration.

Chapter 11 Referring and Evaluating for Special Education

Bailey, D. B., & Henderson, L. W. (1993). Traditions in family assessment: Toward an inquiry-oriented, reflective model. In D. Bryant & M. Graham (Eds.), *Implementing early intervention: From research to effective practice.* New York: Guilford.

Bailey, D. B., & Simeonsson, R. J. (1988). Assessing needs of families with handicapped infants. *Journal of Special Education, 22,* 117–127.

Blacher, J. (1984a). Sequential stages of adjustment to the birth of a child with handicaps: Fact or artifact? *Mental Retardation, 22,* 55–68.

Blacher, J. (Ed.). (1984b). *Severely handicapped young children and their families: Research in review.* New York: Academic Press.

Carter, J., & Sugai, G. (1989). Survey on prereferral practices: Responses from state departments of education. *Exceptional Children, 55*(5), 298–302.

Child Development Resources. (1989). How can we get help? In B. H. Johnson, M. J. McGonigel, & R. K. Kaufmann (Eds.), *Guidelines and recommended practices for Individualized Family Service Plan* (pp. D9–D11). Washington, DC: Association for the Care of Children's Health.

Coleman, M. R., Gallagher, J., & Foster, A. (1994). *Updated report on state policies related to the identification of gifted students* [Report]. Chapel Hill: University of North Carolina, Gifted Education Policy Studies Program.

Das, M. (1995). Tough decisions: One family's experience crosses cultures and continents. *Volta Voices, 2*(3), 5–7.

Dunst, C. J., Cooper, C. S., Weeldreyer, J. C., Snyder, K. D., & Chase, J. H. (1988). Family needs scale. In C. J. Dunst, C. M. Trivette, & A. G. Deal (Eds.), *Enabling and empowering families: Principles and guidelines for practice.* Cambridge, MA: Brookline.

Flood, J., & Lapp, D. (1989, March). Reporting reading progress: A comparison portfolio for parents. *Reading Teacher,* 508–515.

Friesen, B. J., & Poertner, J. (Eds.). (1995). *Case management to service coordination for children with emotional, behavioral, or mental disorders.* Baltimore: Brookes.

Fuchs, D., Fuchs, L. S., & Bahr, M. W. (1990). Mainstream assistance teams: A scientific basis for the art of consultation. *Exceptional Children, 57,* 128–139.

Fuchs, D., Fuchs, L. S., Bahr, M. W., & Stecker, P. M. (1990). Prereferral intervention: A prescriptive approach. *Exceptional Children, 56,* 493–513.

Fulmer, R. H., Cohen, S., & Monaco, G. (1985). Using psychological assessment in structural family therapy. *Journal of Learning Disabilities, 18*(3), 145–150.

Garshelis, J. A., & McConnell, S. R. (1993). Comparison of family needs assessed by mothers, individual professionals, and interdisciplinary teams. *Journal of Early Intervention, 17*(1), 36–49.

Graden, J. E., Casey, A., & Bonstrom, O. (1985). Implementing a prereferral intervention system. Part II: The data. *Exceptional Children, 51*, 487–496.

Graden, J. E., Casey, A., & Christenson, S. L. (1985). Implementing a prereferral intervention system. Part I: The model. *Exceptional Children, 51*, 377–384.

Hadaway, N., & Marek-Schroer, M. F. (1992). Multidimensional assessment of the gifted minority student. *Roeper Review, 15*(2), 73–77.

Halperin, L. (1989). Encounters of the closest kind: A view from within. *National Association of School Psychologists Communiqué, 17*, 6.

Halpern, R. (1982). Impact of PL. 94-142 on the handicapped child and family: Institutional responses. *Exceptional Children, 49*, 270–272.

Harry, B. (1992). Making sense of disability: Low-income, Puerto Rican parents' theories of the problem. *Exceptional Children, 59*(1), 27–40.

Harry, B., Allen, N., & McLaughlin, M. (1995). Communication versus compliance: African-American parents' involvement in special education. *Exceptional Children, 61*(4), 364–377.

Henderson, L. W., Aydlett, L. A., & Bailey, D. B. (1993). Evaluating family needs surveys: Do standard measures of reliability and validity tell us what we want to know? *Journal of Psychoeducational Assessment, 11*, 208–219.

Hepner, P., & Silverstein, J. (1988). Seeking an independent evaluation. Part II: What will the assessment involve? *Exceptional Parent, 18*(2), 48–53.

Hirsch, G. P. (1981). *Training developmental disability specialists in parent conference skills.* Unpublished doctoral dissertation, University of Kansas, Lawrence.

Individuals with Disabilities Education Act (IDEA). 20 U.S.C., Secs. 1400–1485 (Supp. 1996).

Liebman, R. (1975). *Constructing a workable reality* [Videotape]. Philadelphia: Philadelphia Child Guidance Clinic.

Malekoff, A., Johnson, H., & Klappersack, B. (1991, September). Parent-professional collaboration on behalf of children with learning disabilities. *Families in Society*, pp. 416–424.

McGrew, K. (1992). A review of scales to assess family needs. *Journal of Psychoeducational Assessment, 10*, 4–25.

McLaughlin, M. J., & Warren, S. H. (1994). Authentic assessments: The key to increased participation of students with disabilities in accountability systems. *Coalition Quarterly, 12*(1), 7–11.

Mehan, H. (1993). Beneath the skin and between the ears: A case study in the politics of representation. In S. Chaiklin & J. Lave (Eds.), *Understanding practice:*

Perspectives on activity and context (pp. 241–268). Cambridge: Cambridge University Press.

Menchetti, B. M., & Bombay, H. E. (1994). Facilitating community inclusion with vocational assessment portfolios. *Assessment in Rehabilitation and Exceptionality, 1*(3), 213–222.

National Council on Disability. (1995). *Improving the implementation of the Individuals with Disabilities Education Act: Making schools work for all of America's children.* Washington, DC: Author.

Pugach, M. C., & Seidl, B. L. (1995). From exclusion to inclusion in urban schools: A new case for teacher education reform. *Education and Urban Society, 27*(4), 379–395.

Pugach, M. C., & Wesson, C. L. (1995). Teachers' and students' views of team teaching general education and learning-disabled students in two fifth-grade classes. *Elementary School Journal, 95*(3), 279–295.

Rockowitz, R. J., & Davidson, P. W. (1979). Discussing diagnostic findings with parents. *Journal of Learning Disabilities, 12*(1), 11–16.

Sandel, A., McCallister, C., & Nash, W. R. (1993). Child search and screening activities for preschool gifted children. *Roeper Review, 16*(2), 98–102.

Sattler, J. M. (1988). *Assessment of children.* San Diego: Author.

Sexton, D., Snyder, P., Rheams, T., Barron-Sharp, B., & Perez, J. (1991). Considerations in using written surveys to identify family strengths and needs during the IFSP process. *Topics in Early Childhood Special Education, 11*(3), 81–91.

Shea, V. (1984). Explaining mental retardation and autism to parents. In E. Schopler & G. Mesibov (Eds.), *The effects of autism on the family* (pp. 265–288). New York: Plenum.

Sindelar, P. T., Griffin, C. C., Smith, S. W., & Watanabe, A. K. (1992). Prereferral intervention: Encouraging notes on preliminary findings. *Elementary School Journal, 92*(3), 245–259.

Smith, M. J., & Ryan, A. S. (1987). Chinese-American families of children with developmental disabilities: An exploratory study of reactions to service providers. *Mental Retardation, 25*(6), 345–350.

Switzer, L. S. (1985). Accepting the diagnosis: An educational intervention for parents of children with learning disabilities. *Journal of Learning Disabilities, 18*(3), 151–153.

Teglasi, H. (1985). Best practices in interpreting psychological assessment data to parents. In A. Thomas & J. Grimes (Eds.), *Best practices in school psychology* (pp. 415–430). Kent, OH: National Association of School Psychologists.

Thousand, J. S., Villa, R. A., & Nevin, A. I. (1994). *Creativity and collaborative learning: A practical guide to empowering students and teachers.* Baltimore: Brookes.

Turbiville, V. P., Turnbull, A. P., Garland, C. W., & Lee, I. M. (1996). Development and implementation of IFSPs and IEPs: Opportunities for empowerment. In S. L. Odom & M. E. McLean (Eds.), *Early intervention/ early childhood special education: Recommended practices* (pp. 77–100). Austin, TX: Pro-Ed.

Van Reusen, A. K., Bos, C. S., Schumaker, J. B., & Deshler, D. D. (1994). *The self-advocacy strategy for education and transition planning: Preparing students to advocate at education and transition conferences*. Lawrence, KS: Edge Enterprises.

Villa, R. A., Thousand, J. S., Stainback, W., & Stainback, S. (Eds.). (1992). *Restructuring for caring and effective education: An administrative guide to creating heterogeneous schools*. Baltimore: Brookes.

Ware, L. P. (1994). Contextual barriers to collaboration. *Journal of Educational and Psychological Consultation, 5*(4), 339–357.

Wright, L., & Boyland, J. H. (1993). Using early childhood developmental portfolios in the identification and education of young, economically disadvantaged, potentially gifted students. *Roeper Review, 15*(4), 205–210.

Chapter 12 INDIVIDUALIZING FOR APPROPRIATE EDUCATION

Abeson, A., & Weintraub, F. (1977). Understanding the individualized education program. In S. Torres (Ed.), *A primer on individualized education programs for handicapped children* (pp. 3–8). Reston, VA: Foundation for Exceptional Children.

Able-Boone, H. (1993). Family participation in the IFSP process: Family or professional driven? *Infant-Toddler Intervention, 3*(1), 63–71.

Bailey, D. B., Winton, P. J., Rouse, L., & Turnbull, A. P. (1990). Family goals in infant intervention: Analysis and issues. *Journal of Early Intervention, 14*, 15–26.

Barber, L., & Brophy, K. (1993). Parents' views on school placement procedures for their children with special needs. *Journal on Developmental Disabilities, 2*(1), 100–111.

Beckman, P. J., & Bristol, M. M. (1991). Issues in developing the IFSP: A framework for establishing family outcomes. *Topics in Early Childhood Special Education, 11*(3), 19–31.

Bernstein, M. E., & Martin, J. (1992). Informing parents about educational options: How well are we doing? *American Annals of the Deaf, 137*(1), 31–39.

Campbell, P. H., Strickland, B., & La Forme, C. (1992). Enhancing parent participation in the individualized family service plan. *Topics in Early Childhood Special Education, 11*(4), 112–124.

Clatterbuck, C. C., & Turnbull, H. R. (1996). The role of education and community services in supporting families of children with complex health needs. In G. H. S. Singer, L. E. Powers, & A. L. Olson (Eds.), *Redefining family support: Innovations in public-private partnerships* (pp. 389–412). Baltimore: Brookes.

Davis, B. (1985). IEP management programs. *Reports to Decision Makers, 7*. (ERIC Document Reproduction Service No. ED 266 610)

DeGangi, G., Royeen, C. B., & Wietlisbach, S. (1992). How to examine the Individualized Family Service Plan process: Preliminary findings and a procedural guide. *Infants and Young Children, 5*(2), 42–56.

Enell, N. C., & Barrick, S. W. (1983). *An examination of the relative efficiency and usefulness of computer-assisted individualized education programs*. Carmichael, CA: San Juan Unified School District. (ERIC Document Reproduction Service No. ED 236 861)

Federal Register. (1981, January 19). Washington, DC: U.S. Government Printing Office.

Ferguson, D. L. (1984). Parent advocacy network. *Exceptional Parent, 14*, 41–45.

Gerber, P. J., Banbury, M. M., Miller, J. H., & Griffin, H. D. (1986). Special educators' perceptions of parental participation in the individual education plan process. *Psychology in the Schools, 23*, 158–163.

Goldstein, S., Strickland, B., Turnbull, A. P., & Curry, L. (1980). An observational analysis of the IEP conference. *Exceptional Children, 46*(4), 278–286.

Goldstein, S., & Turnbull, A. P. (1982). The use of two strategies to increase parent participation in IEP conferences. *Exceptional Children, 46*(4), 360–361.

Harry, B., Allen, N., & McLaughlin, M. (1995). Communication versus compliance: African-American parents' involvement in special education. *Exceptional Children, 61*(4), 364–377.

Jones, D. E., Clatterbuck, C. C., Marquis, J., Turnbull, H. R., & Moberly, R. L. (in press). Educational placements for children who are ventilator assisted. *Exceptional Children*.

Katzen, K. (1980). To the editor: An open letter to CEC. *Exceptional Children, 46*(8), 582.

Lewis, C. L., Busch, J. P., Proger, B. B., & Juska, P. J. (1981). Parents' perspectives concerning the IEP process. *Education Unlimited, 3*(3), 18–22.

Lynch, E. W., & Stein, R. (1982). Perspectives on parent participation in special education. *Exceptional Children, 3*(2), 56–63.

Marion, R. (1979). Minority parent involvement in the IEP process: A systematic model approach. *Focus on Exceptional Children, 10*(8), 1–16.

McGonigel, M. J., Kaufmann, R. K., & Johnson, R. H. (Eds.). (1991). *Guidelines and recommended practices for the Individualized Family Service Plan* (2nd ed.). Bethesda, MD: Association for the Care of Children's Health.

Minke, K. M., & Scott, M. M. (1993). The development of Individualized Family Service Plans: Roles for parents and staff. *Journal of Special Education, 27*(1), 82–106.

Morissey, P. A., & Safer, N. (1977). The Individualized Education Program: Implications for special education. *Viewpoints, 53*, 31–38.

Morningstar, M. E., Turnbull, A. P., & Turnbull, H. R. (1995). [Unpublished raw data]. Lawrence, KS: University of Kansas, Beach Center on Families and Disability.

Nadler, B., & Shore, K. (1980). Individualized Education Programs: A look at realities. *Education Unlimited, 2*, 30–34.

National Council on Disability. (1995). *Improving the implementation of the Individuals with Disabilities Education Act: Making schools work for all of America's children*. Washington, DC: Author.

Parker, D., (with Moore, C.). (1991). *Achieving inclusion through the IEP process: A handbook for parents*. Hanover, MD: Maryland Coalition for Integrated Education.

Pyecha, J. N., Cox, J. L., Dewitt, D., Drummond, D., Jaffe, J., Kalt, M., Lane, C., & Pelosi, J. (1980). *A national survey of Individualized Education Programs (IEPs) for handicapped children* (5 vols.). Durham, NC: Research Triangle Institute. (ERIC Document Reproduction Service Nos. ED 199 970–974)

Rainforth, B., York, J., & Macdonald, C. (Eds.). (1992). *Collaborative teams for students with severe disabilities*. Baltimore: Brookes.

Rogers, J. J. (1994). Is special education free? *Remedial and Special Education, 15*(3), 171–176.

Ryan, L. B., & Rucker, C. N. (1986). Computerized vs. non-computerized Individualized Education Programs: Teachers' attitudes, time, and cost. *Journal of Special Education Technology, 8*(1), 5–12.

Smith, S. W. (1990, September). Individualized Education Programs (IEPs) in special education-—From intent to acquiescence. *Exceptional Children,* pp. 6–14.

Turbiville, V. P. (1995). *Parent handbook for individualized family service plans*. Lawrence, KS: University of Kansas, Beach Center on Families and Disability.

Turbiville, V. P., Lee, I. M., Turnbull, A. P., & Murphy, D. L. (1993). *Handbook for the development of a family-friendly IFSP* (2nd ed.). Lawrence, KS: University of Kansas, Beach Center on Families and Disability.

Turbiville, V. P., Turnbull, A. P., Garland, C. W., & Lee, I. M. (1996). Development and implementation of IFSPs and IEPs: Opportunities for empowerment. In S. L. Odom & M. E. McLean (Eds.), *Early intervention/early childhood special education: Recommended practices* (pp. 77–100). Austin, TX: Pro-Ed.

Turnbull, A. P., Strickland, B., & Hammer, S. E. (1978). The Individualized Education Program. Part 1: Procedural guidelines. *Journal of Learning Disabilities, 11*, 40–46.

U.S. Department of Education. (1981). *Assistance to states for education of handicapped children: Interpretation of the Individualized Education Program (IEP)*. Washington, DC: U.S. Government Printing Office.

Vacc, N. A., Vallecorsa, A. L., Parker, A., Bonner, S., Lester, C., Richardson, S., & Yates, C. (1985). Parents' and educators' participation in IEP conferences. *Education and Treatment of Children, 8*(2), 153–162.

Van Reusen, A. K., & Bos, C. S. (1990). I PLAN: Helping students communicate in planning conferences. *Teaching Exceptional Children, 22*(4), 30–32.

Van Reusen, A. K., & Bos, C. S. (1994). Facilitating student participation in Individualized Education Programs through motivation strategy instruction. *Exceptional Children, 60*(5), 466–475.

Van Reusen, A. K., Bos, C. S., Schumaker, J. B., & Deshler, D. D. (1987). *The education planning strategy*. Lawrence, KS: Edge Enterprises.

Van Reusen, A. K., Deshler, D. D., & Schumaker, J. B. (1989). Effects of a student participation strategy in facilitating the involvement of adolescents with learning disabilities in the Individualized Educational Program planning process. *Learning Disabilities, 1*(2), 23–34.

Vaughn, S., Bos, C., Harrell, J., & Lasky, B. (1988). Parent participation in the initial placement/IEP conference ten years after mandated involvement. *Journal of Learning Disabilities, 21*(2), 82–89.

West, J. S. (1990). Educational collaboration in the restructuring of schools. *Journal of Educational and Psychological Consultation, 1*(1), 23–40.

Witt, J. C., Miller, C. D., McIntyre, R. M., & Smith, D. (1984). Effects of variables on parental perceptions of staffings. *Exceptional Children, 51*(1), 27–32.

York, J., & Tundidor, M. (1995). Issues raised in the name of inclusion: Perspectives of educators, parents, and students. *Journal of the Association for Persons with Severe Handicaps, 20*(1), 31–44.

Ysseldyke, J. E., Algozzine, B., & Mitchell, J. (1982). Special education team decision making: An analysis of current practice. *Personnel and Guidance Journal, 60*(5), 308–313.

Chapter 13 EXTENDING LEARNING INTO HOME AND COMMUNITY

Alameda, T. (1993–1994). The healthy learners' project. *Family Resource Coalition Report, 12*(3 & 4), 20–21.

Billingsley, B. S., & Cross, L. H. (1991). Teachers' decisions to transfer from special to general education. *Journal of Special Education, 24*, 496–511.

Billingsley, F. F. (1993). Reader response in my dreams: A response to some current trends in education. *Journal of the Association for Persons with Severe Handicaps, 18*(1), 61–63.

Brown, K. R. (1993–1994). Building Beacons for children and families in New York City. *Family Resource Coalition Report, 12*(3 & 4), 39–41.

Bulgatz, M., & O'Neill, R. E. (1994). *Teacher perceptions and recommendations concerning students with challenging behaviors in the regular classroom: An initial survey.* Unpublished manuscript.

Burchard, J., Burchard, S., Sewell, C., & VanDenBerg, J. (1993). *One kid at a time: Evaluative case studies and description of the Alaska Youth Initiative Demonstration Project.* Juneau: State of Alaska, Division of Mental Health and Mental Retardation.

Chapley, G. D., Trimarco, T. A., Crisci, P., & Capobianco, M. (1986–1987). School-parent partnerships in gifted education: From paper to reality. *Education Research Quarterly, 11*(3), 37–46.

Chesapeake Institute. (1994, September). *National agenda for achieving better results for children and youth with serious emotional disturbance.* Washington, DC: Department of Education, Office of Special Education and Rehabilitative Services, Office of Special Education Programs.

Children's Defense Fund. (1995). *The state of America's children yearbook, 1995.* Washington, DC: Author.

Cooper, H. M. (1989a). *Homework.* White Plains, NY: Longman.

Cooper, H. M. (1989b). Synthesis of research on homework. *Educational Leadership, 47*(3), 85–91.

Crowson, R. L., & Boyd, W. L. (1993, February). Coordinated services for children: Designing arks for storms and seas unknown. *American Journal of Education, 101,* 140–179.

Eber, L. (1994). *The wraparound approach toward effective school inclusion.* Alexandria, VA: Federation of Families for Children's Mental Health.

Eber, L., Wilson, L., Notier, V., & Pendell, D. (1994). The wraparound approach. Inclusion: A many-sided issue. *Illinois Research and Development Journal, 30*(2), 17–24.

Epstein, J. L. (1987). Parent involvement: What research says to administrators. *Education and Urban Society, 19,* 119–136.

Epstein, M. H., Polloway, E. A., Foley, R. M., & Patton, J. R. (1993). Homework: A comparison of teachers' and parents' perceptions of the problems experienced by students identified as having behavioral disorders, learning disabilities, or no disabilities. *Remedial and Special Education, 14*(5), 40–50.

Gajria, M., & Salend, S. (1995). A comparison of homework practices of students with and without learning disabilities. *Journal of Learning Disabilities, 28,* 291–296.

Goetz, K. (1994, Spring–Summer). Kaleidoscope: Hope at the end of the road. *Family Resource Coalition Report,* pp. 20–21.

Horner, R. H., Diemer, S., & Brazeau, K. (1992). Educational support for students with severe problem behaviors in Oregon: A descriptive analysis from the 1987–1988 school year. *Journal of the Association for Persons with Severe Handicaps, 17*(3), 154–169.

Horner, R. H., Dunlap, G., & Koegel, R. L. (1988). *Generalization and maintenance: Lifestyle changes in applied settings.* Baltimore: Brookes.

Horner, R. H., Dunlap, G., Koegel, R. L., Carr, E. G., Sailor, W., Anderson, J., Albin, R. W., & O'Neill, R. E. (1990). Toward a technology of "nonaversive" behavioral support. *Journal of the Association for Persons with Severe Handicaps, 15*(5), 125–132.

Jayanthi, M., Sawyer, V., Nelson, J. S., Bursuck, W. D., & Epstein, M. H. (1995). Recommendations for homework-communication problems. *Remedial and Special Education, 16*(4), 212–225.

Kagan, S. L., & Neville, P. R. (1993a). Family support and school-linked services. *Family Resource Coalition Report, 12*(3 & 4), 4–6.

Kagan, S. L., & Neville, P. R. (1993b). *Integrating services for children and families: Understanding the past to shape the future.* New Haven, CT: Yale University Press.

Kay, P. J., Fitzgerald, M., Paradee, C., & Mellencamp, A. (1994). Making homework work at home: The parent's perspective. *Journal of Learning Disabilities, 27*(9), 550–561.

Koegel, L. K., Koegel, R. L., & Dunlap, G. (Eds.). (1996). *Community, school, and social inclusion through positive behavioral support.* Baltimore: Brookes.

Koyanagi, C., & Gaines, S. (1993). *A guide for advocates for "all systems failure": An examination of the results of neglecting the needs of children with serious emotional disturbance.* Alexandria, VA: Federation of Families for Children's Mental Health.

Lyytinen, P., Rasku-Puttonen, H., Poikkeus, A. M., Laakso, M. L., & Ahonen, T. (1994). Mother-child teaching strategies and learning disabilities. *Journal of Learning Disabilities, 27*(3), 186–192.

McLaughlin, M. J., Leone, P., Warren, S. H., & Schofield, P. F. (1994). *Doing things differently: Issues and options for creating comprehensive school-linked services for children and youth with emotional or behavioral disorders.* College Park, MD: University of Maryland and Westat.

Melaville, A. I., & Blank, M. J. (with Asayesh, G.). (1993). *Together we can: A guide for crafting a profamily system of education and human services.* Washington, DC: U.S. Government Printing Office.

Mount, B., & Zwernik, K. (1988). *It's never too early, it's never too late: A booklet about personal planning for persons with developmental disabilities, their families and friends, case managers, service providers, and advocates.* St. Paul, MN: Metropolitan Council.

Polloway, E. A., Epstein, M. H., & Foley, R. (1992). A comparison of the homework problems of students with learning disabilities and nonhandicapped students.

Learning Disabilities, 7, 203–209.

Risley, T. (1996). Get a life! Positive behavioral intervention for challenging behavior through life arrangement and life coaching. In L. K. Koegel, R. L. Koegel, & G. Dunlap (Eds.), *Community, school, family, and social inclusion through positive behavioral support* (pp. 425–623). Baltimore: Brookes.

Sailor, W. (1996). School-linked services. In National Council on Disability, *Improving the implementation of the Individuals with Disabilities Education Act: Making schools work for all of America's children.* Supplement (pp. 661–684). Washington, DC: National Council on Disability.

Salend, S. J., & Schiff, J. (1989). An examination of the homework practices of teachers of students with learning disabilities. *Journal of Learning Disabilities, 22,* 621–623.

Sheffield, B. E. (1994). Watts/Jordan school-based health clinic: Promoting health and preventing violence in Los Angeles. *Family Resource Coalition Report, 13*(1 & 2), 12.

Smull, M., & Harrison, S. B. (1992). *Supporting people with severe reputations in the community.* Alexandria, VA: National Association of State Mental Retardation Program Directors.

Soderlund, J., Bursuck, B., Polloway, E. A., & Foley, R. (1995). A comparison of the homework problems of secondary school students with behavior disorders and nondisabled peers. *Journal of Emotional and Behavioral Disorders, 3*(3), 150–155.

Stanford Research Institute (SRI) International. (1990). *National longitudinal transition study of special education students.* Menlo Park, CA: Author.

Turnbull, A. P. (1993, December). *Belonging: A dimension of human development.* Paper presented at Zero to Three Eighth Biennial National Training Institute, Washington, DC.

Turnbull, A. P., & Ruef, M. (in press). Family perspectives on problem behavior. *Mental Retardation.*

Turnbull, A. P., & Turnbull, H. R. (1996). Group Action Planning as a strategy for providing comprehensive family support. In L. K. Koegel, R. L. Koegel, & G. Dunlap (Eds.), *Community, school, family, and social inclusion through positive behavioral support* (pp. 99–114). Baltimore: Brookes.

Turnbull, A. P., Turnbull, H. R., & Blue-Banning, M. J. (1994). Enhancing inclusion of infants and toddlers with disabilities and their families: A theoretical and programmatic analysis. *Infants and Young Children, 7*(2), 1–14.

U.S. Department of Education. (1990, January 9). Reading and writing proficiency remains low. *Daily Education News,* pp. 1–7.

U.S. Department of Education. (1992). *Fourteenth annual report to Congress on the implementation of Public Law 94-142: The Education for All Handicapped Children Act.* Washington, DC: Author.

U.S. Department of Education & American Educational Research Association. (1995). *School-linked comprehensive services for children and families: What we know and what we need to know.* Washington, DC: Authors.

Wahlberg, H. J., Paschal, R. A., & Weinstein, T. (1985). Homework's powerful effects on learning. *Educational Leadership, 42*(7), 76–79.

Chapter 14 ATTENDING AND VOLUNTEERING AT SCHOOL

Bailey, D., & Winton, P. (1989). Friendship and acquaintance among families in a mainstreamed day care center. *Education and Training of the Mentally Retarded, 24,* 107–113.

Barbetta, P. M. (1995). Emotional or behavioral disorders. In A. P. Turnbull, H. R. Turnbull, M. Shank, & D. Leal, *Exceptional lives: Special education in today's schools* (pp. 186–235). Englewood Cliffs, NJ: Merrill/Prentice Hall.

Blacher, J., & Turnbull, A. P. (1983). Are parents mainstreamed? A survey of parent interactions in the mainstreamed preschool. *Education and Training of the Mentally Retarded, 18,* 10–16.

Block, M. E. (1994). *A teacher's guide to including students with disabilities in regular physical education.* Baltimore: Brookes.

Comer, J. P., & Haynes, N. M. (1991). Parent involvement in schools: An ecological approach. *Elementary School Journal, 91*(3), 271–277.

Dauber, S. L., & Epstein, J. L. (1993). Parents' attitudes and practices of involvement in inner-city elementary and middle schools. In N. F. Chavkin (Ed.), *Families and schools in a pluralistic society.* Albany: State University of New York Press.

Falvey, M., Coots, J., & Terry-Gage, S. (1992). Extracurricular activities. In S. Stainback & W. Stainback (Eds.), *Curriculum considerations in inclusive classrooms: Facilitating learning for all students* (pp. 229–238). Baltimore: Brookes.

Gallimore, R., Weisner, T. S., Kaufman, S. Z., & Bernheimer, L. P. (1989). The social construction of eco-cultural niches: Family accommodation of developmentally delayed children. *American Journal of Mental Retardation, 94,* 216–230.

Harris, L., Kagay, M., & Ross, J. (1987). *The Metropolitan Life survey of the American teacher: Strengthening links between home and school.* New York: Louis Harris and Associates.

Harris, T. (1994). Christine's inclusion: An example of peers supporting one another. In J. S. Thousand, R. A. Villa, & A. I. Nevin (Eds.), *Creativity and collaborative learning: A practical guide to empowering students and teachers* (pp. 293–304). Baltimore: Brookes.

Keenan, J. W., Willett, J., & Solsken, J. (1993). Focus on research. Constructing an urban village: School/home collaboration in a multicultural classroom. *Language Arts, 70,* 204–214.

Luetke-Stahlman, B., Luetke-Stahlman, B., & Luetke-Stahlman, H. (1992). Yes, siblings can help. *Perspectives, 10*(5), 9–11.

Lynn, L. (1994). Building parent involvement. *National Association of Secondary School Principals Practitioner, 20*(5), 1–4.

Moles, O. C. (1993). Collaboration between schools and disadvantaged parents: Obstacles and openings. In N. F. Chavkin (Ed.), *Families and schools in a pluralistic society* (pp. 21–51). Albany: State University of New York Press.

Moll, L. C. (1992). Bilingual classroom studies and community analysis: Some recent trends. *Educational Researcher, 21*(2), 20–24.

Rich, D. (1993). Building the bridge to reach minority parents: Education infrastructure supporting success for all children. In N. F. Chavkin (Ed.), *Families and schools in a pluralistic society* (pp. 235–244). Albany: State University of New York Press.

Santelli, B., Turnbull, A. P., Marquis, J. G., & Lerner, E. P. (1995). Parent to parent programs: A unique form of mutual support. *Infants and Young Children, 8*(2), 48–57.

Stayton, V. D., & Karnes, M. B. (1994). Model programs for infants and toddlers with disabilities and their families. In L. J. Johnson, R. J. Gallagher, M. J. LaMontagne, J. B. Jordan, J. J. Gallagher, P. L. Hutinger, & M. B. Karnes (Eds.), *Meeting early intervention challenges: Issues from birth to three* (pp. 33–58). Baltimore: Brookes.

Stouffer, B. (1992, April). We can increase parent involvement in secondary schools. *National Association of Secondary School Principals Bulletin*, pp. 5–8.

Timm, M. A. (1993). The regional intervention program: Family treatment by family members. *Behavioral Disorders, 19*(1), 34–43.

Vatterott, C. (1994, February). A change in climate: Involving parents in school improvement. *Schools in the Middle*, pp. 12–16.

Wheeler, P. (1992, October). Promoting parent involvement in secondary schools. *National Association of Secondary School Principals Bulletin*, pp. 28–35.

Chapter 15 ADVOCATING FOR SYSTEMS IMPROVEMENT

Allen, R. I., & Petr, C. G. (1996). Toward developing standards and measurements for family-centered practice in family support programs. In G. H. S. Singer, L. E. Powers, & A. L. Olson (Eds.), *Redefining family support: Innovations in public-private partnerships* (pp. 57–86). Baltimore: Brookes.

Bergman, A. I., & Singer, G. H. S. (1996). The thinking behind new public policy. In G. H. S. Singer, L. E. Powers, & A. L. Olson (Eds.), *Redefining family support: Innovations in public-private partnerships* (pp. 435–464). Baltimore: Brookes.

Board of Education of Sacramento Unified School District v. Holland, 14 F. 3d 1398 (9th Cir., 1994).

Board of Education v. Rowley, 458 U.S. 176, 102 S. Ct. 3034, 73 L. Ed., 2d 690 (1982).

Buswell, B. (1993, November). *School reform and students with disabilities. Discussions about school reform: Strategies for families of students with disabilities.* Washington, DC: U.S. Department of Education, Office of Special Education and Rehabilitative Services.

Buswell, B., & Schaffner, B. (1994). Parents and school reform. *Coalition Quarterly, 12*(1), 16–20.

Clatterbuck, C., & Turnbull, H. R. (1996). The role of education and community services in supporting families of children with complex health care needs. In G. H. S. Singer, L. E. Powers, & A. L. Olson (Eds.), *Redefining family support: Innovations in public-private partnerships* (pp. 389–412). Baltimore: Brookes.

Daniel R. R. v. State Board of Education, 874 F. 2d 1036 (5th Cir. 1989).

Epstein, J. L. (1995, May). School/family/community partnerships: Caring for the children we share. *Phi Delta Kappan*, pp. 701–712.

Fiedler, C. R. (1985). *Conflict prevention, containment, and resolution in special education due process disputes: Parents' and school personnel's perception of variables associated with the development and escalation of due process conflict.* Unpublished doctoral dissertation, University of Kansas, Lawrence.

Fisher, R., & Ury, W. (1991). *Getting to yes: Negotiating agreement without giving in* (2nd ed.). Boston: Houghton Mifflin.

Greer v. Rome City School District, 762 F. Supp. 936 (N. D. Ga. 1990).

Irving Independent School District v. Tatro, 468 U.S. 883, 104 S. Ct. 3371, 82 L. Ed. 2d 664 (1984).

Jones, T. M., Garlow, J. A., Turnbull, H. R., & Barber, P. A. (1996). Family empowerment in a family support program. In G. H. S. Singers, L. E. Powers, & A. L. Olson (Eds.), *Redefining family support innovations: Innovations in public-private partnerships* (pp. 87–114). Baltimore: Brookes.

McGinley, K. H. (1987). *Evaluating the effectiveness of mediation as an alternative to the sole use of the due process hearing in special education.* Unpublished doctoral dissertation, University of Kansas, Lawrence.

Mills v. DC Board of Education, 348 F. Supp. 866 (D. D.C. 1972); *contempt proceedings*, EHLR 551: 643 (D. D.C. 1980).

Mlawer, M. A. (1993). Who should fight? Parents and the

advocacy expectation. *Journal of Disability Policy Studies, 4*(1), 105–115.

National Council on Disability. (1995). *Improving the implementation of the Individuals with Disabilities Education Act: Making schools work for all of America's children.* Washington, DC: Author.

Oberti v. Board of Education, 789 F. Supp. 1322 (D. N.J., 1992).

Pennsylvania Association for Retarded Citizens (PARC) v. Commonwealth of Pennsylvania, 334 F. Supp. 1257, 343 F. Supp. 279 (E. D. Pa. 1971, 1972).

Powers, L. E. (1996). Family and consumer activism in disability policy. In G. H. S. Singer, L. E. Powers, & A. L. Olson (Eds.), *Redefining family support: Innovations in public-private partnerships* (pp. 413–434). Baltimore: Brookes.

Prestby, J. E., Wandersman, A., Florin, P., Rich, R., & Chavis, D. (1990). Benefits, costs, incentive management and participation in voluntary organizations: A means to understanding and promoting empowerment. *American Journal of Community Psychology, 18*(1), 117–149.

Roncker v. Walters, 700 F. 2d 1058 (6th Cir. 1983), *cert. den.* 464 U.S. 864, 104 S. Ct. 196, 78 L. Ed. 2d 171 (1983).

Turnbull, A. P., & Turnbull, H. R. (1982). Assumptions concerning parent involvement: A legislative history. *Educational Evaluation and Policy Analysis,* 4(3), 281–291.

Turnbull, A. P., & Turnbull, H. R. (1996). The synchrony of stakeholders: Lessons for early care and education from the disability rights movement. In S. L. Kagan & N. Cohen (Eds.), *American early care and education.* San Francisco: Jossey-Bass.

U.S. Department of Education. (1995). *The community action toolkit.* Washington, DC: Author.

Wade, S. M. (1994). *Focus group survey of parents of children with disabilities w ho are members of school improvement teams* [Report]. Tampa: University of South Florida, Florida Diagnostic and Learning Resources System.

Yuan, S., Baker-McCue, T., & Witkin, K. (1996). Coalitions for family support and the creation of two flexible funding programs. In G. H. S. Singer, L. E. Powers, & A. L. Olson (Eds.), *Redefining family support: Innovations in public-private partnerships* (pp. 357–388). Baltimore: Brookes.

Zirpoli, T. J., Wieck, C., Hancox, D., & Skarnulis, E. R. (1994). Partners in policymaking: The first five years. *Mental Retardation, 32*(6), 422–425.

Reprint
Acknowledgments

(Additional reprint acknowledgments appear in the text.)

Cover Art
Cindy Higgins, Copyright © 1995, Beach Center on Families and Disability, University of Kansas, used by permission.

Chapter 1

From pages 16-17 from *Head Start* by Edward Zigler and Susan Muenchow. Copyright © 1992 by Edward Zigler and Susan Muenchow. Reprinted by permission of BasicBooks, a division of HarperCollins Publishers, Inc.

Chapter 2

From Comer, J. P., & Haynes, N. M. (1991). Parent involvement in schools: An ecological approach. *The Elementary School Journal, 91*(3), 271–277. Published by The University of Chicago Press. Copyright © 1991 by The University of Chicago. All rights reserved.

From "Parent Attitudes About Special Education and Reintegration: What is the Role of Student Outcomes?" by S. K. Green and M. R. Shinn, *Exceptional Children, 61,* 1995, 269–281. Copyright © 1995 by the Council for Exceptional Children. Reprinted with permission.

From Harry, B. (1992). An ethnographic study of cross-cultural communication with Puerto Rican-American families in the special education system. *American Educational Research Journal, 29*(3), 471–494. Copyright © 1992 by the American Educational Research Association. Reprinted by permission of the publisher.

From Harry, B., & Kalyanpur, M. (1994). Cultural underpinnings of special education: Implications for professional interaction with culturally diverse families. *Disability & Society, 9*(2), 145–165. Published by Carfax Publishing Company, 875–81 Massachusetts Avenue, Cambridge, MA 02139.

From Lindle, J. C. (1989). What do parents want from principals? *Educational Leadership, 47*(2), 13. Reprinted with permission of the Association for Supervision and Curriculum Development. Copyright © 1989 by ASCD. All rights reserved.

From "Special Education in the Restructured School" by Wayne Sailor, 1991, *Remedial and Special Education, 12,* 8–22. Copyright © 1991 by PRO-ED, Inc. Reprinted by permission.

From "Examining the Individualized Family Service Plan Process: What are Family and Practitioner Preferences?" by J. A. Summers, C. Dell'Oliver, A. P. Turnbull, H. A. Benson, E. Santelli, M. Campbell, & E. Siegel-Causey, 1990, *Topics in Early Childhood Special Education, 10*(1), 78–99. Copyright © 1990 by PRO-ED, Inc. Reprinted with permission.

Chapter 3

From Jones, T. M., Garlow, J., Turnbull, H. R., & Barber, P. A. (1996). Best practices: Empowerment in a family support program. In G. H. S. Singer, L. E. Powers, & A. L. Olson (Eds.), *Redefining family support: Innovations in public-private partnerships* (pp. 87–114). Baltimore: Paul H. Brookes Publishing Company, P.O. Box 10624, Baltimore, MD 21285–0624. Reprinted by permission.

From Lonsdale, G. (1978). Family life with a handicapped child: The parents speak. *Child Care, Health, and Development, 4,* 99–120. Reprinted by permission of the publisher, Blackwell Science, Ltd.

From Singer, G. H. S., & Nixon, C. (1996). A report on the concerns of parents of children with acquired brain injury. In G. H. S. Singer, A. Glang, & J. Williams (Eds.), *Children with acquired brain injury: Educating and supporting families* (pp. 23–52). Baltimore: Paul H.

Brookes Publishing Company, P.O. Box 10624, Baltimore, MD 21285-0624. Reprinted by permission.

From "Family Perspectives on Inclusive Lifestyle Issues for Persons with Problem Behavior" by A. P. Turnbull and M. Ruef, *Exceptional Children,* in press. Copyright © by The Council for Exceptional Children. Reprinted with permission.

Chapter 4

Excerpts of *The Seven Habits of Highly Effective People: Restoring the Character Ethic* used with permission of Covey Leadership Center, Inc., 3507 N. University Ave., P. O. Box 19008, Provo, Utah 84604-4479. Phone (800) 331-7716.

From Crago, M., & Eriks-Brophy, A. (1993). Feeling right: Approaches to a family's culture. *The Volta Review, 95,* 123–129. Reprinted with permission from *The Volta Review.* Copyright © 1993 by the Alexander Graham Bell Association for the Deaf, 3417 Volta Place, NW, Washington, DC 20007.

From Harry, B. (1992). An ethnographic study of cross-cultural communication with Puerto Rican-American families in the special education system. *American Educational Research Journal, 29*(3), 471–494. Copyright © 1992 by the American Educational Research Association. Reprinted by permission of the publisher.

From "Making Sense of Disability: Low-Income Puerto Rican Parents' Theories of the Problem" by Beth Harry, *Exceptional Children, 59,* 1992, p. 31. Copyright © 1992 by The Council for Exceptional Children. Reprinted with permission.

From Kalyanpur, M., & Rao, S. S. (1991). Empowering low-income black families of handicapped children. *American Journal of Orthopsychiatry, 61*(4), 523–532. Reprinted, with permission, from the *American Journal of Orthopsychiatry.* Copyright © 1991 by the American Orthopsychiatric Association, Inc.

From *Positive Illusions: Creative Self-Deception and the Healthy Mind* by Shelley E. Taylor. Copyright © 1989 by BasicBooks, a division of HarperCollins Publishers, Inc.

From Vohs, J. (1993). A place to stand—A gift to give. In A. P. Turnbull, J. M. Patterson, S. K. Behr, D. L. Murphy, J. G. Marquis, & M. J. Blue-Banning (Eds.), *Cognitive coping, families, and disability* (pp. 61–66). Baltimore: Paul H. Brookes Publishing Company, P. O. Box 10624, Baltimore, MD 21285-0624. Reprinted by permission.

From Yates, A. Current status and future directions of research on the American Indian child. *American Journal of Psychiatry, 144*(9), 1135–1142, 1987. Copyright © 1987, the American Psychiatric Association. Reprinted by permission.

Chapter 5

From Chan, S. (1992). Families with Asian roots. In E. W. Lynch & M. J. Hanson (Eds.), *Developing cross-cultural competence: A guide for working with young children and their families* (pp. 181–258). Baltimore: Paul H. Brookes Publishing Company, P. O. Box 10624, Baltimore, MD 21285-0624. Reprinted by permission.

From Joe, J. R., & Malach, R. S. (1992). Families with Native American roots. In E. W. Lynch & M. J. Hanson (Eds.), *Developing cross-cultural competence: A guide for working with young children and their families* (pp. 89–119). Baltimore: Paul H. Brookes Publishing Company, P.O. Box 10624, Baltimore, MD 21285-0624. Reprinted by permission.

From Hanson, M. J. (1992). Families with Anglo-European roots. In E. W. Lynch & M. J. Hanson (Eds.), *Developing cross-cultural competence: A guide for working with young children and their families* (pp. 65–87). Baltimore: Paul H. Brookes Publishing Company, P.O. Box 10624, Baltimore, MD 21285-0624. Reprinted by permission.

From "Making Sense of Disability: Low-Income Puerto Rican Parents' Theories of the Problem" by Beth Harry, *Exceptional Children, 59,* 1992, p. 31. Copyright © 1992 by The Council for Exceptional Children. Reprinted with permission.

From Kozol, J. (1988). *Rachel and her children: Homeless families in America.* New York: Fawcett-Columbine/Crown. Copyright © 1988.

From Sharifzadeh, V. S. (1992). Families with Middle Eastern roots. In E. W. Lynch & M. J. Hanson (Eds.), *Developing cross-cultural competence: A guide for working with young children and their families* (pp. 319–352). Baltimore: Paul H. Brookes Publishing Company, P.O. Box 10624, Baltimore, MD 21285-0624. Reprinted by permission.

From Spradley, T. S., & Spradley, J. P. (1978). *Deaf like me.* New York: Random House. Copyright © 1978.

From "Examining the Individualized Family Service Plan Process: What Are Family and Practitioner Preferences?" by J. A. Summers, C. Dell'Oliver, A. P. Turnbull, H. A. Benson, E. Santelli, M. Campbell, & E. Siegel-Causey, 1990, *Topics in Early Childhood Special Education, 10*(1), 78–99. Copyright © 1990 by PRO-ED, Inc. Reprinted with permission.

Chapter 6

From Chan, S. (1992). Families with Asian roots. In E. W. Lynch & M. J. Hanson (Eds.), *Developing cross-cultural competence: A guide for working with young children and their families* (pp. 181–258). Baltimore: Paul H. Brookes Publishing Company, P.O. Box 10624,

Baltimore, MD 21285-0624. Reprinted by permission.

From *A Difference in the Family* by Helen Featherstone. Copyright © 1980 by BasicBooks, Inc. Reprinted by permission of BasicBooks, a division of HarperCollins Publishers, Inc.

From Hanson, M. J. (1992). Families with Anglo-European roots. In E. W. Lynch & M. J. Hanson (Eds.), *Developing cross-cultural competence: A guide for working with young children and their families* (pp. 65–87). Baltimore: Paul H. Brookes Publishing Company, P.O. Box 10624, Baltimore, MD 21285-0624. Reprinted by permission.

From Joe, J. R., & Malach, R. S. (1992). Families with Native American roots. In E. W. Lynch & M. J. Hanson (Eds.), *Developing cross-cultural competence: A guide for working with young children and their families* (pp. 89–119). Baltimore: Paul H. Brookes Publishing Company, P.O. Box 10624, Baltimore, MD 21285-0624. Reprinted by permission.

From Sharifzadeh, V. S. (1992). Families with Middle Eastern roots. In E. W. Lynch & M. J. Hanson (Eds.), *Developing cross-cultural competence: A guide for working with young children and their families* (pp. 319–352). Baltimore: Paul H. Brookes Publishing Company, P.O. Box 10624, Baltimore, MD 21285-0624. Reprinted by permission.

From Singer, G. H. S., & Nixon, C. (1996). A report on the concerns of parents of children with acquired brain injury. In G. H. S. Singer, A. Glang, & J. Williams (Eds.), *Children with acquired brain injury: Educating and supporting families* (pp. 23–52). Baltimore: Paul H. Brookes Publishing Company, P.O. Box 10624, Baltimore, MD 21285-0624. Reprinted by permission.

From Traustadottir, R. (1991). Mothers who care: Gender, disability, and family life. *Journal of Family Issues, 12*(2), 211–228. Copyright © 1991 by Sage Publications, Inc. Reprinted by permission of Sage Publications, Inc.

From Yates, A. Current status and future directions of research on the American Indian child. *American Journal of Psychiatry, 144*(9), 1135–1142, 1987. Copyright © 1987, the American Psychiatric Association. Reprinted by permission.

Chapter 7

From "Time as a Resource and Constraint for Parents of Young Children with Disabilities: Implications for Early Intervention Services" by M. J. Brotherson and B. L. Goldstein, 1992, *Topics in Early Childhood Special Education, 12*(4), 508–527. Copyright © 1992 by PRO-ED, Inc. Reprinted by permission.

From Chan, S. (1992). Families with Asian roots. In E. W. Lynch & M. J. Hanson (Eds.), *Developing cross-cultur-*

al competence: A guide for working with young children and their families (pp. 181–258). Baltimore: Paul H. Brookes Publishing Company, P.O. Box 10624, Baltimore, MD 21285-0624. Reprinted by permission.

Excerpts from *A Difference in the Family* by Helen Featherstone. Copyright © 1980 by BasicBooks, Inc. Reprinted by permission of BasicBooks, a division of HarperCollins Publishers, Inc.

From "Enhancing Integration During the Summer: Combined Educational and Community Recreation Options for Students with Severe Disabilities" by S. Hamre-Nietupski, L. Krajewski, R. Riehl, K. Sensor, J. Nietupski, J. Moravec, J. McDonald, & P. Cantine-Stull, *Education and Training in Mental Retardation, 27*(1), 1992, p. 73. Copyright © 1992 by the Council for Exceptional Children. Reprinted by permission.

From Kalyanpur, M., & Rao, S. S. (1991). Empowering low-income black families of handicapped children. *American Journal of Orthopsychiatry, 61*(4), 523–532. Reprinted, with permission, from the *American Journal of Orthopsychiatry.* Copyright © 1991 by the American Orthopsychiatric Association, Inc.

From "Families with Chronically Ill Young Children" by S. S. Martin, M. P. Brady, & J. A. Kotarba, 1992, *Remedial and Special Education, 13*(2), 6–15. Copyright © 1992 by PRO-ED, Inc. Reprinted by permission.

From Rousso, H. (1984). Fostering healthy self-esteem. *Exceptional Parent, 8*(14), 9–14. Reprinted with the expressed consent and approval of *Exceptional Parent,* a monthly magazine for parents and families of children with disabilities and special health care needs. Subscription cost is $28 per year for 12 issues. Call 1-800-247-8080. Offices at 120 State Street, Hackensack, NJ 07601.

From Sharifzadeh, V. S. (1992). Families with Middle Eastern roots. In E. W. Lynch & M. J. Hanson (Eds.), *Developing cross-cultural competence: A guide for working with young children and their families* (pp. 319–352). Baltimore: Paul H. Brookes Publishing Company, P.O. Box 10624, Baltimore, MD 21285-0624. Reprinted by permission.

From Willis, W. (1992). Families with African American roots. In E. W. Lynch & M. J. Hanson (Eds.), *Developing cross-cultural competence: A guide for working with young children and their families* (pp. 121–150). Baltimore: Paul H. Brookes Publishing Company, P.O. Box 10624, Baltimore, MD 21285-0624. Reprinted by permission.

Chapter 8

From Brantlinger, E. (1992). Professionals' attitudes toward the sterilization of people with disabilities. *Journal of the Association for Persons with Severe Handicaps,*

17(1), 4–18. Copyright © 1992 by *Journal of the Association for Persons with Severe Handicaps.*

From Gallivan-Fenlon, A. (1994). "Their senior year": Family and service provider perspectives on the transition from school to adult life for young adults with disabilities. *Journal of the Association for Persons with Severe Handicaps, 19*(1), 11–23. Copyright © 1994 by *Journal of the Association for Persons with Severe Handicaps.*

From "Parent Attitudes About Special Education and Reintegration: What is the Role of Student Outcomes?" by S. K. Green and M. R. Shinn, *Exceptional Children,* Vol. 61, 1995, 269–281. Copyright © 1995 by the Council for Exceptional Children. Reprinted with permission.

Chapter 9

From "Using Videotape to Communicate with Parents of Students with Severe Disabilities" by P. A. Alberto, L. Mechling, T. A. Tabor, & J. Thompson, *TEACHING Exceptional Children, 27*(3), 18–21. Copyright © 1995 by The Council for Exceptional Children. Reprinted with permission.

From Finders, M., & Lewis, C. (1994). Why some parents don't come to school. *Educational Leadership, 51*(8), 12–14. Reprinted by permission of the Association for Supervision and Curriculum Development. Copyright © 1994 by ASCD. All rights reserved.

From Lindle, J. C. (1989). What do parents want from principals? *Educational Leadership, 47*(2), 13. Reprinted with permission of the Association for Supervision and Curriculum Development. Copyright © 1989 by ASCD. All rights reserved.

Chapter 11

From Das, M. (1995). Tough decisions: One family's experience crosses cultures and continents. *Volta Voices, 2*(3), 5–6. Reprinted with permission from *The Volta Review.* Copyright © 1995 by the Alexander Graham Bell Association for the Deaf, 3417 Volta Place, NW, Washington, DC 20007.

From "Using Psychological Assessment in Structural Family Therapy" by R. H. Fulmer, S. Cohen, & G. Monaco, 1985, *Journal of Learning Disabilities, 18*(3), 145–150. Copyright © 1985 by PRO-ED, Inc. Reprinted by permission.

From "Making Sense of Disability: Low-Income Puerto Rican Parents' Theories of the Problem" by Beth Harry, *Exceptional Children, 59,* 1992, p. 31. Copyright © 1992 by The Council for Exceptional Children. Reprinted with permission.

From "Communication Versus Compliance: African-American Parents' Involvement in Special Education" by B. Harry, N. Allen, and M. McLaughlin, *Exceptional Children, 61*(4), 1995, 364–377. Copyright © 1995 by The Council for Exceptional Children. Reprinted with permission.

From Wright, L., & Boyland, J. (1993). Using early childhood development portfolios in the identification and education of young, economically disadvantaged, potentially gifted students. *Roeper Review, 15*(4), 205–210. Reprinted with the permission of the *Roeper Review,* Vol. 15, Copyright © 1993, P.O. Box 329, Bloomfield Hills, MI 48303-0329.

Chapter 12

From "Communication Versus Compliance: African-American Parents' Involvement in Special Education" by B. Harry, N. Allen, and M. McLaughlin, *Exceptional Children, 61*(4), 1995, 364–377. Copyright © 1995 by The Council for Exceptional Children. Reprinted with permission.

From "To the Editor: An Open Letter to CEC" by K. Katzen, *Exceptional Children, 46*(8), 1980, p. 582. Copyright © 1980 by The Council for Exceptional Children. Reprinted with permission.

Chapter 13

From Horner, R. H., Dunlap, G., Koegel, R. L., Carr, E. G., Sailor, W., Anderson, J., Albin, R. W., & O'Neill, R. E. (1990). Toward a technology of "nonaversive" behavioral support. *Journal of the Association for Persons with Severe Handicaps, 15*(3). Copyright © 1990 by *Journal of the Association for Persons with Severe Handicaps.*

From "Recommendations for Homework-Communication Problems" by M. Jayanthi, V. Sawyer, J. S. Nelson, Bursuck, W. D., and M. H. Epstein, 1995, *Remedial and Special Education, 16*(4), 212–225. Copyright © 1995 by PRO-ED, Inc. Reprinted by permission.

From "Making Homework Work at Home" by P. J. Kay, M. Fitzgerald, C. Paradee, and A. Mellencamp, 1994, *Journal of Learning Disabilities, 27*(9), 550–561. Copyright © 1994 by PRO-ED, Inc. Reprinted by permission.

Chapter 14

From Comer, J. P., & Haynes, N. M. (1991). Parent involvement in schools: An ecological approach. *The*

Index